Handbook of Latin American Studies: 1950

A SELECTIVE AND ANNOTATED GUIDE TO

MATERIAL PUBLISHED IN 1950

ON

ANTHROPOLOGY, ART, ECONOMICS, EDUCATION,

GEOGRAPHY, GOVERNMENT, HISTORY,

INTERNATIONAL RELATIONS, LABOR

AND SOCIAL WELFARE, LANGUAGE

AND LITERATURE, LAW, MUSIC,

PHILOSOPHY, AND

SOCIOLOGY

Advisory Board

HANDBOOK OF
LATIN AMERICAN STUDIES: 1950

No. 16

PREPARED BY

THE HISPANIC FOUNDATION

IN

THE LIBRARY OF CONGRESS

●

FRANCISCO AGUILERA, *Editor*

ELSIE BROWN, *Acting Assistant Editor*

1953
UNIVERSITY OF FLORIDA PRESS
GAINESVILLE

A UNIVERSITY OF FLORIDA PRESS BOOK

Copyright, 1953, University of Florida

L. C. Card Catalogue Number: 36–32635

MANUFACTURED BY CONVENTION PRESS, JACKSONVILLE, FLORIDA

Contributing Editors

Francisco Aguilera, *The Library of Congress,* LITERATURE

José Juan Arrom, *Yale University,* LITERATURE

Harold Benjamin, *George Peabody College for Teachers,* EDUCATION

Harry Bernstein, *Brooklyn College,* HISTORY

Manoel Cardozo, *The Catholic University of America,* HISTORY

Phyllis Carter, *The Library of Congress,* STATISTICS

Asher N. Christensen, *University of Minnesota,* GOVERNMENT

Helen L. Clagett, *The Library of Congress,* LAW

Howard F. Cline, *The Library of Congress,* HISTORY

Mercer Cook, *Howard University,* LITERATURE

Benjamín Cornejo, *Economic Commission for Latin America, United Nations,* ECONOMICS

Raymond E. Crist, *University of Florida,* GEOGRAPHY

Ralph Edward Dimmick, *Pan American Union,* LITERATURE

Dirección de Investigaciones Económicas, Nacional Financiera, S. A., *Mexico City,* ECONOMICS

Carl H. Farman, *Department of Health, Education, and Welfare,* LABOR AND SOCIAL WELFARE

Ángel Flores, *Queens College,* LITERATURE

Arch C. Gerlach, *The Library of Congress,* CARTOGRAPHY

Wendell C. Gordon, *The University of Texas,* ECONOMICS

Roscoe R. Hill, *The National Archives* (retired), HISTORY

Preston E. James, *Syracuse University,* GEOGRAPHY

Charles E. Kany, *University of California, Berkeley,* LANGUAGE

Irving A. Leonard, *University of Michigan,* LITERATURE

M. B. Lourenço Filho, *Universidade do Brasil,* EDUCATION

George McCutchen McBride, *University of California, Los Angeles,* GEOGRAPHY

Robert E. McNicoll, HISTORY

Concha Meléndez, *Universidad de Puerto Rico,* LITERATURE

Irving Rouse, *Yale University,* ANTHROPOLOGY

John Howland Rowe, *University of California, Berkeley,* ANTHROPOLOGY

Aníbal Sánchez Reulet, *Pan American Union,* PHILOSOPHY

v

Contents

Editor's Note

AMONG THE FORTY-TWO Contributing Editors in the present number of the *Handbook of Latin American Studies* there appear four new names.

Thomas Lynn Smith assumes responsibility for the newly-created section entitled *Sociology,* whose establishment was recommended by the Advisory Board in November, 1950, and approved by the Librarian of Congress.

Aníbal Sánchez Reulet is now in charge of philosophy; he succeeds Risieri Frondizi, who served without interruption since the establishment of that section in No. 5 to No. 15 inclusive, regardless of where he was teaching at the time—Tucumán, Caracas, New Haven, or Río Piedras.

The subsection on Mexican economics has now a corporate byline (Dirección de Investigaciones Económicas, Nacional Financiera, S. A.) in recognition of the fact that its compilation is done on an institutional basis by the above-mentioned research organization in Mexico City.

Benjamín Cornejo would not be listed here as a new name if we had not incorrectly attributed to Raúl Prebisch the authorship of the subsection on Argentine economics in No. 15. For our error, caused by an unavoidable misunderstanding, we herewith apologize both to Dr. Cornejo and to Dr. Prebisch.

It will be noticed that Roland D. Hussey resumes in this issue the work in history which he interrupted for one year, after serving continuously from Nos. 6 to 14.

The addition of sociology as a distinctive field of interest in Latin American studies has enlarged the main body of the *Handbook.* The expansion of the subsection on statistics has had the same effect. We have high hopes that such an increase in size will represent a corresponding improvement in quality and usefulness.

Another increase in the size of the *Handbook* resulted from developing the customary *author* index into an *author-and-subject* index. At a meeting held in March, 1953, the Advisory Board recommended "that the Editorial Office of the *Handbook* be authorized to experiment with a combined author-subject index to No. 16, in dictionary form." We have experimented within rigid space and time limitations on the assumption that an index can be very helpful without attempting to be exhaustive. Suggestions for the improvement of the index would be welcomed by the editorial staff.

A rearrangement of the History section has been put into effect after consultation with the Contributing Editors most concerned and with the Advisory Board. The customary subsections, under Spanish America and Haiti, entitled "The Revolutionary Period" and "The National Period," have been combined to form a single unit called "The Nineteenth and Twentieth Centuries." The historians in charge of the Colonial Period may at their pleasure extend the concept of "colonial" a few years beyond 1800. It was felt that the new arrangement would obviate the problem, often moot, of setting bounds to the revolutionary period, and facilitate the allocation of nineteenth-century Cuban material and nineteenth- and twentieth-century Puerto Rican material. An arrangement similar to this was adopted in No. 14 for the Spanish American Literature section, and has proved satisfactory.

The contributions of Arch C. Gerlach, on cartography, and Roscoe R. Hill, on archival materials, are scattered under various headings according to subject, area, and period.

The resignation of George M. Foster from the Advisory Board was reported at the meeting held by this body last March. Dr. Foster was one of the five members of the Advisory Board established by the Librarian of Congress in 1947, after the Library of Congress assumed responsibility for the maintenance and operation of the Editorial Office of the *Handbook* as an integral part of the Hispanic Foundation. Dr. Foster's contribution to *Handbook* planning during 1947-1952 is highly regarded by the Library of Congress, on whose behalf the editor expresses regret for Dr. Foster's departure and deep appreciation for his continued support and assistance.

Numerous persons and institutions have demonstrated their interest in the *Handbook*. The Pan American Union, as usual, has placed its resources and facilities at the service of the Editorial Office and the Contributing Editors. The editor is glad to have this opportunity to express his special thanks for the assistance received from Marian Forero and José Gómez Sicre, of the Pan American Union's Columbus Memorial Library and Division of Music and Visual Arts respectively. Magnus Mörner, Librarian of the Ibero-American Library and Institute, School of Economic Sciences, Stockholm, Sweden, has graciously favored us with titles from Scandinavian publications which we believe are especially useful.

The appointment of Howard F. Cline as Director of the Hispanic Foundation, beginning September 1, 1952, has given the *Handbook* unit the benefit of his scholarly and editorial experience. It is gratifying to recall that Dr. Cline has served as Contributing Editor in charge of one of the History sections in Nos. 11-16.

Charmion Shelby, Assistant Editor of the *Handbook,* was on leave during most of the period of preparation of the present number. Her responsibilities were taken over by Elsie Brown, whose name appears on the title page. The editor would like to pay special tribute to Miss Brown and to Consuelo G. Talkington and Mercedes G. Balco who, as members of the staff, have borne more than their share of the burden of editing the manuscript and seeing it through the press.

The Library of Congress continued its practice of inviting those editors who live outside the Washington area to spend as many as three days in the *Handbook* offices to work on some of the materials needed for their sections, with the aid of a modest consultant's fee. It is a pleasure to report that twelve of the twenty-two out-of-town editors invited found it possible to come to Washington. In many of the cases the editor himself or the institution with which he is affiliated helped to defray the transportation expenses.

One of our Contributing Editors, Dr. Hussey, noted in the introductory statement to his History section a problem that is of general interest; we have taken the liberty of transferring his comment here. Dr. Hussey writes: "One other aspect of publication, in this and recent years, poses a problem chiefly for bibliographers, and incidentally is a major reason for the length of the addenda in recent volumes of the *Handbook*. But it can affect scholars who consume instead of listing history. A large number of periodicals, and some books, are appearing appreciably later than the dates on their title pages. The 1950 *Boletín de la Sociedad Mexicana de Geografía y Estadística* actually came out only in 1952. Other "1950" items did not appear until 1951 or carried over into 1952. The Sociedad de Geografía e Historia de Guatemala solved the problem by omitting the 1950 volume of its *Anales* entirely—volume 24 was for 1949, volume 25 for 1951. One wishes that others would imitate the example.

No rule can handle the bibliographical problem satisfactorily, but in general the official date has been accepted unless a corrective colophon or other printed indication appears in the publication itself. In that case, it has been incorporated into the entry (for instance, '1949, i.e. 1950'), though sometimes the entry appears in the officially correct *Handbook,* and sometimes in that for the year of real publication."

To the Chairman and associate members of the Advisory Board of the *Handbook of Latin American Studies,* to the Contributing Editors, and to Lewis F. Haines, Director of the University of Florida Press, and his staff the Library of Congress owes a growing debt of gratitude which the editor takes pleasure in acknowledging upon closing this rather long "note."

N. B. Readers ought to bear in mind that all items in this volume were published in 1950 unless otherwise indicated.

FRANCISCO AGUILERA

THE HISPANIC FOUNDATION
THE LIBRARY OF CONGRESS
WASHINGTON, D. C.

Handbook of
Latin American Studies: 1950

General

BIBLIOGRAPHIES

CHARMION SHELBY

1. **Andrade Chiriboga, Alfonso.** Hemeroteca azuaya. T. 1-2. Cuenca, Ecuador, El Mercurio. 287, 245 p.
Information on 128 periodicals published in the province of Azuay during the 19th century.

2. ANUARIO BIBLIOGRÁFICO URUGUAYO DE 1947. Con un suplemento al anuario uruguayo de 1946. Montevideo, Biblioteca Nacional. xi, 47 p.
Classified lists of 383 publications for 1947 and 26 supplementary titles for 1946, with author indexes and lists of publishers and presses. A welcome resumption of the Uruguayan national bibliography, excellently presented.

2a. ANUARIO BIBLIOGRÁFICO VENEZOLANO, 1947-1948. Caracas, Biblioteca Nacional. 408 p.
Books, pamphlets, and magazines appearing during the two-year period, to the number of 2400 titles. Includes a supplementary list for 1945-1946. The section "Escritores venezolanos fallecidos en 1949" gives biobibliographical information on 22 authors.

3. **Argentina. Ministerio de Educación. Universidad de Buenos Aires. Instituto Bibliotecológico.** Catálogo de las publicaciones de la Universidad de Buenos Aires editadas durante el período 1945-1950, con motivo de la Exposición Feria del Libro Argentino. Buenos Aires, Universidad de Buenos Aires. 67 p.
Publications of the *Rectorado* and eight Faculties of the University. 205 titles. Indexed.

4. BIBLIOTECA DEL DOCTOR RICARDO OLIVERA. Obras selectas de literatura, arte e historia. Ediciones originales. Encuadernaciones lujosas. Buenos Aires, Compañía Impresora Argentina. 269 p.
Catalogue of 2395 titles, mostly Spanish and French literary works, of a private library offered for sale at auction. Includes several 17th-century editions of *Don Quixote*.

5. BIBLOS. Buenos Aires, Cámara Argentina del Libro. Año 8, no. 37, primer bimestre –no. 42, sexto bimestre.

6. BOLETIM BIBLIOGRÁFICO. São Paulo, Biblioteca Pública Municipal, v. 16-17.
Special articles on library science, literature and art; topical bibliographies; and classified accession lists of the Library.

7. BOLETÍN BIBLIOGRÁFICO. Algunas publicaciones nacionales correspondientes al año 1948. San José, Biblioteca Nacional. 16 p.

8. BOLETÍN BIBLIOGRÁFICO. Algunas publicaciones nacionales correspondientes al año 1949. San José, Biblioteca Nacional. 20 p.
Two issues continuing the Costa Rican national bibliography, listing books, pamphlets, magazines, and newspapers appearing in these years.

9. BOLETÍN BIBLIOGRÁFICO. Lima, Universidad Nacional Mayor de San Marcos, Biblioteca Central. Año 23, v. 22, no. 1-2, julio.
Contains sections listing books and pamphlets appearing in Peru, 1949-1950; selected articles, Nov. 2, 1949-June 2, 1950; and bibliography of law and political science, 1936-1950. Author indexes for each section.

10. BOLETÍN BIBLIOGRÁFICO ARGENTINO. Buenos Aires, Ministerio de Educación, Dirección General de Cultura. No. 23-24, enero-diciembre, 1948, i.e. 1950. 114 p.
Classified list of 1544 publications, followed by an author index and addresses of institutions, publishers, and book dealers.

11. **Horta, Maria Helena de Castro, and Diva de Campos Lennon.** Índice do *Dicionário bio-bibliográfico sergipano* do Dr. Armindo Guaraná (*Bol. bibliog.*, São Paulo, v. 14, p. 125-156).
Alphabetical index, greatly increasing the usefulness of a much consulted reference work. [R. E. Dimmick]

12. **Kimsa, Antanas.** Bibliografía del R. P. Félix Restrepo, S. J. (*Bol. inst. Caro y*

Cuervo, t. 5, no. 1-3, 1949, i.e. 1950, p. 478-548).

Listing of publications (707 titles) on a diversity of topics: literature, linguistics, religious and educational problems, history, biography, book reviews. The rest of the volume consists of articles contributed in honor of Father Restrepo by his friends and students.

13. Metford, J. C. J. British contributions to Spanish and Spanish-American studies. New York, Longmans, Green for the British Council. 86 p., illus., ports.

This is an entertaining narrative bibliography of British writings on Spain and Spanish America from the 16th century to the mid-20th. [B. Wood]

14. Peraza Sarausa, Fermín. Anuario bibliográfico cubano, 1949. Habana, Ediciones Anuario Bibliográfico Cubano. 167 p.

Classified list of 1187 titles for 1949, plus some 200 supplementary titles for 1937-1948, all with complete bibliographical information; dictionary index. The thirteenth number of this excellent guide, published continuously since 1938.

15. ————. Bibliografía Martiana, 1949. Habana, Municipio de La Habana, Departamento de Educación (Publ. de la Biblioteca Municipal de La Habana, serie C: Guías Bibliográficas 17). 26 p.

Continuation. See also item 89.

15a. United Nations Educational, Scientific, and Cultural Organization. Centro de Cooperación Científica para América Latina. Artículos científicos publicados en América Latina. V. 3. Montevideo. 323 p.

16. Velázquez, Gonzalo (comp.). Anuario bibliográfico puertorriqueño. Índice alfabético de libros, folletos, revistas y periódicos publicados en Puerto Rico durante 1948. Río Piedras, Puerto Rico, Biblioteca de la Universidad. 71 p.

Well prepared and most useful bibliography for an important field. Dictionary listing by author and subject of current Puerto Rican production, with lists of publishers and dealers appended. The contents represent chiefly current acquisitions in the Library of the University of Puerto Rico.

18. Villaseñor y Villaseñor, Ramiro. Bibliografía de José López-Portillo y Rojas, 1850-1923. Guadalajara, Mexico (Suplemento a la revista *Et Caetera,* año 1, no. 4, oct.-dic.). 20 p.

Books, pamphlets, articles and book reviews in a number of fields, with indication of private or public libraries in which the publications may be found.

19. Williams, Edwin B. Spanish and Portuguese language and literature (PMLA, v. 65, no. 3, April, p. 90-95).

United States publications on Spanish and Portuguese language and literature (including Latin America) for the year 1949. [Ed.]

20. YEAR BOOK OF CARIBBEAN RESEARCH. 1949 SUPPLEMENT. Agriculture, fisheries and forestry. Building, engineering, technology. Medicine and public health. Natural sciences. Social sciences. Port-of-Spain, Trinidad, Caribbean Commission. 296, 40, 65, 37, 82 p.

Annotated bibliographies prepared as surveys of research and investigation in the Caribbean and adjoining countries. [Ed.]

BIOGRAPHIES

21. Hilton, Ronald (ed.). Who's who in Latin America. Third edition, revised and enlarged. Part 5. Argentina, Paraguay, and Uruguay. Stanford, Calif., Stanford University Press. xvii, 258 p.

The third edition of this work, published in sections, began to appear in 1945. In 1950 Part 3 (Colombia, Ecuador, Venezuela) and Part 7 (Cuba, Dominican Republic) remained to be published. An appreciative biographical sketch of Bailey Willis opens Part 5. [Ed.]

22. Marbán y Escobar, Edilberto. Don Emilio Blanchet. Educador, historiógrafo y moralista. Habana, Academia de la Historia de Cuba. 77 p.

Cuban educator who left Cuba in 1861 and returned to Matanzas as professor in 1899. Taught American history among other subjects and published popular biographies and histories. [R. E. McNicoll]

23. Polillo, Raul de. Santos Dumont, gênio. São Paulo, Companhia Editôra Nacional. 319 p.

A somewhat padded biography of a pioneer in aviation. The author refers very sensibly to the Wright brothers. Filled with philosophical drivel. [M. Cardozo]

24. QUIEN ES QUIEN EN LA ARGENTINA. Biografías contemporáneas. Quinta edición. Buenos Aires, Kraft. 628 p.

Fifth edition of the Argentine *Who's Who.* A list of deaths among names in the fourth edition is provided. A standard reference tool. [H. F. Cline]

25. Solari, Juan Antonio. Emilio Frugoni, su magisterio político-social, su mensaje lírico. Buenos Aires, La Vanguardia. 70 p.

An Argentine tribute to a Uruguayan political leader and poet on his seventieth birthday. Biography and political analysis. [F. Aguilera]

DESCRIPTION AND TRAVEL

26. Argentina. Ministerio de Obras Públicas de la Nación. Administración General de Parques Nacionales y

Turismo. Visión de Argentina. An outline of Argentina. Buenos Aires, 1949, i.e. 1950. 196 p.
Well illustrated tourist description. P. 177-196 are devoted to *An outline of Argentina*, in English. [Ed.]

27. ————. **Presidencia de la Nación. Control de Estado.** La Nación Argentina, justa, libre, soberana. 3. edición. Buenos Aires, Peuser. 802 p., charts, maps, tables.
A graphic presentation in color of many material aspects of Argentina; Luis Guillermo Bähler, editor-in-chief. [Ed.]

28. **Backhouse, Hugo.** Among the gauchos. London, Jarrolds. 208 p., illus.
Country life in Argentina described by a long-time resident. [Ed.]

30. **Barros Prado, Eduardo.** Glückliche Jahre am grossen Strom. Ein Amazonasbuch. Ins Deutsche übertragen von Ludwig Schönfeldt. Wien [Austria], Ullstein, 1950? 247 p., illus.
Personal impressions, related in an interesting and informing fashion, of life in Manaos and other places in the Amazon valley, during the past half-century. Translation of *Yo ví el Amazonas* (Buenos Aires, 1948). [H. W. Spiegel]

31. **Carnelutti, Francesco.** America. Padova [Italy], Antonio Milani. 88 p.
Impressions of an intelligent Italian who visited Brazil, Uruguay, Argentina, and Chile. [M. Cardozo]

32. **Chile. Ferrocarriles del Estado.** Guía del veraneante, 1950. Revista anual de turismo. Santiago. 338 p., maps.

33. **Dargan, Ena.** The road to Cuzco. A journey from Argentina to Peru. London, Andrew Melrose. 215 p., illus.
Description into which is woven much of history and tradition. [G. M. McBride]

34. **Davies, Howell** (ed.). The South American handbook, 1950. 27th annual edition. A year book and guide to the countries and resources of South and Central America, Mexico, and Cuba. London, Trade and Travel Publications (distributed by the H. W. Wilson Co., New York). 766 p.

35. **Fermor, Patrick Leigh.** The traveller's tree. A journey through the Caribbean Islands. Illustrated by A. Costa. London, John Murray. 403 p.
The author's description of this volume, which covers Guadeloupe, Martinique, Haiti, and the British West Indies in the great tradition of British travellers, is correct: "The scope of this book thus reduces itself to a personal random account of an autumn and winter spent in wandering through these islands, and it has all the fallibility implicit in such a charter. Its ultimate purpose, if it must be defined, is to retransmit to the reader whatever interest and enjoyment we encountered. In a word, to give pleasure." Another volume, to recount experiences in Puerto Rico and Central America, is forecast. [H. F. Cline]

36. **Figueiredo, José de Lima.** Terras de Matto-Grosso e da Amazonia. Rio de Janeiro, A Noite, 1950? 347 p.
A rather fascinating travel book. Observations interspersed with history. [M. Cardozo]

37. **García, Rubén.** Rincones y paisajes del México maravilloso. Prólogo por José Vasconcelos. México, Talleres Gráficos de la Nación. 451 p., illus.
Travel notes, with much useful information and numerous interesting photographs, touching many out-of-the-way places in Mexico as well as some more familiar ones visited by General García. [H. F. Cline]

38. **Katz, Richard.** Mein Inselbuch. Erste Erlebnisse in Brasilien. Erlenbach-Zürich, Switzerland, Eugen Rentsch. 239 p.

39. **Kerr, John Graham.** A naturalist in the Gran Chaco. Cambridge, England, University Press. xi, 234 p., 24 plates, map.
Interesting detailed account of travels in the Chaco and along the Paraguay and Pilcomayo rivers—half a century ago. [G. M. McBride]

40. **Lelong, M. H.** En Patagonie et Terre de Feu. Édition illustrée de 9 photographies et 1 carte. Paris, René Julliard (La Croix du Sud). 273 p.
General description and observations. [G. M. McBride]

41. **Luke, Harry.** Caribbean circuit. London, Nicholson & Watson. 262 p.
A British traveller's account. Good on Lesser Antilles. [R. E. McNicoll]

42. **Mestas, Alberto de.** El Salvador, país de lagos y volcanes. Madrid, Ediciones Cultura Hispánica. vii, 672 p.
A sympathetic Spanish diplomat collects all available data on the economic geography, history, government, and cultural activities of El Salvador, making of this guide a meritorious pioneer effort, despite its profuseness. [F. Aguilera]

43. **Morton, Friedrich.** Xelahuh. Abenteuer im Urwald von Guatemala. Salzburg, Austria, Otto Müller. 338 p., illus.
An Austrian's jungle travels in Guatemala. [R. E. McNicoll]

44. THE NEW WORLD GUIDES TO THE LATIN AMERICAN REPUBLICS. V. 1-3. Editor-in-chief, Earl Parker Hanson; associate editors, Charlotte Leeper Hanson and Mary C. Mahoney. 3rd edition, completely re-

vised. New York, Duell, Sloan and Pearce. Various pagings, illus., maps.

45. Paniagua Serracante, J. Del San Juan místico y heroico. Crónicas. San Juan, P. R., Biblioteca de Autores Puertorriqueños. 119 p.

Evocation of capital of Puerto Rico: landscape, buildings, etc. [A. Flores]

46. Prado, Cid. Viagem à Bahia. Reportagens do *Correio Paulistano*. São Paulo, Martins. 91 p.

Account of an automobile trip from São Paulo to Bahia over the new highway. [M. Cardozo]

47. Quénard, Gervais. Les deux Amériques à vol d'oiseau. Paris, Bonne Presse. 114 p.

A French Assumptionist missionary's impressions of the two Americas' spiritual resources vis-à-vis their economic wealth. Deals mostly with Mexico, Colombia, Peru, Chile, Argentina, and Brazil. [F. Aguilera]

48. Toor, Frances. New guide to Mexico. Completely revised and augmented with maps and illustrations. New York, Crown. 270 p.

A handy compilation of up-to-date travel information, with many other bits of utilitarian knowledge. [H. F. Cline]

49. Uruguay. Oficina Nacional de Turismo. Uruguay. Guía oficial. Montevideo. 152 p.

50. Von Hagen, Victor Wolfgang. A guide to Guayaquil. New York, F. Farnam Associates (Guides to Ecuador), 1950? 32 p., illus., map.

One of the best of these guides. [G. M. McBride]

51. ——————. Huancayo and Ayacucho. New York, F. Farnam Associates (Guides to Peru), 1950? 32 p., illus., maps.

Brief, well illustrated description. [G. M. McBride]

STATISTICS

PHYLLIS CARTER

With the exception of the national statistical yearbooks, that is, the annual compilations of data issued for the purpose of providing convenient summaries of the most recent statistics of the areas, publications consisting of tabular and graphic statistics on Latin American countries are not listed separately in the *Handbook*. The bibliographies listed below systematically covered various types of statistical publications in 1950, and taken together constitute an adequate guide to the basic data available.

STATISTICAL BIBLIOGRAPHIES

52. Costa Rica. Dirección General de Estadística. Bibliografía estadística de Costa Rica, por Manuel García Valverde . . . . San José. Processed.

52a. Great Britain. Colonial Office. Library Reference and Research Section. Monthly list of official colonial publications. London. January-December, no. 1-12. Processed.

Brief listing of publications received, including those of the British colonies in the Western Hemisphere. Each issue has a separate section on government gazettes, in which statistical supplements and sections in the gazettes are indicated by title or by notes.

52b. Inter American Statistical Institute. Estadística. Quarterly journal. Washington. V. 8, no. 26-29.

Each issue contains a selected annotated bibliography of recent Latin American statistical publications, with special emphasis on census volumes and statistical yearbooks and other major compilations of statistical data of the American Republics. The first issues of new bulletins and journals are listed, but no succeeding issues; however, articles and sections of special interest are shown under their proper subject headings. A section of news notes immediately preceding the bibliography contains information on statistical studies and publication programs launched by statistical agencies.

52c. ——————. Monthly accession list of publications received . . . . Washington. January-December. Processed.

Brief entries, not annotated; principally of the statistical publications of the American Republics. The coverage is more comprehensive than in the bibliography published in *Estadística,* and new titles appear much sooner. Each issue of each periodical received is listed.

52d. International Statistical Institute. Revue de l'Institut International de Statistique. Review of the International Statistical Institute. The Hague. V. 18, no. 1-4.

Each issue contains a bibliography on all types of statistical publications from all countries of the world.

52e. POPULATION INDEX. Office of Population Research, Princeton University, and Population Association of America, Inc. Princeton, N. J. V. 16, no. 1-4.

Annotated bibliography of statistical publications on population, vital statistics, and related subjects, of all areas of the world.

52f. United Nations. Demographic yearbook—Annuaire démographique, 1949-50. Second issue. Department of Social Affairs, Population Division; Department of Economic Affairs, Statistical Office of the United Nations. New York. 558 p.

Bibliography at end presents citations to the most recent population census and other sources of official demographic statistics including general statistical annuals and bulletins in each major political area of the world. Full bibliographic citations, no annotations.

52g. United States. Bureau of the Census. Publications on foreign countries. Annotated accession list. Washington. January-December. Processed.

A quarterly list of statistical publications received from all countries of the world, chiefly through exchange agreements with other national statistical offices. Brief entries, not annotated, but listing separately titles of articles and sections of special interest. Each issue of each publication received is listed.

STATISTICAL YEARBOOKS

52h. Brazil. Instituto Brasileiro de Geografia e Estatística. Conselho Nacional de Estatística. Anuário estatístico do Brasil. Ano 10, 1949. Rio de Janeiro, Serviço Gráfico do IBGE. 792 p.

Contains the latest data available on each subject at the time of publication. Sections on: 1, physical situation (territory and climate); 2, demographic situation (population, vital statistics, migration); 3, economic situation (mining, agricultural, and industrial production; transportation, communication; property; money; stocks and bonds; banking; foreign and domestic commerce, and prices; wages; consumption); 4, social situation (urban improvements; medical and social assistance, insurance, savings and loan banks, cooperatives; labor); 5, cultural situation (education, libraries, museums, etc.); 6, administrative and political situation (public finance, police and defence, criminals, justice, electoral statistics); 7, appendix, international statistics. Two more recent numbers of the yearbook have since appeared: ano 11, 1950, published 1951, and ano 12, 1951, published 1952.

52i. Chile. Dirección General de Estadística. V. 3-8. Santiago.

The general statistical yearbook of Chile appears as eight separate volumes without a common single title for the series, but with different individual titles. Description and comments for the six volumes published in 1950 follow:
V. 3. Agricultura e industrias agropecuarias. Año agrícola 1946-1947. 54 p.
A later issue covering 1947-1948 appeared in 1952.
V. 4. Minería. Año 1947. 42 p.
Two later issues: Año 1948, published 1951, and Año 1949, published 1952.
V. 5. Industrias. Año 1947. 63 p.
Two later issues: Año 1948, published 1951, and Año 1949, published 1952.
V. 6. Finanzas, bancos y cajas sociales. Año 1948. 109 p.
A later issue, Año 1949, published 1951.
V. 7. Comercio interior y comunicaciones. Año 1947. 151 p.
A later issue, Año 1948, published 1951.
V. 8. Comercio exterior. Año 1948. xv, 302 p.
Two later issues: Año 1949, published 1951, and Año 1950, published 1952.

Volumes 1 and 2 (dealing respectively with "Demografía y asistencia social" and "Educación, justicia, política y administración") were not published in 1950. Two issues of the former appeared later: Año 1947, published 1951, and Año 1948, published 1952. Of the latter there appeared an issue for Año 1948 in 1951.

52j. Colombia. Dirección Nacional de Estadística. Anuario general de estadística, 1947. Bogotá. xii, 765 p.

52k. ―――. ―――. Anuario general de estadística, 1948. Bogotá. xii, 779 p.

Data on area, geography, climatology, population, vital statistics, education, health, justice and crime, wages, labor accidents, livestock slaughter, banking and credit, communication and transportation, business, retail prices and cost of living, foreign commerce, manufacturing, mining, construction in cities, and public finance.

52kk. El Salvador. Dirección General de Estadística. Anuario estadístico de la República de El Salvador correspondiente al año de 1948. T. 1, Sección demográfica y judicial. T. 2, Sección de comercio exterior e interior. T. 3, Sección de producción y consumo. San Salvador, Imprenta Nacional. 299, vi p., unpaged folded leaves; iii, 420 p.; 256, v p.

T. 1: data on area, geography, climatology, urban and rural population, vital statistics, migration, education, and justice and crime. T. 2: data on livestock consumption, banking and credit, communication and transportation, retail and wholesale prices, foreign commerce, and public finance. T. 3: data on agriculture and livestock, manufacturing, mining, construction, and other industrial activity.

52m. Honduras. Secretaría de Gobernación, Justicia, Sanidad y Beneficencia. Informe de los actos realizados por el Poder Ejecutivo en los ramos de gobernación, justicia, sanidad y beneficencia. Año fiscal de 1948 a 1949. Tegucigalpa. 329 p.

Includes the report of the Dirección General de Estadística and constitutes the general statistical yearbook of Honduras. Data on population, vital statistics, migration, health, justice and crime, public assistance, livestock, real estate transactions, manufacturing, mining, and public finance.

52n. Mexico. Dirección General de Estadística. Anuario estadístico de los Estados Unidos Mexicanos, 1943-1945. México. 833 p.

Data on area, geography, climatology; 1940 census by nationality, urban-rural distribution, etc.; vital statistics; migration; education; justice and crime; labor statistics; housing, 1939; social assistance; other social statistics; agriculture, livestock, forestry, fishery; banking and credit; communication and transportation; domestic commerce; retail and wholesale prices and cost of living; foreign commerce; consumption; other economic statistics. Data for the years 1943-1945 except where otherwise noted.

52o. ————. ————. Compendio estadístico, 1950. México. 332 p.
Includes the latest data available for the same subjects as appear in the 1943-1945 *Anuario*. Therefore the information is in many cases several years more recent though not as detailed as that in the *Anuario*.

52p. Netherlands. Ministerie voor Uniezaken en Overzeese Rijksdelen. Curaçaos verslag, 1947. I, Tekst van het verslag van bestuur en staat van Curaçao over het jaar 1946. 's-Gravenhage, Staatsdrukkerijen Uitgeverijbedrijk. 174 p.
Part 1 contains summary data scattered through the text on Curaçao, Aruba, Bonaire, St. Martin, St. Eustatius, and Saba. Part 2 (*Statistisch jaaroverzicht van Curaçao over het jaar 1946*) was published in 1951. Also published in 1951: *Curaçaos verslag, 1948*, parts 1 and 2, covering the year 1947; *Verslag Nederlandse Antillen, 1949* (note change of title), part 1 covering 1948; and *Verslag Nederlandse Antillen, 1950*, part 1 covering 1949. Part 2 of the last two yearbooks appeared in 1952.

52q. ————. ————. Surinaams verslag, 1947. I, Tekst van het verslag van bestuur en staat van Suriname over het jaar 1946. II, Statistisch jaaroverzicht van Suriname over het jaar 1946. 's-Gravenhage. 71, 169 p.
Part 1 contains summary data scattered through text. Part 2, the statistical yearbook proper, contains data on meteorology, population, vital statistics, migration, education, health, justice and crime, agriculture and livestock, banking and credit, communication and transportation, retail prices, foreign commerce, mining, public finance, and electoral statistics. Two later reports have since appeared: the 1948 *verslag* covering the year 1947, parts 1 and 2, published 1951, and the 1949 *verslag* covering 1948, parts 1 and 2, published 1952.

52r. Nicaragua. Dirección General de Estadística. Anuario estadístico de la República de Nicaragua. Año 1947. Managua, Talleres Nacionales. 379 p.
Data on area, geography, climatology, population, vital statistics, migration, education, cultural statistics (libraries, museums, theaters), justice and crime, banking and credit, communication and transportation, foreign commerce, domestic commerce and prices, public finance, industrial statistics, agriculture.

52s. Panama. Dirección de Estadística y Censo. Extracto estadístico. Años 1941, 1942, 1943. V. 1: Comercio exterior. V. 2: Estadística general. Panamá. 357; xvi, 346 p.
V. 2 contains data on area, climatology, population, vital statistics, education, hospital statistics, justice and crime, social security, vaccination and slaughter of livestock, banking and credit, communication and transportation, retail prices, index of cost of medical care; production of sugar, condensed and evaporated milk, and alcoholic beverages; consumption of energy;

value of construction of private homes; public finance. A later edition of v. 1, *Comercio exterior, 1944-1946*, has since appeared.

52t. Puerto Rico. Department of Agriculture and Commerce. Bureau of Commerce. Annual book of statistics of Puerto Rico, fiscal year 1947-1948. San Juan, P. R. 293 p.
Data on area, geography, climatology, population, vital statistics, migration, education, health, justice and crime, labor statistics, social security, social assistance, accidents, agriculture, banking and credit, transportation, wholesale and retail prices and cost of living, foreign commerce, production of cigarettes, construction, public finance. Two later editions for fiscal years 1948-1949 and 1949-1950 have been issued, the latter by the Department of Agriculture and Commerce in collaboration with the Economic Development Administration.

52u. Venezuela. Dirección General de Estadística. Anuario estadístico de Venezuela, 1948. Caracas. xxxii, 559 p.
Data on area, geography, climatology, population, vital statistics, migration, education, health, justice and crime, labor accidents and indemnities, libraries, public spectacles, traffic accidents, fires, agriculture and livestock, fishery, forestry, banking and credit, communication and transportation, wholesale and retail prices, cost of living, foreign commerce, manufacturing, mining, energy, construction, public finance, and consumption. The volume for 1949 was published in 1952.

The countries not mentioned above failed to publish general statistical yearbooks in 1950. The latest information available for these countries follows:

Argentina. The first general statistical yearbook of Argentina since *Anuario geográfico argentino* (published in 1941 by the Comité Nacional de Geografía) and its *Suplemento 1942* (published in 1943) was published in 1951 by the Dirección General del Servicio Estadístico Nacional under the title *Anuario estadístico de la República Argentina. Tomo 1. Compendio.* It contains data pertaining to 1948.
Bolivia. No general statistical yearbook has been published since *Extracto estadístico de Bolivia* for 1936, issued by the Dirección General de Estadística. The most recent statistics are found in *Revista mensual* of the Dirección General de Estadística y Censos.
Costa Rica. The issue for 1949 of *Anuario de la Dirección General de Estadística* appeared in 1951.
Cuba. There has been no general statistical yearbook since *Anuario estadístico de la República de Cuba*, 1914, of which only the one issue was ever published.
Dominican Republic. The *Anuario estadístico de la República Dominicana*, v. 11-12, for 1946-1947, was published in 1951. V. 13-14, for 1948-1949, was published in 1952.
Ecuador. There has been no compilation of annual data since *Ecuador en cifras, 1938 a 1942*, published in 1944 by the Dirección General de Estadística. Current statistics appear in *El trimestre estadístico del Ecuador*, issued by the same agency.

Guatemala. The *Memoria de las labores del Poder Ejecutivo en el ramo de Hacienda y Crédito Público* . . . , issued by the Ministerio de Hacienda y Crédito Público, constitutes the general statistical yearbook of Guatemala. There has been none published since the *Memoria* for 1943 issued in 1945. Current statistical data are published in the *Boletín* of the Dirección General de Estadística.

Haiti. There is no general statistical yearbook. Current data are found in *Bulletin trimestriel de statistique,* published by the Institut Haïtien de Statistique.

Paraguay. The latest yearbook is *Anuario estadístico de la República del Paraguay, 1946-1947,* published in 1948 by the Dirección General de Estadística.

Peru. The issue of *Anuario estadístico del Perú* (published by the Dirección Nacional de Estadística) for 1948-1949 appeared in 1951.

Uruguay. The latest numbers of *Anuario estadístico de la República Oriental del Uruguay* (published by the Dirección General de Estadística) are: t. 49, v. 1, 1942, and t. 48, v. 2, 1941-1943.

1950 Census of the Americas

Lists of the available results of the hemispheral 1950 census of population, housing and agriculture in the Americas are prepared from time to time by the Inter American Statistical Institute, Washington, D. C. The following are the most recent:

Censuses of the American nations: scope of programs and selected information on population census results. March, 1953, release no. 1440A. 11 p. (Also issued in Spanish, release no. 1440B.)

Agricultural censuses of the American nations since 1946: selected information (*Estadística,* v. 11, no. 38, March, 1953, p. 27-29).

Illiteracy in the American nations: results of population censuses taken since 1946 (*Estadística,* v. 11, no. 40, Sept., 1953).

Housing censuses of the American nations since 1946: selected information (*Estadística,* v. 11, no. 40, Sept., 1953).

OTHER TOPICS

53. Argentina. Ministerio de Educación de la Nación. Primer ciclo anual de conferencias organizado por la Subsecretaría de Cultura de la Nación (Serie 3, no. 4). V. 1. Buenos Aires. 265 p.
Contains text of lectures as follows:
1. Óscar Ivanissevich. La medicina avanza constantemente invadiendo el campo de la cirugía.
2. Agustín Eduardo Riggi. La Antártida Argentina. Su geografía y su geología.
3. Tomás D. Bernard, hijo. La historiografía. La crónica. La historia erudita. El ensayo.
4. Carlos Astrada. Ideal humanista y formación política.

5. Carlos Vega. La música popular. Canciones y danzas nativas.
6. Ernesto Soto Avendaño. La escultura. Los iniciadores de la post-emancipación.
7. Juan H. Bossio. La divisa. Su sentido y su valor en el intercambio financiero.
8. Leopoldo Marechal. La poesía lírica. Lo autóctono y lo foráneo en su contenido esencial.
9. José Imbelloni. Antropología. Investigadores e investigaciones. Etapas de esta ciencia en nuestro país.
10. Rafael Jijena Sánchez. El folklore. Sus métodos y sus conquistas.
11. Carlos Suffern. La música. Su influencia en la formación estética nacional.

54. Boletín de filología. Montevideo, Instituto de Estudios Superiores, Sección de Filología y Fonética Experimental. T. 6, no. 43-45, marzo-sept. 272 p.
Entire issue is devoted to the Guaraní-Tupí language. It includes papers submitted to the Primer Congreso de la Lengua Guaraní-Tupí, held at Montevideo in February, 1950. This conference attracted *guaranistas* and *tupinólogos* from Argentina, Bolivia, Brazil, Paraguay, and Uruguay. [F. Aguilera]

55. Boletín de la Junta Auxiliar Jalisciense de la Sociedad Mexicana de Geografía y Estadística. Guadalajara, Jalisco, Mexico. T. 9, no. 1, mayo-junio-no. 3, sept.-dic.
These issues represent the beginning of a "new cycle" in the life of the publication, which has appeared irregularly since 1919. Contain articles and texts of documents dealing with local history, geography, and related subjects. [C. Shelby]

56. Dávila, Carlos. Nosotros, los de las Américas. Santiago, Editorial del Pacífico. 403 p.
A thought-provoking book on inter-American relations. Much of it is devoted to inter-American economic questions, and there is some consideration of Canada's place in the American system. English edition appeared in 1949. See *HLAS, no. 51, 1949, item 100.* [A. N. Christensen]

57. González, Juan Vicente. Historia y pasión de Venezuela. Selección, prólogo y notas de Arturo Uslar-Pietri. Washington, Unión Panamericana (Escritores de America). 102 p.
Well edited anthology of major items by an important Venezuelan *pensador* (1811-1866), little known beyond his national borders. As a journalist and historian González reflects many contemporary intellectual currents. Here included are parts of his biography of Ribas, his *Mesenianas* and sketches of or essays on Páez, Rojas, Pinto, Bello, Toro. Selected bibliography. [H. F. Cline]

58. Goytía, Víctor F. Unidad y poder en la paz de América. Prólogo de Gustavo Méndez P. Panamá, Hernández. 163 p., illus.
A discussion of the idea of geokinetics—the

dynamic relationship between geography and the human mind—and its application to the future of Panama and of America. [B. Wood]

59. Grossmann, Rudolf. Das geistige Ibero-Amerika von heute. Hamburg, Germany, H. H. Nolke, 1950? 31 p.

60. HISPANIC AMERICAN REPORT. A monthly report on developments in Spain, Portugal, and Latin America. Stanford University, Stanford, Calif. V. 3, no. 1, Jan.-no. 12, Dec.

61. Instituto Francés de Estudios Andinos. Lima. Travaux de l'Institut Français d'Études Andines. V. 1. Paris-Lima, 1949, i.e., 1950.
Divided into three sections: biology, geography, human sciences. Seems to deal almost exclusively with field results rather than historical items. [H. F. Cline]

62. INTER-AMERICAN COOPERATION. Cultural and economic aspects. Papers and discussions of the Inter-American Conferences held at the University of Delaware, June 28-29, 1949. Newark, Del., University of Delaware Press. vi, 91 p.
Addresses, with little discussion, about diverse topics in the fields of cultural and economic relations. [B. Wood]

63. Mayol, Josefina. Ex-libris cubanos. Habana, Úcar García. 195 p., illus.
Description, with illustrations, of bookplates found in public and private libraries of Cuba. Reprinted, with additions, from *Bol. asoc. cub. bibl.*, v. 1, no. 3-4, dic., 1949. [C. Shelby]

64. Mielche, Hakon. After you, Columbus. London, William Hodge. 273 p., illus.
Chatty story of a Norwegian's 1948 voyage in the track of Columbus. [W. Stewart]

65. Pan American Institute of Geography and History. Sección Nacional [de la República Argentina]. Catálogo de las obras exhibidas en la exposición de libros y materiales de geografía e historia americana. Buenos Aires. Unpaged.
The exhibition at the Institute's Fifth Congress (Santiago, Chile, 1950) included maps, books, and other materials of geographic and historic interest. [C. Shelby]

65a. ————. Sección Nacional [de la República Argentina]. Informe nacional de actividades . . . Comisiones de Cartografía . . . Geografía . . . Historia . . . para ser presentado a la Quinta Asamblea General que se celebrará en Santiago de Chile del 16 al 27 de octubre de 1950. Buenos Aires. 105 p., sketch maps, tables.
Useful list of achievements in recent years by the several commissions. It shows decided ac-

tivity in the several fields and indicates contributions of individuals. [G. M. McBride]

66. Pan American Union. Department of Cultural Affairs. Guía de instituciones, 2. parte. América Latina (Publ. de la Oficina de Ciencias Sociales, Guía de Instituciones, 2). Washington. vi, 126 p.
The term "social sciences" is broadly interpreted. List includes 396 institutions and societies, arranged by country, with address, date of founding, purpose, names of officers. Index of names. The first part covers the U. S. [C. Shelby]

67. Pilkington, Frederick. Daybreak in Jamaica. London, The Epworth Press. 220 p.
A description of the Methodist missionary effort in Jamaica with considerable historical and social data interwoven; interesting photographs. [H. F. Cline]

68. Pinto, Juan. Diccionario de la República Argentina; histórico, geográfico, biográfico, literario. Buenos Aires, Mundo Atlántico. 753 p.

69. Rodríguez Piñeres, Eduardo (ed.). Selección de escritos y discursos de Santiago Pérez. Bogotá, Academia Colombiana de Historia (v. 81). 347 p.
Speeches, articles, and essays on political and historical subjects by the liberal statesman Santiago Pérez (1830-1900), who became President of Colombia. [A. Flores]

70. Rosales, Hernán. Nicaragua. Película de una vida. México, Gráficos Guanajuato. 262 p.
Memoirs of a Nicaraguan now living in Mexico, journalistically portraying various aspects of life in his native country between 1893 and 1910. [F. Aguilera]

71. Rubio, Ángel. Panamá. Monumentos históricos y arqueológicos. México, Instituto Panamericano de Geografía e Historia, Comisión de Historia (Publ. 23). 121 p., illus.
Primarily of value for the fairly recent legislation protecting antiquities, but the bibliographies and the maps and other illustrations have direct value for the historian of Panama. [R. D. Hussey]

72. TRIMESTRAL. Santa Fe, Argentina, Instituto Social de la Universidad Nacional del Litoral. Año 1, no. 1, enero-no. 3, junio.
Devoted to university and regional cultural activities—literature, art, folklore. Contains original articles, notices of lectures, concerts and exhibitions, book reviews. Illustrated. [C. Shelby]

73. United Nations Educational, Scientific, and Cultural Organization. Centro de Cooperación Científica para

América Latina. Instituciones científicas y científicos latino-americanos. Argentina. V. 2. Montevideo. 103 p.
This list is one of a series for Latin America. For V. 1, see *HLAS, no. 15, 1949,* item 1018. [H. Benjamin]

74. ————. ————. Instituciones científicas y científicos latinoamericanos. Bolivia. V. 1. Montevideo. 99 p.

75. ————. ————. Instituciones científicas y científicos latinoamericanos. Brazil. V. 1-2. Montevideo. 139, 305 p.

76. ————. ————. Instituciones científicas y científicos lationamericanos. México. V. 1. Montevideo. 214 p.

77. **Valle-Arizpe, Artemio de.** En México y en otros siglos. 2. edición. Buenos Aires, Espasa-Calpe Argentina (Col. Austral). 143 p.
Popular edition of a collection of charming anecdotes by a gifted Mexican writer: "Why was Bolívar expelled from Mexico?"; legends and traditions about the cathedral of Mexico City; glimpses of the colonial period, etc. The first edition appeared in 1948. [A. Flores]

78. **Vasconcelos, José.** Discursos, 1920-1950. México, Botas. 318 p.
As the title indicates, these are speeches delivered on a variety of literary, educational, and political themes by an outstanding Mexican educator, a busy politician, and a Mexican *pensador.* For full meaning, they should be read in conjunction with appropriate sections of his four-volume autobiography, *Ulises criollo* (1935). The *discursos* are a minor contribution to material on the Mexican Revolution by one of its chief actors. [H. F. Cline]

79. **Von Hagen, Victor Wolfgang.** Frederick Catherwood Arch^t. Introduction by Aldous Huxley. New York, Oxford University Press. xix, 177 p., illus.
"Professionally speaking," says the introduction, "Catherwood belongs to a species—the artist—archaeologist—which is all but extinct." He is best known to Americanists for his drawings of Maya ruins, which illustrate John Lloyd Stephens' *Incidents of Travel in Central America, Chiapas, and Yucatán.* [Ed.]

80. **Yáñez, Agustín.** Don Justo Sierra. Su vida, sus ideas y su obra. México, Universidad Nacional Autónoma de México, Centro de Estudios Filosóficos. 218 p., illus.
The editor of the 15-volume edition of Maestro Justo Sierra's *Obras completas* has written a companion piece, with the avowed object of inducing further reading of Sierra's works. Illustrated with contemporary cartoons, this is a readable summary of many phases of the great educator, author, and politician. [H. F. Cline]

81. **Zubillaga Perera, Cecilio.** La voz del común. Selección, prólogo y notas de Guillermo Morón. Caracas, Ávila Gráfica (Col. Los Combatientes, 3). 305 p.
A book of selections from letters and other writings of a Venezuelan liberal thinker (1886 to 1948). [W. Stewart]

82. **Zuculin, Bruno.** America latina: Bolivia, Cile, Colombia, Ecuador, Paraguay, Perù, Uruguay. Firenze [Italy], Le Lingue Estere. 200 p., illus.
A former Italian consular officer and travel expert offers a survey of conditions in seven South American countries. His special concern is the immigration possibilities of each of them. [F. Aguilera]

ADDENDA

83. **Altamirano, Ignacio Manuel.** Obras completas. T. 1. Discursos. Edición, prólogo y notas de Agustín Yáñez. México, Secretaría de Educación Pública, Departamento de Divulgación, 1949. xvi, 313 p.
First of a projected 20-volume series that will bring together the many productions of this important Mexican figure, a full-blooded Indian. Politician and patriot, Altamirano is perhaps best remembered as a writer of the first rank. He took much care with his speeches, of which a good portion here appear. A well edited beginning of an important enterprise. [H. F. Cline]

84. **Barros y Arango, Francisco de los.** Los últimos escritores de Indias. Biobibliografía de españoles del siglo XIX que escribieron sobre países de fuera de Europa ó viajaron por ellas (*Bol. real soc. geog.,* t. 83, no. 7-12, julio-dic., 1947, p. 587-643; t. 84, no. 1-6, enero-junio, 1948, p. 205-230; t. 85, no. 1-3, enero-marzo, 1949, p. 33-102; no. 4-6, abril-junio, 1949, p. 191-223; no. 7-9, julio-sept., 1949, p. 398-427).
A valuable list, alphabetically arranged, of men mostly of the second half of the century, who wrote travel and scientific accounts, rather than history as such. Africa and the Philippines are included. [R. D. Hussey]

85. BOLETÍN DE LA BIBLIOTECA NACIONAL. Guatemala, Ministerio de Educación Pública. 4. época, año 1, no. 1, dic., 1948, i.e. 1949.
Publication is resumed with this number after a lapse of four years. Bibliography of Guatemalan publications appearing 1945-1948; brief essays on library science, art, literature, history. [C. Shelby]

86. **Congreso Internacional de Americanistas. XXVI, Sevilla, 1935.** Reseña y trabajos científicos. T. 1. Antecedentes y discursos generales del Congreso. Sección primera: arqueología y arte. Sección segunda: religión, geografía, antropología, etnografía y lingüística. T. 2. Sección ter-

cera: descubrimiento, conquista y colonización. Madrid, 1948. 488, 492 p., illus.

87. ESCRITORES VENEZOLANOS FALLECIDOS ENTRE 1942 Y 1947. Caracas, Biblioteca Nacional (Alcance al *Anuario Bibliográfico Venezolano*), 1948. 72 p.

Bibliography of sixty Venezuelan historians, composers, and writers who died between 1942 and 1947. [A. Flores]

88. Hanson, Earl Parker. New worlds emerging. New York, Duell, Sloan and Pearce, 1949. xix, 366 p.

An explorer-geographer's views and reports on a series of "underdeveloped" countries and areas from a quarter century of personal experiences on frontier assignments in the Arctic, Liberia, Alaska, and Latin America. Chapters 1-9 deal with tropical Latin America: the Amazon, Puerto Rico, and a general survey (ch. 8). [H. F. Cline]

89. Peraza Sarausa, Fermín. Bibliografía Martiana, 1948. Habana, Municipio de la Habana, Departamento de Educación

(Publ. de la Biblioteca Municipal de la Habana, serie C: Guías Bibliográficas, 16), 1949. 23 p.

Continuation.

90. PRIMERA EXPOSICIÓN BIBLIOGRÁFICA POTOSINA. San Luis Potosí, 2-18-IV, 1949. San Luis Potosí, Mexico, Editorial Universitaria, 1949. 48 p.

Catalogue of an exhibition of books from the University of San Luis Potosí library bearing the San Luis Potosí imprint, and beginning with the establishment of the first press in 1817. Also magazines, engravings, and lithographs, manuscripts and other memorabilia. [C. Shelby]

90a. Sabor Vila, Sara. La Biblioteca del Congreso de la Nación Argentina (*Rev. hist. amer.,* no. 27, junio, 1949, p. 77-99).

Includes a useful list of 35 publications issued between 1918 and 1935 under the auspices of the Argentine Congressional Library (Roberto Levillier, general editor). Based on documentation at the Archives of the Indies, they cover the bibliographical, historical, and legislative fields. [F. Aguilera]

Anthropology

GENERAL

91. Acosta Saignes, Miguel. Tlacaxipeualiztli. Un complejo meso-americano entre los caribes. Palabras iniciales de Domingo Casanovas. Caracas, Universidad Central, Facultad de Filosofía y Letras, Instituto de Antropología y Geografía. 48 p.

Links various traits of human sacrifice (such as flaying, the cardiac sacrifice, arrow "Morning Star" sacrifice, communion and ritual cannibalism, importance of the thigh) in a Tlacaxipeualiztli complex, distributed from the Andes to North America, with Carib occurrences midway between the former and Mexico. [R. Wauchope]

91a. Arnold, J. R., and **W. F. Libby.** Radiocarbon dates. Chicago, University of Chicago Institute of Nuclear Studies. 15 p.

Includes fourteen Middle American samples, chiefly from the Valley of Mexico and Monte Albán, as well as dates from Argentina and Peru. Several are surprising to most archaeologists. [R. Wauchope]

92. B.B.A.A. BOLETÍN BIBLIOGRÁFICO DE ANTROPOLOGÍA AMERICANA. México, Instituto Panamericano de Geografía e Historia, Comisión de Historia. V. 12, partes 1-2, enero-dic., 1949, i.e. 1950.

A comprehensive review of Americanist anthropology in 1949. It contains summaries of anthropological activities throughout the Americas and in Europe, bibliographical studies, summaries of the contents of anthropological journals from all over the world, a list of recently published books and monographs, reviews, obituaries, and bibliographies of anthropologists. The obituaries commemorate the following scholars: Leonard Bloomfield (with bibliography), John M. Cooper (with bibliography), Arthur Ramos (with bibliography), and Salvador Toscano. In an attempt to give fuller coverage, the B.B.A.A. appears this year for the first time in two parts. [J. H. Rowe]

93. Barreis, David A. Comments on South American-Archaic relations (*Amer. antiquity*, v. 16, no. 2, Oct., p. 165-166).

Comparison of implement types on the lower Paraná River with those of the Archaic in the Southeastern United States. There is enough similarity, according to the author, to suggest the existence of historical contacts at an early period. [I. Rouse]

94. Canals Frau, Salvador. Prehistoria de América. Buenos Aires, Editorial Sudamericana. 589 p., 12 plates, 118 figs.

Not a review of the data in this complex field but an attempt to explain American culture history in terms of succesive migrations from the Old World. The theory bears no relationship to archaeological and ethnographic fact. [J. H. Rowe]

95. Chard, Chester S. Pre-Columbian trade between North and South America (*Kroeber Anthropological Society Papers*, no. 1, Berkeley, California, p. 1-27).

Careful, critical review of historically recorded and archaeological evidence with the conclusion that, except for local trade in the circum-Caribbean area, there was very little of inter-continental scope and it appears to have been late. [D. B. Stout]

96. Comas, Juan. Bosquejo histórico de la antropología en México (*Rev. mex. estud. antrop.*, t. 11, p. 97-192).

Summary of institutional and individual activities. An important contribution to the history of the modern discipline. See item 434.

97. Curry, Hilda J. Negative painted pottery of Angel Mounds Site and its distribution in the New World (*Ind. univ. publ. anthrop. ling.*, Memoir 5, p. 33-90).

Angel Mounds, in Indiana, is the center for negative painted pottery in the United States. The author uses it as a base from which to discuss the distribution of negative painting throughout the New World. She adopts the theory that it spread northward from Central America or northern South America but notes that none has been found in the Antilles, which are on the direct route into the United States. 11 figs., 3 maps, 15 plates. [I. Rouse]

98. Disselhoff, Hans-Dietrich. Altamerikanische Kulturen (*Saeculum*, Band 1, Heft 1, p. 137-162).

Review of the status of prehistoric studies and new discoveries, concluding with biographical information on recently deceased Americanists: Walter Lehmann, Robert Lehmann-Nitsche, Konrad Theodor Preuss, Karl Sapper, Paul Schellhas, Emil Heinrich Snethlage, and Max Uhle. [R. Wauchope]

99. ————. Una exposición moderna de arte antiguo americano (*Rev. Indias,* Madrid, año 10, no. 41, julio-sept., p. 597-602).
Popular account of an exposition at Munich (May, 1950). See item 108. [J. H. Rowe]

100. **Driver, Harold E.,** and **S. H. Riesenberg.** Hoof rattles and girls' puberty rites in North and South America (*Ind. univ. publ. anthrop. ling.,* Memoir 4, p. 1-31).
Critical examination of the distribution evidence on these two culture traits. Though previously interpreted as being linked traits surviving from the earlier periods of New World culture history, the authors conclude that they are not in fact truly associated even though each may be of considerable antiquity. Four maps. [D. B. Stout]

101. **Gilmore, Raymond M.** Fauna and ethnozoology of South America (*Handbook of South American Indians,* v. 6, p. 345-465).
Discussion of the history and present character of the South American fauna with particular reference to the use the Indians have made of it. Both wild and domesticated animals are included. [I. Rouse]

102. **Johnson, Frederick.** American archaeology, 1949 (*Amer. jour. arch.,* v. 54, no. 3, July, p. 235-253).
A summary of achievements in American archaeology in 1949 compiled from information submitted by the editorial staff of *Amer. antiquity* and other sources. [J. H. Rowe]

103. **Krickeberg, Walter.** Ancient America. With photographs by K. Peter Karfeld. London, B. T. Batsford. 15 p. plus plates.
About half of the short introduction and fourteen of the forty-seven magnificent photographic reproductions in full color are of Middle American archaeological subjects. [R. Wauchope]

104. **Leach, Maria** (ed.). Dictionary of folklore, mythology and legend. V. 2, J-Z. New York, N. Y., Funk and Wagnalls. 1196 p.
The final volume of the *Dictionary.* See *HLAS, no. 15, 1949,* item 141. [D. B. Stout]

105. **Lévi-Strauss, Claude.** The use of wild plants in tropical South America (*Handbook of South American Indians,* v. 6, p. 465-487).
Believing that all Tropical Indians originally lived in the forest and used domesticated as well as wild plants, the author argues that those Indians who now subsist only on wild plants must have been forced to do so by being pushed into areas of savanna. He gives a comprehensive survey of the present use of wild trees and plants. [I. Rouse]

106. **Lussagnet, Suzanne.** Bibliographie américaniste (*Jour. soc. amér.,* n. s., t. 39, p. 273-367).
Covers mainly 1949, with some items for earlier years; contains titles for physical anthropology, ethnography, ethnology, linguistics, history, human geography, reprints and translations, bibliographies, and miscellaneous. [D. B. Stout]

107. **Morgan, Lewis Henry.** Montezuma's dinner. An essay on the tribal society of the North American Indians. New York, N. Y., Labor News Company. 79 p.
New edition of Morgan's well-known attack on the validity of concepts of "royalty" and "empire" applied to the social organization of the American Indians, particularly the Aztecs. [R. Wauchope]

108. **Munsing, Stefan P.** Frühe Kunst Amerikas. Aus den Sammlungen des Staatlichen Museums für Völkerkunde, München, und Privatbesitz. München [Germany]. Unpaged, 36 plates.
An exhibition catalogue. [J. H. Rowe]

109. **Pérez de Barradas, José.** Drogas ilusiónogenas de los indios americanos (*Antrop. etnol.,* t. 3, enero-dic., p. 9-107).
Thorough compilation of data on narcotics used by American Indians. [D. B. Stout]

110. ————. Los médicos brujos en los pueblos aborígenes americanos (*Bol. real acad. hist.,* t. 127, cuad. 1, julio-sept., p. 253-308).
A stimulating discussion which, however, loses some of its possible value by carelessness about the time element and about indicating sources. The bibliography (p. 305-306) is strongest for the colonial period. [R. D. Hussey]

111. **Pessoa, Marialice Moura.** O mito do dilúvio nas Américas. Estudo analítico e bibliográfico (*Rev. mus. paulista,* n.s., v. 4, p. 7-47).
Comprehensive distributional study with excellent bibliography. Text in Portuguese and English. [D. B. Stout]

111a. **Sauer, Carl O.** Cultivated plants of South and Central America (*Handbook of South American Indians,* v. 6, p. 487-543).
Very full summary of the domestication of plants by the Indians, including the few available archaeological data. Bitter manioc is found to be the staple food in Brazil, the Guianas, Venezuela, and the West Indies, in contrast to maize elsewhere, and it thus links together this entire region. [I. Rouse]

112. **Stern, Theodore.** The rubber-ball games of the Americas (*Mon. amer. ethnol. soc.,* no. 17).
A comprehensive study, based mainly on ethno-

logical data. The author tentatively concludes that the rubber-ball game had its origin in the cir-cum-Caribbean area, whence it spread north into Meso-America and south into the tropical for-ests of South America, a conclusion that is contrary to the archaeological evidence in the Antilles that the game is late there. [I. Rouse]

113. **Steward, Julian H.** (ed.). Handbook of South American Indians. V. 6. Physi-cal anthropology, linguistics and cultural geography of South American Indians. Washington, U. S. Government Printing Office (Smithsonian Institution, Bureau of American Ethnology, Bull. 143). 715 p., 3 figs., 18 maps, 47 plates.
The final volume of text in this monumental work, containing syntheses for the whole con-tinent of data on linguistics, and several aspects of physical anthropology, ethnozoology, ethno-botany, and geography. The individual contri-butions in this volume are reviewed in the ap-propriate sections, below. (See *HLAS, no. 12, 1946,* item 105; *no. 14, 1948,* item 113; and *no. 15, 1949,* item 145). [D. B. Stout]

114. **Zapater, Horacio A.** D'Orbigny y la clasificación del aborigen sudamericano

(*An. inst. étnico nac.,* t. 2, 1949, i.e. 1950, p. 111-130).
Reviews the contributions to racial classification of D'Orbigny, Imbelloni, and Canals Frau. Gives comparative maps and calls attention to the group "Huárpidos" described by Canals Frau in 1944. [T. D. Stewart]

ADDENDA

115. **Congreso Indigenista Interameri-cano.** Segundo, 24 de junio–4 de julio de 1949, Cusco, Perú. Anales. Lima, Lu-men, 1949. 389 p., illus.
Contains 198 pages of official proceedings and 181 pages of abstracts of papers presented to the Congress. [D. B. Stout]

116. **Zelinsky, Wilbur.** The historical geog-raphy of the Negro population of Latin America (*Jour. negro hist.,* v. 34, no. 2, April, 1949, p. 153-221).
A comprehensive summary presented in three sections: 1, the historical background of the Negro population in Latin America; 2, the dis-tribution of Negroes in Latin America; and 3, the Negro population geography of Cuba and Puerto Rico. Maps, tables. [D. B. Stout]

ARCHAEOLOGY: MIDDLE AMERICA

ROBERT WAUCHOPE

THE news of perhaps most general interest to Middle American archaeologists in 1950 was the release, by W. F. Libby of the Institute of Nuclear Studies, University of Chicago, of three lists of provisional dates for prehistoric specimens, as determined by the relatively new technique of radiocarbon (carbon 14) measurement. Among the specimens were several from representative periods of Middle America; their possible bearing on the correlation problem and on matters of culture growth and relationships with other areas makes this field of research a promising one for archaeology.

In past issues of this *Handbook* we have noted the growing trend toward syn-thesis and anthropological interpretation of archaeological data. The year 1950 saw no particular increase in the proportion of such publications, but among the relatively few of this type several are outstanding, notably J. E. S. Thompson's *Maya hierogly-phic writing: introduction* and Tatiana Proskouriakoff's *A study of Classic Maya sculpture,* both published by the Carnegie Institution of Washington. Among other monographs and papers I call attention to such studies as Carmen Cook's study of deities represented in Tlatelolco figurines (see item 217), Burland and Nowotny's study of figurine symbolism, José García Payón's paper on types and functions of ambassadors represented in Aztec codices, and two works on human sacrifice by Miguel Acosta S. and Laurette Séjourné, respectively. The various writings of A. V. Kidder and E. M. Shook continue to show a lively interest in the developmental and other broader aspects of their materials; my short study of pre-Classic ceramics devotes considerable space to speculations of this nature; S. K. Lothrop's latest book on Panama presents a picture of this region's role as a sort of refuge area of static culture during at least one epoch of prehistory; Virgilio Rodríguez Beteta offers hy-potheses regarding the abandonment of lowland Classic Maya sites.

Scholars treating of native sources and early documents again appear to be, as a group, the outstanding contributors of the year, in part because of the ethnic nature of their material and in part because of their consistent prolific production. At the risk of omitting important examples, I call attention to the impressive list of publications by Caso, Barlow, Berlin, Mengin, Hernández, Rodríguez, Jiménez Moreno, Recinos, Roys, J. E. S. Thompson, Makemson, Anderson and Dibble, Aguirre, and the Vargas Rea editions. And in this connection, Stephen F. de Borhegyi wrote an interesting report on his attempt to identify an historical site, Santiago de los Caballeros, by archaeological methods.

A few papers treat of ancient man in Middle America. Richard S. MacNeish's excavations in Tamaulipas went back to pluvial times there; Luis Aveleyra Arroyo de Anda assembled much of the material on ancient man in Mexico, and Howel Williams reexamined the subject of ancient footprints in Nicaragua. Important new data continue to come to light on the pre-Classic Formative stages; at least eight items in the lists that follow present materials and discussion of the Formative.

As for 1950 activities: In Mexico, the Instituto Nacional de Antropología e Historia and related institutions continued a widespread program, including excavation and reconnaissance at Tlatilco, Tula, Xochicalco, Tepantla, and Tajín, and at other sites in the states of Morelos, Veracruz, Guerrero, Puebla, Michoacán, and Oaxaca. Work was also resumed at Palenque, where important new discoveries in sculpture, hieroglyphic texts, and architectural features are being made. Frans Blom and Gertrude Duby continued exploration in the Lacandón forest and in the Comitán and Jatate river region.

The Carnegie Institution of Washington embarked upon its new project in Yucatán with mapping of the Mayapán site and environs by Morris R. Jones of the U. S. Geological Survey, and with the many administrative and routine activities accompanying a shift of staff and facilities from Guatemala. With A. V. Kidder's retirement as Chairman of the Division of Historical Research, H. E. D. Pollock became Director of the Institution's newly named Department of Archaeology.

A. V. Kidder, Gordon Ekholm, and Gustav Stromsvik cruised the coasts of Honduras and British Honduras, examining sites and collections on the cays and the mainland. In the spring, Linton Satterthwaite, Jr., University of Pennsylvania Museum, made valuable, and in some cases spectacular, discoveries at Cahal Pech, Caracol, and Benque Viejo, British Honduras. C. W. Meighen and J. A. Bennyhoff excavated during the summer at Potts Creek, north of Belize.

In the Central American highland, Carnegie Institution staff members were preparing final reports on their investigations of the past years; E. M. Shook managed, in addition, to continue some work in the earlier Formative remains of the region. Stephen F. de Borhegyi, with a grant from the Viking Fund, organized the study collections in the Guatemalan National Museum and made several comparative typological studies. The now excavated and restored site of Zaculeu, Guatemala, was turned over to the government by the United Fruit Company. In El Salvador, Stanley H. Boggs continued the government's long-term excavation, restoration, and museum building at Tazumal, San Andrés Campana, and Cihuatán.

The great importance of the southern Central American area in relationships between Middle and South America has long been realized, but so far archaeological work there is rare. In past issues of the *Handbook* we have noted the work of the Smithsonian Institution, the National Geographic Society, and the Peabody Museum of Harvard University. Doris Z. Stone was preparing a publication on Honduras.

GENERAL

117. Carter, George F. Plant evidence for early contacts with America (*Southw. jour. anthrop.,* v. 6, no. 2, p. 161-182).
Useful summary and review of the distribution and possible history of the sweet potato, *Hibiscus tiliaceus,* yam, bottle gourd, cotton, maize, and certain cosmopolitan weeds, concluding that frequent and long continued prehistoric contacts took place both ways across the Pacific, between Asia and the New World. "Surely our picture of the origin and growth of the Middle American high cultures can no longer rest on the easy assumption of absence of extensive and ancient Old World contacts."

118. Kidder, Alfred Vincent. Annual report of the Chairman of the Division of Historical Research (In *Carnegie Institution of Washington year book no. 49, 1949-1950,* p. 191-208).
Résumé of the Division's activities and future plans, with the following special reports on archaeology:
1. Morris R. Jones, *Survey and base map at Mayapán, Yucatán.*
2. Tatiana Proskouriakoff, *Middle American art.* Stages in the development of Classic Maya sculpture.
3. Edwin M. Shook. *Guatemala.* New discoveries of pre-Classic and Classic period materials in the highland and on the Pacific coastal plain.
4. Raymond H. Thompson. *Ceramic studies.* Representations of vessels in Maya codices, murals, sculptured stone, and painted pottery.
5. Howel Williams. *Nicaragua.* Further discussion of the antiquity of the El Cauce footprints.

119. Rainey, Froelich G. The Museum takes inventory (*Univ. mus. bull.,* v. 15, no. 4, p. 3-18).
Administrative report of University Museum activities, including the Middle American archaeological program and new discoveries at Cayo X, Caracol, and Benque Viejo, British Honduras. Illus.

120. Sterling, M. W. Sixty-sixth annual report of the Bureau of American Ethnology to the Secretary of the Smithsonian Institution. Washington, D. C., Government Printing Office. 34 p.
Report of activities for 1948-1949, including notices of the excavations at Utivé in the province of Panamá, at Barriles and Palo Santo in the province of Chiriquí, and at three sites between Santiago and Soná, Veraguas.

121. Vela, David. Noticias del maíz. Su origen, distribución y relaciones con las culturas indígenas de América (*Antrop. hist.,* v. 2, no. 1, enero, p. 30-42).
History of research on this topic, from about 1900 to 1943 (Mangelsdorf and Reeves).

ARCHAEOLOGY

122. Armillas, Pedro. Pozuelos en peñas en el estado de Guerrero (*Mesoamer. notes,* 2, p. 118-124).
Describes pitted rocks in Guerrero which author believes were mortars used in the preparation of food. Presents some brief comparative material, from Argentina and Chile to California and Kentucky.

123. ————. Teotihuacán, Tula y los toltecas. Las culturas post-arcaicas y pre-aztecas del centro de México. Excavaciones y estudios, 1922-1950 (*Runa,* v. 3, p. 37-70).
History of investigations at Teotihuacán and adjacent or related sites. Accounts of the most recent years of work are more detailed, and include excellent illustrations of newly discovered murals, façade friezes, and pottery. The last section presents the phase names for Teotihuacán cultural chronology and their characteristics.

124. ————. Visita a Copán (*Cuad. amer.,* año 9, v. 52, no. 4, julio-agosto, p. 143-152).
General description of Copán, particularly its stelae, relative to the general development of Maya prehistoric culture.

126. Aveleyra Arroyo de Anda, Luis. Prehistoria de México. Revisión de prehistoria mexicana. El hombre de Tepexpan y sus problemas. Prólogos de W. Du Solier y Pablo Martínez del Río. México, Ediciones Mexicanas. 167 p., plates, tables.
Description of the various discoveries related to the matter of pre-Formative period "ancient man" in Mexico.

128. Barberena, Santiago I. La gruta de Corinto (*An. mus. nac.,* t. 1, no. 3, julio-sept., p. 68-71).
Consists chiefly of the author's interpretation of the symbolic significance of the hands which appear as petroglyphs at this site in the Department of Morazán, El Salvador.

129. Bassetti, Gian. L'aquila e il serpente nell' America degli indios. Milano [Italy], Ceschina. 230 p.
Essentially a travel book, but with a considerable portion devoted to what the author himself calls a "superficial" account of the prehistory and archaeological remains of Mexico and Guatemala.

130. Bernal, Ignacio. Compendio de arte mesoamericano. México, Ediciones Mexicanas (Enciclopedia Mexicana de Arte, no. 7). 52 p.
One of the few books on Middle American art with an adequate introductory text on archaeology; in fact, one finds actually very little art analysis *per se.* Excellent photographic reproductions.

132. ————. The "Q complex" as seen from Monte Albán (Mesoamer. notes, 2, p. 87-93).
Resurrects the old "Q Complex" to check it against traits at Monte Albán and reaches, of course, a negative correlation, since the generalized traits are not examined for what is now known of their chronologically and geographically distinct sub-varieties.

133. Blom, Frans. A polychrome Maya plate from Quintana Roo (Notes middle amer. arch. ethnol., no. 98, Dec. 1, p. 81-84).
Description of a remarkable ceramic specimen, depicting two figures using blowguns, the Moan bird, and the Earth Monster.

134. Boggs, Stanley H. Archaeological excavations in El Salvador (For the Dean, p. 259-276).
History of investigations and summary descriptions of various archaeological sites in the Republic.

135. ————. "Olmec" pictographs in the Las Victorias Group, Chalchuapa Archaeological Zone, El Salvador (Notes middle amer. arch. ethnol., no. 99, Dec. 5, p. 85-92).
Group of pictographs with interesting resemblances to the style of certain La Venta sculptures.

136. Borhegyi, Stephen F. de. Estudio arqueológico en la falda norte del volcán de Agua (Antrop. hist., v. 2, no. 1, enero, p. 3-22).
Very interesting attempt to determine the site of Santiago de los Caballeros de Guatemala through archaeological methods. Included are ceramic studies and discussion of stone sculpture, the Pipil distribution, and other important problems.

137. ————. A group of jointed figurines in the Guatemala National Museum (Notes middle amer. arch. ethnol., no. 100, Dec. 30, p. 93-99).
Description, comparative data, and discussion of pre-Classic doll-like jointed figurines from Kaminaljuyu and Tazumal.

138. ————. Notas sobre sellos de barro existentes en el Museo Nacional de Arqueología y Etnología de Guatemala (Antrop. hist., v. 2, no. 2, junio, p. 16-26).
Classification of seal types, probably from the Alta Verapaz and from Salcajá, Quezaltenango. Although both cylindrical and flat types are believed to have been made in proto-Classic times, the latter survived to post-Classic times and Borhegyi favors priority of appearance by the cylindrical.

139. ————. Rim-head vessels and cone-shaped effigy prongs of the pre-Classic period at Kaminaljuyu, Guatemala (Notes middle amer. arch. ethnol., no. 97, July 28, p. 60-80).
Interesting new interpretations of the form and function of certain ceramic forms.

140. ————. Tlaloc effigy jar from the Guatemala National Museum (Notes middle amer. arch. ethnol., no. 96, July 10, p. 55-59).
Description and archaeological significance of an anthropomorphic jar believed to have come from Kaminaljuyu.

141. Burland, C. A., and Karl Anton Nowotny. Further comments on the wooden figurine from Mexico (Amer. antiquity, v. 15, no. 3, Jan., p. 251-252).
Suggestions regarding the symbolism and provenience of the Vienna Ethnographic Museum specimen described by Nowotny in 1949. See HLAS, no. 15, 1949, item 184.

143. Covarrubias, Miguel. Tlatilco. El arte y la cultura preclásica del Valle de México (Cuad. amer., año 9, v. 51, no. 3, mayo-junio, p. 149-162).
Sees Tlatilco as a Zacatenco site which later came under "Olmec"-style cultural influence. Believes that this Tlatilco-"Olmec" culture is expressed in the Chavín of Peru.

144. Du Solier, Wilfrido. La plástica en las cabecitas arcaicas del Valle de México y la Huaxteca. México, Ediciones Mexicanas (Enciclopedia Mexicana de Arte, no. 2). 45 p.
Detailed typological study leading to the conclusion that the Huaxteca Archaic developed independently of that in the Valley of Mexico.

146. Franco Torrijos, Enrique. Odisea en Bonampak. Narración inédita de una azarosa expedición. México, Artes Gráficas. 154 p.
Expedition adventures.

147. Galicia, Remberto I. Petrograbados en una gruta a orillas del Torola (An. mus. nac., t. 1, no. 2, abril-junio, p. 65-66).
Note on petroglyphs in the Department of Morazán, El Salvador.

148. García Payón, José. Castillo de Teayo. Noticias sobre su arqueología (Uni-Ver, año 2, t. 2, no. 16, abril, p. 155-164).
Tula-type sculpture (stalking jaguars) and certain clay figurines persuade the author that this region, of Huaxtec speech when conquered by the Texcocanas and Aztecs, was formerly a Toltec colony.

149. ————. Elementos físicos que contribuyeron a la gran inundación de la ciudad de México, en los años 1499 ó 1500 (Uni-Ver, año 2, t. 2, no. 20, agosto, p. 309-319).

Attributes the disastrous flooding of Tenochtitlán to Aztec defense works, which did not permit the flood waters to escape into the lake.

150. ————. "Palmas" y "hachas" votivas (*Uni-Ver,* año 2, t. 2, no. 14, feb., p. 63-66).
Further evidence on the nature of palmate stones and thin stone heads.

151. ————. Restos de una cultura prehistórica encontrados en la región de Zempoala, Ver. (*Uni-Ver,* año 2, t. 2, no. 15, marzo, p. 90-130).
Archaeological report on excavations at El Trapiche, Veracruz; the earliest remains correspond in time with Early Zacatenco, but the author sees the latter (and earliest Teotihuacan) as marginal expressions, possibly of an earlier and richer Formative culture on the Gulf. 26 figs.

152. ————. Las tumbas con mausoleos de la región central de Veracruz (*Uni-Ver,* año 2, t. 2, no. 13, enero, p. 7-23).
This article, with superior reproductions of the photographs, appeared in English translation in 1945 in the Carnegie Institution's *Notes on Middle American Archaeology and Ethnology,* no. 59. See *HLAS, no. 11, 1945,* item 185.

153. Gifford, E. W. Surface archaeology of Ixtlán del Río, Nayarit (*Univ. Calif. publ. amer. arch. ethnol.,* v. 43, no. 2, p. 183-302).
Report on a surface reconnaissance; sets up three chronological periods corresponding in general to the previously known Early Chametla through Late Culiacán sequences. 50 figs.

154. González, Darío. Ruinas de Tehuacán (*An. mus. nac.,* t. 1, no. 2, abril-junio, p. 60-63).
Brief description of surface remains at Tehuacán. Says that pottery is of Mexican style.

155. Healey, Giles Greville. The Lacanja valley (*Archaeology,* v. 3, no. 1, spring, p. 12-15).
Excellent photographs of additional unpublished ruins in the Lacandón country of Chiapas.

156. Hewes, Gordon W. Some Lake Cuitzeo sites, Michoacán, Mexico (*Masterkey,* v. 24, no. 6, Nov.-Dec., p. 179-182).
Results of a reconnaissance on the shoreline of Lago de Cuitzeo, with indications that remains of early man may underlie Early Formative there.

157. Irigoyen, Renán. Los mayas y el henequén. Mérida, Mexico (Publ. de los Henequeneros de Yucatán). 24 p.
Reprinted from *Rev. estud. yucatecos,* no. 3, dic., 1949.

158. Jakeman, M. Wells. An expedition to Central America (*Impr. era,* v. 53, no. 2, Feb., p. 112-114, 144-147).
Popular account of itinerary, experiences, and results of an expedition to the Xicalango district of western Campeche. Notes a large earthen embankment, possibly a dyke or fortification, at Aguacatal. The author believes that the main period at Aguacatal is pre-Classic.

159. Jennings, Jesse D. On the validity of Tepexpan Man (*Bull. Texas arch. paleon. soc.,* v. 21, p. 105-110).
Critical examination of the methodology and recording of the Tepexpan Man and related discoveries.

160. Kidder, A. V. Certain archaeological specimens from Guatemala. II (*Notes middle amer. arch. ethnol.,* no. 95, July 6, p. 46-54).
Continuation of a useful series of descriptions of incidental finds, purchases, and gifts to the Guatemala National Museum through the Carnegie Institution.

161. Kirchhoff, Paul. The Mexican calendar and the founding of Tenochtitlan-Tlatelolco (*Trans. New York acad. sci.,* ser. 2, v. 12, no. 4, Feb., p. 126-132).
Examines the year counts of various native sources relative to the founding of the twin cities, equating Mexican dates with the Christian calendar, and selects 1369-1370 as the most probable date. (The traditional date has been 1325.)

162. Krickeberg, Walter. Bauform und Weltbild im alten Mexico (In *Mythe, Mensch und Umwelt,* Adolf Ellegard Jensen [ed.], p. 294-333, Bamberg, Germany, St. Otto-Verlag).
Religious and mythological symbolism in the form and decoration of ancient architectural forms, particularly the stepped or terraced pyramid. (The book cited is also v. 4 of *Paideuma.*)

163. ————. Olmeken und Tolteken: nach den jüngsten Ergebnissen der mexikanischen Archäologie. I (*Zeit. ethnol.,* Band 75, p. 13-35).
Reviews in considerable detail all the archaeological data related to the so-called Olmec style, and various aspects of the Olmec chronological position and relationships. Makes the results of the Tuxtla Gutiérrez "Mesa Redonda" available for the first time in German, with summaries of the discoveries of Olmec style from Central Mexico to the Pacific Coast of Guatemala; suggests possible relationships in South America (San Agustín and Chavín).

164. Lardé, Jorge. Cronología arqueológica de El Salvador (*An. mus. nac.,* t. 1, no. 3, julio-sept., p. 72-79).
Discussion of the antiquity of remains covered by volcanic deposits in the valley of San Salvador Cuzcatlán.

165. ————. El Salvador antiguo. San Salvador, Ministerio de Cultura (Biblioteca del Pueblo, 10). 158 p.

Collection of articles, including seven on archaeology.

166. ————. Índice provisional de los lugares del territorio salvadoreño en donde se encuentran ruinas u otros objetos de interés arqueológico (*An. mus. nac.*, t. 1, no. 1, p. 44-50).
Location of 132 archaeological sites, listed alphabetically.

167. **Lothrop, Samuel Kirkland.** Archaeology of Southern Veraguas, Panama. With appendices by W. C. Root, Eleanor B. Adams, and Doris Stone (*Mem. Peabody mus. arch. ethnol.*, v. 9, no. 3, 116 p.).
Introduction contains extensive historical and ethnological background material. Main report treats of the archaeological remains, stone artifacts, pottery, and metal work, with exhaustive comparative material and a thoughtful discussion of intercontinental contacts and trade. Concludes that during much of the prehistoric period Panama was a refuge area of static cultures. 150 figs., 10 tables.

168. **MacNeish, Richard S.** A synopsis of the archaeological sequence in the Sierra de Tamaulipas (*Rev. mex. estud. antrop.*, t. 11, p. 79-86).
Sequence of cultures in Tamaulipas cave excavations, from possibly Late Pluvial times to 1785. Chart suggests correlation of chronologies in Valley of Mexico, Tampico-Pánuco, Sierra de Tamaulipas, northern Tamaulipas coastal plain, and the Río Grande Delta.

170. **Médioni, Gilbert.** Art maya du Mexique et du Guatémala. Ancien Empire. Paris, Éditions de la Cyme. 113 p.
Numerous and for the most part excellent photographic reproductions, chiefly of Maya sculpture; the eight-page introduction is badly out of date, based on the Old Empire-New Empire concept, the teocentli origin of corn agriculture, and the *Popol Vuh* version of ethnic origins. Appendices summarize various aspects of Maya culture, following Morley.

171. **Noguera, Eduardo.** El horizonte tolteca-chichimeca. México, Ediciones Mexicanas (Enciclopedia Mexicana de Arte, no. 4). 48 p.
Cultural manifestations in Cholula, Tizatlán, Tula, Tenayuca, Calixtlahuaca, Totonacapan, Yucatán, Mixteca Puebla, and northwestern Mexico are briefly summarized. Well illustrated, sometimes in color.

172. **Paz, J. Rufino.** La gruta de Corinto (*An. mus. nac.*, t. 1, no. 2, abril-junio, p. 64).
Brief notes on surface remains in the Department of Morazán, El Salvador.

173. **Piña Chan, Román.** Estratigrafía en los terrenos adyacentes a la catedral metropolitana (*Mem. acad. mex. hist.*, t. 9, no. 2, abril-junio, p. 199-224).
Stratigraphy of Mixteca-Puebla wares at Tlatelolco.

174. **Proskouriakoff, Tatiana.** A study of Classic Maya sculpture. Washington, Carnegie Institution of Washington (Publ. 593). 209 p., 111 figs.
Establishes style characteristics, based on epigraphy and comparative sculptural studies from all Classic Maya sites. An important monograph, revealing "a certain coherence of development, perhaps not entirely free of outside influences but surely selective of them. . . . This development has an inherently dramatic structure, in which the tendency to more complex organization of the pattern is followed by the opposite trend of disintegration."

175. **Rodríguez Beteta, Virgilio.** La caída y desaparición del "Primer Imperio" maya (*Antrop. hist.*, v. 2, no. 2, junio, p. 54-67).
Reviews all previous hypotheses and presents a new one: that deforestation for agriculture altered the rainfall, and that the droughts of deforested areas on the one hand, and the torrential (and destructive) rains of the untouched areas on the other, so upset weather predictions and agricultural instructions by the priests that socio-political upheavals resulted.

176. **Ruppert, Karl.** Gallery-patio type structures at Chichen Itza (*For the Dean*, p. 249-259).
Description and distribution of an architectural type. Five pages of floor plans.

177. **Satterthwaite, Linton, Jr.** Plastic art on a Maya palace (*Archaeology*, v. 3, no. 4, winter, p. 215-222).
Photographs and preliminary description of important new relief sculptures in British Honduras.

178. ————. Reconnaissance in British Honduras (*Univ. mus. bull.*, v. 16, no. 1, p. 21-36).
Summary and excellent photographs of the important discoveries at Cahal Pech, Xunan Tunich (Benque Viejo), and Caracol.

180. **Shook, Edwin M.** Tiquisate UFERS scoop archaeological world. Find ruined city on farm (*Unifruitco*, Aug., p. 62-63).
Account of discoveries and excavations at Sin Cabezas, a Late Classic site in the Tiquisate area of western Guatemala. Illus.

181. ————, and **Robert E. Smith.** Descubrimientos arqueológicos en Poptún (*Antrop. hist.*, v. 2, no. 2, junio, p. 3-15).
Results of a four-day visit, the architecture described by Shook and the pottery and artifacts by Smith. Poptún itself is a Late Classic period ruin, but the general region was occupied in Formative period (Chicanel) times. Copper rattles from La Hortaliza suggest also a post-Classic occupation.

182. **Smith, A. Ledyard.** Uaxactún, Guatemala. Excavations of 1931-1937. Washington, Carnegie Institution of Washington (Publ. 588), xii, 108 p., 143 figs.
Beautifully illustrated and concisely written report of the important Uaxactún excavations, tracing the growth of the city, the evolution of stone-vaulted structures over a period of six hundred years, and related ceramic, epigraphic, burial, and cache information. Excellent introduction by A. V. Kidder.

183. **Stromsvik, Gustavo.** Las ruinas de Asunción Mita. Informe de su reconocimiento (*Antrop. hist.*, v. 2, no. 1, enero, p. 23-29).
Preliminary survey occasioned by destruction in 1949 of important units of this ruin by the new Roosevelt highway. Records details of structures already damaged or threatened, with notes on pottery and other artifacts, indicating occupation in Formative, Classic, and proto-historic periods.

184. **Von Hagen, Victor Wolfgang.** The forgotten Catherwood (*Art news*, v. 48, no. 10, Feb., p. 30-32, 62-63).
Modern photographs of Maya ruins compared with Catherwood's drawings of the 1840's, with text extracts from Von Hagen's book on Catherwood. See item 79.

185. **West, Robert C., and Pedro Armillas.** Las chinampas de México (*Cuad. amer.*, año 9, v. 50, no. 2, marzo-abril, p. 165-182).
The so-called "floating gardens" of Mexico, including their pre-Conquest history.

NATIVE SOURCES, EARLY HISTORY, AND EPIGRAPHY

187. ANALES DE TLALTILOLCO. Número uno. Anónimo indígena, traducido al español por Porfirio Aguirre. México, Vargas Rea (Col. Amatlacuilotl). 46 p.
Spanish and Nahuatl in parallel columns.

188. **Barlow, Robert H.** Codices and Mesoamerican picture writing. A note on civil books (*Mesoamer. notes*, 2, p. 107-117).
Brief and elementary classification of pictorial manuscripts, apparently written for the beginning student.

189. **Berlin, Heinrich.** La historia de los Xpantzay (*Antrop. hist.*, v. 2, no. 2, junio, p. 40-53).
Documents relating to a noble Cakchiquel family of Tecpán, parts of which contain genealogical and geographical (place names) data of interest comparable to those of the *Annals of the Cakchiquels*, the Totonicapán *Título*, and the *Popol Vuh*. The translation is by Adrián Recinos. See item 205.

190. **Carrasco Pizana, Pedro.** Los otomíes. Cultura e historia prehispánicas de los pueblos mesoamericanos de habla otomiana. México, Instituto de Historia. 355 p., illus.
History, economy and material culture, social organization, religion, and geographical distribution of Otomí-speakers in prehistoric times. A most useful reference book, well indexed and with many illustrations from codices.

191. **Caso, Alfonso.** De la necesidad de la crítica histórica para interpretar los eclipses de sol en los manuscritos mexicanos (*Rev. mex. estud. antrop.*, t. 11, p. 15-22).
Reply to Weitzel's article on the correlation of Aztec and Christian calendars as tested by eclipse data in codices. See item 219.

192. ———. Explicación del reverso del Codex Vindobonensis (*Mem. col. nac.*, t. 5, no. 5, p. 9-46).
Explanation and commentary for the thirteen pages that contain illustrations. An excellent summary of the historical data on the first three dynasties of Tilantongo, corroborating similar sections of the Codices Bodley and Nuttall. Contains photographic reproductions of the 1929 facsimile edition and two useful tables of genealogy and chronology.

193. **Chimalpain, Domingo.** Diferentes historias originales de los reynos de Culhuacan y México, y de otras provincias. Übersetzt und erläutert von Ernst Mengin. Hamburg, Germany, Museum für Völkerkunde in Hamburg (Mitteilungen, 22). 47 p.
Transcription and German translation of the Chimalpain Nahuatl manuscript in the Bibliothèque Nationale, Paris, with an historical and bibliographical introduction and a useful index of person, place, and ethnic names.

194. **Dávila Garibi, José Ignacio.** Los cazcanes. México, Cultura. 40 p.
Protohistory and cultural-linguistic relationships of the Cazcanes of Jalisco and Zacatecas.

195. **Du Solier, Wilfrido.** Indumentaria antigua mexicana. Prólogo de Manuel Toussaint. México, Ediciones Mexicanas. 110 p., illus.
Thirty-two excellent illustrations, in color, of prehistoric Middle American costumes, based on information in chronicles, codices, and mural and ceramic paintings. Full explanatory notes with detailed drawings. Issued (1950) in English by the same publisher under the title *Ancient Mexican costumes*.

196. **García Payón, José.** De la calidad y deberes de los embajadores entre los aztecas (*Uni-Ver*, año 2, t. 2, no. 21, sept., p. 357-368).
Assembles data on the functions of Aztec ambassadors, from codices and other early accounts.

197. HISTORIA CHICHIMECA. Manuscrito copiado por F. Galicia Chimalpopoca y

traducido al castellano. México, Vargas Rea (Col. Amatlacuilotl). 53 p.
Spanish and Nahuatl in parallel columns, with glyphs reproduced in color.

198. Hunter, Milton R., and Thomas Stuart Ferguson. Ancient America and the Book of Mormon. Oakland, California, Kolob Book Co. 450 p.
Correlation of passages from *The Book of Mormon* with extracts from the works of Ixtlilxochitl, the *Popol Vuh*, the *Título de Totonicapán*, and others. Postulates three groups of colonizers migrating from the Fertile Crescent to Middle America, and identifies Quetzalcoatl as the resurrected Messiah.

199. Jiménez Moreno, Wigberto. The importance of Xaltocan in the ancient history of Mexico (*Mesoamer. notes*, 2, p. 133-138).
Brief outline of Toltec, Chichimec, and Mexica history and Xaltocan's place in this story, with notes on the Xaltocan dynasty and sources for its history.

200. Lens, Hans. El papel indígena mexicano. Historia y supervivencia. México, Cultura, 1948, i.e. 1950. 281 p., figs., maps, plates.
De luxe edition, with numerous illustrations and eleven actual samples of ancient Mexican papers. Discusses the technical, religious, and social aspects of paper manufacture.

202. Makemson, Maud W. The Katun calendar of the *Book of Tizimin* (*Amer. antiquity*, v. 16, no. 2, Oct., p. 166-168).
Data supporting the author's contention that the Katun 5 Ahau which began in 1594 1 Muluc (*Book of Tizimin*) was not fictitious, and that it coincides with a certain Katun 5 Ahau of the Makemson Correlation.

204. Melgarejo Vivanco, José Luis. Historia de Veracruz. Época prehispánica. T. 1. Jalapa-Enríquez, Mexico, Talleres Gráficos del Gobierno de Veracruz, 1949, i.e. 1950. 518 p., illus., maps.
Profusely illustrated book assembling largely documentary history of various Indian groups and data on subject categories (agriculture, houses, food, clothing, etc.) gleaned from archaeological, historical, and modern ethnological sources. Excellent color plates; poor halftones.

205. MEMORIAL DE SOLOLÁ. ANALES DE LOS CAKCHIQUELES. Traducción directa del original, introducción y notas de Adrián Recinos. TÍTULO DE LOS SEÑORES DE TOTONICAPÁN. Traducción del original quiché por el P. Dionisio José Chonay; introducción y notas de Adrián Recinos. México, Fondo de Cultura Económica (Biblioteca Americana, Serie de Literatura Indígena). 303 p.

Excellent translations of two famous Guatemala highland Indian records, one by the distinguished scholar and diplomat Adrián Recinos, admired for his earlier *Popol Vuh;* the other by Dionisio José Chonay.

206. MORLEYANA. A collection of writings in memoriam Sylvanus Griswold Morley, 1883-1948. Santa Fe, N. Mex., The School of American Research and the Museum of New Mexico. 268 p.
Collection of informally written anecdotes, bibliography, and other records from the unusually rich life of this famous authority on the Maya. Included is Morley's own report on the Guatemala-British Honduras border skirmishing in 1916, in which Dr. Lafleur and the guide of a Morley-Carpenter expedition were killed.

207. POPOL VUH. The sacred book of the ancient Quiché Maya. English version by Delia Goetz and Sylvanus G. Morley, from the Spanish translation by Adrián Recinos. Norman, Okla., University of Oklahoma Press (The Civilization of the American Indian). xix, 267 p.
First English translation of this important native document, based on what is by far the best translation to date, that of Recinos, whose introduction is exhaustive and scholarly.

208. QUALI AMATL. CHICOME CALLI. CONQUISTA DE TLALTILOLCO. Anónimo nahuatl, traducido al castellano por Porfirio Aguirre. México, Vargas Rea (Col. Amatlacuilotl). 42 p.
Spanish and Nahuatl in parallel columns; glyphs are illustrated in color.

209. Roys, Ralph L. Guía para el Códice Pérez. Traducción de Gustavo Vega Ibarra. México, Ediciones de la Liga de Acción Social. 14 p.
Translated extract from Carnegie Institution of Washington's *Contributions to American Anthropology and History*, no. 49 (see HLAS, no. 15, 1949, item 223), with additional notes by the translator of the codex, Ermilo Solís Alcalá.

210. Rubio, Ángel. Panamá. Monumentos históricos y arqueológicos. México, Instituto Panamericano de Geografía e Historia, Comisión de Historia (Publ. no. 109, Monumentos Históricos y Arqueológicos, 1). 121 p.
Chapter 3 reviews the history of archaeological research in Panama.

211. Sahagún, Bernardino de. General history of the things of New Spain. Florentine Codex. Book I, The Gods. Translated from the Aztec into English, with notes and illustrations, by Arthur J. O. Anderson and Charles E. Dibble. Santa Fe, N. Mex., School of American Research (Monograph no. 14, part 2).

The first of the Sahagún manuscripts translated from the Aztec into English by Anderson and Dibble, with parallel passages in double columns and reproductions of the original illustrations.

212. —————— (comp.). Primeros memoriales de Tepeopulco. Anónimos indígenas. Traducidos del nahuatl al español por Porfirio Aguirre. Partes 1-3. México, Vargas Rea (Col. Amatlacuilotl). Unpaged.
Reproductions, both black-and-white and in colors, with Spanish and Nahuatl text in parallel columns.

214. Séjourné, Laurette. Ensayo sobre el sacrificio humano (Cuad. amer., año 9, v. 53, no. 5, sept.-oct., p. 165-171).
Aztec human sacrifice viewed in the light of native mythology and native concepts of social structure.

215. Thompson, J. Eric S.   Maya hieroglyphic writing. Introduction. Washington, Carnegie Institution of Washington (Publ. 589). xviii, 347 p., 64 figs., 22 tables.
The importance of this definitive "introduction" to Maya hieroglyphic writing cannot be over-emphasized. It is the best and most authoritative treatment yet published, with new approaches and new interpretations too numerous to mention here. After an excellent outline of Maya civilization and history and the sources of glyphic material, there are twelve chapters and five appendices treating of the principles of Maya glyphic writing, the 260-day cycle and 365-day year, methods of recording numbers, the Long Count, distance numbers, period endings, anniversaries, and katun counts, ritualistic and astronomical cycles, the moon, soulless mechanisms and magical formulae, aids to decipherment, interpretation, divinatory almanacs, the correlation problem, determinants, and many other subjects. A monumental publication.

216. ——————. Rubber in America before 1492. Boston, Mass., Godfrey L. Cabot, Inc. 9 p.
Brief account of the production and uses of rubber in prehistoric America.

217. TLATELOLCO A TRAVÉS DE LOS TIEMPOS. XI (Mem. acad. mex. hist., t. 9, no. 1, 118 p.).
Eleventh group of a long series of articles by historians, linguists, and anthropologists concentrating on a single locality in Mexico. Contains the following:
1. Antonieta Espejo. Resumen de los trabajos arqueológicos. Includes a map of the site and four plates.
2. James B. Griffin and Antonieta Espejo. La alfarería correspondiente al último período de ocupación nahua del Valle de México: II. Description, discussion, and bibliography of four Lago de Texcoco pottery types.
3. Román Piña Chan. Estratigrafía en los terrenos adyacentes a la Catedral Metropolitana. Description and discussion of pottery types by strata.

4. Carmen Cook. Figurillas de barro de Santiago Tlatelolco. Figurines from the excavations, including a discussion of the identity of various deities represented.
5. Rosaura Hernández Rodríguez. Documentos relacionados con San Bartolomé Tlatelolco. 16th- and early 17th-century documents relative to the colonization of the Valle de Toluca by the Mexica Axayacatl, father of Moctezuma II, and to the foundation of San Miguel Tlatelolco.

218. Weber, Richard. Neue Untersuchungen zum Korrelationsproblem der Mayazeitrechnung (Zeit. ethnol., Band 75, p. 90-102).
A lengthy summary in German of the Makemson correlation as presented in The Maya correlation problem. See HLAS, no. 12, 1946, item 182.

219. Weitzel, R. Boland. Mexican manuscripts and solar eclipses (Rev. mex. estud. antrop., t. 11, p. 5-13).
Tests the Spinden, Caso, and "Revised" correlations of Aztec and European calendars by means of solar eclipse data in three Nahuatl codices. See also item 191.

ADDENDA

219a. Aveleyra Arroyo de Anda, Luis. Sobre dos notables puntas de proyectil de la cuenca de México (Mex. antiguo, t. 7, dic., 1949, p. 514-521).
Description and speculations concerning the age and relationships of two pressure-flaked obsidian points from the vicinity of Chalco and Tepechpan, respectively; they have Yuma-like and Folsom-Clovis-like features.

219b. Bernal, Ignacio. Distribución geográfica de las culturas de Monte Albán (Mex. antiguo, t. 7, dic., 1949, p. 209-216).
Series of maps showing the distribution of Monte Albán pottery over four main periods. The first shows strong Gulf Coast and Olmec connections, the second Mayance, the third Teotihuacán and IIIb and IV native Zapotec.

219c. Caso, Alfonso. Una urna con el dios mariposa (Mex. antiguo, t. 7, dic., 1949, p. 78-95).
Excellent analysis of the butterfly god motif in Middle America, with particular attention to a specimen from Atlatlauca, Mexico.

219d. Franco C., José Luis. Algunos problemas relativos a la cerámica azteca (Mex. antiguo, t. 7, dic., 1949, p. 162-208).
Classification of Aztec pottery, its chronological distribution, and critical examination of other classifications.

220. Lehmann, Walter. Sterbende Götter und christliche Heilsbotschaft. Stuttgart, W. Kohlhammer Verlag (Quellenwerke zur alten Geschichte Amerikas aufgezeich-

net in den Sprachen der Eingeborenen, III), 1949. 134 p.

A posthumous work, the third in this series of German translations of important Indian source materials. Includes, in an introduction, speculations on absolute dating, trans-Pacific prehistoric contacts, and conditions prior to and just after the Spanish conquest of this region. Since it was written many years ago, this work contains some now out-of-date hypotheses, but in several places it is curiously prophetic.

220a. Maldonado-Koerdell, Manuel, and Luis Aveleyra Arroyo de Anda. Nota preliminar sobre dos artefactos del pleistoceno superior hallados en la región de Tequixquiac, México (*Mex. antiguo,* t. 7, dic., 1949, p. 155-161).

Bone point, possibly of human workmanship, from the Upper Becerra and a flint point of certain human manufacture from the underlying Upper Pleistocene conglomerate, said to have been found *in situ.*

220b. Mateos, Salvador. Códice Valeriano (*Mex. antiguo,* t. 7, dic., 1949, p. 315-321).

Post-Conquest (1574) Nahuatl codex fragment.

220c. Schulz, R. P. C. Los llamados números de serpiente del Código Maya de Dresde y el punto cero de la cuenta larga maya (*Mex. antiguo,* t. 7, dic., 1949, p. 322-342).

Interpretation of the calendrical glyphs associated with the winding serpents in the Dresden Codex.

220d. Seler-Sachs, Caecilie. Fragmentos de vasijas de barro con decoración en relieve (*Mex. antiguo,* t. 7, dic., 1949, p. 96-118).

Specimens described are chiefly from Puebla, Veracruz, and Oaxaca.

220e. Winning, Hasso von. Shell designs on Teotihuacán pottery (*Mex. antiguo,* t. 7, dic., 1949, p. 126-153).

Describes Classic and post-Classic Teotihuacán techniques of representing shells on pottery. They probably symbolized water and possibly were part of the ritual in which gods were petitioned for water.

ARCHAEOLOGY: WEST INDIES, VENEZUELA, AND BRAZIL

IRVING ROUSE

FOUR 1950 publications reflect continued interest in the problem of prehistoric cultural relationships among North, Central, and South America, although without positive results so far as the area covered here is concerned. Theodore Stern's study of the distribution of the rubber-ball game (item 112) and Hilda J. Curry's of negative painted pottery (item 97) both indicate contact among the three Americas, but via the Isthmus of Panama rather than the Antilles.

Excavation during the year was largely confined to Cuba and Venezuela. Members of the Grupo Guamá in Habana dug several Ciboney (non-ceramic) sites near Cienfuegos in western Cuba. The Grupo Caonabo of Morón worked at both Ciboney and sub-Taino (ceramic) sites in central Cuba, while in the east, Orencio Miguel Alonso trenched a large midden in the sub-Taino site of Potrero del Mango near Banes. None of the results of this work is out of the ordinary; and they are overshadowed in importance by the announcement of previous finds by Dr. Bernardo Utset in Ciboney shell heaps near Manzanillo, which give indications of contact with both sub-Taino and Spanish cultures and thereby open up the possibility of establishing a Ciboney chronology by means of the direct historical approach.

Further evidence was obtained in Cuba of the association of the ground sloth with both Ciboney and sub-Taino cultures; this was of interest because the sloth had become extinct in the time of Columbus. It is to be hoped that, as more attention is paid to chronology in Cuba, it will be possible to determine at what point during the archaeological sequence the extinction took place.

In Venezuela, Prof. J. M. Cruxent, Director of the Museo de Ciencias Naturales at Caracas, and Irving Rouse, of the Yale Peabody Museum, undertook excavations at Manicuare on the Peninsula of Araya, Barrancas on the lower Orinoco, and Quibor in the state of Lara. The Manicuare excavations revealed the first non-ceramic culture to be found archaeologically in northern South America, one which has interesting similarities with Ciboney culture in Cuba. On the Orinoco, an early, Saladero style of pottery was discovered underlying pottery of the classic Barrancas style. There is reason to believe that this early pottery is ancestral to the first ceramics in the Antilles and hence may mark the northward spread of the Arawak Indians, who seem to have introduced pottery and agriculture into the Antilles.

Prof. Cruxent and Dr. León Croizat also made an archaeological survey of the llanos south of Valle de Pascua, and Alfredo Boulton, of the Museo de Ciencias Naturales, explored a cave site on the Río Parguaza in Venezuelan Guiana. Drs. Eduardo Fleury and Hans Tanner collected artifacts on the Guajira Peninsula and visited a number of caves with paintings on the walls. An expedition which attracted great popular interest among Venezuelans was one from the Universidad Central in Caracas, under the direction of Miguel Acosta Saignes, which succeeded in locating the site of the colonial city of Nueva Cádiz on the island of Cubagua near the Peninsula of Araya.

So far as is known, no significant projects of excavation or survey were initiated during the year in either the Guianas or Brazil. H. V. Walter, however, continued his survey of pre-ceramic occupations in the caves of the Lagoa Santa Region of Minas Gerais.

In September, 1950 the Junta Nacional de Arqueología of Cuba sponsored a Round Table in Habana, which was attended by archaeologists from all parts of the region under consideration and from the western part of the Caribbean as well. It was decided to set up an Association of Caribbean Archaeologists with J. M. Cruxent of Venezuela as President, Oswaldo Morales Patiño of Cuba as Secretary, and Irving Rouse of the United States as Editor. This association plans eventually to publish a bulletin on the archaeology of the Caribbean.

The area suffered a great loss in 1950. Juan A. Cosculluela, dean of Cuban archaeologists and the first to make extensive excavations in Ciboney sites, died at Habana on May 16.

THE CARIBBEAN ISLANDS

CUBA

222. Aguayo, C. Guillermo. Observaciones sobre algunos mamíferos cubanos extinguidos (*Bol. hist. nat. soc. F. Poey*, v. 1, no. 3, nov., p. 121-134).
Review of the evidence for the association of extinct sloths and insectivores with the Indians of Cuba. It is suggested that the Indians may have been responsible for the extinction of these mammals.

223. Febres Cordero G., Julio. Balance del indigenismo en Cuba (*Rev. bibl. nac.*, Habana, 2. serie, t. 1, no. 4, agosto, p. 61-204).
Summary and evaluation of research on the Indians of Cuba. Extensive bibliography.

224. García y Grave de Peralta, Fernando. Excursiones arqueológicas. VII y VIII (*Rev. arqueol. etnol.*, 2. época, año 5, no. 10-11, enero-dic., p. 35-67).
Continuation of the author's account of his archaeological explorations in eastern Cuba. See *HLAS, no. 4, 1938*, item 146 c, and *no. 15, 1949*, item 334.

225. Herrera Fritot, René. Arquetipos zoomorfos en las Antillas Mayores (*Bol. hist. nat. soc. F. Poey*, v. 1, no. 3, nov., p. 140-149).
Brief but comprehensive survey of the occurrence and kinds of zoomorphic and anthropomorphic designs in the archaeology of the Greater Antilles. The author points out that, in Cuba, they are limited to the latest of the three known cultural complexes (sub-Taino and Taino). Illustrated with material from Cuba and the Dominican Republic.

226. Miguel Alonso, Orencio. Discovery of a pre-Columbian gold figurine in Cuba (*Amer. antiquity*, v. 15, no. 4, April, p. 340-341).
Description of a gold figurine in Central or South American style found near an Indian village site in eastern Cuba. This is the first such specimen to be reported from the Antilles.

227. Morales Patiño, Oswaldo. La antigüedad de los asientos indocubanos (*Rev. arqueol. etnol.*, 2. época, año 5, no. 10-11, enero-dic., p. 115-133).
Survey of the various methods of determining the age of dwelling sites, and a critique of Irving Rouse's approach to this problem in his *Archaeology of the Maniabón Hills, Cuba* (see *HLAS,*

no. 8, 1942, item 206). The author favors Rouse's use of estimates based upon the rate of refuse accumulation.

228. ————. Arqueología cubana. Relación de actividades durante el año 1949 (*Rev. arqueol. etnol.*, 2. época, año 5, no. 10-11, enero-dic., p. 5-34).

Summary of archaeological activities in Cuba during 1949, with a brief, illustrated description of the principal finds. The excavations of Dr. Bernardo Utset near Manzanilla in Oriente Province are worthy of note. At the site of Carnero, Dr. Utset found artifacts typical of the Cayo Redondo form of Ciboney (non-agricultural) culture accompanied by stone vessels, "Carib" stones, and unspecified "objects resulting from Spanish-Indian transculturation." At Leonero and the Loma del Indio, Cayo Redondo type artifacts were instead accompanied by crude Indian pottery which, it is suggested, may be the result of transculturation with the neighboring sub-Taino (agricultural) Indians.

230. **Núñez Jiménez, Antonio.** Descubrimiento de pictografías en Caleta Grande, Isla de Pinos (*Univ. Habana*, no. 82-87, enero-dic., 1949, i.e. 1950, p. 357-365).

Account of a fourth discovery of painted pictographs on the Isle of Pines, with an illustrated description.

231. ————. Un viaje arqueológico a Mayarí (*Carteles*, año 31, no. 39, sept. 24, p. 43-45).

Report of excavations in Ciboney and Taino sites at Mayarí, with illustrations of the specimens found.

232. **Pichardo Moya, Felipe.** Los Jardines de la Reina (*Bohemia*, año 42, no. 22, mayo 28, p. 28-29, 111-112).

Brief summary of the archaeology and ethnohistory of islands on the south coast of Cuba.

233. ————. Presencia en Cuba de un monstruo prehistórico (*Bohemia*, año 42, no. 7, feb. 12, p. 8-9, 138-139).

Association of bones of an extinct sloth with Indian remains in central Cuba.

234. **Vivanco, Julián.** Los indios palafíticos de Cuba y los dujos o metates. Habana, Belascoaín. 16 p.

Unconvincing attempt to prove that the Taino, rather than the Ciboney, built the pile dwellings of Cuba, and that they are also responsible for the Central American-type metates found in the island.

OTHER ISLANDS

235. **Alegría, Ricardo E.** Historia de nuestros indios. San Juan, P. R. 52 p., illus.

Textbook for elementary school children on the Indians of Puerto Rico. Archaeological data are utilized but, despite the title, the emphasis is on ethnology.

236. **Bullbrook, J. A.** The aborigines of Trinidad (*Ubotimes,* Port-of-Spain?, v. 2, no. 6, p. 17-20).

A semi-popular account of the history of archaeological research in Trinidad and of the nature of the remains.

237. **O'Reilly, Pamela.** Arawak relics. A new burial-ground unearthed in Tobago by Mr. Tom Cambridge (*Guardian weekly,* Port-of-Spain, Trinidad, July 30, p. 3, 8-9).

Account of the discovery of a burial site near Plymouth, Tobago. The pottery found appears to resemble that of Erin in Trinidad and of Barrancas in Venezuela.

VENEZUELA

238. **Acosta Saignes, Miguel.** Arqueología para aficionados. Caracas. 19 p., 9 plates.

Brief explanation of archaeology for the amateur. Includes the author's theory that Venezuela was populated by four successive groups of Indians: 1, primitive hunter-gatherers; 2, advanced hunter-gatherers; 3, Arawak; and 4, Carib.

239. **Cruxent, José María.** Archaeology of Cotua Island, Amazonas Territory, Venezuela (*Amer. antiquity,* v. 16, no. 1, July, p. 10-16).

Description of a village and workshop site on the upper Orinoco River. The pottery at this site has some resemblances to that of Barrancas on the lower Orinoco.

240. ————. Las bateítas de Aguirre (*Mem. soc. cien. nat. La Salle,* t. 10, no. 27, sept.-dic., p. 175-186).

Description of a unique series of rock basins in west central Venezuela. It is suggested that they may have been either vessels, tombs, crucibles, or shrines.

241. **Galtsoff, Paul S.** The pearl fishery of Venezuela. Washington, Government Printing Office (U. S. Department of the Interior, Fish and Wildlife Service, Fisheries, no. 26, p. 1-26).

This report begins with a brief account of the prehistory and history of pearl fishing, which was in the hands of the Indians until the middle of the 16th century.

BRAZIL

242. **Barata, Frederico.** A arte oleira dos Tapajó. I. Considerações sobre a cerâmica e dois tipos de vasos característicos. Belém, Brazil, Instituto de Antropologia e Etnologia do Pará (Publ. no. 2). 47 p., illus.

Well illustrated description of Santarem pottery in Brazilian collections. A series of these descriptions is planned.

243. Drumond, Carlos. Notas sôbre cerâmica brasílica. São Paulo, Universidade de São Paulo, Faculdade de Filosofia, Ciências e Letras (Bol. 107, Etnografia e lingua Tupi-Guarani, no. 18). 8 p.
Description of a unique, painted neck of a jar from the State of São Paulo and of a cylindrical pottery stand from Marajó Island. The former is identified as Tupi-Guarani.

244. Evans, Clifford, Jr. A report on recent archaeological investigations in the Lagoa Santa region of Minas Gerais, Brazil (*Amer. antiquity,* v. 15, no. 4, April, p. 341-343).
Brief account of preceramic material being excavated from two caves by H. V. Walter. This material, which is characterized by small hand axes polished only on the bit, appears to be later than the Pleistocene fauna of the region.

245. ————, and Betty J. Meggers. Preliminary results of archaeological investigations at the mouth of the Amazon (*Amer. antiquity,* v. 16, no. 1, July, p. 1-9).
Deals with 1949 excavations sponsored by Columbia University. Seven phases of local, tropical-forest type culture are recognized, in addition to the more advanced Marajoara phase. The last is shown to be late and probably intrusive from up-river, contrary to some previous theories, which have assumed that it originated at the mouth of the Amazon. A very important piece of research.

246. Palmatary, Helen C. The pottery of Marajó Island, Brazil (*Trans. amer. philos. soc.,* n. s., v. 39, part 3, p. 261-358).
The author has studied the extensive Marajó material in the University Museum, Philadelphia, as well as four other collections in the United States and two in Brazil. She presents a detailed, well illustrated description and makes comparisons with material from other parts of the New World. 112 plates.

247. Pereira, José Anthero, Jr. Nótulas e comentários arqueológicos e etnográficos (*Rev. arq. mun.,* ano 17, v. 136, set., p. 35-94).
Miscellaneous comments on subjects ranging from petroglyphs to the origin of the American Indian.

ADDENDA

248. Barata, Frederico. Os maravilhosos cachimbos de Santarem (*Estud. bras.,* ano 7, v. 13, no. 37-39, julho-dez., 1944, p. 270-294).
It is suggested that floral designs on pipes associated with Santarem pottery are the result of Jesuit influence.

249. Bigarella, João José. Nota prévia sôbre a composição dos sambaquís de Paraná

e Santa Catarina. Contribução ao estudo de planicie sedimentar da parte norte da ilha de Santa Catarina (*Arq. biol. tecnol.,* v. 4, art. 15, 16, 1949, p. 95-106, 107-140).
All 150 *sambaquís* examined by the author in the States of Paraná and Santa Catarina appear to be artificial, although there are also natural banks of shell in the area. The flora and fauna of these middens, their chemical composition, and their geological situation are discussed in some detail.

250. Biocca, Ettore. I "sambaquís" del litorale paulista (Brasile) (*Riv. antrop.,* v. 35, 1947, p. 335-347).
Not seen.

251. Díaz Niese, Rafael. La alfarería indígena dominicana. Ciudad Trujillo, 1945. 34 p., illus.
Classification and description of pottery bottles in the Museo Nacional de Ciudad Trujillo. Those illustrated are all of the Boca Chica style and Taino culture.

252. Hatt, Gudmund. Had West Indian rock carvings a religious significance? (In *Ethnological studies published on the occasion of the Centenary of the Ethnographical Department, National Museum* [Copenhagen], *National-museets Skrifter, Etnografisk Raekke,* no. 1, 1941, p. 165-202).
The author describes and interprets petroglyphs observed by him in the Dominican Republic and the Virgin Islands, including a number associated with ball courts and pillar stones. He correlates them with both Igneri and Taino cultures.

253. Josselin de Jong, J. P. B. de. Archaeological material from Saba and St. Eustatius, Lesser Antilles. Leiden [Holland], E. J. Brill (*Mededelingen van het Rijksmuseum voor Volkenkunde,* no. 1, 1947, 54 p.).
Report of archaeological excavations which the author undertook in 1923 at a site on Saba and another on St. Eustatius. The pottery from the former site is cruder and less finely incised and painted than at the latter, but the significance of this difference remains to be determined.

254. Mangones, Edmond, and Louis Maximilien. L'Art pré-colombien d'Haïti. Port-au-Prince, n.d., 30 p., 62 plates.
Catalogue of an archaeological exhibition held during the Third Caribbean Congress in 1941. Many fine, hitherto unpublished Haitian artifacts are illustrated.

255. Mason, J. Alden. New pottery types from Santarem, Brazil (In *Reseña y trabajos científicos del XXVI Congreso Internacional de Americanistas* [Sevilla, 1935], Madrid, t. 1, 1948, p. 55-69).
Both painting and modeling-incision are found

to be included in the Santarem ceramic complex, contrary to Nordenskiöld, who held that the former preceded the latter in the Amazon Basin. Tracing the distribution of the elements of the Santarem complex, the author concludes that it is as closely linked with the pottery of Marajó and Central America as with that of the West Indies.

256. Onorate, Ettore. Descrizione dei sambaquí da Cabeçuda (*Riv. antrop.*, v. 35, 1947, p. 349-350).
Not seen.

257. Oramas, Luis R. La civilización de Venezuela precolombina (In *Reseña y trabajos científicos del XXVI Congreso Internacional de Americanistas* [Sevilla, 1935], Madrid, t. 1, 1948, p. 431-447).
Description of archaeological remains in Venezuela, particularly of the *calzadas* on the western llanos. The author cites an historical record which indicates that an Arawak tribe, the Caquetía, built the *calzadas*.

258. Ortiz, Fernando, J. A. Cosculluela, René Herrera Fritot, Fernando Royo Guardia, and Oswaldo Morales Patiño. Las culturas pre-colombinas de Cuba (In *Actas y Documentos del Primer Congreso Histórico Municipal Interamericano*, Instituto Interamericano de Historia Municipal e Institucional, Habana, 1943, p. 192-356).

Important series of papers outlining the Indian cultures of Cuba and discussing some of their diagnostic traits. Well illustrated.

259. Padilla d'Onís, Luis. Historia de Santo Domingo. Primera parte. Prehistoria dominicana. México, Instituto Panamericano de Geografía e Historia (Publ. no. 71), 1943. 315 p., illus., maps.
Beginning with the history of the earth and the prehistory of mankind, the author proceeds to discuss the Indian tribes in the Antilles and the culture of the local Taino. He also describes a series of caves which the Taino may have used as shrines and proposes the theory that the Ciguayo, a divergent group on the island, were an offshoot of the Maya.

260. Palm, Erwin Walter. Excavations of La Isabela, white man's first town in the Americas (*Acta amer.*, v. 3, 1945, p. 298-303).
Preliminary account of excavations in ruins of Columbus' first settlement. Both Indian and Spanish pottery were found, but it is not known whether they are contemporaneous.

261. Pichardo Moya, Felipe. Los indios de Cuba en sus tiempos históricos. Habana, Muñiz, 1945. 52 p.
Authoritative account of the history of the Cuban Indians from the discovery until their extinction during the present century. Archaeological evidence is used in discussing population and acculturation.

ARCHAEOLOGY: WESTERN AND SOUTHERN SOUTH AMERICA

JOHN HOWLAND ROWE

THE year 1950 brought substantial additions to knowledge in the form of published archaeological reports and studies, while the field and research projects undertaken promise even more important contributions for the future. Wendell C. Bennett upheld his distinguished record of prompt publication of his work by getting out the second report resulting from the Virú Valley Project of 1946, *The Gallinazo Group, Virú Valley, Peru.* Henry and Paule Reichlen published a second preliminary report on their explorations in northern Peru, this one dealing with the Chachapoyas area. In Colombia, the Banco de la República published a handsome picture book of outstanding specimens in its Museo del Oro in Bogotá, easily the finest thing of its kind ever done in Latin America. A number of other publications of outstanding importance are so noted in the bibliography below.

A review of field work and excavation in the several countries follows.

Colombia. Gerardo Reichel-Dolmatoff terminated his campaign of excavations in the Santa Marta area with a series of excavations in the Ranchería and César valleys which produced the longest archaeological sequence yet reported for any part of Colombia. Four successive pottery styles were found in the Ranchería valley, the chronological relationships being worked out chiefly at the stratified sites of El Horno and Portacelli. Following the termination of this work, Reichel-Dolmatoff resigned from the directorship of the Instituto Etnológico del Magdalena to devote himself to the publication of his extensive archaeological and ethnographic notes.

An extensive archaeological survey of the Bogotá area, with test excavations in three sites, was undertaken jointly by Emil W. Haury of the University of Arizona and Julio C. Cubillos of the Instituto Etnológico Nacional. The rubbish deposits located were all thin and yielded only late materials, but it was possible to make some chronological and regional distinctions in the objects found. Following the work near Bogotá, Cubillos spent two months trenching the habitation site of Monte Alto in the Tumaco area near the Ecuadorean border, in continuation of a survey undertaken the previous year. A cemetery with shaft graves was also found. Eliecer Silva Celis dug an extensive cemetery at Guicán in Boyacá which was discovered during highway construction.

Ecuador. Ecuador lost through death one of its most distinguished scholars, Jacinto Jijón y Caamaño, author of many important works on the history and archaeology of Ecuador and Peru and owner of one of the finest private collections and libraries in South America.

Peru. The most important field work of the year was Wendell C. Bennett's excavations at Huari, near Ayacucho. Huari is one of the largest and least known highland sites and has been recognized for some years as a place where excavation was urgently needed. Earlier work at the site is described in an article by Rowe, Collier, and Willey reviewed in the bibliography below. Bennett dug some fifteen test pits looking for refuse stratigraphy and was able to distinguish two successive styles, a good Coast Tiahuanaco style stratigraphically earlier than one of Nazca Y affiliations. The results are especially interesting as most Peruvianists expected the reverse order. Bennett also made a survey of sites in the Mantaro basin.

Richard P. Schaedel continued his extensive survey of North Coast architecture, and carried out further excavations in ruins near Chanchan of the Middle and Late periods.

Ross T. Christensen, a collaborator of the Instituto de Antropología at Trujillo, made an extensive reconnaissance in the Departments of Piura and Tumbes, with an excursion to the Ecuadorean province of El Oro. He chose the village site of Chusís in the lower Piura valley for intensive study and made a series of stratigraphic tests in it. The place appears to have been a small and comparatively poor settlement throughout its long history and the remains are of a sort that will be difficult to relate to established sequences further south.

New light was thrown on an old excavation when J. H. Rowe laid out the collection excavated by Max Uhle at Cemetery F at Moche in 1899-1900 and preserved at the University of California. Rowe took Rafael Larco's suggestion that the Early Chimu style could be subdivided chronologically on the basis of spout shapes and tested it against Uhle's grave lots. Larco's sequence was corroborated, opening the way to a much more detailed study of Early Chimu culture history than has ever been possible before.

The city of Cuzco was severely shaken by earthquake on May 21 and a number of the Inca ruins in the city were further damaged, although on the whole the Inca walls stood the shock better than the Spanish ones. Several previously unknown walls were revealed by the destruction of Colonial and modern constructions. The museum collections were not damaged.

Argentina. Osvaldo Menghin and various collaborators made a series of field trips to identify and excavate Early Man sites. Menghin visited the Sierra de Córdoba, caves in Tandilia, Buenos Aires Province, and camp sites in the Territories of La Pampa and Misiones. Menghin's dating methods are chiefly typological and many of the sites he reports may turn out to be relatively recent. Ciro R. Lafón dug at the Humahuaca site of La Huerta in Jujuy to secure information for the proposed restoration of the Pucará of Tilcara.

GENERAL

262. Imbelloni, José. La extraña terracota de Rurrenabaque (noreste de Bolivia) en la arqueología de Sudamérica (*Runa*, v. 3, partes 1-2, p. 71-169).
Describes a seated figure urn in the Museo Nacional, La Paz, and traces its traits and related ones over most of South America. Since the chronological relationships of most of the pieces discussed are unknown, the network of influences which Imbelloni reconstructs is of dubious value.

263. Iribarren Charlín, Jorge. Notas preliminares sobre la dispersión continental de un adorno del labio en los pueblos aborígenes, el bezote, labret o tembeta. Ovalle, Chile, El Tamaya. [6], x, 117 p., 1 fig., 12 plates.
A distribution study of lip plugs, using archaeological and ethnographic data. Iribarren Charlín's study is preceded by an article by O. F. A. Menghin, *Observaciones sobre la arqueología del bezote en el viejo mundo*, p. [5-6], i-vi.

ARGENTINA

265. Becker-Donner, Etta. Die nordwestargentinischen Sammlungen des Wiener Museums für Völkerkunde (*Archiv für Völkerkunde*, Band 5, p. 1-103).
Contents: 1, *Die Quebrada de Humahuaca*, p. 2-64; 2, *Die Calchaquí-Täler*, p. 64-100. An important museum study, continued in the next issue of the same journal.

266. Bórmida, Marcelo. Curioso objeto lítico de la península Valdés (*Runa*, v. 3, partes 1-2, p. 231-235).
A cylindrical stone object with incised markings, from the Allende Collection in Tandil. It is unique and the author has no idea what it was used for.

267. Canals Frau, Salvador. Exploraciones arqueológicas en el antiguo Valle de Uco (Mendoza). Córdoba, Universidad Nacional de Córdoba (Publ. del Instituto de Arqueología, Lingüística y Folklore Dr. Pablo Cabrera, no. 22). 29 p., 18 figs.
The Valle de Uco is a dry valley south of Mendoza where archaeological remains are found in spite of the fact that the area could not have been very attractive for Indian occupation. The author distinguishes two periods of occupation in the pottery, and sees Inca influence in the later pottery type. No Inca influence is visible in the pieces illustrated.

268. Casanova, Eduardo. Restauración del Pucará. Buenos Aires, Universidad de Buenos Aires, Facultad de Filosofía y Letras, Instituto de Antropología. 55 p., 3 plans, 16 plates.
A brief description of the archaeological site of Pucará de Tilcara in Jujuy, with an account of the excavations made there by Ambrosetti and Debenedetti and the plans of a museum and residence to be built there by the University of Buenos Aires.

269. Frenguelli, Joaquín. The present status of the theories concerning primitive man in Argentina (*Handbook of South American Indians*, v. 6, p. 11-17).
A partisan review of theories, mostly Argentine.

270. Gaspary, Fernando. Investigaciones arqueológicas y antropológicas en un "cerrito" de la Isla Los Marinos (Provincia de Entre Ríos). Córdoba, Universidad Nacional de Córdoba (Publ. del Instituto de Arqueología, Lingüística y Folklore Dr. Pablo Cabrera, no. 23). 67 p., 49 figs., 3 tables.
Excavation of a habitation site and cemetery at the partly artificial mound of Cerro Grande, near Rosario. The report discusses the resulting collection without giving any data about the associations of the specimens. The material found is attributed to the Chaná-Timbú, the historic inhabitants of the area.

271. Ibarra Grasso, Carlos. La cultura draconiana (*Cien. nueva*, año 1, t. 1, no. 1, p. 49-56).
A brief sketch of the Draconian or Barreales pottery style.

272. Ibarra Grasso, Dick Edgar. El Museo Arqueológico Calchaquí (*Cien. nueva*, año 1, t. 1, no. 1, p. 39-48).
An introduction written for the forthcoming catalogue of the museum established and directed by P. Salvador Narváez in Catamarca. The collection consists of nearly 5,000 specimens from all over the Province of Catamarca.

273. ————. Nueva interpretación sobre la arqueología del Noroeste Argentino (*Cien. nueva*, año 1, t. 1, no. 1, p. 11-37).
A review of some of the better known literature on Northwest Argentina and Bolivia leading to an ambitious reconstruction of the cultural history of these areas based on technical and stylistic resemblances to the surrounding regions. The author has Imbelloni's misplaced enthusiasm for reconstruction from distribution.

274. ————, and Honoria Bini Frías. Cerámica tucumana con picos-trompa (*Cien. nueva*, año 1, t. 1, no. 2, p. 55-59).
Discusses four modelled specimens, each with a feature which the authors interpret as an exaggerated beak or trunk. The pieces are so different that there is no reason to assume that they represent the same animal or bird.

275. ————, and Carlos Ibarra Grasso. La colección arqueológica Paz Posse (*Cien. nueva*, año 1, t. 1, no. 2, p. 21-54).
A large private collection from Northwest Ar-

gentina and Bolivia acquired by the Universidad de Tucumán in 1948. The Bolivian specimens, from San Lucas, Department of Chuquisaca, are particularly important. Unfortunately, the illustrations are so poorly reproduced that the article is nearly unusable.

276. Menghin, Osvaldo F. A., and Marcelo Bórmida. Investigaciones prehistóricas en cuevas de Tandilia (Provincia de Buenos Aires) (*Runa,* v. 3, partes 1-2, p. 5-36).

On the basis of five nondescript flakes, not clearly implements, Menghin defines a very primitive culture which he dates to the early postglacial. The sites are small rockshelters.

277. Pertierra y Polo, Roberto A. Una corneta humahuaquense. Contribución a la arqueología argentina (*Americanista,* año 1, no. 1, enero-julio, p. 14-17).

278. Serrano, Antonio. Los primitivos habitantes de Entre Ríos. Paraná, Provincia de Entre Ríos, Ministerio de Educación (Biblioteca Entrerriana General Perón, Historia, 2). x, 181 p., 75 figs.

A systematic review of the archaeology and ethnography of the province. The temporal relationships are inferred from distributions and scanty historical data.

CHILE

279. Cornely, Francisco L. Prehistoria del territorio diaguita chileno (Provincias de Coquimbo y Atacama) (*Publ. soc. arqueol. La Serena,* Boletín no. 5, dic., p. 3-18).

A systematic summary of the archaeological history of the area, forming a valuable introduction to the subject. The author sets up a sequence of four periods, plus the unplaced El Molle culture.

280. Hornkohl, Herbert. Un ídolo lítico hallado en Tilama, Provincia de Coquimbo, Chile (*Publ. soc. arqueol. La Serena,* Boletín no. 5, dic., p. 19-20).

Part of a small stone figurine; only six comparable specimens are known from Chile.

281. Iribarren Charlín, Jorge. La Urna de Chellepín y algunas correlaciones arqueológicas (*Publ. soc. arqueol. La Serena,* Boletín no. 5, dic., p. 21-27).

Description of a famous piece from the Department of Illapel now in the Museo de Antropología de Buenos Aires. The author relates it to other Chilean specimens and discusses its relationships (distant, if any) with Northwest Argentine urns.

282. Montandón, Roberto. Apuntes sobre el pukara de Lasana. Introducción de Leopoldo Pizarro, Director del Museo Histórico Nacional. Santiago, Consejo de Monumentos Nacionales (Cuadernos del Consejo de Monumentos Nacionales, no. 1). 23 p., 20 plates.

283. Rowe, John Howland. Influencia incaica en la alfarería diaguita-chilena (*Publ. soc. arqueol. La Serena,* Boletín no. 5, dic., p. 28-29).

A discussion of the amount and nature of Inca influence on Elqui Valley ceramics, as shown in illustrations published by Cornely in *Boletín* no. 4. See *HLAS, no. 15, 1949,* item 252.

COLOMBIA

284. Arcila Vélez, Graciliano. Actualidad etnológica de Antioquia (*Univ. Antioquia,* v. 25, no. 100, agosto-oct., p. 515-524).

A summary of anthropological problems in Antioquia. The remarks on archaeology include a list of private collections.

285. Gómez Picón, Rafael. San Agustín, santuario de América (*Rev. América,* v. 21, no. 65, junio, p. 179-183).

Brief historical review of the explorations carried out at San Agustín through 1937.

286. Lehmann, Henri. Le civiltà precolombiane della Colombia (*Vie del mondo,* v. 12, no. 6, p. 599-612).

287. Margain, Carlos R. Estudio inicial de las colecciones del Museo del Oro del Banco de la República. Bogotá, Imprenta del Banco de la República. 3-62 p., 9 plates.

A study made in 1945. The author first defines a series of terms for describing metallurgical processes and then reviews the collections of the museum, noting the characteristics of each Colombian area. He is somewhat handicapped by the fact that only 1.5 percent of the objects have reliable provenience data.

288. El Museo del Oro. Bogotá, Banco de la República (Ediciones conmemorativas de la fundación del Banco de la República en su XXV aniversario, 1923-1948), 1948, i.e. 1950. 64 unnumbered pages, 2 maps, 101 colored plates.

Contents: Introduction, by Gustavo Santos, p. [3-5]; *El oro indígena,* by Gregorio Hernández de Alba, p. [7-21]; *Origen de la industria del oro en América,* by Paul Rivet, p. [23-27]; *El trabajo indígena del oro,* by Bernardino de Sahagún (quoted from *El oro de Indias,* by Luis Alberto Acuña), p. [29-37]. An earlier catalogue of this gold collection was published in 1944; this album contains twice as many plates as the 1944 one and the reproductions are much better. Stunning illustrations of ancient Colombian gold work.

289. Reichel-Dolmatoff, Gerardo. Actividades antropológicas de Colombia en el período 1945-1950 (*Runa,* v. 3, partes 1-2, p. 278-282).

A good summary of the extensive field work done in the years covered. The text is headed: *Colombia. Las ciencias del hombre en el período 1945-1950.*

290. Royo y Gómez, José. Las Piedras de Tunja de Facatativá y el cuaternario de la sabana de Bogotá. Bogotá, Instituto Etnológico Nacional. 14 p., 1 fig., 2 plates.

The geological report on a cut made by Haury and Cubillos in a rock shelter at Facatativá. No human remains of any geological antiquity are reported, but this study gives a useful summary of the Pleistocene geology of the area.

291. Trimborn, Hermann. Die Caldas-kultur (*Zeit. ethnol.,* Band 75, p. 36-42).

A classification of the 16th-century cultures of the Cauca Valley from historical sources.

292. ————. Herrentum und Herrengestalten im vorkolumbischen Caucatal (*Paideuma,* Band 4, p. 335-347).

Another in Trimborn's series of studies in historical ethnology; illustrated with archaeological specimens.

PERU AND BOLIVIA

294. Bennett, Wendell C. Cultural unity and disunity in the Titicaca basin (*Amer. antiquity,* v. 16, no. 2, Oct., p. 89-98).

The author emphasizes the fact that the Titicaca basin was not a cultural unit in archaeological terms through most of its history. The article includes a review of the chief sites on which data are available.

295. ————. The Gallinazo Group, Viru Valley, Peru. New Haven, Yale University Press (Yale University Publications in Anthropology, no. 43). 127 p., 27 figs., 12 plates, 8 tables.

The report on Bennett's excavations at the Gallinazo mounds in 1946. Describes structures, burials, and pottery of the Gallinazo period.

296. Bingham, Hiram. La ciudad perdida de los Incas (Lost city of the Incas). Historia de Machu Picchu y sus constructores. Traducción de María Romero. Santiago, Zig-Zag (Col. Historia y Documentos). 283 p., plates.

298. Horkheimer, Hans. Guía bibliográfica de los principales sitios arqueológicos del Perú (*Bol. bibliog.,* Lima, año 23, v. 20, no. 3-4, dic., p. 181-234).

A bibliography of references to some of the better known Peruvian sites. The titles are listed alphabetically by author, with a geographical key and an index of sites. A useful tool.

299. ————. El Perú prehispánico. Intento de un manual. T. 1. Lima, Cultura Antártica. 295 p., 75 figs.

A review of theories about ancient Peru rather than a review of data. Its most valuable feature is a directory of people active in Peruvianist studies.

300. Kinzl, Hans, and Erwin Schneider. Cordillera Blanca (Perú). Innsbruck, Universitäts-Verlag Wagner. [iv], 167 p., 119 plates, folding map.

A magnificent album of pictures and a fine map of the Callejón de Huaylas and neighboring areas at a scale of 1:200,000. Plates 160-167 show antiquities of Chavín and Callejón sites, including some pottery in a new style. The authors are mountain climbers. German text; abridged text in Spanish and English.

301. Kroeber, Alfred Louis. A local style of lifelike sculptured stone heads in ancient Peru (In *Beiträge zur Gesellungs- und Völkerwissenschaft; Festschrift zum achtzigsten Geburtstag von Professor Richard Thurnwald,* Berlin, Gebr. Mann, p. 195-198).

Calls attention to a group of sculptures from the Huamachuco-Cabana region of northern Peru. Many of them have tenons and were set in the walls of buildings.

302. Kutscher, Gerdt. Chimu: eine altindianische Hochkultur. Berlin, Gebr. Mann. 112 p., 74 figs., 80 plates.

A popular account of the Early Chimu culture with emphasis on the intuitive interpretation of representations on pottery. The illustrations are especially valuable.

303. ————. Iconographic studies as an aid in the reconstruction of Early Chimu civilization (*Trans. New York acad. sci.,* series 2, v. 12, no. 6, p. 194-203).

Examples of interpretations of Early Chimu pottery designs.

304. ————. Sakrale Wettläufe bei den frühen Chimu (Nord-Peru) (In *Beiträge zur Gesellungs- und Völkerwissenschaft; Festschrift zum achtzigsten Geburstag von Richard Thurnwald,* Berlin, Gebr. Mann, p. 209-226).

Kutscher interprets certain Early Chimu pottery designs as representing ritual races. This interpretation is certainly preferable to Larco's guess that they represent messengers.

305. Lafón, Ciro René. El aríbalo incaico. Ensayo de clasificación tipológica (*Runa,* v. 3, partes 1-2, p. 211-217).

Gives a typological shape classification without regard to archaeological data; an effort of scant utility. Lafón includes some interesting data on the history of the name *aryballos.*

306. Lilien, Rose. Tripod vessels from the Virú Valley (*Amer. antiquity,* v. 15, no. 4, April, p. 339-340).

Discusses three tripod specimens of the Gallinazo period found in the Virú Valley by the

Columbia University expedition in 1946. This is the earliest reported occurrence of tripod vessels in the area. A modelled stirrup spout vessel, the bottom of which is pushed out to make four supports, is described and assigned to the same period.

307. Lothrop, Samuel Kirkland. Metalworking tools from the central coast of Peru (*Amer. antiquity,* v. 16, no. 2, Oct., p. 160-164).
A description of 15 specimens in the Peabody Museum, Cambridge, chiefly stone hammers and embossing tools. An important contribution to Andean culture history.

308. Mariátegui Oliva, Ricardo. Cuzco imperial. Lima, Instituto de Investigaciones de Arte Peruano y Americano (Documentos de Arte Peruano, no. 9). 71 p., 31 illus.
Familiar pictures of Cuzco architecture.

309. ————. Macchu-Picchu [sic]. Lima, Instituto de Investigaciones de Arte Peruano y Americano (Documentos de Arte Peruano, no. 10). 32 p., 12 plates.
Familiar pictures, poorly reproduced. The author still suffers from the delusion that the ruins of Machu Picchu are pre-Inca.

310. Núñez del Prado, Óscar. Exploración arqueológica (*Tradición,* año 1, v. 1, no. 1, enero-feb., p. 71-76).
Description of a well preserved building at Raqc'i, Province of Urubamba, which the author dates to the Early Inca period because only Killke Series sherds are found there. An excellent study.

311. ————. Exploración arqueológica en Raqc'i (Urubamba). Cuzco, [The author]. 11 p., 2 plates, 1 fig.
Printed by Empresa Editorial Cuzco, S. A. Though labelled as a reprint from *Tradición* (see the preceding item), this version is paged differently and has illustrations of pottery not found in the periodical edition.

312. ————. El "khipu" moderno (*Tradición,* año 1, v. 2, no. 3-6, mayo-dic., p. 42-57).
Describes 10 modern quipus from Paucartambo in the perspective of what is known about ancient ones.

313. Osborne, Carolyn M. Shaped breechcloths from Peru. Berkeley, University of California Press (University of California, Anthropological Records, v. 13, no. 2). iv, 157-164 p., figs., plates.
Technical analysis of 22 specimens from the Rimac, Chincha, Cañete and Pisco valleys, all attributed to the Late period. The pieces were garments and show signs of wear. The shaping was done by spacing the warps; no warps were added or subtracted.

314. Reichlen, Henry. Illustration d'un rite précolombien de divination (*Jour. soc. amér.,* n.s., v. 39, p. 258-259).
Describes a modelled figure, probably Middle Period, from Moche Valley, showing a man blowing into a pair of lungs—a form of divination known from historical sources.

315. ————, and **Paule Reichlen.** Recherches archéologiques dans les Andes du haut Utcubamba. Deuxième rapport de la Mission Ethnologique Française au Pérou Septentrional (*Jour. soc. amér.,* n.s., v. 39, p. 219-246).
A very important report giving preliminary results of surface exploration at 39 sites and excavations at four. The authors define three local cultures: Revash, Kuelape, and Chipurik. The three have different distributions, but at the site of Kuelape there is a Chipurik occupation later than the Kuelape one. Kuelape pottery is plain with plastic ornament; Chipurik pottery is painted with red and black. Neither style has close resemblances to other known Peruvian types.

316. Rowe, John H., Donald Collier, and Gordon R. Willey. Reconnaissance notes on the site of Huari, near Ayacucho, Peru (*Amer. antiquity,* v. 16, no. 2, Oct., p. 120-137).
History of previous work at this important highland site and description of a visit made to it in 1946. A tentative classification of sculpture and pottery is proposed. While this paper was in press, excavations were undertaken at Huari by Wendell C. Bennett (see p. 29).

317. Schaedel, Richard P. Schaedel report (*Archaeology,* v. 3, no. 3, autumn, p. 186).
A brief account of Schaedel's study of North Coast architecture, in progress at the time.

318. Tschopik, Harry, Jr. An Andean ceramic tradition in historical perspective (*Amer. antiquity,* v. 15, no. 3, Jan., p. 196-218).
In one of the most stimulating papers ever done in Andean studies, the author, making full use of archaeological and historical data, describes the modern pottery-making industry of Chucuito in southern Peru as part of a long tradition going back to prehistoric times.

319. Wassén, Henry. Tre föremål från Paracas, Peru (*Göteborgs Musei Arstryck* 1949 och 1950, p. 213-222).
Describes three interesting specimens from Paracas: 1, a trophy head jar in the Cavernas style, painted after firing; 2, a carved and painted staff in the Necropolis (Early Nazca) style, showing masked figures; 3, a small figurine, probably Cavernas.

ADDENDA

319a. Disselhoff, Hans-Dietrich. Grabungen und Funde im Canton Sta. Elena

(Ecuador) (*Méx. antiguo,* t. 7, dic., 1949, p. 343-410).
A report on excavations made in 1938 between La Libertad and La Entrada in the Province of Guayas. Several different styles were found in the area, but the relations between them are not clear. This article is purely descriptive; the author promises another one with conclusions.

319b. Hissink, Karin. Gedanken zu einem Nazca-Gefäss (*Méx. antiguo,* t. 7, dic., 1949, p. 411-438).
An interpretation of a Nazca vase illustrated many years ago by Uhle, in terms of A. E. Jensen's theories about primitive religion.

ETHNOLOGY: MIDDLE AMERICA

SOL TAX

RESEARCHES continued in 1950 at about the usual pace, the main tendency being the continued increase of activity of action organizations, particularly the Indianist Institutes in Guatemala and Mexico, and the development of community surveys in Puerto Rico and in Costa Rica. The publications of the Office of Social Sciences of the Pan American Union, particularly its studies of the middle class in Latin America are noteworthy additions (see item 3347). *B.B.A.A.,* v. 12, partes 1-2, enero-dic., 1949, i.e. 1950, is an excellent source of information on many of the research activities in the area. The editor was assisted in the preparation of this section by Mrs. June Nash. For this year as previously he has depended for advice on linguistic publications upon Dr. Norman A. McQuown.

GENERAL

320. Barlow, Robert H. Codices and Mesoamerican picture writing. A note on civil books (*Mesoamer. notes,* 2, p. 107-117).
See item 188.

321. Du Solier, Wilfredo. Ancient Mexican costumes. Translated by W. Du Solier and John Roberts. México, Ediciones Mexicanas.
See item 195.

322. Hernández, Francisco J. El juguete popular en México. Estudios de interpretación. México, Ediciones Mexicanas (Enciclopedia Mexicana de Arte, 10). 158 p., illus.

323. Hoyos Sancho, Nieves de. Folklore de Hispanoamérica. La quema de Judas (*Rev. Indias,* Madrid, año 10, no. 41, p. 561-587).
Survey of studies on customs and folklore of Latin America and their European counterparts. Sections on Mexico and ten other Latin American countries.

324. Mintz, Sidney W., and **Eric R. Wolf.** An analysis of ritual coparenthood (compadrazgo) (*Southw. jour. anthrop.,* v. 6, p. 341-368).
Review of historical antecedents and present day functional correlates based on a comparison of *compadrazgo* in five modern Latin American communities: San José and Barrio Poyal, Puerto Rico; Tusik, Yucatán; Moche, Peru; and Pascua,

Arizona. Authors have done some field work in Puerto Rico.

MEXICO (EXCEPT THE YUCATÁN PENINSULA)

325. Angulo, Andrés. Barrios de la antigua república de Tlaxcala. Topoyanco (*Orientación musical,* v. 9, no. 101, p. 10-11, 13).

326. Barrios E., Miguel. Textos de Xaltocan. Parts 1-2 (*Mesoamer. notes,* 1, p. 1-25; 2, p. 68-85).

327. Carrasco Pizana, Pedro. Los otomíes. Cultura e historia prehispánicas de los pueblos mesoamericanos de habla otomiana. México, Universidad Nacional Autónoma de Mexico, Instituto de Historia en colaboración con el Instituto Nacional de Antropología e Historia (Publ. del Instituto de Historia, primera serie, no. 15). 355 p.
Culture and pre-Hispanic history of the Otomiana-speaking pueblos of Mesoamerica: the Otomí, Mazuai, Matlatzinca, and Ocuilteca. Author uses primarily sources written in the century after the Conquest but also archaeological and recent ethnographic. Gives a distribution of the Indians, their relations with other groups, and a description of the material culture, social organization, war, religion, cosmogony, calendar, ceremonies.

328. Christensen, Bodil. Oraciones del culto del volador (*Rev. mex. estud. antrop.,* t. 11, p. 23-26).

Reproduction of a short text from Xicotepec, in Nahuatl and Spanish.

330. Horcasitas Pimentel, Fernando (ed.). Textos modernos de *La llorona* (*Mesoamer. notes,* 1, p. 34-52, and 2, p. 53-59).
Accounts of several informants on the myth of *La llorona* dating from colonial days in the valley of Mexico.

331. Leal, Mary. Patterns of tone substitution in Zapotec morphology (*Int. jour. amer. ling.,* v. 16, no. 3, July, p. 132-133).

332. Mak, Cornelia. A unique tone perturbation in Mixteco (*Int. jour. amer. ling.,* v. 16, no. 2, April, p. 82-86).

332a. MEMORIAS DEL INSTITUTO NACIONAL INDIGENISTA. V. 1, no. 1. Densidad de la población de habla indígena en la República Mexicana. Prólogo de Alfonso Caso. Introducción de Manuel Germán Parra. México, Ediciones del Instituto Nacional Indigenista. 76 p., maps.

333. Mendoza, Vicente T. Una adoración de pastores en Chilpancingo (*An. inst. invest. estét.,* no. 18, p. 35-62).
See item 3191.

334. Newman, Stanley, and **Robert Weitlaner.** Central Otomian I: Proto-Otomí reconstructions. Central Otomian II: Primitive Central Otomian reconstructions (*Int. jour. amer. ling.,* v. 16, no. 1, Jan., p. 1-19; no. 2, April, p. 73-81).

335. Peña, Moisés T. de la. Problemas sociales y económicos de las Mixtecas. México, Instituto Nacional Indigenista (Memorias, v. 2, no. 1). 182 p., illus., maps.
See item 2424.

336. Ross, Patricia Fent. The Mejicanos of Cuetzalan (*Mesoamer. notes,* 2, p. 94-100).

337. Spicer, Edward H. The military organization in Yaqui culture (*For the Dean,* p. 171-187).
Based on field work in Sonora.

338. Stanislawski, Dan. The anatomy of eleven towns in Michoacán. Austin, Texas, University of Texas, Institute of Latin-American Studies (Latin-American Studies, 10). 77 p., photos, maps.
A first-hand study and analysis which divides the towns into *Hispanic* (Pátzcuaro, Ario de Rosales, Tacámbaro, Purépero, Apatzingán, Buena Vista, Churumuco, and Arteaga), *dual-character* (Erongarícuaro and Chilchota), and *Indian* (Pichátaro), all fully described, with maps, and analyzed.

339. Waterhouse, Viola, and **May Morrison.** Chontal phonemes (*Int. jour. amer. ling.,* v. 16, no. 1, Jan., p. 35-39).

THE YUCATÁN PENINSULA

340. Nida, Eugene U., and **Moisés Romero C.** The pronominal series in Maya (Yucatec) (*Int. jour. amer. ling.,* v. 16, no. 4, Oct., p. 193-197).

341. Redfield, Robert. A village that chose progress. Chan Kom revisited. Chicago, University of Chicago Press. xi, 187 p.
Discussion, based on field work in 1948, of changes since the author's previous visit in 1933. A notable shift of theoretical views and approach from *Chan Kom, a Maya village* (1934).

342. Weathers, Nadine. Morphological analysis of a Tzotzil (Mayan) text (*Int. jour. amer. ling.,* v. 16, no. 2, April, p. 91-98).

CENTRAL AMERICA

343. ALFABETOS PARA LOS CUATRO IDIOMAS INDÍGENAS MAYORITARIOS DE GUATEMALA: QUICHÉ, CAKCHIQUEL, MAM Y KEKCHÍ. Guatemala, Ministerio de Educación Pública, Instituto Indigenista Nacional (Publ. especiales, no. 10). 29 p.

344. Heath, G. R. Miskito glossary with ethnographic commentary (*Int. jour. amer. ling.,* v. 16, no. 1, Jan., p. 20-34).
Extracts from lexicon on terms of flora and fauna, medicinal terms, folklore items, and social organization.

345. Paul, Benjamin D. Life in a Guatemalan Indian village (In *Patterns for Modern Living,* Division 3, Cultural Patterns, Chicago, The Delphian Society, p. 468-515).
Mainly life cycle material, based on intensive field work in San Pedro La Laguna.

346. ———. Symbolic sibling rivalry in a Guatemalan Indian village (*Amer. anthrop.,* v. 52, no. 2, April-June, p. 205-218).
Description and analysis of a family ritual in San Pedro La Laguna with underlying cultural beliefs.

347. Samayoa Chinchilla, Carlos. Madre Milpa. Guatemala, Tipografía Nacional de Guatemala. 462 p.
Examples of pre-Columbian and modern tales. Extensive glossary of indigenous words and expressions included. See also item 2622.

348. Stone, Doris. Notes on present-day pottery making and its economy in the

Ancient Chorotegan area (*Middle amer. research records,* v. 1, no. 16, Dec., p. 269-280).

THE WEST INDIES

349. Alpenfels, Ethel J. (and others) (eds.). Virgin Islands, U. S. A. (*Jour. educ. soc.,* v. 24, no. 4, Dec., p. 185-248).
An issue of the journal devoted to the Virgin Islands, including articles: Antonio Jarvis, "The people of the Virgin Islands"; Carol Kohler, "The godmother concept—its place in the socio-economic structure"; Pauline Kupcok, "A brief history of the Virgin Islands, U.S.A."; Elinor Doryk, "Dancing in the Virgin Islands"; and Emmabelle S. Boyles, "Music in the Virgin Islands."

350. Ames, David W. Negro family types in a Cuban solar (*Phylon,* v. 11, no. 2, second quarter, p. 159-163).
Brief description based on summer field work in Habana.

351. Bascom, William R. The focus of Cuban santeria (*Southw. jour. anthrop.,* v. 6, no. 1, spring, p. 64-68).
The worship of African deities and their significance in religion.

352. Gordon, Maxine W. Cultural aspects of Puerto Rico's race problem (*Amer. soc. rev.,* v. 15, no. 3, June, p. 382-392).

353. Hawkins, W. Neil. Patterns of vowel loss in Macushi (Carib) (*Int. jour. amer. ling.,* v. 16, no. 2, April, p. 87-90).

355. Marcelin, Milo. Mythologie voudou. Rite arada. Illustrations de Hector Hyppolite. V. 2. Port-au-Prince, Les Éditions Haïtiennes. 198 p.
See *HLAS, no. 15, 1949,* item 2569, for v. 1.

356. Taylor, Douglas. The meaning of dietary and occupational restrictions among the island Carib (*Amer. anthrop.,* v. 52, no. 3, July-Sept., p. 343-349).

357. LES TEMPS MODERNES. Paris. 5. année, no. 52, fév., p. 1345-1536.
P. 1345-1416 of this number are devoted to a section called on the table of contents "Textes antillais." It begins with an essay, *Martinique, Guadeloupe, Haïti,* by Michel Leiris (p. 1345-1368). Next is a selection of poems by various authors (p. 1369-1385). *Chants voudous* are presented by Alfred Métraux (p. 1386-1393). These are followed by *Trois chansons guadeloupéennes* (p. 1394-1396); *Biguines et autres chansons de la Martinique* (1397-1407); *Noms de véhicules terrestres dans les Antilles de langue française* (p. 1408-1413); and *L'Homme vert* (account of a dream, by Albert Mangonès). [Ed.]

ADDENDA

358. Barrera Vásquez, Alfredo. Noticias acerca de la investigación de la lengua maya de Yucatán (*Méx. antiguo,* v. 7, dic., 1949, p. 217-237).
Review of studies of Yucatec from the notations of Columbus to the present.

359. Canales, José Alberto. Los nicarindios (*An. soc. geog. hist. Guatemala,* t. 24, año 24, no. 3-4, sept.-dic., 1949, p. 283-297).
Brief history; groupings of indigenous peoples with differences described.

360. Cook, Carmen, and Don Leonard. Costumbres mortuorias de los indios huaves (*Méx. antiguo,* v. 7, dic., 1949, p. 439-513).
Field work undertaken for the Instituto Indigenista and the Museo Nacional de Oaxaca. Data on ceremony for the dead including texts, grave goods, and significance of the dead in religion. Illus.

361. Jiménez Moreno, Wigberto. Seler y las lenguas indígenas de México (*Méx. antiguo,* v. 7, dic., 1949, p. 16-21).
Appraisal of Seler's linguistic work.

362. Larsen, Kay. Huastec baby talk (*Méx. antiguo,* v. 7, dic., 1949, p. 295-298).
Vocabulary mainly of one family near Valles, San Luis Potosí, with notes on processes by which some words are derived from adult vocabulary.

362a. LENGUAS INDÍGENAS DE GUATEMALA EN EL SIGLO XVIII. Manuscritos que se conservan en el Archivo de Sevilla, España. Con la ortografía del original (*An. soc. geog. hist. Guatemala,* t. 24, año 24, no. 1-2, mayo-junio, 1949, p. 107-158).
Kekchí, Quiché, Pokonchí, Cakchiquel, Zutuhil, Pocomán and Popoluca, Chol, Zotzil, Tzeltal, and Mam vocabulary.

363. Monzón, Arturo. El calpulli en la organización de los tenochca. México, Universidad Nacional Autónoma de México, Instituto de Historia, 1949. 112 p.
Social organization, social stratification, division of work, land ownership.

364. Pike, Eunice Victoria. Texts on Mazatec food-witchcraft (*Méx. antiguo,* v. 7, dic., 1949, p. 287-294).
Description of ceremonies: marriages, baptism, attitudes in mourning, offerings to dead, and other ceremonies in connection with religious feasts of mestizo type.

365. Schoembs, Jakob. Aztekische Schriftsprache. Grammatik (mit Lautlehre). Text und Glossar. Heidelberg, Carl Winter Universitätsverlag, 1949. 212 p.

A grammar of 16th-century literary Náhuatl (p. 9-74), a reproduction of the Náhuatl text of the twelfth book of Sahagún's *Historia general de las cosas de Nueva España* (p. 79-123), and a Náhuatl-German vocabulary (p. 124-211). Excellent manual for literary Náhuatl. The grammatical section is based on Molina and Carochi, but with modern terminology. [C. E. Kany]

366. Verschueren, J. La République d'Haïti. Paris, P. Lethielleux, 1948. 3 v. 539, 514, 467 p.

The three volumes are entitled respectively *Panorame d'Haïti, Echos d'Haïti,* and *Le culte du voudou en Haïti.* See *HLAS, no. 14, 1948,* item 341.

367. Waterhouse, Viola. Oaxaca Chontal. Sentence types and text analysis (*Méx. antiguo,* v. 7, dic., 1949, p. 299-314). Data from field work in Santiago Astata.

ETHNOLOGY: SOUTH AMERICA

D. B. STOUT

IN this, the sixth number of the *Handbook* for which this contributing editor has prepared a section, it seems appropriate to repeat the exhortations first voiced in the volume for 1945, *viz.:* "that more of our South American colleagues expend their energies—and their printing space—on the living Indian cultures around them. All too few of the items listed below contain a new ethnographic fact or an original ethnologic interpretation or synthesis." Only in Brazil is there a consistent annual output, of a substantial volume, by ethnologists of professional competence. Peru, Colombia, and Venezuela remain promising, as was observed in 1946 and 1948; the ethnologists of each have published excellent studies from time to time, but they remain too few, and too much effort is still spent on secondary and tertiary sources with little solid contribution to the science of man. For the remaining South American nations this annual round-up of selected entries is little short of discouraging, despite occasional exceptions which are too often the product of immigrant or visiting scholars.

There appeared one publication during the year which merits special mention: the sixth, and final, volume of the *Handbook of South American Indians* (see items 113, 1129), devoted to articles on physical anthropology, linguistics, and cultural geography, and edited by Julian H. Steward.

For details of meetings, research activities, changes in personnel, and the work of the Institute of Social Anthropology in the various South American nations, see: *B.B.A.A.,* v. 13, part 1, 1950, i.e. 1951; *Bol. indig.,* v. 10, no. 1-4; and the *Sixty-seventh* and *Sixty-eighth annual report of the Bureau of American Ethnology,* Smithsonian Institution, Washington, 1951, 1952.

It is our unhappy duty to report the deaths in 1950 of two scholars who were leaders in the study of South American Indians: Jacinto Jijón y Caamaño of Ecuador and Max Schmidt of Paraguay.

GENERAL

368. Mason, J. Alden. The languages of South American Indians (*Handbook of South American Indians,* v. 6, p. 157-318).
A careful, indeed generally meticulous and successful, attempt to bring into adjustment the previous proposed classifications "presented without any pretense of finality," for what is generally regarded as the region of the greatest linguistic diversity in the world. The bibliography is extraordinarily complete; the map (in color, in pocket), excellently drafted and printed, shows locations as of time of first record. See also item 372a.

369. Métraux, Alfred. The contribution of the Rev. Father Cooper to South American ethnography (*Primitive man,* v. 23, no. 3, July, p. 39-48).

370. ————. Les Peaux-rouges de l'Amérique du Sud. Paris, Éditions Bourrelier (Col. La Joie de Connaître). 123 p., illus.
Popular survey of the principal varieties of South American Indian cultures.

371. ————. South American Indian folklore (In *Dictionary of folklore, mythology and legend,* p. 1052-1058).

Comprehensive summary describing the major types of myths and tales and their distributions. See item 104.

372. Rydén, Stig. A study of South American Indian hunting traps (*Rev. mus. paulista*, n. s., v. 4, p. 247-352).
An exhaustive, and valuable, distributional study, based on a wealth of sources. Illustrations and maps.

372a. Tribal and linguistic distributions of South America, 1:9,000,000. Tribal locations after Julian H. Steward and linguistic distributions after J. Alden Mason (*Handbook of South American Indians*, v. 6).
This map (no. 18), prepared to illustrate and accompany the *Handbook of South American Indians*, v. 6, was printed at the Government Printing Office, Washington. It shows the distribution of 42 tribes and 72 languages by means of colors, numbers, and symbols. The map, which goes in a pocket inside the back cover, was inadvertently omitted in the early manufacture of the publication. [A. C. Gerlach]

BRAZIL

373. Ayrosa, Plínio. Nomes dos membros do corpo humano e outros designativos na língua brasílica. Mss. do séc. XVIII. São Paulo, Universidade de São Paulo, Faculdade de Filosofia, Ciências e Letras (Bol. 114, Etnografia e Língua Tupi-Guarani, no. 19). 40 p.

374. ————. Orações e diálogos da doutrina cristã na língua brasílica. Mss. do séc. XVIII, transcritos e anotados . . . . São Paulo, Universidade de São Paulo, Faculdade de Filosofia, Ciências e Letras (Bol. 106, Etnografia e Língua Tupi-Guarani, no. 17). 96 p.

375. Baldus, Herbert. A alimentação dos índios do Brasil (*Sociologia*, v. 12, no. 1, março, p. 44-58).
Suggestions for research on dietary, beliefs about food, and cooking methods of Brazilian Indians, with directions for preparation of specimens for laboratory study and analysis.

376. ————. Bebidas e narcóticos dos índios do Brasil. Sugestões para pesquisas etnográficas (*Sociologia*, v. 12, no. 2, maio, p. 161-169).

377. ————. Lendas dos índios Tereno (*Rev. mus. paulista*, n. s., v. 4, p. 217-232).
Four tales, collected in 1947, with commentaries and summaries in English and German.

378. Fernandes, Eurico. Medicina e maneiras de tratamento entre os índios Pariukur

(Aruak) (*Amér. indígena*, v. 10, no. 4, oct., p. 309-320).

379. Ferreira, Manoel Rodrigues. Terras e índios do Alto Xingu. São Paulo, Edições Melhoramentos, 1950? 158 p., illus.
Brief notes and excellent photographs of considerable ethnographic value.

380. Galvão, Eduardo. O uso do propulsor entre as tribus do Alto Xingu (*Rev. mus. paulista*, n. s., v. 4, p. 352-368).
Detailed description of a ceremonial game in which the spearthrower is employed. 14 plates.

381. Lamartine, Oswaldo. Notas sôbre a pescaria de açudes no Seridó (*Bol. mus. nac.*, Rio, n. s., Antropologia, no. 10, 22 out., 13 p., 11 figs.).

382. Lima, G. C. Bierrenbach. A origem do homem americano e tribus indígenas do Brasil (*Rev. arq. mun.*, ano 17, v. 135, set., p. 3-36).
A list of 481 tribes in Brazil, compiled from secondary and tertiary sources.

383. Lima, Pedro E. de. A canoa de casca de jatobá entre os índios do Xingu (*Rev. mus. paulista*, n. s., v. 4, p. 369-380).
Detailed description of the manufacture of bark canoes. 12 plates.

384. ————. Os índios Waurá. Observações gerais. A cerâmica (*Bol. mus. nac.*, Rio, n. s., Antropologia, no. 9, 8 maio, p. 1-25).
Brief notes, mainly on pottery-making as done by a community of 95 Waurá who live on the Rio Batovi, an affluent of the Xingu. 19 plates.

385. Loukotka, Čestmír. Les langues de la famille Tupi-Guarani. São Paulo, Universidade de São Paulo, Faculdade de Filosofia, Ciências e Letras (Bol. 104, Etnografia e Lingua Tupi-Guarani, no. 16). 42 p.
Classification, with concordance of variant names, based on intensive comparative studies and on the author's hypotheses concerning Tupi-Guarani tribal migrations. Contains exhaustive bibliography, with many entries for unpublished manuscripts.

386. Meggers, Betty J. Caboclo life in the mouth of the Amazon (*Primitive man*, v. 23, no. 1-2, Jan.-April, p. 14-28).
Brief description of economic, social and religious life of the rural and town folk on Marajó, Caviana, and Mexiana islands.

387. Nimuendajú, Curt. Reconhecimento dos rios Içána, Ayarí e Uaupes (*Jour. soc. amér.*, n. s., t. 39, p. 126-182).
Posthumous publication of valuable notes on a number of Indian communities in the states of Amazonas and Acre, in the form of a report, dated 1927, to the Serviço de Proteção aos Índios.

388. **Ribeiro, Darcy.** Religião e mitologia Kadiuéu. Rio de Janeiro, Serviço de Proteção aos Índios (Publ. no. 106). 222 p., plates and musical scores.
Comprehensive account, based on field work.

389. **Schultz, Harold.** Lendas dos índios Krahó (*Rev. mus. paulista*, n. s., v. 4, p. 49-162).
Brief ethnographic notes and 18 myths and tales, collected in 1947, with résumés.

390. **Silva, F. Altenfelder.** O estado de *uanki* entre os Bakairi (*Sociologia*, v. 12, no. 3, agôsto, p. 259-271).
Brief description of Bakairi culture, with emphasis on the state of *uanki*, a ritualistic seclusion undergone in periods of crisis during the life cycle.

391. **Wirth, D. Mauro.** Lendas dos índios Vapidiana (*Rev. mus. paulista*, n. s., v. 4, p. 165-216).
Sixty-five myths and tales collected in 1937-1939.

BRITISH, DUTCH, AND FRENCH GUIANA

392. **Aubert de la Rüe, E.** Quelques observations sur les Oyampi de l'Oyapock (*Jour. soc. amér.*, n. s., t. 39, p. 85-96, 4 plates).

CHILE

393. **Emperaire, J.** Évolution démographique des indiens Alakaluf (*Jour. soc. amér.*, n. s., t. 39, p. 187-218).
Excellent demographic data, based on field investigations in 1946-1948. Two plates, two tables.

394. **Mostny, Greta.** Transculturación de las tribus fueguinas (*Amér. indígena*, v. 10, no. 3, julio, p. 221-232).
Comparison of the rates of culture change among the Ona, Yámana (Yaghan) and Alacaluf, using language as the principal index. This paper, presented at the II Congreso Indigenista Interamericano, was published in a somewhat more extended form in *Rev. geog. Chile*, año 3, no. 3, julio, 1950, p. 37-60. See item 455.

COLOMBIA

396. **Gutiérrez de Pineda, Virginia.** Organización social en la Guajira (*Rev. inst. etnol. nac.*, v. 3, entrega 2, 1948, i.e. 1950, p. 1-255).
Excellent, comprehensive ethnographic report based on field work carried out in 1947.

396a. **Pérez de Barradas, José.** Los muiscas antes de la conquista. V. 1. Madrid, Consejo Superior de Investigaciones Científicas (Pueblos Indígenas de la Gran Colombia, t. 1). 610 p., illus., map.
Comprehensive social and cultural description, based on extensive use of the early sources.

397. **Pineda Giraldo, Roberto.** Aspectos de la magia en la Guajira (*Rev. inst. etnol. nac.*, v. 3, entrega 1, 1947, i.e. 1950, p. 1-163).
Comprehensive account, based on field work carried out in 1947.

398. **Reichel-Dolmatoff, Gerardo.** Los kogi, una tribu de la Sierra Nevada de Santa Marta, Colombia (*Rev. inst. etnol. nac.*, v. 4, entregas 1-2, 1949-1950, p. 1-314).
The first of two volumes of a detailed and comprehensive ethnography, based on field work carried out in 1946 and 1949. The Kogi are more usually known in the previous literature as the Kágaba. 23 plates, 1 map.

399. ———, and **Alexander L. Clark.** Parentesco, parentela y agresión entre los iroka (*Jour. soc. amér.*, n. s., t. 39, p. 97-109).

400. **Rivet, Paul,** and **Cesáreo de Armellada.** Les Indiens motilones (*Jour. soc. amér.*, n. s., t. 39, p. 15-57).
Detailed analysis and vocabulary comparisons based on a 1738 manuscript.

PERU

401. **Indians of Peru.** Photographs by Pierre Verger, captions and text by Luis E. Valcárcel. Lake Forest, Illinois, Pocahontas Press. Distributed by Pantheon Books, New York. 199 p., 1 map, 87 plates.
English edition; original appeared in Spanish, 1945. See *HLAS, no. 11, 1945*, item 346.

402. **La Barre, Weston.** Aymara folktales (*Int. jour. amer. ling.*, v. 16, no. 1, Jan., p. 40-45).
Several examples illustrating the violence and hostility which characterize Aymara behavior.

403. **Matos Mar, José.** Marco geográfico del área cultural del kauke en el Perú. Lima, Universidad Nacional Mayor de San Marcos, Facultad de Letras, Instituto de Etnología (Publ. no. 1). 44 p., illus.
Survey report on the Kauke language community, Yauyos province. Reprinted from *Letras*, primer semestre, no. 44, 1950, p. 133-174.

404. **Radicati di Primeglio, Carlos.** Introducción al estudio de los quipus (*Documenta*, año 2, no. 1, 1949-1950, p. 244-339).
A review of literature and outline of the problems connected with unravelling mysteries

abounding in the study of the knotted cords or quipus used by the Peruvian Indians, in an attempt to take them out of polemics and dilettantism. This extends the work of Locke, Nordenskiöld, Cipriani, and Altieri, whose scientific writings form a foundation. This first installment of a projected long investigation consists of four chapters concerning the present state of the problem, the general characteristics of quipus, a chronological catalogue of the known examples (including eight not hitherto published) and, finally, remarks on various aspects, especially concerning the probable use and function of quipus. The author arrives at no specific positive conclusions. Illus. [H. F. Cline]

405. Rowe, John Howland. Sound patterns in three Inca dialects (*Int. jour. amer. ling.*, v. 16, no. 3, July, p. 137-148).
Description of differences between two of the larger extant Quichua dialects (Cuzco and Ayacucho) and a discussion of their relation to Classic Inca as known from early sources.

406. Shell, Olive A. Cashibo I: Phonemes (*Int. jour. amer. ling.*, v. 16, no. 4, Oct., p. 198-202).
The phonemic structure of this Pano language of Peru, Brazil, and Bolivia.

407. Tibesar, Antoine S. The salt trade among the Montaña Indians of the Tarma area of eastern Peru (*Primitive man,* v. 23, no. 4, Oct., p. 103-108).

OTHER COUNTRIES

408. Hawthorn, H. B. The Quechua Indians near Sucre, Bolivia (*Can. geog. jour.,* v. 41, no. 1, July, p. 44-53).
Brief, neat description of Sucre Indian life. Illus., map. [G. M. McBride]

409. Holmberg, Allan R. Nomads of the long bow. The Siriono of eastern Bolivia. Prepared in cooperation with the U. S. Dept. of State as a project of the Interdepartmental Committee on Scientific and Cultural Cooperation. Washington, U. S. Govt. Printing Office (Smithsonian Institution, Institute of Social Anthropology, Publ. no. 10). iv, 104 p., 7 plates, 4 charts, 1 map.
Succinct, comprehensive account, based on field research carried out in 1940-1941 in which the main interest was to investigate the relationship between the psychological principles of learning and cultural forms and processes in a perennially hungry society; to this end the author has achieved a successful study.

410. Lares, José Ignacio. Etnografía del Estado Mérida. Tercera edición. Mérida, Venezuela, Universidad de los Andes, Dirección de Cultura (Publ. no. 7). 37 p.
Republication of the 1907 edition, which in turn was a corrected version of the first, 1883, edition.

411. Paz y Miño, Luis Telmo. Las lenguas indígenas del Ecuador. Diccionario toponímico (*Bol. acad. nac. hist.,* Quito, v. 30, no. 75, enero-junio, p. 57-74; no. 76, julio-dic., p. 172-189).
To be continued. See *HLAS no. 14, 1948,* item 543, and *no. 15, 1949,* item 459.

ADDENDA

412. Anchieta, José de. Auto representado na festa de São Lourenço. Peça trilingüe do século XVI, transcrita, comentada e traduzida, na parte tupi, por M. de L. de Paula Martins. São Paulo, Museu Paulista (Bol. 1, ano 1, Documentação Linguística, 1), 1948. 142 p., illus.
See items 2916, 2921.

413. Catálogo geral das publicações da Comissão Rondon e do Conselho Nacional de Proteção aos Índios. Rio de Janeiro, Ministerio da Agricultura, Conselho Nacional de Proteção aos Índios (Publ. no. 96), 1946. 32 p.
Complete list, containing many items treating of Brazilian Indian ethnography.

414. Guasch, Antonio. El idioma guaraní. Gramática. Lecturas. Vocabulario doble. Segunda edición, mejorada y acrecentada. Buenos Aires, Ediciones del Autor, 1948. 536 p.
Reedition; it first appeared in 1944.

415. Loukotka, Čestmír. Klassifikation der südamerikanischen Sprachen (*Zeit. ethnol.,* Band 74, 1942, p. 1-69).
Extensively revised edition of the author's *Clasificación de las lenguas sudamericanas* and *Roztřídění jihoamerických Jazyků* which appeared in the Colección Lingüística Sudamericana, no. 1 and 3, Prague, 1935 and 1941. The German edition increases the author's earlier list of South American Indian language families from 94 to 114. (One map.) A large part of this edition of *Zeitschrift für Ethnologie* was destroyed in the course of air raids on Berlin during World War II, hence copies are scarce and the article has only now come to this editor's attention. A very helpful and extensive synopsis of Loukotka's classification is given in a review in the *Int. jour. amer. ling.,* v. 17, no. 4, Oct., 1951, p. 259-266.

416. ———. Sur quelques langues inconnues de l'Amérique du Sud (*Lingua posnaniensis,* t. 1, 1949, p. 53-82).
Brief notes and vocabularies on 15 languages, based mainly on information contained in nine unpublished manuscripts.

417. Nimuendajú, Curt. Os Tapajó (*Bol. mus. paraense Emilio Goeldi,* t. 1, 1949, p. 93-106).

Brief notes, based on early sources, taken from unpublished manuscript left by Nimuendajú.

418. Olivares Figueroa, R. Diversiones pascuales en Oriente y otros ensayos. Caracas, Ardor, 1949. 191 p., illus.
Detailed descriptions of customs, songs, dances, and the like, in celebration of Easter.

419. Schaden, Francisco S. G. Índios e caboclos. Páginas de etnografia e folclore

(*Rev. arq. mun.*, ano 15, v. 125, junho, 1949, p. 23-64).

420. Titiev, Mischa. Social singing among the Mapuche. Ann Arbor, Michigan, University of Michigan (Museum of Anthropology, Anthropological Papers, no. 2), 1949. 17 p.
Several Araucanian songs, analyzed for the light they shed on the interrelations of social organization and personality development.

PHYSICAL ANTHROPOLOGY

T. D. STEWART

AFTER 1949, a year characterized by so many major international conferences, 1950 seems almost uneventful. Yet this year, too, had an international gathering that attracted American anthropologists: the Fifth International Congress of Anatomists held in Oxford, England, from July 24 to 28. Two papers from the program of this Congress should be mentioned here: 1, Carlos Henckel, of Concepción, Chile, reported the finding among the Mapuche Indians in the province of Cautín of "White Indians" characterized by white skin, reddish hair, and gray or blue eyes; 2, W. F. Harper, of the University College of the West Indies, Jamaica, demonstrated a number of artificially deformed Arawak skulls. (See *Man*, v. 50, Nov., art. 237, p. 149.)

It is noteworthy also in connection with international conferences that one of the main results of the 1949 UNESCO Conference on Race became generally available in 1950: the so-called "Statement on Race." In the rush to publish this statement the initial, unpolished version was used. (For example, in *B.B.A.A.*, v. 12, pt. 1, 1949, i.e. 1950, p. 12-15; *Bol. Indig.*, v. 10, no. 1, marzo, p. 10-19.) Later, attention was called to some corrections suggested by a group of experts serving as editors. (See *El Correo de la UNESCO*, v. 3, no. 6-7, agosto, p. 8-9.)

International cooperation in physical anthropology appeared also this year in the form of a large section (156 p.) in the sixth volume of the *Handbook of South American Indians,* published in Washington by the Bureau of American Ethnology. Contributors are divided equally between Latin Americans and North Americans. (One of the North American contributors, Morris Steggerda, died March 15, 1950.) In addition to a compilation of facts about the physical characteristics of the Indians, past and present, the volume contains a large relevant bibliography.

Reports of a few local activities may also be mentioned. At the Instituto de Antropología in Buenos Aires students and professors of the sections of history and philosophy of the Faculty of Philosophy and Letters held a series of "sesiones de comunicaciones" at one of which (September 6) Marcelo Bórmida talked on *Craneología patagónica.* Later, Bórmida went to Patagonia to extend the observations of the 1949 expedition (see *HLAS, no. 15, 1949,* p. 46), especially as regards blood groups and physical measurements. This is noted in *B.B.A.A.*, v. 13, pt. 1, 1950, i.e. 1951, p. 28-29.

At the Instituto de Antropología in Tucumán the director, Branimiro Males, was completing his first reports on the racial origin of the peoples of northwest Argentina. The titles of some of the manuscripts that he and his associates have prepared in this connection are as follows: *El origen étnico de la población de la ciudad de Salta; Antropometría de algunos tipos raciales indígenas y de sus derivaciones criollas; El índice cefálico de la población de la ciudad de Tucumán;* and *Un aporte al estudio de la criminalidad de la Provincia de Tucumán.* (See Universidad

Nacional de Tucumán. *Memoria correspondiente al año 1950.* Tucumán, Argentina, 1951, p. 34.)

From Colombia comes the promise of a craniological study as the result of an accidental discovery of burials in the course of building a new road. The find was made near the town of Guicán in the northern part of the Department of Boyacá and was investigated by Eliécer Silva Celis and Eginhard Menghius. Fourteen skulls with cultural associations were recovered in the initial excavations. (See *B.B.A.A.,* v. 13, part 1, 1950, i.e. 1951, p. 41).

At the Museo Nacional de Antropología y Arqueología in Lima, Peru, dental studies were made on prehistoric skulls by Drs. Marcelo A. Obando and Alessandra Dabbert. Dr. Obando found evidence of dental fluorosis among the remains from Ancón. At this museum also further studies on prehistoric cranial surgery were carried out by Drs. Esteban D. Rocca, Luis Graña R., and Petronio Garaycochea. (*Ibid.*, p. 139-140.)

Finally, in Mexico, Eusebio Dávalos Hurtado lectured at the Universidad Nacional Autónoma on September 27 on *Perspectivas de la antropología física en México.* (See *Bol. indig.*, v. 10, no. 4, dic., p. 348.)

GENERAL

421. Boyd, William C. Blood groups of South American Indians (*Handbook of South American Indians*, v. 6, p. 91-95).
Classification by A-B-O and M-N blood groups. The distribution of genes p and q is shown on a map. Bibliography.

422. Comas, Juan. En memoria de Franz Weidenreich, 1873-1948 (*Rev. mex. estud. antrop.*, t. 11, p. 297-313).
Analysis of Weidenreich's contributions, especially in the field of fossil man. Includes a photograph but no bibliography.

423. Imbelloni, José. La "tabla clasificatoria de los indios" a los trece años de su publicación (*Runa,* v. 3, partes 1-2, p. 200-210).
Reviews briefly the criticisms offered during the period 1937-1950 regarding details of the author's racial map of the Americas. Given especial attention are the views of Dembo, Biasutti, Vivó, Newman, Sauer, Canals Frau, and Zapater.

424. McCown, Theodore D. The antiquity of man in South America (*Handbook of South American Indians*, v. 6, p. 1-9).
Reviews the history of research on this subject and in general agrees with Hrdlička's claim that most of the putatively ancient remains are recent intrusions into older strata. Large bibliography.

425. Oetteking, Bruno. Sacropelvimetry (*Rev. mex. estud. antrop.*, t. 11, p. 27-77).
Discusses each of the component parts in terms of landmarks or measuring points and their definitions, the respective measurements (including angles and indices), and the resulting linear reconstructions. The treatment attempts to be more precise than that found in available handbooks. Table 1 includes measurements on 21 male sacra from the Bahamas. 16 figures.

426. Steggerda, Morris. Anthropometry of South American Indians (*Handbook of South American Indians*, v. 6, p. 57-69).
Lists a large number of observations on stature and cephalic index by sex, tribe, and linguistic group. Photographs of 48 physical types. Bibliography.

427. ————. Mestizos of South America (*Handbook of South American Indians*, v. 6, p. 105-109).
Reviews the few available studies on human hybrids in this area, showing the degrees of mixture and the effect on physique.

428. ————. The pigmentation and hair of South American Indians (*Handbook of South American Indians*, v. 6, p. 85-90).
A compilation of descriptions from the writings of anthropologists who had seen the Indians in question.

429. Stewart, T. D. Deformity, trephining, and mutilation in South American Indian skeletal remains (*Handbook of South American Indians*, v. 6, p. 43-48).
Briefly outlines the areas where these practices occurred and describes the peculiarities of the practice according to area. Large bibliography.

430. ————. Investigaciones periódicas de la calidad física de las poblaciones americanas (*II cong. indig. inter-amer.*, p. 256).
Abstract of a paper read at the Congress recommending that tests of population quality be combined from time to time with census enumeration.

431. ————. Pathological changes in South American Indian skeletal remains (*Handbook of South American Indians*, v. 6, p. 49-52).
Reviews the subject under two headings: 1, chronic infectious diseases, such as syphilis,

leprosy, and tuberculosis; and 2, degenerative changes such as arthritis, dental decay, and tumors and exostoses. Few illustrations. Bibliography.

432. ――――, and **Marshall T. Newman.** Anthropometry of South American Indian skeletal remains (*Handbook of South American Indians,* v. 6, p. 19-42).
Lists 43 cranial series and locates their sources on a map. For each of 11 measurements and 4 indices the series are arranged by the descending order of the means in the males. When the means are based on 25 or more specimens they are accompanied by their probable errors and standard deviations. The range is given in every case. The generalized distributions of average mean height index and the average cranial module are shown in maps. Illustrations of cranial types. Large bibliography.

433. **Wilson, Elsie A.** The basal metabolic rates of South American Indians (*Handbook of South American Indians,* v. 6, p. 97-104).
Reviews the findings according to tribe and purity of race. The complications caused by race-mixture, climate, and nutrition are stressed.

MIDDLE AMERICA

434. **Comas, Juan.** Bosquejo histórico de la antropología en México (*Rev. mex. estud. antrop.,* t. 11, p. 97-192).
Amplified and corrected edition of item 579, *HLAS, no. 14, 1948.* Large bibliography.

435. **Dávalos Hurtado, Eusebio, and Javier Romero.** Dictamen de los antropólogos físicos [acerca del hallazgo de Ichcateopan, Guerrero] (*Rev. mex. estud. antrop.,* t. 11, p. 204-225).
Part of a larger report by numerous experts directed toward the identification of a burial claimed by Srta. Eulalia Guzmán to be that of Cuauhtémoc. The partly burned skeletal remains are carefully itemized and shown to include at least 5 individuals. Two are subadults. Photographs of the material are included. See also item 1606.

436. **Keeler, Clyde E.** An attempt to eliminate a genetic syndrome in man (*Eugen. news,* v. 35, no. 3, Sept., p. 40-44).
Maintains that the albinistic "moon-children" of the Caribe-Cuna Indians (Panama) represent "not merely a pigment variation, but rather a pleiotropic syndrome affecting morphology, physiology, and psychosomatic behavior." Now that these individuals are allowed to breed, the earlier eugenic measures of the Cuna are being weakened.

437. ――――, and **Luis Prieto.** The Caribe-Cuna moon-child. A demonstration of pigment-gene pleiotropy in man (*Bull. Ga. acad. sci.,* v. 8, no. 3, p. 3-6).
Considers the albinistic Indians of Panama ideal for demonstrating the side effects resulting from the genes that modify melanic pigmentation. Cites physical, physiological, and mental peculiarities in 37 of these children observed by Prieto.

438. **Terra, Helmut de.** Radiocarbon age measurements and fossil man in Mexico (*Ciencia,* México, v. 10, no. 7-8, Oct. 15, p. 209-210).
Calls attention to the finding by Arnold and Libby of a radiocarbon date of $11,300 \pm 500$ years for the Becerra peat at the Tepexpan Man site. The younger marl above the bone-bearing caliche layer gave a date of $4,118 \pm 300$ years. Published in English and Spanish.

ARGENTINA AND BRAZIL

439. **Avila, José Bastos d'.** Anthropometry of the Indians of Brazil (*Handbook of South American Indians,* v. 6, p. 71-84).
Gives some of the findings of individual investigators, both on skulls and on the living, according to region.

440. **Bergna, Luis María.** Estudio antropométrico de escolares de ascendencia araucano argentina (*An. inst. étnico nac.,* t. 2, 1949, i.e. 1950, p. 131-142).
43 males and 56 females between the ages of 7 and 12 years were measured in Los Toldos. The following measurements are given by age group: Stature; sitting height; bi-acromial, bi-iliac, and bi-trochanteric diameters; lengths of upper and lower extremities; length, breadth, and height of head.

441. **Canals Frau, Salvador.** Algunos rasgos antropológicos de la población argentina (*An. inst. étnico nac.,* t. 2, 1949, i.e. 1950, p. 15-27).
Reviews the beginnings of physical anthropology in Argentina, the population increase because of immigration, and the changes in stature. Problems for future study are indicated.

442. **Dávalos Hurtado, Eusebio.** Datos antropológico-físicos de la región de Icaño de Santiago del Estero (*Jour. soc. amér.,* n. s., t. 39, p. 59-71).
Anthropometric description of the Wagner osteological collection preserved in the Musée de l'Homme, Paris. Comparison of the bones from single, multiple, and urn burials failed to reveal differences in physical type. Figures reported are limited to 19 males, mostly deformed ("tabular erecta"). Stature calculated by means of the Manouvrier tables is higher than that reported earlier by Ten Kate and Imbelloni.

443. **Frenguelli, Joaquín.** The present status of the theories concerning primitive man in Argentina (*Handbook of South American Indians,* v. 6, p. 11-17).
Presents a modification of the Ameghinian theory, placing the whole series of Argentine fossil humans in a more recent time scale.

Frenguelli still believes "there was a Paleolithic age in the pampas region . . . in an epoch probably contemporary with . . . the site where the *Sinanthropus* was found in Asia."

444. Imbelloni, José. Cephalic deformations of the Indians in Argentina (*Handbook of South American Indians,* v. 6, p. 53-55).

Brief summary of the picture as presented in the author's many writings on the subject.

445. Lima, Pedro E. de. Grupos sanguíneos dos índios do Xingu (*Bol. mus. nac.,* Rio de Janeiro, n. s., Antropologia, no. 11, dez. 20, 4 p.).

Presents data on blood groups O, A, B, and AB in a sample of 377 Indians from the Upper Xingu River, State of Mato Grosso. The following tribes are represented: Kamaiurá, Waurá, Mehinako, Kalapalo and Bakairí. All were group O except one Bakairí woman, who was an Indian-White cross. Comparative figures are given.

446. ————. Nivéis tensionais dos índios Kalapalo e Kamaiurá (*Rev. bras. med.,* v. 7, no. 12, dez., p. 787-788).

Mean systolic and diastolic pressures are reported by age group (10-50 years) for 124 Indians from the Upper Xingu River, State of Mato Grosso. The observations were made very early in the morning and probably before the Indians had eaten. Their diet is free from salt, but contains considerable potassium.

447. Pourchet, Maria Julia. Brazilian mestizo types (*Handbook of South American Indians,* v. 6, p. 111-120).

White-Negro-Indian crosses have long been a subject of study in Brazil. Some of these findings are here summarized.

448. Puig, Alberto Andrés. Crecimiento demográfico en la República Argentina. Período 1927-1947 (*An. inst. étnico nac.,* t. 2, 1949, i.e. 1950, p. 101-110).

Compares the population by province and territory at the beginning and end of this 20-year period. Emphasizes with two graphs the very great relative increase in territorial population compared with that of the provinces.

CHILE, COLOMBIA, PERU, AND URUGUAY

449. Álvarez Segura, Juan. La población aborigen en el Perú y el censo de las Américas en 1950 (*II cong. indig. interamer.,* p. 238-242).

Gives racial subdivisions of the census of 1940 and argues for improving the 1950 census records from the standpoint of Indian coverage.

450. Chávez Ruiz, Alejandro. Objeto de las trepanaciones en el antiguo Perú (*Rev. mus. reg. Ica,* año 2, no. 3, p. 31-35).

Review of literature with two illustrations.

451. Esguerra Gómez, Alfonso. El biotipo universitario colombiano (*Rev. acad. col. cien.,* v. 8, no. 29, nov., p. 4-15).

Presents statistical correlations between stature and weight in a series of 992 students between 17 and 23 years of age, and in a series of 520 newborn males (Clínica de Marly). Using 168 cm. and 58 kg. as adult means, the study makes subdivisions of range in terms of x/s.d. Discusses these findings in terms of Viola's biotypes.

452. Henckel, Carlos. The anthropometry of the Indians of Chile (*Handbook of South American Indians,* v. 6, p. 121-135).

The somatology, craniology, and osteology of the main tribes and groups are summarized. Four plates. Large biblography.

453. ————. The physical anthropology of the internal organs among the races of Chile (*Handbook of South American Indians,* v. 6, p. 145-152).

Considers the racial differences in myology, angiology, splanchnology, the nervous system, and the organs of sense. Bibliography.

454. Herzog, Ernesto. The geographical pathology of Chile (*Handbook of South American Indians,* v. 6, p. 137-144).

The patterns of a number of disease entities are discussed, with especial attention to the racial factor.

455. Lipschütz, Alejandro, and Greta Mostny. Cuatro conferencias sobre los indios fueguinos (*Rev. geog. Chile,* año 3, no. 3, julio, p. 13-60, and no. 4, oct., p. 63-86).

Final summation of the results of the Misión Científica Chilena para el Estudio del Indio Fueguino. Of especial interest to physical anthropologists are the lectures dealing with the racial classification of the Fuegians (I), ethnic mutation in Fuegian tribes (III) and the origin of the American Indian and the Fuegian problem (IV). There is an introduction by General Ramón Cañas Montalva. Also issued as a separate, xv, 86 p., illus., maps.

456. Pretto, Julio C., and María Gómez Calderón. Antropometría en alumnos de los colegios nacionales de Lima (*Bol. inst. psicoped. nac.,* año 9, no. 2, dic., p. 41-99).

Analyzes 28 measurements on 1165 males and 1755 females, 13 to 21 years of age, from four schools. The measurements, collected in 1947, 1948, and 1949, are defined and listed by age with the usual statistical constants.

457. Ramón Guerra, Alfredo U. Peso y talla de nuestros recién nacidos y lactantes hasta el año de edad (*Arch. pedia. Uruguay,* v. 21, no. 2, feb., p. 81-97).

Reports the weight and height of 135 male and 120 female newborns over 2500 g. birth weight. In addition like data are given by monthly interval (less than 100 subjects each) up to the end of the first year. These figures occupy the middle channel of the Wetzel grid. Other comparisons are made.

458. ———— (and others). Peso y talla de nuestros niños de primera infancia (*Arch. pedia. Uruguay*, v. 21, no. 3, marzo, p. 173-175).

The data of the previous study (item 457) are extended by three-month intervals to three years. Total number of children examined is 1668.

ADDENDA

460. **Arauco Camacho, Florencio.** La deformación en los cráneos Khollas (*Gac. méd. bol.*, año 7, no. 21, sept., 1949, p. 101-102).

Reply to the criticism of Eusebio Dávalos Hurtado (item 461). Claims to be misunderstood and is unwilling to argue the case.

461. **Dávalos Hurtado, Eusebio.** Morfología humana (*Gac. méd. bol.*, año 6, no. 18-19, nov., 1948, p. 183-185).

Refutes some of the concepts and assertions contained in item 396, *HLAS, no. 13, 1947*.

462. **Henckel, Carlos, and Próspero Arriagada.** Estudios somatológicos en recién nacidos (*Rev. asoc. méd. arg.*, v. 62, no. 640, oct. 30, 1948, p. 575-580).

Reports the following measurements and observations on 241 male and 222 female "native" infants having a birth weight of above 2500 g. (twins excluded): Stature, weight, index of Rohrer; absolute and relative length of thorax; absolute and relative circumference of thorax; circumference, maximum length, and maximum breadth of head, cephalic index; color of iris; color of hair; color of skin; presence or absence of Mongolian spot. The data are treated statistically.

463. **Imbelloni, José.** De historia primitiva de América. Los grupos raciales aborígenes (*Cuad. hist. prim.*, año 3, no. 2, 1948, p. 71-88).

Part of the article listed as item 379 in *HLAS, no. 4, 1938* is here revised in accordance with the author's recent discussion of this subject in *Runa* (item 423).

464. **Lima, Pedro E. de.** Notas antropológicas sôbre os índios do Xingu. Rio de Janeiro, Museu Nacional (Publ. Avulsas, no. 5, 1949, p. 21-29).

General statement of the physical status of five tribes: Kamaiurá, Auety, Trumaí, Iawalapití, and Mehinaku. From these and other mixed groups in the region, the author obtained measurements on 54 males, 41 females, and 34 children; dermatoglyphic records on 88; and blood group records on 60. The details will be reported later. Accompanying plates show physical types.

465. **Quevedo A., Sergio A.** Crecimiento y alimentación de los aborígenes de Anta. Cuzco, Col. Antropología Peruana, 1949. 208 p., 18 graphs, 13 photographs.

Detailed observations, mostly metrical, on 120 males and 85 females between the ages of four and 24, from the native community of Marcko located 30 kilometers northwest of Cuzco in the Province of Anta. The altitude here is 2997 meters. Nonmetrical observations include pulse, respiration, temperature, blood pressure, hair form, denture, tooth decay, and diet. Comparisons are mostly national but sometimes include other races. English summary. Bibliography.

466. **Quintana Augspurg, Guillermo.** Investigación trofológica sobre la clase 1925 convocada en Salta. Estado de nutrición (*Rev. asoc. arg. diet.*, v. 7, no. 26, abril-junio, 1949, p. 128-134).

In 1603 conscripts the percentages of the various constitutional types which had low, normal, and high weights according to "standard" weight-height-age tables were as follows: Normosomic, 15, 76, 9; leptosomic, 20, 72, 8; athletic, 6, 65, 29; tall asthenic, 25, 64, 11; short asthenic, 26, 42, 20; pyknic, 12, 63, 25. Some of the conscripts were grouped according to origin into a general group (596) composed of those from urban, tropical, and fertile valley regions, and a mountain group (147). Thoracic deformations were found among 48.6 per cent of the general group and 45.8 per cent of the mountain group. The Knudsen-Schiötz sign was false for this military group. In the mountain group alone was there a correlation between poor dental condition and thoracic deformation.

467. **Salazar Mallén, M.** El aglutinógeno Lewis en la sangre de los mexicanos (*Bol. inst. estud. méd. biol.*, v. 7, no. 1-6, enero-dic., 1949, p. 25-28).

The blood of 81 Otomí Indians and 199 mestizos of Mexico City tested with anti-Le[a] serum showed agglutination in 9.87 per cent and 11.42 per cent (frequency of gene Le[a] = 0.3142 and 0.3380), respectively. These results are significantly lower than those reported for the English.

467a. **San Martín F., Mauricio (and others).** La herencia del sabor al fenil-tio-carbamida (*II cong. indig. interamer.*, p. 250-251).

Tasters were found as follows: 68.9 per cent of 288 Huancayo Indians, 64.0 per cent of 325 Huancayo mestizos, 89.4 per cent of 2754 Lima mestizos.

468. **Varela, Casper de Campos.** Projeção de medidas craniométricas em "norma lateralis" (*An. fac. farm. odont.*, v. 4, 1944-1945, p. 43-50).

Describes a method based on the Pythagorean theorem for projecting face measurements onto the median plane. For example, a triangle is constructed using the bi-auricular distance and the auriculo-nasion distance. From this the distance from nasion to the mid bi-auricular point is read off or computed by formula.

469. ————, and **Guilherme Oswaldo Arbenz.** Projeção de medidas craniométricas em "norma lateralis" (*An. fac. farm. odont.*, v. 7, 1948-1949, p. 461-465).

Supplements previous theoretical paper of same title (item 468). The bi-auricular and auriculo-vertical distances are given for 135 cases. From these figures bi-auricular height is measured graphically and also computed. Differences range up to 1.7 mm.

Spanish American Art

HAROLD E. WETHEY

THE major contribution in 1950 to the study of Latin American art was the appearance of the second volume of the comprehensive survey of the colonial field, *Historia del arte hispanoamericano,* written chiefly by Diego Angulo Íñiguez, with the collaboration of Enrique Marco Dorta and Mario Buschiazzo. Muthmann's monograph on colonial silverwork in South America was a significant addition to the understanding of this rich and abundant material, which is still so little explored. The first general study of the architecture of Paraguay came from the pen of the experienced architect and scholar Professor Juan Giuria of Montevideo. Trent Elwood Sanford's readable popular account of the *Architecture of the Southwest* was devoted in large part to the colonial period. After several years of preparation Mrs. Elizabeth Weismann's subjective work *Mexico in Sculpture* appeared. Articles included Erwin Walter Palm's four studies on a variety of aspects of Spanish American treasures in Santo Domingo, while the architectural history of the southern hemisphere was further clarified by Rubén Vargas Ugarte's publication of new documents on the cathedral of Huamanga, Peru, and through research by Buschiazzo, Furlong, Martín Noel, and others.

In the field of contemporary art Orozco continued to hold the public eye in 1950 as a result of his death the preceding year. Baldinger's account of Orozco's last murals and the tributes by Charlot, Fernández, and Toussaint provided further proof of his pre-eminence among masters of the twentieth century. Publications on Mexican painting were in general less numerous, however, than in recent years. Although Charlot treats a great variety of subjects in his new book, the chief interest centers upon the Mexicans. The 19th century received attention in Salteraín y Herrera's exhaustive biography of the Uruguayan painter Blanes.

GENERAL

471. ART IN LATIN AMERICA. Washington, Pan American Union (Club and Study Fine Arts Series). 91 p., illus.
This is a popular booklet intended to interest the general public. Most of the short articles had previously been published in the *Bulletin of the Pan American Union* and *Américas.* It includes material on pre-Columbian, colonial, and modern art. A brief bibliography of works in English is included.

472. BIBLIOGRAFÍA DE LAS ARTES POPULARES DE MÉXICO. Prólogo de Alfonso Caso. México, Instituto Nacional Indigenista (Memorias, v. 1, no. 2, p. 83-132).
Well organized list of books and articles.

473. Carrillo y Gariel, Abelardo. Las Galerías de San Carlos. México, Ediciones Mexicanas (Enciclopedia Mexicana de Arte, 6). 53 p., illus.
An illustrated account, not a catalogue, of the

gallery of painting in Mexico City. The collection consists largely of works by Mexican painters of the colonial period and the 19th century and by European masters. Often the paintings are optimistically attributed.

474. Giuria, Juan. La arquitectura en el Paraguay. Buenos Aires, Instituto de Arte Americano e Investigaciones Estéticas. 137 p., 57 illus.

Prof. Giuria's book includes studies of the abandoned Jesuit missions, the churches of Asunción, and domestic architecture. His comprehensive history of the colonial period and the 19th century is well documented, and it is illustrated with plans as well as photographs. It is the first major work upon the architecture of Paraguay.

476. Montenegro, Roberto. Retablos de México. Mexican votive paintings. Translated by Irene Nicholson. México, Ediciones Mexicanas. 75 p., illus.

An interesting collection of votive pictures of the past two centuries, exemplifying typically Mexican popular art.

477. Nucete-Sardi, José. Notas sobre la pintura y la escultura en Venezuela. Segunda edición. Caracas, Ávila Gráfica (Col. Arte). 111 p., illus.

After a few words about the colonial period, the author makes a survey of the eclectic school of Venezuela, where romanticism prevailed in the past century and in the present the artists are largely traditional. The first edition was published in 1940.

479. LA PINTURA COLONIAL EN CUBA. Exposición en el Capitolio Nacional, marzo 4 a abril 4 de 1950. Organizada por la Corporación Nacional del Turismo con la cooperación del Patronato Pro-Museo Nacional y bajo los auspicios del Ministerio de Educación. Habana, Corporación Nacional del Turismo. 212 plates.

This well illustrated catalogue is devoted largely to portraits, landscapes, and scenes of daily life, dating from the 18th and 19th centuries.

480. Sanford, Trent Elwood. The architecture of the Southwest. New York, W. W. Norton. 312 p., 64 plates.

An enthusiastic and readable popular account, most of which is devoted to the Spanish colonial period.

481. Villanueva, Carlos Raúl. La Caracas de ayer y de hoy. Su arquitectura colonial y la reurbanización de El Silencio. Con dos artículos de Carlos Manuel Möller y Maurice E. H. Rotival. Paris, Draeger Frères. Unpaged, illus.

Valuable for pictures of the past and present.

COLONIAL

GENERAL

482. Angulo Íñiguez, Diego. Historia del arte hispanoamericano. T. 2. Los capítulos 3, 6, 9 y 12 por Enrique Marco Dorta. El capítulo 7 por Mario J. Buschiazzo. Barcelona, Salvat. 930 p., 837 illus.

The second volume of this monumental work includes 13 chapters by Diego Angulo dealing in whole or in part with Mexican art in the 17th and 18th centuries. Architecture, sculpture, and painting are studied and much of the material is published in a methodical historical fashion for the first time. Marco Dorta contributes the following chapters: 3, "La arquitectura del siglo XVII en Panamá, Colombia y Venezuela"; 6, "La arquitectura barroca del siglo XVII en el Perú y en Bolivia"; 9. "La escultura en Colombia, Venezuela, Ecuador, Perú y Bolivia"; and 12, "La pintura en Colombia, Ecuador, Perú y Bolivia." Chapter 7, by Buschiazzo, is called "La arquitectura de los siglos XVI y XVII en el Brasil." New documentation from the Archivo de Indias helps to clarify the architectural chronology of Bolivia, and considerable new light is thrown upon colonial painting. The importance of this publication, so vast in its scope, can hardly be exaggerated. Two more volumes now in preparation will complete the first comprehensive survey of Latin American art. For v. 1, see *HLAS, no. 11, 1945,* item 506.

483. ————. Orfebrería de Guatemala en el Museo Victoria y Alberto de Londres (*Arch. esp. arte,* t. 23, p. 351-354).

Data on silverwork in connection with a handsome silver receptacle of the 18th century. Illus.

484. Muthmann, Friedrich. L'Argenterie hispano-sud-américaine à l'époque coloniale. Genève [Switzerland], Éditions des Trois Collines. 236 p., 40 plates.

A most significant scholarly contribution to the study of the minor arts, important because of relationships to textiles and architectural decoration.

ARGENTINA

485. Buschiazzo, Mario J. Dos monasterios de clausura en Córdoba (*An. inst. arte amer. invest. estét.,* no. 3, p. 26-37).

An important study of the Carmelite and Dominican nunneries with new documentation and excellent drawings as well as photographs. 19 illus.

486. Furlong, Guillermo. Juan Manuel López. Arquitecto e ingeniero (*An. inst. arte amer. invest. estét.,* no. 3, p. 72-101).

An important study based upon extensive archival research relative to an architect (active 1773-1812) who worked upon the cathedral of Córdoba, Argentina, and upon the fountains and aqueducts of the city. Two illus.

487. Trostine, Rodolfo. Tomás Cabrera. Pintor colonial salteño (*Estud. acad. lit. Plata,* t. 83, no. 446, oct.-dic., p. 386-394).
Well documented study of a provincial late colonial artist who is known by a group of signed pictures and one signed statue. Illus.

BOLIVIA

488. DOCUMENTOS DE ARTE COLONIAL SUD-AMERICANO. Cuaderno 7. El santuario de Copacabana. De La Paz a Tiahuanaco. Introducción de Martín S. Noel. Buenos Aires, Ministerio de Educación de la República Argentina (Publ. de la Academia Nacional de Bellas Artes). xlix p., 136 plates.
For the first time this great Bolivian church of the 17th century is made known to the public. Martín S. Noel provides an excellent scholarly introduction and the plates are magnificent, although by some curious oversight there is no general view of the interior. Churches in some small towns between La Paz and Tiahuanaco are also mentioned and illustrated.

489. Noel, Martín S. Réplica que el presidente de la Academia Nacional de Bellas Artes . . . hace a los reparos formulados a los prólogos por él suscriptos de los cuadernos 4 y 5 de arte colonial sudamericano . . . . Buenos Aires, Academia Nacional de Bellas Artes. 29 p.
Noel's reply to Buschiazzo's criticism in *An. inst. arte amer. invest. estét.,* no. 2, 1949, p. 131-132.

490. Schenone, Héctor. Notas sobre el arte renacentista en Sucre, Bolivia (*An. inst. arte amer. invest. estét.,* no. 3, p. 44-65).
In his notes on architecture the author contributes a drawing of the floor plan of San Agustín and analyses of Gothic vaults. A miscellany of pictures includes a large *Pietà,* which Schenone recognizes as Flemish. It is a modified copy of Willem Key's picture in the Henkel Collection at Unkel, a town on the Rhine. The painting of the Magdalen signed "Antonio Mermejo, Limae 1626" is an interesting discovery. 18 illus.

491. Wethey, Harold E. Retablos coloniales en Bolivia (*An. inst. arte amer. invest. estét.,* no. 3, p. 7-14).
The development of altars from the Renaissance works of the 16th century through the baroque and rococo of the 18th century is traced. The author publishes the drawing and contract

(1604) for the lost high altar of Sucre cathedral by the artist José Pastorelo. 11 illus.

CHILE

492. Benavides, Alfredo. The art of Chile. Architecture in the colonial period (*Studio,* v. 139, no. 686, May, p. 134-139, 160).
A brief popular résumé with illustrations.

493. ————. La iglesia de Algarrobo (*An. inst. arte amer. invest. estét.,* no. 3, p. 66-71).
A wooden church of colonial style built in 1837. Nine illustrations.

494. Montandón, Roberto. Iglesias y capillas coloniales en el desierto de Atacama. Santiago, Imprenta Universitaria (Cuadernos del Consejo de Monumentos Nacionales, 2), 1950? 31 p., illus., map, plans.
These churches belong in the same category as the provincial monuments of neighboring Argentina.

DOMINICAN REPUBLIC

495. Palm, Erwin Walter. Arte colonial en Santo Domingo, siglos XVI-XVIII. Exposición organizada por la Universidad de Santo Domingo y la Secretaría de Estado de Educación y Bellas Artes. Ciudad Trujillo. 51 p., one illus.
Painting, sculpture, and metal work with full data about each work.

496. ————. Los hospitales antiguos de la Española. Ciudad Trujillo, Secretaría de Estado de Sanidad y Asistencia. 57 p., 25 illus.
Dr. Palm makes a documentary study of the hospitals of San Nicolás, San Andrés and San Lázaro in Ciudad Trujillo and compares them with European prototypes and other colonial hospitals of Spanish America. See also item 1630.

497. ————. The treasure of the cathedral of Santo Domingo (*Art quart.,* v. 13, no. 2, spring, p. 120-139).
A scholarly presentation of silver ecclesiastic objects dating from the 16th through the 18th centuries. 22 illus.

498. ————. A vault with cosmotheological representations at the "Imperial Monastery" of the Dominicans on the island of Hispaniola (*Art bull.,* v. 32, no. 3, Sept., p. 219-225).
After a highly complicated and scholarly discussion, Dr. Palm comes to the conclusion that the vault is late mediaeval in iconography and 18th century in date. Eight illus.

ECUADOR

499. La Orden Miracle, Ernesto. Elogio de Quito. Madrid, Cultura Hispánica (Cuadernos de Arte, serie B, 1). 122 p., 200 plates, 16 plans.
A magnificent collection of large photographs, splendidly printed. The text in Spanish and English is descriptive and enthusiastic rather than scholarly. Description of plates (p. 111-122) by Luis M. Feduchi.

500. Pareja Díez-Canseco, Alfredo. De la vida y legenda de Miguel de Santiago, pintor de Quito, siglo XVII (*Cuad. amer.*, año 9, vol. 49, no. 1, enero-feb., p. 192-202).
Purely romantic essay.

MEXICO

501. Almela Vives, Fernando, and Antonio Igual Ubeda. El arquitecto y escultor valenciano Manuel Tolsá (1757-1816). Con un estudio preliminar de Felipe María Garín. Valencia, Spain, Diputación Provincial. 142 p., illus.
The first fully documented study of the Valencian artist who migrated to Mexico City, where he became the leading figure of his day in artistic circles.

502. Carrillo y Gariel, Abelardo. Imaginería popular novo-española. México, Ediciones Mexicanas (Enciclopedia Mexicana de Arte, 1). 45 p., 44 plates.
Interesting examples of popular art: small paintings on wood and also sculpture. The dates suggested are too early in many cases.

503. Ferrán Salvador, Vicente. El escultor y arquitecto español Manuel Tolsá en Méjico (*Rev. Indias*, Madrid, año 10, no. 40, abril-junio, p. 311-325).
New biographical material extracted from the archives of Valencia, Spain.

504. Kuri Breña, Daniel. La cantera que canta. San Agustín en un relieve de Zacatecas. México, Ábside. 34 p., illus.
A curious appreciation of the former Augustinian monastery, a work of the 17th and 18th centuries.

505. Maza, Francisco de la. Dibujos y proyectos de Tresguerras (*An. inst. invest. estét.*, no. 18, p. 27-33).
Here are published some drawings for Stations of the Cross as well as projects for altars and architectural details.

506. ————. Un pintor colonial desconocido (*An. inst. invest. estét.*, no. 18, p. 89-90).
On Mariano Morelos, a hitherto unknown painter, whose signature appears on a picture

(1806) of the Immaculate Conception. Four illustrations.

507. ————. Los retablos dorados de Nueva España. México, Ediciones Mexicanas (Enciclopedia Mexicana de Arte, 9). 43 p., 61 plates.
A brief popular discussion of an extensive and complex development.

508. Mercadillo Miranda, José. La pintura mural del santuario de Atotonilco. Versión inglesa de Gladys J. Bonfiglio. México, Jus. 117 p., plus 91 plates.
Written by a non-professional in a rather naïve manner, the text identifies the iconography of a series of late colonial murals.

509. Mora, Joaquín A. El palacio de Nuestra Señora de Guadalupe (*Universidad,* Monterrey, no. 8-9, julio, p. 203-234).
After a sketch of the colonial history of the city of Monterrey, the author describes the fine episcopal palace (1787-1788), which has lately been restored. Illus.

510. R. T. Un retablo de Gregorio Cañas (1795) (*An. inst. arte amer. invest. estét.*, no. 3, p. 109-111).
Publication of a new document.

511. Rodríguez Barragán, Nereo. El palacio de gobierno de San Luis Potosí. San Luis Potosí, Mexico, Editorial Universitaria. 37 p., illus.
The documentary history of a late colonial structure, now much rebuilt.

512. Romero de Terreros, Manuel. La iglesia y convento de San Agustín. México, Instituto de Investigaciones Estéticas (Ediciones del IV Centenario de la Universidad de México, v. 2), 1951, i.e. 1950. 48 p., illus., plan.
A brief monograph on this important structure, now used as the National Library. Documents for the high altar and choir stalls are transcribed, and the illustrations include interesting prints and photographs of the 19th century.

513. Toussaint, Manuel. Vitruvio interpretado por un arquitecto de Nueva España en el siglo XVII (*An. inst. invest. estét.*, no. 18, p. 85-88).
Díaz de Aguilera, chief architect of the Mexico City cathedral, made notes upon his copy of Vitruvius.

514. Weismann, Elizabeth Wilder. Mexico in sculpture. Cambridge, Massachusetts, Harvard University Press. 224 p., 167 illus.
In this picture book Mrs. Weismann gives a poetic and interpretative description of each plate. She emphasizes the survival of Indian motives in architectural ornament of the 16th century and devotes much attention to folk

images. Less space is given to the principal monuments of ecclesiastical sculpture. Comprehensive bibliography and factual data are included in the notes.

515. ———. Stone sculpture of colonial Mexico (*Mag. art.*, v. 43, no. 3, March, p. 106-110).
In this short excursion in pursuit of colonial sculpture the author proposes the abandonment of standard methods of art history and suggests "looking at the stuff itself and trying to see what it is." Illus.

PERU

516. Harth-terré, Emilio. Una iglesia mudéjar del siglo XVI (*El Comercio*, Lima, enero 15).
A documentary account of the nunnery of the Concepción in Lima, previously studied by Rubén Vargas Ugarte.

517. Mariátegui Oliva, Ricardo. La catedral de Puno (*An. inst. arte amer. invest. estét.*, no. 3, p. 38-43).
A brief description of this well-known church. Five illus.

518. ———. Chiguata y su iglesia del Espíritu Santo. Lima, Instituto de Investigaciones de Arte Peruano y Americano (Documentos de Arte Peruano, 11). 26 p., illus.

519. ———. Zepita. Templo de San Pedro y San Pablo. Lima, Instituto de Investigaciones de Arte Peruano y Americano (Documentos de Arte Peruano, 12). 28 p., illus.
Two more descriptive booklets, like others in the series, with poorly printed photographs.

520. Vargas Ugarte, Rubén. La catedral de Huamanga (*Mar del sur*, v. 4, no. 11, mayo-junio, p. 15-20).
Padre Vargas' investigation of the archives of the cathedral of Huamanga (Ayacucho) has brought forth important new data. The plans of 1630 are shown to have been prepared by the famous Jesuit architect of Lima, Martín de Aizpitarte. Furthermore, the altars of the transept, finished in 1764, prove to have been begun in the second quarter of the century.

521. Villanueva Urteaga, Horacio. San Agustín de Cuzco (*El Comercio*, Cuzco, marzo 18).
Dr. Villanueva publishes the text of the contract for the cloister of the Augustinians, rebuilt in 1670 by the architect Juan Esteban Alvarado.

522. Wethey, Harold E. La arquitectura colonial de Arequipa (*El Deber*, Arequipa, julio 27, p. 9-12).
A Spanish translation of chapter 8 of *Colonial Architecture and Sculpture in Peru*. See *HLAS, no. 15, 1949*, item 580.

NINETEENTH AND TWENTIETH CENTURIES

ARGENTINA

523. Baliari, Eduardo. Vicente Forte. Creador de libertades. Buenos Aires, Ollantay. 26 p., illus.
Illustrations of a contemporary abstract painter influenced by Picasso; philosophical introductory essay.

524. Pettoruti, Emilio. Exposición retrospectiva de la obra del pintor . . . , organizada bajo los auspicios del Ministerio de Educación Pública y de la Universidad de Chile por el Instituto de Extensión de Artes Plásticas . . . agosto de 1950. Santiago, Museo Nacional de Bellas Artes. 15 p., plates.
The catalogue and critical evaluation are by the well known writer Julio Payró.

525. PINTORES ARGENTINOS. HÉCTOR BASALDÚA, HORACIO BUTLER, RAQUEL FORNER, RAÚL SOLDI. Buenos Aires, Pampa. 16 color plates.
A moderately good collection of color reproductions in folio size accompanied by an explanatory paragraph by each of the artists represented.

526. SALÓN SANMARTINIANO DE ARTES PLÁSTICAS, 10 AL 31 DE OCTUBRE DE 1950. Buenos Aires, Comisión Nacional de Homenaje al Libertador General San Martín (Ley 13661). 129 plates.
Well illustrated catalogue of official historical painting in Argentina, which is in the style of the past century.

CHILE

527. Eyzaguirre, Jaime. José Gil de Castro. Pintor de la independencia americana. Santiago, Sociedad de Bibliófilos Chilenos. xiii, 38 p., 76 plates.
Carefully compiled catalogue of historical portraits, well printed.

528. Letelier, Jorge. The art of Chile. Contemporary painting and sculpture (*Studio*, v. 139, no. 686, May, p. 140-149).
This well illustrated article outlines contemporary trends in Chilean painting.

COLOMBIA

529. VIII SALÓN ANUAL DE ARTISTAS COLOMBIANOS, OCTUBRE 12, 1950. Bogotá, Ministerio de Educación Nacional, Extensión Cultural y Bellas Artes. Plates.
A small exhibition catalogue.

530. II Congreso Interamericano de Estadística. Catálogo de las exposiciones de pintura colombiana. Pintura contemporánea. Carteles para los censos de 1950. Bogotá, Contraloría General de la República, Dirección Nacional de Censos. Unpaged.

CUBA

531. Fernández Castello, Jesús. Desarrollo actual de la pintura en Cuba (*Cuad. hispanoamer.*, no. 13, enero-feb., p. 129-136).
A brief evaluation of leading painters. Six illus.

532. Ortiz, Fernando. Wifredo Lam. Habana, Ministerio de Educación, Dirección de Cultura (Cuadernos de Arte, 1). 22 p., 19 plates.
A metaphysical explanation of Lam, one of the most interesting abstract surrealists of the Picasso tradition in Latin America.

533. Valderrama, Esteban. Leopoldo Romañach y Guillén, maestro de todos (*Arquitectura*, Habana, año 18, no. 201, abril, p. 156-168).
Homage to a contemporary Cuban painter (1862-1951), a portraitist in the impressionist tradition.

MEXICO

534. Alfaro Siqueiros, David. El muralismo de México. México, Ediciones Mexicanas (Enciclopedia Mexicana de Arte, 8). 35 p., illus.
This essay is significant chiefly because the author is one of the leaders of the contemporary movement, which he explains in vague and sweeping statements of doubtful validity.

535. Baldinger, Wallace S. Orozco's last murals (*Mag. art*, v. 43, no. 2, Feb., p. 43-47).
Mr. Baldinger gives an account of Orozco's last days at work upon the murals as well as an iconographic and stylistic analysis of them.

536. Charlot, Jean. Art-making from Mexico to China. New York, Sheed and Ward. 308 p., illus.
The book contains a statement of this painter's artistic theories and his opinions on a variety of subjects, but it is most valuable for the firsthand material on the contemporary Mexican movement in painting.

537. ————. Diego Rivera at the Academy of San Carlos (*College art jour.*, v. 10, no. 1, fall, p. 10-17).
Rivera's years as a student of painting.

538. ————. Orozco's stylistic evolution (*College art jour.*, v. 9, no. 2, winter 1949-1950, p. 148-157).
Some interesting data on the artist's early career.

539. Fernández, Justino. Catálogo de las exposiciones de arte en 1949 (*An. inst. invest. estét.*, suplemento del no. 18). 43 p.

540. ————. Diego Rivera, antes y después (*An. inst. invest. estét.*, no. 18, p. 63-82).
An excellent critical review of Rivera's career, inspired by the exhibition of 50 years of his work (1949).

541. ————. Orozco, genius of America (*College art jour.*, v. 9, no. 2, winter 1949-1950, p. 142-147).
An English translation of an article published in *Cuad. amer.*, nov.-dic., 1949.

542. ————. La transcendencia en la obra de Orozco (*An. inst. invest. estét.*, no. 18, p. 19-26).
A fine tribute to the great painter after his death (1949).

543. Gual, Enrique F. (ed.). Drawings by Tamayo. México, Ediciones Mexicanas. 5 p., 43 plates.
Facsimiles of drawings, including studies for the mural at Smith College. Summary text.

544. ———— (ed.). 50 years of Diego Rivera. Oils, water colors, 1900-1950. Text by . . . . México, Fischgrund. 4 p., 14 color plates.
These color plates of fair quality are unusual in that many are little known works of Rivera's early career.

545. ———— (ed.). Rufino Tamayo. México, Fischgrund. 3 p., 10 plates.
Color plates of small format but good quality considering the reasonable price.

546. HOMENAJE DE EL COLEGIO NACIONAL AL PINTOR JOSÉ CLEMENTE OROZCO, 14 DE DICIEMBRE DE 1949. México, Ediciones de El Colegio Nacional. 25 p., illus.
Speeches by Silvio A. Zavala and Manuel Toussaint.

547. Islas García, Luis. Las pinturas guadalupanas de Fernando Leal en el Tepeyac. México, Ediciones Mexicanas (Enciclopedia Mexicana de Arte, 5). 64 p., illus.
Descriptive explanation of an illustrative set of murals on the Virgin of Guadalupe.

548. Orendáin, Leopoldo I. Pintores jaliscienses del siglo XIX: José Ma. Zepeda Estrada (*Et caetera*, año 1, no. 2, abril-junio, p. 95-99).

Discussion, description, and reproduction of the main works of this Jaliscan portraitist, rescued from oblivion in 1937. [H. F. Cline]

549. ————. Pintura popular. Guadalajara, Mexico. 23 p., illus.

A short discussion of ex-votos of the 19th century, as typical of Mexican piety.

550. Pijoán, José. Adiós a Orozco (*Rep. amer.*, no. 1104, feb. 15, p. 65-66).

URUGUAY

551. Salteraín y Herrera, Eduardo de. Blanes. El hombre, su obra y la época. Montevideo, Impresora Uruguaya. 301 p., illus.

A detailed biography of a famous 19th century Uruguayan painter. Many small illustrations.

ADDENDA

551a. Cotter, C. S. The discovery of the Spanish carvings at Seville (*Jamaican hist. rev.*, v. 1, no. 3, Dec., 1948, p. 227-233).

Concerns a discovery at the ruins of Sevilla Nueva, existent in Jamaica from 1510 to 1534. The fine renaissance carved stones found there have also been discussed by Diego Angulo in *El gótico y el renacimiento en las Antillas* (see *HLAS, no. 14, 1948,* item 655). Cotter differs from Angulo as to some interpretations. [R. D. Hussey]

552. IV CONGRESO HISTÓRICO MUNICIPAL INTERAMERICANO. Exposición de estampas. Buenos Aires, 1949. 35 p., illus.

Other booklets issued in connection with this congress, which was devoted to city planning and other municipal problems, were concerned with the *Exposición de Obras Públicas Municipales* (24 p., illus.) and the *Exposición de la Vivienda* (18 p., illus.). In addition there were a *Sinopsis* (121 p.) and an *Acta final* (49 p.). See also *HLAS, no. 15, 1949,* item 525a.

553. Vargas, José María. El arte quiteño en los siglos XVI, XVII y XVIII. Quito, Romero, 1949. 238 p., 54 illus.

This popular study might serve as a guide book, but it is completely deficient in documentation and understanding of artistic styles and shows no knowledge of previous publications on the subject.

Brazilian Art

ROBERT C. SMITH

ALTHOUGH the 1950 bibliography in the field of Brazilian art is not so large as it has sometimes been in former years, almost every aspect of the subject is represented by at least one first-rate publication.

Students of pre-Cabralian art recognized at once the worth of Helen Palmatary's work on the pottery of Marajó (item 246), which comes as close to being a definitive piece of research as any publication on Brazilian culture. They will congratulate the American Philosophical Society for sponsoring this study and making possible its publication with so many illustrations.

In the field of colonial art Dom Clemente Maria da Silva-Nigra's book on the building of the Benedictine monastery in Rio de Janeiro has proved a model of exhaustive research in a great body of documents applicable not only to the construction itself but to the general activity of many of its craftsmen as well. The same type of research, though in a much more limited way, is represented by Robert C. Smith's study of the parish records of Santo Antônio of Recife at the close of the 18th and beginning of the 19th century. An excellent illustration of another kind of approach to the study of colonial art is John Bury's paper on the Jesuit churches. He is concerned not with documenting the history of surviving or destroyed buildings but rather with their stylistic significance, which he shows to be an outstanding manifestation of the architecture of Mannerism, a style which is just beginning to be recognized and understood.

The International Colloquium on Luso-Brazilian Studies, held at Washington in October as one of the events commemorating the hundred fiftieth anniversary of the Library of Congress, devoted one of its sessions to the baroque art of Portugal and Brazil. Attention of scholars from a number of countries, all specialists in different aspects of the culture of the area, was directed to the main characteristics of Portuguese 17th- and 18th-century architecture through the lecture by Dr. Reynaldo dos Santos, president of the Academia Nacional de Belas Artes of Portugal, and by a lecture on the colonial architecture of Brazil by the editor of this section. These addresses and the remarks of the official commentators, Dr. Rodrigo Melo Franco de Andrade, director of the Brazilian Diretoria do Patrimônio Histórico e Artístico Nacional, Germain Bazin, chief curator of painting at the Louvre, and Mario J. Buschiazzo, professor of the history of American architecture at the University of Buenos Aires, were incorporated in the proceedings of the Colloquium, which appeared in 1953.

For 19th-century art in Brazil the paper by Professor David James of Brown University and Francisco Marques dos Santos of Rio de Janeiro on the painter Monvoisin is an outstanding contribution. In the domain of contemporary art, architecture leads as the topic of greatest interest in Brazil and abroad and the one which has elicited most publication. Much of this is to be found in the pages of the new quarterly *Habitat*, edited by Lina Bo Bardi, wife of the director of the Museu de Arte, São Paulo, which began with its first issue in 1950 a continuing policy of wide and thorough reporting of important new examples of contemporary architecture in Brazil. *Habitat* is also interested in other aspects of Brazilian art, especially the little known folk art of the country, a topic represented admirably by the catalogue of the Museu Folclórico of São Paulo (items 554 and 3174). Contemporary paintings and sculptures in the Brazilian section of the Biennale exhibition at Venice proved that they can be favorably compared with the best of the art of any other country at this time.

FOLK ART

554. Alvarenga, Oneyda. Catálogo ilustrado do Museu Folclórico. V. 2. São Paulo, Prefeitura do Município, Discoteca Pública Municipal. xviii, 295 p., illus.

The folk art of Brazil is still relatively little known. Nevertheless it is extremely interesting, without being really distinguished. Outstanding are the fetishes of various materials made for African cults implanted in Brazil and the wooden ex-voto heads formerly set up in rural chapels of the State of Paraíba. Both groups are amply illustrated in this voluminous collection of 235 photographs. Each object is fully described and the catalogue ends with a glossary of artifacts. See also item 3174. The first volume of this catalogue is devoted to a listing of recordings of folk music belonging to the Discoteca Pública Municipal.

555. Os BARCOS MASCARADOS DO SÃO FRANCISCO (*Ilus. bras.*, ano 41, no. 187, nov., p. 24-25).

An article dealing lightly with the handsome bowsprits of the São Francisco river boats, carved in the form of human figures. They have the same direct and powerful effect of the wood-carved ex-votos of northeastern Brazil. Illus.

556. Duarte, Eustáquio. São Francisco, o rio vagabundo (*Sombra*, ano 10, no. 107, nov.-dez., p. 62-65, 112).

Especially interesting because of the fine photographs of buildings, people, and objects of popular art.

557. Ex-VOTOS DO NORDESTE (*Habitat*, no. 1, out.-dez., p. 72-74).

Photographs of wooden heads and bodies collected in Pernambuco by Augusto Rodrigues.

COLONIAL

558. Bury, John B. Jesuit architecture in Brazil (*The month*, v. 5, no. 6, Dec., p. 385-408).

In this very interesting illustrated paper an English architectural historian considers the principles of Mannerist architecture as developed in Italy between about 1525 and 1600 and shows how they were reflected in the buildings of the Jesuits in Portugal, the Portuguese colonies of the East, and Brazil. The Brazilian buildings are studied not only in relation to their own interior and exterior architecture but also in regard to their influence on subsequent churches in the same country.

559. Iria, Alberto. A Bahia no Arquivo Histórico Colonial de Lisboa (*IV cong. hist. nac.*, v. 2, p. 15-30).

Contains a catalogue of 22 maps and topographical drawings of the 17th and 18th centuries referring to Bahia. Some are of importance for the history of colonial architecture. Illus.

560. Leite, Serafim. Francisco Dias, jesuita português, arquitecto e piloto no Brasil, 1538-1633 (*Brotéria*, v. 51, fasc. 4, out., p. 257-265).

The most complete biography to date of the first Jesuit architect in Brazil, who is credited with the introduction to that country of the principles of formal church building in the Portuguese Mannerist style. Born at Merceana (Alenquer) in 1538, here misprinted 1638, he served as master of the works of the Jesuit church of São Roque in Lisbon under Afonso Álvares before 1573. Two years later Dias planned the Jesuit church and college at Angra in the Azores and in 1575 embarked for Brazil. Father Leite, the distinguished historian of the Jesuits in Brazil, here offers documentary proof that Dias' mission to America was considered by his superiors a matter of short duration. In spite of the General's order to return, however, he was permitted to remain in Brazil for the remaining 56 years of his life. This important article concludes with a brief account of his work in Bahia, Rio de Janeiro, and Olinda.

561. Mattos, Waldemar. Palácio da Associação Comercial da Bahia. Bahia, Tipografia Beneditina. 316 p.

One of the great monuments of Bahia's past. [M. Cardozo]

562. PEQUENO GUIA DAS IGREJAS DA BAHIA. No. 5, Convento do Desterro. No. 6, Ordem Terceira de São Domingos. No. 7, Igreja da Ajuda e a devoção dos passos. No. 8, Mont-Serrat, o forte e a igreja. Salvador, Prefeitura.

Extremely useful small, well illustrated monographs varying from 18 to 26 pages of text based on documents. They try, wherever possible, to discover basic dates of construction and the identity of craftsmen.

563. Rebêlo, E. de Castro. As inscrições lapidares da Igreja da Vitória e o local da Vila Velha (*IV cong. hist. nac.*, v. 4, p. 221-242).

Inscriptions concerning the erection and subsequent rebuildings of one of Bahia's oldest churches.

564. Rodrigues, José Wasth. Documentário arquitetônico relativo à antiga construção civil no Brasil. Fasc. 1-2. São Paulo, Martins. 1-20, 21-40 plates.

These are the last volumes, of which there are eight in all, dealing with details of colonial construction by means of drawings made by the author. The work was begun in 1918. The present volumes refer to São Paulo and Minas Gerais. This is an extremely useful source of reference.

565. Silva-Nigra, Clemente Maria da. Construtores e artistas do Mosteiro de São Bento do Rio de Janeiro. Salvador, Tipografia Beneditina. 309 p., illus., some in color.

A sumptuously printed and superbly documented history of the Benedictine monastery of Rio de Janeiro with special reference to the details of its construction and the identity of a large number of craftsmen who worked upon it. This is a monumental work, a great contribution to Luso-Brazilian studies. It is to be hoped that it will lead the way to other publications, so badly needed, in this genre.

566. Smith, Robert C. The Portuguese woodcarved retable, 1600-1750 (*Belas artes*, 2. série, no. 2, p. 14-56).

A first attempt to trace the stylistic development of this essential aspect of the baroque art of Portugal. There are references to Brazilian examples.

567. ————. Santo Antônio do Recife (*An. mus. imperial*, 1946, i.e. 1950, p. 141-176).

On the basis of account books and other old records the author has assembled material which makes it possible to identify a number of specific craftsmen who labored in this church, one of the greatest in Recife, during the period 1790-1815. Of particular interest are the master carpenter Manuel Ferreira da Costa, the sculptor Alexandre da Silva, and the painters Manuel de Jesus Pinto and José Eloi. Wherever possible their work is described and illustrated and its stylistic significance discussed.

NINETEENTH CENTURY

568. Acquarone, Francisco. Mestres da pintura no Brasil. Rio de Janeiro, Paulo de Azevedo. 253 p., illus., some in color.

A series of essays on the work of pre-eminent painters of the second half of the 19th century preceded by brief statements on pre-Cabralian, colonial, romantic, and contemporary painting in Brazil. The numerous illustrations include sketches and minor works not hitherto published.

569. Antunes, Paranhos. Os prateiros do Rio Grande do Sul (*IV cong. hist. nac.*, v. 5, p. 557-568).

The local tradition of silver-working in Rio Grande do Sul is here traced back to the late 17th century. Illustrations of silver stirrups, maté cups, knives, etc., are provided.

570. Carneiro, Newton. Iconografia paranaense. Curitiba. 40 p., illus.

A selection of diverting drawings, paintings, and prints concerning Paraná, many of which are from the collection of the Biblioteca Nacional. Outstanding in interest are the early 19th century portraits by F. G. Vermond, the topographical paintings of J. H. Elliot, and the *costumista* studies of Franz Keller.

571. Cruz, Mário da Silva. Vitor Meireles e Pedro Américo (*An. mus. imperial*, 1946, i.e. 1950, p. 207-230).

The curator of the Museu Imperial describes and documents two important 19th century paintings belonging to the museum, *Princess Isabel taking the oath of regency*, by Vitor Meireles, 1875, and *The battle of Campo Grande*, painted by Pedro Américo in 1871. Illus.

572. GRADES E SOMBRAS (*Rio*, no. 127, jan., p. 80-83).

Good photographs by Käzmer of fine iron balconies of the 19th century in Rio de Janeiro.

573. Jack. Arquitetura de glacê e de açucar candi (*Rio*, no. 127, jan., p. 96-99).

Amusing examples of elaborate Moorish, Gothic revival and neo-baroque architecture, like the Café Mourisco building and the Martinelli-Barreto Pinto house in Rio, are compared with the sober small houses of the present-day architects Miranda and Roberto. Illus.

574. James, David, and Francisco Marques dos Santos. Raimundo Augusto Quinsac de Monvoisin (*An. mus. imperial*, 1946, i.e. 1950, p. 29-52).

This is an admirably documented account of the activity of the French painter Monvoisin (1790-1870) in Brazil between the years 1847 and 1858. The article is illustrated with a considerable number of his portraits, drawings, and genre paintings. It is one of the best contributions to the examination of French contacts with Latin America. See *HLAS, no. 15, 1949*, item 628.

575. Oliveira, Carlota Cardozo de. Pedro Américo. Milionário de glórias (*Ilus. bras.*, junho, p. 22-25).

Biographical details and critical comments concerning the great Brazilian battle painter of the late 19th century. Eight illus.

576. PAULISTÂNIA. São Paulo. No. 34, maio-junio.

Contains a group of articles commemorating the hundredth anniversary of the birth of the great 19th century realist José Ferraz de Almeida Júnior (1850-1899). They add little to our knowledge of him and his work.

577. Sodré, Alcindo. Museu Imperial. Rio de Janeiro, Imprensa Nacional. 205 p., illus.
The museum devoted to the art and history of the former imperial family is in Petrópolis. This extremely informative history and catalogue was written by the museum's late director.

TWENTIETH CENTURY

578. Bardi, L. Bo. Casas de Vilanova Artigas (*Habitat*, no. 1, out.-dez., p. 2-16).
A thorough examination, with many plans, elevations, and diagrams, of the small and elegant houses which Artigas has been building for over a decade in São Paulo.

579. Bento, Antônio. A retrospectiva de Bruno Giorgi (*Sombra*, ano 10, no. 107, nov.-dez., p. 80-81).
Recent work of the sculptor included in this exhibition shows him moving in the direction of Henry Moore. Illus.

580. Byden, Alf. Report on Brazil (*Architect. rev.*, v. 108, no. 646, Oct., p. 221-222).
A Swedish associate of the Brazilian architect Oscar Niemeyer offers his conclusions on the new style so widely admired and discussed since the publication of Philip L. Goodwin's *Brazil builds* (*HLAS, no. 9, 1943*, item 849). Byden points out that the modern style is far from being universally accepted in Brazil, that it is associated with government and luxury buildings and that it is not concerned with working class housing and city planning. He calls attention to the "fundamentally simple approach," which is a basic characteristic of the new Brazilian style and to a relative freedom from restrictive regulations, which permits the modern architect great freedom of execution.

581. Catálogo do Segundo Salão Bahiano de Belas Artes, 1950. Bahia, Secretaria de Educação e Saúde. 44 p., illus.
A well made catalogue with clear reproductions of interesting prize-winning exhibits.

582. Deinhard, Hanna. Modern tile-murals in Brazil (*Craft hor.*, spring, p. 6-10).
The art of tile decoration, so popular in the colonial period, revived for modern architecture in Brazil largely through the efforts of Cândido Portinari. Illus.

583. Djanira expõe na Bahia (*Rio*, no. 131, maio, p. 56-57).
Portraits exhibited in Salvador by a well-known modern painter of abstractionist tendencies. Illus.

584. O estranho caso da arquitetura brasileira (*Rio*, no. 127, jan., p. 60-73).
Principally photographs of outstanding young architects of the contemporary movement with occasional sketches from their work. Those included are: Affonso Eduardo Reidy, Henrique Mindlin, Aldary Henrique Toledo, Francisco Bolonha, Marcelo and Maurício Roberto, Er-

nani Vasconcelos, Alcides Rocha Miranda, Firmino Saldanha, José Sousa Reis, and Oscar Niemeyer.

585. Ferraz, Geraldo. O Brasil na Biennale de Venezia (*Sombra*, ano 10, no. 102, junho, p. 48-53, 98).
Excellent reproductions of the paintings and sculptures exhibited by Brazilian artists at an international exposition in Venice.

586. Fonseca, José Paulo Moreira da. Cândido Portinari (*Rev. branca*, ano 2, no. 12, maio-agôsto, p. 26).
The pathetic and baroque elements in the painter's work. Illus.

587. Immeuble d'appartements à São Paulo; Rino Levi et Roberto Cerqueira César (*Architect. d'aujourd'hui*, no. 20, sept., p. 16-17).
Plans and photographs of a 14-story apartment house.

588. Lopes, Napoleão Agostinho. Mário Cravo (*Rio*, no. 131, maio, 2 p.).
Comments on an abstract sculptor of ability. Illus. See also item 592.

589. M. M. Lasar Segall (*Cult. aliment.*, ano 1, no. 1, p. 54-55).
A note about the great expressionist master of São Paulo illustrated exclusively with still-life paintings. *M.M.* stands for Murilo Miranda.

590. Meireles, Cecília. Rebollo (*Trópico*, ano 1, no. 2, maio, p. 36-37).
A short note on a São Paulo painter by an eminent Brazilian poetess.

591. Papadaki, Stamo. The work of Oscar Niemeyer. New York, Reinhold. 220 p., illus.
A picture book with brief text discussing the outstanding buildings of this very important contemporary architect. There is a foreword by a distinguished pioneer of modern architecture in Brazil, Lúcio Costa.

592. Rocha, Mário Augusto da. Um escultor nos Estados Unidos (*Sombra*, ano 10, no. 103, julho, p. 84-85, 93).
On the recent work of Mário Cravo Júnior. Illus. See also item 588.

593. ————. Um pintor brasileiro em New York (*Sombra*, ano 10, no. 98, fev., p. 82-83, 98).
An enthusiastic account of the work of a youthful and as yet little known Bahian painter, Carlos Frederico Bastos. Illus.

594. Santa Cruz, Luiz. Burle Marx, o pintor e o jardineiro (*Sombra*, ano 10, no. 97, jan., p. 46-49).
A brief but informative text about Brazil's foremost landscape architect accompanied by photographs of corners of his exotic tropical gardens Illus.

595. Three houses in Brazil (*Architect. rev.*, v. 108, no. 647, Nov., p. 303-306).
The article describes briefly two houses in São Paulo, by Rino Levi and D. Calabi respectively, built around courtyards in the contemporary style of that city. Reference is also made to a house at Cataguazes by A. H. Toledo, constructed on a sloping site and containing present-day reflections of colonial elements in plan and construction. A number of such houses have been erected in various parts of Brazil.

596. XXV Biennale di Venezia. Catalogo. 2. edizione. Venezia. P. 221-226, illus.
The Brazilian section of the Italian international exhibition of contemporary art with a brief introduction by Sérgio Milliet.

597. Zélia Nunes, uma nova escultora brasileira (*Sombra,* ano 10, no. 104, agôsto, p. 46-47, 88).
The sculptress seems to have been influenced somewhat by Bruno Giorgi. Illus.

ADDENDUM

598. Exposição do mural Tiradentes de Cândido Portinari destinado ao Colégio de Cataguazes. Rio de Janeiro, Museu de Arte Moderna, 1949. 16 p., illus.
Contains a great many details of this important painting about the Inconfidência Mineira.

Economics

GENERAL

599. Armas Arias, Guillermo. Planificación económica regional. Su proyección a países no industrializados. México. 140 p.
An academic dissertation (University of Mexico) on regional planning, well documented, with emphasis on public administration and foreign experience. [H. W. Spiegel]

600. Export-Import Bank of Washington. Ninth and tenth semiannual reports to Congress for the period July-December 1949 and . . . January-June 1950. Washington. 72, 64 p., tables.
These reports contain a wealth of material on the Bank's lending to the various Latin American countries. [W. C. Gordon]

601. Flota Mercante Grancolombiana. Informe de labores, 1949. Bogotá, Imprenta del Banco de la República. 17 p., tables.
The annual report on the joint Colombia-Ecuador-Venezuela merchant fleet. [W. C. Gordon]

602. Foreign agriculture. Washington, U. S. Department of Agriculture, Office of Foreign Agricultural Relations. V. 14, no. 1, Jan.-no. 12, Dec.
Has frequent articles and notes on Latin America. [Ed.]

603. Foreign commerce weekly. Washington, United States Department of Commerce, Office of International Trade. V. 38, no. 1, Jan. 2—v. 41, no. 13, Dec. 25.
Current economic information from all parts of the world, including Latin America. [Ed.]

604. Gordon, Wendell Chaffee. The economy of Latin America. New York, Columbia University Press. xi, 434 p., tables.
This important volume fills a long-felt need: a general survey of Latin America as an economic unit endowed with special forms of economic institutions and practices often overlooked, and a basic text for university courses on Latin American economics. The major thesis, around which a vast body of carefully organized material is grouped, is: "The Latin-American economic system and the present measures being taken to change that system can be judged by whether or not they tend to lead to a distribution of income which will give at least a decent sufficiency to everyone. The great historic controversies over foreign investments, foreign trade, the ownership of property, and the like are merely side issues." With a wealth of new ideas and data and a helpful bibliography this is an indispensable volume for the general reader and the specialist. [H. F. Cline]

605. Informe al gobierno de la Delegación de Cuba a la III Reunión de la Comisión Económica para América Latina [de las Naciones Unidas], por conducto del Dr. Ernesto Dihigo, Ministro de Estado. Habana. 184 p.

606. Inter-American economic affairs. Washington, Institute of Inter-American Studies. V. 3, no. 4, spring–v. 4, no. 3, winter.
Established review whose scope is sometimes wider than its title. [H. F. Cline]

607. Inter-American Institute of Agricultural Sciences. Informe sobre el desarrollo del programa cafetero del Instituto Interamericano de Ciencias Agrícolas. Washington, Unión Panamericana. 34 p.
The Institute, an inter-governmental project, is located at Turrialba, Costa Rica. [Ed.]

608. Latin American business highlights. A quarterly digest. New York, The Chase National Bank, Nov. 33 p., graphs, tables.
The first issue of this quarterly contains a general statement on Latin American business conditions followed by short statements on most of the individual countries. [W. C. Gordon]

609. Noticias. New York, Council for Inter-American Cooperation, Inc., affiliated with the National Foreign Trade Council. V. 6, no. 1, Jan. 3–no. 52, Dec. 26.
Weekly summary in English of information on Latin America appearing in the United States press. Deals with all aspects of Latin America, especially trade. [H. F. Cline]

609a. **Organization of American States. Food and Agriculture Organization of the United Nations.** Manual for the use of the delegates to the Fourth Inter-American Conference on Agriculture and the Second Latin American Regional Meeting on Food and Agricultural Programs and Outlook. Montevideo, Uruguay, Dec. 1, 1950. Washington, Pan American Union–FAO. 185 p., tables.

Contents: Antecedents, p. 1-35; Agricultural and economic situation of the Latin American countries, and reports on selected basic commodities, p. 36-123; Report on conservation of renewable resources in Latin America, p. 124-155; Agricultural statistics—production, consumption, and commerce, p. 156-185. [Ed.]

610. ————. **Inter-American Economic and Social Council.** Actas de las sesiones del Consejo Interamericano Económico y Social. V. 20-22. Washington, Pan American Union. xiv, 3667-3845; v, 3847-4015; iv, 4017-4199 p.

These minutes contain the text of the Council debates. [W. C. Gordon]

611. ————. ————. Informe del Secretariado sobre las condiciones económicas y los problemas de desarrollo de América Latina. Washington, Unión Panamericana. 157 p., diagrams, tables.

Report prepared by Loreto M. Domínguez. Contents: 1, Estado actual de las economías latinoamericanas; 2, Características del proceso de crecimiento económico; 3, Bases de crecimiento económico; 4, La necesidad de planeamiento económico. Appendices: 1, Resumen de las medidas de intervención y planeamiento gubernamental en América Latina; 2, Notas sobre índices de precios y términos de comercio exterior. Publication also appeared in English. [Ed.]

612. ————. ————. La política marítima de los países latinoamericanos. Washington, Unión Panamericana. 99 p.

Report prepared by Marcos Falcón Briceño. [Ed.]

614. **Sánchez Meza, Guillermina.** Diagnós-

tico económico de América Latina. México. 329 p.

An academic dissertation, University of Mexico. The first part treats of the economic geography of Latin America, the second of its structural characteristics, the third of economic policies. In the concluding part, the author formulates a number of policy proposals. [H. W. Spiegel]

615. **United Nations. Department of Economic Affairs.** Agricultural requisites in Latin America. Report of the Joint ECLA/FAO Working Party. Lake Success, N. Y. xvii, 156 p., tables.

Technically useful data on farm machinery, fertilizers, fisheries, and the increasing of the land area under cultivation. [W. C. Gordon]

616. ————. ————. **Economic Commission for Latin America.** Trade trends and policies of Latin American countries (E/CN. 12/165, 1 May, 1950). 132 p., graphs, tables.

617. **United States. Department of State. Division of Library and Reference Services.** Economic studies of underdeveloped countries. Latin American and Caribbean area (Bibliography no. 52). Washington. ii, 90 p.

A general bibliography of material on Latin American economic problems, classified by countries. There is also a general section of books on the Latin American economy as a whole. [W. C. Gordon]

618. ————. ————. ————. Point four. Latin America and European dependencies in the Western Hemisphere. A selected bibliography of studies on economically underdeveloped countries (Bibliography no. 55). Washington. 110 p.

Mostly references to basic economic studies issued within the last 10 years. [F. Aguilera]

ADDENDUM

619. **Pan American Union.** Economic survey of inter-American agriculture. V. 1-2. Washington, 1949. 228, 113 p., maps.

LATIN AMERICA (EXCEPT ARGENTINA, BRAZIL, AND MEXICO)

WENDELL C. GORDON

AGENCIES which publish a variety of reports, yearbooks, and magazines containing economic and statistical information include the Caribbean Commission, with headquarters in Port-of-Spain, the central banks, finance and *economía* ministries, statistical offices, and development banks and corporations, which exist in many of the countries. Inclusion of statistical materials in this section is based upon the plan outlined under "Statistics" (p. 6).

The chief criterion used in deciding whether to include an item has been an effort to appraise its usefulness to a scholar interested in studying some aspect of the economy of one of the countries covered. This has meant that in some cases non-scholarly works which express a point of view have been included, because the nature of the viewpoints of people, whether completely rational or not, is important for certain types of studies. However, it has been the intention to exclude purely hack writing that seems to express merely the viewpoint of the author.

CENTRAL AMERICA

COSTA RICA

620. Banco Nacional de Costa Rica. Trigésima quinta memoria anual. Informe del décimotercero ejercicio. San José. 224 p., graphs, tables.
Offers not only a summary of the activities of the bank during the year but also a description of economic developments in the economy as a whole plus a variety of public documents and decrees pertaining to economic matters.

621. BOLETÍN ESTADÍSTICO MENSUAL. San José, Banco Central de Costa Rica. No. 1, enero-no. 12, dic.
A monthly magazine containing statistics on Costa Rican money, banking, insurance, financial reserves, exchange rates, foreign trade (including a balance of payments statement), price levels, and public finance.

622. ECONOMIC REVIEW OF COSTA RICA, 1949 (*Int. ref. serv.*, v. 7, no. 85, Aug., 4 p.).

623. Facio, Rodrigo. El problema de las divisas (*Rev. banco cent. Costa Rica*, no. 2, junio, p. 78-96).
An analysis of the Costa Rican foreign exchange problem made in connection with discussion of a proposed foreign exchange control law.

624. REVISTA DEL BANCO CENTRAL DE COSTA RICA. San José. No. 1, marzo–no. 4, dic.
This quarterly, which began publication in March, has in each issue a general economic survey, analytical articles, statistical series on money, credit, and price levels, and the texts of recent laws on such matters.

625. SOLIDARISMO Y RACIONALISMO. San José, Oficina de Coordinación Económica. Año 3, no. 15-16, enero-abril–no. 20, nov.-dic.
A bimonthly magazine containing articles on problems connected with economic development in Costa Rica.

EL SALVADOR

626. Armour Research Foundation. Estudio tecnológico preliminar para el desarrollo industrial de El Salvador (*Rev. econ. El Salvador*, t. 1, no. 1-4, enero-dic., p. 373-457).

A general study of industrial development possibilities in El Salvador, containing specific sections on coffee, cotton, henequen, vegetable oils, sugar, leather, salt, etc. Also appeared as a reprint.

627. Banco Central de Reserva. XVI ejercicio, 1949. Memoria presentada por la Junta Directiva a la Junta General de Accionistas el 23 de febrero de 1950. San Salvador. 37 p., graphs, tables.
Statistics and descriptive material on the operations of the Bank during 1949.

628. Clarke, Rufus R. Informe sobre reorganización del Banco Hipotecario de El Salvador. San Salvador, Ministerio de Economía, Instituto de Estudios Económicos. 15 p.
A report recommending measures to reestablish public confidence in the bank, to form a stable market for the bank's securities, and to create a stable source of short term funds to finance crop harvesting.

629. REVISTA DE ECONOMÍA DE EL SALVADOR. T. 1, no. 1-4, enero-dic. San Salvador, Ministerio de Economía, Instituto de Estudios Económicos. 612 p., graphs, tables.
Gives texts of laws and decrees on economic matters, a plan for studying the Salvadorean economy, and information on the activities of various government agencies associated with economic development, plus extensive statistical tables on finance, trade, production, and transportation.

630. REVISTA MENSUAL DEL BANCO CENTRAL DE RESERVA DE EL SALVADOR. San Salvador, enero-dic.
This monthly magazine contains statistical data on a wide variety of financial matters.

631. United Nations. Economic and Social Council. Economic Commission for Latin America. Agricultural credit in El Salvador (E/CN.12/167/Add. 2). New York. 59 p., tables.
A document issued first by the Economic Commission for Latin America, third session, Montevideo. It has three chapters: "Sources of credit," "The trends of long and short term loans," and "Survey of the manner in which agricultural production is financed in El Salvador." An appendix (p. 39-59) is devoted to the principal branches of Salvadorean agriculture.

GUATEMALA

632. Banco de Guatemala. Memoria anual de 1949. Guatemala. 182 p., graphs, tables.
Contains discussions of general economic developments, of money, banking, and credit control, and of Guatemala's international balance of payments.

633. Collart Valle, Ángel Antonio. Problemas económico-sociales de Guatemala. México. 317 p.
A comprehensive descriptive survey of the economy of Guatemala, organized on a functional basis. The book contains little analysis of problems. Thesis, University of Mexico.

634. Cosenza Gálvez, Francisco. Notas sobre la planeación económica de la república de Guatemala (*Rev. econ.*, México, v. 13, no. 10, oct., p. 357-369).
An appraisal of the resources to be found in Guatemala, with primary regard to their relation to industrialization.

635. ECONOMIC REVIEW OF GUATEMALA, 1949 (*Int. ref. serv.*, v. 7, no. 37, June, 4 p.).

636. GUATEMALA. SUMMARY OF BASIC ECONOMIC INFORMATION (*Int. ref. serv.*, v. 7, no. 19, May, 4 p.).

637. León Aragón, Óscar de. Los contratos de la United Fruit Company y las compañías muelleras en Guatemala. Estudio histórico-jurídico. Prólogo de Manuel Galich. Guatemala, Editorial del Ministerio de Educación Pública. 301 p.

638. EL MES ECONÓMICO Y FINANCIERO. Guatemala. V. 3, no. 13, enero–no. 24, dic.
A monthly economic news magazine published in newspaper format.

639. TÓPICOS ECONÓMICOS. Guatemala, Universidad de San Carlos. Época 2, no. 1, marzo–no. 8, oct.?
This monthly magazine, published by the Facultad de Ciencias Económicas of the Universidad de San Carlos, contains scholarly articles on economic problems.

640. United Nations. Economic and Social Council. Economic Commission for Latin America. Agricultural credit in Guatemala. Lake Success, N. Y. 77 p.

641. Villacorta Escobar, Manuel. Investigación para la economía agrícola (*Tópicos econ.*, época 2., no. 7, sept., p. 5-10).
A brief general analysis of the agricultural economy of Guatemala.

642. Villagrán, Francisco. Deuda externa de Guatemala. Historia de la deuda inglesa (*Rev. fac. cien. jur. soc. Guatemala*, 4. época, no. 6-7, enero-junio, p. 3-24).
A brief history of English lending to Guatemala.

HONDURAS

643. BOLETÍN MENSUAL DEL BANCO CENTRAL DE HONDURAS. Tegucigalpa. V. 1, no. 1, julio–no. 6, dic.
This monthly magazine, which began publication in July, contains statistics on finance and the text of certain legislation on economic matters.

644. ECONOMIC REVIEW OF HONDURAS, 1949 (*Int. ref. serv.*, v. 7, no. 13, May, 4 p.).

645. United Nations. Economic and Social Council. Economic Commission for Latin America. Agricultural credit in Honduras. Lake Success, N. Y. 38 p.

NICARAGUA

646. Food and Agriculture Organization. Report of the FAO Mission for Nicaragua. Washington-Rome. x, 200 p., illus.
Information on agriculture, forestry, and cattle raising and the problems connected with their development.

647. Ministerio de Hacienda y Crédito Público. Presupuesto general de egresos e ingresos correspondiente al año fiscal de 1950-1951. Managua. 448 p., tables.
The budget and also the text of attached explanatory documents.

648. Recaudador General de Aduanas. Memoria del . . . por el período del 1. de enero al 31 de diciembre de 1949. Managua. 163 p.
Descriptive material on the operation of Nicaraguan customs and statistical material on foreign trade.

649. REVISTA TRIMESTRAL DEL BANCO NACIONAL DE NICARAGUA. Managua. V. 9, no. 36-37, enero-marzo–no. 39, oct.-dic.
This quarterly contains some analytical text and the text of some laws and decrees, plus statistical tables on the operations of the bank, prices in Managua, public finance, and the public debt.

PANAMA

650. Contraloría General de la República. Dirección de Estadística y Censo. Extracto estadístico de la República de Panamá. V. 1. Comercio exterior, años 1941-1943. Panamá, 1950? xi, 357 p., tables.
Detailed statistics on Panama's imports and exports during 1941, 1942, and 1943. There is no accompanying explanatory text. See item 52s.

651. ESTADÍSTICA PANAMEÑA. Panamá, Dirección de Estadística y Censo. V. 9, no. 1, enero–no. 12, dic.
This monthly magazine contains statistics on social assistance, public finance, finance, prices, transportation, production, commerce, and international trade.

THE CARIBBEAN ISLANDS

GENERAL

652. CARIBBEAN ECONOMIC REVIEW. Port-of-Spain, Trinidad, Caribbean Commission. V. 2, no. 1, May–no. 2, Nov.
Publication began with v. 1, no. 1-2, Dec., 1949. [Ed.]

653. THE GRAIN TRADE OF THE CARIBBEAN. Port-of-Spain, Trinidad, Caribbean Commission, Central Secretariat (External Trade Bulletin no. 8). 155 p., map.

654. MONTHLY INFORMATION BULLETIN. Port-of-Spain, Trinidad, Caribbean Commission. V. 3, no. 6, Jan.–v. 4, no. 5, Dec.

655. Scott, Walter. The industrial utilisation of sugar cane by-products. Port-of-Spain, Trinidad, Caribbean Commission, Central Secretariat. ix, 121 p.
This report contains a considerable amount of technical data on the processing of cane by-products—bagasse, molasses, sugar cane wax, etc.

656. Zeidenfelt, Alex. Transportation in the Caribbean during World War II (*Int.-amer. econ. affs.,* v. 4, no. 3, winter, p. 75-96).
The difficulties of providing adequate shipping among the islands because of wartime conditions and the Nazi submarine campaign.

BRITISH WEST INDIES

657. Great Britain. Colonial Office. Annual Report on Jamaica for the year 1948. Report on Jamaica for the year 1949. London, His Majesty's Stationery Office. 148 p., map, tables.
A general report on developments in Jamaica during the two years.

CUBA

658. Alienes y Urosa, Julián. Características fundamentales de la economía cubana. Habana, Banco Nacional de Cuba (Biblioteca de Economía Cubana). 405 p., graphs, tables.
"This is an important book. It represents a courageous effort to relate Cuba's economic problems to economic theory. Relationships discussed include: Population and national income, the utilization of the factors of production, the size of the business unit, the monoculture problem, the balance of payments, and the relationship between the Cuban problem and the foreign trade multiplier."

659. ———. Evolución de la economía cubana en la postguerra (*Trim. econ.,* v. 17, no. 2, abril-junio, p. 186-213).
An analysis of the Cuban economy made on the assumption of imminent deflation.

660. ANUARIO AZUCARERO DE CUBA. CUBA SUGAR YEAR BOOK. 1950. Habana, Editora Mercantil Cubana, 1950? 222 p., tables.
A bilingual annual containing a wealth of information about the sugar industry and Cuba in general.

661. EL BANCO NACIONAL DE CUBA (*Rev. banco rep.,* Colombia, v. 23, no. 271, mayo, p. 503-508).
A short factual description of the organization and functions of the new Cuban central bank.

662. Banco Nacional de Cuba. Qué es y cómo opera el . . . . Habana. 19 p.
A brief summary of the organization and functions of the Cuban central bank.

663. BOLETÍN DE ESTADÍSTICAS. Habana, Dirección General de Estadística. V. 6, no. 1, enero-abril-no. 4, sept.-dic.
A quarterly publication giving statistical tables and charts on Cuban prices, money, banking, public finance, securities markets, foreign trade, and transportation.

664. CUBA ECONÓMICA Y FINANCIERA. Habana. V. 25, no. 286, enero–no. 297, dic.
A monthly economic news magazine containing a very considerable amount of information on a wide range of subjects, especially Cuba.

665. Dirección General de Estadística. Comercio exterior, 1948-1949. Habana. 551 p., tables.
Detailed statistics on Cuban foreign trade.

666. ECONOMIC REVIEW OF CUBA, 1949 (*Int. ref. serv.,* v. 7, no. 48, June, 8 p.).

667. ESTABLISHING A BUSINESS IN CUBA (*Int. ref. serv.,* v. 7, no. 121, Dec., 12 p.).

668. Great Britain. Board of Trade. Commercial Relations and Exports Department. Cuba. Economic and commercial conditions in Cuba. London, His Majesty's Stationery Office (Overseas Economic Surveys). 89 p., tables.
A factual report by T. Brimelow.

669. Gutiérrez, Gustavo. Presente y futuro de la economía cubana. Habana, Junta Nacional de Economía (Publicaciones, 4). 84 p.

Contains a considerable amount of factual information on Cuban economic developments in 1950.

670. Junta Nacional de Economía. El acuerdo de Ginebra sobre aranceles y comercio (Estudios e Investigaciones Económicas, Publ. 7). Habana. 224 p., tables.
A study of the significance for Cuba of the General Agreement on Tariffs and Trade.

671. Menocal, Juan Manuel, II. The Cuban tax system (*Nat. tax. jour.*, v. 3, no. 2, June, p. 165-172).
A general survey of the taxes in effect in Cuba. It is descriptive rather than analytical.

672. Nelson, Lowry. Rural Cuba. Minneapolis, Minnesota, University of Minnesota Press. 285 p.
A careful study of Cuban agriculture, land tenure, and rural life, done by a sociologist. See item 3327.

673. Vivó, Hugo. El empleo y la población activa de Cuba. Habana, Asociación Nacional de Industriales de Cuba. 88 p., graphs, tables.
Poses the Cuban employment problem as being especially acute because of the highly seasonal nature of the sugar industry. Diversification of the economy is recommended.

674. Wallich, Henry C. Monetary problems of an export economy. The Cuban experience, 1914-1947. Cambridge, Mass., Harvard University Press. 357 p.
This is an important book—both as a factual study of monetary changes in Cuba during the last fifty years and as a theoretical analysis of the special monetary problems which plague the country.

DOMINICAN REPUBLIC

675. Banco Central de la República Dominicana. Memoria anual. Tercer ejercicio: 1949, enero 1. a diciembre 31. Ciudad Trujillo. ii, 98 p., tables.
Descriptive material on banking developments during 1949 plus data on individual banks and some general statistical series on trade and prices.

676. Banco de Reservas de la República Dominicana. Informe anual, año 1949. Ciudad Trujillo. 12, 11 p.
A short summary of the activities of the bank during the year. Spanish and English text.

677. Boceto económico de la República Dominicana (*Cuad. inform. econ.*, año 2, no. 3, abril, p. 3-13).
Much factual and statistical information on the economy of the Dominican Republic.

678. Boletín de hacienda. Ciudad Trujillo, Secretaría de Estado del Tesoro y Crédito

Público. V. 4, no. 1, enero-junio–no. 2, julio-dic.
A semi-annual publication containing much statistical information and the texts of governmental decrees on public finance.

679. Economic review of the Dominican Republic, 1949 (*Int. ref. serv.*, v. 7, no. 7, April, 7 p.).

680. Estadística bancaria. Ciudad Trujillo, Dirección General de Estadística. V. 14, no. 2.
A 71-page number giving banking information for 1949.

681. Secretaría de Estado del Tesoro y Crédito Público. Memoria del año 1949. Ciudad Trujillo. 1114 p., tables.
Information on Dominican taxes and other government receipts in 1949.

682. Viau, Alfred. La era de Trujillo. Economía y finanza. Ciudad Trujillo? 125 p.
Eulogy of Trujillo, which nevertheless contains considerable data on Dominican production, trade, and finance.

HAITI

683. Apunte económico de la República de Haití (*Cuad. inform. econ.*, año 2, no. 4, mayo-junio, p. 3-16).
Contains much useful factual and statistical information on the Haitian economy.

684. Banque Nationale de la République d'Haïti. Annual report of the Fiscal Department for the fiscal year, October, 1948–September, 1949. Port-au-Prince, 1950? 131 p., tables.
A general survey of foreign trade, government finance, and money and banking, accompanied by statistical tables. Also in French.

685. Economic review of Haiti, 1949 (*Int. ref. serv.*, v. 7, no. 51, June, 4 p.).

686. Establishing a business in Haiti (*Int. ref. serv.*, v. 7, no. 97, Oct., 4 p.).

687. Hubert, Giles A. Some problems of a colonial economy. A study of economic dualism in Haiti (*Int.-amer. econ. affs.*, v. 3, no. 4, spring, p. 3-30).
A commendable effort to develop a theory to describe the nature of the capitalistic pressures working on a colonial-type economy.

688. Monthly bulletin of the Fiscal Department. Port-au-Prince, Banque Nationale de la République d'Haïti. V. 27, no. 1, Jan.–no. 12, Dec.
Descriptive material and statistical tables on Haitian finance and commerce.

689. PREPARING SHIPMENTS TO HAITI (*Int. ref. serv.*, v. 7, no. 14, May, 4 p.).

690. **Young, Chester W.** Some aspects of Haiti's population and national territory significant in census considerations (*Estadística*, v. 8, no. 26, March, p. 69-86; no. 27, June, p. 204-216; no. 28, Sept., p. 388-399).
Considerable information on the population distribution and sociology of Haiti.

NETHERLANDS WEST INDIES

691. NETHERLANDS WEST INDIES. SUMMARY OF BASIC ECONOMIC INFORMATION (*Int. ref. serv.*, v. 7, no. 112, Sept., 4 p.).

PUERTO RICO

692. **Bureau of the Budget. Division of Statistics.** Balance of external payments of Puerto Rico. Fiscal years 1941-1942 to 1947-1948. San Juan. v, 29 p., v, 29 p., tables.
Valuable compilation of statistics on the balance of payments, including statistics on export prices, prepared by Belén H. Cestero. English and Spanish.

693. **Department of Finance.** Financing economic development in Puerto Rico, 1941-1949. San Juan. 39 p.
An encouraging but not uncritical survey of the measures being taken to promote development in Puerto Rico. The edition in Spanish is called *El financiamiento del desarrollo económico en Puerto Rico*. The report was prepared by Sol Luis Descartes.

694. **Descartes, Sol Luis.** [Domestic financing and economic development] in Puerto Rico (In *Domestic financing and economic development*, United Nations, Department of Economic Affairs, New York, p. 193-219).
The article deals primarily with the financing of economic development in Puerto Rico.

695. **Di Venuti, Biagio.** Money and banking in Puerto Rico. Río Piedras, University of Puerto Rico Press. 307 p.
A thorough and comprehensive analysis of the money and banking system in Puerto Rico. It was designed as a text for use at the University of Puerto Rico.

696. **Land Authority.** Informe, año económico 1948-1949. Report, fiscal year 1948-1949. San Juan. 38, 39 p.
Describes activities of the Land Authority, including those related to its sugar mills and "proportional farms," as well as its land reclamation and land redistribution programs. Spanish and English.

697. **Perloff, Harvey S.** Puerto Rico's economic future. A study in planned development. Chicago, University of Chicago Press. xviii, 435 p., illus., maps.
A thorough and scholarly economic survey of Puerto Rico. Among topics discussed are the sugar industry, manufacturing, external trade, income analysis, and the problem of planning.

698. **Planning Board.** 8. informe anual, 1949-1950. Santurce. 145 p., illus. Spanish and English text.

699. **Water Resources Authority.** Annual report, fiscal year 1949-1950. San Juan. 101 p., illus., maps.
The Authority is active, especially in the electric power and irrigation fields.

700. **Zorrilla, Frank, Rafael Freire Meléndez** (and others). La industria de la leche en Puerto Rico. Estudio estadístico realizado por . . . . San Juan, Minimum Wage Board, Research and Statistics Division. 117 p.

SOUTH AMERICA (EXCEPT ARGENTINA AND BRAZIL)

BOLIVIA

701. **Banco Agrícola de Bolivia.** Octava memoria correspondiente al año 1949. La Paz. 65 p., tables.
Statement as to the 1949 operations of the Agricultural Credit Bank, accompanied by statistical tables.

702. **Banco Central de Bolivia.** 21. memoria anual, correspondiente a la gestión del año 1950. 100 p., graphs, tables.
Contains an appraisal of economic conditions in Bolivia, plus extensive statistical tables.

703. **Banco Minero de Bolivia.** Trigésima memoria anual, correspondiente a 1949. La Paz. 26 p., tables.
Brief survey of Bolivian mineral production and trade and of the Banco Minero's activities in 1949.

704. ECONOMIC REVIEW OF BOLIVIA, 1949 (*Int. ref. serv.*, v. 7, no. 57, July, 7 p.).

705. **Griess, Phyllis R.** The Bolivian tin industry (*Econ. geog.*, v. 27, no. 3, July, p. 238-250).
A critical discussion of the industry which accounts for at least 60 per cent, and usually 70 per cent or more, of the total value of Bolivian exports. However, the foreign credit thus obtained is used to buy foodstuffs from abroad, while too little effort is made to "valorize" the fertile area of the eastern foothills. Bolivia has neglected both agriculture and manufacturing in favor of mining. The imbalance that has ensued

should be corrected while there is still an income from tin mining, for, as the author concludes, "Bolivia's situation will be most unfortunate when its tin ores have been exhausted if the country has failed in the meantime to develop other national resources." [R. E. Crist]

706. **Hallowell, Burton C.** Tin control and exchange depreciation in Bolivia, 1931-1939 (*Int.-amer. econ. affs.*, v. 4, no. 1, summer, p. 71-84).
The third in a series of articles by Professor Hallowell on the place of the tin mining industry in the Bolivian economy. For the first two, see *HLAS, no. 15, 1949*, items 891 and 892.

707. **Villalpando M., Juan.** El pensamiento económico en Bolivia (*Estud. econ.*, año 4, no. 5, dic., p. 140-190).
A brief but comprehensive economic history of Bolivia.

CHILE

708. **Alessandri Palma, Arturo.** Las cuestiones económicas, el régimen parlamentario y la cuestión social en Chile, desde 1891 hasta 1925 (*Atenea*, v. 97, no. 299, mayo, p. 140-161).
Comments by an ex-President on monetary developments in Chile about the turn of the century.

709. BOLETÍN MENSUAL. Santiago, Banco Central de Chile. Año 23, no. 263, enero– no. 274, dic.
Each issue of this monthly magazine contains charts, statistical tables, and a summary of recent economic developments in Chile; also brief summaries of recent laws.

710. **Banco Central de Chile.** Vigésima cuarta memoria anual, presentada a la Superintendencia de Bancos. Año 1949. Santiago. 87 p., tables.
Descriptive material covering economic developments during 1949, the texts of important decrees affecting the economy, and extensive statistical tables.

711. ————. Sección de Estadística e Investigaciones Económicas. Balanza de pagos de Chile, 1949. Santiago. 67 p., graphs, tables.
A comprehensive survey of Chilean foreign trade during recent years, with especial reference to 1949.

712. ————. ————. Inversiones extranjeras en Chile en 1948. Santiago. 80 p.
An impressive statistical study of foreign investment in Chile. The statistics are compiled both by industries and by countries of origin.

713. **Bustamante Pérez, Mario.** El problema de la carne en Chile (*Mem. licenciados*, v. 5, p. 121-160).

A comprehensive study of the production, distribution, and consumption of meat in Chile.

714. **Caja Autónoma de Amortización de la Deuda Pública.** Informe que presenta la . . . al Ministerio de Hacienda sobre las operaciones realizadas en el año 1949. Santiago. 53 p., tables.
Detailed data on operations affecting the public debt during 1949.

715. **Caja de Crédito Agrario.** Memoria correspondiente a los años 1948 y 1949. Santiago. 64 p., graphs, tables.

716. **Caja de Crédito Minero.** Memoria correspondiente al año 1949. Santiago. 62 p. plus tables.
Summary of the minerals situation and a statement as to the activities of the various divisions of the Caja.

717. **Caja Nacional de Ahorros.** Sexagésima quinta memoria anual, año 1949. Valparaíso, 1950? 42 p., graphs, tables.
A detailed statement of the operations of the National Savings Bank during the year.

718. **Carvallo Hederra, Sergio.** Las cooperativas de electrificación rural en Chile. Washington, Unión Panamericana, Departamento de Asuntos Económicos y Sociales, División de Asuntos Sociales y de Trabajo. 23 p.
A discussion of the manner in which the Chilean government's Empresa Nacional de Electricidad has been encouraging the establishment of cooperatives of rural consumers of electric power.

718a. ————. El cooperativismo en Chile. Washington, Unión Panamericana, Departamento de Asuntos Económicos y Sociales, División de Asuntos Sociales y de Trabajo, Sección de Cooperativas. vi, 62 p.
Reviews briefly the development of cooperatives in Chile, including consumer and other types. Has the texts of important legislation and a useful bibliography. [C. Farman]

719. CHILE. SUMMARY OF BASIC ECONOMIC INFORMATION (*Int. ref. serv.*, v. 7, no. 88, Aug., 8 p.).

720. **Cifuentes Betancourt, Claudio.** El impuesto a las cifras de los negocios (*Mem. licenciados*, v. 8, p. 107-170).
Discussion of the law and administration of the tax on total volume of business in industry and commerce (the so-called *cifra de los negocios*).

721. **Contraloría General de la República.** Memoria de . . . correspondiente al año 1949 y balance general de la Hacienda Pública en 31 de diciembre de 1949. Santiago. 381 p., tables.

Discusses the activities of the Contraloría during 1949 and contains statistics on Chilean public debt, revenues, and expenditures. Gives financial statements for many semi-autonomous government entities.

722. Contreras Lara, Ramiro. Coordinación de los medios de transporte en Chile (*Mem. licenciados,* v. 4, p. 73-158).
An analysis of the Chilean highway, railway, river and lake, ocean, and air transportation systems, with a concluding discussion on overall coordination.

723. Corporación de Fomento de la Producción. Fundación Pedro Aguirre Cerda. Geografía económica de Chile. T. 1-2. Santiago. xxx, 428 p.; xvii, 545 p., tables, maps.
A comprehensive work covering a wide range of material from geographical resources through population, standard of living, and finance, to the role of the government in the promotion of economic development. A third volume will follow. See item 1207.

724. ECONOMÍA Y FINANZAS. Santiago. Año 14, no. 159, enero–no. 176, dic.
A monthly magazine containing both scholarly articles and current news items on Chilean economic problems.

725. ECONOMIC REVIEW OF CHILE, 1949 (*Int. ref. serv.,* v. 7, no. 26, May, 7 p.).

726. Ferdman Fischer, Jorge. De la instalación y funcionamiento de industrias, bajo el punto de vista legal (*Mem. licenciados,* v. 3, p. 433-486).
Considerable data on the legal requirements which must be met to establish a business in Chile.

727. Franco Amaro, Raúl. Las cooperativas agrícolas (*Mem. licenciados,* v. 3, p. 305-432).
Contains a considerable amount of information on the operation of cooperatives, especially in Chilean agriculture.

728. Fraustaedter, Hans. Problemas del comercio exterior de Chile (*Economía,* Santiago, año 11, no. 36, 3. trimestre, p. 121-126).
A concise analysis of the direction of Chile's foreign trade.

729. García, Desiderio. [Domestic financing and economic development] in Chile (In *Domestic financing and economic development,* United Nations, Department of Economic Affairs, New York, p. 91-112).
The article deals primarily with the financing of economic development in Chile.

730. Herrera Lane, Felipe. Política económica. Santiago, Editorial Jurídica de Chile

(Col. de Apuntes de Clases, no. 4). 242 p.
A general, largely factual, survey of the economy of Chile, with major sections on natural resources, population, government relations with business, mining, agriculture, and manufacturing.

731. Job (pseud.). Apuntes sobre la estructura económica chilena (*Atenea,* año 27, t. 97, no. 300, junio, p. 364-386).
A thoughtful study of Chilean mining, agriculture, and industry, in the light of the economic implications of the present organization of those industries.

732. Kaltwaser Passig, Jorge. Naturaleza jurídica de las cooperativas y en especial de las cooperativas agrícolas (*Mem. licenciados,* v. 3, p. 273-303).
Information on the place of cooperatives in the Chilean economy.

733. Le-Bert Espinoza, Rafael. Régimen impositivo de los bienes raíces (*Mem. licenciados,* v. 8, p. 327-377).
A study of the legal aspects of the tax on real property in Chile.

734. Le-Bert Sotomayor, Fernando. La industria de la betarraga azucarera y sus posibilidades económicas (*Mem. licenciados,* v. 8, p. 253-291).
A survey of the possibility of developing a sugar beet industry in Chile.

735. Lietti, Mario. Problemas chilenos. 2. edición. Santiago, Tipografía Chilena. 29 p.
Chiefly notable for advocacy of the development of olive oil and natural silk industries in Chile.

736. Ministerio de Hacienda. Exposición sobre el estado de la Hacienda Pública. Presentada por el Ministro de Hacienda don Raúl Yrarrázaval Lecaros a la Comisión Mixta de Presupuestos en 9 de noviembre de 1950 (Oficina del Presupuesto y Finanzas, folleto no. 74). Santiago. 52 p., tables.
A comprehensive survey of the Chilean budgetary situation.

737. Mora Venegas, Alfonso. Los bosques en la economía chilena. Santiago. 98 p.
A statement with regard to the economic importance of forests, followed by a summary of the Chilean legislation on forests. Thesis, University of Chile.

738. Ochoa Romani, Juan. El problema agrario de la provincia de Coquimbo. Santiago. 87 p.
A factual description of the geography and crops of the province of Coquimbo, accompanied by a proposed program for agricultural reform containing suggestions on the land tenure system. Thesis, University of Chile.

739. **Olate Vásquez, Hugo.** Industria del arroz en Chile y sus proyecciones económicas (*Mem. licenciados,* v. 5, p. 161-222).
Much information on the rice industry both in Chile and on the world scene.

740. **Rencoret Bravo, Álvaro.** Derecho tributario. El impuesto sobre la renta. Santiago, Editorial Jurídica de Chile. 404 p.
A study of Chile's income tax.

741. **Runco González, Alejandro.** Chile y Perú a través de su producción económica (*Mem. licenciados,* v. 4, p. 159-287).
A survey first of Peruvian production, then of Chilean production, followed by a discussion of trading relations between the two countries, which is supported by an abundance of statistical data.

742. **Santa Bahamondes, Arnoldo.** Chiloé económico (*Mem. licenciados,* v. 4, p. 289-344).
Descriptive study of the economy of an interesting Chilean region.

743. **Sepúlveda Parada, Mario.** El Consejo Nacional de Economía (*Mem. licenciados,* v. 4, p. 15-71).
Analyzes the Chilean government's economic planning council, set up in 1946, in the light of the functioning of similar agencies in other countries and also by comparison with previous similar agencies in Chile.

744. **Silva Silva, Clemente.** Sociedades anónimas nacionales civiles comerciales ante la legislación tributaria. Santiago, 1950? 88 p.
Description of the Chilean tax system in relation to forms of corporate organization. Thesis, University of Chile.

745. **Subercaseaux, Guillermo.** La situación monetaria en Chile durante la primera guerra mundial (*Economía,* Santiago, año 11, no. 36, 3. trimestre, p. 107-120).
Financial and foreign trade developments in Chile during World War I.

746. **United Nations. Economic and Social Council. Economic Commission for Latin America.** Plan para detener la inflación en Chile. Santiago, Editorial Universitaria. 63 p.
The report of a United Nations economic mission to Chile, composed of Carl Iversen, Simeon E. Leland, and Erik Lindahl. It contains a comprehensive plan for controlling inflation. Published in English by the United Nations, New York, 1951, as *Report of the United Nations Economic Mission to Chile, 1949-1950* (ST/TAH/K/Chile/1).

747. **Vega Muñoz, René.** Industria química pesada en Chile y sus posibilidades (*Mem. licenciados,* v. 5, p. 223-263).

A general survey of the Chilean chemical industry, discussing various other aspects of the industry in addition to nitrates.

748. **Vodnizza Fernández, Juana.** La marina mercante nacional y el crédito naviero (*Mem. licenciados,* v. 8, 171-252 p.).
Comprehensive survey of the Chilean merchant marine, giving especial attention to its financing.

COLOMBIA

749. ANALES DE ECONOMÍA Y ESTADÍSTICA. Bogotá, Contraloría General de la República. 2. época, año 6, no. 61-66, enero-junio–no. 70-72, oct.-dic.
This magazine, which is ostensibly monthly, is actually published at irregular intervals, and one issue may contain several numbers. The publication contains statistical material on the budget, foreign trade, mining, industry, and transportation, although not all of the series are carried in every issue.

750. **Banco de la República.** XXVII informe anual del Gerente a la Junta Directiva, julio 1. de 1949–junio 30 de 1950. Bogotá, 1950? 232 p., graphs, tables.
A comprehensive survey of Colombian trade and finance.

751. ————. **Departamento de Investigaciones Económicas.** La minería en Colombia. El petróleo (Bol. Gráfico no. 11). Bogotá. 31 p., tables.
An informative survey of the petroleum industry in Colombia with maps, tables, and analytical text.

752. BOLETÍN DE LA SUPERINTENDENCIA BANCARIA. Bogotá. No. 143, enero–no. 150, agosto-dic.
This bulletin, which is published most months, contains the texts of new decrees on banking matters and extensive statistical tables.

753. **Caja de Crédito Agrario, Industrial y Minero.** Informe presentado por el gerente general al Excmo. Sr. Presidente de la República en 30 de junio de 1950. Bogotá, 1950? 232 p., graphs, illus., tables.
A variety of information on the financing of agriculture, industry, and mining in Colombia.

754. **Contraloría General de la República.** Estadística fiscal y administrativa, 1948. Anexo al informe financiero. Bogotá. x, 437 p., graphs, tables.
A brief commentary, followed by voluminous tables on sources of revenue and expenditures, broken down into sections on the national government, departments, and municipalities.

755. ————. Informe financiero. Vigencia fiscal de 1949. Bogotá. 529 p., tables.
Information on government revenue, expenditures, and public debt in 1949.

756. Dirección Nacional de Estadística. Anuario de comercio exterior, 1948. Bogotá. 824 p., tables.
Detailed information on exports, imports, and tariffs during 1948.

757. Echavarría Olózaga, Hernán. El problema del cambio. Bogotá, Editorial Litografía Colombia, 1950? 99 p.

758. ECONOMIC REVIEW OF COLOMBIA, 1949 (*Int. ref. serv.*, v. 7, no. 45, June, 8 p.).

759. Emiro Valencia, Luis. Política del cambio exterior. Bogotá, Iqueima. xxxii, 140 p.
A plea for the establishment of a scientific, carefully prepared foreign exchange budget by the Colombian government.

760. Great Britain. Board of Trade. Commercial Relations and Export Department. Colombia. Economic and commercial conditions in Colombia. London, His Majesty's Stationery Office (Overseas Economic Surveys). 42 p., tables.
A report by L. A. Scopes giving a wide range of information on the Colombian economy.

761. Instituto de Fomento Industrial. Informe del gerente, junio 30 de 1950. Bogotá. 107 p.
Describes the activities of the Instituto in connection with Colombia's economic development. Most important probably are the activities related to the Paz de Río steel mill.

762. International Bank for Reconstruction and Development. The basis of a development program for Colombia. Report of a mission headed by Lauchlin Currie and sponsored by the International Bank for Reconstruction and Development in collaboration with the government of Colombia. Washington. 642 p.
A comprehensive survey of Colombian economy, which contains recommendations for the development of almost all its phases. The recommendations on the steel industry are especially controversial.

763. Morales Pradilla, Próspero. Inmigración. Una necesidad de Colombia. Bogotá, A.B.C., 1950? 72 p.
In this short study it is assumed that immigration is desirable, and there is discussion of a variety of procedures to make it more orderly and to ease the adjustment of the immigrant to the new environment.

764. Ospina B., Sebastián. Perspectivas de la industria cafetera en Colombia (*Rev. banco rep.*, Colombia, v. 23, no. 272, junio, p. 604-609).
A general appraisal of the coffee situation, with especial regard to Colombia, prepared by the Colombian Consul General in San Francisco.

765. REVISTA DEL BANCO DE LA REPÚBLICA. Bogotá. V. 23, no. 267, enero–no. 278, dic.
Monthly magazine containing analytical articles on economic problems, current notes, and an extensive section of statistical data.

ECUADOR

766. Banco Nacional de Fomento. Informe anual de labores, 1949. Quito. 25 p., tables.
Annual statement of the activities of the National Development Bank.

767. BOLETÍN DEL BANCO CENTRAL DEL ECUADOR. Quito. Año 23, no. 270-271, enero-feb.–año 24, no. 280-281, nov.-dic.
Each issue of this monthly magazine, which is sometimes published as two issues in one, contains the text of new legislation affecting banking, articles on economic matters, and statistics on a wide variety of economic problems.

768. BOLETÍN DEL MINISTERIO DEL TESORO. Quito. No. 21-22, 1.-2. trimestres–no. 23-24, 3.-4. trimestres.
A bulletin, ostensibly a quarterly, containing the text of official documents and numerous statistics on tax matters.

769. COMERCIO EXTERIOR ECUATORIANO. Quito, Banco Central del Ecuador. No. 29, enero–no. 39, dic.
This monthly (with occasional lapses) magazine contains statistical data on Ecuador's foreign trade.

770. Corporación de Fomento. Informe anual de labores, 1949. Quito. 163 p.
Report on the assistance given by this government-sponsored Development Corporation to agriculture and industry.

771. ECONOMIC REVIEW OF ECUADOR, 1949 (*Int. ref. serv.*, v. 7, no. 72, July, 4 p.).

772. ECUADOR. SUMMARY OF BASIC ECONOMIC INFORMATION (*Int. ref. serv.*, v. 7, no. 24, May, 4 p.).

773. Estrada, V. E. El momento económico en el Ecuador. Procurando hacer país. La tragedia monetaria pasada y la futura. Sus causas, sus narcóticos y sus remedios. Guayaquil, La Reforma. 86 p.
A polemic against the policies which author says have been causing a decline in the value of the sucre.

774. Great Britain. Board of Trade. Commercial Relations and Export Department. Ecuador. Economic and commercial conditions in Ecuador. London, His Majesty's Stationery Office (Overseas Economic Surveys). 47 p., map, tables.
A wide variety of information, reported by J. E. M. Carvell.

775. MERCHANT SHIPPING AND SHIPBUILDING. ECUADOR (*World trade commod.,* v. 8, part 1, no. 4, March, 4 p.).

776. Ministerio del Tesoro. Informe a la nación, 1950. Quito. 99 p.
This report, submitted by the Minister of the Treasury José Araújo Luna, contains much information on recent tax developments, especially developments in tax law and the organization of tax collections. It also contains information on the operation of the government monopolies.

777. PREPARING SHIPMENTS TO ECUADOR (*Int. ref. serv.,* v. 7, no. 18, May, 8 p.).

778. Superintendente de Bancos. Informe del . . . al H. Congreso Nacional, 1949-1950. Quito, 1950? 106 p., graphs, tables.
This report, submitted by the Superintendent Manuel Romero Sánchez, contains a wide variety of data on money and credit in Ecuador.

FRENCH GUIANA

779. FRENCH GUIANA. SUMMARY OF BASIC ECONOMIC INFORMATION (*Int. ref. serv.,* v. 7, no. 123, Dec., 4 p.).

PARAGUAY

780. ECONOMIC REVIEW OF PARAGUAY, 1949 (*Int. ref. serv.,* v. 7, no. 54, July, 4 p.).

781. Ferreira, Jorge E., and Elvin A. Duerst. Costo de producción del arroz en el Paraguay, cosecha 1948-1949. Estudio sobre diez arroceros comerciales de la región oriental del Paraguay . . . . Asunción, Servicio Técnico Interamericano de Cooperación Agrícola. 4 p., illus.

782. PARAGUAY INDUSTRIAL Y COMERCIAL. Asunción, Ministerio de Economía. Año 7, no. 65, enero–no. 76, dic.
Miscellaneous data on economic developments during the period covered plus the texts of government decrees.

PERU

See also item 741.

783. Banco Central de Reserva del Perú. Memoria, 1949. Lima, 1950? 116 p., tables.
Considerable factual information with statistical tables on the operation of the Peruvian economy in 1949.

784. Banco de Crédito del Perú. Oficina de Estudios Económicos. Vademécum del inversionista, 1950-1951. Lima. 532 p., tables.

An annual publication containing data on the securities issues of the national government, banks, and leading private corporations in Peru.

785. Banco Industrial del Perú. Décimotercera memoria, año 1949. Lima. 28 p., 12 anexos.
General data on Peruvian trade, production, and cost of living, as well as information on the activities of the bank in financing industrialization.

786. Banco Minero del Perú. Memoria, año 1949. Lima. 31 p., tables.
Much information on Peruvian mining during 1949. The general observation is made that the industry was in a difficult situation during that year because of low prices.

787. BOLETÍN DEL BANCO CENTRAL DE RESERVA DEL PERÚ. Lima. Año 20, no. 218, enero–no. 229, dic.
Each issue of this monthly magazine contains a general survey of recent economic developments in Peru plus statistical tables.

788. BOLETÍN DEL INSTITUTO NACIONAL DE INVESTIGACIÓN Y FOMENTO MINEROS. Lima. Año 1, no. 1.
This new publication is a continuation of the *Boletín del Cuerpo de Ingenieros de Minas* and of the *Boletín del Instituto Geológico del Perú.* Its second number (oct., viii, 278 p.) is devoted to the *Anuario de la Industria Minera en el Perú, 1949.*

789. Comisión Ejecutiva del Inventario del Potencial Económico. Inventario del potencial económico de la Nación. Fascículo 1. 1948-1949. Lima, 1950? 120 p., chart, tables.
Text of decrees setting up the Commission and a statement of its plans for appraising the economic potential of Peru.

790. Fuentes Irurozqui, Manuel. Síntesis de la economía peruana. Lima, Sanmartí. 268 p.
A comprehensive factual survey. The economy of Peru is described industry by industry. There are additional chapters on foreign trade, banking, and government finance.

791. INFORMACIONES COMERCIALES. Lima, Ministerio de Hacienda y Comercio del Perú, Dirección de Asuntos Comerciales. Año 1, no. 1, enero–no. 12, dic.
This monthly magazine contains articles on foreign and domestic trade problems and the texts of many government decrees.

792. Moll, Bruno. La reforma monetaria en el Perú (*Trim. econ.,* v. 17, no. 4, oct.-dic., p. 636-654).
An article on the implications of the Peruvian currency devaluation of 1949.

793. Pan American Union. Division of Economic Research. The Peruvian econ-

omy. A study of its characteristics, stage of development, and main problems. Washington. 279 p.
Considerable factual and statistical material on the economy of Peru.

794. Superintendencia de Bancos. Memoria de la . . . y estadística bancaria, de seguros y capitalización correspondientes al año 1949. Lima. 650 p., tables.
A statement of developments among banks in Peru (such as bankruptcies and liquidations) during the year; government decrees affecting banking; and 420 pages of banking statistics.

795. Velarde Morán, Ernesto (ed.). Índice geográfico e industrial de los pueblos del Perú. Con los últimos decretos sobre legislación industrial. Lima, Imprenta Americana. xi, 270 p., tables.
A wide range of factual information on the stage of industrial development in Peru, accompanied by the texts of numerous governmental decrees on the subject.

Uruguay

796. Banco de la República Oriental del Uruguay. Memoria y balance general. Ejercicio 1949. Montevideo. 152 p., graphs, tables.
A comprehensive survey which covers not only the operations of the Bank during 1949 but also many of the more general economic activities of Uruguay, such as foreign trade.

797. Banco Hipotecario del Uruguay. Memoria correspondiente al 57. ejercicio, año 1948. Montevideo. 99 p., graphs.
The bank has financed urban and rural housing, colonization projects, and hotels.

798. Boletín del Banco Hipotecario del Uruguay. Montevideo. 2. época, no. 36, enero-feb.–no. 42, dic.
This magazine, published monthly or bimonthly, contains a variety of data on the Uruguayan economy as well as leading articles on a range of economic problems.

799. Bregman, Samuel. El presupuesto general de gastos de la república en el período pre-constitucional (*Rev. fac. cien. econ. admin.,* época 2, no. 1, sept., p. 31-48).
Information on Uruguayan public finance about 1830.

800. Delegación Permanente del Uruguay en las Naciones Unidas. Oficina de Información y Prensa. El Uruguay y su desarrollo económico. Algunos índices representativos. Montevideo, Imprenta América. 73 p., maps, tables.

801. Economic review of Uruguay, 1949 (*Int. ref. serv.,* v. 7, no. 55, July, 8 p.).

802. Great Britain. Board of Trade. Commercial Relations and Export Department. Uruguay. Economic and commercial conditions in Uruguay. London, His Majesty's Stationery Office (Overseas Economic Surveys). 34 p., map, tables.
This report, by C. G. Harris, contains a considerable amount of detailed factual information.

803. Informativo. Montevideo, Ministerio de Hacienda. Enero-dic.
A monthly publication containing a wide variety of information on Uruguayan public finance.

804. Iniciativas y realizaciones de carácter económico, financiero y social (*Rev. fac. cien. econ. admin.,* época 2, no. 1, sept., p. 67-106).
A proposed change in the organic law of the Banco de la República, which would provide for the creation of a monetary department and a rural and industrial credit department. The proposed law and accompanying comment are submitted by Nilo R. Berchesi.

805. Ministerio de Relaciones Exteriores. El tratado de amistad comercial y desarrollo económico de 23 de noviembre de 1949. Montevideo. 76 p.
This document contains the text of the important recent treaty signed by the United States and Uruguay, which has "model" provisions dealing with foreign investments. It also contains an extensive commentary by Ariosto D. González. See also item 2310.

806. Recopilación de la estadística agropecuaria del Uruguay. Montevideo, Ministerio de Ganadería y Agricultura, Dirección de Agronomía, Sección Economía y Estadística Agraria (Publ. no. 102). 167 p., tables.
This report, prepared under the direction of Ricardo Christopherson, contains a wide variety of statistics on agriculture and cattle raising, including both production and trade.

807. Revista del Banco de la República Oriental del Uruguay. Montevideo. Año 8, no. 32, enero-año 9, no. 35, dic.
A quarterly publication giving information on many phases of economic activity in Uruguay. Statistical supplement.

Venezuela

808. Arcila Farías, Eduardo. El capital extranjero. Caracas, Industrias Gráficas. 45 p.
Argues that the Venezuelan economy is of the colonial type and that industrialization financed in part by a carefully controlled import of capital is desirable to change this situation.

809. Banco Central de Venezuela. Memoria correspondiente al ejercicio anual 1949. Caracas, 1950? 126 p., tables.

Analysis of Venezuelan economic developments in 1949, accompanied by extensive statistical tables.

810. BOLETÍN DE LA CÁMARA DE COMERCIO DE CARACAS. Año 35 (37?), no. 434, enero–no. 445, dic.
A monthly magazine giving a variety of current information on economic matters.

811. BOLETÍN DEL BANCO CENTRAL DE VENEZUELA. Caracas. Año 10, no. 59-60, enero-feb.-no. 69-70, nov.-dic.
Each issue of this magazine contains a general survey of recent economic developments in Venezuela and statistical tables.

812. BOLETÍN INFORMATIVO DEL MINISTERIO DE HACIENDA. Caracas. Año 12, no. 101, enero-no. 103, julio.
This periodical contains a variety of information on Venezuelan public finance and the texts of numerous decrees.

813. Cárdenas Becerra, Humberto. El impuesto sobre la renta en Venezuela (Tópicos econ., época 2., no. 8, oct., p. 3-19).
A discussion of Venezuela's income tax law.

814. Consejo de Economía Nacional. Informe de las actividades realizadas por el . . . durante el año de 1948. Caracas. 27 p.

815. ————. Informe de las actividades realizadas por el . . . durante el año de 1949. Caracas. 43 p.
The council makes recommendations on various economic problems at the request of other branches of the government. These recommendations are summarized in the report.

816. Corporación Venezolana de Fomento. Memoria y cuenta del ejercicio 1. de enero a 30 de junio de 1949. Caracas. 240 p., graphs, plans, product maps, tables.
This very informative publication contains first a policy statement emphasizing the desire of the Corporation to encourage private enterprise followed by detailed discussion of the measures taken to promote particular enterprises.

817. ————. Memoria y cuenta correspondiente al ejercicio 1. de julio 1949 al 30 junio de 1950 y presupuesto para el ejercicio 1950-1951. Caracas. 168 p., graphs, illus., tables.
Detailed description of developments, especially in agriculture and manufacturing, which are being encouraged by this government-sponsored corporation.

818. CUADERNOS DE INFORMACIÓN ECONÓMICA. Caracas, Corporación Venezolana de Fomento. Año 2, no. 1, enero-no. 8, dic.
This magazine, which appears sometimes monthly, sometimes bimonthly, contains both scholarly articles and current information on the economy. It offers a wealth of data, including a regular statistical appendix.

819. ECONOMIC REVIEW OF VENEZUELA, 1949 (Int. ref. serv., v. 7, no. 12, May, 8 p.).

820. ESTUDIO SOBRE LOS TRANSPORTES DE GUAYANA (Cuad. inform. econ., año 2, no. 4, mayo-junio, p. 75-94).
The transportation situation in the Guiana region of Venezuela.

821. Lippert, T. W. Cerro Bolívar. Saga of an averted iron ore crisis (Venezuela-up-to-date, no. 4, March, p. 4-5, 10-13).
The story of the exploration work in connection with the discovery of Cerro Bolívar.

822. LA MINERÍA EN VENEZUELA (Cuad. inform. econ., año 2, no. 4, mayo-junio, p. 23-49).
Appraisal of the mineral resources of Venezuela.

823. PANORAMA INDUSTRIAL DE VENEZUELA (Cuad. inform. econ., año 2, no. 6, agosto-sept., p. 36-56; no. 7, oct.-nov., p. 19-47).
A useful survey of the Venezuelan economy, containing much statistical information.

824. LA PESCA EN VENEZUELA (Cuad. inform. econ., año 2, no. 8, dic., p. 22-30).
Brief history of the fishing industry in Venezuela and description of its current organization.

825. PREPARING SHIPMENTS TO VENEZUELA (Int. ref. serv., v. 7, no. 115, Dec., 7 p.).

826. EL PRESUPUESTO EN VENEZUELA (Cuad. inform. econ., año 2, no. 5, julio, p. 19-44).
A comprehensive statement of the background of budget preparation in Venezuela, made in connection with analysis of the 1950-1951 budget.

827. Ruggeri Parra, Pablo. Fundamentos constitucionales del sistema rentístico venezolano. Milano [Italy], Magnani. 96 p.
A general analysis of the Venezuelan tax system.

828. Superintendencia de Bancos. Informe relativo a las actividades en el año de 1949. Caracas. 44 p., tables.
Description of measures affecting Venezuelan banking taken in 1949; statistical tables.

829. TRANSPORTES FLUVIALES, MARÍTIMOS Y AÉREOS DE VENEZUELA (Cuad. inform. econ., año 2, no. 3, abril, p. 19-37).
Much factual and statistical information on water and air transportation.

830. LOS TRANSPORTES TERRESTRES EN VENEZUELA (Cuad. inform. econ., año 2, no. 2, feb.-marzo, p. 32-59).
Contains much factual and statistical information on transportation by land.

831. **Van Sickle (Paul G.) Corporation.**
Ferrocarril del Este, Venezuela. Economic,
engineering, construction study. Denver?
vii, 285 p., illus., maps.
An engineer's detailed report on the project for
building a railroad to bring out Cerro Bolívar
iron ore to Barcelona.

832. VENEZUELA. SUMMARY OF BASIC ECO-
NOMIC INFORMATION (*Int. ref. serv.*, v. 7,
no. 98, Oct., 7 p.).

833. **Wharton, Clifton R., Jr.**   C. B. R. in
Venezuela (*Int.-amer. econ. affs.*, v. 4, no.
3, winter, p. 3-15).
Discussion of the program of the Consejo de
Bienestar Rural for the improvement of the
standard of living in rural Venezuela.

ADDENDA

834. **Bird, Esteban A.** El financiamiento de
la industrialización de Puerto Rico. Bound
with *La expansión industrial en Puerto
Rico*, by Santiago Díaz Pacheco. San
Juan, Puerto Rico, Departament of Education, 1949.
Two short lectures delivered at the University
of Puerto Rico.

835. **Dominican Republic. Banco de Reservas.** Informe anual. Año 1948. Spanish and English texts. Ciudad Trujillo,
Imprenta Arte y Cine, 1949. 12, 10 p.

836. ————. Secretaría de Estado de
Economía Nacional. Memoria . . . correspondiente al año 1948. Ciudad Trujillo, Editora Arte y Cine, 1949. 186 p.

837. **Paraguay. Ministerio de Hacienda.**
Dirección General de Estadística. Anuario
estadístico de la República del Paraguay,
1946-1947. Asunción, 1948. 336 p., tables.

838. **Pflucker Pedemonte, Luis A.** Economía minera. Lima, Universidad Nacional
Mayor de San Marcos, Facultad de Ciencias Económicas y Comerciales, 1949.
92 p.

ARGENTINA

BENJAMÍN CORNEJO

DURING 1950 Argentine literature on economic subjects has maintained the level
of the previous year. It appears mainly in the numerous technical reviews which are
published and in a number of books.

The bulk of the production is given over to editorial articles which tend to extol
and disseminate the policy followed by the government as regards industrialization,
with the object of securing the economic independence of the country; for this reason
they must obviously be excluded from this account.

On the other hand, a large part of the literary output which can be classed as
"academic" also seems to be influenced in the same way. Apart from one or two
articles and a few books whose merits are discussed below, this literature carries little
scientific weight. It consists for the most part of either purely descriptive work or
elementary syntheses based on the theories and teachings of the leading contemporary
economists.

As far as subjects are concerned, no particular predilection can be noted. A good
deal of the work published, however, continues to revolve around the inflationary
tendency that became acute in 1950 and resulted in a considerable rise in the cost
of living.

Reviews and periodical publications, including those edited by the various Argentine universities, continue to be published regularly. These are usually statistical and
informative in nature.

GENERAL ECONOMIC THEORY

839. **Bustos, Alfredo O.** Algunos aspectos
de economía agraria (*Horiz. econ.*, no. 55,
abril, p. 309-313; no. 56, mayo, p. 362-
366; no. 58, julio, p. 26-33; no. 60, sept.,
p. 125-135).

Starting with elementary concepts of agrarian
economy and the characteristics distinguishing
it from industrial economy, the author discusses
the land ownership system and its influence on
agrarian economy. He mentions the individualist
standards enshrined in legislation influenced by
18th- and 19th-century doctrines, among them
the Argentine Constitution of 1853. He refers

to the 1949 Argentine Constitutional reforms and to the concept of the "social function" of property therein adopted. He then discusses the factors in agrarian production and indirect influences affecting it; among these he mentions the State, producers' organizations, and ways of marketing the products. He analyzes methods of exploitation with particular reference to systems and theories of land ownership and to factors determining such methods and the size of the enterprise. He concludes by referring to the Argentine system of rural labor and to recent government policy.

840. León, Félix. La publicidad en la teoría económica del valor (*Rev. inst. econ. téc. publ.*, v. 6, no. 1-2, p. 51-63).
After reflecting briefly on advertising activity in the modern world of business, the author points out the omissions of the classical schools of thought in this respect, since the hypothesis of perfect competition does not admit of advertisement or publicity influencing the demand of the individual seller. He further points out how the new theories of Chamberlin and Mrs. Robinson, based on the differentiation of the product and the imperfection of the market, clearly place publicity primarily within the theory of prices. The discussion concludes with an elementary exposition of the influence of publicity on the sales graph of the entrepreneur, accentuating the monopolistic elements of his market. The author admits the new theories represent a considerable theoretical advance, but doubts their ultimate fruitfulness.

841. Martini, Óscar S. Economía, riqueza y humanismo. Buenos Aires, El Ateneo. 70 p.
Within the framework of present-day ethics or rules of conduct, the author seeks a "humanization" of economy inspired by Roman Catholic philosophy.

842. Piñón Filgueira, Evaristo M. El estado y la empresa (*Rev. fac. cien. econ.*, Buenos Aires, año 3, no. 28, oct., p. 956-973).
Advocates a corporative economy as the middle-of-the-road policy between liberalism and collectivism.

843. Prados Arrarte, Jesús. Problemas básicos de la doctrina económica. Buenos Aires, Editorial Sudamericana. 180 p.
The author has collected in this book various essays on theoretical subjects and present-day world economies. They deal with the Keynesian theories, planning, State control and free enterprise, Malthus, the industrialization of underdeveloped countries, the Soviet economy, etc. Inspired, as the author confesses, by the schism threatened today between the principles of economic science and the viewpoints of public and government opinion, the book undertakes to explain, in simple, non-technical language, the basic principles of modern economic science and the present state of its problems. The author has succeeded in this objective and, without sacrificing simplicity, has written a brilliant exposition.
The various problems with which this book

deals are linked by the author's liberal principles and by his adherence to a strictly scientific approach. Since he wished to give this work a popular nature, he has used ingenious modes of exposition, but these have not obscured the critical wisdom and acute observation brought to bear on the latest and most advanced concepts of economic theory.

844. Roza Igarzábal, Hugo de la. Ensayo sobre una reclasificación de los factores productivos (*Rev. econ.*, Córdoba, año 2, t. 2, no. 2, julio-dic., p. 164-179).
This article deals fundamentally with the ideas of capital and interest, indicating the theoretical discrepancies which have arisen from the inclusion (or exclusion) of money in the concept of capital. The author, who gives sound references to the opinions of the leading contemporary economists dealing with these problems, believes that money should occupy a separate place in the classification of factors of production; and that physical goods and land should be lumped together in a single category as capital, so that the traditional threefold character of such factors would be preserved in a classification similar to that of J. B. Clark, which the author believes compatible with the opinions, *inter alia*, of Keynes and Hayek: namely, capital, labor, and money. In order to underline the significance of this classification, de la Roza points out that it would eliminate the Wicksellian distinction between the natural rate and the rate of equilibrium of interest.

845. Smolensky, Pedro. Economía libre y economía dirigida (*Rev. cien. econ.*, Buenos Aires, año 38, 3. serie, no. 25, p. 363-374).
A short essay on forms of State intervention with special references to United States legislation and policy. It poses the conflict between economic planning and the political system of a democracy.

CURRENCY AND BANKING; INFLATION

846. Bogliolo, Rómulo. La moneda y los problemas económicos. Buenos Aires, La Vanguardia. 113 p.
Defends the traditional principles of a healthy currency and attacks inflationary policies and certain monetary policies in particular, as instruments of political power-seeking and demagogy. Polemic in nature, it also deals with the recent monetary reforms in Argentina, the devaluation of the peso, and the rise in the cost of living, and declares that the policy followed has not succeeded in increasing available resources.

847. Correa Ávila, Carlos. Las teorías de los economistas acerca de la estabilidad del poder adquisitivo del dinero (*Rev. fac. cien. econ. com. pol.*, no. 60-61, sept., 1949-abril, p. 489-521).
The author starts with the assumption that a certain degree of stability in the value of money is indispensable for the effective exercise of its

function. After referring to the methods used for measuring its purchasing power and its variations, the author discusses the theories of Cassel and of Fisher's compensated dollar among those that propose to achieve stabilization within the gold standard system. He also considers the theories of Gesell, Marshall-Pigou, Keynes, Graham, and the U. S. Federal Reserve System among those advocating measures for stabilizing monetary value within a paper currency system. The author concludes that there is no sure stabilization policy, and that actual stabilization is not in itself a condition which ensures economic stability, as it is probable that price stabilization militates against economic activity and the maintenance of a high level of employment.

848. Coscia, Adolfo A. Incremento del patrimonio nacional y el costo de la vida (*Rev. econ. arg.*, año 33, t. 49, no. 388-390, oct.-dic., p. 201-210).
Describes the following characteristics of Argentina today: industrialization; full employment; displacement of productive factors; increase in means of payment; rise in the cost of living; increase in wages; and redistribution of wealth and of income. After recalling how in Argentina the diversification of production has not meant replacing some activities by others but adding the new to the old thanks to the country's abundant natural resources, the author maintains that the recent process of industrialization can be carried out without detriment to the traditional agricultural and stock-raising activities. But this process has, for the author, the unpleasant aspect of inflation and a rise in the cost of living. Coscia believes that the cause of both is to be found in the increase in the production of capital goods and producer goods out of proportion to consumer goods, although in the long run the cost of living should come down and the welfare of society be improved.

849. Schettini, José Adolfo. La incidencia de las variaciones de los precios sobre los balances sucesivos de una misma empresa (*Rev. cien. econ.*, Buenos Aires, año 38, 3. serie, no. 24, julio-agosto, p. 277-311; sept.-oct., p. 387-413).
A study of a mathematical and accountancy nature in which the author endeavors to pose the precise problem created for accountancy by changes in prices, whether changes in certain price sectors or alterations in the general price level during periods of monetary inflation. The article refers particularly to the analysis of the circulating capital of businesses in relation to costs.

PUBLIC FINANCE

850. Ahumada, Guillermo. Productividad e improductividad de los servicios en general y en particular de los servicios públicos (*Rev. cien. econ.*, Buenos Aires, año 38, 3. serie, no. 21, enero-feb., p. 3-13).
After some historical references to the concept of the productivity of public services, the author alludes to the principle according to which the

attitude of the State towards the choice of expenditure, i.e. in the selection of the collective needs which it must satisfy, is, like that of individuals, bound to be based on calculations of the satisfactions to be derived, but with the fundamental difference of a political content in State activity. The introduction of this principle allows the author to establish that there is a limit beyond which public services cease to be socially and economically productive and may even degenerate into an unjust redistribution of the national income when the tax contributions of all, or of the majority, are turned into advantages for the few who benefit by certain social services. There is also a reference to anticyclical expenditure rates founded on the theory of the multiplier and to the pernicious effects which can occur when the policy of spending to create employment is practiced anti-economically in periods of prosperity. The nationalization of the great public utilities (which the author supports) does not mean that the cost problem can be ignored and in reality represents a strong tendency towards the extension of bureaucracy.

851. Broide, Julio. Anotaciones a la economía de guerra y de paz (*Rev. fac. cien. econ.*, Buenos Aires, año 3, no. 25, julio, p. 531-606).
An excellent summary of the questions and problems involved in the financing of war, with particular reference to the Second World War and the policy of the United States, especially its economic effects. The theories of Pigou and Keynes are mentioned, with the latter's plan of compulsory savings. The financial and economic repercussions which this financing produced in other countries are discussed, together with the problems arising at the end of the conflict. The monetary vicissitudes of the post-war period are the object of special comment, as well as the policy of the United States with regard to reconstruction.

852. Trevisán, Egidio C. Repercusión e incidencia del impuesto (*Rev. fac. cien. econ.*, Buenos Aires, año 3, no. 23, mayo, p. 296-365).
A summary of the theory of the repercussion and incidence of taxes, taking into consideration the problems of competition and monopoly, the elasticity and rigidity of demand, the nature of the product, and costs.

FOREIGN TRADE

853. Llorens, Emilio. Notable cambio de frente (*Rev. econ. arg.*, año 33, t. 48, no. 386-387, agosto-sept., p. 165-170).
This short study revolves around what has been called the Decalogue of Montevideo, formulated at the Third Meeting of the U. N. Economic Commission for Latin America (CEPAL) in Montevideo, June, 1949, and based on studies prepared under the direction of Professor Raúl Prebisch. For the author, the "notable change in front" consists in the frank adoption of a realistic policy of protection for industry in the Latin American countries, embracing the control of foreign trade and the doctrine that theoretical systems have no universal and permanent valid-

ity, but a temporary one limited by the situation, interests, and realities of each country or group of countries, as opposed to the liberalism traditionally proclaimed by theoreticians and statesmen, though not faithfully followed in Latin American practice. The great importance of this change lies, for Llorens, in the decisive adoption of a doctrine which has long pervaded the subconscious of writers and governments but which has been prevented from coming to the surface by the weight of entrenched liberal traditions and the influence of the great industrial countries.

ECONOMIC CYCLE

854. Llorens, Emilio. Sugerencias para una política argentina de ocupación integral (*Rev. econ. arg.*, año 32, t. 48, no. 383, mayo, 67-72).
Deals with the problem of the most suitable policy for absorbing each year's new labor force, calculated on the basis of those reaching the age of 15, and taking into account labor losses and unabsorbed labor. The author calculates the accrued annual manpower total at 100,000, males and females together, and considers the hypothesis of their incorporation into agriculture and stock-raising (70,000, and 30,000 in allied services), into industry (50,000, and 50,-000 in allied services), or their absorption in proportions similar to the present distribution of the working population. The latter solution, which seems to him to be the most acceptable, would require an investment of some 2,000 million pesos.

855. López Francés, Miguel. Carácter del ciclo económico (*Hac. econ. prev.*, año 2, no. 6, mayo-junio, p. 13-28).
A summary of cyclical theories and of the theories referring to longer cyclical waves as expounded by the great present-day economists. It refers to the theories denying the existence of the cycle and, inspired by Keynes, the author concludes by maintaining that "if precise characteristics such as regularity in sequence of time and duration have to be included in the definition of economic cycles, they must not be based on a more or less mechanical explanation but on a real and concrete appreciation of the factors of different economic variables."

ECONOMIC DEVELOPMENT

856. Ferrari, Horacio Carlos. La industria lechera en la economía agraria argentina. Buenos Aires, El Ateneo. 187 p.
This analysis of the dairy industry is placed in the framework of the agricultural and cattle-raising economy of Argentina and ends with a comparative study of other producer countries. The methods of milk production, processing, and marketing are examined. The author proposes legislation which would allow the dairy industry to be developed in closer accordance with favorable natural factors.

857. Moyano Llerena, Carlos, Roberto Marcenaro, and Emilio Llorens. Ar-

gentina social y económica. Buenos Aires, Depalma. 448 p.
This book has three aspects of unequal merit: 1, elementary principles of economics; 2, linked to these, a summary of the Argentine economy; and 3, orientation of Argentine social and economic policy in the last few years. In all these aspects the work is an excellent summary, forming a useful primer for economic studies and research; but the extremely elementary character of the first part, and the political nature of the third, serve to emphasize the greater merits of the second. With the help of some brief historical references and the latest available statistics the authors have given a fairly complete picture of the Argentine economy and its evolution. The study does not confine itself strictly to economics but extends, as its title implies, to social policy. This is analyzed in chapters whose subjects range from the historical formation and ethnic background of the Argentine people, the present distribution of population, the family unit, natural resources, and factors of productivity, etc., to social and political problems and trade relations with foreign countries. The statistics used are excellent, while comparisons are drawn which allow one to assess the position of Argentina and its importance within the overall picture of America and the world.

NATURAL RESOURCES

858. Mozo, Sadí H. El petróleo argentino en el siglo XIX. Actividades desarrolladas en las provincias de Jujuy y Salta. Bahía Blanca. 123 p.
Essay of a historical nature dealing with the first petroleum discoveries and explorations carried out in northern Argentina beginning in the early 19th century. It contains much information regarding the first companies and provincial legislation affecting this type of activity. The author provides a full bibliography on the subject and in an appendix gives the text of the above-mentioned legislation.

STATISTICS AND DEMOGRAPHY

859. Correa Ávila, Carlos. El decrecimiento de la natalidad y sus causas (*Rev. econ. arg.*, año 33, t. 48, no. 384, junio, p. 101-107; año 34, t. 48, no. 385, julio, p. 137-143).
Alludes briefly to population theories down to Malthus and refers to the present demographic situation of the world and of Argentina, which would appear to reveal a dangerous decrease in the birthrate. Studies the demographic, economic, and family factors responsible for this phenomenon, which is considered environmental and sporadic, and then analyzes a different type of causes which the author classifies as biological and psychological. The article gives a philosophical interpretation of Neo-Malthusianism and believes that a definite solution can come only with a return to Christianity.

860. Llorens, Emilio. Se debe mejorar el nivel alimenticio (*Rev. econ. arg.*, año 31, t. 48, no. 367-368, enero-feb., p. 5-16).

Deals with the problem of nutritional deficiency of the great mass of humanity, notwithstanding the productive potential of capitalist society, which has not achieved a fair distribution of wealth. Includes statistical tables of annual per capita income in the most important countries, of the relationship between the intake of calories, mortality rates, and average life expectancy, and of land utilization. Refers to capitalist "solutions" for the problem of over-production —destruction of goods and reduction of output —which have helped to bring the system into disrepute; to food distribution plans tried out in the United States; and to the policy of the present Argentine government.

ADDENDUM

860a. **García Vázquez, Enrique.** El concepto de ahorro a través de Keynes y Robertson (*Rev. cien. econ.*, Buenos Aires, 3. serie, año 37, no. 17-18, oct., 1949, p. 641-650).

An excellent short paper comparing the theories of the authors named in the title, in particular the ideas of the equivalence of savings and investment in Keynes and of inequivalence in Robertson, and outlining the connections between both concepts. The author also refers to the theories advanced in Sweden (Ohlin) and by Hawtrey.

OTHER WORKS *

861. Argentina. Summary of basic economic information (*Int. ref. serv.*, v. 7, no. 93, Aug., 7 p.).

862. Economic review of Argentina, 1949 (*Int. ref. serv.*, v. 7, no. 9, Apr., 12 p.).

863. **Ministerio de Agricultura y Ganadería. Dirección General de Pesca y Conservación de la Fauna.** Producción pesquera de la República Argentina, años 1943-1944-1945 (Publ. miscelánea no. 333). Buenos Aires. 328 p., tables.

864. **Ministerio de Asuntos Técnicos. Dirección Nacional de Servicios Técnicos del Estado. Dirección General del Servicio Estadístico Nacional.** Servicio Estadístico Oficial de la República Argentina. La actividad industrial argentina desde 1937 a 1949. Buenos Aires. 72 p., graphs, tables.

865. **Ministerio de Economía de la Nación. Instituto Argentino de Promoción del Intercambio.** Memoria anual. Ejercicio 1949. Buenos Aires. 86 p., tables.

866. **Ministerio de Finanzas. Banco Central de la República Argentina.** Memoria anual. 15. ejercicio, 1949. Buenos Aires. 122 p., tables.

867. ————. **Banco de Crédito Industrial Argentino.** Memoria y balance. Sexto ejercicio, 1949. Buenos Aires, 101 p., graphs, tables.

868. ————. **Banco de la Nación Argentina.** Memoria y balance general del 57. ejercicio correspondiente al año 1948. Buenos Aires. 206 p., graphs, tables.

869. ————. **Banco Hipotecario Nacional.** Memoria anual, 63. ejercicio, 1948. Buenos Aires. 69 p., graphs, tables.

870. ————. ————. Memoria anual, 64. ejercicio, 1949. Buenos Aires. 67 p., graphs, tables.

871. **Ministerio de Hacienda.** La coordinación económica, financiera y administrativa como fundamento de la prosperidad nacional. Buenos Aires. 51 p.

872. ————. Cuarta conferencia de Ministros de Hacienda. Buenos Aires, 1949, i.e. 1950. 242 p.

873. ————. Mensaje del Poder Ejecutivo e informe del Ministerio de Hacienda. Cuenta de inversión, ejercicio de 1949. Buenos Aires. 173 p.

874. ————. **Dirección General Impositiva.** Memoria, año 1948. Buenos Aires. 252 p., graphs, tables.

875. **Ministerio de Industria y Comercio. Dirección General del Gas del Estado.** El gasoducto Presidente Perón a través del periodismo nacional y extranjero. Buenos Aires, 1949, i.e. 1950. 187 p., illus.

876. **Presidencia. Subsecretaría de Informaciones. Dirección General del Registro Nacional.** Abastecimiento y represión del agio. V. 1. Buenos Aires. 628 p.

See item 3075.

877. **United States. Tariff Commission.** Recent developments in the foreign trade of Argentina. Washington. v, 185 p.

---

*The items in this section were supplied by the *HLAS* office.

BRAZIL

HENRY WILLIAM SPIEGEL

IN the economic history of Brazil, the year 1950 marks the turning point which divides the attempts at liquidating the difficulties generated by the Second World War from the new tasks created by the outbreak of hostilities in Korea. Much of the economic literature was devoted to the urgent questions of the day. A few items were of fundamental importance. Outstanding among these was the new issue of the reference work compiled by the British Chamber of Commerce of São Paulo and Southern Brazil, *Facts about the State of São Paulo.* Few persons are better acquainted with the economy of Brazil in general, and of São Paulo specifically, than Gilbert Last, the able Secretary of the British Chamber of Commerce. Mr. Last, the compiler of this reference work, has a well deserved reputation among students of Brazilian affairs as the author of an important biweekly newsletter.

The Abbink Report (See *HLAS, no. 15, 1949,* item 669) continued to be a subject of lively discussions. Comments by Dr. Bulhões, outstanding economist and head of the Brazilian delegation to the Abbink Commission, were an especially significant contribution to this discussion.

A new economic periodical issued by the Association of Manufacturers contained a number of interesting studies (item 887). Furthermore, Andrade's study of the development of various public policies is bound to be of great help to the student of economic affairs.

In the field of social insurance, Alim Pedro's comprehensive report (item 2353) provides a wealth of information which goes far beyond the limits of its title. As for specific commodities, much attention is given to oil, and the discussion of the proper form of organization of the petroleum industry continued with unabated vigor (items 904 and 905).

GENERAL

879. Andrade, Almir de. Contribuição à historia administrativa do Brasil, na república, até o ano de 1945. V. 1-2. Rio de Janeiro, Olympio. 242, 377 p.

This work is divided into 31 chapters. Each chapter is devoted to a topic of economic importance: agriculture in general, coffee, sugar, rice, wheat, timber, oil, iron and steel, etc. A typical chapter, that on rice, for example, begins with a historical survey, quoting verbatim presidential messages and other pertinent public documents. This is followed by references to public policies relevant to the subject and by a bibliography. The student of economic policies will find this an invaluable aid in tracing various government activities affecting the Brazilian economy.

880. Banco do Brasil. Relatório apresentado à assembléia geral dos acionistas realizada em 27 de abril de 1950. Rio de Janeiro. 397 p., graphs, tables.

This report is an indispensable reference work.

881. ————. Resenha econômica mensal. Rio de Janeiro. Ano 3, no. 1, jan.-no. 12, dez.

A periodical survey of current statistical information and foreign trade notes; bibliography appended.

882. Big time in São Paulo (*Fortune*, v. 42, July, p. 65-70, 136-141).

Business and industry in the heart of Brazil; information on the Matarazzo empire. [P. E. James]

883. El Brasil. Recursos. Posibilidades. Rio de Janeiro, Ministerio de las Relaciones Exteriores. 143 p., illus.

A new edition in Spanish, reduced in size, of the reference work published for many years under the auspices of the Ministry of Foreign Affairs.

884. British Chamber of Commerce of São Paulo and Southern Brazil. Facts about the State of São Paulo. Second edition. São Paulo, 1950? 228 p., illus.

Over twenty years have passed since the publication of the first edition of this important reference work. No other book supplies a similar wealth of well selected and reliable information. The contents were assembled by Gilbert Last, the Chamber's able Secretary.

885. Bulhões, Octavio Gouvêa de. À margem de um relatório. Texto das conclusões da Comissão Mista Brasileiro-Americana de Estudos Econômicos. Missão Abbink. Rio de Janeiro, Edições Financeiras. 348 p.

The Portuguese text of the final report of the

Joint Brazil-United States Technical Commission (see *HLAS, no. 15, 1949,* item 669), with a valuable introduction of some 50 pages by Dr. Bulhões, the head of the Brazilian delegation. This introduction contains important chapters on foreign investment and on monetary problems.

886. Conjuntura econômica. Rio de Janeiro, Centro de Análise da Conjuntura Econômica do Núcleo de Economia da Fundação Getúlio Vargas. Ano 4, no. 1, jan.-no. 12, dez.

As before, this important monthly contains a number of indexes as well as brief articles, generally of high quality, devoted to current economic problems. One series treats of foreign investments in Brazil.

887. Estudos econômicos. Rio de Janeiro, Departamento Econômico da Confederação Nacional da Indústria. Ano 1, no. 1, março-no. 3-4, set.-dez.

A new economic periodical, sponsored by the manufacturers' association. There are a number of noteworthy articles on the value of industrial production, anti-trust legislation, profit sharing, the Brazilian textile industry, and other matters.

888. Pan American Union. Division of Economic Research. Economic developments in Brazil, 1949-1950. Washington. 69 p., tables.

Compilation of statistical and other data.

889. Presidente da República. Mensagem apresentada ao Congresso Nacional por ocasião da abertura da sessão legislativa de 1950 pelo General Eurico Gaspar Dutra . . . . Rio de Janeiro. 349 p.

A presidential message on the state of the Union, discussing numerous economic problems.

890. Renner, A. J. Assuntos econômicos e sociais. Pôrto Alegre, Globo. 294 p.

A collection of nearly a hundred short articles on miscellaneous topics, reprinted from the *Diário de Notícias* of Pôrto Alegre and from other sources.

891. Revista do Serviço Público. Rio de Janeiro, Departamento Administrativo do Serviço Público. Ano 13, v. 1, no. 1, jan.-v. 4, no. 3, dez.

As before, this important periodical carries articles on public affairs and documentation relating to administrative matters.

892. Tejo, Limeira. Retrato sincero do Brasil. Pôrto Alegre, Globo. 284 p.

A study of Brazil's development, largely from the economic point of view. [T. L. Smith]

893. Temas cooperativos. Rio de Janeiro, Centro Nacional de Estudos Cooperativos. 124 p.

Essays on cooperation and on the cooperative movement.

PUBLIC FINANCE

894. Bouças, Valentim F. História da dívida externa. Segunda edição. Rio de Janeiro, Edições Financeiras. 372 p., tables.

New edition of a work first published in 1946. See *HLAS, no. 12, 1946,* item 1100.

895. Orçamento para o exercício de 1950. Rio de Janeiro, Departamento de Imprensa Nacional. 423 p., tables.

Owing to the growth of public functions, the Brazilian budget estimates, presented here for 1950, are indispensable for the study of economic affairs in Brazil.

896. São Paulo (state). Secretaria da Fazenda. Contadoria Central do Estado. Orçamento geral do Estado para o exercício de 1950. São Paulo. 224 p., tables.

The state budget of São Paulo for 1950.

BANKING AND INSURANCE

897. Balanço econômico. Mesa redonda: Alvaro Brandão. Rio de Janeiro, Edições Financeiras (Finanças em Debate, 2), 1950? 109 p., illus.

Round table, devoted largely to problems of accounting.

898. Banco do Rio Grande do Sul, S. A. Relatório da diretoria correspondente ao ano de 1949. Pôrto Alegre, Globo. 141 p., graphs, tables.

Annual report of an outstanding bank in southern Brazil.

899. Pereira, Mozart Emygdio. Economia e finanças. Bahia, Bolsa de Mercadorias e Valores da Bahia, Serviço de Divulgação (Publ. no. 1). 74 p.

Thoughts on miscellaneous financial matters, with especial reference to organized exchanges and relevant law.

900. Pinto Ariosto. A Caixa Econômica Federal do Rio de Janeiro em 1949. Relatório. Rio de Janeiro, Gráfica Olímpica. 402 p., graphs, tables.

An account of the farflung activities of the Rio de Janeiro Savings Bank.

901. Revista do IRB (Instituto de Resseguros do Brasil). Rio de Janeiro. Ano 10, no. 59, fev.-ano 11, no. 64, dez.

The bimonthly periodical of the public reinsurance organization.

PUBLIC UTILITIES

902. Lloyd Brasileiro. Patrimônio nacional. Relatório apresentado ao Exmo.

Snr. Ministro de Estado para os Negócios da Viação e Obras Públicas, 1948. Rio de Janeiro. 358 p., tables.
The Brazilian merchant marine in 1948.

903. Ministério da Fazenda. Tesouro Nacional. Serviço de Estatística Econômica e Financeira. Movimento marítimo e fluvial do Brasil, 1946-1947. Rio de Janeiro. 165 p., tables.
Shipping statistics.

PETROLEUM

904. Carvalho, Estevão Leitão de. Petróleo. Salvação ou desgraça do Brasil? Rio de Janeiro, Centro de Estudos e Defesa do Petróleo e da Economia Nacional. 245 p.
A contribution to the discussion, going on for several years, as to the form of organization under which oil prospecting, drilling, and refining is to take place. Author favors a public monopoly.

905. Presidência da República. Conselho Nacional de Petróleo. Relatório de 1949. Rio de Janeiro. 222 p., illus., maps, tables.
A detailed account of the activities of the National Petroleum Council, with special reference to work in progress in the State of Bahia.

MISCELLANEOUS COMMODITIES

906. Departamento Nacional de Produção Mineral. Actividades em 1948. Rio de Janeiro. 83 p.

907. Fonseca, Cassio. A economia da borracha. Aspectos internacionais e defesa da produção brasileira. Rio de Janeiro, Comissão Executiva de Defesa da Borracha. xii, 255 p., illus.
Rubber in the Brazilian economy and in international trade. [Ed.]

908. Instituto do Açúcar e do Álcool. I Congresso Açucareiro Nacional. Anais. V. 1. Rio de Janeiro. 243 p.

909. Ministério da Agricultura. Instituto de Óleos. Atividades do I.O., janeiro, 1949–junho, 1950. Rio de Janeiro. 524 p.
Report of the work of the government institute in the important field of vegetable oils. [Ed.]

910. Ponce Filho, Generoso. Junta deliberativa do Instituto Nacional do Mate. Relatório. Rio de Janeiro. 130 p.
Current activities of the maté cartel.

911. U. S. Senate. Subcommittee of the Committee on Agriculture and Forestry. 81st Congress, First Session. Hearings pursuant to S. Res. 36. Utiliza-

tion of farm crops. Price spreads. Part 2. Washington. P. 465-1160.
In these hearings before the "Gillette Committee" considerable attention was paid to the rise of coffee prices, especially for Brazilian coffee. The activities of the committee caused much comment in Brazil. (The discussion of the coffee situation begins on p. 787.)

REGIONAL AFFAIRS

912. Azevedo, Fernando de. Um trem corre para o oeste. Estudo sobre o Noroeste e seu papel no sistema de viação nacional. São Paulo, Martins. 375 p., illus., fold. maps.
A useful monograph on the role and history of the railroads as a cultural and economic factor in the development of Brazil, with special reference to the E. F. Noroeste. Well documented, with photographs and maps. The area involved is the triangle from Campo Grande to Corumbá on one side, to Cuiabá on the other. [H. F. Cline]

913. MENSAGEM APRESENTADA À ASSEMBLÉIA LEGISLATIVA DE MINAS GERAIS EM SUA SESSÃO ORDINÁRIA DE 1950 PELO GOVERNADOR MILTON SOARES CAMPOS. Belo Horizonte. 384 p.
Message of the State Governor of Minas Gerais, containing survey of regional economic affairs.

914. Minas Gerais. Departamento Estadual de Estatística. Anuário estatístico de Minas Gerais. Ano 3. Belo Horizonte, 1949, i.e. 1950. xvi, 433 p., tables.

915. Pedroso, José, and Adolpho Porto. Rio de Janeiro. O estado e o município. Rio de Janeiro, Departamento de Imprensa Nacional. 754 p., tables, illus.
Basically a reference work, this socio-economic summary provides a detailed picture of each of the municipalities in the State, preceded by summary discussions of social and economic factors creating and influencing present problems. The statistical material, including complete appendices, generally comes from the years 1945-1948. [H. F. Cline]

ADDENDA

916. BOLETIM DO IMPÔSTO DE CONSUMO. Impóstos em geral. Rio de Janeiro. Ano 1, no. 1, nov., 1949.
A new periodical, devoted exclusively to the problems relating to sales and excise taxes: legislation, court decisions, administrative rulings.

917. Ferreira, Evaldo Osorio. Jazimentos de minerais metalíferos do Brasil. Rio de Janeiro, Ministerio da Agricultura, Departamento Nacional da Produção Mineral, Divisão de Geologia e Mineralogia (Bol. no. 130), 1949. 122 p.

Brief statements on location of deposits of 31 minerals. Bibliography for each one. [Ed.]

918. **Ministério da Agricultura. Instituto de Óleos.** Carnaúba. Seus problemas

econômicos e extrativos (Bol. no. 5). Rio de Janeiro, 1949. 238 p., tables.

An authoritative study of the production and marketing of carnaúba wax. Close attention is paid to the development of substitutes in the U. S. market.

MEXICO

DIRECCIÓN DE INVESTIGACIONES ECONÓMICAS, NACIONAL FINANCIERA, S. A.

LA bibliografía económica mexicana de 1950, como la del año precedente, es en buena parte producto de la reflexión sobre los problemas más actuales de esa índole del país, y del estudio y crítica de los mismos. Si en años anteriores el problema de la industrialización nacional matizó el major número de los trabajos publicados, en 1950, aunque es posible advertir en todos los estudios el trasfondo de esa misma inquietud, aparentemente hubo motivos de mayor preocupación para los estudiosos de la economía mexicana. Así, a los temas relativos al comercio exterior, en general, y en particular a la discusión del tratado comercial de 1942 entre México y Estados Unidos, recientemente denunciado, corresponde una buena porción de la bibliografía. A los primeros pertenece la ya vasta serie de monografías que informan sobre el comercio entre México y otros países y que ha publicado el Consejo Superior de Comercio Exterior, destacándose de ellas la relativa al comercio mexicano-norteamericano. El tratado fué estudiado por su naturaleza (no. 1001a) y se explicaron las repercusiones del mismo (no. 928a, 988a, 1016), apuntándose también la política que en esa materia debe seguirse (no. 952). Otros temas de estudios, dentro de este mismo sector, los proporcionaron: las relaciones de intercambio (no. 920, 986), la balanza de pagos (no. 956), la devaluación (no. 963), la Carta de la Habana y el Acuerdo Arancelario (no. 1001), la V Reunión del Consejo Interamericano de Comercio y Producción (no. 975a), y la nueva estructura comercial (no. 1017g). Finalmente, se produjo un estudio de orden institucional (no. 988) y hubo una excelente aportación al conocimiento histórico del comercio entre México y Venezuela (no. 925).

De la orientación que siguió la política económica, se pueden hallar buenos testimonios en el informe presidencial (no. 922) y en los discursos pronunciados por los Secretarios de Hacienda (no. 936) y de Economía (no. 983) en la Convención Nacional de Banqueros. Han de considerarse también en este capítulo: el alegato del Subsecretario de Hacienda en pro del establecimiento de un plan de arbitrios (no. 939, 939a), la declaración sobre desarrollo económico del delegado mexicano ante la IV Asamblea de las Naciones Unidas y las conferencias del Lic. Antonio Carrillo Flores sobre el progreso económico alcanzado en el último decenio y sobre la responsabilidad de la iniciativa privada en el desarrollo económico; de este mismo estadista, cabe recordar la publicación en español, con correcciones y adiciones, de su concienzudo estudio sobre financiamiento del desarrollo económico, que originalmente apareció en inglés en 1949, y que revela muchos de los puntos de vista oficiales ante problemas económicos concretos.

Acaso sea éste el sitio más adecuado para recordar los estudios de Mosk y de Tannenbaum, pues en sus abundantes y, en general, bien informadas y perspicaces páginas, discuten lo acertado o desacertado de la política mexicana de los últimos años, proponiendo incluso las soluciones que en consecuencia del estudio realizado les parecieron pertinentes; estos libros si no fuera más que por este último hecho, que produciría saludables respuestas por parte de los economistas mexicanos, son instrumentos imprescindibles para acercarse al conocimiento del México contemporáneo.

El mérito de haber producido obras fundamentales sobre México, en 1950, no correspondió exclusivamente a investigadores extranjeros. Los estudios de Alanís Patiño sobre tierras de riego, de Moisés T. de la Peña sobre problemas demográficos y agrarios y sobre las Mixtecas, de Edmundo Flores sobre los braceros, de González Santos sobre crédito, de José Domingo Lavín sobre petróleo, y de Salas Villagómez sobre deuda pública, aunque abordan temas particulares, son aportaciones de considerable importancia, fundamentales cada una en su materia.

El grupo de trabajos sobre historia de la economía es también considerable. Aparte del mencionado estudio sobre historia del comercio mexicano-venezolano, se produjo un interesante ensayo sobre feudalismo y capitalismo en México (no. 1590) y se produjeron varios ensayos sobre historia de las ideas económicas (no. 980, 980a, 981, 1788) y uno, erudito y penetrante, sobre la vinculación de las ideas y la economía de un período determinado (no. 1625).

Los estudios pequeños y artículos sobre distintas actividades económicas fueron muy abundantes y diversos, lo que hace difícil intentar una clasificación de los mismos. Sin embargo, es conveniente hacer notar que la industria eléctrica mereció un amplio trabajo, que la industria petrolera mereció otro, ya mencionado (no. 978), y que sobre las pesquerías mexicanas se hizo una completa monografía (no. 960). En este grupo cabe también la crítica que un grupo de técnicos mexicanos hizo al estudio de Higgins Industries, Inc. sobre transportes marítimos (no. 921a).

919. **Aguilar Uranga, Manuel.** Caminos vecinales (*Rev. econ.,* México, v. 13, no. 6, junio 15, p. 187-189).

919a. ————. Cómo incrementar el ingreso neto de operación en los ferrocarriles (*Rev. econ.,* México, v. 13, no. 3, marzo 15, p. 84-87).

919b. ————. Los ingresos de la Federación y los ingresos de los Ferrocarriles Nacionales en la primera mitad del siglo (*Rev. econ.,* México, v. 13, no. 1, enero 15, p. 6-10).
Afirma que en la misma forma en que el Gobierno ha tomado medidas para evitar la disminución del poder de compra de sus ingresos, es preciso que se autorice a los Ferrocarriles a tomar medidas similares.

920. **Ahumada, Jorge,** and **A. Nataf.** La relación de intercambio de los países de América Latina (*Trim. econ.,* v. 17, no. 3, julio-sept., p. 396-415).
Este estudio se publicó en inglés en *Staff Papers,* revista cuadrimestral, Washington, v. 1, no. 1, February. Contiene datos relativos a México.

921. **Alanís Patiño, Emilio.** Las tierras de riego (*Prob. agríc. indust. México,* v. 2, no. 2, abril-junio, p. 49-167, graphs, tables, illus.).
El subtítulo, "El destino de los 2,206 millones de pesos invertidos por el Gobierno de México en obras para riego," resume satisfactoriamente el tema. En la introducción se hace una reseña se trata de los aprovechamientos hidráulicos y los la materia; posteriormente, en capítulos distintos, se trata de los aprovechamientos hidráulicos, y los axiomas en la política de riego del Distrito de

Riego de Tula, Hgo., y se examina el programa de obras para riegos en 1947-1952, dando cuenta de lo que en el período 1947-1949 se ha realizado. Útiles apéndices. Las 16 conclusiones a que llega el autor son dignas de ser tomadas en cuenta para meditar la política que establezca el Gobierno mexicano.

921a. ————, **Roberto Mendoza Franco, Alfonso Poiré Ruelas,** and **Francisco Ávila de la Vega.** Comentarios al estudio sobre México de Higgins Industries, Inc. México, Banco de México. 335 p., maps, tables.
Véase *HLAS, no. 15, 1949,* no. 789.

922. **Alemán, Miguel.** Informe presidencial. Política económica (*Mercado val.,* año 10, no. 36, sept. 4, p. 4-7).

923. ANUARIO FINANCIERO DE MÉXICO. V. 10, 1948. México, Cultura (Asociación de Banqueros de México). 1400 p., tables.

924. **Arce Ibarra, Roxana.** La rehabilitación y la coordinación de los ferrocarriles en la economía de México (*Invest. econ.,* v. 10, no. 4, 4. trimestre, p. 427-455).
Con el objeto de que el país participe de una efectiva economía de intercambio, el Gobierno debe coordinar ciertos aspectos de su política que ha manejado independientemente (transportes, agricultura, industria y comercio), tomando como base los transportes y particularmente los ferrocarriles.

925. **Arcila Farías, Eduardo.** Comercio entre Venezuela y México en los siglos XVII y XVIII. México, El Colegio de México. 324 p., maps.

Un exhaustivo y competente estudio, basado en documentos de primera mano, provenientes en su mayor parte del Archivo General de la Nación.

926. Asociación de Banqueros de México. Informe del Consejo. Balance, abril de 1950. México, Cultura. 33 p.

926a. Asociación Nacional de Cosecheros. Memoria de la IX Asamblea Plenaria Extraordinaria . . . en la C. de Morelia, Mich., los días 10, 11 y 12 de noviembre de 1950. n. p. Unpaged.

927. ASPECTOS DEL DESARROLLO ECONÓMICO DE MÉXICO (*Rev. econ.*, México, v. 13, no. 3, marzo 15, p. 81-84).
Información proporcionada por el Departamento de Estudios Financieros de la Nacional Financiera.

928. Attolini, José. La industria eléctrica y la Cuenca del Papaloapan (*Rev. ind.*, v. 4, no. 40, enero, p. 102-103, 141-143).

928a. ————. El tratado de comercio méxico-americano (*Invest. econ.*, v. 10, 3. trimestre, no. 3, p. 337-360).

929. Ayala Vergara, Helio. Política económica en materia de grasas (*Rev. econ.*, México, v. 13, no. 9, sept. 15, p. 311-314).
Antecedentes sobre la situación de las grasas en México y sobre la política gubernamental a ese respecto.

930. Banco Capitalizador de Monterrey. Informe y estadísticas correspondientes al ejercicio social de 1949 . . . . Monterrey. 20 p.

930a. Banco de México, S. A. Vigésima-octava Asamblea General Ordinaria de Accionistas. México. 231 p., tables, graphs.

930b. Banco de Nuevo León. Asamblea Ordinaria de Accionistas, 1949. Monterrey. 19 p.

930c. Banco Industrial de Jalisco. Informe del Consejo de Administración y documentos . . . , presentados a la XV Asamblea de Accionistas verificada el 17 de mayo de 1950. Guadalajara. 21 p., graphs, tables.

930d. Banco Mercantil de Monterrey, S. A. Informe anual. Monterrey. 32 p.

930e. Banco Nacional de Crédito Ejidal. Informe que rinde el Consejo de Administración a la XIV Asamblea General de Accionistas, sobre las operaciones realizadas en el ejercicio de 1949. n. p. 49 p., tables.

930f. Banco Nacional de México, S. A. Asamblea General Ordinaria de 19 de abril de 1950. n. p. 43 p., illus., graphs.

930g. Banco Nacional del Comercio Exterior. Informe del Consejo de Administración a la XIII Asamblea General de Accionistas. México. 94 p.

930h. Banco Nacional del Ejército y la Armada, S. A. Informe, Primera Asamblea Ordinaria de Accionistas. n. p. 27 p.

930i. Banco Nacional Hipotecario Urbano y de Obras Públicas. Décimoséptima Asamblea General de Accionistas, 1949. n. p. 86 p.

930j. Banco Regional del Norte, S. A. Asamblea General Ordinaria, marzo 20 de 1950. Monterrey. Unpaged.

931. Barnetche, Alfonso, and Manuel Rodríguez Aguilar. Las reservas petroleras de la República Mexicana (*Rev. min. petrol.*, v. 16, no. 197, feb.-marzo, p. 17-19).

932. BASIC INDUSTRIES IN TEXAS AND NORTHERN MEXICO. Austin, Tex., The University of Texas Press (Institute of Latin-American Studies, Latin-American Studies, 9). 193 p., tables, maps.
Estudios por diferentes autores, presentados a la Conferencia celebrada del 9 al 11 de junio de 1949. Referentes a México: Práxedes Reina Hermosillo, *The role of Nacional Financiera in the development of industry in Northern Mexico;* H. R. Pape, *Five years of achievement at Altos Hornos Steel Company;* José Antonio de Silva, *Problems of utilizing coal resources in the industrialization of Northern Mexico;* Ed Nunnally, *Problems of Texas-Mexico trade;* Virgilio Garza, Jr., *Brief sketch of the industrial development of Monterrey;* Antonio J. Bermúdez, *The oil industry in the Northeast of Mexico;* Antonio Rodríguez L., *Mexico's irrigation possibilities along the northeastern zone bordering the State of Texas;* Alejandro Páez Urquidi, *Planning the hydroelectric development of Northern Mexico;* José Ch. Ramírez, *The El Mante Refinery in the national sugar industry.*

933. Behrendt, Richard F. Factores que afectan el actual estado económico de los indios en Latinoamérica (*Amér. indígena*, v. 10, no. 3, julio, p. 195-214).
Contiene varios datos relativos a las formas de participación del indio en la actividad económica mexicana actual.

934. Bernstein, E. M. El precio del café y la política monetaria (*Trim. econ.*, v. 17, no. 3, julio-sept., p. 416-438).
Contiene datos relativos a México.

935. **Bervera Alba, Horacio.** La producción de algodón en la República Mexicana (*Rev. econ.*, México, v. 18, no. 5, mayo 15, p. 145-150).

936. **Beteta, Ramón.** Discurso del Sr. Lic. . . . , Secretario de Hacienda y Crédito Público ante la XVI Convención Bancaria (*Carta mensual,* no. 48, abril, p. 566-580).
Texto del discurso pronunciado en la XVI Convención Nacional Bancaria, celebrada en Monterrey en abril de 1950. Aparece también en *Rev. econ.*, México, v. 18, no. 4, abril 15, p. 118-123, y en *Mercado val.*, año 10, no. 18, mayo 1, p. 3-6.

937. **Blanco, Gonzalo.** El abastecimiento de agua a la ciudad de México; su relación con los recursos naturales renovables (*Rev. econ.*, México, v. 13, no. 2, feb. 15, p. 63-65; no. 3, marzo 15, p. 93-95).

938. **Boletín Estadístico.** Secretaría de Hacienda y Crédito Público, Comisión Nacional Bancaria. México. T. 14, no. 129, enero-feb.-no. 134, nov.-dic.
Contiene datos relativos a las instituciones de crédito. Véase también *Directorio de instituciones de crédito y organizaciones auxiliares* (148 p.), publicado el mismo año por la Comisión Bancaria.

939. **Bustamante, Eduardo.** El plan nacional de arbitrios (*Rev. econ.*, México, v. 13, no. 2, feb. 15, p. 45-47; no. 3, marzo 15, p. 79-80).
Se examina el conjunto de normas que dentro de la organización federal mexicana se requiere para el establecimiento de un sistema nacional de tributación que tome en cuenta la coexistencia legal de la Federación, los Estados y los Municipios como entidades económicas. Véase también no. 6, junio 15, p. 198-200.

939a. ———. Los sistemas tributarios de los Estados (*Rev. econ.*, México, v. 13, no. 4, abril 15, p. 124-127; no. 15, mayo 15, p. 151-153).
Demuestra cómo dentro del sistema vigente no se logra una repartición general y uniforme de la carga fiscal. Insiste en la necesidad de un plan nacional de arbitrios, y concluye que dicho plan persigue la distribución de la carga fiscal de un modo más equitativo, la coordinación de la acción impositiva de la Federación, los Estados, los Municipios y el Distrito y los Territorios Federales, y el establecimiento de acuerdos entre los mismos para determinar las proporciones en las que han de ser atribuídos y distribuídos los ingresos.

940. **Camposortega, Carlos, and José María Arteaga.** Industrialization and standardization (*Mex. amer. rev.*, v. 18, no. 5, May, p. 12-13, 30-31).

Exposición de los motivos que el Gobierno tuvo para establecer la Dirección General de Normas y del funcionamiento de la misma, evolución y resultados.

941. **Cardoso, Alfonso.** Posición de la Cámara Nacional de la Industria de Transformación ante los últimos ordenamientos y reformas legales (*Jorn. indus.*, año 2, t. 2, no. 15, enero-feb., p. 10-21).
Informe que examina dos acuerdos gubernamentales, de 24 de diciembre de 1949, que significan cierta intervención económica del Estado, así como otras reformas a leyes de contenido principalmente económico.

942. **Carrillo Flores, Antonio.** Financiamiento del desarrollo económico de México, prácticas, métodos y problemas (*Prob. agríc. indus. México,* v. 2, no. 1, enero-marzo. p. 11-47).
La primera parte se ocupa de examinar el desarrollo económico de México en sus aspectos generales; la segunda examina el mercado de capitales en México, describe las instituciones dentro de las cuales éste opera y los títulos, operaciones y métodos de financiamiento; finalmente, tras analizar en la tercera parte las repercusiones del desarrollo económico de México, establece una serie de 46 conclusiones, que bien pueden servir de base para un programa de política económica nacional.

942a. ———. La responsabilidad de la iniciativa privada en la industrialización de México. México, Cultura. 28 p.
Conferencia dictada dentro del ciclo organizado por el Consejo Directivo del Movimiento Económico Nacional. Explica la necesidad de que la industrialización se realice de una manera equilibrada. Se publicó también en *Mercado val.*, año 10, no. 37, sept. 11, p. 3-7, y en *Rev. econ.*, México, v. 13, no. 9, sept. 15, p. 304-308; no. 10, oct. 15, p. 352-357.

943. **Castro Estrada, Rubén, and Óscar Fuentes del Valle.** Fomento del cultivo del olivo (*olea europaea*). Coahuila, Escuela Superior de Agricultura Antonio Narro. Unpaged.

944. **Centro Bancario de Guadalajara.** Panorama de la situación económica de Jalisco. Guadalajara. 12 p.

945. **Clark, Lew B.** Begin decade with record of progress (*Mex. amer. rev.*, v. 18, no. 2, Feb., p. 8-11, 22, 24-26).
El consejero de asuntos económicos de la Embajada de Estados Unidos en México hace un examen de las perspectivas de la economía mexicana para 1950, con base en las condiciones generales durante 1949, a las que considera favorables. Examina los beneficios que la industria manufacturera alcanzó de la devaluación del peso, la estabilidad del mismo; la política arancelaria; exhibe datos relativos al

comercio exterior, producción agrícola, minería, petróleo, desarrollo de la industria eléctrica, transportes y comunicaciones y trabajo. Este artículo apareció primero en *For. com. weekly*, v. 38, no. 4, 23 de enero, 1950, p. 3-5, 43.

945a. ————. Improved conditions brighten Mexico's outlook (*For. com. weekly*, v. 40, no. 9, Aug. 28, p. 3-5, 36-38).

El autor examina aquí los efectos de la estabilidad del peso mexicano, durante el primer semestre de 1950, en el incremento de los negocios; se ocupa de la situación financiera, el turismo, el comercio exterior y la balanza de pagos, el desarrollo de la agricultura y la ganadería, etc., y concluye que el primer semestre de 1950 fué bueno para la economía mexicana.

946. Cobos, José Antonio. Aspectos del movimiento cooperativo en México (*Invest. econ.*, v. 10, no. 3, 3. trimestre, p. 361-369).

Establece un plan de acción, después de reseñar históricamente la existencia de las cooperativas en México, de aludir a las leyes vigentes sobre la materia y de explicar los diversos tipos de cooperativas que funcionan.

947. Colina, Rafael de la. Mexico's expanding economy (*Mex. amer. rev.*, v. 18, no. 12, Dec., p. 24-28, 124).

Discurso pronunciado por el Embajador de México en Estados Unidos en la National Foreign Trade Convention, Nueva York, octubre de 1950. Panorámica del desarrollo económico de México en los años más recientes.

949. Consejo Superior Ejecutivo de Comercio Exterior. Secretaría General. Monografía sobre las relaciones comerciales de México con . . . .

Los números de esta ya vasta serie, correspondientes a 1950, tratan del comercio de México con los siguientes países: Bélgica, Canadá, Checoeslovaquia, Chile, Dinamarca, Francia, Noruega, Polonia, Suecia, Suiza (por Jorge Daesslé Segura); Cuba, Holanda (por Armando Amador y Jorge Daesslé S.); Brasil (por Enrique Vélez Villaseñor y Jorge Daesslé S.); Gran Bretaña, Guatemala (por José L. Ballesteros); Estados Unidos (por Francisco J. Castellanos). Número de páginas variable.

950. Dávila, José María. El crédito agrícola y la banca privada. México, La Impresora. 19 p.

951. Declaración mexicana sobre desarrollo económico ante la IV Asamblea de las Naciones Unidas, 1949 (*Trim. econ.*, v. 17, no. 1, enero-marzo, p. 125-132).

Declaración del Delegado de México, Lic. Alfonso Cortina.

952. Denuncia del tratado comercial méxico-americano (*Jorn. indus.*, año 2, t. 2, no. 17, mayo-junio, p. 1-9).

Puntos de vista de la Cámara Nacional de la Industria de Transformación sobre el tratado de comercio méxico-americano ante la entonces probable denuncia del mismo por los Estados Unidos.

954. Díaz Arias, Julián. Monopolio (*Rev. econ.*, México, v. 13, no. 12, dic. 15, p. 418-423).

Crítica al artículo de Gustavo R. Velasco, *El problema de los monopolios*, contiene un apartado en el que examina el Artículo 28 Constitucional. Véase no. 1017d.

955. Díaz Garza, Alfonso. Efectos de la devaluación en la economía mexicana (*Carta mensual*, no. 46-47, feb.-marzo, p. 493-497).

956. Espinosa de los Reyes, Jorge. La balanza de pagos de México (*Rev. econ.*, México, v. 13, no. 7, julio 15, p. 242-245).

Examen de la política monetaria y comercial adoptada por México a partir de 1947 y de la balanza de pagos para 1949.

957. Espinosa Olvera, René. El censo de población y el nivel de empleo (*Rev. econ.*, México, v. 13, no. 6, junio 15, p. 193-198).

Comentario sobre el Censo de Población 1950, en el que además habla de la población futura del país y del empleo total y las estadísticas de empleo, tanto en términos generales como por lo que toca a los mexicanos, para concluir con una provisión de lo que será la oferta de trabajo futura en México.

957a. ————. Fuerza de trabajo y desocupación (*Invest. econ.*, v. 17, no. 3, julio-sept., p. 355-395).

Este trabajo es parte de una tesis titulada *Comparative analysis of the agrarian problems of Peru and Mexico*, que el autor presentó en la Universidad de Wisconsin para optar al grado de doctor en economía. Contiene algunos datos relativos a México.

957b. ————. El mercado de trabajo norteamericano y los braceros (*Rev. econ.*, México, v. 13, no. 11, nov. 15, p. 389-393).

958. Flores, Edmundo. Los braceros mexicanos en Wisconsin (*Trim. econ.*, v. 17, no. 1, enero-marzo, p. 23-80).

Examina los más diversos aspectos relativos a la estancia de un grupo de trabajadores mexicanos en Wisconsin.

959. Food canning industry grows (*Mex. amer. rev.*, v. 18, no. 10, Oct., p. 13, 32, 34-35).

Extracto de un informe sobre esta importante y reciente industria mexicana preparado por Fred Hajjar, de la Embajada de Estados Unidos en México, que publicó el Departamento de Comercio de Estados Unidos. Concluye con un examen de las escasas perspectivas que industrias estadunidenses similares pueden tener en el mercado mexicano. El informe completo apareció bajo el título *Canned fruits and vegetables—Mexico* (*World trade commod.*, v. 8, part 6-8, no. 17, May, 4 p., cuadros).

960. Ford, Bacon & Davis, Inc. Las pesquerías de México (*Prob. agríc. indus. México*, v. 2, no. 1, enero-marzo, p. 51-118, tables, graphs, illus.).
Se recomienda que México emprenda la investigación científica de sus recursos pesqueros. Se estudia la industria pesquera por lo que se refiere al personal, métodos, equipos y facilidades portuarias. Se analiza la industria pesquera en su aspecto de conservación; las necesidades en cuanto a transportes; el consumo doméstico y las posibilidades de abrir o ampliar el mercado exterior.

961. FOREIGN INVESTMENTS IN MEXICO (*Mex. amer. rev.*, v. 18, no. 12, Dec., p. 52, 92, 94, 96, 98, 100, 102, 104, 106, 108, 110-112).
Extracto de un estudio provisional hecho por la CEPAL, que incluye un examen de las inversiones por el país de origen, de las inversiones directas de Estados Unidos, de la importancia de las inversiones extranjeras en la economía mexicana y, finalmente, de la distribución de las mismas por industrias.

962. Fouqué, Agustín. Inversiones extranjeras (*Jorn. indus.*, año 2, t. 2, no. 17, mayo-junio, p. 25-27).
Declaraciones del presidente de la Cámara Nacional de la Industria de Transformación. Hace hincapié en que se dicte una legislación sobre inversiones extranjeras que permita el control de éstas de una manera provechosa para el desarrollo económico del país.

963. Galván E., José. Hacia dónde vamos en política económica (*Rev. econ.*, México, v. 13, no. 1, enero 15, p. 23-25).
Examen de las medidas respectivas puestas en práctica por el Gobierno en materia de comercio exterior y de los fenómenos consecutivos a la devaluación de la moneda mexicana.

964. Gálvez, Enrique. El crédito para la electrificación de México (*Rev. econ.*, México, v. 13, no. 5, mayo 15, p. 158-159).
Se refiere al que le otorgó el BIRF a la Cía. Mexicana de Luz y Fuerza para la compra de equipo, por la cantidad de Dls. 26 millones.

964a. ———. El desarrollo económico de Puebla (*Rev. econ.*, México, v. 13, no. 11, nov. 15, p. 393-395).

964b. ———. Jalisco en la vida económica de México (*Rev. econ.*, México, v. 13, no. 8, agosto 15, p. 271-273).

965. Gómez, Marte R. Los riegos en México (*Prob. agríc. indus. México*, v. 2, no. 2, abril-junio, p. 35-45).

966. Gómez S. Gordoa, José. La organiza-

ción jurídica del ahorro en México (*Carta mensual*, v. 5, no. 53-55, sept.-nov., p. 259-275).

967. González, Fernando A. Estructura del sistema bancario en México (*Carta mensual*, v. 5, no. 46-47, feb.-marzo, p. 498-507).

968. González Santos, Armando. Situación del crédito en el Noroeste de México (*Prob. agríc. indus. México*, v. 3, no. 1, enero-marzo, 121-164).
Estudia en particular la situación del crédito en los Estados de Nayarit, Sinaloa y Sonora y en el Territorio Norte de Baja California. El estudio contiene gráficas, cuadros y mapas. Se ocupa de la magnitud, volumen y origen del crédito y de los problemas peculiares al mismo en cada una de las entidades territoriales mencionadas.

969. GOVERNMENT INVESTMENT IN INDUSTRY (*Mex. amer. rev.*, v. 18, no. 6, June, p. 18).
Examen sucinto de las inversiones que el Gobierno de México ha hecho en algunas industrias a través de la Nacional Financiera.

970. Guevara Ramírez, Simón. Situación nacional e internacional del café (*Rev. econ.*, México, v. 13, no. 6, junio 15, 190-193).
A propósito del Informe Gillette se hacen algunas aclaraciones sobre los motivos que produjeron el alza de los precios del café. Contiene datos relativos a México.

971. Harrar, J. G. Programa agrícola mexicano. New York, Fundación Rockefeller. 36 p.
Informe sobre las actividades de la Fundación Rockefeller que a partir de 1943 inició trabajos destinados a mejorar la productividad de la agricultura mexicana.

972. Hope, Pablo H. El valor de la técnica en el movimiento económico nacional (*Mercado val.*, año 10, no. 35, agosto 28, p. 4-7).
Conferencia dictada por el Director de la Escuela de Ingeniería del Instituto Tecnológico de Monterrey.

973. Hopkins, John A. Los salarios y la productividad del trabajo agrícola en México (*Prob. agríc. indus. México*, v. 2, no. 2, abril-junio, p. 173-186, graphs, tables, maps, illus.).
En la primera parte el autor examina la proporción de la mano de obra ocupada en la agricultura, los salarios agrícolas, la capacidad adquisitiva de la mano de obra agrícola y la productividad de la misma; hace un estudio sobre la mano de obra utilizada en algunos cultivos mexicanos seleccionados; en la segunda parte estudia la dimensión de los predios, y en la tercera el crédito agrícola.

974. Índice general de las tesis profesionales, 1934-1942, Universidad Nacional
Autónoma de México, Escuela Nacional de Economía (*Invest. econ.*, v. 10,
no. 4, 4. trimestre, p. 533-541).
Útil bibliografía de tesis sobre temas económicos,
entre los que abundan los mexicanos.

975. Informe del Banco Nacional de
Crédito Agrícola y Ganadero sobre
las actividades desarrolladas durante
el ejercicio de 1949. n. p. 58 p., tables,
graphs.

975a. Informe sobre la V Reunión plenaria del Consejo Interamericano de
Comercio y Producción (*Jorn. indus.*,
año 2, t. 2, no. 17, mayo-junio, p. 10-
24).
Este informe, suscrito por Jesús Reyes Heroles,
versa sobre la reunión celebrada en Brasil en
abril de 1949 y contiene puntos interesantes que
revelan la actitud de los miembros de esta importante cámara industrial mexicana.

976. Iturbide, Aníbal de. El estado de la
agricultura y de la industria a partir del
régimen del Presidente Alemán (*Carta
mensual*, v. 5, no. 46-47, feb.-marzo, p.
511-519).

977. Johnston, Gale F. Thrift and the building of a greater Mexico. Remarks concerning Mexico's savings plan. St. Louis,
Mo., Mercantile Commerce Bank and
Trust Co. 6 p.

978. Lavín, José Domingo. Petróleo. Pasado, presente y futuro de una industria
mexicana. México, EDIAPSA. 401 p.

979. López González, Julieta. La mecani-
zación de la agricultura en México (*Rev.
econ.*, México, v. 13, no. 8, agosto 15,
261-264 p.).

980. López Rosado, Diego. Las ideas liberales del Dr. José Ma. Luis Mora (*Rev.
econ.*, México, v. 13, no. 8, agosto 15, p.
273-275).

980a. —————. Las ideas sobre industrialización en la primera mitad del siglo XIX
(*Rev. econ.*, México, v. 13, no. 12, p. 427-
430).
Reseña histórica de las ideas económicas que
prevalecieron en México en el período indicado
y de los organismos e instituciones que bajo su
signo se crearon.

981. Loyo, Gilberto. El Dr. Mora, político
economista (*Rev. econ.*, México, v. 13, no.
7, julio 15, p. 239-242).

981a. Madigan-Hyland. Market survey of

electrical sales and requirements of the
Mexican Light and Power Company, Ltd.,
and its subsidiary companies. December
12, 1949. México, Comisión Federal de
Electricidad. Unpaged.

982. Maitland, John. Dollars pour into
Mexico (*Mex. amer. rev.*, v. 18, no. 12,
Dec., p. 32-33).
Afirma el autor que a resultas de la guerra de
Corea cerca de 320 millones de dólares pene-
traron a México en el lapso de 4 meses; esa
suma incluye grandes cantidades de capital
refugiado.

982a. —————. Foresee economic upswing
(*Mex. amer. rev.*, v. 18, no. 9, Sept., p.
28-29, 61-62).
Reseña el optimismo que suscitó en México la
noticia del aumento de sus reservas monetarias
y el préstamo del Eximbank por 150 millones de
dólares a mediados de 1950.

982b. —————. Open new highway (*Mex.
amer. rev.*, v. 18, no. 6, June, p. 14-17).
Calibra el estímulo que para el desarrollo económico del Noroeste significa la apertura de la
sección que completa la Carretera Panamericana
dentro de México.

983. Martínez Báez, Antonio. Discurso del
Sr. Lic. D . . . , Secretario de Economía,
ante la XVI Convención Bancaria (*Carta
mensual*, v. 5, no. 48, abril, p. 580-588).

984. Mass, Eduardo E. La industria del
sulfato de cobre en México. n. p. 61 p.

985. Medina Mora, Alejandro. Costos ban-
carios departamentales. n. p. 57 p.

986. Mendoza Olguín, Salvador. El intercambio comercial de México (*Rev. econ.*,
México, v. 13, no. 8, agosto 15, p. 268-
271).

986a. —————. Situación ocupacional 1941-
1950 (*Rev. econ.*, México, v. 13, no. 4,
abril 15, p. 115-117).
Tras estudiar la ocupación industrial durante la
última década en México, concluye el autor que
se ha operado en ella un aumento apreciable,
que la nómina de salarios ha crecido aún más
que la ocupación, que si bien el salario medio
nominal ha aumentado, ello ha sido en proporción inferior a la nómina y que el poder de
compra real del sector obrero ha disminuido.

987. Meza A., Manuel. Los sistemas agrícolas de Chiapas (*Rev. econ.*, México, v.
13, no. 4, abril 15, p. 110-114).
Forma parte de un estudio económico más
amplio, de Moisés T. de la Peña, sobre ese
mismo Estado. Véase no. 996.

988. Mora Ortiz, Gonzalo. El Banco Nacional de Comercio Exterior. Prólogo de

Enrique Parra Hernández. México, Ruta. 111 p.

988a. ————. La denuncia del tratado de comercio: principales efectos sobre las exportaciones mexicanas (*Trim. econ.*, v. 17, no. 4, oct.-dic., p. 541-569).

989. **Mosk, Sanford Alexander.** Industrial revolution in Mexico. Berkeley, Calif., University of California Press. xii, 331 p.
El libro de Mosk, redactado en la atmósfera de los primeros años de trasguerra, se inclina a considerar que las industrias manufactureras tuvieron auge durante la guerra, en México, a expensas del desarrollo de otras actividades; este criterio, tan discutible, no impide que la obra sea de una importancia notable por la abundancia de información minuciosa y ordenada que contiene y de la cual el autor extrajo conclusiones inteligentes y, con frecuencia, acertadas en lo particular.

990. **Nacional Financiera, S. A.** Décima-sexta Asamblea General Ordinaria de Accionistas. México, Cultura. 124 p.

990a. ————. Departamento de Estudios Financieros. Empréstitos exteriores de México (*Mercado val.*, año 10, no. 21, mayo 22, p. 5-7).
Resumen de la deuda pública exterior mexicana. Cuadros.

991. **Oliván Palacín, F.** Estudio minero sobre el Estado de Coahuila (*Rev. min. petrol.*, v. 16, no. 197, feb.-marzo, p. 42-47).

991a. ————. La industria de guanos y fertilizantes en la República Mexicana (*Rev. min. petrol.*, v. 16, no. 200, junio-julio, p. 16, 48).

991b. ————. Las industrias lácteas en México (*Rev. ind.*, v. 4, no. 47, agosto, p. 79-134).

991c. ————. Orientación minera del Estado de Zacatecas (*Rev. min. petrol.*, v. 16, no. 199, mayo, p. 27-29, 42-43).

991d. ————. La riqueza minera en el Estado de Michoacán (*Rev. min. petrol.*, v. 16, no. 200, junio-julio, p. 28-31, 45).

992. **Ortega, C. A.** El marquesado de Sierra Nevada y condados de Buena Vista y San Miguel. Orizaba, La Calandria. Unpaged.
Contiene datos sobre el molino de harina de Orizaba, fundado por la Marquesa doña Antonia María de Noroña, que ya en 1555 proveía de dicho artículo a la comarca orizabeña, a Veracruz y a la propia capital del virreinato.

993. **Ortega Mata, Rolfo.** El ajuste del ingreso nacional con el censo de población 1950 (*Rev. econ.*, México, v. 13, no. 8, agosto 15, p. 281-285).

994. **Padilla, Enrique.** Causas determinantes del aumento de precios (*Rev. econ.*, México, v. 13, no. 12, dic. 15, p. 424-425).
Considera el autor que las tres fuerzas que determinan, en diciembre de 1950, la orientación de los precios mexicanos con mayor fuerza son la devaluación de la moneda mexicana, la guerra de Corea y el programa de obras públicas.

994a. ————. La revalorización del peso (*Rev. econ.*, México, v. 13, no. 8, agosto 15, p. 264-267).
Con motivo del rumor de que el peso sería revalorado, el autor expone ciertas consideraciones con el objeto de no acarrear perjuicios a la economía.

995. **Pando Baura, José L.** Posibilidades económicas de México (*Rev. econ.*, México, v. 13, no. 5, mayo 15, p. 153-156).
Examen de la economía mexicana desde el punto de vista de su industria.

996. **Peña, Moisés T. de la.** Problemas demográficos y agrarios (*Prob. agríc. indus. México*, v. 2, no. 3-4, julio-nov.).
Este bien documentado estudio—el mejor publicado sobre la materia en épocas recientes—ocupa todo el volumen (324 p.) del no. 3-4 de la revista arriba señalada. Mapas, gráficas e ilustraciones.

997. **Pérez Guerrero, Fernando.** Obtención de cera de la caña de azúcar. n. p. 83 p.

998. **Petróleos Mexicanos.** Informe del Director General. n. p. 24 p.

999. PONENCIA A LA III CONVENCIÓN NACIONAL DE CAUSANTES (*Jorn. indus.*, año 2, t. 2, no. 18, julio-sept., p. 15-23).
Exhibe los puntos de vista de la Cámara Nacional de la Industria de Transformación sobre los problemas que afronta el causante en México y sobre la manera como pueden resolverse.

1000. RESEÑA DE LA III CONVENCIÓN NACIONAL DE CAUSANTES (*Jorn. indus.*, año 2, t. 2, no. 18, julio-sept., p. 12-14).

1001. **Reyes Heroles, Jesús.** La Carta de La Habana y el acuerdo arancelario general: actualidad y perspectiva (*Trim. econ.*, v. 17, no. 4, oct.-dic., p. 595-635).
El autor hace una reseña de las opiniones favorables y contrarias que suscitó la carta de La Habana; establece el significado del acuerdo general sobre aranceles aduaneros y comercio, examinando su origen y estructura general; examina asimismo la naturaleza de los cuadros y el funcionamiento del acuerdo, todo ello con notable objetividad. Concluye que sólo puede darse un juicio definitivo sobre la posición de un país en relación con el acuerdo después de

analizar sus intereses de exportador y la necesidad que tenga de mantener niveles arancelarios protectores, en relación con los renglones y niveles tarifarios en concreto comprendidos en los cuadros incorporados al convenio.

1001a. ————. Naturaleza del tratado comercial mexicano-americano de 1942 (*Invest. econ.*, v. 10, no. 4, 4. trimestre, p. 395-407).
En esta conferencia el agudo jurista y economista mexicano examina la política económica exterior de los Estados Unidos, principalmente durante el período gubernamental de Roosevelt, el contenido económico del tratado, la estructura jurídica del mismo y, finalmente, las tendencias del momento en la política comercial exterior norteamericana, recomendando cautela a los mexicanos en el tratado de acuerdos nuevos con aquel país.

1002. Rodríguez Aguilar, Manuel. Los problemas de la exploración en México (*Rev. min. petrol.*, v. 16, no. 198, abril, p. 29-30, 42-44).
Reseña de la exploración petrolera mexicana durante los últimos años.

1003. Saavedra, Mario M. La producción agrícola bajo la reforma agraria (*Invest. econ.*, v. 10, no. 1, 1. trimestre, p. 97-114).
Estudio sobre las fuentes estadísticas relacionadas con la producción agrícola.

1004. Sáenz, Josué. Progreso y productividad (*Mercado val.*, año 10, no. 38, sept. 18, p. 3-7).
Conferencia dictada dentro del ciclo organizado por el Consejo Directivo del Movimiento Económico Nacional. Examina las cifras del ingreso nacional de México y el gran incremento que se ha operado de 1929 a 1950; señala las características de la economía mexicana: grandes necesidades insatisfechas, producción insuficiente, productividad baja, desocupación oculta, capitalización suficiente, condiciones de intercambio desventajosas en el comercio internacional. Publicóse también en *Rev. econ.*, México, v. 13, no. 10, oct. 15, p. 344-348; no. 11, nov. 15, p. 395-400, y en traducción inglesa en *Mex. amer. rev.*, v. 18, no. 12, Dec., p. 41-43, 114, 116.

1005. Sáenz Nieves, Salvador. Determinación de la potencia de las plantas hidroeléctricas de México (*Revista mexicana de electricidad*, v. 10, no. 119, agosto, p. 6-8).

1006. Salas Villagómez, Manuel. La deuda pública. Un estudio general. El caso de México. México. 155 p.
El capítulo 5, "La deuda pública interior," se reprodujo en *Invest. econ.*, v. 10, no. 2, 2. trimestre, p. 177-211.

1007. Santaella, Joaquín. Los impuestos mineros (*Rev. min. petrol.*, v. 16, no. 198, abril, p. 17, 37, 38).

1008. Schelbach Sánchez, Enrique. Mejoramiento ganadero (*Prob. agric. indus. México*, v. 3, no. 1, enero-marzo, p. 167-179).
Proyecto para la realización de una campaña a base de inseminación artificial y transplante de óvulos fecundados. El autor estudia el capital que representa la ganadería y define un plan de acción para resolver los problemas más importantes de esta actividad económica.

1009. Schoen, Abbey. Business in Mexico (*Mex. amer. rev.*, v. 18, no. 1, Jan., p. 19-21).
Extracto de un informe del autor, miembro de la Embajada de Estados Unidos en México.

1010. Secretaría de Agricultura y Ganadería. Informes de labores de . . . del 1. de septiembre de 1949 al 31 de agosto de 1950. México. 222 p., plates, tables, graphs.

1010a. Secretaría de la Economía Nacional. Memoria de la . . . presentada al H. Congreso de la Unión por el Secretario Lic. Antonio Martínez Báez. Septiembre, 1949-agosto, 1950. México. 541 p.

1010b. Secretaría de Hacienda y Crédito Público. Dirección de la Casa de Moneda. Memoria de la Dirección de la Casa de Moneda de México correspondiente al año fiscal 1949. México. 159 p.

1011. Solís Ogarrio, Jorge. Ensayo nacional con el maíz (*Rev. econ.*, México, v. 13, no. 6, junio 15, p. 184-187).
Reseña las actividades de la Comisión Nacional del Maíz.

1012. Sotomayor Arciniegas, Miguel. Los Ferrocarriles Nacionales y las tarifas de carga (*Jorn. indus.*, año 2, t. 2, no. 17, mayo-junio, p. 28-42).
Considera el autor que las causas que provocan el aumento de las tarifas ferrocarrileras son: la desorganización de la empresa y su desequilibrio económico, la devaluación de la moneda y la competencia de la carretera a través de los servicios público y privado de transportes.

1013. Tannenbaum, Frank. Mexico. The struggle for peace and bread. New York, Knopf. xiv, 293, xi p.
Esta obra es la culminación del interés que el autor tiene por México desde hace varios años. Está dividida en dos partes, la primera de carácter sociológico y la segunda de carácter económico; ésta ha sido considerada por la crítica deficiente con respecto a la primera. La importancia de la obra consiste en el trazo panorámico que hace del México actual en sus diversos aspectos. Si los juicios y opiniones del autor pueden y deben ser discutidos, es indudable que esta obra, por su aportación al conocimiento y comprensión de los problemas mexi-

canos, ha de ocupar un lugar destacado dentro de la bibliografía y será de consulta obligatoria para quienes quieran estudiar a México. La angustiosa visión que de los problemas de México da y la proposición de que se utilice la pequeña comunidad como medida de salvación suscitaron una interesante polémica y varias respuestas airadas y bien documentadas. Véase no. 1810.

1014. TEXTILE OUTPUT HIGH (*Mex. amer. rev.*, v. 18, no. 12, nov., p. 17-36).
Artículo extractado de un informe de Fred Hajjar, publicado por el Departamento de Comercio de Estados Unidos, sobre la producción de la industria manufacturera textil de artículos de algodón que es la principal de México, y que satisface todas las necesidades locales, teniendo además un remanente considerable para la exportación. El informe completo apareció bajo el título *Cotton industry, Mexico, and cotton piece goods, Canada* (*World trade commod.*, v. 8, part 19, no. 19, May, 4 p., cuadros).

1015. Torón Villegas, Luis. Los carbones minerales y sus posibilidades de utilización (*Rev. min. petrol.*, v. 16, no. 202-203, sept.-oct., p. 10-14).
Síntesis de un estudio presentado en el primer Congreso Nacional Minero; se trata en particular del caso de México.

1016. Torres Gaytán, Ricardo. Repercusiones de la denuncia del tratado de comercio méxico-norteamericano (*Invest. econ.*, v. 10, no. 4, 4. trimestre, p. 511-532).
Acucioso examen de todas las posibilidades, positivas y negativas, que para México significaría el reanudar el tratado comercial con Estados Unidos o el ingresar al GATT; propone el autor que por el momento se continúe sin formular un nuevo tratado y sin ingresar al GATT, y recomienda que a partir de enero de 1951 se eleven los aranceles mexicanos con fines proteccionistas.

1017. Ugarte, Salvador. Mexico's Central Bank (*Mex. amer. rev.*, v. 18, no. 1, Jan., p. 16-18, 38, 40-42).
Conferencia del director general del Banco de Comercio sobre el instituto bancario central y su desarrollo histórico.

1017a. Unión Nacional de Productores de Azúcar, S. A. Estudio sobre la industria azucarera nacional; plan para fomentar su desarrollo; programa para llevar la producción del país a 1.000,000 de toneladas de azúcar en el quinquenio 1951-1955. México. Unpaged, charts.

1017b. U. S.'s EXPORT-IMPORT BANK AND MEXICO (*Mex. amer. rev.*, v. 18, no. 5, May, p. 17-18, 28-30).
Trata de los créditos concedidos a México por esta institución, especialmente para transportes e industrias básicas.

1017c. Velasco, Gustavo R. El mayor peligro, el Estado. México, Asociación de Banqueros de México. 17 p.

1017d. ————. El problema de los monopolios (*Rev. econ.*, México, v. 13, no. 9, sept. 15, p. 321-325; no. 11, p. 407-412).
El autor da una definición general del monopolio, describe el mecanismo de los precios y explica el funcionamiento de los monopolios en México. Concluye que la única solución para combatir los monopolios es la restauración de la concurrencia.

1017e. Velasco Torres, Raúl. El auge petrolero de México (*Rev. econ.*, México, v. 13, no. 2, feb. 15, p. 57-62).
Examen de los progresos logrados por la industria petrolera a partir de su nacionalización y consideraciones sobre la situación de la misma dentro del panorama internacional.

1017f. Viniegra O., Francisco. Breve análisis geológico de la llamada Cuenca de Veracruz. Sus posibilidades petrolíferas (*Rev. min. petrol.*, v. 16, no. 197, feb.-marzo, p. 20-21).

1017g. Zamora, Fernando. La nueva estructura comercial (*Rev. econ.*, México, v. 13, no. 1, enero 15, p. 5-6).

Education

GENERAL

1018. Aguilar Paz, Jesús, and **Rafael Bardales B.** Informes del Seminario Interamericano de Alfabetización y Educación de Adultos y de la I Reunión Panamericana de Consulta sobre Geografía, celebrados en Petrópolis y Rio de Janeiro, Brasil, del 27 de julio al 2 de septiembre y del 12 al 24 de septiembre de 1949, respectivamente. Presentados por los delegados de la República de Honduras . . . . Tegucigalpa, Talleres Tipográficos Nacionales. 81 p.
The first report emphasizes the function of the elementary school in the reduction of illiteracy. [H. Benjamin]

1019. Altoberro, María Celia (and others). El Seminario Interamericano de Alfabetización y Educación de Adultos celebrado en Petrópolis, Brasil, bajo los auspicios de la UNESCO y la Unión de los Estados Americanos (*An. instr. prim.,* época 2, t. 13, no. 6, junio, p. 6-73).
Complete report on all topics and conclusions of the seminar, presented to the National Council on Elementary and Teacher Education in Montevideo by the Uruguayan delegation. [H. Benjamin]

1020. Bravo Mejía, Gonzalo (and others). Informe que presentan los Directores de Educación al señor Ministro del ramo sobre la observación hecha en las escuelas, colegios y universidades de los Estados Unidos de Norte América, a donde viajaron en misión especial (*Rev. educ. nac.,* no. 3, p. 12-72).
Reports on elementary, secondary, higher, technical, and vocational education and on teacher training institutions, with general observations on United States systems as they appeared to five Peruvians. [H. Benjamin]

1021. Hall, Robert King. La educación en crisis. Tucumán, Argentina, Universidad Nacional de Tucumán, Instituto de Pedagogía y Ciencias de la Educación (Cuadernos de Pedagogía, 4). 211 p.

Series of lectures on topics of particular interest to students of comparative education, given at the University of Tucumán in July, 1948. [H. Benjamin]

1022. Mastache Román, Jesús. El libro de texto. Técnica de su manejo. México, Cosmos. 166 p.
A how-to-study manual, with special reference to the textbook as a source of information. [H. Benjamin]

1023. Nannetti, Guillermo. La Organización de los Estados Americanos y la campaña continental de educación. Washington, Unión Panamericana, División de Educación. 20 p., illus., 3 appendices.
Describes seminars, libraries, textbook expositions, cultural interchange, cooperation with UNESCO, and other educational services with which the Organization of American States is concerned. The appendices are as follows: 1, a list of bilateral and multilateral inter-American treaties and conventions of a cultural character; 2, the general agreement for cooperation between OAS and UNESCO; and 3, the agreement between OAS and UNESCO on the training of personnel and the preparation of fundamental education material for Latin America. [H. Benjamin]

1024. Nelson, Ernesto. Una revolución inconclusa y sus efectos sobre la educación (*Nueva era,* Quito, v. 19, p. 50-56).
Relationship of the Renaissance to modern educational philosophy. [H. Benjamin]

1025. Ornague, Enrique E. Fundamentos de los institutos superiores de pedagogía (*Rev. educ.,* La Plata, no. 6, p. 41-47).
The goals and curricular sections of these new schools are described by the director of the first one to be established, the Institute at Bahía Blanca.

1026. Pan American Union. Department of Cultural Affairs. Division of Education. La educación universal en América y la escuela primaria fundamental. El Plan de Montevideo. Washington, 34 p., illus., charts.
Report of the Inter-American Seminar on Ele-

mentary Education held in 1950 at Montevideo on the topic of universal, free, and compulsory schooling. Presented to the First Regional Meeting of UNESCO National Committees of the Western Hemisphere, Habana, 1950. [H. Benjamin]

1027. ————. ————. ————. Opportunities for summer study in Latin America, 1950. Washington. 23 p.
An annual publication. [Ed.]

1028. Romero, Fernando. Inter-American cooperation in vocational education. Washington, Pan American Union, Department of Cultural Affairs, Division of Education (Series M on Vocational Education, no. 7). xvi, 188 p.
Detailed and organized information of interest to all vocational teachers in Latin America and to many in North America. Also in Spanish. [H. Benjamin]

1029. ————. Organización de escuelas y de cursos de educación vocacional. Partes 1-2. Washington, Unión Panamericana. xxvi, 167, 310 p., illus.
Excellent summary of efforts in this field with application to Latin American problems. [H. Benjamin]

1030. ————. Planteamiento del problema de la educación vocacional. Washington, Unión Panamericana, Departamento de Asuntos Culturales, División de Educación (Serie M de Educación Vocacional, no. 1). xi, 52 p.
Purposes, planning, and organization of vocational education. [Ed.]

1031. ————. Trabajo manual y orientación vocacional. Washington, Unión Panamericana, Departamento de Asuntos Culturales (Serie M de Educación Vocacional, no. 2). x, 40 p.
On job analysis; need and purpose of vocational orientation; vocational counselors. This and the three preceding are among the documents prepared for the Inter-American Seminar on Voca-

tional Education, sponsored by the Organization of American States and UNESCO and held at the University of Maryland in 1952. [Ed.]

1032. Teixeira, Anisio. Educação progressiva. Uma introdução à filosofia da edução. São Paulo, Companhia Editora Nacional (Biblioteca Pedagógica Brasileira, Atualidades Pedagógicas). 175 p.
Fundamentos da educação progressiva; a educação e a sociedade em face da educação progressiva. [M. B. Lourenço Filho]

1033. Tejada, Carmela. The Inter-American Seminar on Literacy and Adult Education, Rio de Janeiro. Washington, Pan American Union, Department of Cultural Affairs, Division of Education. iii, 48 p., illus.
Report of the seminar sponsored in 1949 by the OAS, UNESCO, and the government of Brazil. [Ed.]

1034. Tirado Benedí, Domingo, and Santiago Hernández Ruiz. Compendio de la ciencia de la educación. México, Atlante. 394 p.
Textbook on principles of education with emphasis on psychology and method of teaching. [H. Benjamin]

1035. United Nations Educational, Scientific, and Cultural Organization. Fundamental education, regional training and production centre for Latin America (UNESCO/Ed/80). Paris. 26 p.
Historical background, agreement, and budget of joint training and production enterprises of UNESCO and the Organization of American States. See items 1019, 1023, 1026 and 1033. [H. Benjamin]

1036. Verdesio, Emilio. Los ideales de la educación popular. Montevideo, Talleres Gráficos 33. 201 p.
Philosophical, sociological, and psychological principles of modern education, with a sketch of comparative education in the Americas. [H. Benjamin]

SPANISH AMERICA AND HAITI

HAROLD BENJAMIN

EDUCATIONAL articles, reports, and books published in 1950 reveal a rising interest and activity in fundamental education, vocational training, and the teaching of history and geography. Statements of general philosophical objectives in terms of national sentiments, although still represented in the literature, are now falling into the minority.

The influence of the United Nations Educational, Scientific, and Cultural Organization, working in cooperation with the Organization of American States, was particularly apparent in the reports of seminars operated by the two organizations. The Inter-American Seminar on Elementary Education in Montevideo was having an increased impact in 1950. The establishment of a joint regional training and production center by UNESCO and the OAS showed that both these international agencies were prepared to act practically on their views. The 1949 Inter-American Seminar on Literacy and Adult Education further emphasized the international character of efforts to improve education in the countries of the Western Hemisphere. The Pan-American Institute of Geography and History in Mexico continued its fruitful investigations of the teaching of those subjects. The Institute of Inter-American Affairs in Washington, through its cooperative arrangements with various Latin American countries, was stimulating excellent writing on educational topics.

ARGENTINA

1037. **Bono, Humberto Miguel.** Investigaciones sobre la capacidad intelectual en argentinos hijos de nativos e hijos de extranjeros (*An. inst. étnico nac.*, t. 2, 1949, i.e. 1950, p. 75-99).
Children of foreign-born residents were generally found to have average mental capacities superior to those of children of native-born parents. This difference was greater in the interior than in the federal capital.

1038. **Dirección General de Enseñanza Primaria.** Educación común en la capital, provincias y territorios nacionales, 1947-1948. Buenos Aires, 1949-1950.

1039. **Vitalone, Mario C., and María Renée Chaves.** Escuelas primarias especiales para adultos (*Rev. educ.*, La Plata, no. 1, p. 71-77).
Description of current educational programs in prisons.

CHILE

1040. **Bunster, César.** En torno de la docencia. Santiago, Imprenta Universitaria. 209 p.
Collection of essays and addresses on such diverse topics as the teaching of literary history, the teaching of Spanish in secondary schools, the relationship between secondary schools and parents, and the 1942 education law in Brazil.

1041. **Concepción (prov.). Inspección Provincial de Educación Primaria.** Escuelas primarias de Concepción (Cuarto centenario de Concepción, 1550-1950. Folleto histórico pedagógico). Concepción. 157 p., illus.
Contains material on history of education and on industries and social welfare agencies of the province.

1042. **Sociedad Constructora de Establecimientos Educacionales.** Memoria, 1948-1949. V. 1-2. Santiago. 10 p., tables; 12 p., tables.
Laws, decrees, regulations, and statistics of school building in Chile.

1043. **Stuardo Ortiz, Carlos.** El liceo de Chile. Antecedentes para su historia,

1828-1831 (*Rev. chil. hist. geog.*, no. 114, julio-dic., 1949, p. 48-91; no. 115, enero-junio, 1950, p. 162-217).
Materials for a history of this institution, including programs of study, personnel lists, regulations, addresses, and official correspondence.

COLOMBIA

1044. **Ospina Vásquez, Luis.** Estructura de la universidad. Medellín, Universidad de Antioquia, 1950? 27 p.
Recommendations on the proper university objectives, enrollment, curriculum, and faculty employment.

1045. RÉGIMEN DE LA ENSEÑANZA PRIMARIA EN COLOMBIA, 1903-1949. Bogotá, Ministerio de Educación Nacional. 449 p.
Codification of laws, decrees, and regulations affecting elementary education, with chronological index.

CUBA

1046. **Aguayo, Jorge** (comp.). Bibliografía de Alfredo M. Aguayo. Habana, Cultural. 119 p.
Classified bibliography of the works of the former director of the School of Education, University of Habana.

1047. LEY Y ESTATUTOS DE LA UNIVERSIDAD DE ORIENTE. Santiago, Universidad de Oriente, Departamento de Relaciones Culturales. 39 p.
Acts, resolutions, and regulations of the reorganized university, October 10, 1947, to March 23, 1949.

DOMINICAN REPUBLIC

1048. LEY DE ORGANIZACIÓN UNIVERSITARIA, CON SUS MODIFICACIONES HASTA EL 12 DE DICIEMBRE DE 1949. Ciudad Trujillo, Imprenta San Francisco. 35 p.

1049. **Sánchez y Sánchez, Carlos.** Por los fueros de las dos universidades de La Española. Ciudad Trujillo, Universidad de Santo Domingo (Publ., v. 79, serie 3, Derecho y Ciencias Sociales, no. 1). 32 p.

Argument, with supporting documentation, that the University of Santo Domingo was established by papal bull in 1538; the University of Santiago de la Paz y de Gorjón, also in Santo Domingo, by the crown in 1540 as an *Estudio* with the same rights as that of Salamanca, and in 1558 as a university; and the University of San Marcos in Lima, Peru, in 1571.

GUATEMALA

1050. Fuentes J., María Cristina. Guía didáctica para la enseñanza de párvulos. Guatemala, Ministerio de Educación Pública. 103 p., illus.

Designed for teachers of children in three age groups, 3-4, 5-6, and 6-7, on the basis of chronological age in the youngest group and mental age in the two older groups. Based on classification of interests as physical, intellectual, moral, and esthetic.

1051. Ministerio de Educación Pública. Departamento de Educación Rural. Servicio Cooperativo Interamericano de Educación. Acuerdos gubernativos que dan base legal a la organización de Núcleos Escolares Campesinos. Programas mínimos básicos para las escuelas comprendidas en los Núcleos Escolares Campesinos. Guatemala. 43 p.

Legal and educational bases of new rural school centers operated under a cooperative arrangement between the government of Guatemala and the Institute of Inter-American Affairs. The agreement expired in 1950.

MEXICO

1053. Castañeda Alderete, Margarita. Antecedentes, comentario y crítica de la legislación sobre cooperativas escolares. México. 112 p.

The general history and principles of cooperative societies and a brief account of their development in primary, secondary, normal, and technical schools. Thesis, University of Mexico.

1055. Pineda, Salvador (ed.). Problemas universitarios y agonía de la Escuela Nacional Preparatoria. México, Stylo. 286 p.

Collection of articles by a dozen authors, published in the Mexico City newspaper *Excélsior* in the two years ending July 22, 1950 to explain or criticize the autonomy, legal bases, curriculum, and teaching methods of the preparatory section of the national university.

1056. ———. El signo de la Universidad. Ensayo de revisión orgánica. México. 127 p.

Critical essay on the constitutional and legislative bases of the work of the National University, 1910-1950.

1057. Secretaría de Educación Pública. Memoria, 1949-1950. México. 633 p.

The usual comprehensive report. [Ed.]

PERU

1058. Biery, Donald H. Plan, organización y objetivos del programa de orientación y educación prevocacional en el Perú *(Nuevo educ.,* año 6, no. 8, mayo, p. 16-18).

Industry-school cooperation is a feature of this plan.

1059. Eguiguren, Luis Antonio (ed.). La Universidad Nacional Mayor de San Marcos. Cuarto centenario de la fundación de la Universidad Real y Pontificia y de su vigorosa continuidad histórica. Lima, Imprenta Santa María. 282 p., illus., facsims.

Chief events in the history of the university, 1551-1950, with a list of rectors, 1553-1950.

1060. Ministerio de Educación Pública. Plan de educación nacional, aprobado por Decreto Supremo del 13 de enero de 1950. Lima. 179 p., maps, tables.

This plan, developed by the National Council of Education, stresses a 3-3-4 organization with increased financial support and better education of teachers.

PUERTO RICO

1061. Columbia University. Teachers College. Institute of Field Studies. Public education and the future of Puerto Rico. A curriculum survey, 1948-1949. New York. 614 p.

Comprehensive study of curriculum in light of the island's needs.

1062. Department of Education. Annual report of the Commissioner of Education, 1949-1950. San Juan. 205 p., illus.

In addition to the usual statistical summaries, this report describes the organization and services of the Department of Education. Also in Spanish.

1063. ———. La enseñanza de lectura y escritura en los grados primarios. San Juan. 47 p.

1064. ———. Official list of accredited and approved private schools of Puerto Rico, 1949-1950. San Juan, 1950? 14 p.

Complete, well annotated directory.

1065. Insular Board for Vocational Education. Towards a better life through vocational education. San Juan. 72 p., illus., maps.

Copiously illustrated description of the new vocational education program.

URUGUAY

1066. Abbate, María. La educación de los padres y su influencia en la educación de los hijos (*An. instr. prim.*, época 2, t. 13, no. 1, enero, p. 11-36).
Detailed exposition of the uses and problems of educating parents in connection with the learning of their children.

1067. Ardao, Arturo. La Universidad de Montevideo. Su evolución histórica. Montevideo, Centro Estudiantes de Derecho. 109 p.

VENEZUELA

1068. Grisanti, Ángel. Resumen histórico de la instrucción pública en Venezuela. Época colonial. La independencia y primeros años de la República. Época actual. Prólogo de don Francisco García Calderón. Segunda edición. Bogotá, Iqueima. 253 p.
The first edition appeared in 1933.

1069. López Orihuela, D. Nuestra universidad. Caracas, Universidad Central, Facultad de Filosofía y Letras. 33 p.

OTHER COUNTRIES

1070. Hernández, Ángel G. Problemas de la educación primaria. Tegucigalpa, Talleres Tipográficos Nacionales. 303 p., tables.
Historical materials and legal documentation on the national system of education in Honduras.

1071. LEY DE ALFABETIZACIÓN Y EDUCACIÓN DE ADULTOS. Decreto no. 736 y reglamentos. San Salvador, Ministerio de Cultura. 5, 12 p.
Anti-illiteracy and adult education law of El Salvador.

1072. Panamá. Comisión de Estudio de la Educación Nacional. Informe, 1947-1950. Panamá. 256 p.
Report of study made by a commission of the Panamanian Ministry of Education with advice and technical assistance from the Inter-American Educational Foundation and the United States Office of Education.

1073. Pressoir, Catts. L'Enseignement de l'histoire en Haïti. México, Instituto Panamericano de Geografía e Historia (Publ.

no. 102, Comisión de Historia, 16. Memorias sobre la Enseñanza de la Historia, no. 3). xiii, 83 p.
One of the series of reports on this subject by representatives of the Pan American countries.

ADDENDA

1074. Coirolo, Hipólito. Temas de educación. Montevideo, Casa Editora Uruguay, 1949. 269 p.
Collection of 23 speeches and articles by one of the leading teachers of the country, ranging from discussions of national conscience to specific proposals for educational reorganization.

1075. Cuba. Secretaría de Educación. Información ante el Senado, ofrecida por el Dr. Aureliano Sánchez Arango, Ministro de Educación, diciembre 15 de 1948. Habana, 1948. 101 p., illus., facsims.
Detailed report of Senate inquiry into causes of dismissal of teachers, number and quality of teaching staff, and general effectiveness of school system.

1076. Hart, Estellita (comp.). Courses on Latin America in institutions of higher education in the United States, 1948-1949. Introduction by Jorge Basadre. Washington, Pan American Union, Department of Cultural Affairs, 1949. 291 p.
Designed to help Latin Americanists in the United States to know one another better, to serve as a list of prospects for textbook publishers, and to furnish students with a guide to possible places in which to study Latin American topics.

1077. México. Dirección General de Alfabetización y Educación Extraescolar. Departamento de Alfabetización. Memoria. 1944-1948. México, Secretaría de Educación Pública, 1949.

1078. Nivar Ramírez, Consuelo. Sistema educativo en la República Dominicana. Ciudad Trujillo, Universidad de Santo Domingo, 1949. 119 p.
The national history of education is treated in chapters on the colonial, the republican, the North American intervention, and the contemporary periods. A fifth chapter proposes reforms in the present system of education. Thesis.

1079. Saralegui, José. La escuela y la salud. Montevideo, Imprenta Nacional, 1949. 443 p., illus.
Textbook for the preparation of teachers, supervisors, attendance officers, and visiting nurses.

BRAZIL

M. B. LOURENÇO FILHO

See also item 1040.

1080. Almeida, Manoel José de. Escola Caio Martins. Desenvolvimento de seu programa de ação. Belo Horizonte, Imprensa Oficial. 90 p.
Descrição do programa e realizações de uma granja-modêlo para educação de menores abandonados, no município de Esmeraldas, estado de Minas Gerais.

1081. Andrade, Raimundo Ozanan. A reforma social nos colégios (*Formação,* ano 12, no. 145, agôsto, p. 21-29).
Necessidade de estudos sôbre os problemas sociais nas escolas secundarias.

1082. Congresso Nacional de Educação de Adultos, Primeiro. Promovido em feve150reiro de 1947 pela Secretaria de Educação e Cultura da Prefeitura do Distrito Federal com a cooperação do Centro de Professores do Ensino Noturno Municipal, sob os auspicios do Ministério da Educação e Saúde. Rio de Janeiro, Ministério da Educação e Saúde. 222 p.
Contem doze pequenas monografias sôbre alfabetização de adultos, métodos e processos de educação fundamental, e emprêgo de recursos audio-visuais.

1083. Conselho Nacional de Educação. Anais. Ano de 1949. Rio de Janeiro, Ministério da Educação e Saúde. 412 p.
Debates e pareceres do Conselho, que funciona como orgão consultivo do Ministro da Educação.

1084. ————. Fundamentos e metodologia do ensino supletivo. Curso de orientação pedagógica promovido pela Fundação Getúlio Vargas em cooperação com o Departamento Nacional de Educação (Serie Campanha de Educação de Adultos, publ. no. 12). Rio de Janeiro, Ministério da Educação e Saúde. 263 p.
Resumos das lições ministradas no curso pelos professores M. B. Lourenço Filho, Noemy S. Rudolfer, Luiz Alves de Matos, Juraci Silveira e J. Elidio Silveira, respectivamente, sôbre pedagogia de adultos, psico-pedagogia de adultos analfabetos, didática geral, metodologia da leitura e escrita, da aritmética e de conhecimentos gerais.

1085. Fonseca, Anita. Clubes de leitura. Belo Horizonte, Imprensa Oficial (Publ. da Secretaria de Educação do Estado de Minas Gerais). 69 p.
Normas para organização e funcionamento de clubes de leitura nas escolas primárias.

1086. Hall, Robert King. El servicio nacional de aprendizaje industrial del Brasil (*Nueva era,* Quito, v. 19, p. 232-236).
Describes the significant educational experiment being carried on by the National Service of Industrial Apprenticeship. [H. Benjamin]

1087. Hsin-Pao, Yang. A educação de adultos nas comunidades rurais (*Rev. bras. estud. ped.,* v. 14, no. 38, jan.-abril, p. 1-24).
Estudo apresentado ao Seminário de Alfabetização e Educação de Adultos, realizado no Rio de Janeiro em agôsto de 1949 por iniciativa da UNESCO e Organização dos Estados Americanos. Trata do papel da educação na reorganização das comunidades rurais.

1088. Instituto Nacional de Estudos Pedagógicos. Aperfeiçoamento de professores. Bolsas de estudo oferecidas ao magistério primário brasileiro para aperfeiçoamento e especialização. Rio de Janeiro, Ministério da Educação e Saúde (Publ. no. 60). 55 p.
Informações sôbre a organização, funcionamento e finalidades dos cursos mantidos pelo Instituto Nacional de Estudos Pedagógicos.

1089. ————. Atividades econômicas da região no curso primário. Sugestões para organização e desenvolvimento de programas. Rio de Janeiro, Ministério da Educação e Saúde (Publ. no. 50). 29 p.
Objetivos de estudo, mínimos a alcançar, orientação metodológica.

1090. ————. Canto orfeônico no curso primário. Sugestões para organização e desenvolvimento de programas. Rio de Janeiro, Ministério da Educação e Saúde (Publ. no. 51). 57 p.
O ensino musical nas escolas primárias e seus objetivos; instruções metodológicas.

1091. ————. Educação física no curso primário. Sugestões para a organização e desenvolvimento de programas. Rio de Janeiro, Ministério da Educação e Saúde (Publ. no. 49). 46 p.
Tipos de atividades aconselháveis e instruções metodológicas.

1092. ————. Jornadas de educação. Debates de temas educacionais organizados pelo IDORT com a cooperação do INEP. Rio de Janeiro, Ministério da Educação e Saúde (Publ. no. 48). 182 p.

Monografias sôbre doze temas relativos a trabalho e educação, apresentadas a uma reunião de estudos, promovida pelo Instituto de Organização Racional do Trabalho (São Paulo) em cooperação com o Instituto Nacional de Estudos Pedagógicos.

1093. ————. A nova escola primária brasileira. Rio de Janeiro, Ministério da Educação e Saúde (Publ. no. 64). 32 p.
Relatório do prof. Robert King Hall, da Columbia University, Nova York, depois de uma viagem de observação pelo interior de vários estados brasileiros.

1094. ————. Oportunidades de preparação no ensino de enfermagem e serviço social. Rio de Janeiro, Ministério da Educação e Saúde (Publ. no. 46, i.e. 49). 169 p.

1095. ————. Oportunidades de preparação no ensino industrial. Informações para orientar a escolha de uma atividade profissional. Rio de Janeiro, Ministério da Educação e Saúde (Publ. no. 43, 2. tiragem). 317 p.
Estrutura geral do ensino de artesanato, técnico-profissional, de comunicações, transportes, e pesca; relação das escolas e cursos.

1096. ————. Oportunidades de preparação no ensino superior. Informações para orientar a escolha de uma atividade profissional. Rio de Janeiro, Ministério da Educação e Saúde (Publ. no. 56). 306 p.
Estrutura geral do ensino superior no Brasil; descrição dos diferentes cursos; relação das escolas.

1097. ————. Organização do ensino primário e normal. Estado da Paraíba. Rio de Janeiro, Ministério da Educação e Saúde (Publ. no. 62). 38 p., map, tables.

1098. ————. Organização do ensino primário e normal. Estado de Santa Catarina. Rio de Janeiro, Ministério da Educação e Saúde (Publ. no. 53). 80 p., map, tables.

1099. ————. Organização do ensino primário e normal. Estado de Sergipe. Rio de Janeiro, Ministério da Educação e Saúde (Publ. no. 54). 50 p., map, tables.

1100. ————. Organização do ensino primário e normal. Estado do Espírito Santo. Rio de Janeiro, Ministério da Educação e Saúde (Publ. no. 57). 53 p.
Orgãos de administração do ensino no estado; estrutura do ensino primário e normal; inspeção escolar e carreira do professor.

1101. ————. Organização do ensino primário e normal. Estado do Piauí. Rio de Janeiro, Ministério da Educação e Saúde (Publ. no. 52). 49 p.
Descreve a organização geral do ensino no estado, expondo a estrutura do ensino primário e normal, a inspeção escolar e a carreira do professor.

1102. ————. Problemas de educação rural. Curso promovido em 1949 a cargo do professor Robert King Hall, da Columbia University, N. Y. Rio de Janeiro, Ministério da Educação e Saúde (Publ. no. 47). 105 p.
A escola primária e a comunidade rural; formação dos professores; papel da escola na segurança nacional.

1103. ————. Subsídios para a história da educação brasileira. Ano de 1947. Rio de Janeiro, Ministério da Educação e Saúde (Publ. no. 46). 231 p.
Registro sistemático de atos de administração pública referente ao ensino; noticiário geral.

1104. ————. Subsídios para a história da educação brasileira. Ano de 1948. Rio de Janeiro, Ministério da Educação e Saúde (Publ. no. 65).

1105. ————. Subsídios para a história da educação brasileira. Ano de 1949. Rio de Janeiro, Ministério da Educação e Saúde (Publ. no. 66). 164 p.
Registro dos atos de administração federal, estadual e municipal sôbre o ensino; noticiário geral.

1106. Kemper, Werner. Problemas das anormalidades no desenvolvimento psíquico (*Rev. bras. estud. ped.*, v. 14, no. 40, set.-dez., p. 58-78).
Estudo das anomalias de desenvolvimento atribuidas ao ambiente social; relações com o processo educativo.

1107. Leão, Antonio Carneiro. Adolescência e sua educação. São Paulo, Companhia Editôra Nacional (Biblioteca Pedagógica Brasileira, Atualidades pedagógicas). 248 p.
Fatores biológicos e sociais; integração social do adolescente; o ensino secundário e a educação dos adolescentes.

1109. Lisboa, H. Marques. Didática das ciencias naturais. Belo Horizonte, Imprensa Oficial (Publ. da Secretaria de Educação do Estado de Minas Gerais). 114 p.
As ciencias naturais no ensino primário; escolha de métodos; planos de lições.

1110. Lourenço Filho, M. B. Alguns elementos para estudo dos problemas de ensino secundário (*Rev. bras. estud. ped.*, v. 14, no. 40, set.-dez., p. 79-97).
Posição do ensino secundário na situação geral

do ensino brasileiro; movimento de matrícula e evasão escolar nos últimos quinze anos; problemas de organização e de objetivos.

1111. ————. La educación en el Brasil. Rio de Janeiro, Ministério das Relações Exteriores, Divisão Cultural. 38 p.

Princípios políticos; normas de organização e de administração do ensino brasileiro; situação estatística em 1950; campanha de educação de adultos; tendências da educação no país.

1112. As mensagens presidenciais e a educação (*Rev. bras. estud. ped.,* v. 14, no. 38, jan.-abril, p. 73-109).

Trechos das mensagens anuais do Presidente da República ao Congresso Nacional, nos anos de 1947, 1948, 1949 e 1950, referentes à educação.

1113. **Prefeitura do Distrito Federal.** Anuário estatístico do Distrito Federal. V. 4. Estatística cultural. Rio de Janeiro. 134 p., graphs, tables.

1114. **Serviço de Educação de Adultos e Serviço de Informação Agrícola.** Missão rural de educação de adultos. Rio de Janeiro, Ministério da Educação e Saúde e Ministério da Agricultura. 20 p.

Descrição geral de um projeto-piloto realizado no município de Itaperuna, estado do Rio de Janeiro, com uma equipe de educadores e técnicos de agricultura.

ADDENDUM

1115. **Instituto Brasileiro de Geografía e Estatística. Conselho Nacional de Estatística.** Estudos de estatística teórica e aplicada. Estudos sôbre a alfabetização e a instrução da população do Brasil, conforme às apurações do censo demográfico de 1940 (Estatística Cultural no. 1). Rio de Janeiro, Serviço Gráfico do Instituto Brasileiro de Geografía e Estatística, 1948. 104 p., graphs, tables.

Geography

GENERAL

1116. AMÉRICA DEL SUR, 1:8,000,000. Milano [Italy], Società Cartográfica G. De Agostini.
This is one of a series of continental maps newly published by De Agostini, suitable for classroom or lecture use. Shows altitudes in seven colors, ocean depths in five colors, cities in four categories, national boundaries, and highly generalized drainage. It is a colorful map, somewhat competitive with Haack and Westermann maps, but with less attention to detail; probably less expensive. [A. C. Gerlach]

1117. AMÉRICA DEL SUR, 1:8,000,000. Paris, Casa Forest.
This political-economic map shows countries in colors, with state or province boundaries in Brazil and Argentina only. City names are numerous, and symbolized in five categories. An inset table indicates the area, population, and population density of each country. Major imports and exports are named along red arrows leading into or from each country. The names of minerals and of agricultural and forest products are given in Spanish. [A. C. Gerlach]

1118. AMÉRIQUE DU SUD: INDUSTRIES ET TRANSPORTS, 1:10,000,000. Paris, Direction de la Documentation.
Symbols show up to 10 or 12 leading industries in more than 100 cities of South America and the source areas for 30 different minerals. These are too many items for accurate location or good graphic presentation, but the relation of industries, transportation, and industry becomes obvious. Transportation lines are also schematic in pattern, but complete in coverage for railroads, air lines, and shipping lines. French air and shipping lines are distinguished from all others. [A. C. Gerlach]

1119. Ashton, Edwin George. South America. An introductory survey. London, Harrap (Harrap's New Geographical Series). 271 p., diagrams, illus., maps.
Treatment is by political divisions, but with an introductory consideration of general natural conditions. This text (apparently intended for students of secondary education in Great Britain) is mainly economic geography. [G. M. McBride]

1119a. Carpenter, Frances. Caribbean lands: Mexico, Central America, and the West Indies. New York, American Book Company. x, 392 p.
"One of a series of geographical readers for use in the upper grades of elementary schools." Of its type, an excellent, over-simplified summary, replete with illustrations and maps, and reasonably accurate. [H. F. Cline]

1120. Fletcher, Robert D. Modern trends in the tropical meteorology of the Americas (*Rev. acad. col. cien.*, v. 7, no. 28, mayo, p. 552-556, map).

1121. Fosberg, F. R. Ecological notes on the Upper Amazon (*Ecology*, v. 31, no. 4, Oct., p. 650-653).

1122. James, Preston E. Latin America. Revised edition. New York, Odyssey Press. xvi, 848 p., illus., maps.
Brought up to date, with four very useful general maps of South America added. [G. M. McBride]

1123. ————. Programa para un relevamiento geográfico de América. Buenos Aires, Ministerio de Educación, Universidad de Buenos Aires (Instituto de Geografía, serie A, no. 15). 23 p.

1124. MAPA TURÍSTICO DE AMÉRICA DEL SUR. Approximately 1:9,000,000. Convent Station, N. J., Esso Standard Oil Co. of Chile.
This is an excellent (for its scale) and reliable (for its date) road map of the continent, showing national and state boundaries, air routes, shipping routes, and roads in three categories plus those under construction. Insets include a locational table for cities, a schematic relief map in color, and island enlargements. The back of the map is a panoramic presentation at the same scale, showing pictorially the distribution of commodities and commercial activities. Based on the American Geographical Society's 1:5,000,000 map of the Americas, and carefully field checked, this is far above average in both accuracy and design. Prepared and copyrighted by the General Drafting Co., Convent Station, New Jersey. [A. C. Gerlach]

1125. National Research Council. Division of Geology and Geography. Report of the Committee on Latin American Geography, 1948-1949, including report of the Subcommittee on the West Indies and report of the Subcommittee on Mexico. Washington. 62 p.

1125a. Pan American Institute of Geography and History. Commission on Geography. Final act. First Pan American Consultation on Geography. Rio de Janeiro, September 12-24, 1949. Resolutions and recommendations. 11 p.
Official English text. Mimeographed.

1126. Pohl, Frederick. The Pesaro map, 1505 (*Imago mundi,* v. 7, p. 82-83, folding map).
Discusses a map of the Old World and part of America, regarded as being closely associated with Vespucci, as its maker or source of knowledge. E. L. Stevenson, in the *An. assoc. amer. geog.* (v. 17, 1927, p. 43, 51) regarded it as made in 1508. Pohl thinks it could be as early as 1505, and incidentally reproduces it in much more usable size than did Stevenson. [R. D. Hussey]

1127. Pratt, Wallace E., and Dorothy Good (eds.). World geography of petroleum. Princeton, N. J., Princeton University Press (American Geographical Society). 464 p.
Contains the definitive discussion of the petroleum industry in Latin America, with especial emphasis on the human factors in the geographic and technological equation. Attention is called to the fact that in most Latin American countries "ownership of all subsoil minerals is vested in the nation, and that its control is effected through the government," but mention is also made of the serious restrictions of exploratory activity which have grown out of the recent nationalization policies of many governments. This volume is "must" reading for all interested in the inter- and intra-national implications of strategic raw materials. [R. E. Crist]

1128. Riccardi, Riccardo. L'America meridionale. Lineamenti geografici. Roma, Perrella. 199 p.
Formal text-book; continent maps only; no photographs; little detail. [G. M. McBride]

1129. Steward, Julian H. (ed.). Handbook of South American Indians. V. 6. Physical anthropology, linguistics, and cultural geography of South American Indians. Washington, U. S. Government Printing Office (Smithsonian Institution, Bureau of American Ethnology, Bull. 143). 715 p., illus., maps.
Of most interest to geographers are the two chapters by Sauer: Part 4, "Geography of South America," p. 319-340, and "Cultivated plants of South and Central America," p. 487-543. Both are summaries, of course, but thoughtful summaries, based on wide knowledge of the literature and some personal observation. The former is illustrated by well selected photographs (by Jonathan Sauer) and both carry useful maps. See also item 113. [G. M. McBride]

1130. Stose, George Willis. Geologic map of South America, 1:5,000,000. New York, Geological Society of America.
This colored map in two sheets shows the distribution of 48 geological formations. It gives an excellent overview of continental geology, but is not to be substituted for more detailed country and regional maps, even of earlier dates, when interest is focused on only a part of South America. [A. C. Gerlach]

1131. United Nations. Secretariat. Department of Economic Affairs. World iron ore resources and their utilization. With special reference to the use of iron ores in under-developed areas. Lake Success, N. Y. (ST/ECA/6). viii, 74 p., map, tables.
An appraisal of the factors of: 1, known iron ore reserves; 2, ton-mile transportation requirements, and 3, markets for steel, in evaluating actual and potential steel industries in Latin America and other under-developed areas. [R. E. Crist]

THE CARIBBEAN AREA

RAYMOND E. CRIST

AN outstanding work in 1950 is the *Geografía de Cuba* by Leví Marrero, who was born in Santa Clara. He took his doctorate at the University of Habana, was in newspaper work for a number of years, and has travelled extensively all over the New World. He is Professor of Geography in the Institute of Secondary Education of La Víbora, Habana, and Superintendent of Secondary Education of the Ministry of Education. In 1951 the Guggenheim Foundation awarded him a grant which will enable him to continue his field and library research in the United States.

Professor Marrero admirably achieves what he proposes to do, as set forth in the preface to this monumental work: "We have tried to achieve a balance in these chapters in the exposition of the elements which make up the landscape, so that it is possible to understand how the physical background of Cuba has influenced Cuban destiny and how the population of Cuba, by its continuous efforts, generation after generation, has modified this natural landscape, adjusting to it at the same time, to create the present geographic landscape in which nature and culture are so intimately associated." Professor Marrero brought to his task not only complete familiarity with the subject, resulting from many years' work in the field as well as in the library, but also style, *esprit,* and a keen sense of humor.

MEXICO

1132. Atl, Dr. Cómo nace y crece un volcán, el Parícutin. México, Stylo. 152 p. plates.

A de luxe volume with sketches, photographs, and reproductions of oil paintings of Parícutin, at various stages in its evolution. The accompanying text gives a detailed account, year by year, of its growth and the devastation it has wrought. "Dr. Atl" is the pseudonym of Gerardo Murillo.

1133. Pérez Siliceo, Rafael, and David Gallagher. Geología del distrito mercurial de Huahuaxtla, estado de Guerrero, por . . . . Traducción del inglés hecha por Salvador Ulloa. Informe preparado en colaboración con el Geological Survey, United States Department of the Interior. México, Talleres Gráficos de la Nación (Publ. del Instituto Nacional para la Investigación de Recursos Minerales, 27). iv, 30 p., maps.

1134. Tamayo, Jorge L. Geografía de Oaxaca. México, Comisión Editora de El Nacional. 133 p.

An excellent primary text book on this interesting region of southern Mexico. Unfortunately the photographs did not print well.

PANAMA

1135. METEOROLOGÍA. TEMPERATURA, HUMEDAD, VELOCIDAD DEL VIENTO Y PRECIPITACIÓN PLUVIAL. Año 1949, por mes (*Estad. panameña,* v. 9, no. 5, mayo, p. iv, 1-97).
Valuable data on Panama for the climatologist.

1136. Rubio, Ángel. La ciudad de Panamá. Panamá, Banco de Urbanización y Rehabilitación (Publ. no. 17). 238 p., illus., maps.

A historical sketch of the evolution of the city of Panamá, well illustrated with "period" maps. The analysis of the expansion of the city during the past two decades is especially revealing. See item 1453.

COLOMBIA

1137. Alvarado, Benjamín, and Roberto Sarmiento Soto. Los yacimientos de carbón en Colombia (*Bol. minas petról.,* Bogotá, no. 154, agosto, p. 7-37).
A timely article on coal deposits in Colombia. The deposits in the Cauca Valley alone, between Cali and Popayán, are conservatively estimated at 406,500,000 tons. National production has increased from 421,965 tons in 1937 to 1,015,000 tons in 1949, a criterion of the drive toward industrialization in the country.

1138. Bueno, Jesús A. Informe sobre un yacimiento de manganeso en el municipio de Mallama, departamento de Nariño (*Bol. minas petról.,* Bogotá, no. 153, marzo, p. 79-94).
The author concludes that although the quality of this Colombian ore is satisfactory, it has not yet been found in quantities that would make it commercially profitable.

1139. Contraloría General. Censos nacionales, 1:50,000-1:200,000. Bogotá, 1950?
More than 115 *municipio* maps were completed for the northwest part of the country, and others were being prepared. They show contours, drainage, roads, railroads, mines, and minor civil boundaries, and give tables of information about crop production, historic sites, etc., for the area of each sheet. [A. C. Gerlach]

1140. Crist, Raymond E. The personality of Popayán (*Rural soc.,* v. 15, no. 2, June, p. 130-140).
A study of a religious, intellectual, and political capital in a little-known corner of southwestern Colombia, where prestige landholding is in full flower. The dearth of enterprising capital-accumulating business men and of small independent owner-operator farmers has been a decisive factor in investing Popayán with its personality of arrested development.

1141. Girard, E. (ed.). Mapa de la República de Colombia, 1:2,000,000. Paris, Girard, Barrère et Thomas.
Departments, shown in contrasting colors, are named. Physical features are very subdued and generalized, but the rivers are clear and numerous. An inset shows relief in five colors. Product names detract from the utility of the map and obscure the pattern of roads and railroads. [A. C. Gerlach]

1142. MAPA DE LA REPÚBLICA DE COLOMBIA, 1:2,500,000. Preliminary edition. Bogotá, Instituto Geográfico Militar y Catastral.
A map designed and reproduced for use in the schools of Colombia. Copies are not for sale. It is, nevertheless, one of the few good general

reference maps of the country. It is based on sheets of the Millionth Map by the American Geographical Society, modified from air photos and data supplied by the Texas and Socony Vacuum oil companies. The map shows roads in four categories, railroads, pipelines, departmental boundaries, altitudes by hypsometric tints, and a detailed drainage pattern. [A. C. Gerlach]

1143. Ministerio de Obras Públicas. Atlas vial.
This is essentially an official road atlas that devotes one page to each of the 24 departments, showing detailed drainage, roads in four categories, railroads, airports, and settlements. Distances between towns along the railroads are shown in kilometers. [A. C. Gerlach]

1144. REPÚBLICA DE COLOMBIA, 1:25,000. Bogotá, Instituto Geográfico Militar y Catastral, 1948-1950.
This set of maps shows departmental boundaries, roads in three categories, mines, churches, cemeteries, bridges, drainage, and contours at 50-meter intervals. For detailed information on the topography of Colombia, it is not surpassed. [A. C. Gerlach]

VENEZUELA

1145. Arnal, Pedro. Atlas escolar de Venezuela. Milano [Italy], Società Cartográfica G. De Agostini. 95 p.
The author has presented a comprehensive survey of the geography of Venezuela by means of maps, text, and pictures, suitable for use in elementary schools. In 95 pages (7½ x 9 in.) the atlas covers physical features, climate, vegetation, crops, transportation, communications, minerals, population, industries, and trade. About half the atlas is devoted to maps and textual treatment of the individual states and territories of Venezuela. [A. C. Gerlach]

1146. Corporación Venezolana de Fomento. Plan nacional de electrificación, 1:2,000,000. Caracas.
Shows both existing and planned power plants, substations, and transmission lines of various voltages, in the electrification program of Venezuela. Available only as ozalid copies of a manuscript map. [A. C. Gerlach]

1147. MAPA FÍSICO Y POLÍTICO DE VENEZUELA, 1:1,000,000. Caracas, Dirección de Cartografía Nacional.
The best general reference map of Venezuela. Compiled and published by the official mapping agency of that country, it shows international and state boundaries, all the major cities classified by population groups, roads, railroads, pipelines, ports, airports, navigable waterways and other rivers, and relief by 500-meter contours. [A. C. Gerlach]

1148. MAPA GEOLÓGICO-TECTÓNICO DE LOS ESTADOS UNIDOS DE VENEZUELA, 1:1,000,-000. Caracas, Ministerio de Fomento, Instituto Nacional de Minería y Geología.

This map, compiled by Dr. Walter Bucher of Columbia University, is the best available geological map of Venezuela. [A. C. Gerlach]

1149. Ministerio de Obras Públicas. Comisión Nacional de Vialidad. Plan preliminar de vialidad. 2. edición. Caracas.
As an unbound atlas, this group of maps is far more valuable as an agricultural or economic atlas than as a group of road maps. For example, plate 13 is a map of agricultural production, showing by symbols eight major crops plus cattle-grazing and irrigated areas; plates 14, 15, and 16 show at 1:3,500,000 the distribution of agricultural production, cattle, and livestock products by sectors. Other plates show production, in the hinterland of Puerto Cabello, of commodities such as coffee, corn, bananas, etc. Plate 23 is a map of Venezuelan ports and port movements. [A. C. Gerlach]

1150. Vila, Marco Aurelio. Las regiones naturales de Venezuela. Caracas, Universidad Central, Facultad de Filosofía y Letras. 202 p., map.
A description of the salient features of the natural regions of Venezuela, based on investigations in the field and an intensive survey of the literature.

THE WEST INDIES

1151. Bonnet, J. A., and **M. A. Lugo López.** Soil studies in the projected Coamo irrigation area. Río Piedras, P. R., Agricultural Experiment Station (Bull. no. 88). 59 p., illus.

1152. ———, and P. Tirado Sulsona. Soil studies in Lajas Valley. Río Piedras, P. R., Agricultural Experiment Station (Bull. no. 86). 64 p., illus.

1153. Butterlin, Jacques. Contribution à l'étude de la géologie de la bordure sud du Cul-de-Sac (*Rev. soc. haïtienne hist. géog.*, v. 21, no. 76, jan., p. 3-80).
A detailed geological study of the southern edge of the Cul-de-Sac Plain, accompanied by an exhaustive bibliography. Unfortunately the photographs did not print well.

1154. Cuba. Ministerio de Hacienda. Dirección General de Estadística. Clave numérica de la división política del territorio nacional. Habana, P. Fernández. 129 p.

1155. Cucurullo, Óscar, Jr. Rasgos sobre la orogénesis y la topografía de Santo Domingo. Ciudad Trujillo, Editora del Caribe (Publ., Universidad de Santo Domingo, v. 84, serie 4, no. 2), 1950? 26 p., illus.
A delimitation of the natural regions of the Dominican Republic, based largely on the extensive field investigations of the author, Di-

rector of the Institute of Geography and Geology. References are made to the works of Vaughan and Weyl and to the recent studies of the geologists of the Standard and Seaboard oil companies.

1156. MAPA OFICIAL DE CARRETERAS DE PUERTO RICO, 1:2,000,000. Santurce, P. R., Commissioner of the Interior.

In addition to showing roads in three categories, railroads, airports, rivers, and generalized relief features, this map has a locational index and contains large scale insets on the back for the eight largest urban centers in Puerto Rico. Printed by the American Map Co., Inc., no. 8831, 1950. [A. C. Gerlach]

1157. Marrero, Leví. Geografía de Cuba. Cartografía por Gerardo Canet. Habana, ALFA. 736 p., illus.

A significant interpretation of the physical and cultural landscapes of Cuba, indispensable to those who are interested in Latin America. There is a lavish use of superb photographs on excellent paper; and there are numerous reproductions of the military map of Cuba, of relief maps, and of block diagrams. This volume will also be welcomed by non-professional readers, for Professor Marrero elicits the delicate nuances as well as the highlights in the panorama of life on the exotic and exciting island of Cuba.

1158. Picó, Rafael. The geographic regions of Puerto Rico. Río Piedras, P. R., University of Puerto Rico Press. 256 p., illus.

A balanced study of the economic and social forces operative in Puerto Rico, viewed in historical perspective against the physical background of the island, in the evolution of the present cultural landscape. A rapidly increasing population is exerting great pressure on the agricultural resources of the island, to relieve which per acre yields of crop land are being increased, industries are being fostered and migration is being encouraged to areas where migrants will be well received.

1159. Salivia, Luis Alfredo. Historia de los temporales de Puerto Rico. San Juan, P. R. xix, 393 p.

Eye-witness accounts, excerpted from newspapers and journals, of the devastation wrought by the hurricanes in Puerto Rico, listed in chronological order.

ADDENDA

1160. CARTA GEOGRÁFICA DE VENEZUELA, 1:100,000. Caracas, Dirección de Cartografía Nacional, 1948.

This set, when completed, will be the basic map of Venezuela. Approximately 20 sheets were drawn in 1948, and annual production of new sheets will eventually expand the set to 296 sheets, covering the entire country. It is a high grade topographic series, showing contours in areas of accurate surveys, formlines in other areas, roads in four categories, railroads, settlements, and state boundaries. [A. C. Gerlach]

1161. ESTADOS UNIDOS MEXICANOS, 1:100,000. México, Secretaría de la Defensa Nacional, Comisión Cartográfica Militar, 1949—.

To cover all Mexico at this scale will take more than 650 sheets, of which approximately 20 have been published to date. These are detailed maps of the area near the capital city, showing contours at 50-meter intervals, drainage and canals, railroads in eight categories, roads of five classes, communication lines, six categories of airports, pipelines, mines, cultivated areas, all known settlements, and state boundaries in detail. For detailed reference work this map set is excellent. Printed by the American Book and Printing Co., Mexico. [A. C. Gerlach]

1162. Garfias, Valentine Richard, and **Theodore C. Chapin.** Geología de México. México, Jus, 1949. 202 p., maps.

Following a discussion of different sections of Mexico there is a bibliography of 588 items. [Ed.]

1163. Nery Fernández, Felipe. Geografía de Centroamérica para los institutos y escuelas normales. 3. edición. Corregida y adaptada a las nuevas normas metodológicas de la geografía. Guatemala, Tipografía Nacional, 1949. 408 p., illus.

1164. Núñez, Enrique Bernardo. Una ojeada al mapa de Venezuela. 2. edición. Caracas, Ávila Gráfica (Col. Nuestra Tierra), 1949. 238 p.

A collection of short, pithy newspaper articles that have appeared over a period of years. The series under the general heading "Agrarian reform" is especially pertinent. In 1943 the President of Venezuela, in his message to Congress, said: "It is necessary to find land for the people, but it is just as necessary to have farmers who know how to get the most out of the land." In other words, the peasant must be educated if he is to be lifted out of his present state of poverty and stagnation.

1165. Venezuela. Ministerio de Fomento. Oficina Central del Censo Nacional. Municipio de . . . , 1:50,000–1:200,000. Caracas, 1949—.

Available only as ozalids from the worksheets, these 649 *municipio* maps cover the country. They show all known population centers, haciendas, railroads, roads and trails, as well as department, district, and *municipio* boundaries. They were prepared as bases for taking the 1950 census. A complete set is held in the Library of Congress Map Division. [A. C. Gerlach]

SOUTH AMERICA (EXCEPT BRAZIL, COLOMBIA, AND VENEZUELA)

GEORGE McCUTCHEN McBRIDE

THE year's work in the geography of this field is notable less for the number of contributions than for the substantial character of several. In Argentina, the eight-volume work on the geography of that country being sponsored by the Sociedad Argentina de Estudios Geográficos Gaea is the most ambitious undertaking of its kind yet attempted. It will probably be for many years the standard reference work, particularly on the physical aspects of the country. Volumes on human geography are to follow. The set of publications being issued on the soils of the various sections of Argentina (see items 1188, 1194) add details not found elsewhere. For Chile, the *Geografía económica*, while far less extensive than the Argentine study, will be a good reference work. Sauer's interpretation of the geography of the continent offers a condensed statement that will be useful to all serious students (see item 1129.)

In particular regions, the papers on the Amazon Hylaea (items 1223 and 1228), those on the Bolivian altiplano (items 1199 and 1201) and the volume of notes on Ecuador add information regarding little-known districts. The mountain-climbing and exploration in the Cordillera Blanca throw much light on that difficult zone. The explorations in the Antarctic by the Rønne expedition are not only spectacular but offer much new information regarding that region where many interests center.

All in all, these works represent greater than normal activity in the field.

GENERAL

1166. Boffi, Jorge Alberto. Los efectos de los Andes en la circulación aérea sobre la parte austral de Sur América (*Rev. meteorol.*, año 9, no. 34, julio, p. 107-112, maps).

1167. Rønne, Finn. Erobring i Antarktis. Historien om Rønne-ekspedisjonen 1946-1948. Oversatt av Jakob R. Sverdrup. Oslo, Norway, Gyldendal. 189 p., illus.
Translation of *Antarctic conquest*, published in 1949 (New York, Putnam, xx, 299 p.); account of notable explorations made during winter spent on Palmer Peninsula.

ARGENTINA

1168. Angelelli, Victorio. Recursos minerales de la República Argentina. 1. Yacimientos metalíferos. Buenos Aires, Ministerio de Educación (Revista del Instituto Nacional de Investigación de las Ciencias Naturales, Ciencias Geológicas, t. 2). xv, 542 p., illus.
A useful reference work for the geographer; arranged by materials, with maps and block diagrams.

1169. Auer, Väinö. Las capas volcánicas como base de la cronología postglacial de Fuegopatagonia. Buenos Aires, Ministerio de Agricultura y Ganadería, Instituto de Suelos y Agrotecnia (Publ. no. 9). 208 p., illus., maps.

1170. Cordini, I. Rafael. Contribución al conocimiento de los cuerpos salinos de Argentina. Colorada Grande; Choiqué; cuerpos salinos en la fosa de Utracán-Acha; salitral y salina de Pocitos; Salinas Chicas y Chasico. Buenos Aires, Ministerio de Industria y Comercio, Dirección General de Industria Minera (Anales, 3). 85 p., maps.

1171. Daus, Federico A. (comp.). Guía de geógrafos de la República Argentina (*Bol. soc. arg. estud. geog. Gaea*, no. 27, sept., p. 25-42).

1172. ———. La supuesta captura del río Fénix. Buenos Aires, Universidad de Buenos Aires, Facultad de Filosofía y Letras, Instituto de Geografía (Serie A, no. 14). 52 p., diagrams, illus., maps.

1173. Díaz Molano, Elías. Rumbo a la Antártida argentina (*Rev. geog. amer.*, v. 33, no. 196-201, enero-junio, p. 83-94).

1174. Echenique, Juan B., and Lindor Novillo Corvalán. Notas de geografía argentina. Córdoba, Imprenta de la Universidad. 214 p., illus.
An attempt to summarize and simplify the geography of the country (including the Falk-

land Islands and a segment of Artarctica) for student use.

1175. Feruglio, Egidio. Descripción geológica de la Patagonia. V. 1-3. Buenos Aires, Ministerio de Industria y Comercio, Dirección General de Yacimientos Petrolíferos Fiscales. V. 1-2, 1949, 334, 349 p.; v. 3, 1950, 431 p.

1176. Gentili, Carlos A. Descripción geológica de la hoja 35c, Ramón M. Castro (Neuquén). Carta geológico-económica de la República Argentina, escala 1:200,-000. Buenos Aires, Ministerio de Industria y Comercio, Dirección General de Industria Minera (Bol. no. 72). 42 p., map, photographs, and profiles.
Some details of topography and hydrology.

1177. González Bonorino, Félix. Descripción de la hoja 13e, Villa Alberdi, Provincia de Tucumán. Carta geológico-económica de la República Argentina, escala 1:200,000. Buenos Aires, Ministerio de Industria y Comercio, Dirección General de Industria Minera (Bol. no. 74). 77 p., map.

1178. ————. Geología y petrografía de las hojas 12d (Capillitas) y 13d (Andalgalá). Carta geológico-económica de la República Argentina, escala 1:200,000. Buenos Aires, Ministerio de Industria y Comercio, Dirección General de Industria Minera (Bol. no. 70). 99 p., plates, maps.

1179. Greca, Alcides. Una nueva capital para la Nación Argentina. Rosario, Ciencia. 140 p.
A plea for the transfer of the capital toward the interior. The growth of Buenos Aires, according to this author, has thrown the entire life of the nation out of balance. A single city acquires too great a dominance when it has more than 3,000,000 out of the nation's 16,000,-000 people, enjoys most of the export and import trade, is the center of railroads, roads, and airlines, and wields commensurate political power. The author advocates the establishment of a new capital in the province of Córdoba and the creation of a new central foreign trade port at Córdoba.

1180. Instituto Geográfico Militar. Anuario. V. 11. Años 1947-1949. Buenos Aires. 101 p., maps.

1181. Lambert, Luis R. Informe geológico sobre un proyecto de embalse del Río Chubut en Colonia Florentino Ameghino (Territorio del Chubut). Buenos Aires, Ministerio de Industria y Comercio, Dirección General de Industria Minera (Bol. no. 71). 39 p., maps, illus., sketches.
Some detailed geographic description.

1182. Luchini, R. Il sud mendozino e la sua agricultura (*Riv. agric. subtrop. trop.,* v. 44, no. 10-12, ott.-dic., p. 229-264).

1183. Manzi, Francisco. Ríos, arroyos y lagunas del interior de Corrientes (*Rev. geog. amer.,* v. 33, no. 196-201, enero-junio, p. 35-38, map).

1184. MAPA DE LA REPÚBLICA ARGENTINA, 1:5,000,000. Buenos Aires, Ejército Argentino, Instituto Geográfico Militar.
This is the third edition of a popular general map of Argentina. It shows the provinces in contrasting colors, a multitude of cities and towns, roads, railroads, canals, rivers, and relief features by means of shading. The utility of the map would be greatly increased by an index to place names. This map is also available at 1:10,000,000. [A. C. Gerlach]

1185. MAPA DE LOS FERROCARRILES ARGENTINOS, 1:2,000,000. Buenos Aires, Ministerio de Transportes.
An eight-color map which shows, in addition to all railroad lines of the country, the provinces in contrasting colors, relief by hachures, drainages, and passes as wide, medium, and narrow. [A. C. Gerlach]

1186. MAPA GEOLÓGICO DE LA REPÚBLICA ARGENTINA, 1:2,500,000. Prepared by the Dirección de Geología, Servicio Geológico. Buenos Aires, Ministerio de Industria y Comercio, Dirección General de Industria Minera.
Although based on data compiled in 1945, this three-sheet map is the most detailed and accurate geological map of the whole country. 35 geological formations are delineated, and a 28-page booklet was also published as Boletín 73 (Ministerio de Industria y Comercio, no. 86) to explain the map and describe the sources of information. [A. C. Gerlach]

1187. Olascoaga, M. J. Some aspects of Argentine rainfall (*Tellus,* v. 2, no. 4, Nov., p. 312-318, maps).

1188. Quevedo, Casiano V. (and others). Problemas agropecuarios del oeste de Formosa. Buenos Aires, Ministerio de Agricultura y Ganadería, Dirección General de Investigaciones Agrícolas, Instituto de Suelos y Agrotecnia (Publ. no. 12). 21 p., illus.

1189. REPÚBLICA ARGENTINA. RED CAMINERA PRINCIPAL. Approximate scale 1:5,000,-000. Buenos Aires, Ministerio de Obras Públicas, Administración General de Parques Nacionales y Turismo; and Automóvil Club Argentino.
The map is designed for tourist use. It shows roads in seven categories, distances in kilometers, drainage, shaded relief, state boundaries, and population centers. On the back is a pictorial

view of Argentina showing the location and names of 20 national parks or recreation centers, with airline distances from Buenos Aires. [A. C. Gerlach]

1190. **Riggi, Agustín Eduardo.** La Antártida argentina. Su geografía y su geología. Buenos Aires, Museo Argentino de Ciencias Naturales Bernardino Rivadavia (Extensión Cultural y Didáctica, no. 4). 32 p., map.

1191. **Sociedad Argentina de Estudios Geográficos Gaea.** Geografía de la República Argentina. Buenos Aires, Coni. T. 1, 1947, xi, 304 p., illus., maps; t. 3, 1946, 360 p., illus.; t. 4, 1946, 542 p., illus.; t. 5, 1946, 498 p., chart, maps, tables; t. 6, 1947, 432 p., maps, tables; t. 8, 1950, 558 p., illus.
Intended to be a complete and authoritative work, eight volumes on physical geography will be published; all were prepared by the leading geographers of the country. The volumes are enriched by well selected photographs and a few good maps. A work on human geography is also to be issued.

1192. **Sparn, Enrique.** Bibliografía de la geología, mineralogía y paleontología de la República Argentina (incluso de la Antártida americana). Parte 11, años 1946-1949 (*Bol. acad. nac. cien.*, Córdoba, t. 39, entregas 1-2, p. 77-210).

1193. ————. Bibliografía de los yacimientos de minerales y rocas de aplicación de la provincia de Córdoba (Argentina) (*Rev. univ. nac. Córdoba*, año 37, no. 3-4, julio-oct., p. 927-964).

1194. **Zaffanella, Marino J. R.,** and **Noel C. Uriona.** Contribución al conocimiento de la fertilidad de algunos suelos de la región de Concordia, por medio de técnicas analíticas rápidas. Buenos Aires, Ministerio de Agricultura y Ganadería, Dirección General de Investigaciones Agrícolas, Instituto de Suelos y Agrotecnia. 8 p., map.

BOLIVIA

1195. **Escobar V., Ismael.** Anteproyecto para el observatorio de física cósmica de Chacaltaya (*Nimbus,* año 2, v. 2, no. 5, enero-marzo, p. 3-23).
Of particular interest is the description of the meteorological observatory maintained at the ski run on Mount Chacaltaya, at an elevation of 5,280 meters, about 25 miles from La Paz.

1196. **Flores, Domingo.** Las aguas potables de Potosí. Potosí, Universidad Mayor

Tomás Frías, Departamento de Cultura (Cuadernos universitarios, serie 3, año 1, v. 1, no. 1, enero). 61 p.

1197. MAPA DE LA REPÚBLICA DE BOLIVIA. RED GENERAL DE CAMINOS, 1: 2,000,000. Drawn by Jorge García Meza C. La Paz, Ministerio de Obras Públicas, Dirección General de Vialidad.
For its size (approximately 30 inches square) this is a good road map. The drainage and shaded relief are generalized and lacking in detail, but features pertinent to the transportation pattern are emphasized. Roads are shown in eight categories, with separate symbols for national and department roads, including route numbers. Railroads, navigable waterways, and ports are also included. An inset of the Americas shows the Pan American Highway's general route. [A. C. Gerlach]

1198. **Ministerio de Agricultura. Dirección General de Tierras y Colonización.** Zonas colonizables de Bolivia. La Paz, Kollasuyo. 47 p.

1199. **Stenz, Edward.** Condiciones climatológicas del altiplano de Bolivia (*Nimbus,* año 2, no. 6-7, abril-sept., p. 3-23).
Gives new climatic data, especially for Oruro.

1200. UNITED NATIONS PRESENTATION MAP OF BOLIVIA, 1:3,000,000. United Nations, Presentation Branch (no. 235).
Based on *Mapa general de la República de Bolivia,* 1:1,000,000, 1934, this map brings down to date the presentation of roads in two categories, railroads, pipelines, and airports. It shows drainage, relief in color, departmental boundaries, and a large number of place names for its scale. It is an excellent general reference map of Bolivia for desk or office use. [A. C. Gerlach]

1201. **Zabaleta, Julio.** La temperatura en la ciudad de Oruro (*Nimbus,* año 2, no. 6-7, abril-sept., p. 41-56).
A plea for the orientation of streets and houses at 45 degrees from the cardinal points so as to provide better insolation, where insolation is, in many cases, the only source of heat.

CHILE

1202. **Almeyda Arroyo, Elías.** Pluviometría de las zonas del desierto y las estepas cálidas de Chile. Santiago, Editorial Universitaria, 1950? 162 p., maps.

1203. **Biese, Walter.** Estudios geomorfológicos de los yacimientos de guano situados entre Arica y Antofagasta. Santiago, Universo. 110 p.

1204. **Brattström, Hans.** Puerto Montt, Chiles Tromsö (*Jorden runt,* årg. 22, no. 12, des., p. 525-540, map).

1205. Brüggen M., Juan. Fundamentos de la geología de Chile. Santiago, Instituto Geográfico Militar. 374 p., figs., illus., map.
Much of this is geomorphology. It is a useful reference work for a geographer.

1206. ———. Geología. 2. edición corregida. Santiago, Nascimento. 510 p., illus., maps.
Much geographic data on Chile.

1207. Corporación de Fomento de la Producción. Fundación Pedro Aguirre Cerda. Geografía económica de Chile. T. 1-2. Santiago, Imprenta Universitaria. xxx, 428 p.; xvii, 545 p., tables, maps.
This three-volume work (of which only the first and second volumes have been published) aims to provide a thorough treatment of the economic geography of Chile. A joint enterprise of several leading Chilean men of science, it is largely the work of Dr. Humberto Fuenzalida Villegas, professor of geography at the University of Chile. The first and second volumes treat of the physical basis, and the third will deal with the several branches of economic activity, and will include a monographic description of each of the six regions into which the authors divide the country. When completed this should constitute the standard modern reference work on the geography of Chile. See item 723.

1208. Cristi, J. M., and H. F. Williams. Bosquejo geológico de Chile, 1:3,000,000. Santiago, Instituto Geográfico Militar.
Nineteen geological formations are shown in color. The map was carefully compiled from the most recent and accurate, detailed studies of Chilean areas and constituted the best available summary of the country's geology at the time of its publication. [A. C. Gerlach]

1209. Guía de Chile. Santiago, Instituto Geográfico Militar, 1949-1950.
Aside from a pictorial, tourist map of central Chile, 32-34 degrees south latitude, showing highways, railroads, airports, amusement centers, and resorts, this guidebook is concerned primarily with three cities. It contains maps of Santiago, Valparaíso, and Viña del Mar, showing street names, parks, public buildings, and transport routes listed in a 200-page gazetteer that accompanies the maps. [A. C. Gerlach]

1210. Instituto Geográfico Militar. Informes técnicos presentados a la V Reunión Panamericana de Consulta sobre Cartografía, en Santiago, 16 al 23 de octubre de 1950. 38 p., maps.

1211. McAllister, J. F., Héctor Flores W., and Carlos Ruiz F. Quicksilver deposits of Chile. Washington, U. S. Government Printing Office (Geologic Investigations in the American Republics, 1949. Geological Survey Bulletin 964-E). P. iv, 361-400, fold. maps.
Published in cooperation with the Departamento de Minas y Petróleo, Chile, under the auspices of the U. S. Interdepartmental Committee on Scientific and Cultural Cooperation.

1212. White, C. Langdon. Chile. Nation with the long reach (*Pac. disc.,* v. 3, no. 6, Nov.-Dec., p. 4-12, illus., maps).
Concluded in v. 4, no. 2, March-April, 1951, p. 22-29.

ECUADOR

1213. Andrade Marín, Luciano. La bibliografía geográfica ecuatoriana y los geógrafos ecuatorianos (*An. univ. cent. Ecuador,* t. 77, no. 328, enero-dic., 1949, i.e. 1950, p. 19-38).
Brief evaluation of the work done by some Ecuadorean geographers, particularly by Maldonado, considered the father of geography in Ecuador.

1214. Ferdon, Edwin N., Jr. Studies in Ecuadorian geography. With the collaboration of Malcolm H. Bissell in "The Climates of Ecuador" and an appendix by William C. Steere, "The Phytogeography of Ecuador." Santa Fe, N. Mex., School of American Research (Monographs, no. 15) and University of Southern California. 86 p., illus., maps.
Three valuable contributions: Ferdon's "notes" are written from an ethnographic angle but are full of geographic details based on careful observations in many out-of-the-way places; the climate study, a good summary; the phytogeographic paper, valuable. Climatic map, based on Koppen classification; ethnic map. Embodies results of war-time exploration for cinchona.

1215. Hearn, Lea T. A geographic study of the village of Cotocollao, Ecuador (*Jour. geog.,* v. 49, no. 6, Sept., p. 225-231).
Intimate description of a little highland Indian town.

1216. Mapa físico-político, 1:800,000. Guayaquil, Büchner Pérez Castro.
Designed for classroom use, this map has altitude layer tints in nine colors and ocean depths in six shades. In addition to relief and drainage, it shows the principal cities, roads, railroads, and passes. There is an inset of the Galápagos Islands at the same scale. [A. C. Gerlach]

1217. Ministerio de Educación Pública. Observatorio Astronómico. Servicio Meteorológico del Ecuador. Resúmenes anuales correspondientes a 1944, 1945, 1946, 1947 (Bol. meteorológico no. 3). Quito. 94 p.

1218. Moore, Robert Thomas. The first ascent of El Sangay (*Nat. hist.,* v. 59, no. 5, May, p. 216-221, 238-239; no. 6, June, p. 272-277, 286-287).

Well told account of a notable achievement. Illus., maps.

1219. Oppenheim, Victor. The structure of Ecuador (*Amer. jour. sci.,* v. 248, no. 8, Aug., p. 527-539).
Geomorphic summary. Map.

1220. Sauer, Walter. Contribuciones para el conocimiento del cuaternario en el Ecuador (*An. univ. cent. Ecuador,* t. 77, no. 328, enero-dic., 1949, i.e. 1950, p. 327-364).
Summary of observations made during many years while the author has been professor of geology in the university at Quito.

1221. Semanate, Alberto D. Sismología del terremoto de Pelileo. Fotografías del autor y de Eduardo Mena. Quito, Casa de la Cultura Ecuatoriana. 103 p.

PERU

1222. Cornejo Bouroncle, Jorge. Introducción a la geografía económica general, de América y del Perú. Cuzco, Universidad Nacional del Cuzco. 665 p.
Intended as a text for students in the Facultad de Ciencias Económicas y Comerciales of the National University of Cuzco, where the study of geography has recently been introduced. 440 of the 658 pages are devoted to world geography, the remainder to Peru. Consequently little new has been introduced, though data are brought fairly well up to date or nearly so (1946). There is some little known information regarding fishing, the growing of tea, and colonization. No maps or illustrations.

1223. Habich, Eduardo de (ed.). Informe sobre el Huallaga. Expedición científica a su cuenca central, emprendida por la UNESCO con acuerdo del Gobierno del Perú. Lima, Ministerio de Relaciones Exteriores, Organismo Coordinador de la Hilea Amazónica Peruana. 224 p., illus., maps.
Contents: Doran, Edwin, Jr., *Informe geográfico.* Weiss H., Pedro, *Informe médico.* Buitrón, Aníbal, *Informe etnológico.* Ferreyra, Ramón, *Informe botánico.* Doran's contribution adds important details to knowledge of region.

1224. Kinzl, Hans, and Erwin Schneider. Cordillera Blanca (Peru). Innsbruck, Austria, Universitäts Verlag Wagner. 167 p., illus., map.
An excellent map (scale, 1:200,000) and a set of over 100 well selected and well taken photographs make this a notable volume. Its brief pages of text add many facts regarding the cordillera itself, its vegetation, its climate, its animal life and its human inhabitants, including also some description of the Callejón de Huaylas. Most striking are its pictures of the numerous snow-covered peaks, glaciers, glacial lakes, and moraines of great variety. Resulting from several years' exploration by members of the Alpenverein, this work contributes greatly to the hitherto scant information regarding this magnificent mountain range. German text. Abridged text in Spanish and English.

1225. McDowell, Bart. Opening the fabled Santa. Beset by danger, vast Peruvian project unlocks isolated, radiant Andean region (*Travel,* v. 94, no. 6, June, p. 14-17).

1226. MAPA DEL PERÚ, 1:1,000,000. Lima, Ministerio de Guerra, Instituto Geográfico Militar.
In eight sheets, this is the most complete, up-to-date map of Peru for general use. It shows drainage in detail, relief by contours at 500-meter intervals, internal administrative boundaries, roads in six categories, railroads, airports, canals, natural resource fields for petroleum, metals, etc., and even the smallest settlements. [A. C. Gerlach]

1226a. Núñez del Prado, Óscar. Aspecto económico de Virú, una comunidad de la costa norte del Perú (*Rev. univ.,* Cuzco, año 39, no. 99, 2. semestre, p. 85-150, map).

1227. Pareja Paz Soldán, José. Geografía del Perú. V. 1-2. Lima, Librería Internacional del Perú. 238, 219 p.
Treated topically rather than regionally. V. 1 is devoted to physical geography and is poor. V. 2 is full of accurate, up-to-date economic data. No illustrations; maps utilize little of excellent cartographic material being developed in Peru.

1228. Ruëgg, Werner, and Douglas Fyfe. Algunos aspectos sobre la estructuración de la cuenca del Alto Amazonas (*Bol. inst. sudamer. petról.,* v. 3, no. 2, mayo, p. 9-29, map).

1229. Schmid, Karl. Eisgipfel unter Tropensonne. Bergfahrten und Reiseerlebnisse in Peru. Bern, Aars-Verlag. 215 p., photos.
Account of mountaineering in the high Andes of central Peru, with a few striking photographs.

1230. Schull, Herman W., Jr. Engineering of the Incas (*Milit. eng.,* v. 42, no. 286, March-April, p. 112-115, map).

1231. Villanueva Urteaga, Horacio. El terremoto del Cuzco (*Rev. univ.,* Cuzco, año 39, no. 98, 1. semestre, p. 233-251).

1232. Waerum, J. Vandkraft omkring Lima (*Kulturgeografi,* 2. årg., Juni, p. 129-133).

URUGUAY

1233. Bergeiro, José María. La influencia marítima en el clima del Uruguay (*Rev.*

meteorol., año 9, no. 35, oct., p. 151-168, maps).

1234. Pochintesta, Alberto. Síntesis de la estructura geológica de la República Oriental del Uruguay (*Rev. uruguaya geog.,* año 1, no. 1, marzo-mayo, p. 58-69).
A promising beginning in the work of this new publication. Map.

1235. Rocchetti, G. Cenni pedologici sull' Uruguay (*Riv. agric. subtrop. trop.,* v. 44, no. 10-12, ott.-dic., p. 265-275, map).

1236. Ureta Martínez, Horacio. Mapa de la República Oriental del Uruguay, 1:800,-000. Montevideo, Impresora Uruguaya.
This is a good transportation map of Uruguay, showing roads in four categories plus those under construction, railroads, and airports, against a strong background of detailed drainage, colorful departmental boundaries, and numerous settlements. [A. C. Gerlach]

ADDENDA

1237. Dagnino Pastore, Lorenzo. La minería argentina en el decenio 1936-1945. Buenos Aires, Universidad de Buenos Aires, Facultad de Ciencias Económicas, Instituto de la Producción (Publ. no. 11), 1949. 26 p.

1238. Egler, Válter Alberto. A colonização no norte da Argentina e sudoeste do Paraguai (*Bol. geog.,* ano 7, no. 81, dez., 1949, p. 931-941, map).

1239. Groeber, Pablo. Resumen preliminar de las observaciones realizadas en el viaje a la región al sur de Bahía Blanca en enero, 1947. La Plata, Argentina, Universidad Nacional de la Plata (Notas del Museo de la Plata, t. 14, Geología, no. 57, p. 239-266), 1949.

1240. Keller, Frank L. Geography of the Lake Titicaca basin of Bolivia. A comparative study of great landed estates and highland Indian communities. 1949. 113 p., illus., maps.
Mainly a description of land tenure, but with much geographical detail and effective use of maps and photographs. Thesis, University of Maryland.

1242. Paulsen Bruna, Carlos. La Cordillera Pelada (provincias de Osorno y Llanquihue) (*Rev. chil. hist. geog.,* no. 114, julio-dic., 1949, p. 151-168).

1243. Pérez, Martín. La explotación de las aguas subterráneas en la provincia de Mendoza (*Bol. estud. geog.,* v. 1, no. 5, 4. trimestre, 1949, p. 11-32).

1244. Pérez-Moreau, Román A. La palabra *pampa* en fitogeografía. Buenos Aires, Ministerio de Educación (Revista del Instituto Nacional de Investigación de las Ciencias Naturales, Ciencias Botánicas, t. 1, no. 5), 1949, p. 131-178.
Summaries in French, English, and German; bibliography; maps.

1245. Rodríguez Z., Manuel. Reconocimiento de los suelos de la provincia de Bío-Bío. (*Agric. técnica,* año 9, no. 2, dic., 1949, p. 134-161).
Sixteen soil series in six broad groups, together with land use, erosion (with map), and conservation, with detailed soil map. Illus. Also issued as a separate.

1246. Szepessy Schaurek, Ali de. Cordillera-Blanca. Expedition, 1948, des akademischen Alpenclubs, Zürich (In *Berge der Welt,* 3. Band, Bern, Schweizerische Stiftung für Alpine Forschungen, Zürich, Switzerland, 1949, p. 159-166).

1247. Velasco, Matilde Irene. La olivicultura en la República Argentina (*Bol. estud. geog.,* v. 1, no. 4, 3. trimestre, 1949, p. 11-27, map).

1248. Vergara y Lara, Eraclides. Estudio geográfico de la campiña de Yungay (Travaux de l'Institut Français d'Études Andines, t. 1, Paris-Lima, 1949, p. 59-106, illus.).

BRAZIL

PRESTON E. JAMES AND HILGARD O'REILLY STERNBERG

THIS section continues to be under the joint authorship indicated above.

Brazilian geography is being actively pursued in Brazil by three groups: the geographers employed in the Conselho Nacional de Geografia, an agency of the Federal Government which is a part of the Instituto Brasileiro de Geografia e Estatística (IBGE); the geographers in university positions, especially at the University of Brazil, Rio de Janeiro; and the active group at the University of São Paulo (chairman, Aroldo de Azevedo). In 1950 Leo Waibel completed his several years in Brazil; Francis Ruellan continued his work; and in 1948 and 1945-1950, Clarence F. Jones and Preston E. James carried on field studies in Central Brazil and in the Northeast as technical consultants. [P. E. James]

PHYSICAL GEOGRAPHY

1249. Ab'sáber, Aziz Nacib, and Miguel Costa Júnior. Contribuição ao estudo do Sudoeste Goiano (*Bol. paulista geog.*, no. 4, março, p. 3-26).
A competent outline of the geomorphology of a region which structurally and geologically represents an extension of the Southern Plateau. Illus. [H. O. Sternberg]

1250. Almeida, Fernando P. M. de. Relevo de "cuestas" na bacia sedimentar do Rio Paraná, Brasil (*Comptes rendus cong. int. géog.*, t. 2, p. 762-771, figs., plates).

1251. Azevedo, Aroldo de. Regiões climato-botânicas do Brasil (*Bol. paulista geog.*, no. 6, out., p. 32-43).
Various climatic systems on very small-scale maps, compared with broad divisions of vegetation. [H. O. Sternberg]

1252. Bittencourt, Agnelo. Esbôço para um perfil da Amazônia (*Bol. soc. bras. geog.*, ano 1, no. 3, nov.-dez., p. 72-81).

1253. Bölau, Edm. Berggrundsstruktur och ytgestaltning samt deras kulturgeografiska betydelse i centrala Minas Gerais, Brasilien (*Svensk geog. årsbok*, årg. 26, p. 84-101).
Geologic structure and morphology and their importance as culture-geographic factors in central Minas Gerais. [P. E. James]

1254. Dansereau, Pierre. Ecological problems of Southeastern Brazil (*Sci. month.*, v. 71, no. 2, Aug., p. 71-84, illus.)

1255. Duque, J. Guimarães. Apreciações sôbre os solos do Nordeste. Conservação da fertilidade e economia da agua (*Bol. geog.*, ano 8, no. 93, dez., p. 1033-1071).

1256. Ferraz, J. de Sampaio. Iminência duma "grande" sêca nordestina (*Rev. bras. geog.*, ano 12, no. 1, jan.-março, p. 3-12, graph, table).

1257. Gomes, Carlos. A Cordilheira Mestra e as planícies fluminenses (*An. geog. estado Rio de Janeiro*, no. 3, p. 49-60).

1258. Guerra, Antônio Teixeira. Contribuição ao estudo da geomorfologia e do quaternário do litoral de Laguna, Santa

Catarina (*Rev. bras. geog.*, ano 12, no. 4, out.-dez., p. 535-561, figs., maps, plates).

1259. Maack, Reinhard. Notas complementares à apresentação preliminar do mapa fitogeográfico do Estado do Paraná, Brasil (*Bol. geog.*, ano 8, no. 87, junho, p. 338-343).
See item 1260.

1260. ————, and Rudolfo Doubek. Mapa fitogeográfico do Estado do Paraná, 1:750,000. Curitiba, Secretaria de Agricultura, Industria e Comércio em colaboração com o Instituto Nacional do Pinho.
21 vegetation associations are mapped in color over a detailed drainage background for the State of Paraná. Roads, railroads, and the principal cities are shown. There is also a profile and geological section from the Paraná River to the Atlantic. [A. C. Gerlach]

1261. Machado, Floriano Peixoto. Contribuição ao estudo do clima do Rio Grande do Sul. Rio de Janeiro, Conselho Nacional de Geografia, Instituto Brasileiro de Geografia e Estatística, Serviço Gráfico. 91 p., maps, tables.

1262. Moraes, João de Mello. Aspectos da escarpa devoniana Paranaense-Paulista (*An. serv. geog. exér.*, no. 2, 1949, i.e. 1950, p. 85-96, illus., map).

1263. Morais, Luciano Jaques de. Os recursos naturais do vale do Rio Doce (*Bol. soc. bras. geog.*, ano 1, no. 3, nov.-dez., p. 67-71).

1264. Oliveira, Lejeune de. Levantamento biogeográfico da Baía da Guanabara (*Mem. inst. Oswaldo Cruz*, t. 48, p. 363-391).
Reprinted in *Bol. geog.*, ano 8, no. 69, agôsto, 1950, p. 534-559, illus. [H. O. Sternberg]

1265. Romariz, Dora de Amarante (and others). Mapa da vegetação original das regiões central, sul e da mata, do Estado de Minas Gerais (*Comptes rendus cong. int. géog.*, t. 2, Travaux des Sections 2 et 3, p. 831-847, maps).

1266. Roque, Jorge Pereira de la. Viagem ao Amapá (*Rev. bras. geog.*, ano 12, no. 2, abril-junho, p. 291-328).

1267. **Ruellan, Francis.** Les surfaces d'érosion de la région sub-orientale du plateau central brésilien (*Comptes rendus cong. int. géog.*, t. 2, Travaux des Sections 2 et 3, p. 659-673, fig., plates).

1268. **Soares, Lucio de Castro.** Observações sôbre a morfologia das margens do Baixo-Amazonas e Baixo-Tapajós, Pará, Brasil (*Comptes rendus cong. int. géog.*, t. 2, p. 748-761, figs., plates).

1269. **Souza, Elza Coelho de.** Águas da Prata, uma estância mineral (*Bol. carioca geog.*, ano 3, no. 4, p. 14-29, illus.).

1270. **Sternberg, Hilgard O'Reilly.** Floods and landslides in the Paraíba Valley, December, 1948 (*Conserv. amer.*, no. 8, April, p. 2-20).
A translation of an important report. See *HLAS, no. 15, 1949*, item 1245. [P. E. James]

1271. ————. Vales tectônicos na planície amazônica? (*Rev. bras. geog.*, ano 12, no. 4, out.-dez., p. 511-529, figs., maps., plates).
Attention is directed to a rectangular drainage pattern in a region of essentially horizontal strata and the possibility of an explanation related to stresses caused by sedimentary loading is advanced. [H. O. Sternberg]

1272. **Wilhelmy, Herbert.** Zur Klimatologie des Alto-Paraná Gebietes in Südamerika (*Pet. geog. mitt.*, 94. Jahrgang, 3. Quartalsheft, p. 130-139).
Discussion of Köppen's system revised by new information, and related to limits of a long list of crops. Frost resistance of crops in centigrade degrees. Two maps: rainfall and climates. [P. E. James]

ECONOMIC GEOGRAPHY

1273. **Araujo, Ely Goulart Pereira de.** Alguns aspectos da paisagem rural no município de Olímpia (*Bol. paulista geog.*, no. 5, julho, p. 12-22).
A type study in the plateau of western São Paulo, area of rapid growth followed by stagnation. [P. E. James]

1274. **Bernardes, Lysia Maria Cavalcanti, and Nilo Bernardes.** A pesca no litoral do Rio de Janeiro (*Rev. bras. geog.*, ano 12, no. 1, jan.-março, p. 17-50, illus.).

1275. **Bondar, Gregório.** Culturas tropicais para o Estado do Rio de Janeiro (*An. geog. estado Rio de Janeiro*, no. 3, p. 135-160).

1276. ————. As possibilidades econômicas do centro do Estado da Bahia (*Rev.*

bras. geog., ano 12, no. 14, out.-dez., p. 614-620).

1277. **Castelo Branco, José M. B.** Economia acreana (*Bol. soc. bras. geog.*, ano 1, no. 2, set.-out., p. 35-40).

1278. **Corrêa, Virgílio.** Cidades serranas. Teresópolis, Nova Friburgo, Petrópolis (*An. geog. estado Rio de Janeiro*, no. 3, p. 61-104).

1279. **Cruz, Ruth Bouchaud Lopes da.** Notas sôbre a ocurrência do caroá no Nordeste (*Bol. carioca geog.*, ano 3, no. 4, p. 30-40, map).

1280. **Gourou, Pierre.** Observações geográficas na Amazônia (*Rev. bras. geog.*, ano 12, no. 2, abril-junho, p. 171-246, plates).
An important contribution to the geographical literature on the Brazilian Amazon. [H. O. Sternberg]

1281. **Jones, Clarence F.** A fazenda Miranda em Mato Grosso (*Rev. bras. geog.*, ano 12, no. 3, julho-set., p. 353-370, graphs, plates, maps; no. 4, out.-dez., p. 587-588).

1282. **Lamego, Alberto Ribeiro.** O homem e a serra. Rio de Janeiro, Conselho Nacional de Geografia (*Bibl. geog. bras.*, série A, Livros, publ. no. 8). 350 p., illus., maps.
With the same thoroughness with which he elaborated his previous monographs, *O homem e o brejo* (1940), *O homem e a restinga* (1946), and *O homem e a Guanabara* (see *HLAS, no. 14, 1948*, item 1553), Lamego brings together in this volume an impressive array of geological and historical materials. His object is to describe and explain the cultural landscapes of the mountainous area which encompasses the middle Paraíba Valley. In contrast with the variety of natural landscapes, coffee played the part of a common denominator in the settlement of the area. [H. O. Sternberg]

1283. **Lopes, Lucas.** O vale do São Francisco. Experiência de planejamento regional (*Rev. bras. geog.*, ano 12, no. 1, jan.-março, p. 122-136, maps).

1284. **Mattos, Dirceu Lino.** Contribuição ao estudo da vinha em São Paulo. A região de São Roque (*Bol. paulista geog.*, no. 4, março, p. 27-47).
The author, professor of economic geography at the University of São Paulo, presents an able sketch of the natural and cultural factors responsible for the presence of an island of vineyards in the traditional landscape of coffee and cotton. Illus. [H. O. Sternberg]

1285. **Melo, Beatriz Célia Correia de.** Interpretação do mapa de produção de café no sudeste do Planalto Central do Brasil (*Rev. bras. geog.*, ano 12, no. 1, jan.-março, p. 73-87, fold. map, plates).

1286. Mendes, Renato da Silveira. Paisagens culturais da Baixada Fluminense. São Paulo, Universidade de São Paulo, Faculdade de Filosofia, Ciências e Letras (Bol. 90, Geografia no. 4). 171 p., illus., maps.
A doctoral dissertation which makes a noteworthy contribution to the cultural geography of the coastal plain in the vicinity of Rio de Janeiro. [H. O. Sternberg]

1287. Oliveira, Beneval de. Contribuição para a divisão regional do Estado do Paraná (*Rev. bras. geog.*, ano 12, no. 1, jan.-março, p. 55-71, maps, plates).

1288. Pendleton, Robert L. Agricultural and forestry potentialities of the tropics (*Agron. jour.*, v. 42, no. 3, March, p. 115-123).
A realistic appraisal of tropical problems, with some material from Brazil's coffee lands. [P. E. James]

1289. Silva, Moacir M. F. Uma estrada de ferro do Nordeste (*Rev. bras. geog.*, ano 12, no. 1, jan.-março, p. 97-121).

1290. Simões, Ruth Matos Almeida. Distribuição da produção do arroz no sudoeste do Planalto Central (*Rev. bras. geog.*, ano 12, no. 2, abril-junho, p. 269-283, fold. map, plates).

1291. ————. Interpretação do mapa de produção de cana de açúcar no sudeste do Planalto Central (*Rev. bras. geog.*, ano 12, no. 3, julho-set., p. 371-378, fold. map, plates).

1292. Streiff-Becker, Rudolph. Neue Entwicklungen in Zentralbrasilien (*Geog. helvetica*, Jahrgang 5, Nr. 3, Juli, p. 171-180).
A report on the Goiás frontier. Summaries in French and Italian. [P. E. James]

1293. Vieira, Flávio. Ferrovias nordestinas (*Bol. soc. bras. geog.*, ano 1, no. 1, julho-agôsto, p. 5-10).

1294. ————. Linhas integrantes do sistema ferroviário brasileiro (*Bol. geog.*, ano 8, no. 86, maio, p. 133-150; no. 87, junho, p. 287-300).

POPULATION AND SETTLEMENT

1295. Azevedo, Aroldo de. Geografia humana do Brasil. São Paulo, Companhia Editôra Nacional. 268 p., illus., maps.

Text, offering a valuable collection of data for a general up-to-date view of the geography of Brazil. [P. E. James]

1296. Bernardes, Lysia Maria Cavalcanti. Distribuição da população no Estado do Paraná em 1940 (*Rev. bras. geog.*, ano 12, no. 4, out.-dez., p. 562-582, maps, plates).

1297. Camargo, Felisberto Cardoso de. Terra e colonização no antigo e novo quarternário da zona da Estrada de Ferro de Bragança, Estado do Paraná (*Agric. pecuária*, v. 21, no. 325, agôsto, p. 16, 18-20, 22-23, illus.).

1298. Cascudo, Luís da Camara. Geografia do Brasil holandês (*IV cong. hist. nac.*, v. 4, p. 243-450).

1299. Conforti, Emilio. Prima conferenza brasiliana di immigrazione e colonizzazione (*Riv. agric. subtrop. trop.*, v. 44, no. 10-12, ott.-dic., p. 276-283).

1300. ————. Lo stato di Minas Gerais (Brasile) in rapporto all' immigrazione italiana (*Riv. agric. subtrop. trop.*, v. 44, no. 4-6, aprile-giugno, p. 103-126; no. 7-9, luglio-sett., p. 178-195).

1302. Cruz, Ruth Bouchaud Lopes da. Distribuição da população no Estado do Espírito Santo, em 1940 (*Rev. bras. geog.*, ano 12, no. 3, julho-set., p. 393-412).

1303. Diégues Júnior, Manuel. Colonização estrangeira no Espírito Santo (*Obs. econ. fin.*, ano 14, no. 169, fev., p. 114-121).

1304. Fortini, Archymedes. 75 anos de colonização italiana (*Cooperativismo*, ano 4, no. 45, março, p. 13-14, 28-32; no. 46, abril, p. 14, 20-21).

1305. Moura, Valdiki. Aspectos de colonização e imigração na Bahia (*Coop.*, v. 9, no. 84, nov., p. 5-6).

1305a. Pereira, José Verissimo da Costa. Expedição a São Paulo, Mato Grosso, Goiás e Minas Gerais (*Rev. bras. geog.*, ano 12, no. 3, julho-set., p. 429-444; no. 4, out.-dez., p. 597-613).

1306. Quattrocchi, Nino. O cooperativismo e a colonização italiana no Brasil (*Cooperativismo*, ano 5, no. 52, out., p. 13-14, 19-20).

1307. Schmidt, Carlos Borges. Povoamento ao longo de uma estrada paulista.

Resultados de um caminhamento realizado entre a Serra da Quebra-Cangalha e a cidade de Cunha (*Bol. paulista geog.,* no. 6, out., p. 44-51, graphs, map).

1308. Waibel, Leo. European colonization in southern Brazil (*Geog. rev.,* v. 40, no. 4, Oct., p. 529-547).
Exploitive and shifting agricultural systems involving land rotation are the dominant type even among the German colonists. Farm sizes are too small to provide a living. [P. E. James]

1309. Weiss, João. Colonos na selva. Conto de um emigrante como colono no sul do Brasil. Rio de Janeiro, edição do autor. 155 p., illus.
A non-technical chronicle of an Austrian family experience in settling forest lands of Rio Grande do Sul in the years 1912-1917. [H. O. Sternberg]

OTHER MATERIALS OF GEO-GRAPHIC INTEREST

1310. Boletim da Sociedade Brasileira de Geografia. Rio de Janeiro. Ano 1, no. 1, julho-agôsto–no. 3, nov.-dez.

1311. Carta geral do Estado de São Paulo, 1:750,000. São Paulo, Instituto Geográfico e Geológico.
An excellent general reference map for desk or office use, showing minor civil divisions (*comarcas*), very detailed drainage, roads in four classes, railroads, and airports in color. An inset lists more than 250 cities in the state, and indicates for each the altitude in meters and the distance in kilometers from the city of São Paulo. [A. C. Gerlach]

1312. Mapa do Brasil, 1:5,000,000. Rio de Janeiro, Conselho Nacional de Geografia, Instituto Brasileiro de Geografia e Estatística.

Contemporary Brazilian cartography is well illustrated by this recent official map of the country. National and state boundaries are officially delineated. Roads and railroads are clearly distinguished, and cities are shown in five categories. Color layers are divided by contours at 200, 600, 1,000, and succeeding intervals of 1,000 meters. Insets show geology, population density, vegetation zones, physical features, Köppen climatic regions, and natural regions of the country. [A. C. Gerlach]

1313. Pedrosa, Carlos. Principais fontes da bibliografia geográfica brasileira (*Bol. geog.,* ano 7, no. 82, jan., p. 1194-1198).

1314. Pinheiro, Irineu. O Cariri. Seu descobrimento, povoamento, costumes. Fortaleza. 288 p.

1315. Waibel, Leo. O que aprendi no Brasil (*Rev. bras. geog.,* ano 12, no. 3, julho-set., p. 419-428).

ADDENDA

1316. Duque, José Guimarães. Solo e água no polígono das sêcas. Fortaleza, Departamento Nacional de Obras contra as Sêcas, Serviço Agro-Industrial (Publ. no. 148, série 1-a), 1949. 135 p., illus., map, tables.
An important study of the Northeast, containing much information on soils, soil destruction, and recommended conservation practices. [P. E. James]

1317. Ferreira, Evaldo Osorio. Jazimentos de minerais metalíferos do Brasil. Rio de Janeiro, Ministério da Agricultura, Departamento Nacional da Produção Mineral, Divisão de Geologia e Mineralogia (Bol. no. 130), 1949. 122 p.
Brief statements on location of deposits of 31 minerals. Bibliography for each one. [Ed.]

Government

ASHER N. CHRISTENSEN

ALTHOUGH the list of publications dealing with constitutional and political affairs in Latin America for the year 1950 is somewhat shorter than the lists of earlier years, the brevity is more than offset by the excellence of many of the publications.

As the readers will note, the 1950 list contains many excellent monographic studies, which come from several countries, and which will measurably expand the information horizon of the student of Latin American government. As examples of these monographs, one may cite those relating to the electoral system of some of the republics, three fine studies on administrative organization (Brazil, El Salvador, and Mexico), and monographs on the Chilean Senate, municipal government in Mexico, and the executive power in Mexico and Uruguay. If this flow of studies continues students of Latin American government the world over will have reason to be pleased.

GENERAL

1318. **Barros Hurtado, César.** América. Penurias de su libertad. El panamericanismo por dentro. Buenos Aires, Artes Gráficas Bartolomé U. Chiesino. 231 p.
This book, dedicated to Alfredo Palacios, contains a number of what are really separate essays all related to the subject of inter-American relations. Chapter IX deals with the evolution of Argentine political parties, and their stand on Pan Americanism. See also item 2222.

1319. **Canabarro, Nemo.** A emancipação. Rio de Janeiro, Borsoi. 402 p.
Concerned with the problem of reconciling the norms of democratic political society in a world in which "capitalism" makes the operation of that society difficult.

1320. **Davis, Harold Eugene.** Government and politics of Latin America. A syllabus and selected readings. Washington, American University. Various pagings.
An extremely helpful and valuable publication. It contains, in addition to the syllabus, basic data on the Latin American republics, suggested research topics, and detail on the governmental organization of seven of the countries: Mexico, Colombia, Peru, Guatemala, Chile, Cuba, and Uruguay.

1321. **Diez de Medina, Fernando.** Siripaka. Ainoka. La Paz, Editorial Artística. 102 p.

A vague analysis of a mildly socialist democratic movement.

1322. **González Uribe, Héctor.** Naturaleza, objeto y método de la teoría general del estado. Nociones introductorias al curso de teoría general del estado. México, Jus. 180 p.
Good general book on what would be called, in the United States, the elements of political science. The social scientist here will find it of interest to note how his Latin American colleagues define and organize the study of politics.

1323. **Pierson, W. W.** (ed.). Pathology of democracy in Latin-America: a symposium (*Amer. pol. sci. rev.,* v. 44, no. 1, March, p. 100-149).
1. Arthur P. Whitaker. A historian's point of view.
2. Russell Fitzgibbon. A political scientist's point of view.
3. Sanford A. Mosk. An economist's point of view.
4. W. Rex Crawford. Discussion: a sociologist's point of view.
One of the finest collections of papers yet published. Each of the participants discusses the influence of a particular conditioning factor upon the contemporary Latin American scene. Additional comments on the papers in this symposium were made by Professor Paul C. Bartholomew, University of Notre Dame, and Professor Federico G. Gil, University of North Carolina.

ARGENTINA

1324. Antoni, Norberto. Los derechos sociales en la Constitución nacional argentina de 1949. Tucumán? Imprenta de la U.N.T. 31 p.
Discusses the significance of the social guarantees incorporated in the reformed constitution.

1325. Ghioldi, Américo. Marxismo, socialismo, izquierdismo, comunismo y la realidad argentina de hoy. Buenos Aires, Ediciones Populares Argentinas. 191 p.
The published version of three lectures, one general and the other two with special reference to Argentina. The subjects are: Marxism in the history of socialism; Juan B. Justo and ideological education; and problems and obligations of contemporary Argentine socialism.

1326. Lafont, Julio B. Historia de la Constitución argentina. T. 1, Período hispánico, revolución, independencia. T. 2, Anarquía, tiranía, organización. 2. edición. Buenos Aires, Editorial F.V.D. xviii, 522; 474 p.
New edition of an excellent and highly important work originally published in 1935. It is amply documented and has an extensive bibliography. The appendices to each volume contain important documentary materials. Chapter 20 of v. 2 is a fine essay on Argentine historiography.

1327. Linares Quintana, Segundo V. The development of political science in the Argentine Republic (In *Contemporary Political Science*, Paris, UNESCO, p. 196-207).
The author critically discusses the contributions of various Argentine writers (arranged chronologically) to the study of politics, and notes their methodology. The article is well footnoted, and includes a bibliography. A welcome addition to our information on this discipline in Latin America.

1328. Martins, Mario. Perón. Um confronto entre o Brasil e a Argentina. Rio de Janeiro, Edições do Povo. 312 p.
A worried and democratic Brazilian looks at the Perón administration. There is a list (for the person interested primarily in Argentina) of the university professors who have been suspended in Argentina, and of the provincial newspapers which have been closed.

1329. Núñez Arca, P. Perón, man of America. Buenos Aires. 142 p.
The author describes this as "documentary political biography." Peronism as interpreted by a Peronist. [W. Stewart]

1330. Pan, Luis. Prensa libre. Pueblo libre. Prólogo de Américo Ghioldi. Buenos Aires, La Vanguardia. 137 p.
Attack on Perón's press policy by a leading Argentine Socialist. Worth reading. [W. Stewart]

1331. Perón, Juan D. The voice of Perón. Buenos Aires, Presidencia de la Nación Argentina, Subsecretaría de Informaciones. 192 p.
Paragraphs from the writings and speeches of President Perón, covering topics ranging from "Aggrandizement" to "Virtue."

1332. Presidente de la Nación Argentina. Mensaje del . . . , General Juan Perón, al inaugurar el 84. período ordinario de sesiones del honorable Congreso Nacional, Mayo 1, 1950. Conceptos doctrinarios. Buenos Aires. 78 p.
In addition to outlining the work of the administration in the preceding year, the message contains a considerable amount of discussion of internal political affairs.

1333. Sammartino, Ernesto E. La verdad sobre la situación argentina. Montevideo. 394 p.
A fairly dispassionate but severe attack on the Perón government. The chapters on "The causes of the Argentine crisis," "The immediate background of June 4, 1943," and "The work of the government" are perhaps the best. An important book for the student of Argentine government and politics.

1334. Secretaría de la Presidencia. Subsecretaría de Informaciones y Prensa. Perón. Cuatro años de su gobierno. Buenos Aires. Unpaged, illus.
Laudatory account of the accomplishments of President Perón and his government in the fields of international relations, national recuperation, social welfare, agriculture, etc.

1335. Valenzuela, Rodolfo Guillermo. Para los argentinos del mañana, justicia social, libertad económica y soberanía política. Exposición de la doctrina revolucionaria ante la honorable Convención Constituyente de 1949. Buenos Aires, Kraft. 172 p.
This collection of speeches by a member of the 1949 Constituent Assembly is a valuable document on Argentine constitutional development.

1336. Vigo, Salvador C. Reforma constitucional argentina. Santa Fe, Editorial Nueva Impresora. 540 p.
A pro-Perón argument for constitutional reform. The author, evidently close to the commission which made the preliminary studies and recommendations, includes details that make the book significant.

1337. Yantorno, Juan Antonio. Males de la política argentina. Buenos Aires, Mastellone, Caruso. 332 p.
Dedicated to the Unión Cívica Radical and *La Prensa*. It contains a good chapter on *caudillismo* and a long and useful one on the practice of electoral fraud in Argentina.

BOLIVIA

1338. Presidente Constitucional de la República, Mamerto Urriolagoitia H. Mensaje al H. Congreso Nacional de 1950. La Paz. 139 p.

In addition to the regular presidential message, and a report on the year's work of each of the major government departments, there is a foreword giving a list of the cabinet officers from May 21 to August 3, 1949 (the interim period) and the cabinet constituted on August 3, 1949.

1339. Trigo, Ciro Félix. Reseña constitucional boliviana. La Paz, Universidad Mayor de San Andrés, Escuela de Derecho y Ciencias Políticas (Publ., Cuad. no. 3). 71 p.

Hardly more than a topic index of Bolivian constitutional history. Useful and valuable, nevertheless.

BRAZIL

1340. Brandão, A. C., and Delcilio Palmeira (eds.). Repertório eleitoral. Rio de Janeiro, A. Coelho Branco. 546 p.

The foreword includes biographical data and photographs of the members of the Supreme and Regional Electoral Tribunals. Then follow a detailed description and analysis of the electoral law of July 24, 1950. The volume has a very useful topical index. This is a "must" for those interested in Latin American political parties.

1341. Carvalho, Orlando M. A crise dos partidos nacionais. Belo Horizonte, Kriterion. 50 p.

Discusses methods for studying political phenomena and suggests the scientific study of Brazil's political institutions.

1342. CÓDIGO ELEITORAL, LEI NO. 1.164 DE 24 DE JULHO DE 1950, SUBSTITUI O CÓDIGO ELEITORAL [de 1946]. São Paulo, Saraiva (Biblioteca da Livraria Acadêmica, Legislação Brasileira). 119 p.

The full text of the electoral code adopted on July 24, 1950. It is well indexed to facilitate its use. It replaces the electoral code of 1946.

1343. Fontenelle, Walter. Uma democracia em pânico. Aspectos da politica brasileira. São Paulo, Editôra Jornal dos Livros. 301 p.

Contains some materials of interest to the student of Brazilian political parties.

1344. Presidência da República. Departamento Administrativo do Serviço Público. Indicador da organização administrativa federal. Rio de Janeiro, Departamento de Imprensa Nacional. 558 p., tables.

An excellent and very useful manual of the administrative organization of the Brazilian federal government, with organizational charts of each of the major departments.

1345. ————. ————. Relatório, 1949. Rio de Janeiro. 126 p., tables.

1346. A RECONSTRUÇÃO DE SÃO PAULO NO GOVERNO FERNANDO COSTA. São Paulo, 1950?

Laudatory account of the activities of Fernando Costa as Interventor Federal in São Paulo during the early forties. [H. W. Spiegel]

CHILE

1347. Blasier, S. Cole. Chile. A Communist battleground (*Pol. sci. quart.*, v. 65, no. 3, Sept., p. 353-375).

A useful and sober review of Chilean politics since about 1936, with backward glances at earlier Communist influences, bringing the story to March, 1949. Concludes, "Communists have always survived previous effort in Chile to destroy the movement. . . . In view of their past record of applying flexible tactics in seeking mass support, it is quite possible that the Communists will some day reassert their former influence in the political life of Chile." [H. F. Cline]

1348. Boizard, Ricardo. Cuatro retratos en profundidad: Ibáñez, Lafertte, Leighton y Walker. Santiago. 298 p.

Biographical essays on four Chilean public figures, Carlos Ibáñez, Elías Lafertte, Bernardo Leighton, and Horacio Walker, which emphasize their political life and activity.

1349. Presidente de la República. Mensaje de S. E. el . . . , don Gabriel González Videla, al Congreso Nacional al inaugurar el período ordinario de sesiones, 21 de mayo de 1950. Santiago. 399 p.

Contains the message of the President and full reports, bulwarked with statistical data, of each of the cabinet departments.

1350. Theoduloz Vásquez, Nahum. Estudio del Senado chileno. Evolución histórica, composición, funciones y atribuciones. Santiago. 115 p.

This very fine thesis (University of Chile) will be extremely useful to students of Chilean government. The chapter titles indicate its scope: "The Senate in earlier Constitutions" (prior to that of 1833); "The Senate under the 1833 Constitution"; "The Senate and the Constitution of 1925." Includes material referring to the Senate's representative function and to its general and special legislative activities. Short bibliography.

COLOMBIA

1351. Gracián, Luis. Laureano Gómez. Bogotá, Ediciones Nuevo Mundo. 90 p.

Biography by an ardent admirer of Gómez who

regards him as "not the exponent of a party but the creation of a race." "Luis Gracián" is the pseudonym of Néstor Forero Morales.

1352. Niño H., Alberto. Antecedentes y secretos del 9 de abril. Bogotá, Pax, 1950? 159 p.
The former chief of the National Department of Security writes about the events of April 9, 1948, in Bogotá. There is considerable discussion of the part played by the Communist party.

1353. Noguera Laborde, Rodrigo (ed.). Constitución de la República de Colombia y sus antecedentes documentales desde 1885. Bogotá, Pontificia Universidad Católica Javeriana (Publ. del Fondo Rotatorio, v. 2). 263 p.
A well edited collection of constitutional documents, including a briefly annotated text of the current Constitution.

1354. LA OPOSICIÓN Y EL GOBIERNO DEL 9 DE ABRIL DE 1948 AL 9 DE ABRIL DE 1950. Dos documentos políticos. Memorial de algunos ciudadanos liberales y respuesta del Excmo. señor Presidente, doctor Mariano Ospina Pérez. Bogotá, Imprenta Nacional. 76 p.
The letter of the Liberals lists and documents the political and other crimes of which they accuse the government. The reply presents a refutation of each of the charges. The defense revolves largely about the necessity of maintaining order and exterminating Communism. Published in English under the title *The political situation in Colombia.*

1355. Ospina Pérez, Mariano. El Gobierno de Unión Nacional. T. 1. La política de unión nacional. El programa. T. 2. Un programa en acción. Mensajes y otros documentos, de agosto a diciembre de 1946. T. 3. Un programa en acción. Mensajes y otros documentos, de enero a julio de 1947. T. 5. Crisis, defensa y consolidación de la democracia. Mensaje y documentos, de enero a diciembre de 1949. T. 6. Historia de un proceso político. Mensajes y otros documentos, de enero a diciembre de 1949. T. 7. La obra administrativa de un gobierno. Mensaje presidencial al Congreso de 1949. T. 8. Últimos meses de gobierno. Documentos de 1950, excepto el mensaje final. Bogotá, Imprenta Nacional, 1946-1950. 228, 264, 187, 496, 427, 335, 503 p.
Speeches and writings of the President of Colombia, including several letters from those who attack his government or its program and in each case the reply or refutation. Also full departmental reports, with statistical data. [In *HLAS, no. 14, 1948,* item 1626, the date for t. 1 was given as 1948 instead of 1946; and in *no. 15, 1949,* item 1320a, t. 6 was entered erroneously as a 1949 publication, although it appeared in

1950. The other volumes have not been listed previously. T. 4, reported to have been published in 1949, has not been seen. (Ed.)]

1356. Villegas, Silvio, and Abel Naranjo Villegas. Panegíricos de Mariano Ospina Pérez y Laureano Gómez. Bogotá, Editorial Nuevo Mundo (Ediciones Orientación), 1950? 64 p.
Although the title indicates the authors are not unbiased, the book is of interest and of some value to students of recent political history in Colombia.

ECUADOR

1357. Presidente. Mensaje del . . . Galo Plaza al Congreso de 1950. Agosto 10, 1950. Quito, Talleres Gráficos Nacionales. 80 p.
Message to the Congress on the state of the nation, including summaries of the activities of the principal governmental departments during the fiscal year and references to plans for the future.

1358. Presidente Constitucional del Ecuador, Galo Plaza. Mensaje al país. Enero 1. de 1950. Resumen de trabajo en 1949; planes para 1950. Quito, Talleres Gráficos Nacionales. 48 p.
New Year's message to the country on the calendar year 1949.

EL SALVADOR

1359. Asamblea Nacional Constituyente. Constitución política de la República de El Salvador. San Salvador, Imprenta Nacional (Secretaría de Información de la Presidencia de la República, no. 8). 45 p.
Official text of the current Constitution, promulgated September 7, 1950.

1360. Public Administration Service. Informe sobre la conveniencia de introducir mejoras en la organización del gobierno de El Salvador. San Salvador, Ministerio de Economía, Instituto de Estudios Económicos. 74 p.
An excellent sort of "Hoover Commission" report by a Chicago group on the organization of the executive-administrative branch of the government. Chapter 2 has a full discussion of the executive power, including its legislative ramifications.

GUATEMALA

1361. LEY ELECTORAL. DECRETOS 255, 313, 324, 538 Y 552. Guatemala, Ministerio de Gobernación. 85 p.
Texts of several decrees which together comprise an electoral code. The usual subjects—suffrage qualifications, party organization, campaign regulation, election administration, etc.—are covered.

1362. **Presidente de la República.** Informe del ciudadano . . . , doctor Juan José Arévalo, al Congreso Nacional en su primer período de sesiones ordinarias del año de 1950. Síntesis de la labor de los ministerios durante el quinto año de gobierno, 1949. Guatemala. 380 p.

This presidential message is accompanied by full and generally well prepared reports of the cabinet departments.

1363. **Ruiz Franco, Arcadio.** Hambre y miseria. Fermentos de lucha. Guatemala, Tipografía Nacional. 226 p.

This volume has much material relating to the fall of General Ubico in 1945, and the early organization of the new government. The author feels that if Communism does come to power in Guatemala it will not be the fault of programs adopted since 1945 but rather of those who oppose needed social changes.

MEXICO

1364. **Araújo Mendizábal, Roberto.** Sufragio efectivo. México. 80 p.

The brevity of this thesis (Law School, University of Mexico) detracts greatly from the contribution it might have made. Nevertheless it does contain data on the development of the suffrage in Mexico. The author proposes the establishment of an electoral tribunal, as in Brazil.

1365. **Barrera Fuentes, Florencio.** Historia y destino del municipio en México. México. 106 p.

A very fine thesis (Law School, University of Mexico) on municipal government in Mexico. There is an interesting introductory chapter on local government in Mexico in pre-Columbian years. This is followed by chapters on local government during the colonial period; local government and Mexican constitutional law; the Revolution and local government; and the future of the city. The work is adequately documented and has a short bibliography.

1366. Constitución política de los Estados Unidos Mexicanos. Texto vigente. Con anotaciones sintéticas concordadas y un índice alfabético por Carlos Vargas Galindo. México, Botas (Col. de Leyes Mexicanas). 183 p.

Unofficial text of the Constitution, with all amendments up to 1950, accompanied by a handy topic index, alphabetically arranged.

1367. Constitución política del estado de Chihuahua. Decreto núm. 356. Chihuahua. 55, ii p.

Official text of the state constitution, with a brief title index. Of importance to those interested in state governmental organization in Mexico.

1368. **González Reyes, Mario F.** El órgano legislativo y su función en el derecho mexicano. México. 79 p.

Chapter 5 of this short thesis (University of Mexico) has some good material on the powers of the Mexican Congress. Undocumented, with a brief bibliography.

1369. **Laguna Arcos, Enriqueta.** El ejecutivo y la promulgación de las leyes. México. 85 p.

Two chapters of this thesis (University of Mexico), one dealing with the legislative process in Mexico, the other with the executive's responsibility for enforcement of the laws, make it a significant contribution. There is a short bibliography, which includes some judicial decisions.

1370. **Loredo Castañeda, Emma.** El Senado en la teoría jurídica del estado federal. México. 104 p.

This thesis (University of Mexico) discusses the development of the Mexican Senate through the various Constitutions, and its general legislative and special powers.

1371. **Palavicini, Félix F.** Política constitucional. México, Beatriz de Silva. 343 p.

Collection of well organized and well written political essays. They cover a wide range of subjects, from "The principles of the Revolution" to "Cuartelazo."

1372. **Presidente de la República.** Informe que rinde al H. Congreso de la Unión el C. . . . , Lic. Miguel Alemán, correspondiente a su gestión del 1. de septiembre de 1949 al 31 de agosto de 1950. México, Secretaría de Gobernación. 94 p.

President Alemán's message is arranged in broad chapter divisions (domestic policy, foreign relations, etc.) and each of the chapters is based on one or more government department reports. The official reply of the Congress is included.

1373. **Secretaría de Bienes Nacionales e Inspección Administrativa. Dirección Técnica de Organización.** Directorio del Gobierno Federal, Poderes Legislativo, Ejecutivo y Judicial, 1950. México, 1950? lxxxix, 591 p.

An extremely valuable publication. It contains the Constitution of the nation, the laws establishing and regulating the major government departments, an organization chart of the federal government, budget data (with "pie" charts), the judicial organization, etc.

1374. **Tiscareño Silva, Rafael.** Interpretación del artículo 78 de la Constitución del Estado de Coahuila de Zaragoza. México. 89 p.

A good thesis (University of Mexico) on federal-state relations in Mexico. The author discusses the article in question (it relates to the term of the state governor) against the background of national constitutional principles.

PARAGUAY

1375. BATALLAS POR LA DEMOCRACIA. T. 1, por Epifanio Méndez. Prólogo de Guillermo Enciso. Asunción. 304 p.
Editorials and articles from *La Razón* which was, in 1947, the organ of the Colorado party. A valuable source for recent political events in Paraguay. A second volume will be published with the same title but by another author.

1376. Centurión, Carlos R. El libro como expresión del Partido Liberal del Paraguay. Buenos Aires, Editorial Asunción, 1950? 62 p.
Brief, but contains considerable historical material referring to the Paraguayan Liberal Party.

PUERTO RICO

1377. Bureau of the Budget. Report on surveys, research projects, investigations, and other organized fact-gathering activities of the Government of Puerto Rico, 1949-1950. San Juan, P. R. 60 p.
Lists 274 projects "completed, in progress, or started during fiscal year 1949-1950." All agencies of the Government contributed items, and the stated intention is to revise this publication at least once a year. [H. F. Cline]

1378. Calderón, Enrique. El dolor de un pueblo esclavo. Nueva York, Azteca Press. 141 p.
This sociological study and plea for statehood is largely concerned with the plight of the Puerto Ricans in New York.

1379. MANUAL OF GOVERNMENT AGENCIES IN PUERTO RICO, EXECUTIVE BRANCH. Río Piedras, University of Puerto Rico (Public Administration Monograph no. 2). 341 p.
A handy manual listing the date of the establishment of each agency, its administrative organization, and its principal activities.

URUGUAY

1380. Aguirre Larreta, Aureliano (comp.). Una vida al servicio de un ideal. Leonel Aguirre. Artículos y discursos. Montevideo, Impresora Uruguaya. 257 p.
Writings and speeches of a prominent political figure. Devoted largely to political matters of the last quarter-century.

1381. Barbagelata, Aníbal Luis. El Consejo de Ministros en la Constitución nacional. Montevideo, Universidad de Montevideo, Facultad de Derecho y Ciencias Sociales (Biblioteca de Publicaciones Oficiales, sección III, liii). 391 p.
Excellent, well documented monograph, with a rich bibliography. Especially significant in view of recent changes in the organization of the executive.

1382. Demicheli, Alberto. El poder ejecutivo. Génesis y transformaciones. Buenos Aires, Depalma. 207 p.
Another very fine monographic study of the executive power in Uruguay. It is well documented and very well planned and organized.

1383. Ravera, Julio M. Apuntes para una biografía de César Mayo Gutiérrez. La Paz, Uruguay. 95 p.
Owing to the long public career of the subject and his great interest in educational programs, this outline for a biography is valuable to the student of government.

1384. Solari, Juan Antonio. Emilio Frugoni. Su magisterio político-social, su mensaje lírico. Buenos Aires, La Vanguardia. 70 p.
Essays on such topics as "Frugoni the Socialist," "Frugoni the legislator and Constitution writer," are important for the student of recent Uruguayan politics.

VENEZUELA

1385. DISCURSOS Y DOCUMENTOS OFICIALES DESDE EL 15 DE ENERO HASTA EL 25 DE MAYO DE 1950. Caracas, Oficina Nacional de Información y Publicaciones. 78 p.
Important speeches, decrees, political statements, etc.

1386. Planas-Suárez, Simón. Páginas de preocupación y patriotismo, 1936-1941. Buenos Aires, J. Pellegrini. 532 p.
A valuable document on the political history and politics of Venezuela, 1936-1941. Most of the book is concerned with governmental programs and action during these years.

1387. PROYECTO DE ESTATUTO ELECTORAL ELABORADO POR LA COMISIÓN ESPECIAL NOMBRADA AL EFECTO Y ENTREGADO A LA JUNTA MILITAR DE GOBIERNO EN EL PALACIO DE MIRAFLORES EL 25 DE MAYO DE 1950. Caracas, Oficina Nacional de Información y Publicaciones. 73 p.
A valuable document referring to Venezuelan political and constitutional history. The preface contains a good discussion of past and present electoral problems of the nation.

1388. Rodríguez, Valmore. Bayonetas sobre Venezuela. México, Beatriz de Silva. 190 p.
A strong, though not unbiased, defense of the administration of Acción Democrática in Venezuela. There is an account of the *coup d'état* of November, 1948. The appendix contains an interesting document relating to the administration of public finances by the Acción Democrática regime.

OTHER COUNTRIES

1389. CONSTITUTION DE LA RÉPUBLIQUE D'HAÏTI. Port-au-Prince, Imprimerie de l'État. 32 p.

Official text of the Constitution promulgated November 25, 1950.

1390. Cuba. Dirección General de Estadística. Clave numérica de la división política del territorio nacional. Habana. 129 p.

An ingenious sort of "Dewey Decimal System" for identifying the political and administrative subdivisions of Cuba.

1391. Dominican Republic. Presidente de la República. Evolución de la democracia en Santo Domingo. Discurso pronunciado por su Excelencia el . . . , Rafael L. Trujillo Molina, al inaugurar la XIII Conferencia Sanitaria Panamericana. Ciudad Trujillo, Editora del Caribe. 67 p.

The speaker lists the social gains attained in his administration. Also published in English translation.

1392. Partido Demócrata. Doctrinas de Dn. Nicolás de Piérola, declaración de principios, bases de organización del Partido i anexo histórico. Lima, La Providencia. 229 p.

Documents of a Peruvian party, containing, among other items, a statement of the party platform, materials relating to the founding and history of the party, its stand on past issues, and its organization and officers.

1393. Stokes, William Sylvane. Honduras. An area study in government. Madison, Wis., University of Wisconsin Press. xii, 351 p., illus., maps, ports.

Excellent monographic study of the development, theory, and practice of government in Honduras.

1394. Zeledón, Marco Tulio. Historia constitucional de Costa Rica en el bienio 1948-1949. San José, Franklin Aguilar. 73 p.

The appendices of this pamphlet contain texts of many important decrees, laws, etc., relating to the political events and disturbances in Costa Rica, in 1948 and 1949.

ADDENDA

1395. Astudillo y Ursúa, Pedro. Las nuevas funciones del poder legislativo. México, 1949. 135 p.

The general thesis of the author is that the complexity of modern policy-making decisions has fundamentally changed the role of legislative bodies. Chapter 3, which deals with the legislative power and process in the Mexican Congress, has some valuable data in it. Thesis, University of Mexico.

1396. CONSTITUCIÓN POLÍTICA DE LOS ESTADOS UNIDOS MEXICANOS. Texto vigente. México, Partido Revolucionario Institucional, 1949. 107, iii p.

This unofficial text of the constitution is published by the P. R. I. The officers of P. R. I. for the ensuing year (1950) are listed in the prefatory pages.

1397. Lara Alemán, Víctor. La representación política dentro del régimen democrático. México, 1949. 72 p.

A few of the brief chapters of this general and discursive thesis (University of Mexico) will be of interest to the student of government in Latin America, especially chapter 4 on the suffrage and 6 on the political parties in Mexico.

1398. Vega Hernández, Jaime. La sucesión presidencial en México. México, 1949. 87 p.

Not much more than a compilation of what the Mexican constitutions from 1824 through 1917 disposed with reference to succession to the presidency. This information is, of course, now handily arranged. The thesis (University of Mexico) has no documentation other than the constitutional clauses, and no bibliography.

History

GENERAL

1399. Academia Colombiana de Historia. Curso superior de historia de Colombia, 1781-1830. T. 1-3. Bogotá, A.B.C. (Biblioteca Eduardo Santos, v. 2-4). xi, 372; 424; 454 p.

An episodic history of Colombia for the 50 years indicated, the work of 25 collaborators. Delivered originally as a series of lectures in celebration of the Golden Anniversary of the founding of the Colombian Academy of History. Of varying excellence. [W. Stewart]

1400. Agraz García de Alba, Gabriel. Esbozos históricos de Tecolotlán, Jalisco. Guadalajara, Mexico. 402 p., illus.

Useful historical notes and documents on a *patria chica* of west central Mexico, from parochial archives, civil administrative documents, and secondary sources. [H. F. Cline]

1401. Alessio Robles, Vito. Las provincias del norte de México hasta 1846 *(Mem. primer cong. hist.,* México, p. 137-151).

A detailed summary by an outstanding authority on Northern Mexico; comprehends geography and history. Map. [H. F. Cline]

1402. Altamira, Luis Roberto. Paso de Ferreira. Historia de la célebre estancia en cuyas tierras fundáronse dos pueblos cordobeses: Villa Nueva y Villa María. Córdoba, Argentina, Universidad Nacional de Córdoba, Facultad de Filosofía y Humanidades, Instituto de Estudios Americanistas (Publ. no. 15). 44 p.

1403. Aragão, Henrique de Beaurepaire. Notícia histórica sôbre a fundação do Instituto Oswaldo Cruz *(Mem. inst. Oswaldo Cruz,* t. 48, p. 1-50).

On the occasion of the 50th anniversary of the scientific research center first known as "Instituto de Manguinhos." [M. Cardozo]

1404. Arias Solís, Enrique. Apuntes para la historia de la región que constituyó el partido del Carmen desde los tiempos primitivos hasta 1843 *(Repr. campechano,* año 7, enero-dic., p. 207-243).

Undocumented but important antiquarian notes on the strategically located island of Carmen and its municipality. The island, long a part of Yucatán, lies at the mouth of the Usumacinta river system, and has been a strategic key to much of southern Mexico and its commerce. [H. F. Cline]

1405. Barahona, Rubén. Breve historia de Honduras. 3. edición. Tegucigalpa. 206 p.

Revised edition of an elementary textbook that first appeared in 1943. Stress is placed on pre-Columbian and colonial periods. [H. F. Cline]

1406. Benítez, Fernando. La ruta de Hernán Cortés. Estampas y viñetas de Alberto Beltrán. México, Fondo de Cultura Económica. 257 p., illus.

An examination of the transformation wrought upon the historic road from Veracruz to Mexico City, through the centuries. [R. D. Hussey]

1407. Brazil. Ministério das Relações Exteriores. Instituto Rio-Branco. Catálogo da Coleção Visconde do Rio-Branco. 2 v. Rio de Janeiro. 508; 508, lxxxiv p.

Titles and descriptions of 5122 manuscripts and publications dating from the 16th century to the last quarter of the 19th. Concerned with many aspects of Brazilian history, catalogue contains as well material relating to the early history of Paraguay, on Artigas, Rosas, and the diplomatic history of the region of La Plata. The collection is in the National Library of Brazil. [C. Shelby]

1408. Butler, Ruth Lapham (ed.). Guide to the *Hispanic American Historical Review,* 1918-1945. Durham, North Carolina, Duke University Press (Duke University Publications). 251 p.

An indispensable substitute for a consolidated index to this valuable periodical. Lists articles under a variety of headings, with cross-references, documents by years, and book reviews by authors of the books, with a general index to the authors and editors of all the items. [R. D. Hussey]

1409. Castillero Reyes, Ernesto J. Leyendas e historias de Panamá la vieja. Pana-

má, Editora Panamá América. 95 p., illus.
Pleasantly written essays, mostly but not entirely
on the colonial era. [R. D. Hussey]

1410. Congreso de Historiadores de México y los Estados Unidos. Primer
Congreso, Monterrey, México, 4-9 septiembre de 1949. Memoria del . . . . México, Cultura. 420 p.
Bilingual presentation of the several papers and
discussions of this epoch-making meeting. The
specialized contributions bearing on various
aspects of Mexico have been separately noted
below. The volume has an analytical index.
[H. F. Cline]

1411. Frías V., Francisco. Manual de historia de Chile. Santiago, Nascimento.
551 p.
Textbook for secondary schools. [W. Stewart]

1412. Furlong, Guillermo. La lepra en la
Argentina (*Arch. ibero-amer. hist. med.,*
v. 2, no. 1, enero-junio, p. 121-136).
Offers considerable amounts upon the disease's
history in other parts of America, although it
emphasizes the history in various parts of
Argentina, ca. 1725-ca. 1837, as revealed by the
Argentine national archives. [R. D. Hussey]

1413. Gautier, José A. En torno a *Biografía del Caribe.* Un capítulo que se olvidó
a Germán Arciniegas (*Rev. cub.,* v. 26,
enero-junio, p. 195-223).
The chapter that Arciniegas forgot, in his well-
known book (*HLAS, no. 11, 1945,* item 59), is
upon the story of Puerto Rico, from the 16th
century to 1898. As contributed by Gautier, it
is not a work of research, but is worth reading,
especially upon the 19th century. [R. D. Hussey]

1414. Geiger, Maynard. The old mission
libraries of California (*Calif. libr. bull.,*
v. 11, no. 4, June, p. 143-144, 177).
Primarily upon the library of Santa Barbara
mission, the oldest in California with a continuous history, 1786 to the present. [R. D.
Hussey]

1415. Grases, Pedro. El doctor Vicente
Lecuna, historiador (*Rev. nac. cult.,* año
12, no. 82-83, sept.-dic., p. 76-91).
Dr. Lecuna is well known for his editorship of
the Bolívar papers and for original studies.
Bibliography, pp. 88-91. See item 2002. [Ed.]

1416. Gschaedler, André. Seventeenth century documents on Spanish navigation in
the Mitchell Library of Sydney, Australia
(*Hisp. amer. hist. rev.,* v. 30, no. 3, Aug.,
p. 397-399).
A volume (bought by the Mitchell Library solely
to get one item) entitled *Papeles varios de
Indias y Portugal, Manuscritos,* has 63 documents, mostly for the period of the Portuguese
captivity. Only the 12 (1619-1674) upon navigation are analyzed here. They concern New
Spain, the Caribbean, the South Seas, and the
Philippines. [R. D. Hussey]

1417. Guía de los tomos i al xxi, 1930-
1950 (*Bol. arch. gen.,* México, t. 21, no.
4, oct.-dic., p. 487-635).
A list of the titles in the *Boletín* named, in the
order of their appearance, with added information upon the contents when the title is not
adequate, followed by an index of names and
some subjects. [R. D. Hussey]

1418. Hammond, George. Manuscript collections in the Bancroft Library (*Amer.
arch.,* v. 13, no. 1, Jan., p. 15-26).
Discussion of the more outstanding collections
for the history of California, chiefly for the
Mexican period and the early United States
period, and as to those more recently received.
[R. D. Hussey]

1419. Hildebrand, Karl-Gustaf. Latinamerika, Sverige och skeppshandeln, 1825
(*Hist. tidskrift,* häfte 4, p. 392-421).
A critical examination and revision of part of
Sven Ola Swärd, *Latinamerika i svensk politik
under 1810-och 1820-talen* (Uppsala, 1949).
Hildebrand discusses a projected transfer (1825-
1830) of ships to Colombia and Mexico, apparently for use against Cuba. Pressure from Russia, as guardian of the Metternich system,
caused Sweden to withdraw from the scheme.
[Ernst Ekman, U.C.L.A., for R. D. Hussey]

1420. Holmes, Vera Lee. A history of the
Americas, from discovery to nationhood.
New York, Ronald Press. xiv, 609 p.,
illus., maps, ports.
A college textbook that surveys the history of
North and South America beginning with early
Indian cultures and continuing to about 1830.
A useful text for a survey course. [H. F. Cline]

1421. Iguíniz, Juan B. (comp.). Guadalajara a través de los tiempos. Relatos y
descripciones de viajeros y escritores desde
el siglo XVI hasta nuestros días. T. 1,
1586-1867. Guadalajara, Banco Refac-
cionario de Jalisco. xvi, 284 p.
A collection of 28 excerpts which provide interesting and informative views of this western
Mexican metropolis as it developed and changed.
Presumably v. 2 will cover the period from
1867 to the present. [H. F. Cline]

1422. Isabelle, Arsène. Emigração e colonização na província brasileira do Rio
Grande do Sul, na República Oriental do
Uruguai e em toda a bacia do Prata.
Tradução de Belfort de Oliveira. Prefácio
de Augusto Meyer. Rio de Janeiro, Souza.
228 p., illus.
First published in Montevideo in French in
1830. There is information on Rio Grande do
Sul, Uruguay, and "tout le bassin de La Plata,"
of interest for the prospective European immigrant of those days. [M. Cardozo]

1423. Jaramillo Pérez, César. Resumen de
historia de América. Quito, La Salle.
562 p.

A valiant attempt by a leading historian of Ecuador to compress for textbook purposes the development of the Western Hemisphere from precolonial times through the United Nations. Designed as a college text, it is schematic and oversimplified in part, but has many virtues, chief of which is a panoramic and continental view of matters and problems common to the New World. An interesting and important South American adaptation of the Bolton thesis and approach, based almost exclusively on Spanish language works. Inadequate maps. [H. F. Cline]

1424. Jones, Tom B., and W. Donald Beatty. An introduction to Hispanic American history. Revised edition. New York, Harper. x, 667 p., illus.

Revised edition of a standard textbook. Part 6, the 20th century, has been completely revised and brought down to 1949. New materials have been incorporated into parts 1-5. [R. L. Tree]

1425. Kraus, H. P. Latin America. A choice selection of important books and manuscripts . . . (Catalog 52). New York. 74 p., 32 facsims.

Excellent description of 265 items, printed almost entirely from the 16th to the early 19th century, and strongly *relaciones* or other ephemera. About one fifth are "not recorded in any bibliography," and some others have been unknown or little known in America. At pages 1 to 4 appears Hans Nachod's *Resettlement of Santa Fé de Nuevo México in 1693-1695*. This is based upon a lengthy manuscript offered as item 104, concerning the work of the leader of the expedition, Capitán Juan Páez Hurtado. [R. D. Hussey]

1426. Libros y folletos del Archivo Histórico de la Secretaría de Hacienda (*Bol. arch. gen.*, México, t. 21, no. 1, enero-marzo, p. 45-115; no. 3, julio-sept., p. 377-413).

The first installment lists imprints upon "economía política" for the second half of the 18th and first half of the 19th centuries. The second, with a title to correspond, analyzes the *Libros de contabilidad*, 1594, under many subject headings. [R. D. Hussey]

1427. Lubin, Maurice A. En marge du recensement en Haïti (*Rev. soc. haïtienne. hist. géog.*, v. 21, no. 76, jan., p. 105-116).

A handy gathering together of various estimates of counts of the population, from Charlevoix's in 1726, to the preliminary census of Port-au-Prince in February, 1949. The text of Dessalines' decree of October 25, 1804, is included. [R. D. Hussey]

1428. McGarry, Daniel D. Educational methods of the Franciscans in Spanish California (*Americas*, v. 6, no. 3, Jan., p. 335-358).

An excellent use of extensive sources, printed and manuscript, upon the whole period from 1769 to 1843. [R. D. Hussey]

1439. Martínez, Manuel Guillermo. Don Joaquín García Icazbalceta. Su lugar en la historiografía mexicana. Traducción, notas y apéndice de Luis García Pimentel y Elguero. México, Porrúa. xvi, 185 p., illus.

Translation of the English original. See *HLAS, No. 13, 1947,* item 1149. [H. F. Cline]

1440. Meeteren, N. van. Bibliografía de la historia de Curaçao (*Rev. hist. amér.,* no. 29, junio, p. 134-138).

List of 28 items published to 1945, and 11 thereafter, including the few that deal with the Spanish aspects. [R. D. Hussey]

1441. Metford, J. C. J. British contributions to Spanish and Spanish American studies. New York, Longmans, Green. 86 p.

A survey of British interest as expressed in books, not a bibliography as such. About one quarter of the whole deals with Spanish America. [R. D. Hussey]

1442. Monsant, Juan N. P. Resumen histórico de la Universidad de los Andes. Mérida, Venezuela, Universidad de los Andes (Dirección de Cultura, no. 3). 47 p.

Brief chronicle of dates and events, divided into three periods: 1785-1810, 1812-1832, 1832-1889. [H. Benjamin]

1443. Munro, Dana Gardner. The Latin American Republics. A history. Second edition. New York, Appleton-Century-Crofts. 605 p., maps.

The second edition of a standard textbook. There has been some revision and the history of each country has been brought down to 1950. [R. L. Tree]

1444. Nath, Dwarka. A history of Indians in British Guiana. London, Thomas Nelson. xvi, 251 p.

A thoroughly scholarly study of every aspect of the history of the East Indian population in the colony from the start of its introduction in 1838. [R. D. Hussey]

1445. Parkes, Henry Bamford. A history of Mexico. Revised and enlarged. Boston, Houghton Miflin. 446 p., illus.

Reissue of a standard text with but few additions or corrections. The history is brought to about 1946, though materials after 1934 are sketchily treated. Recent bibliography has been added. [H. F. Cline]

1446. Plazas, Francisco de Paula. Villavieja. Ciudad ilustre, 1550-1950. Aspecto histórico y genealogías de Villavieja. Neiva, Colombia, Dirección de Educación Pública. 135 p.

An antiquarian and genealogical contribution, heavily weighted on the clerical side. A collection of undigested notes rather than a narrative or analysis. [H. F. Cline]

1447. Pradeau, Alberto Francisco. Historia numismática de México. Desde la época precortesiana hasta 1823. Traducida, corregida y aumentada por Román Beltrán Martínez. México, Banco de México. 223 p., 23 illus.
The original edition appeared in English in Los Angeles, in 1938. This translation has been made with a check of the documents in the original Spanish, and the translator has added four chapters. Bibliography, p. 215-223. [R. D. Hussey]

1448. Ramírez de Arellano, Rafael William. La capital a través de los siglos. San Juan, P. R. Unpaged, illus.
A unique combination of old documents, maps, plans, and description of San Juan. [R. E. McNicoll]

1449. Recaséns Siches, Luis. El pensamiento filosófico, social, político y jurídico en Honduras (*Rev. univ.*, Tegucigalpa, t. 14, no. 2, julio-sept., p. 57-59).
Biobibliographical notes on a long list of *pensadores,* most of whom are still living and writing. Many have produced historical works. [H. F. Cline]

1450. REVISTA DEL ARCHIVO HISTÓRICO. Cuzco, Peru, Universidad Nacional del Cuzco. Año 1, no. 1.
A new publication that may appear annually. This is primarily a catalogue of various collections of documents found in the archive. Includes complete texts for some documents. This publication promises to be quite useful. [R. L. Tree]

1451. REVUE DE LA SOCIETÉ D'HISTOIRE ET DE GÉOGRAPHIE D'HAÏTI. INDEX DE 1925 à 1950 (*Rev. soc. haïtienne hist. géog.*, v. 21, no. 77, avril, p. 60-79).
An indispensable guide to the many articles published in the only Haitian historical review, since its start. Many have not been mentioned in the relevant *HLAS.* [R. D. Hussey]

1452. Rosado Iturralde, Gonzalo de Jesús. Breve historia de Cozumel. T. 1. Cozumel, Mexico, Club del Libro, 1950? 210 p.

1453. Rubio, Ángel. La ciudad de Panamá. Panamá, Banco de Urbanización y Rehabilitación (Publ. no. 17). 238 p., maps.
Discussion of the commercial and political importance of the city from the 16th century, but of independent value chiefly for the 20th. The maps and plates form a valuable series, beginning with the map of 1609. See item 1136. [R. D. Hussey]

1454. Salazar Bondy, Augusto. Hipólito Unanue en la polémica sobre América (*Documenta,* año 2, no. 1, 1949-1950, p. 395-413).
As part of a longer study of the thought of

Unanue, a Peruvian *pensador* of the Enlightenment, the author offers this discussion of his views on the "America vs. Europe" theme, along lines sketched by Gerbi's *Viejas polémicas sobre el Nuevo Mundo* (1946). Unanue took on Buffon and De Pauw in writings following 1794, and this provides an interesting intellectual profile of incipient nationalism. [H. F. Cline]

1455. Santovenia, Emeterio S. Cuarenta años de vida de la Academia. Habana, Academia de la Historia de Cuba. 30 p.
Brief account of the activities of the Cuban Academy of History during its entire existence. [R. E. McNicoll]

1456. Schlarman, Joseph H. L. Mexico, a land of volcanoes. From Cortés to Alemán. Milwaukee, Wis., Bruce. xiv, 640 p.
A pronounced Catholic interpretation of Mexican history, professionally inadequate but containing some new materials. Emphasis falls on the troubles of Church and State after Independence. [H. F. Cline]

1457. Sierra, Justo. Evolución política del pueblo mexicano. México, Fondo de Cultura Económica. xvi, 301 p., port.
Reissue of the great Mexican synthesis, prepared by a leading intellectual for publication first in 1901. This book was reissued by the same firm in 1940. [H. F. Cline]

1458. Tro, Rodolfo (ed.). Cuba. Viajes y descripciones, 1493-1949. Habana. 188 p.
Excellent guide to Cuban travel accounts which suggests that more use might be made of these sources for a broader Cuban history. The writer feels the present guide would have been more usable if a chronological organization had been used along with the alphabetical. Also in *Rev. bibl. nac.,* Habana, 2. serie, t. 1, no. 3, mayo. [R. E. McNicoll]

1459. Trouillot, Henock. Beaubrun Ardouin. L'homme politique et l'historien. Port-au-Prince, Instituto Panamericano de Geografía e Historia (Publ. no. 106, Comisión de Historia, 20, Historiadores de América, 7). 54 p., illus.

1460. Valle, Rafael Heliodoro. Las investigaciones de historia en México y Centroamérica (*Univ. México,* v. 4, no. 48, dic., p. 25-26).
A helpful check-list of the principal institutions, organizations, and periodicals concerned with historical materials. [H. F. Cline]

1461. Vargas, Marco Tulio. Anotaciones históricas del Magdalena. Bogotá, Librería Latina, 1950? 221 p.
Sketches concerning the history of the region of Santa Marta and the lower Magdalena—some of them quite interesting. [W. Stewart]

1462. Whitaker, Arthur P. Developments of the past decade in the writing of Latin

American history (*Rev. hist. amér.*, no. 29, junio, p. 123-133).

In retrospect it appears that the decade of World War II had less effect on the writing of Latin American history than might have been expected. Activity in the United States was most affected and that in Latin America, least. The author notes a continuation of revisionism in regard to the Black Legend and in the rehabilitation of some anti-liberal figures such as Rosas. A wholesome change of emphasis towards development of intellectual history and inter-discipline studies is also set forth as a positive gain in the decade. The author's high position in the field makes his rather optimistic appraisal a significant guide to young historians debating which field to choose for specialization. [R. E. McNicoll]

ADDENDA

1464. **Congreso Histórico Municipal Interamericano. Tercer Congreso, San Juan Bautista de Puerto Rico, 14-18 de abril de 1948.** Actas y documentos. San Juan, P. R. 1948? 343 p.
Not strongly historical, in spite of title. But includes, of some interest to historians: Francisco Pérez de la Riva, *La habitación rural en Cuba* (p. 135-219); and Manuel A. Domínguez, *Genealogía de la vivienda colonial porteña* (p. 263-323). The latter deals with the story from the 16th century, the former is valuable chiefly for the 19th. [R. D. Hussey]

1465. **Dávila Garibi, José Ignacio.** El culto guadalupano en lo que fué la Nueva Galicia. México, Librería San Ignacio de Loyola, 1948. 91 p., port.
Bibliography, p. 69-87. [R. D. Hussey]

1466. ————. Serie cronológica de los prelados . . . antigua diócesis, hoy arquidiócesis de Guadalajara, 1548-1948 . . . . México, Cultura, 1948. 122 p.
Lacks scholarly apparatus except for a bibliography (p. 99-115), but was written by an outstanding scholar in the field, after long study in many archives, including that of the Vatican. [R. D. Hussey]

1467. **Esteban-Infantes y Martín, Emilio.** Expediciones españolas, siglo XIX. Prólogo del Conde de Romanones. Madrid, Instituto de Cultura Hispánica, 1949. 347 p., illus., maps.
The interesting sections for us are those concerning Prim in Mexico (p. 143-174) and the expedition to the Pacific (p. 241-320). Valuable for Spanish view. Good maps. [W. Stewart]

1468. Índice de los Boletines de la Academia Nacional de la Historia. Del Número 1 al Número 124, años de 1912 a 1948. Caracas, Imprenta Nacional, 1949. 75 p.
An excellent research tool. [W. Stewart]

1469. **Reina Valenzuela, José.** Bosquejo histórico de la farmacia y la medicina en Honduras. Tegucigalpa, Ariston, 1947. 233 p.
From pre-Conquest to the present. [R. D. Hussey]

1470. **Rennard, Joseph.** Centenaire de la liberté. Notes pour servir a l'histoire des origines de l'abolition de l'esclavage dans les colonies françaises (*Rev. d'hist. col.*, t. 35, 1. semestre, 1948, p. 27-69).
Useful especially for the governmental attitudes, from the later 18th century to 1848. [R. D. Hussey]

1471. **Vargas, Fulgencio.** Proceso histórico de la metrópoli guanajuatense. México, 1948. 138 p., illus.
Written to commemorate the bicentenary of the founding of Guanajuato. *Fuentes de información:* p. 127-138. [R. D. Hussey]

1472. **Vidal, Salvador.** Estudio histórico de la catedral de Zacatecas. Zacatecas, Mexico, 1949. 36 p.

SPANISH AMERICA AND HAITI: THE COLONIAL PERIOD

ROLAND D. HUSSEY AND HOWARD F. CLINE

MANY good but few really outstanding studies appeared in 1950, upon the colonial history of Middle America and the West Indies. One has the impression that Spanish writers and publications continued to increase in proportional importance, and that Cuban contributions were also weightier, as a whole, than they had been for some time. The influence of the four hundredth anniversary of the death of Hernán Cortés could still be seen, as could that of the active movement for the canonization of Fray Junípero Serra. Both, of course, called forth many articles which add too little to knowledge to require mention, but some even as to Cortés managed to bring out new facets of that many-sided life that are important for more than the narrative and usually eulogistic biographer.

Items now first listed (although they appeared before 1950) and deserving of special mention include Delgado Roig's work on the pioneering of Spain in treatment of psychiatric cases, the work *Estudios hispanoamericanos* (item 1523), Manfredini's biography of the second Revillagigedo and Lantery's *Memorias*. The last is an important item among the regrettably few private and personal records for its general field.

Among the 1950 items, one is tempted to give first place to a pair of articles, those by Connell-Smith and Peraza de Ayala. They are valuable in themselves, but even more in view of what I already know to have appeared in later years. Connell-Smith is a compelling revision of much that has been known—or unknown—about American angles of Anglo-Spanish relations in the 16th century. Peraza de Ayala's article on the Canaries trade with the Indies has been followed by books and articles by others, to be mentioned in future numbers, which will equally compel new evaluations in Spanish American history. Additions to knowledge of slightly less novelty are found in Valle Llano's history of the Jesuits in Santo Domingo, and Velázquez's *Estado de guerra en Nueva España*. And for one reason or another, no one building a basic library upon Spanish American colonial history should overlook the English translation of Motolinía, the augmented edition of Simpson's standard work on the encomienda or the completion of Sánchez Alonso's history of Spanish historiography. The catalogues of manuscript collections in the Spanish Academy of History (items 1506, 1509) are also deserving of attention.

Only one periodical new in 1950 has been analyzed, the *Caribbean historical review,* which appeared in December. Unfortunately, it is not yet clear whether that first issue was still-born. In addition, the addenda sections of this *Handbook* have entries for the first time from three other periodicals: *Jamaican historical review, Revue d'histoire de l'Amérique française* (Montreal), and *Archivos iberoamericanos de historia de la medicina* (Madrid). The first printed many articles of Spanish American interest, but always appeared irregularly and no issue is known to me since 1949. The second naturally concentrates upon Canada, but includes high quality studies upon the French West Indies. The third is sometimes rather pedantic and stresses philosophical aspects of the history of medicine to a degree that may lessen its value for many American historians, but it also prints articles of great factual value, and with proportionate attention to America. [R. D. Hussey]

STATEMENTS about the general items and those touching colonial South America which have appeared in recent *Handbooks* would also cover 1950. It was a rather routine year. Spaniards again demonstrated great talents, while significant work by other European or North American investigators was notable by its absence, so far as South America is concerned. There is a startlingly large output of "novelized history," which usually is really neither novel nor history.

For the northern areas, little noteworthy publication appeared by local hands. The really first class item is J. M. Ots Capdequí's *Instituciones de gobierno . . . durante el siglo XVIII* (item 1708); he is a Spanish exile. Peru, as usual, was prolific, though not especially original, with earlier reported themes still dominant; new data on Inca Garcilaso (item 1730) and 17th century science (item 1731) have more than antiquarian appeal, as do articles on mining (items 1741, 1757) and use of the Rímac River (item 1758).

The Chilean colonial scene is drab this year, with reeditions more notable than original work. As forecast several *Handbooks* ago, the shrivelling process noted for colonial history of the Platine region is virtually complete; with one exception, which is almost 19th-century history (item 1753), no really lasting scholarly work is listed from that once productive center. [H. F. Cline]

GENERAL *

1473. Arcila Farías, Eduardo. Comercio entre Venezuela y México en los siglos XVI y XVII. México, El Colegio de México. 324 p., maps.

The author is an excellent economic historian, who after five years of research in the archives of his native Venezuela spent nearly two years in the Archivo General de la Nación, Mexico City. [R. D. Hussey]

1474. Armas, Fernando de. Iglesia y estado en las misiones americanas (*Estud. amer.,* v. 2, no. 6, mayo, p. 197-217).

Examines manner in which the institutions of the Castilian Crown attracted the American church to itself rather than to Rome. [R. D. Hussey]

1475. Ballesteros y Beretta, Antonio. Historia de España y su influencia en la historia universal. T. 4, 1. parte. 2. edición. Barcelona, Salvat. 1144 p., illus.

First edition appeared in 1922. Work covers the reign of the Hapsburgs in America as well as in Spain. The bibliographies have supplements which bring the entries up to date, but there is probably no other change. [R. D. Hussey]

1476. Bataillon, Marcel. Erasmo y España. Estudios sobre la historia espiritual del siglo XVI. Traducción de Antonio Alatorre. V. 1-2. México, Fondo de Cultura Económica. lxxxv, 503, 545 p., facsims., ports.

First Spanish language version of *Érasme et l'Espagne* (Paris, 1937), revised by the author and augmented with a chapter "Erasmo y el Nuevo Mundo." This chapter was prepublished in *Cuad. amer.,* v. 51, no. 3, mayo-junio, p. 173-195. [R. D. Hussey]

1477. Bayle, Constantino. El clero secular y la evangelización de América. Madrid, Consejo Superior de Investigaciones Científicas, Instituto Santo Toribio de Mogrovejo (Biblioteca Missionalia Hispanica, v. 6). xvii, 350 p.

An important study of efforts made by non-monastical groups in evangelization. As most of the literature on missions is by or about specific orders, this fills a definite gap. The important contributions of the hierarchy (as opposed to the regulars) is reconstructed, principally from familiar materials now reviewed in the light of this important approach. [H. F. Cline]

1478. ————. Los municipios y los indios (*Missionalia hispanica,* año 7, no. 21, p. 409-442).

From cabildo records argues that although in general town governments of the 16th century were made up of encomenderos, they passed a good deal of local protective legislation in favor of Indians to stop or ameliorate the chief abuses

which higher Crown authorities were also combatting. [H. F. Cline]

1479. Boletín del Archivo Nacional de Historia. Quito. Año 1, no. 1, enero-junio.

First issue (238 pages), published under the auspices of the Casa de la Cultura Ecuatoriana. Contains indexes and extracts of documents in the Archivo (director, Carlos Vivanco). [R. L. Tree]

1480. Bonifaz, Miguel. Minería y legislación colonial (*Rev. estud. jur. pol. soc.,* año 10, no. extraordinario, mayo, p. 195-224).

A technical survey of mining legislation in the various areas of Latin America in the colonial period. Includes pre-Hispanic antecedents, labor regulations, and tables showing production in various mines over a period of years. [R. L. Tree]

1481. Chaunu, Pierre. L'Amérique espagnole coloniale. Les grandes lignes de la production historique de 1935 à 1949 (*Rev. hist.,* Paris, 74. année, t. 204, juillet-sept., p. 77-105).

Chiefly on items published in Spain and Spanish America, and therefore better known elsewhere than in France during the troubled years named. But a valuable list and commentary, by one of the younger generation of French Hispanists. [R. D. Hussey]

1482. Connell-Smith, G. English merchants trading to the New World in the early sixteenth century (*Bull. inst. hist. res.,* v. 23, no. 67, May, p. 53-67).

Using chiefly the notarial archives of Seville, the author shows that until the English Reformation and the accompanying bad relations with Spain, English merchants living in Spain had an open and flourishing trade with the Indies. Conditions began to change when Charles V no longer needed the help of Henry VIII against France, and Philip II limited their trade to Spain and to Catholics within Spain. [R. D. Hussey]

1483. Finan, John J. Maize in the great herbals (*Chron. bot.,* v. 13, no. 1-6, 1949-1950, p. 141-191).

Reprinted with introductory matter from v. 35 of the *Annals* of the Missouri Botanical Garden. The author made good use of Spanish American printed accounts. [R. D. Hussey]

1484. García Gallo, Alfonso. La unión política de los Reyes Católicos y la incorporación de las Indias (*Rev. estud. pol.,* año 10, v. 30, no. 50, marzo-abril, p. 179-193).

An examination of the recently much discussed Aragonese and Castilian positions upon the matter of the legal rights to American lands. [R. D. Hussey]

*For Brazilian items see "Brazil," p. 169-179.

1485. Gascón de Gotor, A. Pedro Porter y Casanate. Aventurero genial, soldado, navegante, descubridor, publicista. Zaragoza, Spain, Imprenta Estilo (Aragón en América). 137 p., illus.
Said to be a thorough study of the whole American career of this important figure in Mexico, California, and Chile based upon the Archive of the Indies and manuscripts in the National Library, Madrid. Has not been seen. [R. D. Hussey]

1486. Graham, Gerald S. Empire of the North Atlantic: the maritime struggle for North America. Toronto, Canada, University of Toronto Press. xvii, 338 p.
Although primarily upon the struggle between France and England, and from the sources of those countries, this book should not be overlooked by persons interested in the Spanish American end. [R. D. Hussey]

1487. Guijarro Olivares, José. Historia de los hospitales coloniales españoles en América durante los siglos XVI, XVII y XVIII (*Arch. iberoamer. hist. med.*, v. 2, no. 2, julio-dic., p. 529-599).
A carefully detailed study of the external history of some sixty hospitals in Spanish America, widely scattered. The amount of information furnished upon each differs greatly, aside from the fact that some started very late in the 18th century. (Those founded in the 16th century, however, were numerous.) Sources are poorly indicated, but apparently nearly all the data, and probably all the illustrations, are from the Archive of the Indies. 22 plates. [R. D. Hussey]

1488. Hanke, Lewis. Los primeros experimentos sociales en América (*Rev. bim. cub.*, v. 65, no. 1-3, enero-junio, p. 55-117).
Translation, with introductory note, by Roberto Ezquinazi Mayo, of the booklet of 1935. [R. D. Hussey]

1489. Hobbs, William H. The track of the Columbus caravels in 1492 (*Hisp. amer. hist. rev.*, v. 30, no. 1, Feb., p. 63-73).
The author, emeritus professor of geography of the University of Michigan, uses information upon compass variation, but also arguments from the habits of pelagic birds, etc., to determine that the route of Columbus was farther south (largely within the tropics) than that propounded by Samuel Eliot Morison in 1942. [R. D. Hussey]

1490. Jos, Emiliano. Ciencia y osadía sobre Lope de Aguirre el Peregrino. Sevilla, Consejo Superior de Investigaciones Científicas, Escuela de Estudios Hispano-Americanos (Publ. 53, Serie 2, no. 21). 166 p.
Detailed critique, with new documents on the "Caudillo de los Marañones," aimed chiefly at undermining the work of an Argentine, Burmeister, and the Peruvians Lastres and Seguín,

concerning the early discovery of the Amazon; it succeeds pretty well. [H. F. Cline]

1491. ————. El libro del primer viaje. Algunas ediciones recientes (*Rev. Indias,* Madrid, año 10, no. 42, oct.-dic., p. 719-751).
A careful and critical study of this Columbus document. [R. D. Hussey]

1492. Konetzke, Richard. La condición legal de los criollos y las causas de la Independencia (*Estud. amer.,* v. 2, no. 5, enero, p. 31-54).
An effort at a new evaluation. Points out that creoles received increasing favor under both Charles III and Charles IV. [R. D. Hussey]

1493. Lastres, Juan B. El ejercicio de la medicina durante los siglos XVI, XVII y XVIII (*Rev. univ.,* Cuzco, año 39, no. 98, 1. semestre, p. 88-104).
An important panoramic sketch of the progress in the practice of medicine in the New World from the conquest to the close of the 18th century. The author shows that medical science made considerable progress over the three centuries and that some important medical schools were established quite early. [R. L. Tree]

1494. Lejarza, Fidel de. Fuentes documentales. La historia misionera en *Los americanos en las órdenes nobiliarias* (*Missionalia hispanica,* año 7, no. 21, p. 443-524).
An alphabetical listing of missionaries in the American colonies, and of data about them, revealed in the two-volume work named, published in Madrid, 1947, by Guillermo Lohmann Villena (see *HLAS, no. 13, 1947,* item 1212). As the data appear mostly because the missionary was a witness in another man's *proceso,* and such names were not indexed in the 1947 volumes, the present article is the only easy way to discover them. [R. D. Hussey]

1495. Losada, Ángel. De thesauris. Un manuscrito original e inédito del Padre Las Casas (*Rev. Indias,* Madrid, año 10, no. 42, oct.-dic., p. 769-778).
A manuscript in the Biblioteca del Palacio, Madrid, in a contemporary hand with corrections by Las Casas. Also published in *Miscelánea americanista* (Madrid, 1951). [R. D. Hussey]

1496. Lugo, Américo. Los restos de Colón. Ciudad Trujillo, Librería Dominicana (Ediciones de la Academia Dominicana de la Historia). 129 p.
Standard Dominican viewpoint upon the whereabouts of the remains of Columbus, by a veteran historian. First published in *Clío,* in 1934. [R. D. Hussey]

1497. Majo Framis, Ricardo. Álvar Núñez Cabeza de Vaca. Madrid, Gran Capitán (Col. Milicia de España). 227 p.
Ornamented paraphrase of Cabeza de Vaca's

two well-known accounts of his life in North America and in the Plata region. [R. D. Hussey]

1498. ————. Vidas de los navegantes y conquistadores españoles del siglo XVI. 2. ed. Madrid, Aguilar. 227 p.
Popularized first volume, solely upon "navegantes." The men were active in much territory besides the Americas. [R. D. Hussey]

1499. **Maura, Duque de.** Un testimonio social del siglo XVII (*Bol. real acad. hist.,* t. 126, cuad. 2, abril-junio, p. 327-349).
A commentary upon the *Memorias de Lantery* published in Cadiz in 1949. See item 1528. [R. D. Hussey]

1500. **Molleda, Ma. Dolores G.** El contrabando inglés en América. Correspondencia inédita de la factoría de Buenos Aires (*Hispania,* Madrid, t. 10, no. 39, abril-junio, p. 336-369).
Preceded by an introduction that gives details of the trade and navigation policies in the first third of the 18th century, these letters and memoranda give much detail on the English trading "factory" in Buenos Aires as a smuggling center, in conjunction with the slave trade. The papers, from Simancas, are reports of an Englishman, Mathias Plowe, who in 1723 was suborned by Spanish gold to sell secrets in his possession as secretary of the South Sea Company in 1718. [H. F. Cline]

1501. **Muro Orejón, Antonio.** Cristóbal Colón. El original de la capitulación de 1492 y sus copias contemporáneas (*An. estud. amer.,* t. 7, p. 505-515).
The original having disappeared, the author chooses a copy of 1497 as most "official," and compares it with other early versions. 8 plates. [R. D. Hussey]

1502. **Oviedo y Valdés, Gonzalo Fernández de.** Sumario de la natural historia de las Indias. Edición, introducción y notas de José Miranda. México, Fondo de Cultura Económica (Biblioteca América, Serie de Cronistas de Indias). 279 p.
The first edition of this book appeared in Toledo, 1526. Editor's introduction, p. 7-74. [R. D. Hussey]

1503. **Peraza de Ayala, José.** El régimen comercial de Canarias con las Indias en los siglos XVI, XVII y XVIII (*Rev. hist.,* Islas Canarias, año 23, t. 16, no. 90-91, abril-sept., p. 199-244).
Deals almost entirely with the 16th and early 17th centuries. Much data upon the trade, and upon the Sevillian efforts, partially successful, to restrict it, appears in addition to discussion of the legal aspects. Based upon the Canarian archives. [R. D. Hussey]

1504. **Pulido Rubio, José.** El piloto mayor de la Casa de Contratación. Pilotos mayores, catedráticos de cosmografía y cosmógrafos. Sevilla, Consejo Superior de Investigaciones Científicas, Escuela de Estudios Hispano-Americanos (Publ., serie 2, no. 19). viii, 983 p.
A greatly expanded version of a book of the same title published at Seville in 1923. That presented data to 1620; this one ends with 1717. The institution of the *piloto mayor* is discussed as well as the individual figures. [R. D. Hussey]

1505. **Ramelli, Eda.** Fray Juan de Pineda, humanista, estudiado en la *Agricultura christiana.* México. 192 p.
The *Agricultura christiana* (Salamanca, 1589) of the Franciscan Pineda (ca. 1520-ca.1593) is analyzed in this thesis (University of Mexico), or more properly, rearranged in paraphrase for its ideas. A strong influence from Erasmus and extensive social criticism is revealed, but there is practically nothing about the Indies. [R. D. Hussey]

1506. **Real Academia de la Historia.** Índice de la colección de Don Luis de Salazar y Castro formado por Antonio de Vargas-Zúñiga y Montero de Espinosa, y Baltasar Cuartero y Huerta. T. 1-6. Madrid, 1949-1950.
Salazar y Castro (1658-1734) was *cronista de Castilla* from 1685 and *cronista mayor de Indias* from 1691. His great manuscript collection is notable among genealogists, but has much of general interest for the history of Spain, and to some degree of America. The first six volumes contain indices to papal documents, 590-1670, to Aragonese items, 1213-1516, and to those for the reigns from Charles I (V) to Charles II, 1516-1698. [R. D. Hussey]

1507. **Ricard, Roberto.** La plaza mayor en España y en América española (*Estud. geog.,* año 11, no. 39, mayo, p. 321-327).
For the French original, see *HLAS, no. 13, 1947,* item 1224. [R. D. Hussey]

1508. **Rodríguez Casado, Vicente.** El Pacífico en la política internacional española hasta la emancipación de América (*Estud. amer.,* 2, no. 5, enero, p. 1-30).
A documented essay, starting with the time of Cortés. It ties up the 18th-century question of dominating the South Atlantic, as in the Falklands case or the Spanish-Portuguese boundary questions, with Pacific Ocean designs. [R. D. Hussey]

1509. **Rodríguez Moñino, Antonio.** La colección de manuscritos del Marqués de Montealegre, 1677 (*Bol. real acad. hist.,* t. 126, cuad. 1, julio-sept., p. 307-344; cuad. 2, oct.-dic., p. 561-627).
Part of a contemporary printed catalogue. The rich collection went largely to Luis de Salazar, and is now in the Real Academia de la Historia, Madrid. There are a fair number of Americana. 100 copies of this article were separately printed in 1951 (236 p.). [R. D. Hussey]

1510. Rumeu de Armas, Antonio. El gobernador Manrique de Acuña y la batalla naval de 1552 (*Rev. hist.*, Islas Canarias, año 23, t. 16, no. 89, enero-marzo, p. 1-21).

The battle and its antecedents were closely tied up with foreign interests in the Indies, and incidentally killed off several well-known French corsair captains who had been in the Caribbean. [R. D. Hussey]

1511. Salas, Alberto Mario. Las armas de la Conquista. Buenos Aires, Emecé. 462 p., illus.

Exhaustive and most interesting treatment of weapons, defensive armor, and military practices of both Indians and Spaniards, and, in a final section, discussion of the influence of one people upon the other in the waging of war. Thoroughly documented, with a good bibliography. [C. Shelby]

1512. Salvador y Conde, J. El padre Domingo de la Anunciación y su personalidad misionera (*Missionalia hispanica,* año 7, no. 19, p. 81-162).

An extended eulogy and biobibliographical sketch of an exemplary missionary of the Dominican order in Mexico. He was born in 1510, came to New Spain as a youth and died in 1591. He was a missionary to Nahua-speaking Indians around Mexico City, and organizer of an enterprise to missionarize Florida (1559). [H. F. Cline]

1513. Sánchez Alonso, Benito. Historia de la historiografía española. Ensayo de un examen de conjunto. III, De Solís al final del siglo XVIII. Madrid, Consejo Superior de Investigaciones Científicas. 312 p.

Part I, published in 1941. Part II, in 1944. Part III appears in three chapters, 1684-1727, 1727-1781, and 1781-1808, with a section in each upon the *Historia de las Indias.* There is also a table of contents and an extensive *Índice* (p. 279-304) of the three volumes. Although the whole work is essentially a biobibliography, it includes synthesis, and some information about the content of the various works. [R. D. Hussey]

1514. SIMANCAS. ESTUDIOS DE HISTORIA MODERNA. V. 1. Valladolid, Spain, Asociación Internacional de Amigos de Simancas. xii, 506 p.

Probably actually published only late in 1951, or in 1952. A bookseller's announcement shows articles covering from the 15th to the 18th centuries. They include of American interest: Alicia Gould y Quincy, *Lucio Marineo Siculo (1444-1536)* and [Vicente (?)] Beltrán y Heredia, *Nuevos datos acerca del P. Ninaya y del lic. Calvo de Padilla, compañeros de Las Casas.* [R. D. Hussey]

1515. Verlinden, Charles. Les influences médiévales dans la colonisation de l'Amérique (*Rev. hist. amér.,* no. 30, dic., p. 440-450).

A plea for the need of studying the medieval backgrounds of the mother countries, with valuable footnotes upon relevant studies already made. [R. D. Hussey]

1516. Woodbrige, Hensley Charles. Spanish nautical terms of the Age of Discovery. Urbana, Illinois. 11 p.

Abstract of a Ph. D. thesis at the University of Illinois. Using Fernández de Navarrete's *Colección de viajes* as his base, the author has attempted to discover what terms were in use from 1492 to 1540, and whether they have an earlier recorded history. No direct American influence is revealed by this abstract. [R. D. Hussey]

ADDENDA

1517. Ballesteros y Gaibrois, Manuel (ed.). Escritores de Indias . . . . 2. edición. Zaragoza, Spain, Heraldo (Biblioteca Clásica Ebro, Clásicos Españoles, 7, 25), 1949. 2 v., illus.

Extracts, with biobibliographical notes and an introduction on historical and literary values and on the *leyenda negra,* from many well-known 16th-century *cronistas* of the Indies, plus Rodrigo de Vivero on Japan and Fray Gabriel de San Antonio on Cambodia. V. 1 of the first edition (Zaragoza, 1940) was mentioned but not described in *HLAS, no. 6, 1940,* item 2804. [R. D. Hussey]

1518. Bermúdez Plata, Cristóbal. La cárcel nueva de la Casa de la Contratación (*Rev. Indias,* Madrid, año 9, no. 37-38, julio-dic., 1949, p. 645-649).

Completed in 1613. Article also published in *Miscelánea americanista,* v. 1, Madrid, 1951. [R. D. Hussey]

1519. Carande, Ramón. Carlos V y sus banqueros. La hacienda real de Castilla. Madrid, Sociedad de Estudios y Publicaciones, 1949. xvi, 638 p., illus., maps.

A continuation to the author's work of similar title published in 1943 (*HLAS, no. 12, 1946,* item 1713) and like that includes extensive data upon American aspects. [R. D. Hussey]

1520. Delgado Roig, Juan. Fundaciones psiquiátricas en Sevilla y el Nuevo Mundo. Prólogo de Juan J. López Ibor. Madrid, Paz Montalvo, 1948. 80 p., illus.

Mostly upon the Spanish aspects from ancient days, showing that Spain had world priority in establishing hospitals for the mentally ill, with the idea of helping the *loco,* not merely of protecting society against him. Valencia led the way in 1409; Sevilla was third or fourth in 1436. This was reflected in the New World, starting with the founding of the Order of San Hipólito in Mexico in the 16th century. [R. D. Hussey]

1521. Enciso, Martín Fernández de. Suma de geografía. Madrid, Estades (Col. Joyas Bibliográficas, 1), 1948. xix, 228 p.

Reprint of the first edition (Sevilla, 1519) with a biobibliographical introduction by José Ibáñez Cerdá. Limited edition, 250 copies. [R. D. Hussey]

1522. ESTUDIOS DE HISTORIA SOCIAL DE ESPAÑA. V. 1. Madrid, Consejo Superior de Investigaciones Científicas, 1949. 724 p. The start of what promises to be a valuable series for the Americanist as well as the Hispanicist (v. 2 appeared in 1952.) The articles vary considerably in quality, and have a tendency to expound theory rather than to collect "facts" and adduce their meaning, but as a whole they offer important additions to present knowledge. The two of directly American subject matter are listed separately. [R. D. Hussey]

1523. ESTUDIOS HISPANOAMERICANOS. HOMENAJE A HERNÁN CORTÉS EN EL IV CENTENARIO DE SU MUERTE. Badajoz, Spain, Imprenta de la Diputación Provincial (Revista de Estudios Extremeños, Anejo 1), 1948. 399 p., illus.
Articles on Cortés and other subjects. Among them: *Relación del descubrimiento del Reyno del Perú*, edited by M. Muñoz S. Pedro (p. 29-61), which appears to be the same text elsewhere edited by Raúl Porras Barrenechea (see *HLAS, no. 14, 1948*, item 1966); and *La Santa Ana María en la carrera de las Indias*, by Esteban Rodríguez Amaya (p. 393-399), which includes the text (dated July 22, 1610) of the will of Captain García Pérez de Cáceres, a native of Badajoz engaged in trade with the Indies, listing not only his own property but the cargo of his ship.

1524. Hamilton, Earl J. The role of monopoly in the overseas expansion and colonial trade of Europe before 1800 (*Amer. econ. rev.*, v. 38, no. 2, May, 1948, p. 33-53).
An excellent résumé and synthesis of facts in the modern historical literature of several countries, Portugal (p. 34-40), Spain (p. 40-43), the Netherlands, England, and France. [R. D. Hussey]

1525. Junco, Alfonso. Inquisición sobre la Inquisición. México, Jus (Col. de Estudios Históricos), 1949. 309 p.
A critical examination of the attacks upon, and the truth about, and the historians of, the institution. Strong as to the American aspects. [R. D. Hussey]

1526. Konotzke, Richard. La esclavitud de los indios como elemento en la estructuración social de Hispanoamérica (*Estud. hist. soc. España*, v. 1, p. 441-479).
Discusses the European background of slavery, and the story of Indian slavery, in the 15th and 16th centuries, from well-known printed sources. But uses materials from the Archivo General de Indias for the legal revival of Indian slavery in Chile, 1608 to 1676. [R. D. Hussey]

1527. ―――. Las ordenanzas de gremios como documentos para la historia social de Hispanoamérica durante la época colonial (*Estud. hist. soc. España*, v. 1, p. 481-524).
Using considerable amounts of manuscript from Spanish repositories, presents an ordered text of scraps of pertinent information about the *gremios*. The data are chiefly important for Mexico and the 18th century, but concern also other countries or eras. [R. D. Hussey]

1528. Lantery, Raimundo de. Memorias de . . . , mercader de Indias en Cádiz, 1673-1700. Publícalas Álvaro Ricardo y Gómez. Cádiz, Spain, Escelicer, 1949. xvii, 421 p., illus.
Second volume, the only one extant, of three volumes written by Lantery, a native of Nice, for the use of his family. See item 1499. [R. D. Hussey]

1529. Losada, Ángel. Juan Ginés de Sepúlveda a través de su *Epistolario* y nuevos documentos. Madrid, Consejo Superior de Investigaciones Científicas, Instituto Francisco de Vitoria, 1949. 681 p., port.
A large amount of the material has American value, and has not previously been used. Bibliography, p. 659-670. [R. D. Hussey]

1530. Meisnest, Frederick W. The lost *Book of privileges* of Columbus located and identified (*Hunt. libr. quart.*, v. 12, no. 4, Aug., 1949, p. 401-408).
Mentions the three known copies on parchment and two abridged versions, and discusses the third abridged copy now in the Huntington Library, bought by Mr. Huntington from Maggs Bros., London, in 1924. (Maggs Bros. claimed not to know its provenience.) Meisnest says it is not true, as has been claimed, that the notes on the Huntington codex are in the hand of Columbus. [R. D. Hussey]

1531. Van der Kroef, Justus M. Francisco de Vitoria and the nature of colonial policy (*Cath. hist. rev.*, v. 35, no. 2, July, 1949, p. 129-162).
A masterly summary, guided by and annotated from relevant studies in a half dozen languages. [R. D. Hussey]

1532. Wagner, Henry R. Marco Polo's narrative becomes propaganda to inspire Colón (*Imago mundi*, v. 6, 1949, p. 3-13).
Interesting speculations, built around Marco Polo's account of Cipangu, and mentions of Cipangu by Columbus and 16th-century writers. [R. D. Hussey]

1533. Williamson, James Alexander. Hawkins of Plymouth. A new history of Sir John Hawkins and of other members of his family prominent in Tudor England. London, Black, 1949. xi, 348 p., ports., maps.
Of broader scope than the author's 1927 biography of Sir John alone, and reveals an honest effort to use the Spanish documents that

have been printed in translation by Irene Wright. I nevertheless find little difference in the underlying "all English" viewpoint, but the work is extremely valuable for its critical use of new English sources. [R. D. Hussey]

1534. Wroth, Lawrence C. (ed.). John Carter Brown Library in retrospect, 1923-1949. An exhibition commemorating twenty-six years of service. Providence, Rhode Island, The Library, 1949. vi, 40 p., 16 pls.

Annotated catalog of 113 of the most important items of about 5,000 added during the period. At least a third have direct Hispanic interest. Many are unique or nearly so, or the only copies in the United States. [R. D. Hussey]

1535. Zavala, Silvio. América en el espíritu francés del siglo XVIII. México, El Colegio Nacional, 1949. 315 p.

Should be read in conjunction with the lengthy review article by G. Chinard in *Hisp. amer. hist. rev.*, v. 31, no. 3, Aug., 1951. [R. D. Hussey]

MIDDLE AMERICA AND THE ISLANDS

ROLAND D. HUSSEY

LISTS AND INDICES

1537. BOLETÍN DEL ARCHIVO GENERAL DE LA NACIÓN. México. T. 21, no. 1, enero-marzo–no. 4, oct.-dic.

Continuation of the indexes to the sections entitled *Ramo de tierras, Ramo provincias internas, Ramo criminal,* and *Ramo Universidad,* in no. 2 and 3. In no. 4, *Guía de los tomos I al XXI, 1930-1950,* is a subject and name index of the *Boletín,* with some notes on its history. See also items 1547 and 1572. [R. R. Hill]

1537a. Carrasco Puente, Rafael. Bibliografía de Catarina de San Juan y de la china poblana. México, Secretaría de Relaciones Exteriores, Departamento de Información para el Extranjero (Monografías Bibliográficas Mexicanas, segunda serie, no. 3). 149 p.

Excellently prepared bibliography of 151 items, some with voluminous notes, relative to the 16th-century prototype of the *china.* Catarina de San Juan (so named after Christian baptism) was a native of Delhi, India, and her romantic career, which ended with her death in Mexico in 1688, is part of the nation's folklore. [C. Shelby]

1538. CATÁLOGO DE LOS FONDOS DEL CONSEJO DE ADMINISTRACIÓN DE LA ISLA DE CUBA. T. 3, O-Z. Habana, Archivo Nacional de Cuba (Publ. 28). 252 p.

A subject index of the papers of the Consejo de Administración, a consultive body during the Spanish regime. This volume completes the index. The entries give the document number and its year and subject as well as the *legajo* where it is located. The documents relate to the various subjects considered by the Consejo. There is an index of names and places. [R. R. Hill]

1539. Chávez, Antonio. Some original New Mexico documents in California libraries (*New Mex. hist. rev.,* v. 25, no. 3, July, p. 244-253).

A list of 141 "original Spanish manuscripts" in the Henry E. Huntington Library, the Bancroft Library, and the archives of the Santa Barbara Mission, dated 1681-1837 (chiefly 18th century), with a note upon some others in the Bancroft Library, less examined, and dating between 1562 and 1776.

1540. Delgado, Jaime. Gabriel Méndez Plancarte (*Rev. Indias, Madrid,* año 10, no. 40, abril-junio, p. 241-244).

Obituary, with lengthy bibliography, of the noted humanist and historian, who died on September 19, 1949. See also item 2562.

1541. Dermigny, L. Saint-Domingue aux XVIIe et XVIIIe siècles (*Rev. hist.,* Paris, t. 204, oct.-déc., p. 234-250).

A bibliographical article on the great number of valuable studies and documents published in recent years by Gabriel Debien. Many but not all have been noted in the appropriate numbers of *HLAS.*

1542. ÍNDICE DEL RAMO DE TIERRAS. Volúmenes 1761 a 1804 (*Bol. arch. gen.,* México, t. 21, no. 1, enero-marzo, p. 177-186; no. 2, abril-junio, p. 319-329; no. 3, julio-sept., p. 471-482).

Entries range from the 16th to the late 18th centuries, but are mostly for the late 17th and early 18th. The series is to be continued, but no installment appeared in no. 4. Similar lists of *Provincias internas, Criminal,* and *Universidad* were appended to, but separately paged from, no. 2 and 3 of the same *Boletín.*

1543. Le Riverend Brusone, Julio. Notas para una bibliografía cubana de los siglos XVII y XVIII (*Univ. Habana,* no. 88-90, enero-junio, p. 128-231).

Basically, a transcript of the Cuban parts of the well-known Mexican bibliography of Beristaín y Souza, but extensively annotated. Has a voluminous appendix of documents (p. 177-231) from the Mexican national archive, *Ramo Universidad.*

1544. LIBROS Y FOLLETOS DEL ARCHIVO HISTÓRICO DE LA SECRETARÍA DE HACIENDA (*Bol. arch. gen.,* México, t. 21, no. 1, enero-marzo, p. 45-114).

A classified index of books and pamphlets of the Treasury archive, now in the Archivo General. For preceding part see t. 20, no. 2, abril-junio, 1949, p. 319-349. [R. R. Hill]

1545. Peraza y Sarausa, Fermín. Papel Periódico de la Havana. Continuación (*Rev. bim. cub.*, v. 55, no. 1-3, enero-junio, p. 274-283; v. 66, no. 1-3, julio-dic., p. 277-284).

For previous installments of this subject index to the late colonial periodical, see *HLAS, no. 9, 1943,* and later volumes.

DOCUMENTS

1546. ACTAS DEL CABILDO DE SAN JUAN BAUTISTA DE PUERTO RICO, 1751-1760. San Juan, P. R., Gobierno de la Capital (Publ. Oficial). vii, 342 p.

The volume for 1730-1750 appeared in 1949. See *HLAS, no. 15, 1949,* item 1455.

1547. EL ASTILLERO DEL CARBÓN EN TEHUANTEPEC, 1535-1566 (*Bol. arch. gen.,* México, t. 21, no. 1, enero-marzo, p. 3-20).

Four documents from the Cortés archives (AGN, Mex., *Hospital de Jesús*) upon the "first shipyard on the Pacific coast," founded about 1520. They have value also for the trade between Mexico and Peru.

1548. AUTOS SOBRE EL COMERCIO ILÍCITO EN EL VALLE DE MATINA Y REMATE DE LOS OBJETOS Y NEGROS DECOMISADOS, 1716 (*Rev. arch. nac. Costa Rica,* año 14, no. 7-12, julio-dic., p. 209-230).

Includes details and evaluations of goods seized.

1549. Balli, Juan Bautista. Oración de elogio de la jurisprudencia, pronunciada en la Real Universidad de México en . . . 1596. Comentarios de Daniel Kuri Breña. Noticia bibliográfica de Salvador Ugarte. México, Jus. 89 p.

125 copies printed, of a Mexican incunabulum which was unknown until Señor Ugarte bought it from a New York dealer who got it in Peru. All copies include a facsimile (p. 67-84) of *Oratio in laudem jurisprudentiae* (Mexici, ex officina parentis, 1596). Fifty of the copies are numbered, and in them the facsimile is printed upon paper of approximately the late 16th century.

1550. Carreño, Alberto María. Don Fray Juan de Zumárraga, teólogo y editor, humanista e inquisidor. México, Jus (Documentos Inéditos). 264 p.

Text of three lectures supplemented by important documents. The whole book is valuable for aspects of the great bishop's life not usually emphasized, and especially for facts about his library.

1551. Chávez Orozco, Luis. La irrigación en México (*Prob. agríc. indus. México,* v. 2, no. 2, abril-junio, p. 13-31).

Reseña el problema de la irrigación en las épocas precortesiana y colonial. Reproduce el informe de Diego de Guadalaxara Tello sobre el desagüe de la Vega de Meztitlán. Reproducciones de códices y de otros documentos. [Nacional Financiera, S. A.]

1552. Chevalier, François (ed.). Instrucciones a los hermanos jesuítas, administradores de haciendas. Manuscrito mexicano del siglo XVIII. México, Universidad Nacional Autónoma de México, Instituto de Historia (Publ., primera serie, no. 18). 273 p.

An undated item, not earlier than 1722-1723, and probably of the mid-18th century. Valuable for the history of economic life and ideas in general, as well as for the obvious subjects..

1553. Costanso, Miguel. Diario histórico de los viages de mar y tierra hechos al norte de la California escrito por . . . en el año de 1770. Villa Obregón, Mexico, Chimaltistac. 71 p.

100 numbered, finely printed copies of this well-known book. First printed in Mexico in 1770. The introduction discusses the bibliography of the work, including variants between the printed text and that of a manuscript in the Sutro Library, San Francisco.

1554. CURATO DE TEGUCIGALPA. Estado que demuestra los individuos de esta feligresía, con distinción de calidades, sexos y edades. Fecho, en la Real Villa de Tegucigalpa, a los 30 de enero de 1783 (*Rev. arch. bibl. nac.,* Tegucigalpa, t. 28, no. 9-10, marzo-abril, folding table between p. 388 and 389).

Data on eleven *cofradías,* and on population of the *villa,* three nearby *pueblos,* and a *valle.* The *Estado* as printed here has the appearance of such imprints elsewhere, in the period, but no bibliographical information is given.

1555. Debien, G. Refugiés de Saint-Domingue aux États-Unis (*Rev. soc. haïtienne hist. géog.,* v. 21, no. 77, avril, p. 11-25; no. 78, juillet, p. 30-45; no. 79, oct., p. 19-24).

Conclusion of the work discussed in *HLAS, no. 15, 1949,* item 1464. These installments offer the correspondence of an O'Rourke family, 1780-1802.

1556. Desombrages, Joseph Vezien. Correspondance Garnier-Desombrages (*Rev. soc. haïtienne hist. géog.,* v. 21, no. 79, oct., p. 1-10).

One letter of 1788 and the rest 1796-1797. Edited by Camille Large.

1557. DOCUMENTOS QUE SE REFIEREN A LA CORRESPONDENCIA DEL SECRETARIO DE CÁMARA AL GOBERNADOR DE SANTIAGO DE CUBA, FECHA PUERTO PRÍNCIPE 24 DE OCTUBRE DE 1811, ACOMPAÑANDO TESTIMONIO DE LA REAL CÉDULA ABOLIENDO PARA SIEMPRE EL TORMENTO Y SUS EQUIVALENTES (*Bol. arch. nac.*, Habana, t. 48, enerodic., 1949, i.e. 1950, p. 184-185).

1558. DOCUMENTOS RELATIVOS A LA HISTORIA POLÍTICA DE CUBA, 1796-1802 (*Bol. arch. nac.*, Habana, t. 48, enero-dic., 1949, i.e. 1950, p. 158-194).
Factitious title for a group of documents upon real or fancied dangers from Negroes, foreigners, including Miranda, in 1797, and the Brazilian Pbro. D. Leonardo Correa, 1800-1801, and upon the evacuation of Santo Domingo in 1801.

1559. EMPLEOS, CAMPAÑAS Y ALGUNOS TÍTULOS DE D. TOMÁS DE ACOSTA, ENTRE ELLOS EL DE GOBERNADOR DE COSTA RICA (*Rev. arch. nac. Costa Rica*, año 14, no. 1-6, enero-junio, p. 183-211).
Items dated from 1762 to 1811.

1560. Entrambasaguas, Joaquín de (ed.). Algunos datos acerca de la expulsión de los jesuítas de Méjico en el siglo XVIII (*Cuad. lit.*, t. 7, no. 19-21, enero-junio, p. 5-95).
Edited texts of two items, a body of poetry from the manuscripts of the Biblioteca Nacional, Madrid, deploring the expulsion, and another document (from an unstated source) upon the *sublevación* of San Luis Potosí. The introduction remarks, without documenting the statement, that the expulsion "satisfied confused Masonic intrigues."

1561. GACETAS DE MÉXICO. CASTORENA Y URSÚA (1722). SAHAGÚN DE ARÉVALO (1728 A 1742). Introducción por Francisco González de Cossío. V. 1: 1722 y 1728 a 1731. V. 2: 1732 a 1736. V. 3: 1737 a 1742. México, Secretaría de Educación Pública (Testimonios Mexicanos, Historiadores, 4, 5, 6), 1949-1950. xxiv, 374; xxxiii, 388; xviii, 290, 123 p.
Each volume has an excellent introduction. Added together these introductions amount to a valuable survey of the *Relaciones* and *Gacetas* of the whole colonial era in Mexico. At least two items (1692, 1727) not previously known are brought to attention.

1562. Morfi, Juan Agustín de. Descripción del territorio del Real Presidio de San Juan Bautista del Río Grande del Norte (*Bol. soc. mex. geog. estad.*, t. 70, no. 1-3, julio-dic., p. 287-320).
A previously unpublished manuscript dated at the presidio, now Villa Guerrero, Coahuila, on January 23, 1778. Carefully edited by Jorge Cervera Sánchez.

1563. Motolinía, Toribio. Motolinía's *History of the Indians of New Spain*. Translated and edited by Elizabeth Andros Foster. Berkeley, Calif., The Cortés Society (Documents and Narratives Concerning the Discovery and Conquest of Latin America, n. s., no. 4). x, 294 p.
A smooth and apparently accurate translation, and well edited; the first ever made in English of this well-known chronicle. It is based upon the good Mexican edition of 1858, but apparently without reference to the manuscript, now in the University of Texas Library.

1564. Nunemaker, J. Horace (ed.). The archbishop of Mexico authorizes a wig for a priest, 1777 (*Hisp. amer. hist. rev.*, v. 30, no. 4, Nov., p. 498-500).
A charming example of *rutina oficinesca* in a bygone bureaucracy.

1565. Paso y Troncoso, Francisco del (ed.). Guazapares y otros pueblos . . . . México, Vargas Rea. 38 p.

1566. ————. Ocupán y otros pueblos . . . . México, Vargas Rea. 39 p.

1567. ————. Santa Eulalia Chihuahua . . . . México, Vargas Rea. 90 p.

1568. ————. Sayula . . . . México, Vargas Rea. 38 p.

1569. ————. Tonachic y otros pueblos. Tutuaca y otros pueblos . . . . México, Vargas Rea. 46 p.

1570. ————. Xilotepeque . . . . México, Vargas Rea. 37 p.
The six items above are part of the many accounts written in 1777 and 1778 in compliance with the royal order of October 20, 1776. They were found in manuscript form in the Archivo de Indias, Sevilla, and in the archives of the Real Academia de la Historia, Madrid. They belong in the series entitled "Biblioteca de Historiadores Mexicanos, Relaciones del Siglo XVIII . . . ." All are printed in editions of 100 copies each.

1571. Le Pers, Jean Baptiste. Histoire civile . . . de Saint Domingue (*Bol. arch. gen.*, Ciudad Trujillo, año 13, v. 13, no. 64, enero-marzo, p. 80-103; no. 65, abril-junio, p. 248-267; no. 66, julio-sept., p. 343-361; no. 67, oct.-dic., p. 448-469).
Concluding installments (if one adds v. 14, no. 68, enero-marzo, 1951, p. 73-85) of the valuable contemporary account that has been in course of publication since 1946 (see *HLAS*, no. 12, 1946, item 763). The installments listed here are for the years 1685-1733, during two-thirds of which the author resided in the island.

1572. PROCESO CONTRA MILES PHILIPS. RELACIÓN DE MILES PHILIPS (*Bol. arch. gen.*, México, t. 21, no. 1, enero-marzo, p. 115-

172; no. 2, abril-junio, p. 255-300).
For the start of the *proceso*, see *HLAS, no. 15, 1949*, item 1478. The 1950 installment includes an anonymous *Apéndice* entitled "Relación de lo sucedido en el viaje de la Nueva España a don Martín Enríquez mi señor Virrey de ella" (p. 167-172). The *Relación* in no. 2 of the *Boletín* is the Hakluyt account, as translated and published by García Icazbalceta.

1573. Ramírez, J. Fernando (ed.). California y lenguas que se hablan en Sinaloa, Sonora y California. México, Vargas Rea. 57 p.

1574. Ramos, Roberto (ed.). Historia de la tercera rebelión tarahumara. Chihuahua, Mexico, Sociedad Chihuahuense de Estudios Históricos. 56 p.
Ramos edits the text of an anonymous document of 1691, in the Biblioteca Nacional, Mexico. He ascribes it pretty surely to Padre Tomás de Guadalajara. The rebellion was in 1690.

1575. Ramos de Arizpe, Miguel. Report .... Translation, annotations and introduction by Nettie Lee Benson. Austin, Texas, University of Texas Press (Institute of Latin American Studies, Latin American Studies, 11). 61 p.
First available comprehensive account of the four Eastern Interior Provinces of the Kingdom of Mexico (Coahuila, Nuevo León, Nuevo Santander, and Texas). Presented to the Cortes of Cadiz on November 7, 1811. Printed in Spanish at Cadiz, 1812, and several times thereafter, and in English, with various omissions, at Philadelphia, 1814.

1576. REPRESENTACIÓN DEL GOBERNADOR DE COSTA RICA SOBRE INTENTAR EL CABILDO DE CARTAGO . . . EXERCER JURISDICCIÓN A LA VILLA NUEVA Y VIEJA (*Rev. arch. nac. Costa Rica*, año 14, no. 1-6, enero-junio, p. 47-82).
Legal papers of 1777.

1577. REQUISITORIA PARA LA CAPTURA DE FRANCISCO ANTONIO IBÁÑEZ, SOLDADO DESERTOR DE GUATEMALA, 1771-1772 (*Rev. arch. nac. Costa Rica*, año 14, no. 7-12, julio-dic., p. 241-249).

1578. Romero Solano, Luis. Expedición cortesiana a las Molucas, 1527. México, Jus (Sociedad de Estudios Cortesianos, publ. 6). 315 p.
Documents, p. 71-290; bibliography, p. 291-294. The documentation comes largely from the National Archive of Mexico, and includes some 18th-century items upon financial matters which grew out of the expedition.

1579. SAN MIGUEL EL GRANDE. México, Vargas Rea (Biblioteca de Historiadores Mexicanos, Relaciones del Siglo XVIII relativas a Guanajuato). 114 p.

Belongs to the same series of documents as those mentioned above under Francisco Paso y Troncoso, but the original of this one is in the National Library of Mexico.

1580. Sebastián, Félix de. El padre Rafael Landívar, S. J. (*ECA*, año 5, no. 40, mayo, p. 24-32).
Edited by Manuel I. Pérez A., S. J., from a valuable, contemporary and previously unknown account of the life of the Guatemalan poet and exile. Reprinted in *An. soc. geog. hist. Guatemala*, año 25, no. 3, sept., 1951, p. 276-285.

1581. Smith, Robert S. (ed.). Statutes of the Guatemalan indigo growers society (*Hisp. amer. hist. rev.*, v. 30, no. 3, Aug., p. 336-345).
The statutes were approved Sept. 6, 1782, by Captain General Matías de Gálvez.

1582. SOBRE EL RESTABLECIMIENTO DEL CABILDO DE LA CIUDAD DE CARTAGO, 1774-1778 (*Rev. arch. nac. Costa Rica*, año 14, no. 1-6, enero-junio, p. 16-46).
A legal *proceso* before the Audiencia of Guatemala.

1583. TESTIMONIO DE LA JUNTA DE REAL HACIENDA CELEBRADA POR EL CAPITÁN DON JACINTO DE BARRIOS LEAL, PARA DAR AYUDA ECONÓMICA A LOS VECINOS DE LA VILLA DE SANTA CRUZ DE YORO, PARA LA CONQUISTA DE LOS INDIOS PAYAS, LEONES Y MULIAS, 1690 (*Rev. arch. bibl. nac.*, Tegucigalpa, t. 28, no. 7-8, enero-feb., p. 289-293).

1584. TÍTULO DE ESCRIBANO PÚBLICO DE CABILDO, MINAS, REGISTRO E GOBIERNO A FAVOR DE DON LUIS FERNANDO DE LIENDO Y GOICOECHEA (*Rev. arch. nac. Costa Rica*, año 14, no. 7-12, julio-dic., p. 231-240).
Documents, including a royal cedula, 1735-1736.

1585. Utrera, Cipriano de (ed.). Constituciones del cabildo eclesiástico de Santo Domingo (*Clío*, año 18, no. 88, sept.-dic., p. 85-93).
The nearly complete text of the Constitution of 1652, from the Archive of the Indies. It is not in the Cathedral archives, but was preserved for the historian by being sent to Spain as part of an *expediente* upon lax behavior of the Chapter's clergy.

1586. ————. Documentos para la historia de la moneda provincial de la isla Española (*Bol. arch. gen.*, Ciudad Trujillo, año 13, v. 13, no. 64, enero-marzo, p. 50-79; no. 65, abril-junio, p. 167-219; no. 66, julio-sept., p. 331-342).
For start of this item, see *HLAS, no. 15, 1949*, item 1486. The whole series has 138 documents, 1528-1819, of which 50, from 1659 to 1819,

appear in the 1950 issues. There are large gaps in the years covered. Some documents are in calendar form, and some fully printed.

1587. Wilkinson, Henry C. Spanish intentions for Bermuda, 1603-1615 (*Bermuda hist. quart.*, v. 7, no. 2, April-June, p. 49-89).

Full text, in translation, of the relevant Spanish documents used by the editor in his *Adventurers of Bermuda* (London, 1933) plus two recently discovered items of 1611 that refer to 1603. The Diego Ramírez map of 1603, which was in the 1933 book, is also reproduced. All the items come from the Archive of the Indies.

STUDIES

1588. Alcalá, Manuel. César y Cortés. México, Jus (Publ. de la Sociedad de Estudios Cortesianos, no. 4). 252 p.

An interesting comparison of the two men, with bibliographical data. The plates include a colored frontispiece portrait.

1589. Barón Castro, Rodolfo. Reseña histórica de la villa de San Salvador desde su fundación en 1525, hasta que recibe el título de ciudad en 1546. Madrid, Ediciones Cultura Hispánica. 323 p., illus.

A detailed and important synthesis of the colonial history of El Salvador from 1525, based on familiar printed materials, with additional new documentary sources and copious bibliographical data, together with geographic and onomastic indices. [H. F. Cline]

1590. Bazant, Jan. Feudalismo y capitalismo en la historia económica de México (*Trim. econ.*, v. 17, no. 1, enero, p. 81-98).

A generalized commentary, without new facts, upon four centuries of history. Agrees that the encomienda was feudal, but says that it had been replaced by the hacienda, which was strictly capitalistic, long before the end of the colonial era. Also that capitalism in Mexico was throughout a fair reflection of capitalism in Europe for the same era.

1591. Campos, Leopoldo (ed.). Tabla capitular de la Provincia del Santo Evangelio, año de 1602 (*An. prov. Santo Evangelio de México*, año 7, no. 1, enero-junio, p. 1-11).

An official roster of the clergy, in Latin.

1592. Chauvet, Fidel de J. The church of San Francisco in Mexico City (*Americas*, v. 7, no. 1, July, p. 13-30).

Well documented history of successive buildings, from establishment of the first church and monastery about 1525 to the restoration of the present building—the third, dedicated in 1717—to the Franciscans. Previously published in Spanish, with numerous illustrations, in *An. Prov. Santo Evangelio de México*, año 6, no. 1, enero-octubre, 1949, p. 11-46.

1593. Corbató, Hermenegildo. Hernán Cortés a través de algunos cronistas e historiadores (*Rev. iberoamer.*, v. 15, no. 30, agosto, 1949-enero, 1950, p. 275-285).

A critical essay, based only on well-known information.

1594. Curtin, Philip D. The Declaration of the Rights of Man in St. Domingue, 1788-1791 (*Hisp. amer. hist. rev.*, v. 30, no. 2, May, p. 157-175).

Careful and detailed examination of manner in which the reactions of white colonials, whites in France, and mulattoes and slaves differed.

1595. Dávila Garibi, J. Ignacio. Del Comendador D. Leonel de Cervantes, conquistador de Nueva España, a Ignacio Luis Manuel Dávila Garibi y Camacho. México, Cultura. 48 p.

A genealogical study of an ancestral line of the author, based for its start upon documents in the Archivo General de Indias.

1596. Debien, Gabriel. Gens de couleur libres et colons de St. Domingue avant la Constituante, 1789-mars 1790 (*Rev. d'hist. amér. franç.*, v. 4, no. 2, sept., p. 211-232; no. 3, déc., p. 398-426).

This article, of the author's usual thorough excellence, has introductory material starting in 1685. Concluded in no. 4, mars, 1951, p. 530-549.

1597. Dunne, Peter M. Salvatierra's legacy to Lower California (*Americas*, v. 7, no. 1, July, p. 31-50).

A study of the organization of the missions, 1697 to 1717, with some information about developments to 1730.

1598. Ezquerra, Ramón. Un patricio colonial. Gilberto de Saint-Maxent, teniente gobernador de Luisiana (*Rev. Indias*, Madrid, año 10, no. 39, enero-marzo, p. 97-170).

A study of the life and times of Gilbert Antoine de St. Maxent, who served under Spain after the transfer of the colony by France. Also printed in *Miscelánea americanista*, v. 1, Madrid, 1951.

1599. Fernández y Simón, Abel. Memoria histórico-técnica de los acueductos de la Habana. Primera parte. Habana, Úcar García. 156 p., illus.

1600. Flores Guerrero, Raúl. La educación jesuíta en el noreste de México (*Bol. soc. mex. geog. estad.*, t. 70, no. 1-3, julio-dic., p. 265-280).

A study from printed sources of material aspects, ideas, and methods.

1601. García Icazbalceta, Joaquín. Del Santo Domingo del siglo XVI. Biografías

(*Clío,* año 18, no. 87, mayo-agosto, p. 74-77).

Biographies, reprinted from various earlier locations, of Eugenio de Salazar, Alarcón, Vásquez de Ayllón, and Licenciado Suazo.

1602. Geiger, Maynard. Junípero Serra, O.F.M., in the light of chronology and geography, 1713-1784 (*Americas,* v. 6, no. 3, Jan., p. 290-333).

A thoroughly scholarly compilation for reference, as to places, times, and methods of travel.

1603. Gibson, Charles. The identity of Diego Muñoz Camargo (*Hisp. amer. hist. rev.,* v. 30, no. 2, May, p. 195-208).

A separation of the identities of the four 16th- and 17th-century persons named Diego Muñoz and associated with Tlaxcala, plus another, the best known, named Diego Muñoz Camargo. A genealogical table is fortunately furnished to bewildered readers.

1604. ————. El sistema de gobierno indígena de Tlaxcala, México, en el siglo XVI (*Amér. indígena,* v. 10, no. 1, enero, p. 81-90).

The cabildo government replaced or overlaid that of the "four lordships" from 1545, and the city developed greatly from then until 1591, as attention was given to economic rather than warlike activities. The article has large general value for the story of Hispanicization in the 16th century.

1605. Giraud, Marcel. France and Louisiana in the early eighteenth century (*Miss. valley hist. rev.,* v. 36, no. 4, March, p. 651-674).

From about 1703-1715, Louisiana was regarded by France primarily as a barrier against other nations seeking a foothold at the mouth of the Mississippi, but the economic exhaustion of the mother country made it impossible sufficiently to support the colony.

1606. EL HALLAZGO DE ICHCATEOPÁN. Dictamen que rinde la comisión designada por acuerdo del C. Secretario de Educación Pública, en relación con las investigaciones y exploraciones realizadas en Ichcateopán, Guerrero (*Rev. mex. estud. antrop.,* t. 11, p. 197-295).

Concerns the "finds" reported and debated since 1949, of holographs of Father Motolinía and the bones of Cuauhtémoc. This report of an examination by experts in various fields, including the historian Silvio Zavala, will convince most readers that the advocates of their authenticity have been, to put it most kindly, deceived. The magazines and newspapers of Mexico have many other articles upon the matter, which it has seemed unnecessary to enter in this *Handbook.* Some more than intimate that, without necessarily imputing bad faith to prominent figures involved, the episode was part of an *indianista* reaction to the publicity received by the *hispanistas* from the publicized rediscovery of the location of Cortés' remains in 1946. See *HLAS, no. 13, 1947,* item 1310, and *no. 16, 1950,* item 435.

1607. Herrera Carrillo, Pablo. Fray Junípero Serra, civilizador de las Californias. 2. ed. México. 223 p.

The first edition of this excellent, although popular and eulogistic biography, appeared in 1943.

1608. Hobbs, William H. Verrazano's voyage along the North American coast in 1524 (*Isis,* v. 41, pt. 3-4, no. 125-126, Dec., p. 268-277).

Applying modern knowledge of compass variation to Verrazano's "Magliabecchi map" shows that the navigator made his landfall on the Florida coast about 28 degrees north latitude, and cruised the coast to Cape Breton, before turning back for the Old World.

1609. Jiménez Rueda, Julio. Historia de la cultura en México. El virreinato. México, Cultura. xv, 335 p.

A very valuable and interesting group of essays, though hardly as objective as the author states he intended to make them.

1610. Joyau, Auguste. Belain d'Esnambuc. Paris, Bellenand. iv, 175 p.

A good narrative account of the work of the French pioneer in St. Christophe. No scholarly apparatus; apparently based upon earlier printed materials only.

1611. Keys, James M. Las misiones españolas de California. Madrid, Consejo Superior de Investigaciones Científicas, Instituto Juan Sebastián Elcano. 244 p., illus.

Readable and intelligent synthesis of the printed works standard for historians of the subject, but hardly a critical one. A thesis for the doctorate in philosophy and letters at the University of Madrid.

1612. Le Riverend Brusone, Julio. Carácter y significación de los tres primeros historiadores de Cuba (*Rev. bim. cub.,* v. 65, no. 1-3, enero-junio, p. 152-180).

Examination of the ideas and work of the three colonials (Arrate, Urrutia, and Valdés) whose principal writings were published as *Los tres primeros historiadores de Cuba* in three volumes, Habana, 1876-1877.

1613. Lietz, Paul S. Vasco de Quiroga, *oidor* made bishop (*Mid-America,* v. 32, no. 1, Jan., p. 13-32).

Study of Quiroga's transition from a lay member of the Audiencia of New Spain to that of bishop of Michoacán, with importance for the evolution of the relations of Church and State.

1614. Lindsay, Philip. The great buccaneer. Being the life, death and extraordinary adventures of Sir Henry Morgan, buccaneer and lieutenant governor of Jamaica. London, Peter Nevill. 305 p., illus.

A popular, or "literary," work.

1615. López Sánchez, José. Vida y obra del sabio médico habanero Dr. Tomás Ro-may Chacón. Habana, Editorial Librería Selecta. 420 p., port.

An excellent book in the neglected field of medical history. Well documented, this work gives a good notion of the intellectual climate in Cuba at the end of the 18th and the opening of the 19th centuries. [R. E. McNicoll]

1616. Manfredini, James M. Viceroy Revillagigedo II as vicepatron of the Church (*Americas*, v. 7, no. 1, July, p. 51-62).

A scholarly use of a few good sources, but—like all known studies of the great viceroy—it presents little of the "other side" of those matters about which the viceroy complained or about which he proposed action.

1617. Mejía, Vilma L. La Audiencia de los Confines. Las Nuevas Leyes (*Rev. arch. bibl. nac.*, Tegucigalpa, v. 28, no. 7-8, enero-feb., p. 298-306).

Notes that the Audiencia de los Confines (later of Guatemala) was located at Gracias a Dios.

1618. Mejía Ricart, Adolfo. Historia de Santo Domingo. V. 2-3. Ciudad Trujillo, Pol, 1949-1950. 404, 526 p.

These volumes concern the discovery and conquest. V. 1 (pre-history) appeared in 1948, at which time it was announced as the start of a seven- to eight-volume work. V. 3 announces that there will be nine volumes.

1619. Miralles de Imperial y Gómez, Claudio. Censura de publicaciones en Nueva España, 1576-1591. Anotaciones documentales (*Rev. Indias*, Madrid, año 10, no. 42, oct.-dic., p. 817-846).

19 documents from the first two volumes of the Mexican Inquisition correspondence in the Archivo Histórico Nacional, Madrid. Also published in *Miscelánea americanista*, v. 2, Madrid, 1951.

1620. ———. El madrileño Santiago de Vera, sexto gobernador de las Islas Filipinas (*Rev. arch. bibl. mus.*, 4. época, t. 56, no. 3, p. 557-575).

Data from 1570 to 1607, with a genealogical table. While living in New Spain in 1583, Vera asked appointment as *consultor* to the Holy Office there. Investigation showed that eight ancestors had been condemned or reconciled as *judíos* or *judaizantes*, but his career was not hampered. *Apéndice documental* (from the Archivo Histórico Nacional, Madrid), p. 572-575.

1621. Miró, Rodrigo. La cultura colonial en Panamá. México, Costa Amic, 69 p.

Three essays, on intellectual life in general, on education, and upon *La política del mundo*, a play staged in 1809.

1622. Mora, J. A. Investigaciones históricas sobre el Monterrey antiguo (*Universidad*, Monterrey, no. 8-9, p. 185-234).

Thoroughly documented study, largely of the political and architectural aspects, from 1596 to the late 18th century.

1623. Morales Carrión, Arturo. Eighteenth century Puerto Rico in diplomacy and war (*Carib. hist. rev.*, no. 1, Dec., p. 1-21).

Deals with period from 1711—when Spain would, as a last resort, have ceded Puerto Rico to England to win a peace—until the attack of 1797, but mostly with the period from the time of the Anglo-Spanish war of 1779-1782. Thoroughly scholarly, but solely from printed sources.

1624. Morales Padrón, Francisco. El "Western Design" de Cromwell (*Estud. amer.*, v. 2, no. 6, mayo, p. 181-196).

A good account, from the seizure of Jamaica in 1655 to its cession by Spain in 1670. Author cites no sources.

1625. Motten, Clement G. Mexican silver and the Enlightenment. Philadelphia, Pa., University of Pennsylvania Press. vii, 90 p.

A valuable study of the history of the Enlightenment. Much information upon Mexican mining appears up to about 1788, when a mission was sent from Spain under the Basque metallurgist Elhuyar, but little upon the actual operations thereafter. This book received honorable mention for the Albert J. Beveridge Memorial Fellowship of the American Historical Association for 1948.

1626. Navarro, Bernabé. Descartes y los filósofos mexicanos modernos del siglo XVIII (*Fil. letras*, t. 20, no. 39, julio-sept., p. 133-149).

Deals primarily with the first half of the century, and especially with the Jesuits and with Gamarra's "course of philosophy." The same periodical has several other articles for the history of "modernist" philosophy in Mexico, in the 17th and 18th centuries, which have not been separately noted. See also items 3276-3278.

1627. Noble, Stuart G., and Arthur G. Nuhrah. Education in colonial Louisiana (*La. hist. quart.*, v. 32, no. 4, Oct., 1949, i.e. 1950, p. 759-776).

Rather incomplete data upon the French at New Orleans from 1725, but good coverage of the Spanish era. In both cases, based importantly upon local manuscript records.

1628. Núñez y Domínguez, José de Jesús. La virreina mexicana, doña María Francisca de la Gándara de Calleja. México, Imprenta Universitaria. xviii, 399 p., 83 plates.

Doña María Francisca was born in San Luis Potosí, January 29, 1786. This book is valuable for her family, life, and times, and her viceregal husband's share in Mexican history, but very little emerges from it about her as a person. Except as to the viceroy's acts, it is based upon little more than printed and noncontemporary accounts.

1629. ————, and **Cipriano de Utrera.**
El tapado de México y el de Santo Domingo. Ciudad Trujillo. 171 p.
Combination of separate articles, published by
the two authors in *Clío,* v. 17, 1949. The *tapado*
of Mexico was Antonio de Benavides, Marqués
de San Vicente, who after a career in Santo
Domingo arrived at Veracruz in 1683 and was
executed in 1684, crime still not known but apparently espionage or intended subversion. Núñez
y Domínguez published a book on Benavides in
1945 (see *HLAS, no. 11, 1945,* item 3031). The
tapado of Santo Domingo, confused in popular
legend with Benavides, was Luis Franco de Acevedo, a contrabandist of the early 18th century.
Castro points out that in 1650 Benavides had a
son in Santo Domingo.

1630. **Palm, Erwin Walter.** Los hospitales
antiguos de la Española. Ciudad Trujillo,
Secretaría de Estado de Sanidad y Asistencia Pública. 57 p., illus.
A discussion of the first physician to reach the
Indies, Dr. Diego Álvarez Chanca, and of five
hospitals founded, or projected, in the 16th
century. Especially, points out that although
San Nicolás de Bari was founded in 1503, the
present building (ruins) cannot have been begun before 1533. See also item 496.

1631. **Pinedo Rey, Manuel.** Aparece un retrato de Tirso de Molina en Santo Domingo (*Clío,* año 18, no. 86, enero-abril,
p. 28-32).
Reprinted, with an added note, from the newspaper *Arriba,* Madrid, Nov. 1, 1949. Gabriel
Téllez (Tirso de Molina) was in Santo Domingo,
1616-1618. This portrait, apparently contemporary, is the only one known except one of
doubtful authenticity in the Biblioteca Nacional,
Madrid.

1632. **Powell, Philip W.** The forty-niners
of sixteenth-century Mexico (*Pac. hist.
rev.,* v. 19, no. 3, Aug., p. 235-249).
A sound study of the "rush" for Zacatecas
silver, found in 1546 but "rushed" from 1549,
and of its effect upon the economic development
of the region, settlement of towns, and Spanish
policy, including policy toward the Indian.

1633. RESEÑA DE LA CELEBRACIÓN DEL CEN-
TENARIO DEL SR. PBRO. BR. D. JOSÉ SIMÓN
DE ZELAYA (*Rev. arch. bibl. nac.,* Tegucigalpa, t. 28, no. 5-6, nov.-dic., 1949, p.
224-235, 288; no. 9-10, marzo-abril, 1950,
p. 480).
Zelaya (1714-1775) was the curate of Tegucigalpa when the old parish church burned, and
the leader in the building of the new one, now
the cathedral.

1634. **Romero de Terreros, Manuel.** La
biblioteca de Luis Lagarto. México. 39 p.,
facsims.

A list, with identifications, of 72 books, all but
one printed in the 16th century, that belonged
to Lagarto, illuminator and miniaturist, resident
in Puebla from 1600. The basic information is
preserved in the Inquisition records.

1635. **Rubio Mañé, J. Ignacio.** El archive-
ro del virreinato D. Anastasio Marín de
Duarte, 1817-1818 (*Bol. arch. gen.,* México, t. 21, no. 3, julio-sept., p. 333-354).
The documents, dated from 1811 to 1816, show
Marín de Duarte's preference for remaining in
the Secretaría de Cámara rather than returning
to the office that he had had with the Inquisition.

1636. **Ruiz, Eduardo.** Don Carlos de Si-
güenza y Góngora. México, Vargas Rea
(Biblioteca de Historiadores Mexicanos,
Hombres de México). 34 p.
Reprinted from *Hombres ilustres mexicanos*
(México, Eduardo L. Gallo, publisher, 1873-
1874, 4 t.), t. 2, p. 341-352.

1638. **Schmiedehaus, Walter.** El verdadero
origen del Padre Kino. Vida y obra del
Padre Quino (*Bol. soc. chihuahuense,* t. 7,
no. 2, marzo-abril, p. 389-391; no. 3,
mayo-junio, p. 381-387; no. 4, julio-agosto,
p. 406-412; no. 5, sept.-oct., p. 437-442).
A rehash of well-known information, except
that the first article presents the text of the
death record (1711) from the Church of Santa
María Magdalena.

1639. **Simpson, Lesley Byrd.** The encomienda in New Spain. The beginning of
Spanish Mexico. Revised and enlarged
edition. Berkeley, Calif., University of
California Press. xv, 257 p., map, facsim.
First edition, Berkeley, 1929. The revisions
throughout this second edition are so extensive
that it must be read by everyone interested,
and there is a whole new section upon conditions during the second half of the 16th century.

1640. ————. The population of twenty-
two towns of Michoacán in 1554. A supplement to Cook and Simpson, *The population of central Mexico in the sixteenth
century* (*Hisp. amer. hist. rev.,* v. 30, no.
2, May, p. 248-250).
Data from the report of an official investigation
by *oidor* Lebrón de Quiñones, not known to the
authors of the 1948 book named in the title.

1641. **Sodi de Pallares, María Elena.**
Historia del traje religioso en México.
México, Stylo. 63 p.
Interesting but thin, and only in very small part
directly upon Mexico. Colonial period only.
No illustrations.

1642. **Utrera, Cipriano de.** Juan de Salamanca (*Bol. arch. gen.,* Ciudad Trujillo,

año 13, v. 13, no. 64, enero-marzo, p. 104-108).

Episode of 1529-1530, a dispute between the municipality and the Virreina doña María de Toledo (acting for her son don Luis de Colón) over her power to name an official. The Audiencia ruled against her.

1643. Valle, Rafael Heliodoro. Cristóbal de Olid, conquistador de México y Honduras. México, Jus (Sociedad de Estudios Cortesianos, no. 5). 316 p.

Definitive edition of a thesis published in 1948 (see *HLAS, no. 14, 1948,* item 1911). Useful *Índice onomástico,* p. 283-311.

1644. Valle Llano, Antonio. La Compañía de Jesús en Santo Domingo durante el período hispánico. Ciudad Trujillo, Seminario de Santo Tomás. 376 p.

Based upon the Archive of the Indies and upon the Jesuit archives of Rome and Madrid, among other depositaries of documents. Has some discussion of years from 1566 until into the 19th century, but chiefly upon the period 1650-1767. Biographical and documentary appendices, p. 305-355.

1645. Velázquez, María del Carmen. El estado de guerra en Nueva España, 1760-1808. México, El Colegio de México. 256 p., illus., maps.

Deals with the organization and history of the colonial militia, and with related aspects of the development of colonial life. Based chiefly upon the Mexican national archives. Valuable, though spotty in quality.

1646. Von Winning, Jean Bassford. Forgotten bastions along the Spanish Main. Campeche (*Americas,* v. 6, no. 4, April, p. 415-430).

Touristy comments upon ruins of forts, pirate attacks—highly legendary information—and the museum-library. The last is the only part of value to historians.

1647. Vrastil, Joseph. Brother Boruhradsky, alias de Castro (*Mid-America,* v. 32, no. 1, Jan., p. 33-45).

Translated from the Czech by Father Joseph Roubik, the original being the only article printed by Father Vrastil before his life-long collections were destroyed at Prague in 1939. Boruhradsky was a lay brother in Mexico City, 1680-1697. One of his three letters printed here is a contemporary comment upon the riots of 1692.

1648. Zárate, Julio. Don Luis de Velasco, el segundo, virrey de México. México, Vargas Rea (Biblioteca de Historiadores Mexicanos, Hombres de México). 59 p.

Reprinted from *Hombres ilustres mexicanos* (México, Eduardo L. Gallo, publisher, 1873-1874, 4 t.), t. 2, p. 237-259.

1649. Zavala, Silvio A. Cristianismo y colonización (*Cuad. amer.,* año 9, v. 51, no. 3, mayo-junio, p. 163-172).

An interesting essay, without new data.

ADDENDA

1650. Barras y de Aragón, Francisco de las. Paso de Venus por el disco del sol (*An. univ. hispalense,* año 10, no. 2, 1949, p. 25-53).

Brief résumé of the Spanish-French astronomical expedition to California in 1768-1769, with new data upon the effort by England in 1767 to gain permission to send two English astronomers.

1651. Barri, León (hijo). Proposición de división de la Nueva España en tres virreinatos (*Bol. soc. chihuahuense,* t. 6, no. 7, abril-mayo, 1949, p. 228-235).

A proposal of Captain Pablo Rangel, Madrid, December 30, 1821, connected with the Anglo-Saxon danger. The areas suggested were in present-day terms: Central America and south Mexico; central Mexico; temperate zone Mexico and the Provincias Internas. Folding map included.

1652. BOLETÍN DEL ARCHIVO GENERAL DEL GOBIERNO. Guatemala. T. 11, no. 1-2, marzo-junio, 1946, i.e. 1949?

This 150-page issue of the valuable *Boletín,* which was not published until several years after its date, and is, apparently, the last issue to have appeared up to 1952, has its usual range of items indispensable for the history of the colonial period of Central America.

1653. Cabon, P. Alphonse. Une maison d'education à St. Domingue. "Les Religieuses" du Cap, 1731-1802 (*Rev. d'hist. amér. franç.,* t. 2, no. 4, mars, p. 557-575; t. 3, no. 1, juin, p. 75-80; no. 3, déc., 1949, p. 402-422).

Includes a note on the antecedents from 1653. Based on the colonial archives of France. By error, the first two installments listed G. Debien as the author.

1654. Carrera Stampa, Manuel. Los obrajes de indígenas en el virreinato de la Nueva España (*Actas cong. int. amer.,* t. 2, p. 555-562).

Valuable and precise, though unavoidably spotty, data, chiefly for the 16th century.

1655. Dauvergne, Robert. Les anciens plans ruraux des colonies françaises (*Rev. d'hist. col.,* t. 35, no. 3-4, 1948, p. 231-269).

Solidly documented article, primarily for the French Antilles in the 18th century but with value also for the 17th and 19th centuries and other French colonies. The *plans parcellaires* and *dominaux,* and the *terroirs coloniaux,* are very numerous in the archives, and informative upon far more than land bounds.

1656. Dávila Garibi, J. Ignacio. D. Juan Ruiz Colmenero, meritísimo obispo neo-gallego del siglo XVII. México, 1949. 38 p., port.

1657. Debien, G. Les études historiques sur St. Domingue depuis 1938 (*Rev. d'hist. amér. franç.,* t. 3, no. 1, juin, 1949, p. 135-142).
A list classified in ten groups. Excellent in every aspect, and indispensable for the many items published in out-of-the-way reviews and cities.

1658. Delafosse, M. La Rochelle et les îles au XVIIe siècle (*Rev. d'hist. col.,* v. 36, 3. trimestre, 1949, p. 238-281).
Data, newly available from the provincial archives, chiefly for the period 1660-1692. Under Colbert, the city became the most important center of trade with the French West Indies.

1659. Delgado, Jaime. Una polémica en 1805 sobre los límites de la Luisiana. La misión en España de Jaime Monroe (*Rev. arch. bibl. mus.,* 4. época, t. 54, no. 3, 1948, p. 403-433).
Based especially upon documents in the Archivo Histórico Nacional, Madrid.

1660. Gerard, Raoul. Heráldica, banderas y uniformes de la Capitanía General de Guatemala en los siglos XVI, XVII, XVIII y XIX (*An. soc. geog. hist. Guatemala,* año 24, t. 24, no. 3-4, sept.-dic., 1949, p. 226-242).
Precise, though spotty, data upon the makeup of the Guatemala militia, its ordinances, and the subjects mentioned in the title. Mostly for the 18th century.

1661. Gómez de Orozco, Federico. Italianos conquistadores, exploradores y pobladores de México en el siglo XVI (*Mem. acad. mex. hist.,* t. 8, no. 3, julio-sept., 1949, p. 189-212).
Data on 62 men, a large part of them Genoese.

1662. Gutiérrez Contreras, Salvador. Compostela de Indias, su origen y fundación. Compostela, Mexico, 1949. 77 p.
A study based upon printed works, and chiefly for the 16th century.

1663. Hallenbeck, Cleve. The journey of Fray Marcos de Niza. Dallas, Tex., University Press in Dallas, 1949. 115 p., illus., map.
Translation of Marco da Nizza's *Relación* (p. 15-36). The rest of the book is a historical introduction, with notes and analysis. The author thinks even less of Fray Marco's veracity than most of his critics.

1664. Izquierdo, José Joaquín. Raudon, cirujano poblano de 1810. Aspectos de la cirugía mexicana de principios del siglo XIX. México, 1948. 299 p., facsims.

1665. Jacobs, H. P. French interlopers in 1555 (*Jamaican hist. rev.,* v. 1, no. 3, Dec., 1948, p. 234-245).
The annotated and relevant portions, in Spanish and in English translation, of the letter of Martín Vásquez to the admiral of the Indies, Jamaica, June 24, 1556 [sic], concerning an attack on French *rescate* ships in Feb., 1555.

1666. Landaeta, Martín de. Noticias acerca del puerto de San Francisco (Alta California). México, Robredo (Biblioteca Histórica Mexicana, Obras Inéditas, 22), 1949. 78 p.
Letters by a Franciscan who lived in San Francisco from about 1792 to 1807, now first edited by José C. Valdés. 500 numbered copies only.

1667. Le Maire, François. Louisiana in 1717 (*Rev. d'hist. amér. franç.,* t. 3, no. 1, juin, p. 94-110; no. 2, sept., p. 256-269; no. 3, déc., 1949, p. 423-446).
Account by a missionary among French and Spanish coastal settlements.

1668. Lewis, C. Bernard. Treasure on the Pedro Bank (*Jamaican hist. rev.,* v. 2, no. 1, Dec., 1949, p. 26-32).
Concerns dispute between the Jamaican government, the Asiento Company, and the Spanish officials, over salvage of the wreck (1730) of the Spanish Ship *Genovés* on the Pedro Bank off Jamaica, between 16th Sept., 1730, and 11th May, 1731. Based chiefly upon the minutes of the Legislative Assembly of the island.

1669. Manfredini, James Manfred. The political role of the Count of Revillagigedo, viceroy of New Spain, 1789-1794. New Brunswick, N. J., [The author], 1949. vii, 197 p.
An adaptation and reduction of the author's Ph. D. thesis at the University of Texas, and the first full length and separate study of the great statesman's administration. A valuable study, and critical in technique, although like all other studies of the man it depicts a perfection that cannot have been true of any human being.

1670. Martínez Cosío, Luis. Heráldica de Cortés. México, Jus (Sociedad de Estudios Cortesianos, 2), 1949. 221 p., illus.
Another study of the long debated—and probably unanswerable—question about the relation of the conqueror to the Cortesios of Italy through the Monroy family. Some plates, including a portrait of Cortés, are in color.

1671. May, L. F. Port-au-Prince, 1749-1950 (*Rev. d'hist. col.,* v. 36, 3. trimestre, 1949, p. 225-237).
Includes the text of the *acte de fondation,* June 13, 1749, and reproductions of two plans, a

provisional one of 1753 and a large one of 1785.

1672. Menier, M. A., and Gabriel Debien. Journaux de St. Domingue (*Rev. d'hist. col.*, v. 36, 3. trimestre, 1949, p. 424-475). A compilation of data from a multitude of sources, although the authors claim no definitive value for it.

1673. Morales Albo, Federico. Descubrimiento y conquistas en Centro América. Madrid, Victoriano Suárez, 1948. 186 p. No scholarly apparatus, and apparently no new data.

1674. Nemours, Luc. Pour quelles raisons Toussaint Louverture est-il passé des espagnols aux français? (*An. hist. revol. franç.*, année 20, no. 10, avril-juin, 1948, p. 166-171). Demolishes all the reasons that have been advanced, without offering a substitute. It seems to this reviewer that the data given justify a belief that Toussaint was actuated by distrust, if not jealousy, of his various superiors and associates.

1675. O'Brien, Eric (and others). Padre Junípero Serra and the California missions. Santa Barbara, California, Old Mission Serra Shop, 1949. 65 p. Popularized, but by outstanding authorities using excellent sources, many still unpublished.

1676. AUX ORIGINES DE L'ABOLITION DE L'ESCLAVAGE. Proclamations de Polverel y Santhonax, 1793-1794 (*Rev. d'hist. col.*, v. 36, 1. trimestre, 1949, p. 24-55). Eight documents concerning French Saint Domingue, including paragraphs from the Code Noir of 1685, and instruction from Cayenne of 1785.

1677. Palm, Erwin Walter. Dos relaciones acerca de la Española en el siglo XVII (*An. univ. Santo Domingo*, v. 14, no. 49-52, enero-dic., 1949, p. 213-246). One item is Antonio Vásquez de Espinosa's *Compendio y descripción de las Indias Occidentales, Libro II, El distrito de la Audiencia de Santo Domingo*, which León Pinelo says was printed in the author's lifetime. The second is the relevant portion of Juan Díez de la Calle's *Memorial y noticias* (Madrid, 1646). Both are extensively annotated.

1678. Ramírez López, Ignacio. Tres biografías. Fray Pedro de Gante, Fray Alonso de la Veracruz y Fray Juan Bautista Moya. México, Secretaría de Educación Pública (Biblioteca Enciclopédica Popular, 3. época, 201), 1948. 75 p., illus.

1679. REVISTA DE LOS ARCHIVOS NACIONALES DE COSTA RICA. San José. Año 13, no. 1-6, enero-junio, 1949; no. 7-12, julio-diciembre, 1949. 365 p.

As always, this review prints a considerable number of documents upon the colonial period, individually not of outstanding importance, but summing up to a valuable body of evidence upon official life. No. 1-6 include: two documents (1718, 1724-1725) for the period of Governor Diego de la Haya Fernández; two (1796-1797, 1809) for that of Governor Tomás de Acosta; three upon the Partido de Nicoya, 1804-1807; and *Méritos y servicios de Fray José Antonio de Liendo y Goicoechea, 1784-1787*. No. 7-12 include: documents from the governments of Justicia Mayor y Capitán General Pedro Ruiz de Bustamante (1716) and Governors Valderrama (1727), Gemmir y Lleonhart (1745), and Navas (1762); and one item of 1740 and four of 1744 relevant to military matters during the war with England.

1680. Romero de Terreros, Manuel. La ciudad de México en 1749. Reproducción de un plano de la época. México, Ediciones Arte Mexicano, 1949. 4 p., folding map. The map (in color, 51 x 30 cm.) is by Carlos López, 1749. It is reproduced from the only known copy, a copper engraving. It depicts and identifies some 120 buildings.

1681. Roussier, Paul. François Mesplès et sa fortune, pacotille et maisons de rapport (*Rev. d'hist. col.*, t. 35, 3. et 4. trimestres, 1948, p. 161-199). Study of Gascon who, starting as a youth in 1761, built up before his death in 1789 a fortune and social position in French St. Domingue as merchant and entrepreneur of lodging houses, a theatre, etc.

1682. Saldaño, Juan José. Testimonio del cuaderno y diligencias originales practicadas a la casa y población de varios indios xicaques en el valle de San Juan (*Rev. arch. bibl. nac.*, Tegucigalpa, t. 28, no. 3-4, sept.-oct., p. 97-101; no. 5-6, nov.-dic., 1949, p. 203-208). Documents of 1749 bearing on mission activities.

1683. Sandoval, Fernando B. El correo en las Provincias Internas, 1779. México, Junta Mexicana de Investigaciones Históricas (Col. de Documentos, 1), 1948. 50 p. An *expediente* with much value for social and economic conditions, aside from the obvious subject matter. Reprinted from *Bol. arch. gen.*, México, t. 19, no. 3, julio-sept., 1948, p. 337-386.

1684. Scisco, Louis Dow. Voyage of Vicente González in 1588 (*Md. hist. mag.*, v. 42, no. 2, June, 1947, p. 95-100). A study of a long neglected voyage, from Florida into Chesapeake Bay. The interpretation benefits from the author's intimate knowledge of the pertinent localities. Readers might wish also to see his *Discovery of Chesapeake Bay, 1525-1573*, in the same periodical, v. 40, no. 4, Dec., 1945, p. 276-286.

1685. **Taylor, S. A. G.** Military operations in Jamaica, 1655 to 1660 (*Jamaican hist. rev.*, v. 2, no. 1, Dec., 1949, p. 7-25).
Uses no sources new to specialists but offers a valuable critique upon such matters as geographic problems and troop morale.

1686. **Tompkins, S. R.,** and **M. L. Moorhead.** Russia's approach to America. Part 2, from Spanish sources, 1761-1775 (*Brit. col. hist. quart.*, v. 13, no. 3-4, July-Oct., 1949, p. 231-255).
A thoroughly scholarly presentation of information from the archives at Simancas and Sevilla, annotated partly from Russian sources. Part I ("From Russian sources, 1751-1761") appeared in the preceding issue of the same magazine.

1687. **Troncoso de la Concha, Manuel de Jesús.** Antología. Ciudad Trujillo, Librería Dominicana (Colección Pensamiento Dominicano, 1), 1949. 180 p.
Brief, popularized articles, based, at least, on history, mostly of the colonial period.

1688. **Tulane University. Middle American Research Institute.** Administrative papers. Copies relating to New Spain. New Orleans, The Institute (Miscellaneous series, no. 5), 1948. 28 p.
A list by Marie Hunter Irvine, the librarian, of the manuscripts in 40 bound volumes bought in 1934. Material on many parts of Spanish America, from 1493 to 1865, but chiefly for Mexico and the 18th century (not "16th century," as the work itself claims on p. 4).

1689. **Utrera, Cipriano de.** El Estudio de Gorjón y Ciudad y su erección en Universidad (*Clío*, t. 17, no. 83, enero-abril, 1949, p. 32-39).
Thoroughly documented account of events from 1548 to 1562, with value for local quarrels and for the royal flouting of the local will.

1690. **Zárate, Gerónimo de.** Noticias sacadas de un manuscrito intitulado *Relaciones de todas las cosas que en el Nuevo México se han visto y sabido . . . desde . . . 1538 hasta . . . 1626.* México, Vargas Rea, 1949. 71 p.
From inedited manuscript. 100 copies only.

SOUTH AMERICA (EXCEPT BRAZIL)*

HOWARD F. CLINE **

CIRCUM-CARIBBEAN

1691. ACTAS DEL CABILDO DE CARACAS. T. 3, 1606-1611. Caracas, Concejo Municipal del Distrito Federal. xxv, 367 p.

Useful addition to the large body of Cabildo documents, with introductory summary of the period and a list of governors and other principal administrators for the period covered. Analytical indices.

1692. BOLETÍN DEL ARCHIVO GENERAL DE LA NACIÓN. Caracas. T. 37, no. 146, oct.-dic., 1949, i.e. 1950-no. 149, julio-dic., 1949, i.e. 1950.
Indexes to records in the Archive continued as follows: *Reales cédulas*, t. 7, f. 80-t. 11, f. 147; *Gobernación y Capitanía General*, t. 27, f. 323-t. 29, f. 352; *Reales provisiones*, t. 35, f. 314-t. 37, f. 348; *Ayuntamientos*, t. 25, f. 189-t. 45, f. 351 (end); *Intendencia de ejército y real hacienda*, t. 29, f. 118-t. 32, f. 113; *Gran Colombia, Intendencia de Venezuela*, t. 1, f. 253-t. 3, f. 45; *República de Venezuela, Secretaría del Interior y Justicia*, t. 137, f. 84-t. 149, f. 182; and *Gran Colombia, Papeles de Guerra y Marina*, t. 1, f. 1-t. 2, f. 249. Each issue also contains the text of an important document and lists of publications received. [R. R. Hill]

1693. BOLETÍN DEL ARCHIVO HISTÓRICO DE LA PROVINCIA DE MÉRIDA. Mérida, Venezuela. Año 7, t. 7, no. 33, enero-feb.; no. 34, marzo-abril; no. 35, mayo-junio.
Continues the installments of extracts of documents of *Encomiendas*, t. 5, f. 19-65, 1673-1677. Also has texts of several documents relating to Indians and lands. [R. R. Hill]

1695. **Cisneros, Joseph Luis de.** Descripción exacta de la provincia de Benezuela. Reproducción de las ediciones de Valencia (1764) y Madrid (1912), con introducción de Enrique Bernardo Núñez. Caracas, Ávila Gráfica. xv, 158 p.
First published in 1764, this is a reprint of the 1912 edition, with facsimiles of 3 original pages. The introduction (by Manuel Serrano y Sanz) to the 1912 edition is also included.

1696. **García Chuecos, Héctor.** Una insurrección de negros en los días de la colonia (*Rev. hist. amér.*, no. 29, junio, p. 67-76).
In April, 1749 the Negro slaves of the province of Caracas revolted in an attempt to gain their liberty. This study is based on documents found in the Archivo General, Caracas. The author feels that an intensive study of the 270 folios he has found in the archives would shed considerable light on the whole problem of the relations between the inhabitants of Venezuela and the Guipuzcoana Company. [R. L. Tree]

1697. **Perera, Ambrosio.** Lo que se sabe y lo que no se sabe en orden a la fundación de Barquisimeto. São Paulo. 52 p.
This work is aimed at disproving and correcting the work of Nectario María on the same subject. [R. L. Tree]

*For Brazilian items see "Brazil," p. 167-179.
**The editor desires to acknowledge the assistance of Robert L. Tree in preparing part of this section.

1698. Pérez Embid, Florentino. Diego de Ordás, compañero de Cortés y explorador del Orinoco. Sevilla, Consejo Superior de Investigaciones Científicas, Escuela de Estudios Hispano-Americanos (Publ. no. 58, serie 2, no. 18). 145 p., illus., maps.
Monographic treatment of this typical explorer-conqueror, with much attention to details of the expedition and voyage up the Orinoco, rivalries, and subsequent explorations after Ordás' death in November, 1532. Documentary appendices include exploration contract and other pieces.

1699. Polanco Martínez, Tomás. Esbozo sobre historia económica venezolana. Primera etapa: La colonia, 1498-1810. Caracas, Áncora. 249 p.
A useful attempt to synthesize existing materials on the economic history of colonial Venezuela for teaching purposes. Part 1 deals with commerce, agriculture, and pastoral activities, while a much reduced Part 2 deals with public finance. Based exclusively on printed materials, this is a helpful though by no means definitive summary.

1700. PROYECTOS DEL CAPITÁN GENERAL DON PEDRO CARBONELL ENCAMINADOS AL PROGRESO Y EMBELLECIMIENTO DE LA CIUDAD DE CARACAS (*Bol. arch. gen.*, Caracas, t. 38, no. 150, oct.-dic., p. 1-10).
The complete text, dated June 24, 1793.

1701. REPRESENTACIÓN QUE LOS DIPUTADOS DE LA JUNTA GENERAL DE COMERCIO DE CARACAS HACEN AL REAL CONSULADO SOBRE LA APERTURA DEL COMERCIO NEUTRAL DURANTE LA GUERRA (*Bol. arch. gen.*, Caracas, t. 37, no. 147, enero-marzo, p. 123-135).
The complete text, dated October 19, 1797.

1702. Venezuela. Archivo General de la Nación. Hojas militares. V. 3. Caracas, Imprenta Nacional. 488 p.
This last volume of records of individuals who served in the armed forces of Venezuela during the last years of the colonial period covers the letters P to Z. The documents contain information on the merits and services of the soldiers and give much personal data regarding them. [R. R. Hill]

WEST COAST: NORTH

1703. Ariza, Alberto E. Hagiografía de la Milagrosa Imagen de Nra. Sra. del R°. de Chiquinquirá. Bogotá, Iqueima. xxiii, 307 p., illus.
This work is divided into four parts. The first part deals briefly with origin of the Image and gives a complete chronology of the most important events connected with the Image from its origins to the present day. The second part is the most important historically. This volume is composed almost entirely of documents. [R. L. Tree]

1704. IV CENTENARIO DE LA FUNDACIÓN DEL CONVENTO DE SANTO DOMINGO EN SANTA FE DE BOGOTÁ, 1550-1950 (AGOSTO 26). Bogotá, Voto Nacional. 151 p.
A collection of papers and essays on the history and work of the Dominicans in Colombia and the founding of the Convento de Santo Domingo in Bogotá. [R. L. Tree]

1705. Friede, Juan. Antecedentes histórico-geográficos del descubrimiento de la meseta chibcha por el lic. Gonzalo Jiménez de Quesada (*Rev. Indias,* Madrid, año 10, no. 40, abril-junio, p. 327-348).
A study of the discovery of this meseta and the earliest exploration of the Magdalena river in the 1530's. These explorations are important because they led to the opening up of Peru and facilitated communication with the Caribbean. Article based on new materials found in various Spanish archives. [R. L. Tree]

1706. ————. Creación de la Real Audiencia (*Bol. hist. antig.,* v. 37, no. 423-425, enero-marzo, p. 75-80).
A compilation of documents relating to the creation of the Audiencia of New Granada found in Spanish archives. The compiler concludes that his research has corrected erroneous dates. [R. L. Tree]

1707. Otero D'Costa, Enrique (ed.). Primer libro de actas del cabildo de la ciudad de Pamplona en la Nueva Granada, 1552-1561. Bogotá, Pax (Biblioteca de Historia Nacional, 82). xv, 465 p.
A prologue discusses the bibliographic and paleographic history of this first of two volumes. The records themselves are a useful addition to the many similar collections. A number of antiquarian notes and biographical data on early citizens form appendices.

1708. Ots Capdequí, José María. Instituciones de gobierno del Nuevo Reino de Granada durante el siglo XVIII. Bogotá, Universidad Nacional de Colombia. 379 p.
This is an important contribution to the legal and institutional history of the area and of the period. As its author points out, it is not meant for the general reader but more for the specialist; it is the second part of an important investigation, the first installment of which dealt with municipalities, justice, and economic administration. The present one, based on manuscript materials (with important excerpts given) first sets forth in somewhat general terms the doctrines and main institutions employed by the Bourbons to govern America and reshape the Hapsburg traditions; subsequent chapters examine the audiencia, its relations to viceroys, presidents, corregidores and alcaldes mayores, and terminates with discussion of the legal norms governing public offices in general. This is a pioneering effort to fill in great gaps in our knowledge of regional differentiation of administration during this important transitional epoch between familiar early colonial (Hapsburg) usages and the later republican practices.

1709. Pardo Umaña, Camilo. Tiempos viejos. Prólogo de Roberto García Peña. Bogotá, Editorial Santafé, 1949, i.e. 1950. 302 p.

Colombian tales, half history, half legendary, most of them relating to the colonial period. Interestingly told. [W. Stewart]

1710. Picón-Salas, Mariano. Pedro Claver, el santo de los esclavos. México, Fondo de Cultura Económica. 210 p., illus.

A well-known writer presents in attractive format an interesting and significant sketch of Pedro Claver, evangelist among the Negro slaves of New Granada in the 17th century. As the author says, his work is "an emotional and poetic approximation rather than strictly objective." Around fragmentary published sources he has woven an interesting story, in which it is somewhat difficult to disentangle truth from legend and imagination.

1711. Posada, José Restrepo. Arquidiócesis de Bogotá (*Bol. hist. antig.*, v. 37, no. 423-425, enero-marzo, p. 13-28).

A sketch of the history of the Archdiocese of Bogotá from its founding in 1564 to 1949. Primarily a list of bishops. [R. L. Tree]

1712. Torre, José de la. Juan Tafur (*Bol. hist. antig.*, v. 37, no. 423-425, enero-marzo, p. 29-44).

A list of documents concerning Juan Tafur preceded by a brief biographical sketch. Born in 1495, he was associated with Pedro de los Ríos in the reduction of Nombre de Dios. Later he was with Gonzalo Jiménez de Quesada at the founding of Bogotá. In 1576 he was appointed Contador de la Real Hacienda del Nuevo Reino de Granada. [R. L. Tree]

WEST COAST: MIDDLE

1713. Anda Aguirre, Martín. Primeros vecinos de Loja. Quito, Editorial Fr. Jodoco Ricke. 113 p.

Written by a Dominican monk, the volume deals with four of the principal citizens of this provincial place, founded 1547. Historical-biographical sketches of Captains Pedro de León, Pedro de la Cadena, Pedro de Cianca, and Pedro Pacheco; important supplementary material on early history of the Audiencia de Quito. Appendices list the encomenderos of Loja, a law suit over encomiendas, title of the "Muy noble y muy leal Ciudad" of Loja (1567), and grant of coat of arms to city of Valladolid (1572).

1714. Arroyo, Luis. Comisarios generales del Perú. Edición y prólogo del P. Fidel de Lejarza. Madrid, Consejo Superior de Investigaciones Científicas, Instituto Santo Toribio de Mogrovejo (Biblioteca Missionalia Hispanica, Serie B, v. 3). xxi, 594 p.

Short biographies of the comisarios generales of Peru from 1548 to 1908. The biographies are preceded by a 23-page introduction which traces the history of the establishment of the institution. [R. L. Tree]

1715. Boletín del Archivo Nacional de Historia. Quito, Casa de la Cultura Ecuatoriana. Año 1, no. 1, enero-junio; no. 2, julio-dic.

These first two numbers contain extracts from documents no. 1-462 (years 1600-1699) in the Archivo Nacional de Historia, as well as alphabetical indexes of persons and geographical names. No. 1 has also: *La Real Audiencia de Quito en el siglo XVI*, by Carlos Vivanco, a brief survey listing members of the tribunal and bishops of Quito; and *Correspondencia de la Secretaría General del Libertador Simón Bolívar*, being letters June 13, 1822 to August 6, 1823. No. 2 includes: *La ciudad de Quito en 1808-1810*, a Spanish translation of a chapter from W. Bennet Stevenson's *Historical and descriptive narration of twenty years' residence in South America.* [R. R. Hill]

1716. Calvete de Estrella, Juan Cristóbal. De rebus indicis. Estudio, notas y traducción de José López de Toro. 2 v. Madrid, Consejo Superior de Investigaciones Científicas, Instituto Gonzalo Fernández de Oviedo. 734 p.

A contemporary defense of the acts of Vaca de Castro in Peru. The text, though from two manuscripts, is incomplete. [R. D. Hussey]

1717. Castro Seoane, José. La Merced en el Perú, 1534-1584 (*Missionalia hispanica*, año 7, no. 19, p. 55-80).

A continuation of articles that appeared in numbers 8, 10, and 11 of this periodical, commenting on the *Memorial* of Padre Porres. Based on manuscripts from AGI, Charcas, this contains valuable information on demography of Indians in the care of the Mercedarian Order. The series will continue in later numbers.

1718. Escandell y Bonet, Bartolomé. Aportación al estudio del gobierno del conde del Villar. Hechos y personajes de la corte virreinal (*Rev. Indias*, Madrid, año 10, no. 39, enero-marzo, p. 69-95).

Some data concerning the relationship between the viceroy and the Inquisition in Peru, 1586-1587. The personal secretary of the viceroy, Juan Bello, was brought before the Inquisition on a charge of blasphemy. The viceroy intervened and complained to Philip II of the Inquisition's high-handed activities. [R. L. Tree]

1719. Giménez Fernández, Manuel. Las Casas y el Perú (*Documenta*, año 2, no. 1, 1949-1950, p. 342-377).

The subtitle, "Critical essay concerning the notices and judgments which Fray Bartolomé de las Casas formulated in his writings concerning the discovery and conquest of Peru," sums up the contents of this article. Based on printed sources, it adds but little that is new, although it usefully brings together scattered information and references; ideologically lines up with Lewis Hanke's views on Las Casas.

1720. **Lewin, Boleslao.** El Santo Oficio en América y el más grande proceso inquisitorial en el Perú. Buenos Aires, Sociedad Hebraica Argentina. 224 p.

As might well be expected, this history of the Inquisition does not conform to the "white legend." The author takes Juan A. Llorente's classic exposé as point of departure, leans heavily on printed materials and well-known studies, and adds some documents concerning the *auto de fe* in Lima, 1639.

1721. **Mateos, Francisco.** Constituciones para indios del primer concilio limense, 1552 (*Missionalia hispanica,* año 7, no. 19, p. 5-54).

A survey of the ecclesiastical organization of Peru in 1552, personnel who attended the Council, and the affirmations that emerged, especially regarding doctrinal and other points concerning Indians. Only Part 2 of the "constitution" or agreed material, that concerning Indians, exists, in two manuscript forms which are here critically examined and reproduced.

1722. ————. Segundo concilio provincial limense, 1567 (*Missionalia hispanica,* año 7, no. 20, p. 209-296; no. 21, p. 525-617).

Complete Latin text of the Council, taken from the unique manuscript, located in AGI (Sevilla), Patronato, leg. 189, ramo 24. The document was discussed by the author in the same periodical, año 4 (1947), p. 479-524.

1723. **Meneses, Teodoro L.** El *Usca Paucar,* drama religioso quechua del siglo XVIII (*Documenta,* año 2, no. 1, 1949-1950, p. 1-178).

A detailed analysis, with copious notes and appendices, of a religious drama in the native tongue, based on a new manuscript version in the National Library of Peru, with original text, critical notes, and a Spanish translation.

1724. **Moncayo de Monge, Germania.** Mariana de Jesús, Señora de Indias. Quito, Prensa Católica. 312 p.

Hagiography of the local heroine and saint recently canonized for her 17th-century piety. It is somewhat difficult to learn what she was or did from eulogistic, overwritten account.

1725. **Moreyra Paz Soldán, Manuel.** Cartas y un informe sobre el tribunal mayor de cuentas del virrey Marqués de Montesclaros (*Rev. hist.,* Lima, t. 18, entrega 2, p. 311-330).

Some more important letters from the Montesclaros collection in the Archivo de Indias. These letters throw much additional light on the creation of the Tribunal Mayor de Cuentas in Peru at the beginning of the 17th century. There is an introductory note preceding the letters. [R. L. Tree]

1726. **Pino Ycaza, Gabriel.** El muy magnífico señor don Gonzalo Pizarro. Guayaquil, Universidad de Guayaquil, Departamento de Publicaciones. 287 p.

Undocumented and replete with typographical errors, this "narración novelada" adds nothing to knowledge.

1727. **Pons Muzzo, Gustavo.** Historia del Perú. Texto oficial para educación secundaria. 5 v. Lima.

T. 1, Período autóctono: épocas preincaica e incaica. T. 2, Período de influencia hispánica: épocas del descubrimiento y virreinatos. T. 3, Período de influencia hispánica: época de la emancipación. T. 4, Período independiente: época de la república. T. 5, Historia de la cultura peruana. An inexpensive, capable series of texts that includes much of the recent scholarship.

1728. **Porras Barrenechea, Raúl.** Crónicas perdidas, presuntas y olvidadas sobre la conquista del Perú (*Documenta,* año 2, no. 1, 1949-1950, p. 179-243).

A helpful attempt to assemble data beyond the well-known "standard" chroniclers, rounded up by the author in his *Relaciones primitivas* (Paris, 1938) and subsequent publications. A basic critical-bibliographical contribution by a master of this specialized field.

1729. ————. Jauja, capital mítica, 1534 (*Rev. hist.,* Lima, t. 18, entrega 2, p. 117-148).

An excellent account of the activities of Francisco Pizarro and his men in 1534 and the legends surrounding Pizarro's mythical city of Jauja. [R. L. Tree]

1730. ————. Nuevos documentos sobre el Inca Garcilaso (*Documenta,* año 2, no. 1, 1949-1950, p. 593-613).

Of about 200 new documents discovered in 1950 in the town archives of Montilla, Spain, seven are here printed. The collection gives important new light on the career of the famous Inca from 1561 to 1591, hitherto relatively unknown; with brief trips he was a resident in Montilla during these years. Possibly the most important document of those published is the will of doña Luisa Ponce de León (1586) which left Garcilaso in full possession of a fortune that permitted him to write and publish his work.

1731. **Ramos Cabrejo, Gerardo.** Primeros destellos de la ciencia en el Perú (*Mar del sur,* año 2, no. 11, mayo-junio, p. 58-64).

An informative discussion of the first scientific work published in Lima, *Tratado de cometas* (1665) by Francisco Ruiz Lozano. The author shows that Ruiz Lozano's astronomical studies and findings were of a quality and scope comparable to similar work being done in Europe in the same period. [R. L. Tree]

1732. **Rivera Serna, Raúl.** El primer testamento de Mancio Serra de Leguizano (*Mar del sur,* año 2, no. 11, mayo-junio, p. 24-29).

This article includes the text of the first testament, dated August 1, 1576, together with a very short biographical sketch of Serra de Leguizano. This is apparently the first time this testament has been published, although the second testament of 1589 has been published several times. [R. L. Tree]

1733. Temple, Ella Dunbar. Documentos sobre la rebelión de Tupac Amaru (*Documenta,* año 2, no. 1, 1949-1950, p. 656-662).
Further minor data on the great nativist uprising of 1780-1783, citing earlier treatments and here providing a selection of materials from those copied in the British Museum (Add. 20986, fol. 306 ff.). Four items are printed here: a letter of 16 April 1781 concerning the capture of Tupac Amaru, and three others.

1734. ————. Un informe del obispo don Baltasar Jaime Martínez de Compañón en el juicio de residencia del virrey Amat (*Documenta,* año 2, no. 1, 1949-1950, p. 652-655).
A secret report dated May 20, 1778 in which the bishop praises the viceroy highly.

1735. ————. El jurista indiano don Gaspar de Escalona y Agüero, graduado en la Universidad de San Marcos (*Documenta,* año 2, no. 1, 1949-1950, p. 545-586).
The subtitle, "Notes for the history of ideas in the Peruvian viceroyalty during the 17th century," indicates the approach and scope of this biographical sketch of an important 17th-century thinker and his times. Appendix gives documents on his scholastic career.

1736. ————. Notas sobre el virrey Toledo y los incas de Vilcabamba (*Documenta,* año 2, no. 1, 1949-1950, p. 614-651).
Discussion and text of a letter and a will of the illegitimate son of Manco Inca and his sons: Titu Cusi Yupanqui and Felipe Quispe Titu, a line which followed a bitterly anti-Spanish direction. These documents indicate the political astuteness and methods employed on both sides in an ideological and legal struggle between the viceroy and the Incas of Vilcabamba. Forms another part of the longer work on the Incas under the Spaniards on which this author has been toiling for some years, based on new documentary materials.

1737. ————. Los testamentos inéditos de Paullu Inca, don Carlos y don Melchor Carlos Inca. Nuevos datos sobre esta estirpe incaica y apuntes para la biografía del sobrino del Inca Garcilaso de la Vega (*Documenta,* año 2, no. 1, 1949-1950, p. 630-651).
Carries forward the genealogical studies of the tangled Inca lines into post-Conquest times by a long foreword and printing of wills.

1738. Valcárcel, Daniel. Olavide y la Universidad de San Marcos (*Documenta,* año 2, no. 1, 1949-1950, p. 378-394).
A biobibliographical sketch of Pablo de Olavide, professor of theology at San Marcos in the 18th century, with four documents of 1742-1744. After an important stay in Peru, Olavide had a subsequent career in Europe, where he was a strong advocate of French Enlightenment until his death (1803? 1805?).

1739. Vargas Ugarte, Rubén. Epistolario retrospectivo (*Mercurio peruano,* año 25, no. 277, abril, p. 141-148).
A group of short letters from Peruvian ecclesiastics to Church leaders in Europe, including the Holy See. These letters cover the period 1586-1653 and deal primarily with Church problems. Three of the letters are in Italian. [R. L. Tree]

1740. Vernaza, José Ignacio. Una carta de Belalcázar al Rey de España (*Bol. hist. antig.,* v. 37, no. 429-431, julio-sept., p. 432-434).
This letter shows the intense jealousy of the Spanish conquistadores for their lands. Belalcázar is protesting to the king of Spain over the invasion of his dominions by Gonzalo Pizarro and Hernán Pérez de Quesada in 1543. The letter also demonstrates the inability of the Crown to maintain control over its subjects in Peru. [R. L. Tree]

1741. Villanueva U., Horacio. El mineral de Hualgayoc a fines del siglo XVIII; relación de D. Joaquín Ramón de Iturralde (*Rev. univ.,* Cuzco, año 39, no. 98, 1. semestre, p. 183-323).
An important contribution to the economic history of Peru in the latter part of the 18th century. The manuscript reproduced here was written in 1776 and sent to the Viceroy of Peru. The author of the manuscript was protesting the bad conditions in the mines and offering suggestions as to improvements in operations. The document includes six maps and is a highly detailed study of mining operations and labor conditions. [R. L. Tree]

WEST COAST: SOUTH

1742. Algunos documentos relativos a Don Pedro de Valdivia (*Rev. chil. hist. geog.,* no. 115, enero-junio, p. 16-39).
These documents shed considerable light on the general history of the conquest of Chile. Some show that the conquest of Chile was financed by a larger company than was thought previously. Others deal with commercial activities and the interest of Alonso de Monroy in the expedition of conquest. [R. L. Tree]

1743. Echaiz, René León. Historia de Curicó (*Rev. chil. hist. geog.,* no. 115, enero-junio, p. 40-133).
A highly detailed history of Curicó that has been continued from a previous issue and is still to be continued. This chapter deals primarily with the

problems of land distribution in the 17th and 18th centuries. Attention is paid to civil and military organization and to the influence of the Church. Much valuable information. See *HLAS, no. 15, 1949*, item 1585. [R. L. Tree]

1744. Mateos, F. El Padre Manuel de Lacunza y el milenarismo (*Rev. chil. hist. geog.*, no. 115, enero-junio, p. 134-161).
A biographical essay on Lacunza and a discussion of his writings. Lacunza was a Jesuit and prominent figure in the field of ecclesiastical literature in the 18th century in Chile. This is an able discussion written from the Jesuit point of view. [R. L. Tree]

1745. Montt L., Manuel S. La hacienda de San Jerónimo (*Rev. chil. hist. geog.*, no. 115, enero-junio, p. 270-279).
A continuation of an article that has appeared in previous issues and is to be continued. This particular part covers the latter part of the 17th and early years of the 18th century. An intensive study of hacienda records and a valuable contribution. See *HLAS, no. 15, 1949*, item 1588. [R. L. Tree]

1746. Sarmiento de Gamboa, Pedro. Viajes al estrecho de Magallanes, 1579-1584. T. 1-2. Buenos Aires, Emecé. 344, 507 p.
An excellent edition of this basic work, a documentary appendix of Gamboa's life and voyages, a glossary of maritime and archaic terms employed, and a seemingly comprehensive index. V. 2 contains Relations 5 and 6, together with letters and *memoriales* by Gamboa, an *octava* and three of his sonnets, and various letters about him and the expeditions, as well as lesser documents.

1747. Thayer Ojeda, Tomás, and Carlos J. Larraín. Valdivia y sus compañeros. Santiago, Academia Chilena de la Historia. 118 p.
A study of the regional and social origins of Pedro de Valdivia and his associates. Includes very brief biographical sketches of the men. [R. L. Tree]

1748. Vicuña Mackenna, Benjamín. Los Lisperguer y la Quintrala, doña Catalina de los Ríos. Segunda edición crítica de Jaime Eyzaguirre. Santiago, Zig-Zag (Biblioteca de Escritores Chilenos). 346 p.
A new edition of a work that first appeared in *El Ferrocarril* (Santiago) in 1877. Treats customs and social life in Chile in the 17th century. Extensive appendix of documents. [R. L. Tree]

RÍO DE LA PLATA

1749. Arnaud, Vicente Guillermo. Los intérpretes en el descubrimiento, conquista y colonización del Río de la Plata. Buenos Aires. 141 p.
A valuable historiographic essay surveying the writings on and interpretations of the history of the discovery, conquest, and colonization of the La Plata region. [R. L. Tree]

1750. DIARIO DEL CAPITÁN DE FRAGATA D. JUAN FRANCISCO AGUIRRE. T. 2, 2. parte (*Rev. bibl. nac.*, Buenos Aires, t. 19, no. 47-48, 3. y 4. trimestres, 1948, i.e. 1950, p. 561-1192).
Continuation. T. 1 y 2 (1. parte) appeared in 1949. See *HLAS, no. 15, 1949*, item 1591.

1751. González, Ariosto D., Carlos Pérez Montero, and Octavio C. Assunção (eds.). Diario de Bruno de Zabala sobre su expedición a Montevideo. Prólogo y notas de Ariosto D. González. Montevideo, Instituto Histórico y Geográfico del Uruguay. xv, 57 p., illus., facsims.
Two different versions of this diary exist and both have been reproduced here by facsimile. Both versions are followed by a transcribed text. [R. L. Tree]

1752. Guarnieri, Juan Carlos. Nuestras industrias en la época colonial. Prólogo de Juan Carlos Quinteros Delgado. Montevideo, Florensa y Lafón. 60 p.
A short but valuable survey of industry in Uruguay in the colonial period. [R. L. Tree]

1753. Ruiz Moreno, Aníbal. La fundación del protomedicato de Buenos Aires (*Arch. iberoamer. hist. med.*, t. 2, fasc. 1, enero-junio, p. 3-36).
An excellent synthesis from the extensive printed studies and documents of other writers. Concerns the period 1776-1800. [R. D. Hussey]

1754. Vadell, Natalio Abel. La Estancia de Yapeyú: sus orígenes y antecedentes y la existencia de misiones de ese pueblo en la Banda Oriental (*Estudios*, t. 83, no. 445, julio-sept., p. 225-235).
The Estancia de Yapeyú was established in 1626-1627 and the data collected by the author shows that missionaries from Yapeyú were working in the Banda Oriental at a very early date. [R. L. Tree]

ADDENDA

1755. DOCUMENTOS RELATIVOS A LA INSURRECCIÓN DE JUAN FRANCISCO DE LEÓN. Prólogo de Augusto Mijares. Caracas, Instituto Panamericano de Geografía e Historia, Comisión de Historia, Comité de Orígenes de la Emancipación (Publ. no. 1), 1949. 243 p.
Complete texts of the documents pertaining to the insurrection of Juan Francisco de León in 1749 against the Guipuzcoana Company. [R. L. Tree]

1756. Giménez Fernández, Manuel (ed.). El estatuto de la Tierra de Casas. Estudio

histórico y jurídico del Asiento y Capitulación para pacificar y poblar la Tierra Firme de Paria, concedida por Carlos V a su capellán, micer Bartolomé de las Casas (*An. univ. hispalense,* año 10, no. 3, 1949, p. 27-101).
A critical discussion using new documentation from the Archive of the Indies. Four facsimiles. [R. D. Hussey]

1757. **Moreyra Paz Soldán, Manuel.** Cuatro cartas del Marqués de Montesclaros referentes a la mina de Huancavelica (*Rev. hist.,* Lima, t. 18, entrega 1, 1949, p. 86-105).
Four important letters from the collection of correspondence of the Peruvian viceroy, Montesclaros, to the King of Spain found in the Archivo General de Indias, Sevilla. These letters, which are the first from the collection to be published, deal with various problems at the Huancavelica mine from 1608 to 1614. They contain much

information about this important aspect of the Peruvian economy. [R. L. Tree]

1758. ————.⸱ El oidor Juan de Canseco Quiñones, creador del régimen de aguas del valle del Rímac (*Rev. hist.,* Lima, t. 18, entrega 1, 1949, p. 78-85).
A well documented study of the important problem of the use of the waters of the Rímac river in the 16th and 17th centuries. Particular attention is paid to the work of Canseco Quiñones. He wrote the basic regulations, which continued in force until the end of the 19th century. [R. L. Tree]

1759. **Temple, Ella Dunbar.** Un linaje incaico durante la dominación española: los Sahuaraura (*Rev. hist.,* Lima, t. 18, entrega 1, 1949, p. 45-77).
A highly detailed genealogical study of the family and descendants of don Cristóbal Paullu Inca from the middle of the 16th century to the latter part of the 19th century. [R. L. Tree]

THE NINETEENTH AND TWENTIETH CENTURIES

HOWARD F. CLINE, ROBERT E. McNICOLL, HARRY BERNSTEIN,

AND WATT STEWART

AS always, Mexico holds the spotlight in 1950 over its smaller land neighbors, in number of entries and in scope and quality of the contributions. Central American items cling to familiar and narrow political paths and closely related offshoots. While the weight of Mexican material remains much as reported here for previous years— biography and autobiography, political memoirs, local and military histories—there is notable branching out toward economic and social history *per se.*

From the numerous listings a few can be cited as noteworthy for various reasons. Though at opposite poles ideologically, the general syntheses by Tannenbaum (items 1013, 1810) and Schlarman (item 1456) are alike in their polemic tone and controversial interpretive syntheses; the revised issue of Parkes' standard work proved disappointing (item 1445). Nineteenth-century Mexican material was marked by numerous reprints and reissues, as well as translations, of important source writings, with a continuation of the slowly unfolding Porfirio Díaz papers (item 1762). The American War and the Reforma brought forth useful pieces by Mexicans and Americans alike, while Justo Sierra continues to attract biographers. Twentieth-century Mexico, nearly equivalent to the Revolution, offers many vital themes, nearly all of which remain in highly emotional and polemical stages. Two of the more unusual items in this spate are Beteta's long thoughts and Sánchez Salazar's vivid picture of Trotsky's assassination and Mexico under Cárdenas. Memorable for many reasons was the first gathering in Monterrey, Mexico, of historians of the United States and of Mexico, whose important papers appear bilingually on a broad range of themes of concern to both. In general, 1950 was a fair to good year, and concluded about par for the course. [H. F. Cline]

A COUNTRY'S great men are a continuing source of interest to its scholars. In Argentina, Sarmiento leads the parade with half a dozen items. Chile's biographers produced works on Portales, Rengifo, Errázuriz Zañartu, Riesco, and Alessandri. In Peru appeared a good biography of Nicolás de Piérola. Venezuelans produced works on Antonio Leocadio Guzmán, Guzmán Blanco, and José Gregorio Monagas, while in Uruguay Artigas continued a subject of research.

Dr. Levene has at last terminated the heavy task of editing *Historia de la Nación Argentina desde los orígenes hasta la organización definitiva en 1862,* volume 7 being the last. Encina's compendious history of Chile marched on with volume 15, while in Colombia a group of scholars under the aegis of the National Academy of History produced *Curso superior de historia de Colombia, 1781-1830.* Paraguay offered more studies of the Chaco war. In other countries works of merit were published in considerable number. [W. Stewart]

MEXICO

HOWARD F. CLINE

1760. Albarrán, Antonio. Nicolás Romero, guerrillero de la Reforma. México, Vargas Rea (Biblioteca de Historiadores Mexicanos). 74 p.
Reprint, in limited edition, of a small biographical sketch issued first in 1895. It deals with a martyr of the Reforma, and a wily warrior (1827-1865).

1761. Alessio Robles, Miguel. Contemplando el pasado. V. 3. México, Stylo. 318 p.
Third volume of a continuing set of memoirs (see *HLAS, no. 15, 1949,* items 1671 and 1672) by an important figure in the Mexican Revolution. Covering fall 1921 through winter 1923, "a brief but intense period of my life," it describes travels in Europe and contact with leading writers, and Miguel's return to Mexico as Obregón's Minister of Industry and Commerce. Much data on the turbulent period following Villa's death.

1762. Archivo del general Porfirio Díaz. Memorias y documentos. Prólogo y notas de Alberto María Carreño. V. 3-6. México, Universidad Nacional Autónoma de México, Instituto de Historia (Col. de Obras Históricas Mexicanas, 3), 1947-1950. 402, 390, 490, 380 p.
Continued publication of a major body of source materials on the dominant Mexican figure who gave his name to an era. These letters and miscellaneous documents, chiefly to Díaz, cover the latter part of 1867 and the first six months of 1868, when he broke with Juárez. A basic contribution to Mexican and Latin American history though the prefaces and notes leave much to be desired.

1763. Beteta, Ramón. Pensamiento y dinámica de la Revolución Mexicana. Antología de documentos político-sociales. México, México Nuevo. 579 p., port.
Essays and addresses of the Ministry of Treasury which together provide much insight into the development of his personal and the public credo of the Mexican Revolution. Range in subject matter is great.

1764. Colección de las efemérides publicadas en el Calendario del Más Antiguo Galván desde su fundación hasta

EL 30 DE JUNIO DE 1950. México, Antigua Librería de Murguía. 848 p.
A day-by-day summary of the most notable happenings in Mexico from July 25, 1852, to June 29, 1950, as extracted from the famous almanacs, arranged in chronological order.

1765. Delgado, Jaime. España y México en el siglo XIX. V. 1 (1820-1830). Madrid, Consejo Superior de Investigaciones Científicas, Instituto Gonzalo Fernández de Oviedo. 477 p.
A young Spanish investigator deals with matters between the homeland and Mexico from Iturbide's days until negotiations for peace and recognition were opened. V. 2 promises to continue these matters from 1830 to 1845, and a third from 1845 to the end of the century. A wide selection of documentary material has been employed from Spanish repositories, along with most of the monographic contributions. An important contribution to diplomatic history.

1766. Díaz-Thomé, Hugo (ed.). Cartas al General Vicente Guerrero (*Bol. arch. gen.,* México, t. 21, no. 2. abril-junio, p. 191-234; no. 3, julio-sept., p. 415-470).
A selection from the 511 letters (1828-1829) to Guerrero, a leader in the Mexican liberal movement. To be continued. [R. R. Hill]

1767. Documentos relativos a la Guerra de Castas (*Yikal maya than,* año 11, t. 11, no. 132, agosto, p. 114-115).
Trial of Maya Indians, accused of conspiring to start the "War of Races." Reproduced from a rare periodical, *Miscelánea instructiva y amena* (Mérida).

1768. Dos cartas inéditas de Maximiliano (*Rev. Indias,* Madrid, año 10, no. 42, oct.-dic., p. 857-861).
Two minor pieces dated June 17, 1866, and August 4, 1866, to Ministro Mangino, from archive of Castaño de Bayle family. Interesting data on railways, as well as social notes.

1769. Espinosa de los Reyes, Jorge. Las relaciones económicas entre México y los Estados Unidos en el siglo XX (*Mem. primer cong. hist. México,* p. 103-114).
Despite its title, this well-documented survey deals as much with the late 19th as it does with the 20th century, with special attention to transportation, tariffs, and investments under Díaz.

1770. Fernández Ledesma, Enrique. La gracia de los retratos antiguos. Prólogo de

Marte R. Gómez. México, Ediciones Mexicanas. 156 p.
Posthumous and incomplete work of a meticulous investigator (1888-1939), which carries on the same theme as his other posthumous publication, *Galería de fantasmas* (1940). As the prologuist says, these daguerreotypes and biographical sketches of Mexican "types" of the 1830's to 1860's give an excellent view of "cómo era la vida en ese siglo XIX."

1771. Flores Mena, Carmen. El General Don Antonio López de Santa Anna, 1810-1833. México, Universidad Nacional Autónoma de México, Facultad de Filosofía y Letras. 149 p.
A well worked out doctoral thesis, based on wide use of secondary material and some new manuscripts, that gives details on this stormy petrel's early career. Main conclusions are that Santa Anna was no buffoon, but was in fact a valorous and able military man who quickly learned his political trade between 1810 and 1822. A helpful addition to the mass of writings on Santa Anna. [R. E. McNicoll]

1772. Foix, Pere. Pancho Villa. México, Xochitl (Vidas Mexicanas, 7). 278 p.
A well written, journalistic and "novelized" biography by a well-known Spanish émigré who has performed similar tasks on Juárez and Cárdenas. This is far from definitive, but is lively and reasonably true. [R. E. McNicoll]

1773. Fresco, Mauricio. La emigración republicana española. Una victoria de México. México, Editores Asociados. 190 p.
Summary of the sources of Spanish emigration (as refugees) to Mexico and the cultural and economic benefits that the Mexican nation has derived. Lists and bibliographical material concerning these Republican Spaniards should be increasingly helpful.

1774. Gallo, Joaquín. Un episodio histórico (*Mem. acad. nac. hist. geog.*, II, p. 32-35).
The episode in question dates from 1861, and concerns the battle of Río Verde (San Luis Potosí), in which the uncle of the narrator fell prisoner to General Tomás Mejía but refused his pardon because it would have meant excluding himself from further armed service in behalf of the Liberals.

1775. García V., Rubén. La tortuosa vida de Iturbide. México, 1950? 160 p.
Very Mexican view of Iturbide's *españolismo* and conservatism. [R. E. McNicoll]

1776. Garza, Virgilio, Jr. Brief sketch of the industrial development of Monterrey (In *Basic indust. Texas north. Mexico*, p. 94-113).
A summary of the "origin, the founding, the growth, and development" of this northern industrial city of Mexico, which stresses its economic history in the 19th and 20th centuries, especially after 1860. A valuable contribution to local, economic, and urban histories.

1777. Gómez, Mathilde. Los Abasolo en la independencia de México (*Trib. israelita,* no. 63, feb., p. 13).
A succint sketch of this family and its contributions to Mexican Independence.

1778. ————. La doctora Columba Rivera. Una gran figura mexicana (*Trib. israelita,* no. 68, julio, p. 12-13).
Brief sketch of an outstanding woman scientist in Mexico and one of the first women in the republic to receive a medical degree (1900).

1779. ————. Doña Soledad Solórzano de Regules (*Trib. israelita,* no. 73, dic., p. 45).
Sketch of the wife of General Nicolás Regules, who whipped the French at Tacámbaro (1865).

1780. ————. Una heroína de la independencia de México. Doña Rita Pérez de Moreno (*Trib. israelita,* no. 70, sept., p. 8-9).
Biographical vignette of the wife of Pedro Moreno, hero of Mexican independence.

1781. Gómez Morín, Manuel. Diez años de México. Informes del Jefe de Acción Nacional. Introducción de Efraín González Luna. México, Jus. xviii, 301 p.
Authoritative statements of the positions taken by Mexico's chief "opposition party" (P.A.N.) in its criticisms of the activities of the "official" group representing the Mexican Revolution in power. Covers the first decade (1939-1949) of Acción Nacional's existence, and contains acute analyses of national problems, though the proposed solutions are more controversial.

1782. LA GUERRA DE CASTAS EN YUCATÁN Y EL SR. PBRO. DON MANUEL ANTONIO SIERRA O'REILLEY (*Bol. arch. gen.,* México, t. 21, no. 2, abril-junio, p. 237-253).
Preceded by a useful explanatory note by Jorge Ignacio Rubio Mañé, which gives more data than the documents, this is a refutation of charges against him by the priest, brother of the more famous Justo Sierra.

1783. GUÍA DEL MUSEO NACIONAL DE HISTORIA CASTILLO DE CHAPULTEPEC. México, Secretaría de Educación Pública, Instituto Nacional de Antropología e Historia. 99 p., illus.

1784. Henry, Robert Selph. The story of the Mexican War. Indianapolis, Ind., Bobbs-Merrill. 424 p., illus., maps.
A semi-popular account, based on printed materials and monographic treatments, and generally following Justin Smith's conclusions. Pleasantly readable, this synthesis is basically sound and reasonably objective.

1785. Islas García, Luis. Miramón, caballero del infortunio. México, Jus. 420 p., illus.

Undocumented but soundly based biography of Miguel Miramón, conservative president of Mexico (1860) and companion-in-arms of Maximilian. The author has used manuscripts and periodicals, as well as a large range of printed materials secondary in nature to produce an excellent book.

1786. Jaurrieta, Rómulo. Batalla de Sacramento, 28 de febrero de 1847 (*Bol. soc. chihuahuense*, t. 7, no. 4, p. 413-420).
Written in 1895, apparently by an eyewitness, this gives a technical description of a famous battle in the Mexican War, from the Mexican side.

1787. Lemoine Villacaña, Ernesto. Crónica de la ocupación de México por el ejército de los Estados Unidos. México. 103 p.
From contemporary journalistic sources this chronicle deals with the social impact of United States troops in Mexico City from September 14, 1847, to June 12, 1848. Chief Mexican sources are *El Monitor Republicano* and *Siglo XIX*, supplemented by the army of occupation's *The North-American* and *The American Star*. A minor but interesting monograph, with an amusing chapter on Mexican womanhood at the hands of the invaders.

1788. López Rosado, Diego G. Panorama histórico de la Revolución Mexicana (*Invest. econ.*, v. 10, no. 3, 3. trimestre, p. 269-285).
A "before" and "after" portrait of Mexico which enumerates many of the social and economic gains of the Revolution.

1789. Loret de Mola, Carlos. Ángel sin ojos. Biografía de Monseñor Rafael Guízar Valencia. México, Impresiones Modernas. 204 p.
Eulogistic biography of a recent bishop of Veracruz who is said to have performed miracles and whom the local population wish to be canonized.

1790. Macedo, Miguel S. Mi barrio. Segunda mitad del siglo XIX. Ensayo presentado a la Sociedad de Estudios de Historia Local de la Ciudad de México, en 1927 (*Mem. acad. nac. hist. geog.*, 2. época, año 6, primer boletín extraordinario, 79 p.).
A warm appreciation and interesting antiquarian notes on the neighborhood around the ancient Calle de Reloj (now Avenida República Argentina) in Mexico City. Useful photographs and maps; based on printed and archival material.

1791. Manzano C., Teodomiro. La erección del estado de Hidalgo (*Mem. acad. nac. hist. geog.*, 2. época, año 6, boletín no. 4, p. 9-23).
Detailed geo-historical material, with documents, concerning the erection of the state of Hidalgo from the Distrito Federal (January, 1869).

1792. María y Campos, Armando de. Sarah Bernhardt en México (*Trib. israelita*, no. 73, dic., p. 25-26).
Concerning the great artist's performances in Mexico during February, 1887, and her singular lack of appeal there, financially and artistically.

1793. Méndez Moreno, Rafael. En marcha. Ensayo doctrinario, histórico, dialéctico. México. 318 p.
An essay completed in 1947 but delayed in publication, this seems to be a windy harangue that attempts by historical data "to analyze Life's happenings in all their manifestations, through process of Nature and with subjection to scientific materialism, directed toward awakening inquietude, arousing conscience and reviving enthusiasm" among youth to carry on the work of the Mexican Revolution. Represents a useful Marxian but non-Communist point of view on the Revolution.

1794. Mendieta y Núñez, Lucio. El régimen de la tierra en México en el siglo XIX (*Mem. primer cong. hist. México*, p. 209-222).
A helpful summary of fairly familiar materials, emphasizing the effects of the Reform Laws and Porfirian legislation on the development of latifundia.

1795. Menéndez, Carlos R. (ed.). El archivo privado del General Cepeda Peraza. Anales yucatecos. Mérida, Mexico. 101 p.
Personal papers of Manuel Cepeda Peraza, an important local politico-military figure in Yucatán from 1844 through the Intervention, with emphasis in the documents on years 1857-1867. Contains much of interest on the War of the Castes in Yucatán. Cepeda was a Juarista and a local Liberal.

1796. Mora, José María Luis. México y sus revoluciones. Edición y prólogo de Agustín Yáñez. T. 1-3. México, Porrúa (Col. de Escritores Mexicanos, 59-61). xxv, 479; 372; 466 p.
Reissue of a Mexican political classic, a fundamental work by the godfather if not the father of the Reforma. First appearing in Paris 1836-1838, these volumes have become increasingly significant. Helpful prefatory material aids understanding of this edition.

1797. Morales Jiménez, Alberto. Francisco I. Madero, descendiente de judíos (*Trib. israelita*, no. 71, oct., p. 10-11).
The author discusses this controversial point on the basis of material from familiar secondary sources, then gives a quick profile of Madero.

1798. Núñez y Domínguez, José de J. La República Dominicana fué la que proclamó a Juárez "Benemérito de la América" (*Mem. acad. nac. hist. geog.*, 2. época, año 6, boletín no. 3, p. 42-46).
Author claims that *El Monitor* of Santo Domingo, number 88, for 11 May 1867, and then

again on 27 July 1867, carried notices that the Dominican Congress had proposed naming Juárez "Benemérito." Reproduces article to substantiate this view.

1799. Ocampo, Manuel. Historia de la misión de la Tarahumara, 1900-1950. México, Buena Prensa. 350 p.

An "official" Jesuit history, based on mission papers, as well as personal knowledge of the places gleaned from service therein by this padre since 1924. A latter day chronicle.

1800. Palacios, Porfirio. El plan de Ayala. Sus orígenes y su promulgación. 2. edición. México, Secretaría de Educación Pública, Departamento de Divulgación. 85 p.

A politically inspired and derivative view of Emiliano Zapata and his role in the Mexican Revolution, with numerous long extracts from his correspondence. Fervidly pro-Zapata, it centers attention on his famous agrarian plan, but creates more heat than light.

1801. Pani, Alberto J. Apuntes autobiográficos. 2. edición. 2 v. México, Porrúa (Biblioteca Mexicana, 6-7). 345, 446 p.

The first edition of this work (1943) was primarily for family circulation; this second edition, reduced in size, and with some changes in text, carries out the title's promise by providing more or less the public life of a Mexican Revolutionary intellectual, diplomat, and economic thinker. V. 1 takes the story through Obregón; v. 2 courses through the election of President Manuel Ávila Camacho.

1802. Pérez-Maldonado, Carlos. El Casino de Monterrey. Bosquejo histórico de la sociedad regiomontana. Monterrey, México. 252 p., illus.

A noted local historian has treated the "vida social regiomontana en general," using as the focus the 86-year-old Casino, which he says is the hub of activity in Monterrey. Fairly superficial, but with occasional nuggets of data.

1803. Poinsett, J. R. Notas sobre México (1822). Traducción de Pablo Martínez del Campo. Prólogo y notas de Eduardo Enrique Ríos. México, Jus. 510 p., map.

Translation of a well-known, controversial volume. Neither the prologue nor the notes add very much to the work.

1804. Ramírez, Alfonso Francisco. La soberanía del estado de Oaxaca (*Mem. acad. nac. hist. geog.*, 2. época, año 6, boletín no. 4, p. 25-29).

An interesting decree by the Governor (3 June 1915) declaring Oaxaca self-governing until the Republic of Mexico could be reformed and order reestablished.

1805. Ramírez, José Fernando. Mexico during the war with the United States. Edited by Walter V. Scholes. Translated by Elliott B. Scherr. Columbia, Mo.,

University of Missouri (The University of Missouri Studies, v. 23, no. 1). 165 p.

Annotated translation of José Fernando Ramírez' *México durante su guerra con los Estados Unidos* . . . made from v. 3 of Genaro García's *Documentos inéditos o muy raros para la historia de México* (México, 1905). A detailed view of Mexico under war-time stresses.

1806. Ramírez Arriaga, Manuel. Ponciano Arriaga, exilio y retorno (*Bol. soc. mex. geog. estad.*, t. 69, no. 1-2, enero-abril, p. 10-53).

Detailed and important material on the group of Liberal exiles (Juárez et al.) and their activities in New Orleans. Though undocumented, this seems to be based on hitherto unknown materials.

1807. Redfield, Robert. A village that chose progress: Chan Kom revisited. Chicago, Ill., University of Chicago Press. xiv, 187 p.

Though primarily a sociological follow-up of a monograph published in 1933, this excellent summary contains much case study material of the development of a Maya village under the impacts of the Mexican Revolution and its various efforts to better conditions in places like this.

1808. Ruiz Castañeda, María del Carmen. El periodismo político de la Reforma en la ciudad de México, 1854-1861. México. ii, 112 p.

A mimeographed master's thesis that restricts itself chiefly to political periodicals edited by Mexicans, 14 of which are dealt with in detail, with ample and useful bibliography on Mexican journalism and journalists of other periods as well.

1809. Sánchez Salazar, Leandro A. Murder in Mexico: the assassination of Leon Trotsky. With the collaboration of Julian Gorkin. Translated by Phyllis Hawley. London, Secker and Warburg. xix, 235 p.

The true and exciting narrative of the events immediately preceding and following the violent death of one of the world's and Mexico's most famous political exiles, as told by the chief of the Secret Service. While directly dealing with efforts to protect Trotsky and run down his assailants and murderer, the author indirectly gives a great deal of information about Mexico in the hectic years of Cárdenas.

1810. Tannenbaum, Frank. Mexico. The struggle for peace and bread. New York, Knopf. xiv, 293, xi p.

A survey of Mexican matters, 1910-1946, against an historical background; heavily loaded on the liberal side, the author is pessimistic about the Mexican future since it has begun to swing from an agrarian toward an industrial emphasis. A polemic and controversial volume, it has aroused divided critical comment in Mexico and the United States, and is an important statement of a particular interpretation of Mexican developments, past, present, and future. See item 1013.

1811. Tena Ramírez, Felipe. Don Manuel de la Peña y Peña (*Jus*, t. 24, no. 138, enero, p. 3-8).

Sketch of a 19th-century jurist and orator, including a brief summary of 19th-century political party formations. Peña became a Moderate Party president in 1847.

1812. Terrazas, Silvestre. El verdadero Pancho Villa (*Bol. soc. chihuahuense*, t. 7, no. 1-7, enero-dic., p. 362-365, 377-381, 393-396, 401-405, 429-433, 453-456, 475-478).

An anecdotal set of memoirs by one of Villa's aides; eulogistic and uncritical, but with some new material.

1813. Torrea, Juan Manuel. Leandro Valle (*Mem. acad. nac. hist. geog.*, 2. época, año 6, boletín no. 5, p. 32-39).

Biographical sketch of a famous Liberal general of the Reform period (1833-1861), executed as a traitor (shot in the back) by the competing Conservative government.

1814. Trens, Manuel B. Historia de Veracruz. T. 4, v. 1, 2. Del centralismo a la dictadura santanista, 1834-1852. México, S. Turanzas del Valle. 375, 376-726 p., illus.

1815. ————. Historia de Veracruz. T. 5, v. 1, 2. Dictadura, Reforma y Segundo Imperio, 1852-1867. México, S. Turanzas del Valle. 346, 347-604 p., illus.

1816. ————. Historia de Veracruz. T. 6. De la restauración de la república a las fiestas del centenario, 1867-1910. México, La Impresora. 433 p., illus.

Tomos 4, 5, and 6 listed above cover the period 1834-1910. The account is much broader than the title indicates and in many instances is nearly co-extensive with national history. T. 6 is particularly good in its analysis of Juárez' problems. See *HLAS, no. 13, 1947*, item 1347, and *no. 15, 1949*, item 1622. [R. E. McNicoll]

1817. Valle, Rafael Heliodoro (and others). Seis imágenes de Morelos. Con un pórtico de Salvador Pineda. México, Imprenta de la H. Cámara de Diputados. 55 p.

Interpretative views by six intellectuals, each seeing the hero of independence through a different "window."

1818. Valle-Arizpe, Artemio de. La güera Rodríguez. México, Librería de Manuel Porrúa. 425 p.

"The blonde" doña María Josefa Rodríguez de Velasco y Osorio was the *amiga* of Iturbide in the days of his rise and fall. The biography is too romanticized or "novelized" to create entire confidence among historians, but is based partly on archival records. [R. D. Hussey]

1819. Vázquez Santa Ana, Higinio. La charrería mexicana. México. 130 p.

A valuable little study by a well-known folklorist who treats in some detail the life of the Mexican cowboy and his environment.

1820. Woodman, Lyman L. Cortina, rogue of the Rio Grande. San Antonio, Tex., Naylor. ix, 111 p., illus., ports., map.

Based on published materials, chiefly United States government documents, this informal but complete sketch of Juan Nepomuceno Cortina, a Juarista raider, is readable and probably accurate, though "novelized." The author calls his hero "the Number One Mexican border bandit of all time."

1821. Yáñez, Agustín. Justo Sierra y el porfiriato (*Cuad. amer.*, v. 43, no. 5, sept.-oct., p. 201-213).

Based on the published *Obras* this essay traces don Justo's changing views on Díaz the politician while retaining respect for him as a person.

1822. Zavala, Lorenzo de. Albores de la república. México, Empresas Editoriales (Col. El Liberalismo Mexicano en Pensamiento y en Acción, 13), 1949, i.e. 1950. 288 p.

Reissue of the polemic but indispensable view of Mexican developments, 1822-1829, written by a leading Federalist who later became the Vice President of the Republic of Texas.

1823. ————. Venganza de la colonia. México, Empresas Editoriales. 254 p.

Reprint of a famous text originally issued by one of the stormy petrels of the Mexican independence movement. Lorenzo de Zavala here provides a minute picture of political currents during 1829-1830, terminating his three-volume survey of the wars for independence as seen from an acute Federalist angle.

CENTRAL AMERICA

HOWARD F. CLINE

1825. Anales parlamentarios. Asamblea ordinaria del Estado de Honduras (*Rev. arch. bib. nac.*, Tegucigalpa, t. 28, no. 7-8, enero-feb., p. 321-330; no. 9-10, marzo-abril, p. 404-408).

A continuing item, which in these issues covers the years 1832-1833.

1826. Bayo, Alberto. Tempestad en el Caribe. México. 209 p.

The "Caribbean Legion" herein finds its first formal history written by a soldier of fortune, born in Cuba but who served in Spain where he is reported to have participated in the last duel to the death with *espada francesa*. An "impenitent romantic," the author gives a fairly objective account of the Legion whose amorphous existence was a result of a cross between a hatred for dictators and a love of adventure, profit, and intrigue. The author's statement:

"Con gente tan habladora como ésa no había medio de organizar nada," might stand as a summary of this 20th-century filibustering attempt. [R. E. McNicoll]

1827. Bolaños, Pío. Napoleón III y el nicaragüense licenciado don Francisco Castellón (*Rev. arch. nac. Costa Rica,* año 14, no. 7-12, julio-dic., p. 274-281).
A useful account of canal diplomacy in the 1840's and 1850's, based chiefly on printed materials.

1828. Carles, Rubén Darío. Horror y paz en el Istmo, 1899-1902. Panamá. 148 p., illus., port.
A fairly detailed account of the Guerra de los Mil Días, which reached Panama approximately in 1900, based on memoirs, and personal interviews with surviving participants. Included is a helpful chronological table. This is perhaps the best single monograph available on its topic.

1830. Cavallini Quirós, Ligia. Ricardo Fernández Guardia, historiador (*Rev. arch. nac. Costa Rica,* año 14, no. 1-6, enero-junio, p. 4-9).
Obituary of an important local historian (1867-1950).

1831. Chamberlain, Robert S. Francisco Morazán, champion of Central American federation. Coral Gables, Fla., University of Miami (Hispanic-American Studies, no. 9). 58 p.
The subtitle indicates the stress of this useful summary and appraisal of the life and times of the Central American *prócer,* based on printed material and without major bibliographical apparatus. [R. E. McNicoll]

1832. Cuadra Ch., Pedro J. La nacionalidad centroamericana y la guerra del 63 (*Rev. acad. geog. hist. Nicaragua,* t. 10, no. 2, oct., p. 101-132).
Long discussion of El Salvador under Gerardo Barrios, a Liberal, anti-clerical caudillo, and of negotiations for a Central American union. Based on documents and letters.

1833. El Dr. Molina y don José Barrundia (*An. mus. nac.,* t. 1, no. 2, p. 35-40).
Reprints of obituaries from *Gaceta del Gobierno del Salvador,* 12 October 1854.

1834. Documento sobre el estado de la instrucción pública en Costa Rica, 1857 (*Rev. arch. nac. Costa Rica,* año 14, no. 1-6, enero-junio, p. 144-160).
Administrative correspondence that shows the effects of wars on the local educational system, which served 1,000 elementary school pupils.

1835. Documentos relativos a los asuntos entre Costa Rica i Nicaragua (*Rev. arch. nac. Costa Rica,* año 14, no. 1-6, enero-junio, p. 161-184).

Diplomatic correspondence of 1872 concerning limits and navigation of rivers.

1836. Documentos sobre la revolución de 1869 (*Rev. acad. geog. hist. Nicaragua,* t. 10, no. 2, oct., p. 154-165).
A continued series, of relatively minor value. Chiefly operational documents and papers obviously written for the eye of posterity.

1837. Don Dionisio de Herrera (*Rev. arch. bibl. nac.,* Tegucigalpa, t. 28, no. 7-8, enero-feb., p. 325-330).
This and succeeding numbers of the review are filled with biographical and bibliographical information about this *prócer,* the centenary of whose death (1850) brought forth discourses and essays of varying merit.

1838. Durón, Jorge Fidel. El año bibliográfico y publicitario hondureño (*Honduras rotaria,* año 7, no. 84, marzo, p. 4, 21-23).
Helpful list of writings, for the year 1949. Compiler complains that authors and printers fail to give adequate bibliographical data on their publications.

1839. Figeac, José F. Juan Rafael Mora (*An. mus. nac.,* t. 1, no. 1, p. 19-22).
Brief biographical sketch of a local hero who fought against William Walker in the late 1850's.

1840. Halftmeyer, Gratus. Historia de Managua. Data desde el siglo XVIII hasta hoy. Edición definitiva. Managua, 1950? 256 p., illus.
Written to commemorate the centennial of the raising of Managua from a *villa* to a city, this antiquarian work lacks organization and discrimination, but apparently contains much local lore.

1841. Informe del Jefe del Estado de Nicaragua, Manuel Antonio de la Cerda, al Congreso Federal, sobre la situación de Nicaragua en 1825 (*Rev. acad. geog. hist. Nicaragua,* t. 10, no. 2, oct., p. 133-140).
Documents discussing the capture of several revolutionary chieftains.

1842. Intrigas del Gral. Juan José Flores, ex-Presidente del Ecuador, con el Encargado de Negocios Inglés contra la unión de Centro América y los intereses territoriales centroamericanos (*Rev. acad. geog. hist. Nicaragua,* t. 10, no. 2, oct., p. 182-188).
Apparently a periodical article that appeared originally in *Correo del Istmo de Nicaragua,* 9 January 1851, discussing various intrigues uncovered by E. George Squier. Translation into Spanish of Squier's report is in p. 170-181.

1843. Lardé y Larín, Jorge. Orígenes del periodismo en El Salvador. San Salvador, Ediciones del Ministerio de Cultura (Biblioteca del Pueblo, 11). 158 p.

A very useful résumé of journalism in El Salvador and Central America, since some of the first impulses came from Guatemala. Author deals with *pasquines* and the development of the periodical press during and after independence, and appends a check-list of journals, 1824-1850, with which the text deals in detail; bibliography is good. [R. E. McNicoll]

1844. Magaña Menéndez, Gustavo. Estudios sociales, políticos y económicos. San Salvador. 149 p.

Collected essays of an important *pensador*, many of which have historical interest, especially for the years 1924-1927.

1845. Peralta, Hernán G. El 3 de junio de 1850. San José, Costa Rica. 48 p.

José Manuel Quirós and the revolt of the mentioned date. [R. E. McNicoll]

1846. El prócer doctor Isidro Menéndez. Tres documentos y una biografía (*An. mus. nac.*, t. 1, no. 4, oct.-dic., p. 24-28).

Reprinted obituaries of the 19th-century "padre de las legislaciones de Costa Rica y de El Salvador."

1847. Revista del Archivo y Biblioteca Nacionales. Tegucigalpa. T. 28, no. 7-8, enero-feb.–t. 29, no. 5-6, nov.-dic.

Contains many short documents from the National Archive relating to the history of Honduras. The publication of the *Anales parlamentarios* is continued for 1830-1833. There are also numerous historical and geographical articles. [R. R. Hill]

1848. Salvatierra, Sofonías. Máximo Jerez inmortal. Comentario polémico. Managua. xliv, 340 p., illus.

Heated defense and refutation by a "liberal" of the "conservative" view of this early 19th-century political figure apparently written by Pedro Joaquín Chamorro, under the title *Máximo Jerez y sus contemporáneos* (1940). As the present production rectifies statements of the latter in detail "sin verificar consultas especiales" its value is chiefly polemic.

1849. Sequeiros, Gonzalo S. Vidas ilustres: Rómulo E. Durón (*Rev. arch. bibl. nac.,* Tegucigalpa, t. 29, no. 3-4, sept.-oct., p. 118-125).

Sketch of a locally renowned historian and writer (1865-1942).

1850. Tratado de amistad, navegación y comercio celebrado entre los Estados de Costa Rica y del Istmo, 1841 (*Rev. arch. nac. Costa Rica,* año 14, no. 7-12, julio-dic., p. 263-273).

Text of the treaty.

1851. Tratado de paz y amistad celebrado entre España y República de Costa Rica (*Rev. arch. nac. Costa Rica,* año 14, no. 1-6, enero-junio, p. 130).

Text of treaty and correspondence, March, 1850.

1852. Zambrano, Domingo. Algo sobre nuestro ferrocarril interoceánico (*Rev. arch. bibl. nac.,* Tegucigalpa, t. 29, no. 3-4, sept.-oct., p. 113-118).

Brief and disjointed notes by an engineer, with the object of stimulating further rail development in Honduras.

THE ISLANDS

HARRY BERNSTEIN AND ROBERT E. McNICOLL

Cuba

1853. Bandera, himno y escudo de Cuba. Notas históricas, disposiciones legales, usos. Habana, Ministerio de Estado (Serie Información sobre Cuba, no. 2). 63 p., illus.

1854. Boletín del Archivo Nacional. Habana. T. 48, no. 1-6, enero-dic., 1949, i.e. 1950.

Contains selected groups of documents dealing with the history of Cuba, especially relating to revolutionary activities; *Inventario general del archivo de la Delegación del Partido Revolucionario Cubano en Nueva York (1895-1898),* legajos 41-91; *Índice del libro diez y nueve de reales órdenes (1812);* and information on the activities of the Archive and its publications. [R. R. Hill]

1855. Casasús, Juan J. E. La invasión. Sus antecedentes, sus factores, su finalidad. Estudio crítico-militar. Habana. 142 p.

A military analysis of the campaign of '95. [H. Bernstein]

1856. Cortina, José Manuel. Néstor Leonelo Carbonell. Habana, Lex. 16 p.

Praise of the Cuban liberator who organized a Cuban junta in Tampa before which Martí spoke. [R. E. McNicoll]

1857. Costa, Octavio R. Manuel Sanguily. Historia de un ciudadano. Habana, Unidad. 155 p.

An undocumented but apparently well-researched biography of the Cuban patriot and orator (1848-1925) famous for his defense of the working classes. Useful vignettes of Cuba just before and after its belated independence. [H. F. Cline]

1858. Diario de operaciones del Teniente Coronel Rafael Cañizares y Quirós, de junio 17 de 1895 a 13 de agosto de 1898 (*Bol. arch. nac.,* Habana, t. 48, no. 1-6, enero-dic., 1949, i.e. 1950, p. 104-151).

The record of the activities of a Cuban soldier who enlisted early in the War for Independence and served to its end. [R. R. Hill]

1859. DIARIO DEL TENIENTE CORONEL EDUARDO ROSELL Y MALPICA, 1895-1897. II: En la guerra. Prefacio de Emeterio S. Santovenia. Notas de Benigno Souza. Habana, Academia de la Historia de Cuba. 175 p.
A useful military log of the Cuban War for Independence. [H. Bernstein]

1860. DOCUMENTOS PARA SERVIR A LA HISTORIA DE LA GUERRA CHIQUITA (Archivo de Leandro Rodríguez). V. 2, 3. Habana, Archivo Nacional (Publ. 27, 29). vi, 312; vii, 254 p.
These volumes comprise the final installments of the documents assembled by Leandro Rodríguez Colina, dealing with the Guerra Chiquita of the Cuban revolution. They cover the period 1879-1880 and consist mostly of letters to the revolutionary committee in New York, including accounts and other interesting items in connection with the movement. There are details of the activities of Martí after the Pact of Zanjón. [R. R. Hill]

1861. Entralgo, Elías. La Insurrección de los Diez Años. Una interpretación social de este fenómeno histórico. Habana, Universidad de la Habana, Departamento de Intercambio Cultural (Cursos y Conferencias de Extensión Universitaria, 3). 37 p.
The war of 1868-1878 arrived as a conflict over slavery. [H. Bernstein]

1862. Ferrer, Horacio. Con el rifle al hombro. Habana, El Siglo XX. lii, 403 p.
Personal history of a Cuban who fought against Spain in 1895 and whose last military engagement was the "Battle of the Hotel Nacional" in 1933. Excellent on the Machado period that still must find its objective historians. [R. E. McNicoll]

1863. Franco, José L. La revolución de Yara y la constituyente de Guáimaro. Habana, Publicaciones del Comité Pro-Centenario de la Bandera. 31 p.
A careful and critical résumé upon the ideas and persons behind the rising of 1861, and upon the early years thereafter. Lacking in critical apparatus. [R. D. Hussey]

1864. González, Manuel Pedro. Fuentes para el estudio de José Martí. Ensayo de bibliografía clasificada. Habana, Ministerio de Educación, Dirección de Cultura (Bibliografía Cubana, 1). viii, 517 p.
An extensive and apparently complete listing of Martí's writings. [H. Bernstein]

1865. Guerra y Sánchez, Ramiro. Guerra de los Diez Años, 1868-1878. T. 1. Habana, Cultural. xii, 420 p., illus., maps.

Probably the best history of the Ten Years War. Viewed socially, economically, militarily, and politically. [H. Bernstein]

1866. ÍNDICE DEL LIBRO DIEZ Y NUEVE DE REALES ÓRDENES . . . CORRESPONDIENTE AL AÑO DE 1812 (Bol. arch. nac., Habana, t. 48, enero-dic., 1949, i.e. 1950, p. 199-208).
Installments of a series started several years ago (with the entries for the years 1807 and 1808) and not yet completed. See HLAS, no. 12, 1946, item 1732a. [R. R. Hill]

1867. Le Roy Gálvez, Luis F. Don José Estévez y Cantal, 1771-1841, primer químico cubano (Univ. Habana, no. 88-90, enero-junio, p. 98-103).
Undocumented summary from a larger, inedited, scholarly work. [R. D. Hussey]

1868. ————. Historia de la primera cátedra de química en Cuba (Rev. bim. cub., v. 66, no. 1-3, julio-dic., p. 65-93).
Part of the same inedited larger work as the article just above, but thoroughly documented. The chair was established by the Real Sociedad Patriótica in 1820, for the Italian physician José Tasso. It lasted only six months. The article relates connected facts from 1793 to 1836. [R. D. Hussey]

1869. Llaguno y de Cárdenas, Pablo. Campaña del Mayor General Antonio Maceo en la Provincia de Pinar del Río, enero 8 de 1896 a diciembre 4 de 1896 (Bol. arch. nac., Habana, t. 48, no. 1-6, enero-dic., 1949, i.e. 1950, p. 81-98).
An account of the campaign of Maceo, in which he gave his life for the independence of Cuba. [R. R. Hill]

1870. Mañach, Jorge. Martí, apostle of freedom. Translated from the Spanish by Coley Taylor. Preface by Gabriela Mistral. New York, The Devin-Adair Co. xvi, 363 p.
First published in Madrid, 1933, under the title Martí, el apóstol. A classic as a biography and interpretation. [F. Aguilera]

1871. Marinello, Juan. Homenaje a Rubén Martínez Villena. Habana, Ayón. 30 p.
Homage by the president of the Cuban Communist party to a young Communist poet who died in 1934. [R. E. McNicoll]

1872. Martínez Arango, Felipe. Cronología crítica de la guerra hispano-cubano-americana. Habana, Municipio de la Habana (Cuadernos de Historia Habanera, 43). 150 p.
A calendar of events. [H. Bernstein]

1873. Merino Brito, Eloy G. José Antonio Saco: su influencia en la cultura y en las ideas políticas de Cuba. Habana, Molina y Compañía. 266 p.

A general biography of the great Cuban historian. [H. Bernstein]

1874. **Mesa Rodríguez, Manuel.** Letra y espíritu de Martí a través de su epistolario. Habana, Academia de la Historia de Cuba. 40 p.
An interpretation of some of Martí's letters. [H. Bernstein]

1875. **Roa, Ramón.** Con la pluma y el machete. Compilación, prólogo y notas de Raúl Roa. T. 1-3. Edición auspiciada por el Ministerio de Educación. Habana, Academia de la Historia de Cuba. xxxi, 366; 323; 310 p.
Autobiography through letters, essays and poetry, as well as the narrative of a Cuban patriot. [H. Bernstein]

1876. **Rodríguez Expósito, César.** Finlay ante la historia. Habana, Academia de la Historia de Cuba. 50 p.
Excellent summary of the place in history that Cubans desire for the first man to show the connection between mosquitoes and yellow fever. [R. E. McNicoll]

1877. **Roig de Leuchsenring, Emilio.** Banderas oficiales y revolucionarias de Cuba. Habana, Municipio de la Habana (Col. Histórica Cubana y Americana, 7). 143 p.

1878. **Sanguily, Manuel.** Brega de libertad. Selección y prólogo de Ernesto Ardura. Habana, Ministerio de Educación, Dirección de Cultura (Grandes Periodistas Cubanos, 9). 324 p.
Selections from the writings and speeches of the Cuban patriot Manuel Sanguily, dealing with leading Cuban personalities of the 19th century, the struggle for independence and Sanguily's participation in the formation and administration of Cuban government. [H. Bernstein]

1879. **Tro, Rodolfo,** and **Lilia Castro** (comps.). Índice de documentos existentes en el archivo de Antonio Bachiller y Morales que se conservan en la Biblioteca Nacional. Habana, Biblioteca Nacional (Cuaderno no. 1). 45 p., illus.
A listing of the papers, originals and copies, from the archive of Bachiller y Morales. The entries of the first group are chronological; those of the second are alphabetical by author or subject. There is also a list of biographical notes regarding Dominican personages and a biographical sketch of Bachiller y Morales. [R. R. Hill]

1880. **Williams, Eric.** The negro slave trade in Anglo-Spanish relations (*Carib. hist. rev.*, no. 1, Dec., p. 22-45).
Deals with Cuban history from 1765, but the "relations" are mostly from 1812 to 1866. Based upon extensive sources from both Spanish and English angles. [R. D. Hussey]

DOMINICAN REPUBLIC AND HAITI

1881. **Almoina, José.** Yo fuí secretario de Trujillo. Buenos Aires, Editora y Distribuidora del Plata. 335 p.
A detailed account by a Spanish refugee who was once Ramfis' tutor: one of the laudatory items in the Trujillo bibliography, well laden with official or semi-official information. [R. E. McNicoll]

1882. **Balaguer, Joaquín.** El Cristo de la libertad. Vida de Juan Pablo Duarte. Buenos Aires, Americalee. 205 p.
Useful, though admittedly "not a book of analysis" but "a work of love." [R. E. McNicoll]

1882a. BOLETÍN DEL ARCHIVO GENERAL DE LA NACIÓN. Ciudad Trujillo. Año 13, v. 13, no. 64, enero-marzo-no. 67, oct.-dic.
The continuation of *Índice general de los libros copiadores de la Sección de Relaciones Exteriores* includes items 193-613, Sept. 13, 1867-Aug. 27, 1869. No. 67 contains an index of the articles and names appearing in the volume. See also item 1571. [R. R. Hill]

1883. **Danache, B.** Le président Dartiguenave et les américains. Port-au-Prince, Imprimerie de l'État. 164 p.
A rather harsh critique of United States policy in Haiti, 1915-1925, combined with some notes on Dartiguenave. [R. E. McNicoll]

1884. **Herrera, César A.** La batalla de "Las Carreras." Sus antecedentes históricos y consecuencias trascendentales. 2. edición. Ciudad Trujillo. 105 p.
Winner of historical contest on centenary of battle between Santana and invading Haitian forces of Soulouque. [R. E. McNicoll]

1885. **Laurent, Gerard M.** Six études sur J. J. Dessalines. Port-au-Prince, Les Presses Libres. 142 p.
Summary studies of the controversial hero of independence, aimed at high school students. The first is a brief biographical sketch; the second touches strategic planning; a third deals with "l'affaire Belair," shifting any blame from Dessalines; the fourth deals with Miranda's visit to Haiti; the fifth analyzes the massacre of whites in 1804; the final study deals with Dessalines' death. Semi-popular, with strong nationalistic tinges. [H. F. Cline]

1886. **Léon, Rulx.** Chronologie médicale haïtienne (*Rev. soc. haïtienne hist. géog.*, v. 21, no. 77, avril, p. 26-35).
Another valuable installment of a series which has appeared irregularly since 1947 (see *HLAS, no. 13, 1947*, item 1148). Readers may wish to note that by 1952 the articles were dealing with the 1870's. [R. D. Hussey]

1887. Lescouflair, Arthur. Thomas Madiou, homme d'état et historien haïtien. Port-au-Prince, Instituto Panamericano de Geografía et Historia, Comisión de Historia (Publ. no. 105. Historiadores de América, 6). 34 p.

Haitian historian whose *Aperçu sur l'histoire d'Haïti* (1874) and other works made him one of Haiti's first historians. [R. E. McNicoll]

1888. Lugo Lovatón, Ramón. Cáceres frente a Cabral (*Bol. arch. gen.,* Ciudad Trujillo, año 13, v. 13, no. 64, enero-marzo, p. 12-14).

Documents relating to the siege and surrender of the City of Santo Domingo in January 1868, together with an introductory note. [R. R. Hill]

1889. ——. Tomás Bobadilla Briones (*Bol. arch. gen.,* Ciudad Trujillo, año 13, v. 13, no. 65, abril-junio, p. 142-166; no. 66, julio-sept., p. 273-330; no. 67, oct.-dic., p. 406-447).

A biographical sketch with documents (1816-1849) regarding Bobadilla (1786-1871), a prominent Dominican leader and politician. To be continued. [R. R. Hill]

1890. Magloire, Jean. Dumarsais Estimé. Esquisse de sa vie politique. Port-au-Prince, Imprimerie de l'État. 85 p., port.

Laudatory biography of the former President of Haiti. [R. E. McNicoll]

1891. Trujillo Molina, Rafael L. Evolución de la democracia en Santo Domingo. Discurso pronunciado . . . al inaugurar la XIII Conferencia Sanitaria Panamericana. Ciudad Trujillo. 67 p.

The President's account of Dominican progress. Also in English and French. [R. E. McNicoll]

Virgin Islands

1892. Larsen, Jens. Virgin Islands story. A history of the Lutheran State Church, other churches, slavery, education, and culture in the Danish West Indies, now the Virgin Islands. Philadelphia, Pa., Muhlenberg Press. xii, 250 p.

A history of Lutheran missions in the Virgin Islands under Danish rule. [R. E. McNicoll]

Addenda

1893. Arosemena, Mariano. Apuntamientos históricos, 1801-1840. Biografía del autor, notas e índices de Ernesto J. Castillero R. Panamá, Ministerio de Educación (Biblioteca de Autores Panameños, 1), 1949. xxiii, 293, xxiv p.

A somewhat belated appearance of a work written in the late 1830's as an apologia and polemic,

now completely published for the first time, with a biographical sketch of the Panamanian patriot Mariano Arosemena (d. 1868). Provides useful data and views for the first half of the 19th century. [H. F. Cline]

1894. Balaguer, Joaquín. Dominican reality. Biographical sketch of a country and a regime. Translated into English by Mary Gilland. México, 1949. 219 p.

The preface states, regarding Trujillo, "Never, indeed, has the presidential chair been occupied by a person richer in human experience or better suited for a harmonious representation of social life." [R. E. McNicoll]

1895. Berzunza Pinto, Ramón. Desde el fondo de los siglos. Exégesis histórica de la Guerra de Castas. México, Cultura, 1949. 278 p.

Based on limited printed sources, this synthesis of the War of the Castes in Yucatan (1847-1853) attempts a sociological interpretation, reassessing the role of the Maya. Though it adds no new factual information, it opens up interesting vistas, most of them highly controversial. [H. F. Cline]

1896. Corro R., Octaviano. General Marcos Carrillo Herrera, héroe de cuatro guerras. Cosamaloapan, Mexico, 1949. 52 p., illus.

Biography of a local hero (1837-1892) by a local antiquarian, who provides much data on Carrillo through his military career in the War of Reform, Intervention, Empire, and against the Yaquis. This is rather a series of notes than a finished product. [H. F. Cline]

1897. Díaz Vasconcelos, Luis Antonio. De nuestro antaño histórico. Guatemala, Tipografía Nacional, 1948. 211 p.

Essays on aspects of Guatemalan history. [R. E. McNicoll]

1898. Galich, Manuel. Del pánico al ataque. Guatemala, Tipografía Nacional, 1949. 362 p.

A collection of periodical articles written in 1946, strongly anti-Ubico, giving a view of Guatemalan politics since 1934. [H. F. Cline]

1899. La guerra de los Diez Años. Su sentido profundo en la historia de Cuba. Discursos leídos en la recepción pública del Dr. Ramiro Guerra y Sánchez el día 14 de julio de 1949. Habana, Academia de la Historia de Cuba, 1949. 84 p.

Interpretative material which concludes that the two main new forces from the Ten Years' War (1868-1878) were unification of the Cuban people by social equality and then endowing them with a vision of their own capacity. [H. F. Cline]

1900. Jos, Emiliano. Méjico en la mediación inglesa desde las Cortes de Cádiz a la ominosa década (*Estud. hispanoamer.*, 1948, p. 91-150).

Period of 1811 to 1824, based primarily upon the well-known work of C. K. Webster, plus adequate printed materials upon the Spanish side. [R. D. Hussey]

1901. Laurent, Gérard M. Coup d'oeil sur la politique de Toussaint-Louverture. Port-au-Prince, Éditions Henri Deschamps, 1949. xix, 350 p.

A replete chronicle, based chiefly on printed materials but with new documentary sources, which examines minutely the political aspects of the period 1791-1803. Claims all credits possible for the subject of the biography. [H. F. Cline]

1902. Linares, Julio. Modesto Barrios. Managua, 1949? 162 p., port.

Uncritical biography. [R. E. McNicoll]

1903. Roig de Leuchsenring, Emilio. Cuba y los Estados Unidos, 1805-1898. Historia documentada de la actitud disímil del estado y del pueblo norteamericano en relación con la independencia de Cuba. Habana, Sociedad Cubana de Estudios Históricos e Internacionales, 1949. 279 p.

The historian of the City of Habana belabors the annexationist desires of the United States already so well set forth by his colleague Dr. Portell Vilá. [R. E. McNicoll]

SOUTH AMERICA (EXCEPT BRAZIL) *

HARRY BERNSTEIN AND WATT STEWART

GENERAL

1904. Davis, William Columbus. The last conquistadores. The Spanish intervention in Peru and Chile, 1863-1866. Athens, Ga., University of Georgia Press. 386 p.

Considerable attention is given Spanish internal conditions. A good job. [W. Stewart]

1905. Larrazábal, Carlos Héctor. Sucre, figura continental. Buenos Aires, Juan Pellegrini. 331 p.

A biography awarded honorable mention by the Sociedad Bolivariana of Argentina. [H. Bernstein]

1906. Lastres, Juan B. La viruela, la vacuna y la expedición filantrópica (*Archivos iberoamer. hist. med.*, t. 2, fasc. 1, enero-junio, p. 85-120).

A good discussion, from good but not exhaustive sources, of events and happenings chiefly in Peru, 1803-1822. Prints the texts of a body of *reales órdenes y actas*, 1803-1820. [R. D. Hussey]

*For Brazilian items see "Brazil," p. 167-179.

1907. Magne, Leo. L'Extraordinaire aventure d'Antoine de Tounens. Gentilhomme périgordin, avoué, conquistador, roi d'Araucanie-Patagonie. Préface d'André Maurois. Paris, Éditions Latino-Américaines. 199 p.

Story of the fantastic effort in the years 1858-1874 to establish a "New France" in southern South America. [W. Stewart]

ARGENTINA

1908. Altamira, Luis Roberto. El Deán Gregorio Funes, primer historiador del General San Martín. Córdoba, Argentina, Universidad Nacional de Córdoba, Facultad de Filosofía y Humanidades, Instituto de Estudios Americanistas (Publ. no. 18). 84 p.

Minute monographic analysis of writings of Gregorio Funes to show that he fully appreciated San Martín's accomplishments; the object is to show that Córdoba not only provided Argentina's first university, but also its first historian. [H. F. Cline]

1909. ————. San Martín. Sus relaciones con don Bernardino Rivadavia. Buenos Aires, Pellegrini. 72 p.

Correspondence and narrative on the hostility of Rivadavia towards San Martín. [H. Bernstein]

1910. ANALES DEL INSTITUTO DE HISTORIA Y DISCIPLINAS AUXILIARES. T. 4, 5. Mendoza, Argentina, Universidad Nacional de Cuyo. lvii, 305 p.; xlvi, 344 p.

Two volumes of letters and documents dealing with Chile-Argentine military rules and controls after Rancagua, especially the organization by O'Higgins and San Martín of the invasion of Peru, 1820-1823. [H. Bernstein]

1911. LA AUTENTICIDAD DE LA CARTA DE SAN MARTÍN A BOLÍVAR DE 29 DE AGOSTO DE 1822. Advertencia de Ricardo Levene. Buenos Aires, Academia Nacional de la Historia. 170 p.

Contributions to San Martín year, 1950, by Paraguayan, Uruguayan, Chilean, and Argentine historians, under the auspices of the Academia Nacional de la Historia. A volume of documents, brief essays and indorsements tending to establish the authenticity of San Martín's letter of August, 1822 to Bolívar. [H. Bernstein]

1912. BIBLIOGRAFÍA DE SAN MARTÍN. Buenos Aires, Biblioteca del Congreso de la Nación (Información Bibliográfica, Publ. 7). 83 p.

". . . material bibliográfico que posee la Biblioteca del Congreso de la Nación sobre el general San Martín, excluídos los textos generales de historia y las biografías de sus contemporáneos."

1913. Bischoff, Efraín U. El General San Martín en Córdoba. Córdoba, Argentina, Cervantes. 180 p., illus.
Sketches, based upon archives, of San Martín, Puerreydón, and O'Higgins in the events of 1816, the Tucumán Congress, the problem of Artigas, and the invasion of Chile. [H. Bernstein]

1914. Bunkley, Allison W. Sarmiento and Urquiza (*Hisp. amer. hist. rev.*, v. 30, no. 2, May, p. 176-194).
An intriguing description of the personal relations of two of Argentina's "greats." [W. Stewart]

1915. Busaniche, José Luis. San Martín vivo. Buenos Aires, Emecé. 257 p.
Very readable popular biography by a scholar. [H. Bernstein]

1916. Castro, Antonio P. Diario de gastos. Libreta llevada por Sarmiento en sus viajes, 1845-1847. Reproducción facsimilar. Buenos Aires, Ministerio de Educación de la Nación, Museo Histórico Sarmiento (Serie 4, no. 2). 225 p., illus.
A very concise book and full of interest; enlightening concerning various features of Sarmiento's grand tour. [W. Stewart]

1917. Cocca, Aldo Armando. El Coronel Carlos Tomás Sourigues. Maestro francés en la paz y soldado argentino en la guerra. Apuntes sobre su enseñanza en el país. Buenos Aires, Centro de Historia Mitre (Cuadernos de Historia Argentina y Americana, 10). 111 p., ports., facsims., illus.
Story of a French immigrant to Argentina who in the 1840's and 1850's played a role of some importance in the country of his adoption. [W. Stewart]

1918. Corbellini, Enrique C. La revolución de Mayo y sus antecedentes desde las invasiones inglesas. T. 1: Antecedentes. T. 2: La revolución. Buenos Aires, Lajouane. 397, 417 p.
A general history, containing known materials, and presented in a clear, well-organized narrative. [H. Bernstein]

1919. Dellepiane, Antonio. Rosas. Buenos Aires, Santiago Rueda. 367 p.
Critical study of Rosas, the tyrant. "Those who think that Rosas can be rehabilitated and glorified are greatly mistaken." [W. Stewart]

1920. Dose de Zemborain, Justa. Cinco cartas del General San Martín. Buenos Aires. 43 p., facsims.
Letters, 1823 and 1832, with photostats of originals, and notes. [H. Bernstein]

1921. Estrella Gutiérrez, Fermín (comp.). San Martín. Páginas escogidas sobre el héroe. Buenos Aires, Kapelusz. xxv, 373 p.
Selections from poems and essays in praise of the hero. [H. Bernstein]

1922. Gentiluomo, Federico A. San Martín y la provincia de Cuyo. Precursores de la nación en armas. 2. edición. Tucumán, Argentina, La Raza. 277 p.
Second edition of a military man's theory and practice of war and the leadership of San Martín in waging modern type of war in the Argentine. Studies San Martín in the light of total war, mobilization, and organization of civilian economics. [H. Bernstein]

1923. Ghioldi, Américo A. Actualidad de Juan B. Justo. Sus ideas históricas, sus ideas socialistas, sus ideas filosóficas. Buenos Aires. 164 p.
Justo was a leader of socialism in Argentina. This book is enlightening with respect to his life and his ideas. [W. Stewart]

1924. González Arrili, Bernardo. Mujeres de nuestra tierra. Buenos Aires, La Obra. 143 p.
Brief sketches of 40 women—daughter of San Martín, mother of Sarmiento, and so on. [W. Stewart]

1925. Guerrero, César H. Sarmiento, historiador y biógrafo. Buenos Aires, El Ateneo. 216 p.
An admirable work on the subject. [W. Stewart]

1926. HISTORIA DE LA NACIÓN ARGENTINA DESDE LOS ORÍGENES HASTA LA ORGANIZACIÓN DEFINITIVA EN 1862. Ricardo Levene, director general. V. 7. Rosas y su época. 2. sección. Buenos Aires, Academia Nacional de la Historia. 850 p., maps.
The ultimate volume of the compendious and excellent history of Argentina to 1862. The entire book is a landmark in Argentine historiography. [W. Stewart]

1927. IN MEMORIAM ISMAEL BUCICH ESCOBAR. Buenos Aires. 107 p.
Contains laudatory statements and a bibliography of the works of Bucich (1890-1944) along with a reprint of his *Banderas argentinas de la independencia*. [W. Stewart]

1928. Institución Mitre. Le Général don José de San Martín. Nécrologie. Buenos Aires, Coni. 44 p.
A reprint of the obituary notice of José de San Martín, as it appeared in the journal *L'Impartial* of Boulogne-sur-Mer, August 22, 1850. [H. Bernstein]

1929. Irazusta, Julio. Tomás de Anchorena. Prócer de la revolución, la independencia y la federación, 1784-1847. Buenos Aires, La Voz del Plata. 183 p.
A somewhat belated attempt to rescue from near oblivion Anchorena, "susceptible to a most instructive study for the understanding of the social system to which he belonged." Undocumented, and without scholarly bibliography, this nevertheless does catch a useful glimpse of the La Plata area at the end of the colonial period

and the beginning of the 19th century. [H. F. Cline]

1930. Levene, Ricardo. El genio político de San Martín. Buenos Aires, Kraft. 434 p., facsims.
An interpretative and solidly based summary of Argentina's great hero by one of its outstanding historians. Adds new data to Mitre's classic treatment. The polemical "Interview of Guayaquil" is given thorough treatment, sustaining the "Argentine thesis." This is an important and basic work, admirably symbolizing "The Year of the Liberator General San Martín." [H. F. Cline]

1931. ————. El proceso histórico de Lavalle a Rosas. La historia de un año: de diciembre de 1828 a diciembre de 1829. La Plata, Publicaciones del Archivo Histórico de la Provincia de Buenos Aires (Estudios sobre la Historia y la Geografía Histórica de la Provincia de Buenos Aires). 310 p.
This year in the history of Buenos Aires Province is important as background for the age of Rosas. It possesses the usual excellence of Dr. Levene's work. [W. Stewart]

1932. Martínez Paz, Enrique. El deán Funes. Un apóstol de la libertad. Córdoba, Argentina, Pronsato. 326 p.
Good biography of an Argentine cleric and scholar whose life overlapped the end of the colonial period and the beginning of independence. [W. Stewart]

1933. Medrano, Samuel W. El libertador José de San Martín. Buenos Aires, Espasa-Calpe Argentina (Col. Austral). 225 p.
A popular biography. [H. Bernstein]

1934. Menéndez, José María. San Martín. Sus ideas y su acción en la epopeya de la libertad. T. 1-3. Buenos Aires, El Ateneo. 547, 603, 487 p.
A military-political description of events. [H. Bernstein]

1935. Mitre, Bartolomé. Historia de San Martín y de la emancipación sudamericana. T. 1-3. Buenos Aires, Edición del diario "La Nación." 494, 518, 494 p.
Reprinting of the classic history. [H. Bernstein]

1936. Ortega, Exequiel César. José de San Martín. Doctrina, ideas, carácter y genio. Buenos Aires, La Facultad. 263 p.
A biography dealing with ideas, opinions, and some relations with contemporaries. [H. Bernstein]

1937. Ottolenghi, Julia. Vida y obra de Sarmiento en síntesis cronológica. Buenos Aires, Kapelusz. 387 p.
A book of dates, including publications, in Sarmiento's life. [W. Stewart]

1938. Palcos, Alberto. Hechos y glorias del General San Martín. Espíritu y trayectoria del Gran Capitán. Buenos Aires, El Ateneo. 593 p., illus.
An excellent biographical study. [H. Bernstein]

1939. ————. Rivadavia, iniciador de los adelantos técnicos de la nación (*Bol. acad. nac. hist.*, año 25, v. 23, 1949, i.e. 1950, p. 224-241).
Enlightening comment on the significance of Rivadavia's life for Argentina. [W. Stewart]

1940. Rodríguez, Augusto G. Sarmiento militar. Buenos Aires, Peuser. 433 p., illus.
An excellent book which presents the least known facet of the life and personality of the great Argentine. [W. Stewart]

1941. Rojas, Ricardo. La entrevista de Guayaquil. Buenos Aires, Losada (Obras Completas de Ricardo Rojas, v. 30). 365 p., illus., facsims.
Another contribution to the debate. [H. Bernstein]

1942. SAN MARTÍN EN LA HISTORIA Y EN EL BRONCE. Buenos Aires, Kraft (Publicada por la Comisión Nacional Ley 13661). 247 p., illus.
A detailed account of his military actions published in the anniversary year 1950, with a prologue by Juan Perón, letters, documents. Excellent reproduction and photographs. The material was prepared by Ricardo Piccirilli. [H. Bernstein]

1943. Taboada, Gaspar. Los Taboada. Recuerdos históricos. Luchas de la organización nacional. Documentos seleccionados y comentados. T. 5. Buenos Aires, Imprenta López. 670 p.
A collection of letters and other documents relating to members of the Taboada family, prominent in provincial affairs, Santiago del Estero, etc. The opening date is January 13, 1851, the closing May 10, 1859. [W. Stewart]

1944. Vásquez, Aníbal S. Dos siglos de vida entrerriana. Anales y efemérides, 1730-23 de octubre-1930. Paraná, Argentina, Ministerio de Educación (Biblioteca Entrerriana "General Perón," Serie Historia, 1). 603 p.
Historical notes in diary form. Good regional history. [W. Stewart]

1945. Yaben, Jacinto R. Por la gloria del General San Martín. Buenos Aires. 468 p., maps.
A defense of San Martín by a noted Argentine naval historian. It is well documented, begins with the Guayaquil encounter of 1822, covers many military campaigns, the differences be-

tween San Martín and Cochrane. Has many maps, new documentary materials and photographic reproductions. A valuable contribution to the historical materials on Independence, in terms of the military events and consequences. [H. Bernstein]

BOLIVIA

1946. Carrasco, Benigno. Hechos e imágenes de nuestra historia. La Paz, Editorial Don Bosco. 293 p.
Anecdotes that concern the activities of many Bolivians — Melgarejo, for example — from the 1860's to the 1930's. [W. Stewart]

CHILE

1947. Alessandri, Arturo. Revolución de 1891. Mi actuación. Santiago, Nascimento. 222 p.
Informative interpretation, naturally somewhat partisan, by the recently deceased Chilean ex-president. [W. Stewart]

1948. Barros Barros, Osvaldo. Don Manuel Rengifo, el gran ministro de la era portaliana. Valparaíso, Chile. 94 p.
A thesis sketching the life of Rengifo, with particular attention to his two periods in the Ministerio de Hacienda. [W. Stewart]

1949. Bladh, C. E. La República de Chile, 1821-1828 (*Rev. chil. hist. geog.,* no. 115, enero-junio, p. 349-403).
Translation into Spanish of C. E. Bladh's *Republiken Chile Aren 1821-1828* (Stockholm, 1837). It has considerable value for its description of Chilean life of the time, both rural and urban. Translation by Elisabeth De Vylder de Lundberg, revised by Eugenio Pereira Salas. [W. Stewart]

1950. Bulnes, Alfonso. Errázuriz Zañartu. Su vida. Santiago, Editorial Jurídica de Chile (Universidad de Chile, Facultad de Derecho, Colección de Estudios Jurídicos y Sociales, v. 10). 585 p.
First volume of a projected two-volume study. This volume covers the story of the Chilean educator and statesman to the beginning of his presidency in 1871. An excellent work. [W. Stewart]

1951. Congreso. Homenaje del Congreso Nacional de Chile a la memoria del Honorable Senador Don Arturo Alessandri Palma, presidente del Senado y ex-presidente de la República. Santiago. 104 p.

1952. Cruz, Bernardo A. San Felipe de Aconcagua. V. 2. Aconcagua, Chile, Ediciones Aconcagua. 399 p.
Good local history. This volume begins just after San Martín's crossing to Chile—San Felipe lay on his route—and carries down to about 1900. [W. Stewart]

1953. Encina, Francisco A. Historia de Chile. Desde la prehistoria hasta 1891. T. 15. 1. edición. Santiago, Nascimento. 622 p.
Continuation of a multiple-volume work of importance. This volume covers the decade 1866-1876. [W. Stewart]

1954. ————. Historia de Chile. Desde la prehistoria hasta 1891. T. 16. Santiago, Nascimento. 582 p.
This volume covers the period September 18, 1876-October 8, 1879. Challenging. [W. Stewart]

1955. Feliú Cruz, Guillermo. Alessandri, demoledor, constructor y consolidador de un pueblo (*Atenea,* año 27, t. 98, no. 302-303, agosto-sept., p. 212-250).
A sort of political obituary of the great Chilean who died in 1950 at the age of eighty-two. [W. Stewart]

1956. ————. Chile visto a través de Agustín Ross, 1891-1924. Ensayo de interpretación. Estudio preliminar de Francisco Antonio Encina. Santiago. 207 p.
Biography of a Chilean conservative who "for 50 years had fought for sane and noble ideas inspired by a solid patriotism, none of which prospered according to his aspirations." [W. Stewart]

1957. O'Higgins, Bernardo. Archivo de don Bernardo O'Higgins. T. 7. Santiago, Imprenta Universitaria (Archivo Nacional). xvii, 383 p.
Basic materials from 1814 to 1817. [H. Bernstein]

1958. Pérez Rosales, Vicente. Recuerdos del pasado, 1814-1860. Santiago, Carlos de Vidts. 463 p.
The third edition of a work of social significance to Chilean history. Lengthy sections of the work contain Pérez Rosales' reminiscences concerning his stay in California—when he was a "forty-niner"—and the beginnings of German colonization in South Central Chile. Delightfully written. [W. Stewart]

1959. Riesco, Germán. Presidencia de Riesco, 1901-1906. Santiago, Nascimento. 360 p.
A good, largely factual narrative written by a son. [W. Stewart]

1960. Soto Cárdenas, Alejandro. Guerra del Pacífico. Los tribunales arbitrales, 1882-1888. Santiago, Universidad de Chile, Facultad de Filosofía y Educación, Instituto Pedagógico, Departamento de Historia y Geografía. xx, 279 p.
An excellent presentation of the "mopping up" process that follows wars. [W. Stewart]

1961. Soto-Hall, Máximo. Don Diego Portales. Historia novelada. Guatemala, Ediciones del Gobierno de Guatemala (Col. "Los Clásicos del Istmo"). 254 p.
Good, of its kind. [W. Stewart]

COLOMBIA

1962. Arciniegas, Germán. La dictadura en Colombia (*Cuad. amer.*, año 9, v. 49, no. 1, enero-feb., p. 7-33).
A Colombian intellectual, and a Liberal, describes the election of November, 1949, and comments on its meaning for Colombia and the Americas. [W. Stewart]

1963. McGann, Thomas F. The assassination of Sucre and its significance in Colombian history, 1828-1848 (*Hisp. amer. hist. rev.*, v. 30, no. 3, August, p. 269-289).
A new, and acute, examination of a very controversial point in Colombian history. The author convicts Obando of the crime. [W. Stewart]

1964. Vallejo, Alejandro. Hombres de Colombia. Caracas, Ávila Gráfica (Letras Americanas, Memorias, 1). 223 p.
Primarily a biography of Jorge Eliécer Gaitán by a devoted friend and colleague, this work presents the background of recent Colombian events. [A. Flores]

ECUADOR

1965. Chiriboga N., Ángel Isaac. Campañas de la libertad. Guerra entre Colombia y el Perú, 1828-1829. Campaña de los 30 días, Tarqui. Quito, Talleres Gráficos del Estado Mayor General. 274 p.
The war treated here was in the main an effort of Peru to acquire Ecuador. A useful collection of documents is included. [W. Stewart]

1966. Mera, Alejandro R. Leyendas históricas del Carchi. Quito, Editora Ecuador, 1950? 178 p.
Local history of some value. [W. Stewart]

1967. Stevenson, W. Bennett. La ciudad de Quito en 1808-1810 (*Bol. arch. nac. hist.*, año 1, no. 2, julio-dic., p. 425-442).
Chapter X from Stevenson's *Historical and descriptive narrative of twenty years' residence in South America* (London, 1829), translated into Spanish by Luis Merchán Mora. This chapter describes life in Quito in 1808-1810. Informative and interesting. [W. Stewart]

PARAGUAY

1968. Pitaud, Henri. Paraguay, terre vierge. Paris, F. Chambriand. 198 p., illus., maps.
A general treatment of Paraguay by a Frenchman who found the country much to his liking. [W. Stewart]

1969. Ríos, Ángel F. La defensa del Chaco. Verdades y mentiras de una victoria. Buenos Aires, Ayacucho. 450 p.
Written to prove that Paraguay's liberal governments had not been remiss in preparing the country for war with Bolivia. Much data on the Chaco War. [W. Stewart]

1970. Smith, Willard H. Paraguayan interlude. Scottdale, Pa., Herald Press. 184 p., illus.
Largely concerned with the state of the Mennonite colonists in Paraguay; firsthand account. [W. Stewart]

1971. Warren, Harris Gaylord. Political aspects of the Paraguayan Revolution, 1936-1940 (*Hisp. amer. hist. rev.*, v. 30, no. 1, Feb., p. 2-25).
A good analysis of the state of Paraguayan politics at the period in question. [W. Stewart]

1972. Ynsfran, Pablo Max (ed.). The epic of the Chaco: Marshal Estigarribia's memoirs of the Chaco War, 1932-1935. Austin, Tex., The University of Texas, Institute of Latin-American Studies (Latin-American Studies, 8). xiv, 221 p., photos, maps.
An excellent work for an understanding of this war. [W. Stewart]

PERU

1973. Aguirre Molina, Raúl. El gran mariscal del Perú, Ramón Castilla, y sus vinculaciones con el General San Martín. Buenos Aires, El Ateneo. 154 p.
An interesting item associated with the centenary of the death of San Martín. [W. Stewart]

1974. Diez-Canseco, Ernesto. Los generales Diez-Canseco. Episodios históricos. Lima, Torres Aguirre. 425 p.
The three generals were brothers and were brothers-in-law of Marshal Ramón Castilla; one was a president of Peru. Their lives covered an important period in Peruvian history. [W. Stewart]

1975. Morachimo T., Lorenzo. El héroe de Güeppí (Sgto. 2° Fernando Lores Tenazoa). Biografía. Iquitos, Peru. 58 p.
Güeppí was an engagement between Colombian and Peruvian soldiers in March, 1933. The work is interesting but not important. [W. Stewart]

1976. Ulloa y Sotomayor, Alberto. Don Nicolás de Piérola. Una época de la historia del Perú. Lima. 441 p., illus., ports.
Good biography of one of Peru's great men. [W. Stewart]

1977. Valcárcel, Daniel. Recibimiento de San Martín en la Universidad de San Marcos. Lima, CIP. 16 p.
An interesting academic ceremonial. [H. Bernstein]

URUGUAY

1978. Acevedo, Eduardo. José Artigas. Su obra cívica. Alegato histórico. T. 1-3. Montevideo. 515, 663, 892 p.
An official biography, by one of the great Uruguayan historians, the late Eduardo Acevedo. This is not so much a personal or chronological account of Artigas as it is a dedicated defense of the civic accomplishments of the Uruguayan. It is also a contribution to the historiography of Artigas and the political forces of his day. Originally published in 1909, it has now been reissued by the Uruguayan government as a memorial to the deceased historian. [H. Bernstein]

1979. Aguirre, Leonel. Una vida al servicio de un ideal. Artículos y discursos. Montevideo. 257 p.
A selection from the writings of Leonel Aguirre, political thinker and leader, prepared under the auspices of the Partido Nacional Independiente. [W. Stewart]

1980. Arcas, Juan Antonio. Historia del siglo veinte uruguayo, 1897-1942. Montevideo, "La Casa del Estudiante." 194 p.
Simply written history for schoolboys covering Uruguay's important period of "institutional reform." [W. Stewart]

1981. Blanco Acevedo, Pablo. El federalismo de Artigas y la independencia nacional. 2. edición. Montevideo. 232 p.
Detailed and excellent study of the subject from the rejection of Artigas' delegates at Buenos Aires to the Portuguese occupation. [W. Stewart]

1982. Capurro, Federico E. Una memoria más. Montevideo. 563 p.
Memoirs of a Uruguayan civil engineer, follower of Batlle y Ordóñez. [W. Stewart]

1983. Comisión Nacional Archivo Artigas. Archivo Artigas. T. 1. Advertencia del Dr. Felipe Ferreiro. Montevideo. 626 p.
This is the first volume of a multiple-volume work which celebrates the centenary of Artigas' death. The material of this volume is related almost entirely to the grandfather, Juan Antonio Artigas, and the father, Martín José Artigas, of the great Uruguayan *prócer*. [W. Stewart]

1984. Cusano, Ángel María. Carlos Roxlo. Estilo y destino de su vida. Montevideo, Florensa y Lafón. 179 p.
Comment on the Uruguayan poet, legislator, reformer with a reprint of some of his poems and other works. [W. Stewart]

1985. Durán Cano, Ricardo. Pensamiento y acción de Emilio Frugoni. Montevideo. 47 p.
Presentation by a socialist of the activities of a leading Uruguayan socialist in the period since 1910. [W. Stewart]

1986. Genta, Edgardo Ubaldo. Historia de Artigas. Homenaje al héroe en el primer centenario de su muerte, 1850-1950. Montevideo, Florensa y Lafón. 208 p., illus.
A popular history. [H. Bernstein]

1987. Manacorda, Telmo. Itinerario y espíritu de Jacobo Varela. Montevideo. 347 p.
Biography—not too critical—of a leading Uruguayan, son of José Pedro Varela. The son has, in some sense at least, carried on the liberal, reforming tradition of his eminent father. He was at one time Uruguayan Ambassador to Washington. [W. Stewart]

1988. EL PARAGUAYO INDEPENDIENTE. ASUNCIÓN, 1850. Reproducción facsimilar. Montevideo, Instituto Histórico y Geográfico del Uruguay. 40 p.
This number of *El Paraguayo Independiente* carried news of the death of José Artigas. The present work has an introduction and a bibliography of works relating to Artigas. [W. Stewart]

1989. Peña, José Ma. Eduardo Blanco Acevedo. Historia de una vida integral. Montevideo. 205 p.
Somewhat non-objective presentation of an eminent Uruguayan surgeon and professor as well as statesman and politician. [W. Stewart]

1990. Salteraín y Herrera, Eduardo de. Artigas en el Paraguay, 1820-1850. Montevideo. 42 p.
Enlightening comment on the motives of Francia in granting and of Artigas in requesting, in 1820, asylum in Paraguay, where he spent the remaining 30 years of his life. [W. Stewart]

1991. Schiaffino, Rafael. Los cirujanos de Artigas. Montevideo. 135 p.
A reprint dealing with the army surgeons who served at different times with the Artigas forces. These are documents in the form of correspondence to and from the medical men; a few of them in photostat. A useful contribution to a little known part of Latin American medical archives and history. [H. Bernstein]

VENEZUELA

1991a. ÁLBUM CONMEMORATIVO SOBRE EL LIBERTADOR. Caracas. Unpaged, illus., facsims.
A remarkable volume, with mounted facsimiles of basic documents and photographic reproductions. Edited by "Dr. Dallos H. J." [H. Bernstein]

1992. Biggs, James. Historia del intento de don Francisco de Miranda para efectuar una revolución en Sur América. Traducción del inglés y prólogo por José Nucete-Sardi. Caracas, Ávila Gráfica (Publ. de la Academia Nacional de la Historia). xxiii, 252 p.

The first Spanish translation of Biggs' letters about the ill-fated Miranda expedition of 1806. From the *Boston Record* edition of 1810. [H. Bernstein]

1993. BOLETÍN DE LA ACADEMIA NACIONAL DE LA HISTORIA. Caracas. Edición consagrada a Miranda con motivo del bicentenario de su nacimiento. T. 33, no. 129, enero-marzo; no. 130, abril-junio.

In addition to items on Miranda, including two letters, there are a number of pieces discussing the "Entrevista de Guayaquil" between San Martín and Bolívar. The Miranda material seems to be largely of interest to specialists, with one noteworthy posthumous publication of Antonio Ballesteros y Beretta. [H. F. Cline]

1994. Briceño Perozo, Mario. Don Francisco de Miranda, maestro de libertadores. Trujillo, Venezuela, Imprenta del Estado. 109 p.

Biographical sketches. [H. Bernstein]

1995. EL CENTENARIO DEL NACIMIENTO DEL DOCTOR Y GENERAL JUAN PIETRI. Caracas. 107 p.

Biographical sketch of a supporter of Crespo. Eminent doctor, politician, and military man of much prominence in Venezuela after 1892 until his death in 1925. [W. Stewart]

1996. Cova, J. A. Guzmán Blanco, su vida y su obra. Caracas, Ávila Gráfica. 222 p.

Sketchy biography, but interesting. [W. Stewart]

1998. Díaz Sánchez, Ramón. Guzmán. Elipse de una ambición de poder. Caracas, Ministerio de Educación Nacional, Dirección de Cultura y Bellas Artes (Biblioteca Venezolana de Cultura). 609 p.

Excellent biographical study of the Venezuelan liberal statesman Antonio Leocadio Guzmán, father of Antonio Guzmán Blanco. [W. Stewart]

1999. García Chuecos, Héctor. Catálogo de documentos referentes a historia de Venezuela y de América, existentes en el Archivo Nacional de Washington. Caracas, Imprenta Nacional. 88 p.

A listing of documents relating to Venezuela from the records of the Department of State, now in the National Archives, Washington, D. C. The documents are in "Colombia (New Granada), Notes," parts I, 1810-1820, and II, 1820-1834; "Notes to Foreign Legations," 1810-1821, 1821-1828; and "Special Agent to Venezuela, Baptis Irvine, 1818-1819." [R. R. Hill]

2000. GENERAL JOSÉ GREGORIO MONAGAS, LIBERTADOR DE LOS ESCLAVOS. Ofrenda de sus conciudadanos y admiradores con motivo de la inauguración del parque que lleva su nombre en Aragua de Barcelona, 31 de marzo de 1950. Caracas, Excélsior. 57 p., illus.

A mélange of materials—army records and brief messages of Monagas—and laudatory addresses. [W. Stewart]

2001. Grisanti, Ángel. El precursor Miranda y su familia. Primera biografía general de la familia de Miranda. Caracas, Ediciones del Ministerio de Educación Nacional, Biblioteca Venezolana de Cultura (Col. Andrés Bello). 284 p.

The first study made of the family of Miranda, dealing with his ancestry, parents and children. [H. Bernstein]

2002. Lecuna, Vicente. Crónica razonada de las guerras de Bolívar. T. 1-3. New York, The Colonial Press. xxvii, 545; 487; 662 p.; illus., maps.

A military history based upon a collection of documents, most of them already printed in the known collections and the Bulletin of the Venezuelan Academy of History. A luxury edition with excellent reproductions and map reprints. There is a good deal of material on the conferences, congresses and political actions of Bolívar. The author, already known as a leading authority on the Liberator, has dedicated these volumes to the justification of Bolívar as a general and warrior. [H. Bernstein]

2003. Nucete-Sardi, José. Aventura y tragedia de don Francisco de Miranda. 3. edición. Caracas, Ministerio de Educación Nacional. 326 p.

A third edition of a popular biography. [H. Bernstein]

2004. ————. Cecilio Acosta y José Martí, binomio de espíritus (*An. acad. hist. Cuba,* t. 30, enero-dic., 1948, i.e. 1950, p. 7-22).

Concerned chiefly with the thought of the Venezuelan liberal, Acosta, and opponent of Guzmán's dictatorship. [W. Stewart]

2005. Pighini, Giacomo. Il Venezuela, paese dell' avvenire. Firenze, Italy, Le Lingue Estere. 147 p., illus.

An Italian scientist presents Venezuela as a country with a great future and one that should attract the Italian emigrant. [W. Stewart]

2006. REVISTA NACIONAL DE CULTURA. Edición especial consagrada a don Francisco de Miranda en el bicentenario de su nacimiento. Caracas. Año 11, no. 78-79, enero-abril. 288 p.

Preceded by what appear to be *discursos,* this issue reprints a number of items by Miranda as an anthology, and includes a bouquet of tributes in verse to Miranda by Hispanic poets. [H. F. Cline]

2007. Rodríguez Fabregat (h.), Enrique. Francisco de Miranda. Prólogo de Abelardo B. Giménez Bonet. Buenos Aires, Centro de Historia (Cuadernos de Historia Argentina y Americana, 7). 119 p.
A Uruguayan essay on Miranda and his patriot contribution. [H. Bernstein]

ADDENDA

2008. Arenas Luque, Fermín V. Leonor Tezanos Pinto de Uriburu. Su obra social. Buenos Aires, Claridad, 1949. 127 p.
Some valuable social history. Interesting statements concerning Balmaceda's suicide in the Argentine Embassy, Uriburu being at the time the Argentine Ambassador to Chile. [W. Stewart]

2009. Beltrán, Óscar R. Episodios argentinos. T. 1, 2. Buenos Aires, PROCMO, 1947, 1948. 173, 191 p.
Chatty presentation of important, or interesting, episodes in Argentine history: Sarmiento the soldier, Fray Luis Beltrán, Congress of Tucumán, and so on. [W. Stewart]

2010. Bernal Medina, Rafael. Ruta de Bolívar. Bogotá, Lumen, 1949. 206 p., illus.
Divided into two parts, the first half of each chapter of the monograph provides maps of the Liberator's journeys (poorly drawn and reproduced), while part two gives notes and comments. The latter are based on printed sources. There is an appendix of documents and "appreciations" of Bolívar from various sources. [H. F. Cline]

2010a. Egaña, Juan. Escritos inéditos y dispersos. Edición al cuidado de Raúl Silva Castro. Santiago, Imprenta Universitaria, 1949. 255 p.
The unpublished papers in this effort to complete the record of Egaña's literary contribution

to Chile's early political and social thinking are found in the Santiago National Archives. [F. Aguilera]

2011. Guevara, Darío. Juan Benigno Vela, titán del liberalismo radical ecuatoriano. Ambato, Ecuador, Imprenta Municipal, 1949. 309 p., port.
Informative biography of an Ecuadorean liberal, opponent of García Moreno. [W. Stewart]

2012. Iriarte, Tomás de. Memorias. Historia trágica de la expedición libertadora de Juan Lavalle. Estudio preliminar de Enrique de Gandía. Buenos Aires, Ediciones Argentinas "S.I.A.", 1949. ccliii, 405 p.
Preceded by a 253-page prologue, tendentious in tone, polemic in nature, and controversial in results, the *Memorias* appear in unedited fashion, covering the years of attempted Unitarian "Reconquest" in the 1840's, and defeat at the hands of Rosas. Iriarte's account also gives a view of Chile in 1841, as an exile, and several chapters deal with his stay in Brazil. [H. F. Cline]

2013. Ochoa, Lisandro. Cosas viejas de la villa de la Candelaria. Medellín, Colombia, 1948, i.e. 1949. 304 p.
Local and social history of Medellín, Colombia, since some 75 years ago. [W. Stewart]

2014. Silva Castro, Raúl. Bibliografía de don Juan Egaña, 1768-1836. Santiago, Imprenta Universitaria, 1949. 281 p.
A well organized and exceedingly important item for Chilean historiography. [W. Stewart]

2015. Solari, Juan Antonio. Esteban Echeverría. "Asociación de Mayo." Su ideario. Mar del Plata, Argentina, 1949. 95 p.
Brief biography of an Argentine poet, thinker, liberal and opponent of Rosas. [W. Stewart]

BRAZIL

MANOEL CARDOZO

THE notable increase in historical production in Brazil in 1950 over the previous year, as reflected in the bibliography below, is largely the result of the appearance of several volumes of the proceedings of the two great historical congresses of 1949 at Bahia and at Rio de Janeiro, both held to commemorate the fourth centenary of the founding of the nation's ancient capital of Bahia (items 2034, 2035). The volumes published are surprisingly good. Some of the tinsel that seems to be proper to historical extravaganzas of this kind is to be found in them, but they are also liberally filled with first-rate papers, real contributions, in many instances, to historical scholarship.

The large Portuguese delegation to the congresses came loaded with copies of documents from the archives of Portugal. The impressive collection of source materials from the Arquivo Histórico Colonial (now Ultramarino) of Lisbon bore out again the truth of Pedro Calmon's happy phrase, that the great Lisbon archive is truly the "Casa do Brasil." These documents were often not fully utilized in the papers they illustrate, and their meaning was not always fully understood, but this is not difficult to explain. The study of Brazilian history in Portugal is still pretty much in the hands of amateurs, and there are no scholars who devote themselves exclusively or preeminently to it. Yet the wealth of documents which the Portuguese delegates, in their enthusiastic tribute to Bahia, showered upon the congresses, has made available an enormous amount of new information which is now at the disposal of anybody who wants to use it.

Other birthdays afforded the occasion for other works. The centennials of Blumenau and Petrópolis, the semicentennial of Belo Horizonte, the centennials of the birth of Joaquim Nabuco and Rui Barbosa, the bicentennial of the Treaty of Madrid, the tricentennial of the Battle of Guararapes—all these events were celebrated in writing. The year was also rich in guides, on Rio de Janeiro, São Paulo, Bahia, Belo Horizonte, Ouro Preto. Some obviously are better than others, but in all of them the historian will find facts conveniently sorted out for him.

Two ambitious historical projects were brought to a close during the year. With the publication of his eleventh volume, Dr. Afonso de E. Taunay, the director emeritus of the Museu Paulista and dean of Brazilian historians, has concluded his history of the *bandeiras* of São Paulo. Dr. Serafim Leite's history of the Society of Jesus in Brazil during colonial times was also finished, with the appearance of the tenth volume. Both of these works, one on the geographical expansion, the other on the religious development of Brazil, brilliantly round out our knowledge of fundamental aspects of Brazilian history.

São Paulo has further emphasized its position in scientific historical scholarship with the founding of the new quarterly *Revista de História,* the undertaking of a group of historians of the University of São Paulo, under the editorship of E. Simões de Paula. From the point of view of the modern canons of historical writing and the catholicity of interest, this latest journal is clearly the best thing that has come out of Brazil in recent years. For one thing, quite apart from other considerations, it does not limit itself to the history of Brazil (although the articles in this field are thus far the most competent); it also publishes studies on European history. In still other ways, in its Notes and Comments sections, in its book reviews, it succeeds in keeping the Brazilian historian in touch with the historical craft outside of his country. This, we think, is to be encouraged.

During the year the first number of the *Revista do Instituto Histórico* of Petrópolis made its bow. We hope that it will not turn out to be what so many reviews of local historical institutes are, avenues of publicity for antiquarian tidbits and lectures of parochial interest. The Institute was created in 1938.

Of all the periods of Brazilian history, scholars gave the colonial period the most attention. This was bound to happen particularly in a year when centennials of events that took place in the remoter past were celebrated, but we trust that the charms of the earlier centuries, which are very real, will not make historians forget that the more recent scene must also be investigated, and that a history of the republic, for example, complete and documented, is long overdue. Most of the studies on colonial history were, however, of a monographic character. One of the few exceptions was J. F. de Almeida Prado's history of Bahia during the Golden Age, liberally filled with observations of a moral tone which happily do not detract from the story but rather make it easier to understand. Quite a few items appeared in Brazilian church history, a healthy sign. Historians have unfortunately just scratched the surface of this vast and important field, even though it goes without saying that the evolution of Brazil will never be seen in focus unless we know more about the rôle of religion.

In the United States the year was a good one for Brazilian history. Translations appeared of books by Fernando de Azevedo, Carolina Nabuco, and Sérgio Corrêa da Costa. William J. Coleman published his doctoral dissertation on the Rio nunciature, a significant contribution to Brazilian church history. In honor of the International Colloquium on Luso-Brazilian Studies, an outstanding event of 1950 sponsored jointly by the Library of Congress and Vanderbilt University, the Academy of American Franciscan History of Washington, D. C., devoted to Brazil the October issue of its quarterly review, *The Americas,* with articles by Americans and Portuguese.

GENERAL

2016. Amaral, Max Tavares d'. Contribuição à história da colonização alemã no vale do Itajaí. São Paulo, Instituto Hans Staden. 73 p.

2017. Anais da Biblioteca Nacional. V. 70. Rio de Janeiro, Biblioteca Nacional. 247 p.
Contents: Revolução Praieira, Joaquim Nabuco, Rui Barbosa, Maranhão, index of the *Anais,* v. 1-69.

2018. Araújo, Antônio Gomes de. Concurso da Bahia na formação da gens caririense (*An. prim. cong. hist. Bahia,* v. 3, p. 361-372).

2019. Araújo, Heitor O. História da Diocese da Barra (*An. prim. cong. hist. Bahia,* v. 4, p. 587-621).

2020. O Arquivo Nacional (*Rev. hist.,* São Paulo, ano 1, no. 2, abril-junho, p. 241-251).
A list of codices in the National Archive of Rio de Janeiro of interest for the history of São Paulo.

2021. Azevedo, Fernando de. Brazilian culture. An introduction to the study of culture in Brazil. Translated by William Rex Crawford. New York, Macmillan. xxix, 562 p., illus., ports., maps, facsims.
A lavishly illustrated survey of the development of Brazil in which the various aspects of the culture of the country (in the broad sense) are discussed. An intelligent portrait of Brazil by a man who is at home both in history and in sociology. Original publication, entitled *A cultura brasileira,* appeared in 1943 as "tomo 1 do volume I—Introdução—da Série Nacional das publicações do Recenseamento Geral do Brasil, realizado em 1.° de setembro de 1940" (see *HLAS, No. 9, 1943,* item 109a). The second edition, 1944, was published by Companhia Editôra Nacional, as a separate entity with the subtitle *Introdução ao estudo da cultura no Brasil.*

2022. Barbosa, Manoel de Aquino. O titular e o padroeiro da cidade do Salvador (*An. prim. cong. hist. Bahia,* v. 4, p. 407-440).

The "titular" is Our Lord; the "padroeiro," St. Francis Xavier.

2023. Barbosa, Rui. Rui Barbosa e o exército. Conferência ás classes armadas. Rio de Janeiro, Casa de Rui Barbosa. 184 p.
Two addresses by Rui. The second one is especially autobiographical.

2024. Barreto, Abilio. Resumo histórico de Belo Horizonte, 1701-1947. Belo Horizonte, Imprensa Oficial. 342 p., illus., maps.
An official publication prepared in honor of the fiftieth anniversary of the establishment of the capital of Minas Gerais at Belo Horizonte. There is an introduction to the early history of Minas Gerais.

2025. Bittencourt, Feijó. O grande nome da Independência. Primeira parte. Os amigos de Antônio Meneses Vasconcelos de Drummond (*Rev. inst. hist. geog. bras.,* v. 198, jan.-março, 1948, i.e. 1950, p. 3-27).
Drummond was a friend of José Bonifácio de Andrada e Silva.

2026. ————. O grande nome da Independência. Segunda parte (*Rev. inst. hist. geog. bras.,* v. 199, abril-junho, 1948, i.e. 1950, p. 15-118).
On José Bonifácio de Andrada e Silva.

2027. Bruno, Ernani Silva. Bibliotecas e livreiros na cidade de São Paulo (*Bol. bibliog.,* São Paulo, v. 15, p. 77-79).
Largely on the period of the Empire.

2028. Carneiro, Edison (ed.). Antologia do negro brasileiro. Pôrto Alegre, Globo. 432 p.
The pioneers in African studies; the abolition movement; aspects of life during slavery days; Negro revolts; folklore; religion; Negro leaders; the Negro since 1889. Excerpts from the works of several authors, conveniently put together. See item 3330.

2029. Carneiro, Julio Cesar de Moraes. O catolicismo no Brasil. Memória histórica pelo padre Júlio Maria. Rio de Janeiro, AGIR. 256 p.
First published in the *Livro do Centenário,* this sketch of the Catholic Church in Brazil is still the best general thing of its kind that we have.

2030. Carvalho, Septembrino de. Memórias. Dados para a história do Brasil. Rio de Janeiro. 304 p.
Some information for the history of the Naval Revolt and the Contestado campaign.

2031. CENTENÁRIO DE BLUMENAU, 2 DE SETEMBRO, 1850-1950. Rio de Janeiro, Comissão de Festejos. 492 p., illus., maps.
The many-sided history of this Santa Catarina city that grew out of a settlement of German immigrants.

2032. Cerqueira, Carlos Valeriano de. Histórico da cultura da cana na Bahia. Formação econômica da indústria açucareira da Bahia (*An. prim. cong. hist. Bahia*, v. 4, p. 263-335).

2033. COMISSÃO DE ESTUDO DOS TEXTOS DA HISTÓRIA DO BRASIL. Bibliografia de história do Brasil. 1. e 2. semestres de 1948. Rio de Janeiro, Ministério das Relações Exteriores, Serviço de Publicações. 125 p.
Reviews of important publications, Brazilian and foreign, by competent hands.

2034. Congresso de História da Bahia. Primeiro, Salvador, 1949. Anais do . . . . V. 2, 3, 4. Salvador, Instituto Geográfico e Histórico da Bahia. 499, 482, 621 p.
Many of the individual contributions to these volumes are reviewed below in the appropriate sections.

2035. Congresso de História Nacional. Quarto, Rio de Janeiro, 21-28 abril de 1949. Anais. V. 5, 6, 7. Rio de Janeiro, Instituto Histórico e Geográfico Brasileiro. 587, 607, 605 p.
Many of the individual contributions to these volumes are reviewed below in the appropriate sections.

2036. Costa, Luiz Edmundo da. Recordações do Rio antigo. Rio de Janeiro. 179 p., illus.

2037. Costa, Sergio Corrêa da. Every inch a king. A biography of Dom Pedro I, first emperor of Brazil. Translated from the Portuguese by Samuel Putnam. New York, Macmillan. 230 p., port.
A spirited biography written for the general reader.

2038. Ellis Júnior, Alfredo. O ciclo do muar (*Rev. hist.*, São Paulo, ano 1, no. 1, jan.-março, p. 73-81).
From the beginning of the 17th century to the introduction of railroads.

2039. Felizardo, Jorge Godofredo. Coronel Vicente Ferrer da Silva Freire. Esboço biográfico e descendência (*An. prim cong.*

hist. Bahia, p. 317-352).
A Bahia family in Rio Grande do Sul.

2040. ————. Linhagens baianas no Rio Grande do Sul. Verbetes genealógicos (*An. prim. cong. hist. Bahia*, v. 3, p. 291-316).

2041. Florence, Amador. Coisas de velhos censos paulistas (*IV cong. hist. nac.*, v. 5, p. 79-245).
The censuses of São Paulo, beginning with the first one of 1765. A neglected source of information.

2042. Freitas, Newton. Joaquim Nabuco, homem do litoral (*Cultura*, Rio de Janeiro, ano 1, no. 3, maio-agôsto, 1949, i.e. 1950, p. 127-140).
Nabuco as opposed to the *homem do sertão*, symbolized by Antônio Conselheiro.

2043. Gomes, Alfredo. Achegas para a história do tráfico africano no Brasil. Aspectos numéricos (*IV cong. hist. nac.*, v. 5, p. 25-78).
How many Negroes came to Brazil from Africa? The author does not answer the question, but he does give us a great deal of information on the subject.

2044. Lima Sobrinho, Barbosa (ed.). Documentos do Arquivo Público Estadual e da Biblioteca Pública do Estado sôbre a comarca do São Francisco. Seleccionados, coordenados e prefaciados. V. 4-5. Recife, Secretaria do Interior e Justiça, Arquivo Público Estadual (Documentos do Arquivo). lxxxi, 684 p.
Cartas e ordens régias, portarias, ofícios, patentes militares, correspondência da Côrte, provisões régias, supremos tribunais, câmaras municipais, ouvidores — from the beginning through the period of Independence. There is a preliminary essay on the history of the region; it was separated from the province of Pernambuco in 1824.

2045. Machado, José Carlos Bahiana. As grandes epidemias na Bahia, a peste da bicha de 1686, a cólera morbus de 1855 (*An. prim. cong. hist. Bahia*, v. 3, p. 267-276).

2046. Magalhães, J. B. História da evolução militar do Brasil (*IV cong. hist. nac.*, v. 6, p. 347-607).

2047. Manique, Luís de Pina. O convênio luso-brasileiro de 1867 sôbre cartografia portuguesa (*IV cong. hist. nac.*, v. 4, p. 451-484).
On the exchange of maps between Portugal and Brazil. The maps exchanged by the two countries are listed.

2048. **Mendonça, Renato de.** Breve historia del Brasil. Madrid, Ediciones Cultura Hispánica. xiv, 135 p., photos, map.
To my knowledge the first history of Brazil published in Spain since the translation of Oliveira Lima's *La Formation historique de la nationalité brésilienne.* It was earlier published in Mexico City.

2049. **Ministério da Marinha.** Serviço de Documentação da Marinha. Subsídios para a história marítima do Brasil. V. 8. Extratos do arquivo do Almirante Tamandaré. Rio de Janeiro, Imprensa Naval. 291 p.
Documents for the study of the life of Joaquim Marques Lisboa, Marquês de Tamandaré, with preliminary remarks by Admiral Dídio Iratim Afonso da Costa.

2050. **Nabuco, Carolina.** Joaquim Nabuco. O defensor dos escravos. São Paulo, Melhoramentos. 53 p., illus.
A brief biography, competently done, obviously written for the younger reader.

2051. ————. The life of Joaquim Nabuco. Translated and edited by Ronald Hilton in collaboration with Lee B. Valentine, Frances E. Coughlin, and Joaquim M. Duarte, Jr. Stanford, Calif., Stanford University Press. xxv, 373 p., port., map.

2052. **Nabuco, Joaquim.** Acción y pensamiento. Traducción, prólogo y notas de Armando Correia Pacheco. Washington, Unión Panamericana (Escritores de América). 107 p.
An excellent preface introduces a number of well chosen excerpts from the writings of Joaquim Nabuco.

2053. ————. Discursos parlamentares. Publicação comemorativa do 1. centenário do nascimento do antigo deputado por Pernambuco. Iniciativa da mesa da Câmara dos Deputados. Seleção e prefácio do deputado Gilberto Freyre. Introdução do deputado Munhoz da Rocha. Rio de Janeiro, Imprensa Nacional. 534 p.
A great deal on the Church-State problem, from the point of view of an anti-cleric, and also on the abolition of slavery.

2054. **Navarro, Moacyr.** Miguel Couto vivo. Rio de Janeiro, A Noite. 261 p.
The biography of a famous physician (1865-1934) who introduced clinical procedures to Brazilian medicine. A section is devoted to "Pensamentos médicos e outros pensamentos," extracted from Couto's works.

2055. **Neeser, Hermann.** O sêlo, brazão e bandeira da cidade do Salvador (*An. prim. cong. hist. Bahia,* v. 4, p. 13-28).

2056. **Nobre, Freitas.** História da imprensa de São Paulo. São Paulo, Leia. 267 p., illus.
The background material is not absolutely sound, and neither is the concept of democracy as expressed in the book. There is an inventory of newspapers and periodicals published in the state of São Paulo from 1827 to 1944.

2057. **Oliveira, José Teixeira de** (ed.). Dicionário brasileiro de datas históricas. Prefácio de Affonso de E. Taunay. 2. edição. Rio de Janeiro, Pongetti. 423 p.
Largely vital statistics on important Brazilians and other significant figures from abroad who are in some way connected with Brazil. Each entry is ordinarily followed by a quotation from a published work on the person (or event) involved. The sources used have not always been well chosen. In the case of King John V, for example, he is pictured as Oliveira Martins once painted him—a man who spent enormous sums of money to secure privileges he wanted from Rome; yet one cannot dismiss the monarch in so derogatory a fashion. The work, nonetheless, is useful. There is an index.

2058. **Pinheiro, Irineu.** Um baiano a serviço do Ceará e do Brasil (*An. prim. cong. hist. Bahia,* v. 3, p. 353-360).
Notes on José Pereira Filgueiras.

2059. **Pinto, Luiz.** Homens do nordeste e outros ensaios. Rio de Janeiro, Editôra Minerva. 194 p.
Largely on the history of Paraíba.

2060. **Prado, J. F. de Almeida.** A Bahia e as suas relações com o Daomé (*IV cong. hist. nac.,* v. 5, p. 377-439).
A significant contribution to the history of the slave trade.

2061. **Rodrigues, José Honório.** As fontes da história do Brasil na Europa. Rio de Janeiro, Imprensa Nacional. 42 p.
An account of what the author found of interest for the history of Brazil in the archives and libraries of Portugal, Spain, France, the Netherlands, and England. There are suggestions for work to be done.

2062. **Ruas, Eponina.** Ouro Preto. Sua história, seus templos e monumentos. Rio de Janeiro, Imprensa Nacional. 237 p., illus.
An unpretentious guide designed for the tourist, but it will prove useful for the historian also. The author's elaboration on the concept of liberty seems to be out of place in a work of this kind.

2063. **Sampaio, Alde.** Joaquim Nabuco e Joaquim Murtinho. Rio de Janeiro, Olympio. 42 p.
A lecture on Nabuco, the well-known figure of the abolition movement, and another one on Murtinho, a cabinet minister during the first years of the Republic. Both are exceedingly thin.

2064. **São Marino, Gregório de.** Os capuchinhos na Bahia (*An. prim. cong. hist. Bahia*, v. 4, p. 509-586).

2065. **Souza, Eusébio de.** História militar do Ceará. Fortaleza, Instituto do Ceará (Coleção Instituto do Ceará, História do Ceará, monografia no. 15). 359 p.

2066. **Tourinho, Eduardo.** Alma e corpo da Bahia. Rio de Janeiro, Olympio. 278 p.
Sketches of Caramurú, Tomé de Sousa, the Jesuits, the Indians, the Negroes, the São Francisco River, the *entradas*, Frei Vicente do Salvador, Dom Marcos Teixeira, Antônio Vieira, Gregório de Matos, the republican conspiracy of 1798, religious festivals, witchcraft—all evocative rather than rigorously historical.

2067. **Valladão, Alfredo.** Joaquim Nabuco, o evangelista da abolição. Rio de Janeiro, Jornal do Commercio. 40 p.
A lecture which adds nothing to what is already known about the man but which is nonetheless a dignified tribute to his memory.

2068. **Van Leisen, Herbert.** Les États-Unis du Sud: Le Brésil. Genève, Switzerland, Kundig. 203 p.
Light sketches of various aspects of Brazilian life.

2069. **Varela, Alfredo.** O solar brasílico. Remate nos muros austrinos. 2 v. Rio de Janeiro, Edições Instituto América. 415, 243 p.
The first volume is on the settling of southern Brazil; the second, a defense of the author's earlier work, *História da grande revolução*, in six volumes. The work is written in an inflated style which makes it hard to follow. The author has used a wealth of manuscript sources from European archives.

2070. **Vianna, Hélio.** História do Brasil em 1949 (*Verbum*, t. 7, fasc. 4, dez., p. 629-654).
A bibliography of works on Brazilian history published in 1949 in Brazil and abroad.

2071. **Whitaker, Edmur de Aguiar.** A família Aguiar Whitaker. Estudo genealógico. Biografia dos seus fundadores e descendentes, através de documentação escrita, tradição oral e recordações pessoais do autor. São Paulo. 601 p., illus.
The descendants of William Whitaker, a native of Ireland, who arrived in Brazil in 1808.

COLONIAL PERIOD

2072. **Albuquerque, Maria Izabel.** Liberdade e limitação dos engenhos d'açúcar (*An. prim. cong. hist. Bahia*, v. 2, p. 491-499).
Documents from the Arquivo Histórico Ultramarino, Lisbon.

2073. ————. Navegação entre Portugal e a Bahia de 1801 a 1808 (*An. prim. cong. hist. Bahia*, v. 2, p. 465-489).

2074. ————. Quatro documentos do Arquivo Histórico Colonial (*IV cong. hist. nac.*, v. 3, p. 503-513).
They deal with Gomes Freire de Andrade (tio), Marco Antônio de Azevedo Coutinho, Antônio Moniz Barreto, and the Benedictines of Rio de Janeiro.

2075. **Alincourt, Luiz d'.** Memoria sobre a viagem do porto de Santos á cidade de Cuyaba; organizada, e offerecida a sua magestade imperial, o senhor D. Pedro Primeiro, imperador constitucional, e defensor perpetuo do Imperio do Brasil (*An. mus. paulista*, t. 14, p. 253-381).
This valuable work was first published in Rio de Janeiro in 1830. It has since become a collector's item.

2076. **Almeida, Aluísio de.** Bibliotecas paulistas do século XVIII (*Bol. bibliog.*, São Paulo, v. 14, p. 95-102).

2077. **Almeida, Manuel Lopes de.** Um documento sôbre a expedição de Duclerc ao Rio de Janeiro em 1710 (*IV cong. hist. nac.*, v. 7, p. 141-154).
From the library of the University of Coimbra. The report of the committee that passed upon this contribution to the Congress is unusually good.

2078. ————. Relação do levante de Pernambuco em 1710 (*IV cong. hist. nac.*, v. 3, p. 445-502).
New documents of the "Guerra dos Mascates."

2079. **Amaral, Braz do.** Reação do aborígene contra o estrangeiro invasor (*An. prim. cong. hist. Bahia*, v. 3, p. 447-460).

2080. **ANAIS DA BIBLIOTECA NACIONAL. V. 69.** Rio de Janeiro, Biblioteca Nacional. 340 p.
The entire volume is devoted to the Dutch in Brazil.

2081. **Austregésilo, Myriam Ellis.** Estudo sôbre alguns tipos de transporte no Brasil colonial (*Rev. hist.*, São Paulo, ano 1, no. 4, out.-dez., p. 495-516).

2082. ————. Pesquisas sôbre a existência do ouro e da prata no planalto paulista nos séculos XVI e XVII (*Rev. hist.*, São Paulo, ano 1, no. 1, jan.-março, p. 51-71).

2083. **Bello, L. de Oliveira.** Cronologia da vida de Tiradentes, à luz de documentos (*Rev. inst. hist. geog. bras.*, v. 199, abril-junho, 1948, i.e. 1950, p. 3-14).

2084. **Belo, Antônio Raimundo.** Relação dos emigrantes açorianos para os estados do Brasil, extraída dos *Processos de passaportes da Capitania Geral dos Açores* (*Bol. inst. hist. Ilha Terceira*, v. 8, no. 8, p. 35-57).

2085. **Boiteux, Lucas Alexandre.** Bosquejo histórico sôbre a nossa política racial e continental, 1494-1763 (*IV cong. hist. nac.*, v. 7, p. 15-140).
A history of Colônia do Sacramento and expansion in southern Brazil.

2086. **Boxer, C. R.** As primeiras frotas da Companhia do Brasil à luz de três documentos inéditos, 1648-1652 (*IV cong. hist. nac.*, v. 5, p. 299-332).
Points out the rôle played by the Company in the final defeat of the Dutch in Brazil.

2087. **Brandão, Álvaro Soares.** No tempo do cirurgião-mor Antonio Soares Brandão (*IV cong. hist. nac.*, v. 7, p. 239-253).
A contribution to the history of medicine and surgery, based in part on material from the Arquivo Nacional da Torre do Tombo, Lisbon.

2088. **Calmon, Pedro.** Caramuru e o seu episódio (*IV cong. hist. nac.*, v. 4, p. 79-106).
Clarifies many points connected with Caramuru and with the Brazil of his day.

2089. ————. *Cartas econômico-políticas da Bahia.* Inédito que as completam (*An. prim. cong. hist. Bahia*, v. 4, p. 225-232).

2090. ————. O segrêdo das minas de prata. Novos aspectos da conquista da terra. Rio de Janeiro. 181 p.

2091. ————. Vespúcio e o nome da Bahia (*IV cong. hist. nac.*, v. 4, p. 69-78).
Supports the belief that Vespucci named the Bay of All Saints.

2092. **Canabrava, A. P.** A fôrça motriz. Um problema da técnica da industria do açúcar colonial. A solução antilhana e a brasileira (*An. prim. cong. hist. Bahia*, v. 4, p. 337-350).

2093. ————. A lavoura canavieira nas Antilhas e no Brasil, primeira metade do século XVIII (*An. prim. cong. hist. Bahia*, v. 4, p. 351-387).

2094. **Cardozo, Manoel.** Notes for a biography of Salvador Correia de Sá e Benavides, 1594-1688 (*Americas*, v. 7, no. 2, October, p. 135-170).

2095. **Cascudo, Luís da Câmara.** Geografia do Brasil holandês (*IV cong. hist. nac.*, v. 4, p. 243-450).
The Dutch in Brazil, particularly their cultural and economic activities. Illustrated.

2096. **Cidade, Hernâni.** A situação da Bahia na primeira década da restauração. Os "Judas do Brasil" (*An. prim. cong. hist. Bahia*, p. 455-464).

2097. **Cordeiro, J. P. Leite.** A invasão holandesa no Brasil e o bandeirismo paulista (*IV cong. hist. nac.*, v. 3, p. 263-291).

2098. ————. A invasão holandesa no Brasil e os paulistas (*IV cong. hist. nac.*, v. 3, p. 293-443).

2099. ————. A unificação da península ibérica e outros precedentes da invasão holandesa no Brasil (*IV cong. hist. nac.*, v. 3, p. 249-261).

2100. **Corrêa Filho, Virgílio.** Aspectos do rompimento da linha tordesilhana (*IV cong. hist. nac.*, v. 7, p. 167-197).
A general account based on secondary sources, but useful as a summary.

2101. ————. Mato Grosso e Goiás. Seu devassamento e ocupação (*IV cong. hist. nac.*, v. 4, p. 177-213).

2102. **Cortesão, Jaime** (ed.). Alexandre de Gusmão e o tratado de Madrid, 1750. Parte 2, t. 1. Obras várias de Alexandre de Gusmão. Rio de Janeiro, Ministério das Relações Exteriores, Instituto Rio-Branco. 493 p.
A critical edition, fully indexed. A remarkably complete collection.

2103. ————. Alexandre de Gusmão e o tratado de Madrid, 1750. Parte 2, t. 2. Documentos biográficos. Rio de Janeiro, Ministério das Relações Exteriores, Instituto Rio-Branco. 358 p.
The quality of the first volume is fully maintained in the second.

2104. ————. O significado da expedição de Pedro Teixeira à luz de novos documentos (*IV cong. hist. nac.*, v. 3, p. 169-204).
The author shows that the purpose of the expedition was political, i.e., the expansion of Portugal in the Amazon valley.

2105. **Cruz, Ernesto.** O Pará nos séculos XVII e XVIII (*IV cong. hist. nac.*, v. 3, p. 1-62).
A solid study based in part on local archival sources.

2106. **Dias, Eduardo.** Para a história dos Ávilas da Bahia (*An. prim. cong. hist. Bahia*, v. 2, p. 355-387).

Largely documents for the study of the history of this pioneer family.

2107. Diégues Júnior, Manuel. As companhias privilegiadas no comércio colonial (*Rev. hist.,* São Paulo, ano 1, no. 3, julho-set., p. 309-337).
The author concludes that the good brought by the companies was more than offset by the evil.

2108. ————. O engenho de açúcar no século XVI. Produção intensiva, o panorama econômico do açúcar no mundo (*IV cong. hist. nac.,* v. 5, p. 531-552).

2109. DOCUMENTOS HISTÓRICOS. V. 87. SENADO DA CÂMARA, BAHIA, 1696-1726. CONSULTAS DO CONSELHO ULTRAMARINO, BAHIA, 1673. Rio de Janeiro, Ministério da Educação e Saúde, Biblioteca Nacional. 294 p.

2110. DOCUMENTOS HISTÓRICOS. V. 88. CONSULTAS DO CONSELHO ULTRAMARINO, BAHIA, 1673-1683. Rio de Janeiro, Ministério da Educação e Saúde, Biblioteca Nacional. 298 p.

2111. DOCUMENTOS HISTÓRICOS. V. 89. CONSULTAS DO CONSELHO ULTRAMARINO, BAHIA, 1683-1695. Rio de Janeiro, Ministério da Educação e Saúde, Biblioteca Nacional. 294 p.

2112. DOCUMENTOS HISTÓRICOS. V. 90. CONSULTAS DO CONSELHO ULTRAMARINO, BAHIA, 1695-1696, 1724-1732. Rio de Janeiro, Ministério da Educação e Saúde, Biblioteca Nacional. 296 p.

2113. DOCUMENTOS HISTÓRICOS DO ARQUIVO MUNICIPAL. V. 5. ATAS DA CÂMARA, 1669-1684. Bahia, Prefeitura do Município do Salvador. 442 p.
Edited by Antonio Loureiro de Souza. Index.

2114. DOCUMENTOS HISTÓRICOS DO ARQUIVO MUNICIPAL. V. 6. ATAS DA CÂMARA, 1684-1700. Bahia, Prefeitura do Município do Salvador, 1950? 433 p.
Edited by Antonio Loureiro de Souza. Index.

2115. Dourado, Mecenas. A conversão do gentio. Rio de Janeiro. 100 p.
The author's thesis is that the work of Christianizing the Indians was a failure; that the Society of Jesus, quick to realize that little could be done with the Indians along spiritual lines, used them for economic purposes. He feels that an economic history of the Society is needed.

2116. Drumond, Carlos (ed.). A carta de Diogo Nunes e a migração dos tupiguaranis para o Perú (*Rev. hist.,* São Paulo, ano 1, no. 1, jan.-março, p. 95-102).
The letter was written to King John II of Portugal. It has been published before.

2117. Edelweiss, Frederico. Os primeiros vinte anos de extração de ouro documentada da Bahia (*An. prim. cong. hist. Bahia,* v. 4, p. 171-180).

2118. Ellis Júnior, Alfredo. A queda do bandeirismo de apresamento (*Rev. hist.,* São Paulo, ano 1, no. 3, julho-set., p. 301-307).

2119. Ennes, Ernesto. The trial of the ecclesiastics in the Inconfidência Mineira (*Americas,* v. 7, no. 2, Oct., p. 183-213).
One of the moot points of the celebrated conspiracy has finally been cleared up, thanks to the documents that the author found in the Arquivo Histórico Ultramarino, Lisbon.

2120. Falcão, Edgard de Cerqueira. Contestações. São Paulo, Emprêsa Gráfica da Revista dos Tribunais. 51 p.
Mostly the author's answers to certain members of the Instituto Histórico of Bahia on the date of the official founding of Salvador.

2121. Ferreira, Tito Livio. O governo do morgado de Mateus e os censos das ordenanças da capitania de São Paulo (*An. mus. paulista,* t. 14, p. 383-451).

2122. ————. No quarto centenário da chegada à Bahia do fundador de São Paulo (*Bol. bibliog.,* São Paulo, v. 15, p. 7-21).
On Father Manoel da Nóbrega.

2123. Fonseca, Luiza da (ed.). In defense of the Maranhão Indians of colonial Brazil. A report of Frei Christovão de Lisboa, O.F.M., to the Conselho Ultramarino, Lisbon, October 29, 1647 (*Americas,* v. 7, no. 2, Oct., p. 215-220).

2124. ————. Índice abreviado dos documentos do século XVII do Arquivo Histórico Colonial de Lisboa (*An. prim. cong. hist. Bahia,* v. 2, p. 7-353).
A calendar of 4384 papers.

2125. ————. Subsídio para história da cidade da Bahia (*An. prim. cong. hist. Bahia,* v. 2, p. 409-454).
Interesting notes on various aspects of the history of Bahia, followed by documents.

2126. Franco, Francisco de Assis Carvalho. Paulistas e emboabas. Primeiros povoadores de Minas. Manuel Nunes Viana. Govêrno pacificador (*IV cong. hist. nac.,* v. 3, p. 63-168).

2127. **Gomes, Alfredo**. Entradas, bandeiras e monções: característicos (*IV cong. hist. nac.*, v. 5, p. 7-23).
A description of these phenomena.

2128. **Gouveia, Alfredo Mendes de**. Relação dos compromissos de irmandades, confrarias e misericórdias do Brasil, existentes no Arquivo Histórico Colonial de Lisboa, que pertenceram ao cartório do extinto Conselho Ultramarino, 1716-1807 (*IV cong. hist. nac.*, v. 7, p. 201-238).

2129. **Jacques, Paulino**. O estado do Brasil no século XVIII (*IV cong. hist. nac.*, v. 3, p. 525-592).
From the point of view of the concept of power.

2130. **Lamego, Alberto**. As invasões francêsas no Rio de Janeiro. Duclerc e Duguay-Trouin, 1710-1711 (*IV cong. hist. nac.*, v. 6, p. 115-249).
Abundantly documented.

2131. **Lane, Frederick C**. The oceanic expansion of Europe (*Tasks econ. hist.*, supplement 10, p. 19-31).
A stimulating essay upon the rôle of government and of private enterprise in the 16th and 17th centuries, with special reference to governmental use of armed force, and to Portuguese policy in the East Indies and in Brazil. [R. D. Hussey]

2132. **Leite, Bertha**. Dom Pedro Fernandes Sardinha (*IV cong. hist. nac.*, v. 7, p. 433-605).
Magnificently documented study on the first bishop of Brazil. The best account of the man that we now have.

2133. **Leite, Serafim**. História da Companhia de Jesus no Brasil. T. 10. Índice geral. Rio de Janeiro, Instituto Nacional do Livro. xx, 316 p.
The final volume of a remarkable history. Preceding volumes appeared in 1938, 1943, 1945, and 1949. See respective numbers of *HLAS*.

2134. **Lifchitz, Miriam**. O sal na capitania de São Paulo no século XVIII (*Rev. hist.*, São Paulo, ano 1, no. 4, out.-dez., p. 517-526).

2135. **Lima, Américo Pires de**. Nota sôbre a roda dos enjeitados da Bahia no século XVIII (*IV cong. hist. nac.*, v. 5, p. 269-279, and *Brasília*, v. 5, p. 519-525).

2136. —————. Atribulações da Misericórdia da Bahia no século XVIII (*IV cong. hist. nac.*, v. 5, p. 281-297, and *Brasília*, v. 5, p. 527-555).
Documents illustrative of the difficulties of the Santa Casa at the beginning of the 18th century.

2137. —————. Nota sôbre algumas epidemias na cidade da Bahia (*IV cong. hist. nac.*, v. 5, p. 247-268).
A study based on five documents from the Arquivo Histórico Colonial, Lisbon. Also appeared in *Brasília*, v. 5, p. 403-518.

2138. —————. A situação da Misericórdia da Baía no fim do século XVII (*Brasília*, v. 5, p. 557-600).
A series of documents showing how difficult was the situation of the Santa Casa at this time.

2139. **Lôbo, José de Figueiredo**. Fortificações coloniais da Bahia (*An. prim. cong. hist. Bahia*, v. 3, p. 87-132).

2140. **Lopes, Antônio**. A capitania do Cumã (*IV cong. hist. nac.*, v. 4, p. 7-68).
A significant contribution to the history of Maranhão. The captaincy was founded at the beginning of the 17th century and was acquired by the Crown in 1754.

2141. **Luz, Francisco Mendes da** (ed.). Relação das rendas da coroa de Portugal feita em 1593 por Francisco Carneiro, provedor de ementas da Casa dos Contos (*Bol. bibl. univ. Coimbra*, v. 19, p. 44-108).
Transcription of a manuscript in the Royal Academy of History, Madrid. Some information on Brazil.

2142. **Marçal, Heitor**. Marinha e sertão. Fundamentos da economia colonial. Rio de Janeiro, Serviço Gráfico do Instituto Brasileiro de Geografia e Estatística. 126 p.
An essay on the development of the colonial economy in Brazil, beginning with the maritime provinces and continuing with cattle ranching and gold mining in the interior.

2143. **Museu de Angola**. No tricentenário da restauração (1648-1948). Contribuição do Museu de Angola. Luanda, Angola, Imprensa Nacional. 194 p.
Some material on Salvador Correia de Sá e Benavides.

2144. **Neiva, Artur Hehl**. Proveniência das primeiras levas de escravos africanos (*IV cong. hist. nac.*, v. 4, p. 487-523).
The study is limited to the captaincy of São Vicente. The first slaves, from the Congo, arrived after 1559, according to the author.

2145. **Obry, Olga**. A madrinha de Catarina Álvares, a caramurua (*IV cong. hist. nac.*, v. 3, p. 515-524).
Catarina's French godmother was the wife of Jacques Cartier.

2146. **Ott, Carlos**. Os Mataraós (*An. prim. cong. hist. Bahia*, v. 3, p. 277-290).
The story of two Indians, father and son, and the development of Sebastianism in Brazil.

2147. Peres, Damião. Antecedentes históricos da legislação concernente ao ouro do Brasil nos séculos XVI a XVIII (*IV cong. hist. nac.,* v. 5, p. 569-587).

2148. Prado, J. F. de Almeida. A Bahia e as capitanias do centro do Brasil, 1530-1626. História da formação da sociedade brasileira. T. 3. São Paulo, Companhia Editôra Nacional (Biblioteca Pedagógica Brasileira, série 5, vol. 247-b). 351 p.
Roughly speaking, the period covered begins with the administration of Dom Francisco de Sousa and ends with the Dutch conquest of Bahia in 1624. The author calls it the Golden Age of Bahia, when man could still live by himself without the undue interference of government. Essentially an interpretative essay, intelligently written.

2149. Rebêlo, E. de Castro. As inscrições lapidares da igreja da Victória e o local da Vilha Velha (*IV cong. hist. nac.,* v. 4, p. 217-242).
For the history of the founding of Salvador.

2150. Santos, Amilcar Salgado dos. A guerra civil entre paulistas e emboabas, 1708-1709 (*IV cong. hist. nac.,* v. 6, p. 251-346).
Adds very little to what is already known; the approach is from the military point of view.

2151. Silva, Alberto. D. João III e a cidade do Salvador (*An. prim. cong. hist. Bahia,* v. 3, p. 7-71).
In praise of John's policies.

2152. ———. D. João III e a política de colonização do Brasil (*An. prim. cong. hist. Bahia,* v. 3, p. 461-482).

2153. Silveira, Luís. Um episódio da história do comércio luso-brasílico. A fundação da Companhia da Ilha do Corisco (*IV cong. hist. nac.,* v. 5, p. 517-529).
A short-lived company created at the beginning of the 18th century for the purpose of supplying Brazil with Guinea slaves.

2154. ———. Relações da África Portuguesa com a Bahia (*An. prim. cong. hist. Bahia,* v. 2, p. 389-407).
The author publishes transcriptions of many documents.

2155. Soares, Torquato de Sousa. Precursores-bandeirantes (*IV cong. hist. nac.,* v. 4, p. 167-176).
The author tries to show that there were certain European antecedents to the *bandeirante* movement in Brazil.

2156. Sodré, Alcindo. Um govêrno da Bahia. Afonso Miguel de Portugal e Castro, 1779-1783 (*An. prim. cong. hist. Bahia,* v. 4, p. 41-45).

2157. Sousa, Tomás Oscar Marcondes de. O códice de Piero Vaglienti ou 1910 da Biblioteca Riccardiana de Florença (*IV cong. hist. nac.,* v. 4, p. 107-144).
Transcriptions of documents that are of interest for the very beginnings of Brazilian history. Most of the material deals with Vespucci.

2158. ———. A expedição de 1501-1502 e Américo Vespucci (*IV cong. hist. nac.,* v. 4, p. 145-166).
The report of the committee that passed on this contribution to the Congress should also be read.

2159. Spalding, Walter. Governadores e vice-reis do Brasil na Bahia, 1549-1763 (*An. prim. cong. hist. Bahia,* v. 4, p. 47-142).

2160. ———. O Rio Grande do Sul. Os estabelecimentos de fronteira, Santa Catarina, Caminho "dos conventos" (*IV cong. hist. nac.,* v. 6, p. 7-100).
There is a bibliography of 177 items.

2161. Taunay, Affonso de E. História geral das bandeiras paulistas escrita à vista de avultada documentação inédita dos arquivos brasileiros, portuguezes e espanhões. Tomo 11. Os primeiros anos de Goyaz. Monções cuyabanas no século XVIII. São Paulo, Imprensa Oficial do Estado (Edição do Museu Paulista). 219 p.
The last volume of a monumental work. Preceding volumes appeared in 1924, 1936, 1946, 1948, and 1949. See respective numbers of *HLAS*.

2162. Vianna, Hélio. O primeiro brasão de armas do Brasil (*An. mus. imperial,* v. 10, 1949, i.e., 1950?, p. 159, illus.).
In 1675 the Estado do Brasil had, for its coat of arms, on a silver shield a green tree out of whose foliage emerges a brown cross. This was apparently never officially used. Except for this shield, Brazil had no special coat of arms during the colonial period.

2163. Viveiros, Jerônimo de. Alcântara no seu passado econômico, social e político. São Luiz do Maranhão, Imprensa Oficial. 147 p., illus.
The history of one of the oldest regions of Maranhão, with documents.

THE INDEPENDENCE PERIOD

2164. Albuquerque, José Joaquim Pires de Carvalho e. A Bahia e a independência do Brasil (*An. prim. cong. hist. Bahia,* v. 3, p. 185-211).

2165. Andrade, Laércio Caldeira de. O Cel. Felisberto Gomes Caldeira e a independência da Bahia. O Coronel José Bonifácio Caldeira de Andrada e suas

Memórias (*An. prim. cong. hist. Bahia,* v. 3, p. 213-234).

2166. Assumpção, Herculano Teixeira d'. A revolução pernambucana de 1817 e sua repercussão na Bahia (*An. prim. cong. hist. Bahia,* v. 3, p. 133-184).

2167. DOCUMENTOS DO ARQUIVO. PRESIDENTES DE PROVINCIAS, 1820-1821. V. 3. Recife, Secretaria do Interior e Justiça. 439 p.
Correspondence received in Recife during the years 1820-1821 from Piauí, Ceará, Rio Grande do Norte, Paraíba do Norte, Maranhão, Bahia, Alagoas, and Santa Catarina. Some of the documents are of interest for the early years of the revolutionary period. Preliminary note by the director of the Archive, Dr. Jordão Emerenciano.

2168. Herrick, Jane. The reluctant revolutionist. A study of the political ideas of Hipólito da Costa, 1774-1823 (*Americas,* v. 7, no. 2, October, p. 171-181).

THE IMPERIAL PERIOD

2169. Amaral, Braz do. O federalismo na Bahia, 1833-1889 (*An. prim. cong. hist. Bahia,* v. 3, p. 373-396).

2170. CARTAS DE BISPOS A DOM PEDRO II (*An. mus. imperial,* vol. 10, 1949, i.e. 1950?, p. 261-313).

2171. CARTAS DE VARNHAGEN A DOM PEDRO II E OUTROS ESCRITOS (*An. mus. imperial,* v. 10, 1949, i.e. 1950?, p. 159-236).

2172. Coleman, William J. The first apostolic delegation in Rio de Janeiro and its influence in Spanish America. A study in papal policy, 1830-1840. Washington, The Catholic University of America Press. 468 p.
Based almost exclusively on Vatican sources. A doctoral dissertation that exhausts this important subject.

2173. Costa, Sérgio Corrêa da. Pedro I e Metternich. Traços de uma guerra diplomática. Rio de Janeiro, A Noite, 1950? 237 p.

2174. Escragnolle, Luis Affonso d'. Blumenau em 1856 (*Revista do Instituto Histórico de Petrópolis,* vol. 1, p. 40-48). Transcription of a letter, in the Museu Imperial, from H. Blumenau.

2175. ————. O visconde de Camamú e o derrame de moedas falsas de cobre na Bahia (*An. prim. cong. hist. Bahia,* v. 4, p. 143-169).

2176. Lacombe, Lourenço Luís. Dom Pedro I através de suas cartas aos filhos (*An. mus. imperial,* v. 8, 1947, i.e. 1950?, p. 229-271).

2177. ————. D. Pedro II e o Conselheiro Dantas (*An. mus. imperial,* v. 10, 1949, i.e. 1950?, p. 179-259). Letters exchanged by the two men.

2178. ————. Rui Barbosa e o Imperador (*An. mus. imperial,* v. 10, 1949, i.e. 1950?, p. 161-177).

2179. Lamego, Alberto Ribeiro. A aristocracia rural do café na província fluminense (*An. mus. imperial,* v. 7, 1946, i.e. 1950, p. 53-123).

2180. Moraes, Walfrido. O escravo na legislação tributária da província da Bahia (*An. prim. cong. hist. Bahia,* v. 4, p. 181-223).

2181. Morse, Richard M. São Paulo. Raizes oitocentistas da metrópole (*An. mus. paulista,* t. 14, p. 453-487).

2182. O PROGRESSO. REVISTA SOCIAL, LITTERARIA É SCIENTIFICA. Reedição feita pelo govêrno do estado de Pernambuco como parte do programa das comemorações do centenário da Revolução Praieira. Prefácio de Amaro Quintas. Recife, Imprensa Oficial. 920 p.

2184. Sodré, Alcindo. Rui Barbosa anotado por Pedro II (*An. mus. imperial,* v. 10, 1949, i.e. 1950?, p. 151-158).

2185. ————. O sentido político das visitas de Pedro I, Pedro II e Conde d'Eu na Bahia (*An. prim. cong. hist. Bahia,* v. 3, p. 235-266).

2186. ————. Visita de Pedro II à Cachoeira de Paulo Afonso (*An. mus. imperial,* v. 10, 1949, i.e. 1950?, p. 85-150). The visit took place in 1859. A preliminary note is followed by transcriptions from Dom Pedro's diaries. The emperor's notes are interesting for the history of the areas he visited.

2187. Sousa, Otávio Tarquínio de. Um brasileiro adotivo (*Cultura,* Rio de Janeiro, ano 1, no. 3, maio-agôsto, 1949, i.e. 1950, p. 113-120).
A study on Eugène de Monglave.

2188. Taunay, Affonso de E. A Câmara dos Deputados sob o império (*An. mus. paulista,* t. 14, p. 1-253).

2189. TEATRO SANTA ISABEL. DOCUMENTOS PARA A SUA HISTÓRIA. V. 1, 1838-1850. Recife, Prefeitura Municipal do Recife, Directoria de Documentação e Cultura. xiv, 88 p., illus.
Documents concerned with the construction of one of Brazil's great cultural centers, the Teatro Santa Isabel of Recife. [R. E. Dimmick]

2190. Torres, Manuel Júlio de Mendonça. O distrito de Moçâmedes nas fases da origem e da primeira organização, 1485-1859. Lisboa, Agência Geral das Colónias. 535 p.
The author speaks of the Portuguese who left Pernambuco as the result of the Revolução Praieira of 1848 and settled in Moçâmedes, p. 109 et seq.

2191. Vianna, Hélio. Estudos de história imperial. São Paulo, Companhia Editôra Nacional (Biblioteca Pedagógica Brasileira, Série 5, Brasiliana, v. 269). 328 p.
A series of studies, of uneven quality, almost exclusively devoted to the imperial period. The longest study is the biography of Aureliano de Sousa e Oliveira Coutinho (Visconde de Sepetiba). There are letters of Dom Pedro I and the Duque de Caxias; also letters of interest for the history of the Paraguayan War.

THE REPUBLICAN PERIOD

2192. Barbosa, Manoel de Aquino. A primeira reunião do episcopado brasileiro (An. prim. cong. hist. Bahia, v. 4, p. 467-505).
The meeting was held in São Paulo in August, 1890. Its history is given here for the first time.

2193. Barbosa, Rui. Obras completas. V. 18, 1891. T. 4. Anexos ao relatório do Ministro da Fazenda. Rio de Janeiro, Ministério da Educação e Saúde. 1949, i.e. 1950. 545 p.
Rui was the first Minister of Finance of the Republic. There are notes by Oscar Bormann.

2194. ————. Obras completas. V. 20. T. 3, 4. A ditadura de 1893. Jornal do Brasil. Rio de Janeiro, Ministério da Educação e Saúde. 358, 301 p.

2195. Franca, Antônio. Anos de resistência. Rio de Janeiro, Casa do Estudante do Brasil. 163 p.
The struggle against the Integralista movement. The author writes from the Marxist point of view.

2196. Livoni Larco, Felipe. El Instituto Rio Branco (Rev. peruana der. int., t. 10, no. 33, enero-abril, p. 36-52).

2197. Ministério da Marinha. Serviço de Documentação da Marinha. Subsídios para a história marítima do Brasil. V. 9. Almirante Júlio César de Noronha. Programa naval de 1904. Rio de Janeiro, Imprensa Naval. 448 p.
Preliminary remarks by the editor, Admiral Dídio Iratim Afonso da Costa.

2198. Passos, Alexandre. Castro Alves, arauto da democracia e da república. Rio de Janeiro, Pongetti, 1950? 35 p.
Brief account of the democratic movements of the mid-19th century, and of Castro Alves as their herald in Brazil. [R. E. Dimmick]

2199. Silva, Cyro. Pinheiro Machado. Rio de Janeiro, Tupã. 265 p., illus.
An attempt at whitewashing the memory of one of Brazil's great and sordid political bosses, assassinated on September 8, 1915.

2200. Sousa, Maria Mercedes Lopes de. Rui Barbosa e José Marcelino. Rio de Janeiro, Casa de Rui Barbosa. 232 p.

ADDENDA

2201. Araújo, Carlos da Silva. Vieira Fazenda (Cadernos, no. 19, 1949, p. 77-93).
Information concerning a historian of the past century.

2202. Barbosa, Mário de Lima. Ruy Barbosa. São Paulo, Instituto Progresso Editorial (Col. Pantheon Brasileiro, 2), 1949. 247 p., illus.
One of the better biographies of Rui, favorable to the man.

2203. Brasão, Eduardo. O tratado de limites de 1750 e as suas consequências (An. acad. port. hist., 2. série, v. 2, 1949, p. 9-86).
The author uses new documentary sources.

2204. Brito, Manuel Thomaz de Carvalho. O civilismo em Minas. Rio de Janeiro, Casa de Rui Barbosa, 1949. 46 p.
A lecture by a leader of the movement in Minas Gerais.

2205. Castro, Josué de. Fatôres de localização da cidade do Recife. Um ensaio de geografia urbana. Rio de Janeiro, Imprensa Nacional, 1948, i.e. 1947. 84 p., illus.
A great deal on the early history of the region, and on the founding and development of the city.

2206. DOCUMENTOS HISTÓRICOS DO ARQUIVO MUNICIPAL. V. 1. ATAS DA CÂMARA, 1625-1641. Bahia, Prefeitura do Município do Salvador, 1944. 541 p.
Excellent indices.

2207. DOCUMENTOS HISTÓRICOS DO ARQUIVO
MUNICIPAL. V. 2. ATAS DA CÂMARA, 1641-
1649. Bahia, Prefeitura do Município do
Salvador, 1949. 456 p.

2208. DOCUMENTOS HISTÓRICOS DO ARQUIVO
MUNICIPAL. V. 3. ATAS DA CÂMARA, 1649-
1659. Bahia, Prefeitura do Município do
Salvador, 1949. 468 p.

2209. DOCUMENTOS HISTÓRICOS DO ARQUIVO
MUNICIPAL. V. 4. ATAS DA CÂMARA, 1659-
1669. Bahia, Prefeitura do Município do
Salvador, 1949. 463 p.

2210. **Ferreira, Carlos Alberto.** Inventário
dos manuscritos da Biblioteca da Ajuda
referentes à América do Sul. Coimbra,
Portugal, Atlântida (Universidade de
Coimbra, Faculdade de Letras, Instituto
de Estudos Brasileiros), 1946. 682 p.
2310 manuscripts are listed. Except for a few,
they all deal with Brazil. By century: 1-57, 16th;
58-1742, 17th; 1743-2052, 18th; 2053-2150, 19th.
At the end are listed the undated manuscripts,
2151-2310. There is no index.

2211. **Ferreira, Tito Livio.** Documentação
espanhola do Arquivo de Sevilha (*An.
mus. paulista,* t. 13, 1948, i.e. 1949, p.
290A-612).
Documents on the *bandeirante* movement which
Dr. Taunay had copied in Seville.

2212. **Hollanda, Sérgio Buarque de.** Indios e mamelucos na expansão paulista
(*An. mus. paulista,* t. 13, 1948, i.e. 1949,
p. 175-290).
An aspect of the *bandeiras,* competently and
exhaustively studied from the historical and
ethnographical point of view.

2213. **Maranhão, João de Albuquerque.**
História da indústria açucareira no Nordeste. O papel social de Catende. Rio de
Janeiro, Jornal do Commercio, 1949.
127 p.

Family history, the history of sugar, and the
history of a plantation.

2214. **Ministério da Marinha. Serviço de
Documentação da Marinha.** Subsídios
para a história marítima do Brasil. V. 7.
Rio de Janeiro, Imprensa Naval, 1949.
600 p.

2215. **Pintos, Rodolfo Almeida.** Vida y
obra de Antonio Cardoso Fontes. Monte-
video, Instituto de Cultura Uruguayo-
Brasileño (Publ. 6), 1949. 22 p.
Fontes was formerly director of the Instituto
Oswaldo Cruz, Rio de Janeiro.

2216. **Reale, Miguel.** Posição de Rui Barbosa no mundo da filosofia. Rio de
Janeiro, Casa de Rui Barbosa, 1949. 60 p.
The purpose was to place Rui in the current of
thought of his day. Rui was a liberal. He was
a Christian, though his Christianity was affected
by the naturalism of the 19th century. He was
also a humanist, but he was not interested in
philosophy as such, but rather as a point of departure for action. His philosophical view of
life changed, of course, as he grew older. For
one thing he became more spiritual, more concerned with religion.

2217. **Simon, Michel.** Ruy. Avec un message de Paul Claudel. Rio de Janeiro,
Casa de Rui Barbosa, 1949. 240 p.
A biography for foreigners, followed by *pages
choisies* of Rui Barbosa's works.

2218. **Southey, Roberto.** História do Brasil.
Traduzida do inglês por Luiz Joaquim de
Oliveira e Castro e anotada por J. C.
Fernandes Pinheiro. V. 3. 2. edição.
Bahia, Livraria Progresso, 1949. 271 p.

2219. **Souza, Affonso Ruy de.** História política e administrativa da cidade do Salvador. Bahia, Tipografia Beneditina. 1949.
664 p.

International Relations Since 1830

BRYCE WOOD

IN the realm of inter-American political affairs, the year 1950 was marked by the energetic action of the Council of the Organization of American States in dealing with what came to be known as the Caribbean situation. The report of the Investigating Committee (item 2252) is a frank and straightforward document. What threatened to become a dangerous series of incidents was checked, although, as noted by Edgar S. Furniss, Jr. (item 2237), the underlying causes of friction remained unaffected.

In general, there were very few important publications in the field of international relations in 1950. The reasons for this relatively limited output are not entirely clear, although possible contributory factors may be suggested. The tense situation in Europe and the outbreak of the Korean conflict have tended to concentrate interest in those areas; it is also possible that the drawing of sharper internal political lines in some countries has created conditions in which potential writers prefer discretion to publication. Little interest has been shown in the work of the Council of the OAS as a whole, and it does not appear that the Council has whetted many imaginations by concerning itself largely, except in the above case, with organizational matters. It should be noted, however, that it passed a resolution on June 28, 1950, supporting the action of the United Nations in the Korean question. It is to be hoped that the opportunity may be given to list some publications touching on the Council's functions as a forum for the discussion of questions of long-range as well as immediate political significance. There exists some reason for a feeling of uneasiness about the lack of public debate concerning political issues among the American states. One senses that there are issues, but also that there is a reluctance to open them up, at least on an official, multilateral level, and to some extent on a private level. What is the present consistency of "hemisphere solidarity"? It would seem that full and free discussion would be preferable to silence, but we shall have to wait to see whether publicists interested in political dynamics will be more prolific next year than they have been in this one.

GENERAL

2221. ARCHIVO DE ALFONSO REYES. Serie D (Instrumentos), no. 3. La constelación americana. Conversaciones de tres amigos. Buenos Aires: 23 de octubre a 19 de noviembre de 1936. México, Gráfica Panamericana. 45 p.

2222. Barros Hurtado, César. América. Penurias de su libertad. El Panamericanismo por dentro. Buenos Aires, Editorial Crilde. 231 p.

This is a curious book. It is a collection of short essays on inter-American political themes, some of which have been previously published. It is dedicated to Alfredo L. Palacios. It is written as if President Perón had not become the chief executive of his country. It states that "there do not exist, among the 21 American nations, two countries more alike, in their various aspects, than the United States and Argentina." On the Good Neighbor Policy, the author says that it suffered from one error, that of treating despotic and democratic governments alike, thus doing an injustice to peoples who were resisting dictators. See also item 1318.

2223. Cereijo, Ramón Antonio. Por un mayor bienestar económico y social de los pueblos americanos. Discursos pronunciados en la sesión extraordinaria del Consejo Económico y Social de la Organización de los Estados Americanos, reunida en Wáshington. Buenos Aires. 61 p.

Texts of two speeches by the chairman of the Economic and Social Council of the OAS.

2224. Davis, Edward P. Periodicals of international organizations. Part 1. The United Nations and Specialized Agencies. Part 2. Inter-American Organizations. Washington, Pan American Union, Columbus Memorial Library (Bibliographic Series, no. 33). 21 p.

A very useful compilation. Part 2 describes the new publications program of the OAS, and then lists publications of numerous other inter-American bodies. (Reprinted from *LEA*, no. 8, 1949, p. 1-9 and no. 12, 1950, p. 1-12). [C. Shelby]

2225. Gálvez Sarmiento, Luis Antonio. Education for inter-Americanism. Notre Dame, Ind. 196 p.

This Ph.D. dissertation examines the efforts and achievements of the American States in informing their youth about the ideas and ideals of inter-Americanism.

2226. INTER-AMERICAN CONFERENCE FOR DEMOCRACY AND FREEDOM. Resoluciones y otros documentos. Habana. 319 p.

The report of the proceedings at a conference convened jointly by a considerable number of private organizations in various American republics. Among the sponsors were the CIO and AFL from the United States and the Junta Americana de la Defensa de la Democracia, of Uruguay. Representatives from 15 countries and from Puerto Rico attended. The major portion of the text includes resolutions, speeches by the participants, and messages from Mrs. Franklin D. Roosevelt, Senator Herbert H. Lehman, Luis Muñoz Marín and others. The volume provides useful material about the state of liberal thought on inter-Americanism, attitudes toward dictatorial regimes in the Americas, and other subjects. The former president of Venezuela, Rómulo Betancourt, contributed a preface.

2227. INTERNATIONAL ORGANIZATIONS IN WHICH THE UNITED STATES PARTICIPATES. 1949. Washington, Government Printing Office (Department of State, Publ. 3655, International Organization and Conference Series, I, 8). 335 p.

A useful publication for each organization listed, discussing origin and development; membership; purposes, powers, and functions; structure; finances; U. S. relations and relations with other international organizations, and giving a short bibliography, basic texts and publications. Twelve inter-American organizations are in-

cluded as well as many international ones in which the American nations are vitally concerned. [Ed.]

2228. Muñoz Meany, Enrique. El hombre y la encrucijada. Textos políticos en defensa de la democracia. Prefacio de Luis Cardoza y Aragón. Guatemala, Tipografía Nacional. 263 p.

A collection of speeches on diverse subjects by a Guatemalan minister of foreign affairs.

2229. Núñez Arca, P. De Quitandinha a Bogotá passando por Buenos Aires. Reportagens de duas conferências e duas viagens. São Paulo, Letras. 278 p., illus.

Notes and comments of a Brazilian newspaper man on his travels and on two inter-American conferences.

2230. Royal Institute of International Affairs. Documents on regional organizations outside western Europe, 1940-1949. London. vii, 85 p.

Contains agreement establishing Caribbean Commission, 1946; and two documents of the Inter-American System: the Rio Treaty, 1947, and the Charter of the Organization of American States, 1948.

2231. Sánchez Camacho, Baldomera. El problema colonial de América. México. 108 p.

"Every thesis," says the author, "encloses a Utopia." Hers is the hope that mankind may liberate itself from the yoke of slavery. She favors independence for Puerto Rico, now "semi-esclavizado" by U. S. policy. Further, "The fact that the U. S. exercises over all of Latin America a control which is nearly absolute in many of its vital aspects, places the latter in a situation of a semi-colonial character which limits and deforms its development." The Good Neighbor Policy "assuaged some bitterness" in U. S.-Latin American relations, but it ended, she says, in 1945, and there is now a return to the "era of lack of understanding and of abuse." Thesis, Law School, University of Mexico.

INTER-AMERICAN SYSTEM

2232. Andrade, Olímpio de Souza. Joaquim Nabuco e o pan-americanismo. São Paulo, Companhia Editôra Nacional (Biblioteca Pedagógica Brasileira, Série 5, Brasiliana, v. 270). 157 p.

A review of the thought and action of the Brazilian statesman in relation to Pan Americanism. This work won first prize in a contest. sponsored by the Brazilian National Commission of UNESCO.

2233. ANNALS OF THE ORGANIZATION OF AMERICAN STATES. V. 2, no. 1-4.

Record of the official activities of the OAS. [Ed.]

2234. Brigard Silva, Camilo de. La Neuvième Conférence Internationale Américaine de Bogota. Bogotá, 1948. Paris, Recueil Sirey. 29 p.

2235. Corominas, Enrique V. Paz y seguridad americana. Buenos Aires, El Ateneo. 283 p.
An important analysis of the Inter-American Treaty of Reciprocal Assistance of 1947 (the "Rio Treaty") by an Argentine diplomat. The author concludes that Argentina should ratify the treaty.

2236. Ernst, Hermann. Die interamerikanischen Konferenzen von Rio de Janeiro (15. August-2. September 1947) und Bogotá (30. Märs-2. Mai 1948). Mainz [Germany], 1950? iv, 214 p.
A legalistic, strictly descriptive account of the proceedings of the Rio de Janeiro and Bogotá conferences. Texts of the treaties are not appended, but there is a chart of the status of ratification of the Bogotá instruments as of February 15, 1950.

2237. Furniss, Edgar S., Jr. The Inter-American System and recent Caribbean disputes (*Int. organ.*, v. 4, no. 4, Nov., p. 585-597).
An analytical study of the role of the Council of the OAS and its committees. The author points out that the Council's success in the Caribbean situation does not mean that fundamental sources of Caribbean unrest have been affected thereby. See item 2252.

2238. ————. The United States, the Inter-American System, and the United Nations (*Pol. sci. quart.*, v. 65, no. 3, Sept., p. 415-430).
A penetrating exposition of the problems involved in United States bilateral and multilateral commitments, premised on the idea that "it should be plain that security within the hemisphere is only part, and a minor one at that, of the type of world security that United States policy seeks. Policy-makers well know that the crucial focus of American relations lies in Europe and Asia, not buried in the jungles and mountains of Latin America." [H. F. Cline]

2239. Gomes, Luiz Souza. Joaquim Nabuco e o pan-americanismo. Rio de Janeiro, Departamento de Imprensa Nacional. 136 p.
The first half of this study covers Pan American conference developments to 1938. The second half is devoted to Nabuco's participation in the movement.

2240. INTER-AMERICAN COUNCIL OF JURISTS. PRIMERA REUNIÓN, RÍO DE JANEIRO, MAYO 22-JUNIO 15, 1950. INFORME. Presentado por F. V. García-Amador, Representante de Cuba ante el Consejo Interamericano de Jurisconsultos y el Comité Jurídico

Interamericano. Habana, Ministerio de Estado (Conferencias Internacionales, no. 3). 114 p.
This report of the Cuban delegation considers problems of codification of international law, recognition of de facto governments and other questions.

2241. Jameson [sic], Edward A. Keeping peace in the Caribbean Area. Washington, Department of State (Publ. 3918, Inter-American Series 41). P. 18-25.
The author of this enlightening article about the work of the Investigating Committee of the OAS in the Cayo Confites and Luperón affairs was at the time Officer in Charge, Special Political Affairs, Department of State. His name, misspelled on the title page of this reprint, is Edward A. Jamison. Reprinted from the *Department of State Bulletin*, July 3, 1950.

2242. Organization of American States. Council. Acta de la sesión ordinaria (extraordinaria) del Consejo de la Organización de los Estados Americanos celebrada el . . . 1950. Washington, Unión Panamericana. 1187 p.
Verbatim reports of regular and special meetings of the Council. In Spanish only. [Ed.]

2243. ————. ————. Agreement between the . . . and the American International Institute for the Protection of Childhood, signed at the Pan American Union . . . , April 22, 1949. Washington, Pan American Union (Conferences and Organizations Series, no. 4), 1950? Unpaged.

2244. ————. ————. Agreement between the . . . and Directing Council of the Pan American Sanitary Organization, signed at the Pan American Union . . . , May 23, 1950. Washington, Pan American Union (Conferences and Organizations Series, no. 6). Unpaged.

2245. ————. ————. Agreement between the . . . and the Inter-American Statistical Institute, signed at the Pan American Union . . . , April 11, 1950. Washington, Pan American Union (Conferences and Organizations Series, no. 5), 1950? Unpaged.

2246. ————. ————. Agreement between the . . . and the Pan American Institute of Geography and History, signed at the Pan American Union . . . , January 12, 1949. Washington, Pan American Union (Conferences and Organizations Series, no. 3), 1950? Unpaged.

2247. ————. ————. Decisions taken at the meeting of . . . Jan. 6 - Dec. 20,

1950. Washington, Pan American Union. 66 p.
Resolutions and other actions of the Council, without record of debates. Published in English, Spanish, Portuguese, and French. [Ed.]

2248. ————. ————. Standards for study of inter-American organizations. Revised edition. Washington, Pan American Union (Conferences and Organizations Series, no. 1). 6 p.

2249. ————. Inter-American Council of Jurists. First meeting, Rio de Janeiro, Brazil, May 22-June 15, 1950. Final Act. Washington, Pan American Union, Department of International Law and Organization. iv, 29 p. [English, Spanish].
This volume contains the draft statute of the Council of Jurists, and various resolutions. One of the latter concerns the development and codification of international law; another approves further consideration of a proposal for an Inter-American Court for the Protection of the Rights of Man. A table of contents would be helpful.

2250. ————. ————. Report and draft convention on recognition of *de facto* governments. Washington, Pan American Union. 27 p.
This report provides a useful survey of the Tobar and Estrada doctrines and of the practice of American states concerning recognition. The text of the proposed convention on this subject, attached, will no doubt provide material for much debate at the Caracas Conference. Lengthy reservations to the proposal are included, representing the dissident views of Mexico and Venezuela. In general, it appears that solidarity is sought on the principle that each state makes its individual decision about recognition.

2251. ————. Inter-American Economic and Social Council. Estatuto del Consejo Económico y Social, aprobado por el Consejo de la Organización de los Estados Americanos en la sesión del 3 de mayo de 1950. Washington, Unión Panamericana.

2252. ————. Investigating Committee of the Organ of Consultation. Results of its labors. Documents submitted to the Council of the Organization of American States acting provisionally as Organ of Consultation at the meeting of March 13, 1950. Washington, Pan American Union. 72 p.
The important report of the OAS committee which investigated the "Caribbean situation," and reported, among others, on the Cayo Confites and Luperón cases. Names are named, and blame is assessed; the work of this Committee is an example of which the OAS may well be proud, of prompt and effective work in calming a threatening situation. See item 2237.

2253. ————. Secretary General. Annual report . . . for the fiscal year ending June 30, 1950. Submitted to the Council of the Organization at the meeting held on November 15, 1950. Washington, Pan American Union. 199 p.
The activities of the OAS multiply and ramify and become significant. This report, submitted to the Council in mimeographed form, was printed in the *Annals of the Organization of American States*, v. 3, no. 1, 1951, p. 1-108.

2254. Pan American Union. Budget estimates for the financial year ending June 30, 1952. Washington. Various pagings.
This volume deserves book-review space. Of a total OAS budget of $4,790,219 for 1952, the United States provides 68.02 per cent. The other countries supplying more than two per cent of the total are Brazil, Argentina, and Mexico. It is encouraging to find that *Américas* has increased in circulation and now pays one third of its cost.

2255. United States. A decade of American foreign policy. Basic documents, 1941-1949. Prepared at the request of the Senate Committee on Foreign Relations by the Staff of the Committee and the Department of State. Washington, U. S. Government Printing Office (81st Congress, 1st session. Senate document no. 123). xiv, 1381 p.
Part 5 (p. 411-453) is devoted to the Inter-American System. There are selected documents from the Habana Meeting of Ministers of Foreign Affairs of the American Republics, 1940, the Rio de Janeiro Meeting of Ministers of Foreign Affairs, 1942, the Mexico City Conference on Problems of War and Peace, 1945, the Inter-American Conference for the Maintenance of Continental Peace and Security, 1947 (Inter-American Treaty of Reciprocal Assistance), and the Ninth International Conference of American States, 1948 (Charter of the Organization of American States). The section closes with *Waging peace in the Americas*, an address delivered by Secretary Acheson, September, 1949. See *HLAS, no. 15, 1949*, item 1910. [Ed.]

2256. ————. Department of State. Peace in the Americas. A résumé of measures undertaken through the Organization of American States to preserve the peace, with relevant documents. Washington, U. S. Government Printing Office (Department of State, Publ. 3964. International Organization and Conference Series II, American Republics 6). 29 p.
This informative pamphlet deals mainly with the application of the Rio Treaty to "uneasiness in the Caribbean area" in 1949 and 1950. See also items 2237, 2252.

TERRITORIAL QUESTIONS

2257. Arce, José. Las Malvinas. Las pequeñas islas que nos fueron arrebatadas. Madrid, Instituto de Cultura Hispánica. 194 p., illus.

2258. Carrasco, Ricardo. Actos y documentos que legitiman el derecho argentino sobre las islas Malvinas (*An. acad. hist. Cuba*, t. 30, enero-dic., 1948, i.e. 1950, p. 23-62).

2259. Corominas, Enrique V. Cómo defendí Malvinas. Buenos Aires, El Ateneo. 249 p.
Account of the author's activity at the Bogotá Conference in relation to the American Committee on Dependent Territories; with particular reference to the Falkland Islands. Bibliography.

2260. EL CORREDOR BOLIVIANO, LA TÉCNICA Y LA PAZ CONTINENTAL. Foros públicos efectuados el 5 y el 26 de septiembre de 1950, en la sala de conferencias de la Universidad de Chile. Santiago, Círculo de Estudios de Ingenieros, Arquitectos y Técnicos. 67 p.
Technical problems involved in Bolivian access to the Pacific are discussed by engineers and other specialists.

2261. González-Blanco, Pedro. El problema de Belice y sus alivios. México, Galatea. 129 p.
A Mexican finds the solution of the "problem of Belize" in an appeal by "the twenty American Republics" for its "return" by Great Britain to the rightful heir of Spain—Guatemala.

2262. Great Britain. Colonial Office. Report on the Falkland Islands and dependencies for the year 1949. London, His Majesty's Stationery Office (Colonial Reports). 39 p., illus., map.
Pages 18-24 are devoted to a brief history of the Falkland Islands from 1592 to the present, including the reassertion of British sovereignty in 1832. The rest of the report is on present conditions. [Ed.]

2263. Guatemala. Ministerio de Relaciones Exteriores. Puntos capitales que sostiene el gobierno de Guatemala en la controversia anglo-guatemalteca, para reivindicar el territorio de Belice. Edición en español e ingles. Guatemala, Tipografía Nacional. 12 p.
A "white paper" summarizing the Guatemalan position.

TREATIES

2264. Cuadra Ch., Pedro J. Motivos sobre el tratado Chamorro-Bryan. Editoriales de *El Diario Nicaragüense*. Managua, Fondo del Grupo Conservador Tradicionalista. 37 p.

2265. García Samudio, Nicolás (comp.). Tratados y convenios de Colombia, 1938-1948. Edición oficial. Bogotá, Ministerio de Relaciones Exteriores, Comisión Asesora. 772 p., maps.
The international agreements of an active ten-year period are compiled under an alphabetical subject arrangement, and include both multilateral and bilateral instruments. [H. Clagett]

2266. Guerrero Reyes, Ángel. El tratado de aguas internacionales de 1944 y su realización (*Mem. acad. nac. hist. geog.*, 2. época, año 6, no. 2, p. 24-45).

2267. International Conference of American States. Sixth, Habana, January 16-February 20, 1928. Treaties and conventions signed at the . . . . Washington, Pan American Union (Law and Treaty Series, no. 34). 80 p.
This is a timely publication, since it includes the text of the convention on asylum, among others. It is one of the out-of-print documents being reissued by the Pan American Union in the Law and Treaty Series and in the Conference and Congress Series to make them readily available.

2268. McIntee, Patrick G. American historical reappraisal of the Hay-Herrán Treaty. Washington. xi, 165 p.
A doctoral dissertation (Georgetown University) which draws attention to the importance of disunity within Colombia as a reason for the rejection of the treaty.

2269. Pan American Union. Department of International Law and Organization. Division of Legal Affairs. Bilateral treaty developments in Latin America, 1938-1948. Washington, Pan American Union (Law and Treaty Series, no. 32). iii, 154 p.
A list by countries, of dates of signing, ratification, etc., of bilateral treaties to which American States are parties.

2270. STATUS OF PAN AMERICAN TREATIES AND CONVENTIONS. Revised to April 1, 1950, by the Division of Legal Affairs of the Pan American Union. Washington, Pan American Union. 18 p.

2271. United Nations. Treaty Series. Treaties and international agreements registered or filed and recorded with the Secretariat of the United Nations. General Index No. 1 (v. 1-15). Lake Success, N. Y. vii, 206 p.

2272. United States. Air transport services. Agreement and accompanying exchange of notes between U. S. and Dominican Republic, signed Ciudad Trujillo, July 19, 1949. Entered into force July 19, 1949. Washington, Department of State (Treaties . . . Series, 1955). 15 p.

2273. —————. Anthropological research and investigation. Cooperative program in Peru. Agreement between U. S. and Peru, superseding agreement of March 9 and August 4, 1944 . . . ; entered into force March 25, 1949. Operative retroactively from July 1, 1948. Washington, Department of State (Treaties . . . Series, 1960). 9 p.

2274. —————. Educational cooperative program in Paraguay. Agreement between U. S. and Paraguay amending and extending agreement of March 8, 1948 . . . ; entered into force Sept. 1, 1949. Operative retroactively from July 1, 1949. Washington, Department of State (Treaties . . . Series, 1991). 3 p.

2275. —————. Food production. Cooperative program in Costa Rica. Agreement between U. S. and Costa Rica, extending agreement of Feb. 20 and 27, 1948 . . . ; entered into force Oct. 5, 1948. Operative retroactively from June 30, 1948. Washington, Department of State (Treaties . . . Series, 1992). 4 p.

2276. —————. Food production. Cooperative program in Costa Rica. Agreement between U. S. and Costa Rica, amending and extending agreement of August 27 and October 5, 1948 . . . ; entered into force August 22, 1949. Operative retroactively from June 30, 1949. Washington, Department of State (Treaties . . . Series, 1996). 4 p.

2277. —————. Food production. Cooperative program in Peru. Agreement of May 19 and 20, 1943 as modified and extended . . . ; entered into force August 18, 1949. Operative retroactively from June 30, 1949. Washington, Department of State (Treaties . . . Series, 1993). 3 p.

2278. —————. Health and sanitation. Cooperative program in Bolivia. Agreement between U. S. and Bolivia, modifying and extending agreement of July 15 and 16, 1942 . . . ; entered into force July 14, 1948. Operative retroactively from June 30, 1948. Washington, Department of State (Treaties . . . Series, 1999). 3 p.

2279. —————. Health and sanitation. Cooperative program in Colombia. Agreement between U. S. and Colombia, modifying and extending agreement of October 23, 1942 . . . ; entered into force Aug. 4, 1949. Operative retroactively from June 30, 1949. Washington, Department of State (Treaties . . . Series, 1998). 5 p.

2280. —————. Health and sanitation. Cooperative program in Ecuador. Agreement between U. S. and Ecuador, modifying and extending agreement of February 24, 1942 . . . ; entered into force Aug. 20, 1948. Operative retroactively from June 30, 1948. Washington, Department of State (Treaties . . . Series, 2003). 3 p.

2281. —————. Health and sanitation. Cooperative program in Honduras. Agreement between U. S. and Honduras, amending and extending agreement of May 5 and 8, 1942 . . . ; entered into force Aug. 24, 1949. Operative retroactively June 30, 1949. Washington, Department of State (Treaties . . . Series, 1986). 10 p.

2282. —————. Health and sanitary cooperative program in Bolivia. Agreement between U. S. and Bolivia modifying and extending agreement of July 15 and 16, 1942 . . . ; entered into force July 29, 1949. Operative retroactively from June 30, 1949. Washington, Department of State (Treaties . . . Series, 2009). 3 p.

2283. —————. Health and sanitation cooperative program in Brazil. Agreement between U. S. and Brazil, extending and modifying agreement of March 14, 1942 . . . ; entered into force October 4, 1949. Operative retroactively from June 30, 1949. Washington, Department of State (Treaties . . . Series, 2004). 5 p.

2284. —————. Health and sanitary cooperative program in Ecuador. Agreement between U. S. and Ecuador modifying and extending agreement of Feb. 24, 1942 . . . ; entered into force Aug. 26, 1949. Operative retroactively from June 30, 1949. Washington, Department of State (Treaties . . . Series, 2018). 5 p.

2285. —————. Health and sanitary cooperative program in Honduras. Agreement between U. S. and Honduras, extending and modifying agreement of July 8, 1942 . . . ; entered into force July 6, 1948. Operative retroactively from June 30, 1948. Washington, Department of State (Treaties . . . Series, 1980). 10 p.

2286. ————. Health and sanitary cooperative program in Venezuela. Agreement between U. S. and Venezuela extending and modifying agreement of Feb. 18, 1943 . . . ; entered into force March 9, 1949. Operative retroactively from June 30, 1948. Washington, Department of State (Treaties . . . Series, 1974). 8 p.

2287. ————. Health and sanitary cooperative program in Venezuela. Agreement between U. S. and Venezuela, extending and modifying agreement of Feb. 18, 1943 . . . ; entered into force Sept. 30, 1949. Operative retroactively from June 30, 1949. Washington, Department of State (Treaties . . . Series, 2008). 7 p.

2288. ————. Health and sanitation program in Colombia. Agreement between U. S. and Colombia modifying and extending agreement of Feb. 14 and 19, 1946 . . . ; entered into force July 31, 1948. Operative retroactively from June 30, 1948. Washington, Department of State (Treaties . . . Series, 1958). 4 p.

2289. ————. Health and sanitation program in Haiti. Agreement between U. S. and Haiti, extending and modifying agreement of April 7, 1942 . . . ; entered into force June 30, 1949. Washington, Department of State (Treaties . . . Series, 1977). 3 p.

2290. ————. Inter-American Highway. Agreement between U. S. and Guatemala supplementing agreement of May 19, 1943 . . . ; entered into force May 18, 1948. Washington, Department of State (Treaties . . . Series, 2001). 5 p.

2291. ————. Weather stations. Cooperative program in Mexico. Agreement between U. S. and Mexico, superseding previous agreements, effected by exchange of notes signed Mexico March 29 and August 15, 1949; entered into force October 20, 1949. Operative retroactively from July 1, 1948. Washington, Department of State (Treaties . . . Series, 1995). 8 p.

OTHER TOPICS

CHILE

2292. Barros Franco, José Miguel. El caso del *Baltimore*. Apuntes para la historia diplomática de Chile. Santiago. 157 p.
A careful and scholarly study of the *Baltimore* incident. Thesis, University of Chile.

2293. LAS RELACIONES DIPLOMÁTICAS ENTRE CHILE Y ESPAÑA. Criterios expuestos en el Senado y en la Cámara de Diputados de Santiago. Santiago, Talleres Poligráficos Claret. 79 p.
A series of eight speeches favoring resumption of regular diplomatic relations between Chile and Spain.

COLOMBIA

2294. Ministerio de Relaciones Exteriores. Documentos relativos al asilo del Sr. Víctor Raúl Haya de la Torre en la Embajada de Colombia en Lima. Bogotá. 69 p.
First volume in a projected series on this *cause célèbre*.

2295. Vásquez Carrizosa, Alfredo. Plaidoirie pour la République de Colombie dans l'affaire colombo-péruvienne relative a l'asile de Víctor Raúl Haya de la Torre prononcée devant la Cour Internationale de Justice. Paris, A. Pedone. xxiv, 174 p.
See item 3115 on the decision of the Court.

UNITED STATES

2296. Bemis, Samuel Flagg. A diplomatic history of the United States. 3rd edition. New York, Henry Holt. xiii, 994 p.
A newly revised edition of a basic work that appeared in 1936 and was first revised in 1942. Two new chapters cover World War II and after, and a new map illustrates the zone covered by the Rio Pact. The Latin American chapters are essentially untouched. [H. F. Cline]

2297. DEPARTMENT OF STATE BULLETIN. Washington. V. 22, no. 548, Jan. 2–v. 23, no. 599, Dec. 25.
Weekly, containing important addresses by Department of State officials, reports of treaties, and other items of interest in the international relations of the U. S. [Ed.]

2298. Furniss, Edgar S., Jr. American wartime objectives in Latin America (*World pol.*, v. 2, no. 3, April, p. 373-388).
A concise survey of U. S. policy toward Latin America in World War II. Four main aims are described: 1, ending of Latin America's mistrust of the U. S.; 2, acquisition of raw materials; 3, prevention of Nazi use of German minorities in Latin America and 4, forging of close military ties with Latin America.

2299. Gantenbein, James Watson (ed.). The evolution of our Latin-American pol-

icy. A documentary record. New York, Columbia University Press. xxvii, 979 p.
A useful collection of documents for reference or classroom work in the history of American foreign policy.

2300. Guerrant, Edward O. Roosevelt's Good Neighbor Policy. Albuquerque, N. Mex., University of New Mexico, School of Inter-American Affairs (Inter-Americana Studies, 5). viii, 235 p.
A useful review of published materials on the Good Neighbor Policy. The author describes the general course of events, but makes little effort to interpret them or to provide an understanding of policy motives. The Cuban "intervention" in 1933, a vital turning point in policy, is given three unenlightening pages. Was the *policy* really Roosevelt's or is this just a good title?

2301. Hanson, Simon G. Latin America and the Point Four program (*An. amer. acad. pol. soc. sci.*, v. 268, March, p. 66-74).
A useful general summary of objectives, operational problems, and limitations of technical aid to Latin America over a decade before these activities were christened Point Four. Hanson holds that "adoption of the Point Four program as a continuing element in American foreign economic policy will remove much of the uncertainty and distrust in Latin America and make possible the longer range planning, training, and staffing which make for efficiency in the organization of such programs," and the costly mistakes of the past in Latin America need not now be repeated. [H. F. Cline]

2302. Kipp, Laurence J. The international exchange of publications. A report of programs within the United States Government for exchange with Latin America, based upon a survey made for the Interdepartmental Committee on Scientific and Cultural Cooperation, under direction of the Library of Congress. Wakefield, Mass., Murray Printing Co., 1950? 116 p.
The recommendations of this report relate mainly to improvements in technical services for exchange of books and documents.

2303. Stebbins, Richard P. (and others). The United States in World Affairs, 1949. Introduction by George F. Kennan. New York, Harper (Council on Foreign Relations). xviii, 574 p.
A perceptive section on "Politics and revolution in Latin America" is found on p. 469-485. The writer says: ". . . there remains in Latin America a direct correlation between arrested social development, generalized poverty, widespread illiteracy, economic oppression, political violence, and endemic revolution." After noting that the prevalence of these conditions was not uniform, he mentions "the bewildering series of revolutionary uprisings, successful and unsuccessful . . . between 1947 and 1950," and states that Communism was not a major factor, although Communist strength and activity in certain

Latin American countries were not inconsiderable. "Developments in each country had their origin rather in a tangle of local interests and rivalries. . . ." Special attention is devoted to the Dominican-Cuban-Guatemalan crisis and to the tension between Haiti and the Dominican Republic. (See item 2256 on the settlement of these controversies.) Several pages are devoted to an analysis of Secretary Acheson's address on Sept. 19, 1949 (see *HLAS, no. 15, 1949*, item 1910), "in some ways the most important [U.S.] official pronouncement on hemisphere policy in a number of years. . . . The speech itself, however, lacked the imprint of any new and dramatic idea." [Ed.]

2304. United States. U. S. Ambassadors' report on regional conferences in American Republics. Report of the First Regional Conference of U. S. Ambassadors in the Caribbean Area. Washington, Department of State (Publ. 3825, Inter-American Series, 40, April, 1950). P. 160-162.
Reprinted from *Department of State Bulletin*, Jan. 30 and March 20, 1950. The not very informative report of a diplomatic meeting.

2305. ———. Department of State. United States leadership in the Americas. *Waging peace in the Americas*, address by Secretary Acheson, Sept. 19, 1949; *Inter-American faith in United Nations*, remarks by Assistant Secretary Miller, Sept. 19, 1949; *Settling disputes in the Western Hemisphere*, abridgement of address by Ambassador Paul C. Daniels, Dec. 5, 1949; *Inter-American policy objectives*, abridgement of address by Willard F. Barber, Deputy Assistant Secretary for Inter-American Affairs, Dec. 8, 1949; *Economic cooperation in the Americas*, excerpts from an address by Mr. Barber, Dec. 12, 1949. Reprint from the *Department of State Bulletin*. Washington, U. S. Government Printing Office (Department of State Publ. 3750, Inter-American Series, 39). Various pagings.
Reprinted from *Department of State Bulletin*, Sept. 26, 1949, p. 462-466; Dec. 19, 1949, p. 920-925; Dec. 26, 1949, p. 976-980. See also *HLAS, no. 15, 1949*, item 1910.

2306. Y. On a certain impatience with Latin America (*For. affs.*, v. 28, no. 4, July, p. 565-579).
An argument that despite the slowness of Latin Americans to practice democratic principles the United States should continue the fraternal policy of the good neighbor, resisting those who would go back to paternalistic policies. The author weakens his argument at the end by saying that the U. S. should "maintain an attitude of *noblesse oblige.*"

OTHER COUNTRIES

2307. Brazil. Ministério das Relações Exteriores. Serviço de Publicacões. Lista de publicacões, 1826-1950. Rio de Janeiro, 1950? 67 p.
A valuable finding-list for the student of Brazilian foreign relations. [C. Shelby]

2308. Carlés, Fernando J. Algunos aspectos de la geopolítica boliviana. Buenos Aires, Instituto de Derecho Internacional, Facultad de Derecho y Ciencias Sociales (Publ. no. 2). 89 p.
The point of this book by an Argentine army colonel appears to be that Bolivia, frustrated on the Pacific and in the north, should look to cooperation with Argentina as the best means for future economic development. In the introduction, Lucio M. Moreno Quintana, Director of the Institute of International Law of the Faculty of Law and Social Sciences of Buenos Aires, states: "I have always believed that there could be no effective university activities without a fruitful collaboration with the armed forces of the country."

2309. El Salvador. Secretaría de Información de la Presidencia de la República. Política de cordialidad centroamericana. Honduras y El Salvador en un común destino. San Salvador. 34 p., illus.

2310. Quijano, Carlos. El tratado con los Estados Unidos. Montevideo. 43 p.
A critical analysis of the "Treaty of Friendship, Commerce, and Economic Development" between the United States and Uruguay, signed Nov. 23, 1949. The author concludes that the treaty cannot be of much help to Uruguay, and that it looks as though the United States has employed Uruguay as a guinea pig, to test policies which will be tried out later on countries offering more important fields for investment. Ratified by U. S. Senate Aug. 9, 1950. See also item 805.

ADDENDA

2311. Besouchet, Lidia. Rio-Branco e as relações entre o Brasil e a República Argentina. Rio de Janeiro, Ministério das Relações Exteriores, Comissão Preparatória do Centenário do Barão do Rio-Branco (Monografias, 4), 1949. 84 p.

2312. Honduras. Memoria presentada al Congreso Nacional por el Subsecretario de Estado encargado del despacho de Relaciones Exteriores, 1947-1948. Tegucigalpa, Talleres Tipográficos Nacionales, 1949. 237 p., tables.
General survey, country by country, of the foreign relations of Honduras for 1947-1948.

2313. INFORME EXPEDIDO POR LA COMISIÓN MIXTA DE NEGOCIOS INTERNACIONALES RELATIVO A LA CARTA DE LA ORGANIZACIÓN DE LOS ESTADOS AMERICANOS (Rev. jurídica, año 13, no. 50, dic., 1949, p. 26-49).
The Mixed Commission on International Affairs of the Bolivian Congress divided four to three, with the majority favoring adherence to the Charter of the OAS. The majority report is largely of a legal character. The minority report, signed by José Antonio Arze, Faustino Suárez, and Assad Simón, is an important document, indicative of the existing attitudes of a significant sector of Latin American opinion about inter-American affairs. The view is taken that the essence of Pan Americanism is economic imperialism of the United States, and that even during the period of the Good Neighbor Policy imperialism was able to strengthen itself. Pan Americanism is characterized as an association of a wolf and 20 lambs. The minority suggests that the Bolivian Congress should endeavor to encourage elsewhere in Latin America the Revolución Agraria-Antiimperialista, which would be coordinated with the forces of the USSR and "la Nueva China," and concludes with the recommendation that the Bogotá Charter not be ratified but that a League of Latin American Nations be formed.

2314. Levene, Ricardo. La política internacional argentina en 1833 ante la invasión de las Islas Malvinas. Buenos Aires, 1949. 15 p.
Historical note on documents relating to Argentine policy toward the Islas Malvinas question.

2315. Mexico. Secretaría de Relaciones Exteriores. Memoria de la . . . septiembre de 1948-agosto de 1949 presentada al H. Congreso de la Unión por el C. Manuel Tello, Subsecretario Encargado del Despacho. México, 1949. 316 p.
Extensive section on treaties and conventions signed, approved by the Senate, promulgated (with text), or denounced; section on boundaries and international waters, including the Rio Grande and the Colorado; report on conferences and other international activities in which Mexico participated; and other relevant material. [Ed.]

2316. Varela Acevedo, Jacobo. Recuerdos de mi actuación en el Ministerio de Relaciones Exteriores, 1907. Discurso preliminar por Ariosto D. González. Montevideo, Instituto Histórico y Geográfico del Uruguay, 1949. xv, 19 p.

Labor and Social Welfare

CARL H. FARMAN

GENERAL

2317. Alexander, Robert J. Reseña del movimiento obrero en la América Latina. Washington, Unión Panamericana, División de Asuntos Sociales y de Trabajo (Serie sobre Educación Obrera no. 4). 31 p.

Based on Professor Alexander's Fabian Society publication of 1947, this work offers a brief general review, followed by histories of unionism in some Latin American countries where he has directly observed conditions. A useful contribution to an important and a rapidly developing area of activity.

2318. Conferencia Interamericana de Seguridad Social. Manual de instituciones de seguridad social. Ginebra [Switzerland], Oficina Internacional del Trabajo. 356 p.

"This edition of the *Handbook* is a complete revision of the earlier *Inter-American Handbook of Social Insurance Institutions* published in 1945." It covers each country systematically in the language of that country, including constitutional bases for social security, administrative authorities, and each program of social security. Only Honduras and Nicaragua of the Latin American nations are not included.

2319. ————. Comité Permanente Interamericano. Secretaría General. El Comité Interamericano de Seguridad Social. Informe 1. Ginebra [Switzerland], Oficina Internacional del Trabajo. 102 p.

This Committee has been in existence as a permanent body since 1942. Its aim is to provide an interchange of expert information and so to improve standards of social insurance performance in the Western Hemisphere. The present pamphlet is the fullest and best account of its activities up to the Third Conference in Buenos Aires, 1951.

2320. ————. ————. ————. Estatutos y reglamentos. Ginebra [Switzerland]. 18 p.

Presents the text of the organic law of both the Inter-American Conference and its permanent body, the Inter-American Committee on Social Security. The relationship of the two organizations appears, as does the place of the International Labour Organisation.

2321. Congreso Panamericano de la Vivienda Popular. Primer Congreso, celebrado en Buenos Aires, Argentina, del 2 al 7 de octubre de 1939. Resultados. Washington, Unión Panamericana, División de Asuntos Sociales y de Trabajo, Sección de Vivienda y Planificación. 18 p.

"Reimpreso especialmente para los delegados a las discusiones sobre vivienda y planificación de los seminarios regionales sobre asuntos sociales auspiciados por la División de Asuntos Sociales y de Trabajo." A handy source book.

2322. Gropp, Arthur E. La biblioteca y la educación obrera. Washington, Unión Panamericana, Departamento de Asuntos Económicos y Sociales, División de Asuntos Sociales y de Trabajo (Serie sobre Educación Obrera no. 5). 9 p.

A practical guide to further development of libraries as a force in workers' education in Latin America. Includes information on developments in various countries, and has a bibliographic guide to the furtherance of such work.

2323. THE INTERNATIONAL TRADE UNION MOVEMENT (*Ind. lab.*, v. 4, no. 8, Oct. 15, p. 346-356).

Developments at several world congresses are summarized, including those of the World Federation of Trade Unions and of the International Confederation of Free Trade Unions. The meeting of the latter—in 1949—represented a breaking-off of most Western unions from the Communist-dominated W.F.T.U. The importance of issues to labor in Latin America makes the references of value despite the fact that the conferences were not held in this hemisphere and have only slight mention of Latin America.

2324. International Union for Child Welfare. General Council, London, 1950. Reports of member organizations on their activity from 1948 to 1950. Geneva, Switzerland. 49 p.

Of the twenty-five countries that have reports in this brochure, three are from Latin America, namely, Argentina, Bolivia, and Peru. The Bolivian report, though brief, is particularly informative as to general problems.

2325. Méndez, Jorge. Minimum wages in Latin America (Int. lab. rev., v. 62, no. 2, Aug., p. 116-140).

The urgent need of adequate wages throughout Latin America is discussed, with brief summaries of legal provisions in the eighteen countries that have enacted legislation. The survey is authoritative, and constitutes an excellent introduction to this question.

2326. Narasimhan, P. S. Profit-sharing. A review (Int. lab. rev., v. 62, no. 6, Dec., p. 469-499).

Latin America is the only section of the world where several countries have enacted legislation requiring payments to individuals from company profits. This article, which also considers voluntary profit-sharing, offers a useful summary of the compulsory laws in Bolivia, Chile, Colombia, Ecuador, Peru, and Venezuela.

2327. Puelma Salinas, Eduardo. El derecho social en las constituciones americanas. Santiago. 41 p.

Briefly but systematically summarizes basic legislation in the Americas concerning various fundamental social ideas, including private property, freedom to work, work as a social obligation, the labor contract, collective bargaining, wages and hours, work of women and children, social insurance, strikes, and labor unions. Thesis, University of Chile.

2328. REGIONAL TRADE UNION MOVEMENTS (Ind. lab., v. 4, no. 10, Nov. 15, p. 427-431).

Includes summaries of two congresses in the Western Hemisphere—that of the Inter-American Confederation of Workers at Habana, September, 1949, and the Communist-orientated Confederation of Workers of Latin America at Montevideo, March, 1950.

2329. Riega, Alfonso de la. La función de los gremios en el orden nuevo. Santiago, AUCA (Col. Corporativa, año 1, julio, no. 1). 47 p.

A theoretical, somewhat polemical, work which considers trade unions from the corporative viewpoint. The Chilean author follows the Lisbon and Coimbra school of thought on corporative law.

ARGENTINA

2330. THE ARGENTINE NATIONAL EMPLOYMENT SERVICE (Ind. lab., v. 3, no. 1, Jan. 1, p. 12-13).

Summarizes the act of Sept. 29, 1949 (promulgated Oct. 11), setting up under the Ministry of Labor and Welfare a national employment service.

2331. Buenos Aires (prov.). Ministerio de Salud Pública y Asistencia Social. Memoria, 1949-1950. La Plata. 149 p., illus.

The period under review was one of rapid growth in the province. In public health alone, 161 undertakings (hospitals, clinics, etc.) were projected, begun, or finished, for a total cost of 41 million pesos. Corresponding achievements appear for medical social work, mother and child care, and related undertakings.

2332. CONGRESS OF ARGENTINE CONFEDERATION OF LABOUR (Ind. lab., v. 4, no. 7, Oct. 1, p. 322).

Briefly notes some events of the final session of April 19, 1950, including addresses and resolutions by and concerning President Perón and the special position of Argentina as between capitalism and Communism.

2333. ESTATUTO DEL PEÓN. Buenos Aires, Presidencia de la Nación, Subsecretaría de Informaciones, Dirección General del Registro Nacional (Leyes Nacionales y Decretos Reglamentarios, 6). 119 p., tables.

This law of 1944, with amendments, "rige las condiciones del trabajo rural en todo el país." Included in the compilation are detailed wage tables and the text of regulations adopted through 1949. Indexed.

2334. Krotoschin, Ernesto. Curso de legislación del trabajo. Buenos Aires, Depalma. xv, 370 p.

Presents the text of the author's Theoretical and practical courses on labor legislation, given at the Colegio Libre de Estudios Superiores in 1949. Definitions and concepts are expounded, international labor law (ILO and UN) considered, and—in the body of the work—Argentine law and practice in labor matters is extensively reviewed in all its phases.

2335. Landó, Juan Carlos. Hacia la protección integral de la minoridad. Buenos Aires, Depalma. 211 p.

From a varied background in child welfare theory and practice, the author presents his view on personnel training, philosophy of education, policy issues, and similar matters. Cites several cases illustrative of the points developed.

2336. Ministerio de Trabajo y Previsión Social. Instituto Nacional de Previsión Social. Sección Ley 4349. Jubilaciones y pensiones civiles. Memoria correspondiente al año 1949. Buenos Aires. 123 p., graphs, tables.

Text, tables, and charts on the progress of the retirement system for Argentine public employees. In 1949 this program paid 58,000 pensions at a cost of 14 million pesos per month. For the first time, the reserve fund exceeded a billion pesos.

2337. Prado, Pedro F. (ed.). Previsión social argentina. Recopilación ordenada de todas las leyes, decretos y resoluciones sobre jubilaciones, retiros, pensiones, seguros de vida, correspondientes a todas las actividades, públicas y privadas, maternidad, accidentes, ayuda social, mutualidades. Buenos Aires, Alsina. 1012 p.

An exceedingly valuable reference work that contains the text of national legislation in the fields covered, and also has data on the many retirement programs for special groups. Includes provincial acts.

BOLIVIA

2338. Arroba, Gonzalo. Informe preliminar sobre la transformación de los regímenes de pensiones y jubilaciones al sistema del seguro social general obligatorio (*Protec. soc.*, La Paz, año 12, no. 143-144, enero-feb., p. 7-40).

How to achieve the broader social insurance protection demanded in modern times is one of the principal problems of a country with many retirement systems but no central pooling of the risk and no really broad coverage. In this article the author urges Bolivia to change over to a single system, and offers suggestions for merging the various funds, recognizing rights already acquired, and obtaining the necessary factual basis concerning the insured population.

2339. EL SEGURO SOCIAL EN BOLIVIA. Ponencias presentadas al III Congreso Nacional de Facultades de Ciencias Económicas y Financieras. Potosí, Universidad Mayor Tomás Frías, Facultad de Economía y Finanzas. 223 p.

This work has the great value of giving factual data on Bolivia's ten retirement systems as well as recommendations from the congress at which it was presented. Contains also background material on Latin America and Bolivia. The five funds for which membership data are available have 37,000 members.

2340. Unzueta Oblitas, Mireya. Accidentes de trabajo en la industria (*Protec. soc.*, La Paz, año 12, no. 152, oct., p. 9-33).

Offers an evaluation of the Bolivian work accident program presented from the "social service" standpoint, and concludes that it could be greatly strengthened in a number of ways, including broadening the scope of compensable industrial diseases, use of vocational retraining, and extension to fields other than mining and factories. Gives statistics of compensation for 1948-1949.

2341. Villalpando R., Abelardo. Los trabajadores del servicio doméstico. Breve estudio histórico, socio-jurídico y comparativo referido al derecho laboral boliviano (*Rev. trab.*, t. 4, no. 151, agosto, p. 21-45).

The author, a professor of labor legislation in Bolivia, shows the weak economic position of domestic workers there, urges that social insurance be made operative for the group, and considers Bolivian labor laws in relation to domestic servants.

BRAZIL

LABOR

2342. Cesarino Júnior, A. F. (ed.). Consolidação das leis do trabalho (decreto-lei n. 5.452, de 1 de maio de 1943, com as correções ordenadas pelo decreto-lei n. 6.353, de 20 de março de 1944, e as demais alterações). V. 1-2. 3. ed. Rio de Janeiro, Freitas Bastos. 593, 500 p.

The third edition of this standard work; it includes a chapter on earlier related legislation, bibliographical data, court decisions, notes on theory and practice, and detailed indexes.

2343. Figueiredo, Paulo Poppe de (ed.). Estatuto dos funcionarios públicos civis da União, atualizado até junho de 1950. Rio de Janeiro, Aurora. 124 p.

Contains the text of the 1939 decree-law on public officials, extensively annotated and brought up to 1950. The work would be easier to use if, in addition to the alphabetical index, it also had a table of contents.

2344. Menezes, Geraldo Bezerra de. Dissídios coletivos do trabalho. Doutrina, legislação, jurisprudencia. 2. edición aumentada. Rio de Janeiro, Departamento de Imprensa Nacional. 246 p.

Presents the collective labor dispute in Brazil in general, constitutional, and legal aspects. Includes the text of laws, bills, and orders on the subject, and has statistics on strikes and disputes for the years 1941-1949. By the president of the Tribunal Superior do Trabalho.

2345. Mesquita, Luiz José de. Direito disciplinar do trabalho. Uma interpretacão institucionalista do direito do trabalho. São Paulo, Saraiva. 355 p.

According to the author, the disciplinary element in labor law is rooted in the nature of the institution and of the individual as a lower member in the hierarchy than the institution. Hence the disciplinary power is treated in detail, but always basically as an essential, natural part of company administration. Various reader helps such as a bibliography and indexes add to the work's usefulness.

2346. **Neto, Manoel Augusto Vieira** (ed.). Consolidação das leis do trabalho (aprovada pelo decreto-lei no. 5.452, de 1 de maio de 1943) acompanhada das leis, decretos e portarias posteriores. São Paulo, Saraiva (Legislação Brasileira, Biblioteca da Livraria Acadêmica). 925 p.

A third of this work gives the officially authorized text of the 1943 labor code, and later sections provide more recent laws and decrees on minimum wages, agricultural labor courts, the organization of labor tribunals, and related labor matters. With alphabetical and chronological indexes but without annotations.

2347. **Nogueira Júnior, José de Anchieta.** Soluções práticas de direito do trabalho. São Paulo, Livraria Vademecum. 108 p.

A working guide to Brazilian law on questions that include wage increases, expense accounts, holidays, and similar matters. Contains a number of specimen forms.

2348. **Russomano, Mozart Victor.** O empregado e o empregador no direito brasileiro. V. 1. Pôrto Alegre, Livraria Tabajara. 178 p.

Notes the nature and sources of labor law, the parties to the employment relation, employer duties, and various phases of the labor contract. A second volume was issued by another publisher in 1952.

2349. **Serviço de Estatística da Previdência e Trabalho.** Inquérito do salário mínimo. 3 v. Rio de Janeiro, 1949-1950. 80, 61, 77 p.

Provides the results of a 1949 investigation into wages in Brazil. Includes samples of the forms used in making the study, and also existing and proposed legislation on minimum wages.

2350. **Sussekind, Arnaldo.** Duração do trabalho e repousos remunerados. Rio de Janeiro, Freitas Bastos. 629 p.

Doctrine, legislation, and jurisprudence respecting the work day, night work, extraordinary work, weekly and holiday rest, general vacation, and improvement of leisure time.

2351. **Vargas, Getúlio.** A política trabalhista no Brasil. Rio de Janeiro, Olympio. 307 p.

Primarily a campaign document, consisting of collected speeches and Senate debates in which the former and current chief executive of Brazil expressed his viewpoint on labor matters when a member of the Senate in 1946 and 1947.

SOCIAL SECURITY

2352. BENEFÍCIOS DE ASSISTÊNCIA (*Industriários,* no. 13, fev., p. 9-14).

Brazil's Institute for Industrial Workers introduced medical services for its members in 1950. This article has the text of a committee report to the president of the Institute advocating a modest beginning in the Federal District.

2353. **Instituto de Aposentadoria e Pensões dos Industriários.** Relatório-estudio do Ingenheiro Alim Pedro, presidente do IAPI no período de 26-2-46 a 29-1-51. Rio de Janeiro. 477 p., illus., graphs, tables.

This is a well documented and attractively produced report by the director of the social-insurance organization for industrial employees, covering the period from 1946 to 1951. While the bulk of the material relates to the work of this organization, there is a discussion of some 30 pages pertaining to general aspects of social security, and another 130 pages are devoted to an analysis of miscellaneous aspects of Brazilian industry. Many data published in the report are of great interest to sociologists, economists, demographers, and students of housing. [H. W. Spiegel]

2354. **Instituto de Previdência e Assistência dos Servidores do Estado.** Manual do segurado do IPASE (elaborado de acôrdo com a portaria n. 625, de 2 de maio de 1949). Rio de Janeiro, Serviço de Publicidade e Estatística do IPASE. 128 p.

2355. **Oliveira, F. L. Tôrres de,** and **Oswaldo Iório.** Que é feito do seu dinheiro? (*Industriários,* no. 14, abril, p. 30-44).

Text, tables, and charts show in detail what the Industrial Workers' Institute does with its money. A highly informative picture of this phase of a large Latin American social security organization.

2356. A PREVIDÊNCIA SOCIAL NO BRASIL E NO ESTRANGEIRO. Rio de Janeiro, Fundação Getúlio Vargas. 329 p.

It is the purpose of this study (prepared as background information in the drafting of a general social insurance bill) to encompass within relatively small space the main provisions of social insurance legislation in Brazil, the rest of Latin America, and the more important countries elsewhere in the world. This results in a frequent use of charts, first for Brazil, where every institute is thoroughly covered, and then for foreign countries. The study also has the text of a monograph on Brazilian social insurance prepared in terms of an International Labour Office questionnaire, annotated lists of significant legislation, and other helps. A valuable reference work.

2357. PROBLEMAS TÉCNICOS DA ADMINISTRAÇÃO DO SEGURO SOCIAL (*Industriários,* no. 18, dez., p. 7-21).

Considers first the general organization of Brazilian social insurance programs and their principal benefits, and secondly certain technical administrative problems. The paper was read to a European conference of social insurance experts.

2358. Senna, José Rodrigues de. A pesquisa a serviço do IAPI (*Industriários,* no. 17, out., p. 13-52).
Considers the lack of effective management research in Brazil, discusses its functions and usefulness at some length, and urges its adoption by the industrial workers' social insurance institute.

WELFARE

2359. Pinheiro, Maria Esolina (and others). A formação dos trabalhadores sociais (*Bol. inst. intern. amer. protec. infan.,* t. 24, no. 1, marzo, p. 40-58).
Reviews Brazil's social work problems, and discusses the training of social workers in a large country with a low population density.

2360. Ramos, Alberto Guerreiro. Sociologia do orçamento familiar. Rio de Janeiro, Departamento Administrativo do Serviço Público, Imprensa Nacional. 89 p., tables.
A discussion of the Brazilian standard of living, with statistics of actual and recommended food consumption and other health factors. Extensive bibliographic references to authorities in the field.

2361. Serviço Social da Indústria. Departamento Regional da Bahia. O SESI na Bahia, 1948-1950. Salvador. 75 p., illus., ports.
Industrial Social Service (SESI) in Brazil is financed and managed by employers, but is not voluntary, being based on a decree-law of June 26, 1946. The Bahia report shows operations in that state from its creation in 1948 through two years of activity in recreation, aid to children, social medicine, legal aid, and other services.

CHILE

LABOR

2362. Argandoña Olivares, René. El despido colectivo de más de diez asalariados (*Mem. licenciados,* v. 10, p. 205-253).
Chile's Labor Code defines collective dismissals as those affecting ten or more persons. How much legislation is drafted, to whom it applies, which workers can be discharged, and how the procedure may be carried out are the main topics of this study of the subject. Includes information on workers' rights, with compensation for dismissal.

2363. Calás Jamasmi, Armando. Estudio en síntesis del Código del Trabajo chileno y de la previsión social. Santiago. 178 p.
In two main parts: Chilean labor law and Chilean social security. The first summarizes Chilean legislation concerning labor contracts, worker protection, measures for salaried employees, labor unions, labor disputes, and labor

courts and administration. The second part reviews the main social insurance trends in the country.

2364. Díaz Salas, Juan. Compendio alfabético de la legislación social chilena. Guía para su aplicación. Santiago, Editorial Jurídica de Chile. 349 p.
The author's long experience in Chilean labor matters has made possible a superior handy guide to the content of Chilean labor law. The definitions are of use to the student, but with each is given also its practical application and its legal base. An able and a helpful work.

2365. Martínez Amaro, Manuel. Estudio teórico y práctico de las leyes de mejoramiento económico de los empleados particulares (Leyes 6.020, 7.064 y 7.280, refundidas en la ley no. 7.295) (*Mem. licenciados,* v. 1, p. 65-389).
Like Germany and Austria, Chile has special legislation governing the employment of the private white-collar worker as distinct from the wage earner. The present study deals with various aspects of this body of law, including joint wage committees, the living wage, annual adjustments of wages, bonuses for seniority, family allowances, and the unemployment fund for salaried employees. A competent work, unfortunately weakened by the lack of a table of contents or index.

2366. Pizarro Trucco, Rafael. Ley sobre pago de la semana corrida, no. 8961 de 31 de julio de 1948. Valparaíso. 54 p.
By act of July 31, 1948, Chile provided that payment for the wage earner's work week should include Sundays and holidays. The author traces the background of this recent and important law and fully explains its provisions. Thesis, University of Chile.

2367. Vásquez Pérez, Raúl. Situación económico-social del personal ferroviario (Mem. licenciados, v. 2, p. 417-484).
Studies Chile's railroads and the 31,000 workers who operate them. Includes information on wages, "fringe benefits" such as family allowances, and the railway retirement system generally. Also gives a review of railway labor unions in Chile, and has suggestions to improve the economic position of the railway men.

SOCIAL SECURITY

2368. Agüero, Óscar. Ensayo sobre la previsión social en Chile (*Rev. española segur. soc.,* año 4, no. 3, marzo, p. 247-277).
Provides a balanced review of Chilean social security, including not only the wage earners' Caja de Seguro Obligatorio, but also the retirement and other systems for public employees, private salaried employees, merchant marine officers, employees of the State Railways, and members of the armed forces. Also has an account of work accident insurance. Includes statistics of operation.

2369. **Frontaura Gómez, Juan.** Interpretación y aplicación que la Caja de Seguro Obligatorio ha dado a los beneficios que concede la ley 4054 (*Mem. licenciados*, v. 2, p. 285-415).
Briefly analyzes each type of benefit in the Chilean social security program for wage earners, and compares the language and spirit of the law with its manner of administration by the Caja de Seguro Obligatorio.

2370. **Magaña Niedbalski, Jorge.** La ley de previsión para los abogados (*Mem. licenciados*, v. 10, p. 103-157).
Chile's 4,000 lawyers have their own retirement system, which is one of the few in the world designed especially for the profession. This thesis traces the predecessors of the present program, notes the legislative history of the system, and outlines in detail the various provisions that govern the plan.

2371. **Musalem Giacamán, René.** La ley no. 6174 de medicina preventiva y el servicio médico nacional de empleados (*Mem. licenciados*, v. 10, p. 13-102).
Traces the legislative history of the Chilean preventive medicine law—the first of its kind in the world—outlines its general provisions, and discusses in detail the application of the measure to salaried employees. Contains specific suggestions for strengthening the system. Part 2 on salaried employees' medical service includes description and evaluation.

2372. **Pinto, Francisco A.** Seguridad social chilena. Puntos para una reforma. Bound with *Un servicio nacional de salud* por Benjamín Vial V. Santiago, Chile, Editorial del Pacífico. 98 p.
Two professors of the University of Chile here offer comments on Chilean social security, with suggestions for improvement and a discussion of the reformed British system. Prof. Pinto criticizes the existence of many systems and the effects of inflation on benefits. Dr. Vial of the School of Health lists criteria for a national health service.

2373. **Poblete Poblete, Gabriel.** Accidentes del trabajo. Santiago. 66 p.
Explains systematically and in considerable detail the Chilean law, administration, and practice concerning work accidents. The emphasis on Chile is supplemented by a chapter summing up the essentials of legislation elsewhere in Latin America. Well documented. Thesis, University of Chile.

WELFARE

2374. **Escalona Poblete, Hernán.** La Caja de la Habitación y las empresas industriales, mineras y salitreras en la solución del problema de la vivienda (Arts. 16, 17 y 18 de la ley no. 7600). Santiago. 119 p.
Chilean industrial, mining, and nitrate firms are required by law 7600 of 1943 to contribute a percentage of profits to the Housing Fund (Caja de la Habitación). This is the first study of their contribution to solving the country's housing problem, and in the author's view the system has given concrete results. Includes some statistics. Thesis, University of Chile.

2375. **Walker Linares, Francisco.** Panorama del derecho social chileno. Santiago, Editorial Jurídica de Chile (Universidad de Chile, Facultad de Derecho, Col. de Estudios Jurídicos y Sociales, v. 7). 188 p.
A textbook by one of the great authorities of Chile on labor and social matters.

COLOMBIA

2376. **Echeverri Herrera, Carlos.** La grande industria y su afiliación al seguro social (*Segur. soc.*, Bogotá, no. 6-7, enero-junio, p. 9-19).
Excerpts from a letter by the chief administrative officer of the Colombian Social Insurance Fund to the manager of a textile factory, explaining why exemption from the compulsory health insurance program could not be granted.

2377. **Instituto Colombiano de Seguros Sociales.** Cartilla del seguro social obligatorio. 2. edición. Bogotá. 52 p., illus.
The Colombian system of health and maternity insurance began operations in Bogotá in 1949 with coverage of approximately 60,000 commercial, industrial, service, and transport workers. This pamphlet has full information on the practical aspects of the program.

2378. **Martínez Sarmiento, Rafael.** El proyecto de código del trabajo y el seguro social (*Segur. soc.*, Bogotá, no. 6-7, enero-junio, p. 43-53).
Departing somewhat from the conventional interpretation of labor law, this discussion takes the viewpoint that social insurance is more fair to the employer than is a labor code which charges the employer with the full cost of benefits such as pensions or cash sickness payments.

2379. **Muñoz, Laurentino,** and **Leonidas Hurtado.** Alimentación de la clase obrera en Honda. Bogotá, Contraloría General de la República, Dirección Nacional de Estadística (Suplemento a los números 52 a 54 de *An. econ. estad.*). 48 p., tables.
Continues the valuable cost-of-living and nutrition studies carried out by this agency. The study of 112 Honda families with 638 persons show that 24 persons had excellent nutrition and 112 good food, while at the other end of the scale 125 were in a "deplorable" nutritional state.

2380. **Ricardo, Víctor G.** (ed.). Código sustantivo del trabajo. Bogotá, Imprenta Nacional. 177 p.

2381. ————. Una política social en Colombia, 1946-1950. Bogotá, Imprenta Nacional. 91 p.
A report on the work of the Colombian Labor Ministry during the years noted. Has chapters on labor disputes, social insurance (which was established under a law of 1946), special labor legislation, trade union activities, and related matters.

2382. **Vargas Cuéllar, Guillermo.** ¿Qué es el seguro social y qué significa para los colombianos? Medellín, Caribe. 35 p.
Colombia's system of social insurance began operations in 1949, but was preceded by the Labor Code of 1945, which made provision for medical care and cash benefits of various types at the cost of the employers. Activities were extended to Medellín, where this informative pamphlet was published, in 1950.

DOMINICAN REPUBLIC

2383. **Brouwer, Pompilio A.** Breves consideraciones (*Prev. soc.*, Ciudad Trujillo, no. 19, enero, p. 6-9).
A nonstatistical report by the Secretary for Social Welfare in which he explains the legal basis of this department and shows the committees formed and work done.

2384. **Reyes Duluc, Fremio Enrique Efraín.** Seguros sociales totales como base de la seguridad social dominicana (*Segur. soc.*, año 2, no. 10, nov.-dic., 1949, p. 22-23; no. 11, enero-feb., 1950, p. 35-45; no. 12, marzo-abril, p. 41-50; año 3, no. 13, mayo-junio, p. 59-72).
Historical considerations are followed by an exposition of each principal type of insurance (for sickness, maternity, death, old age, invalidity, and unemployment). Each kind of protection is considered in general, but also with special stress on Latin American legislation and the programs of the Dominican Republic.

2385. **Secretaría de Estado de Previsión Social.** Memoria del año 1949. Ciudad Trujillo, ABC-Moya. 303 p., tables.
The extensive activities of the Department are clearly brought out in the report, which is a concise and informative record of institutional and noninstitutional care in the country. Deals with asylums for children and for the destitute aged, school meals, medical services, and low-cost housing. A valuable basic source of information, with extensive statistical data.

2386. SISTEMA DE SEGUROS SOCIALES DE LA REPÚBLICA DOMINICANA (*Prev. soc.*, Ciudad Trujillo, no. 27, nov., p. 11-19).
Reviews the law of December 30, 1948, with provisions concerning coverage, benefits, contributions, and administration of the social insurance program in the Dominican Republic.

2387. **Threan Valdez, Earl R.** Evolución del seguro social dominicano (*Segur. soc.*, año 3, no. 13, mayo-junio, p. 49-58).

Useful original tables and text which show the rapid development of the Dominican Social Insurance Fund in 1948-49. By the chief of the technical-statistical division of the Fund.

2388. TRABAJO. BOLETÍN DE LA SECRETARÍA DE ESTADO DEL TRABAJO. Ciudad Trujillo, año 1, no. 1, enero-junio-no. 2, julio-dic.
This new magazine of about 90 pages per issue includes original articles, the text of labor legislation, international news, and labor statistics. The first issue has the text of the *Reglamento orgánico de la Secretaría de Estado del Trabajo,* December 30, 1949.

ECUADOR

2389. **Caja de Pensiones.** Informe de actividades correspondientes a 1949 (*Bol. inform. estud. soc. econ.*, año 13, no. 48-49, enero-junio, p. 69-81).
The insurance program for public employees, military personnel, and bank workers, which is subordinate to the Instituto Nacional de Previsión, was complicated during 1949 because many cities and other local governments could not pay their social insurance contributions as employers. The Fund, however, continued to operate with a surplus, taking in 67.5 million sucres and spending 22.5 millions. Much of the capital is invested in mortgage loans to members. Signed by Dr. Leonidas García, chairman of the Consejo de Administración. The budget for 1950 appears on p. 92-97.

2390. **Instituto Nacional de Previsión.** Informe presentado por el . . . al Ministerio del Ramo, 1949. Alcance al informe del Instituto (*Bol. inform. estud. soc. econ.*, año 13, no. 48-49, enero-junio, p. 3-11).
The report itself concisely presents salient legislative and administrative developments of the year. The supplement is a reasoned statement why the Institute declined to accept and make operative two decrees of the National Congress, one of which concerned added contributions on the worker's behalf, to be based on company profits, the other attempting to establish social insurance for independent craftsmen.

2391. **Ministerio de Previsión y Trabajo.** Informe a la Nación, 1949-1950. Quito, Editorial Fray Jodoco Ricke. 222 p.
The report of the Minister, Clodoveo Alcívar Zevallos, covers the period May 1, 1949-April 30, 1950, with information on institutions for children in Ecuador, juvenile courts, social service work, medical services, and social insurance.

2392. **Orellana Ricaurte, Rubén.** El seguro social ecuatoriano y el riesgo de la disminución del salario de sus afiliados (*Bol. inform. estud. soc. econ.*, año 13, no. 48-49, enero-junio, p. 12-24).
Contains an excellent summary of the benefits and financial provisions of Ecuador's social insurance system. The author—who is head social insurance actuary—has for his theme the

extent to which social insurance payments offset the worker's wage loss when the risk against which he is insured materializes.

2393. Salgado, Francisco José. El contrato individual de trabajo en la legislatura ecuatoriana (*An. univ. cent. Ecuador*, t. 77, no. 328, enero-dic., 1949, i.e. 1950, p. 177-258).

Thesis, Central University of Ecuador.

EL SALVADOR

2394. Masís, Rodrigo. Proyectos de viviendas económicas para San Salvador. Informe para Mejoramiento Social sobre tipos de viviendas y de colonias . . . . Washington, Unión Panamericana, División de Asuntos Sociales y de Trabajo, Sección de Vivienda y Planificación. 52 p.

Mejoramiento Social, a Salvadorean agency charged with low-cost housing work, entered into a cooperative arrangement with the Pan American Union that resulted in field trips by the author of this study and, for shorter periods, by the chief of the Housing and Planning Section of the Pan American Union, Anatole A. Solow. The resulting work consists of practical, technical advice on housing types to select, land acquisition, and the technical documentation of housing projects.

2395. Pan American Union. Division of Labor and Social Information. La vivienda en El Salvador. Análisis del problema con recomendaciones para un programa nacional de la vivienda. Washington. 36 p., illus.

The result of a study by Public Administration Service (Chicago), which was invited by the Government of El Salvador to undertake a survey. Officials of the Pan American Union participated. Emphasis is on practical aspects—cost and type of dwellings, financing, and adaptation to different populations and environments.

GUATEMALA

2396. Bush, Archer Corbin. Organized labor in Guatemala, 1944-1949. A case study of an adolescent labor movement in an underdeveloped country. Hamilton, New York, Colgate University (Area Studies, Latin American Seminar Reports, no. 2). Various pagings, maps, tables.

"In early 1944," the author points out, "Guatemala had no organized labor movement. By 1950 there were two labor federations, over 150 unions, and nearly 100,000 union members." The volume treats of this development—its background (46 pages), labor accomplishments in agriculture, manufacturing, transport, and other fields, the growth of organization, and the ideology of the labor movement. By its able treatment of a highly important subject, this work fills a great need.

2397. Dittel, J. Walter. La doctrina de presupuesto social como base de los regímenes de previsión social obligatoria. Con nota introductoria de Óscar Barahona Streber. Guatemala, Instituto Guatemalteco de Seguridad Social. ii, 35 p.

Terms such as "social security" and "social budgeting" indicate that new elements have everywhere been added to the "classical" kind of social insurance originally developed in Europe. Here, a Guatemalan official expands on the idea of social budgeting (as developed by W. R. Williamson) in what is termed by Manager Barahona Streber of the Guatemalan Institute a "magnificent synthesis" of the reasons for substituting the newer program for conventional social insurance.

2398. Mazariegos Grajeda, José Gabriel. El contrato de trabajo, suspensión y término del mismo en la doctrina y en nuestra legislación. Guatemala. 42 p.

Treats of labor law and the labor contract in general, with special attention to Guatemala. Emphasis is on methods of suspending or terminating labor contracts. Thesis, University of San Carlos.

2399. Recinos Sandoval, José Abel (ed.). Código de trabajo, contenido en los decretos números 330, 526 y 623 del Congreso de la República. Guatemala, Ministerio de Educación Pública. 378 p.

In addition to the labor code proper, the editor has included other legislative and administrative provisions and decisions in the labor field. Forms of collective contracts are also incorporated in the volume. [H. Clagett]

2400. Reyes Cardona, Julio Antonio. Derechos y acciones de los empleados y trabajadores del estado. Guatemala, Magistratura de Coordinación de Trabajo y Previsión Social. 79 p.

What government employees (including to some measure local government workers as well) can and cannot do under the Guatemalan Constitution and labor code. The points discussed include collective bargaining, union membership, and strikes.

2401. Solow, Anatole A. La vivienda en Guatemala. Análisis del problema . . . . Washington, Unión Panamericana, División de Asuntos Sociales y de Trabajo, Sección de Vivienda y Planificación. iv, 117 p., illus.

"A statement of the problem with recommendations for the program and organization of the Housing Department." The work is based on direct observation and study by the author, who visited Guatemala under a cooperative arrangement between the Government and the Pan American Union. Also published in English.

HAITI

2402. ANNUAL PAID HOLIDAY IN HAITI (*Ind. lab.*, v. 4, no. 4, Aug. 15, p. 182-183).
A summary of the operation of the act of May 5, 1948, which entitles every worker to a paid vacation of 15 days after he has been employed one year.

2403. Kain, Joan. Report on Haiti. Washington, Federal Security Agency, Social Security Administration, Children's Bureau. Various pagings.
A fine statement of Haitian backgrounds affecting health, welfare, and labor, and a useful description of the welfare services that existed in 1949 and 1950. The author was a consultant of the U. S. Children's Bureau in Haiti during a part of each of these years, and has assembled a large body of information on Haitian developments, United Nations assistance, and various United States missions. Appendixes provide additional information on these and related matters.

2404. SOCIAL INSURANCE IN HAITI (*Ind. lab.*, v. 3, no. 12, June 15, p. 474-476).
Summarizes the social insurance act of Oct. 7, 1949, on workmen's compensation and health and maternity insurance.

MEXICO

LABOR

2405. Álvarez, Óscar C. La cuestión social en México. El trabajo. Manual para círculos de estudio. México, Publicaciones Mundiales. xx, 479 p.
Has chapters on labor unions in Mexico, Catholic social action, the federal labor law, and social insurance. Nearly a score of forms intended for trade union practice increase the utility of this work.

2406. Carniado, Enrique. La formación profesional en Méjico. Méjico, Talleres Gráficos de la Nación. 93 p.
Collected materials of somewhat uneven value on the subject of occupational training and apprenticeship. One of the most useful articles —bearing the same title as the book—reviews existing provisions for workers' training in Mexico, as of 1949, and recommends a number of changes.

2407. Carrión Simbrelo, Joaquín. Concepto y naturaleza jurídica del contrato colectivo de trabajo. Algunos de sus aspectos en la legislación mexicana. México. 200 p.
The theoretical material includes various comparative philosophies of trade unionism and the labor contract, together with the author's own viewpoint. In addition, Mexican law, both state and federal, is expounded, with comment on Lombardo Toledano's *Contrato sindical de trabajo.* Thesis, Law School, University of Mexico.

2408. Castro Ruz, Alfonso. Estudio de reforma al procedimiento en los conflictos individuales de trabajo. México. 74 p.
Historical material on Mexico's labor law of 1931 and its predecessors is followed by an account of Mexican procedure in labor disputes and of results in the years 1947-49. Thesis, Law School, University of Mexico.

2409. CONGRESO MEXICANO DE DERECHO DEL TRABAJO Y PREVISIÓN SOCIAL, 19 AL 25 DE JULIO DE 1949. MEMORIA. T. 1-2. México, Secretaría del Trabajo y Previsión Social. viii, 628; xi, 613 p., illus.
Seven committees, each with its own topics, are represented in these proceedings, and the total number of papers is well over one hundred. These include discussions of labor organization and administration, industrial safety, occupational training, work of women and children, and related topics.

2410. Espinosa Olvera, René. Fuerza de trabajo y desocupación. México. 94 p.
Data on employment and unemployment in Mexico, with discussion of the need for further and better statistics of the labor force, and on the formation of an employment service. Has suggestions on what is needed in Mexico to have full employment. Thesis, University of Mexico.

2411. González López, Guillermo. La huelga y el arbitraje en México. México. 47 p.
Briefly reviews the legal authority to strike (or not) in Mexico from colonial times, and includes useful historical notes on labor laws in the various states in 1914-1916, as well as comment on the Constitution of 1917 and later laws. Thesis, University of Mexico.

2412. Lagos Oropesa, Juan. Concepto, evolución y finalidades de la huelga según el derecho mexicano. México. 74 p.
The idea, evolution, and aim of the strike in Mexico, preceded by a discussion of labor disputes. Includes the viewpoint of various authorities, mainly Latin American, and also considers the histories of strikes in Europe. Thesis, University of Mexico.

2413. Mantilla Montiel, Federico. Organización del trabajo. Tendencias modernas del derecho laboral. México. 206 p.
Views labor and capital in Mexico against the background of the importance and desirability of good labor relations. Includes a discussion of collective bargaining and labor unions in Mexico and advocates labor management committees in factories. Thesis, University of Mexico.

2414. Melgar Rueda, Jorge. Naturaleza y elementos del contrato individual de trabajo. México. ii, 61 p.
Emphasis on the viewpoint that the labor contract is unique in nature, looking not only to the interests of both parties but also to social good and human dignity. Thesis, Law School, University of Mexico.

2415. Trueba Urbina, Alberto. Evolución de la huelga. México, Botas. 342 p.

The author, a professor of the University of Mexico and one of the writers who have made Mexican labor law widely known, traces in some detail the history of strikes in Mexico, and fully explains the law and jurisprudence on the subjects. Includes texts of state, federal, and special legislation and of various legal decisions.

2416. ———— (ed.). Ley federal del trabajo reformada, con bibliografía, comentarios y jurisprudencia. 15. edición. México, Porrúa. xvi, 535 p.

A new edition—"corregida y aumentada con nuevas disposiciones sobre trabajo y seguro social, leyes de emergencia conexas, ley sobre contratos colectivos de trabajo de carácter obligatorio y tesis actuales de la Sala del Trabajo de la Suprema Corte de Justicia de la Nación."

2417. United States. Temporary migration of Mexican agricultural workers. Agreement between the United States . . . and Mexico superseding Agreements of April 26, 1943 and March 10, 1947 . . . entered into force February 21, 1948. Washington, Department of State (Publ. 3640, Treaties and Other International Acts Series, 1968). 19 p.

An important document in United States-Mexican relations, and an informative guide to the protection needed and provided in the case of migratory labor.

2418. Velasco Albin, Pedro Enrique. Pago de salarios durante la tramitación de los juicios por despido. México. 74 p.

In comparison with other Latin nations—France, Italy, Spain, Argentina, Brazil—Mexico offers the worker greater job security during a labor dispute. The author considers the Mexican law and discusses decisions of the courts bearing on the worker's right to wages during a legal proceeding. Thesis, Law School, University of Mexico.

SOCIAL SECURITY

2419. Dirección de Pensiones Civiles. Memoria de 25 años de actividades. México. Unpaged, illus.

2420. INSTITUTO MEXICANO DEL SEGURO SOCIAL, 1949. México. 280 p.

Virtually a complete record of Mexican social security during 1949, handsomely prepared with an eye to quick comprehension by the reader and illustrated with hundreds of photographs. The subject matter is primarily medical services, which continued to be the greatest social insurance activity in Mexico.

WELFARE

2421. Banco Nacional Hipotecario Urbano y de Obras Públicas. Memoria de las Conferencias sobre Habitación Popular. México. 231 p., illus., group ports.

This was a national meeting, attended by the representatives of more than twenty official, financial, and professional bodies. The aspects of housing considered in the four sections are: economic and social, financial, architectural, and legal and administrative.

2422. Junta de Asistencia Privada del Distrito Federal. La asistencia privada. T. 1-2. México, Ruta (Temas Mexicanos, 3). 139, 134 p.

From time to time since 1934 the Board of Private Assistance in the Federal District has issued special reports on the diversified activities of the city's many private welfare agencies. The present volume, covering the period 1943-1948, includes brief accounts of the different charities such as hospitals, schools, homes for the aged, loan agencies, school lunches, and other work. Financial statistics for 1948.

2423. Otero Rivero, Ángel. El sistema de asignaciones familiares. Su proyección en el derecho positivo mexicano. México. 125 p.

Advocates the adoption by Mexico of family allowances governed by federal legislation and applicable to persons who work for another, whether in private or public employment. The material is supplemented by a historical survey and by comparative information as of about 1947. Thesis, Law School, University of Mexico.

2424. Peña, Moisés T. de la. Problemas sociales y económicos de las Mixtecas. México, Instituto Nacional Indigenista (Memorias, v. 2, no. 1). 182 p., illus., maps.

Through text and photographs the author gives a full picture of the half million Mixtecs of southern Mexico. Includes recommendations for land use, population shifts, transfers, and other measures to improve conditions.

2425. Valenzuela Kunckel de Sánchez, María. Trabajo social que se desarrolla en algunas dependencias de la Secretaría de Educación Pública. México. 69 p.

Mexican social workers are to be found in the Departments of Health, Education, and National Defense and in the executive offices of the President. The present thesis (University of Mexico) considers the social worker's role in the Education Department—in the cultural missions, National Institute of Pedagogy, and other divisions.

PERU

2426. Bonhomme Seymour Waden, Carlos de. Salario y participación en las utilidades, de acuerdo con la doctrina, con la ley y con la jurisprudencia. Arequipa, Chachani (Col. Derecho del Trabajo en América del Sur, t. 8: Perú). 346 p.

Studies in detail the wage and profit-sharing legislation of Peru, including the special fields of maritime employment, textiles, transport, banking, and others. Profit-sharing, in particular, is treated in detail.

2427. Caja Nacional de Seguro Social. Recopilación de los dispositivos legales del seguro social obligatorio. Lima. 47 p.

Highly useful as a guide to Peruvian social insurance legislation, since it explains the program briefly and systematically and gives the text of legislation as amended to May 30, 1950.

2428. Cuadros E., Raúl. Los derechos del empleado. 2. edición. Arequipa, Escuela Tipográfica Salesiana. 104 p.

Primarily a practical guide, showing the employer his obligations—and the Peruvian white-collar worker his rights—in matters such as wages, hours, summer vacation, discharge, retirement, Christmas and Easter bonuses, and related matters. Contains information on progress under the 1949 law governing social security for salaried employees.

2429. Mar, Juan Manuel del (ed.). Legislación del seguro social del empleado. Corresponde a todos los empleados públicos y particulares incluídos en los beneficios . . . . Lima, Librería Las Américas. 53 p.

2430. REFORM OF COMPULSORY SOCIAL INSURANCE IN PERU (*Ind. lab.*, v. 4, no. 7, Oct. 1, p. 306-307).

By decree of March 24, 1950, Peru raised the wage ceiling to cover workers earning up to 9,000 soles a year (formerly 3,000), and increased benefit rates and contributions. The principal benefit increases were in health and maternity insurance; retirement pensions, however, had increases in dependents' supplements.

2431. Salcedo Fernandini, Manuel. La pediatría en el campo de seguridad social (*Bol. inst. intern. amer. protec. infan.*, t. 24, no. 1, marzo, p. 76-86).

Urges a gradual policy for the adoption of social security programs in Latin America, and discusses Peruvian experience with improving the health level and making medical and dental services more generally available.

URUGUAY

2432. Chans Caviglia, Juan C. El servicio social en la solución de los problemas médico-sociales que afectan a la familia (*Bol. inst. intern. amer. protec. infan.*, t. 24, no. 1, marzo, p. 87-107).

A work presented by the Uruguayan delegation to the Second Pan American Social Service Congress, Rio de Janeiro, 1949. It explains Uruguayan social work practices, both public and private, and proposes a set of resolutions on medical social work for adoption by the Congress. Bibliography.

2433. CONFERENCIA INTERNACIONAL DE SERVICIO SOCIAL. V (*Bol. inst. intern. amer. protec. infan.*, t. 24, no. 3, sept., p. 251-281).

On the occasion of the Fifth International Conference of Social Work, held at Paris in 1950, questionnaires were submitted to the participating countries. This article, which consists of the Uruguayan replies, gives useful information on social work thinking and of the progress of social work in Uruguay.

2434. Jaurena, Eduardo. Frugoni. Una vida consagrada al ideal; y un ideal al servicio de los trabajadores. Con un apéndice de Ricardo Durán Cano. Montevideo, Comisión Ejecutiva Nacional de Homenaje al Doctor Emilio Frugoni. 79 p.

Emilio Frugoni was a lawyer, teacher, Socialist member of Congress, and ambassador to the U.S.S.R. This little book has a brief biography, followed by quotations from Frugoni's speeches in the Chamber of Deputies and from his writings.

VENEZUELA

2435. Arria Salas, Alberto. Ensayo sobre el salario. Anotaciones a la legislación del trabajo venezolano. Caracas, Edime. 395 p.

In two parts, the first being a review of the nature, history, and kinds of wages, and of the history of Venezuelan legislation on the subject; the second, an analysis of the various aspects of wages as treated in Venezuelan law and jurisprudence.

2436. CONVENCIÓN NACIONAL DE INSPECTORES DEL TRABAJO. SEGUNDA, 21 AL 25 DE AGOSTO DE 1950. Caracas, Ministerio del Trabajo, Servicio de Publicaciones. 95 p.

Labor officials here explain and discuss the central labor themes of Venezuela as expressed in legislation. There are ten papers in all (given in full, without discussion) on subjects such as collective bargaining, legal position of unions, paid holidays, and labor disputes.

2437. ESTATUTOS DE MENORES (*Infan. adoles.*, año 2, no. 7-8, enero-feb., p. 49-59).

The text of decree 390, Dec. 30, 1949, on child welfare and protection in Venezuela, dealing with the composition and duties of the Consejo Venezolano del Niño, laws of adoption, foster homes, and juvenile courts.

2438. FREEDOM OF ASSOCIATION AND CONDITIONS OF WORK IN VENEZUELA. REPORT OF THE MISSION OF THE INTERNATIONAL LABOUR OFFICE, 22 JULY–1 SEPT., 1949. Geneva, Switzerland, International Labour Office (Studies and Reports, n.s., no. 21). 185 p., illus., map.

In three parts—one providing a background of economic and political information, another studying labor unions, and the third dealing with general factors in this field, including labor law, collective bargaining, social security, etc. The mission went to Venezuela at the invitation of the Government. Its conclusion reports that several obstacles hinder effective functioning of trade unions, and notes—as to living standards— an improvement in the condition of the workers.

2439. LEY ORGÁNICA DE TRIBUNALES Y DE PROCEDIMIENTO DEL TRABAJO. Edición oficial. Caracas, Ministerio del Trabajo. 42 p.

2440. REVISTA DEL TRABAJO. Caracas, Ministerio del Trabajo, Servicio de Publicaciones. T. 1, no. 1, nov.
This first issue includes a valuable chronology tracing the development of Venezuelan labor law, and has a number of original articles in the general field of labor contracts, unions, and other aspects of labor law.

PUERTO RICO, VIRGIN ISLANDS

2441. Carrero, Telésforo. Housing in Puerto Rico. Santurce, P. R., Puerto Rico Planning Board (Technical paper no. 5). 36 p., illus.
Provides "a comprehensive graphical picture of the existing housing facilities" and housing problems in Puerto Rico. The author is chief of the Urban Development Division of the Puerto Rico Planning Board. Data presented are current as of March 31, 1950.

2442. Helfeld, David M. Materials on labor law in Puerto Rico. [Río Piedras, P. R.] Various pagings.
This is a mimeographed work of great usefulness in view of the lack of materials in English on this particular subject in Puerto Rico. An Institute on Labor Law given for practicing lawyers at the University of Puerto Rico Law School in 1950 and the compilation of materials used in this course resulted in the present volume, which includes United States and Puerto Rican legislation and administrative practice. [H. Clagett]

2443. Puerto Rico. Department of Labor. Bureau of Labor Statistics. Wage Analysis and Special Studies Section. Salarios y condiciones de trabajo en 106 establecimientos dedicados a la manufactura de pan y otros productos de harina en Puerto Rico, feb. de 1950. San Juan, P. R. 8 p.
A short, informative study giving an excellent picture of wages and hours in the Puerto Rican baking industry. The sugar and tobacco industries have been the objects of similar research.

2444. Rottenberg, Simon. Labor cost in the Puerto Rican economy. Río Piedras, P. R., University of Puerto Rico. 66 p.
Considers minimum age legislation and labor union practice in relation to labor cost. Also discusses the wage differential between Puerto Rico and the United States, with comment on the level of productivity on the Island. The

study is a product of the Labor Relations Institute, College of Social Sciences, University of Puerto Rico, and the author is director of the Institute.

2445. United States. Congress. House. Committee on Education and Labor. Investigation of minimum wages and education in Puerto Rico and the Virgin Islands. Hearings . . . (H. Res. 75, 81st Cong., 1st sess.). Washington, U. S. Government Printing Office. viii, 210 p.
This committee, John Lesinski, Michigan, chairman, developed a considerable volume of information on wages and education. The present volume presents much information on industry, labor, and worker incomes through the testimony of persons representing diversified sectors of the population.

OTHER COUNTRIES

2446. Escardó y Anaya, Víctor. Programa de UNICEF en el Paraguay. La colaboración de nuestro instituto (*Bol. inst. intern. amer. protec. infan.*, t. 24, no. 2, junio, p. 149-156).
Reports on a United Nations mission to Paraguay, provision of aid under the International Children's Emergency Fund, and the administrative structure of Paraguayan agencies for aid to children.

2447. Urriola, Cristóbal A. de, Rosa E. Palacio, and Francisco López Fábrega. Cooperativismo. Vivienda. Plan de construcción de colonias agrícolas. Panamá, Banco de Urbanización y Rehabilitación (Publ. no. 19). 45 p.
The most important paper here is that of Ing. López Fábrega on a plan for agricultural housing, complete with financial information and illustrations. The other two papers deal with the findings of the First Seminar on Social Affairs, sponsored at Quito by the Pan American Union.

2448. Vivó, Hugo. El empleo y la población activa de Cuba. Habana, Asociación Nacional de Industriales de Cuba. 88 p., graphs, tables.
Considers in detail Cuba's sugar industry, problems of employment and underemployment, and economic policy generally. Recommends more diversified industrial production and an increase in the number of businesses in the country.

ADDENDA

2449. Confederación Interamericana de Trabajadores. Primer Congreso General, Habana, Cuba, del 6 al 10 de septiembre 1949. Informe del presidente, Bernardo Ibáñez. Santiago, 1949. 47 p.

2450. Dominican Republic. Secretaría de Previsión Social. Memoria, 1948. Ciudad Trujillo, 1949. 363 p., tables.

2451. Fernós-Isern, Antonio. Seguro social para Puerto Rico. Washington, Office of Puerto Rico, 1949. 26 p. Spanish and English.

2452. Haïti. Bureau du Travail. Rapport annuel du Directeur Général. Exercice 1947-1948 (Bull. no. 2). Port-au-Prince, 1949. 59 p.

2453. INFANCIA Y ADOLESCENCIA. Caracas, Consejo Venezolano del Niño. Año 1, no. 1, enero-feb., 1949.
A publication of the Consejo Venezolano del Niño, under the direction of Dr. J. A. Rodríguez Delgado and the editorship of José Carrillo Moreno. Contains articles on child welfare and education in general, with special attention to the people of Venezuela and the services for children in that country. Photographic illustrations.

2454. Inter-American Confederation of Workers. Continental Congress, Second, Habana, Sept. 7-Sept. 11, 1949. Statutes, documents, and resolutions. Habana, Confederation of Workers of Cuba, 1949. Various pagings.

2455. Martí Bufil, Carlos. El seguro social en Hispanoamérica. Madrid, Seminario de Problemas Hispanoamericanos (Cuadernos de Monografías, 4), 1949. 209 p., tables.

2456. Oliveras, Cándido. El salario mínimo en la economía insular. San Juan, P. R., Department of Education, 1949. 19 p.

2457. Panama. Servicio Cooperativo Inter-Americano de Educación. An industrial occupational survey. A study of the needs of industry for skilled and semi-skilled workers with proposals for the development of the vocational education program in the city of Panama. Panamá, 1949. 120 p., illus.

2458. Puerto Rico. Department of Labor. Bureau of Labor Statistics. Patrones ocupacionales para 27 de las principales industrias de Puerto Rico. Compilados y revisados por la Unidad de Investigaciones Ocupacionales de la Sección de Análisis de Salarios y Estudios Especiales. San Juan, P. R., 1949. 351 p.

2459. ————. ————. ————. Wage Analysis and Special Studies Section. Salarios y condiciones de trabajo en 17 establecimientos dedicados a la manufactura de azúcar crudo en Puerto Rico, marzo de 1948. San Juan, P. R., 1949. 21 p.

2460. ————. Labor Relations Board. Fourth annual report for the fiscal year ended June 30, 1949. San Juan, P. R., 1949. 109 p.

2461. Verdiales, Francisco. Actitud oficial del estado hacia las organizaciones obreras. San Juan, P. R., Department of Education, 1949. 21 p.

Spanish American Language

CHARLES E. KANY

THE Instituto de Filología (Universidad de Buenos Aires), which had been divided into Sección Clásica (formerly Instituto de Lenguas Clásicas) and Sección Románica (formerly Instituto de Filología), has been reorganized. The two sections, converted into separate institutions, have been granted complete autonomy. Consequently from May, 1950, the journal *Filología* appears as the organ of the Instituto de Filología Románica.

The former Instituto de Filología (Universidad de Chile) has now become a section of the new Instituto de Investigaciones Histórico-Culturales of the same University. V. 5 of this Instituto's *Boletín de Filología,* covering the two-year period 1947-1949, appeared in 1950 under the editorship of Dr. Rodolfo Oroz. This 435-page tome contains a section on Chilean folklore called "Archivo Folklórico," a continuation of the studies begun years ago by the Sociedad de Folklore Chileno, founded by Rodolfo Lenz.

After a five-year interruption the publication of the *Anales del Instituto de Lingüística* (Universidad Nacional de Cuyo, Mendoza, Argentina) has been resumed with t. 4, appearing in 1950, under the new and capable editorship of Dr. Fritz Krüger. The journal will offer articles on Romance philology, and will stress especially aspects of Spanish American language and culture. A series of *Estudios lingüísticos* (anejos de los *Anales*) will soon appear.

V. 5 (1949, i.e. 1950) of the *Boletín del Instituto Caro y Cuervo* is dedicated to Dr. Félix Restrepo on the occasion of his nomination as honorary president of the Instituto, as decreed in 1948. The volume contains a miscellany of studies on linguistics and literary history by scholars from many countries. To implement the Instituto's activities more efficiently, two separate sections have been formed: that of lexicography (principal purpose: the continuation of Cuervo's *Diccionario de construcción y régimen*) and that of dialectology (purpose: compilation of bibliographical materials for spoken Spanish, particularly that of Colombia). Pedro Urbano González de la Calle, associated with the Instituto for the past ten years, has now transferred his residence to Mexico City, where he occupies a chair at the Colegio de México. In Buenos Aires a new institute of Colombian culture was formed in 1949 with the name of Instituto Caro y Cuervo de la Argentina, an affiliate of the Bogotá Instituto Caro y Cuervo. It proposes to strengthen cultural relations between the two countries and to support their respective literary and philological investigations.

The Uruguayan Dictionary Committee reports its activities and progress, from its inception in 1944 to the present, in *Boletín de la Academia Nacional de Letras* (t. 3, no. 9, junio, p. 3-18). Only words beginning with the letter *a* have apparently been compiled thus far from words current in Uruguay and not registered in the

Spanish Academy dictionary (although they may be equally current in other Spanish American countries).

Outstanding publications of the year are: Alfaro's *Diccionario de anglicismos,* Malmberg's *Études sur la phonétique de l'espagnol parlé en Argentine,* and Pino Saavedra's *Crónica de un soldado.*

Among important reviews of important books are five contributed by Fritz Krüger to *An. inst. ling.,* Mendoza, t. 4. They deal with Tito Saubidet, *Vocabulario y refranero criollo,* tercera edición (see *HLAS, no. 15, 1949,* item 2155); Berta Elena Vidal de Battini, *El habla rural de San Luis,* part 1, 1949 (see *HLAS, no. 15, 1949,* item 2147); J. Vicente Solá, *Diccionario de regionalismos de Salta,* segunda edición, 1947 (see item 2508 on third edition); Joaquín R. Medina, *Cantas del Valle de Tenza* (see *HLAS, no. 15, 1949,* item 2132); and Charles E. Kany, *American-Spanish Syntax,* first edition, 1945 (see *HLAS, no. 11, 1945,* item 2893), in connection with which additional examples were offered of a number of phenomena from popular Catalan speech: nouns of action in *-ada* and *-ida,* adjectives used as adverbs, *devant meu* (=*delante mío*), the use of *no més* (=*no más*), etc.

With the purpose of contributing toward the second edition of Charles E. Kany, *American-Spanish Syntax,* Ángel Rosenblat makes pertinent observations on the first edition in *Nueva rev. filol. hisp.,* año 4, no. 1, enero-marzo. He amplifies phenomena discussed in the book with examples personally noted by him in Argentina, Ecuador, and especially Venezuela, where he now resides. (These observations were duly incorporated in the second edition, University of Chicago Press, 1951).

In later numbers of the *Nueva rev. filol. hisp.,* Ángel Rosenblat treats three other books. In no. 2, abril-junio, he reviews Tomás Navarro, *El español en Puerto Rico* (see *HLAS, no. 14, 1948,* item 2595), suggesting slightly diverging causes for certain local phonetic peculiarities: for instance, a general relaxation of alveolar contact, rather than substratum influence, might explain velar *rr,* velar *n,* and aspirated *s.* In no. 4, oct.-dic., Rosenblat has two short but incisive reviews, with important remarks, on Max Leopold Wagner, *Lingue e dialetti dell' America spagnola* (see *HLAS, no. 15, 1949,* item 2149) and Bertil Malmberg, *L'Espagnol dans le Nouveau Monde: problème de linguistique générale* (see *HLAS, no. 14, 1948,* item 2590). Also Antonio Tovar briefly discussed Wagner's monograph, in *An. inst. ling.,* Mendoza, t. 4.

A second review of Berta Elena Vidal de Battini's *El habla rural de San Luis* appeared in *Romance phil.,* v. 3, no. 2-3, Nov. 1949-Feb. 1950. The reviewer was Yakov Malkiel.

Max Leopold Wagner discussed Georg Friederici, *Amerikanisches Wörterbuch* (see *HLAS, no. 13, 1947,* item 1978) in *Rev. filol. española,* t. 34, cuadernos 1-4.

2462. **Agard, Frederick B.** Present-day Judaeo Spanish in the United States (*Hispania,* v. 33, no. 3, Aug., p. 203-210). Remarks on Sephardic speech in New York and Rochester, with sample texts.

2463. **Alfaro, Ricardo J.** Diccionario de anglicismos. Enumeración, análisis y equivalencias castizas de los barbarismos, extranjerismos, neologismos y solecismos, de origen inglés que se han introducido en el castellano contemporáneo, y advertencias a traductores por . . . . Panamá, Imprenta Nacional. 849 p.
The most complete collection of anglicisms in modern Spanish: some 1300 English terms current in Spanish-speaking countries through news reports, commerce, the cinema, sports, international relations, etc. This present number of anglicisms far surpasses that of gallicisms decried in the last century by Baralt, who managed to collect 851 items. The introduction to the Diccionario (p. 5-34) appeared in *Bol. inst. Caro y Cuervo,* año 4, 1948, no. 1, enero-abril, p. 102-128, with the title *El anglicismo en el español contemporáneo.*

2464. **Andrade C., Abdón.** Contribución al estudio del folklore de Valdivia (*Bol. filol.,* t. 5, 1947-1949, i.e. 1950, p. 267-377).
Contains much popular poetry (*canciones de cuna, zamacuecas, romances,* riddles and legends) gathered from oral tradition in Valdivia and neighboring villages. The abundance of popular forms of speech is of linguistic interest.

2465. Barabino, Américo. English influence on the common speech of the River Plate (*Hispania*, v. 33, no. 2, May, p. 163-165).
English words, with new creations or special meanings, some of them not recorded in available dictionaries.

2466. Barker, George C. Pachuco. An American-Spanish argot and its social functions in Tucson, Arizona (*University of Arizona Bulletin, Social Science Bulletin no. 18*, v. 21, no. 1, Jan., p. 1-38).
Mentions the structure of Pachuco, its origin and spread, its social functions (private language of young groups not fully accepted in society), and gives texts with English translations of Pachuco conversations and songs, and a glossary of common Pachuco terms.

2467. Becco, Horacio Jorge. Don Segundo Sombra y su vocabulario (*Bol. acad. arg. let.*, t. 19, no. 71, enero-marzo, p. 49-80).
A list of 84 items: names of trees and of general fauna, with explanations, and illustrative examples taken from Güiraldes' novel.

2468. Calcaño, Julio. El castellano en Venezuela. Estudio crítico. Caracas, Ministerio de Educación Nacional, Dirección de Cultura (Biblioteca Venezolana de Cultura, Col. Andrés Bello). 571 p.
This government-sponsored reprint of the rare first edition (1897) is prefaced with an appraisal of Calcaño's work by Jesús Semprún, which appeared first in *Cultura venezolana*, año 1, no. 3, agosto, 1918. The work is locally considered a classic, though long ago Lenz characterized it as "un pobre remedo de la obra de Cuervo" and lamented its lack of modern scientific method.

2469. Calderón, Juan F. El barrilete. Notas para el léxico de la artesanía argentina (*Filología*, año 2, no. 1, enero-abril, p. 65-71).
Various kinds of kites and their construction, with drawings and descriptive vocabulary.

2470. Canfield, D. Lincoln. Spanish *ç* and *s* in the sixteenth century: a hiss and a soft whistle (*Hispania*, v. 33, no. 3, Aug., p. 233-236).
Maintains that at the time of the Conquest the letter *ç* represented *s* rather than *ts* as postulated by Amado Alonso.

2471. Coluccio, Félix. Diccionario folklórico argentino. 2. edición. Buenos Aires, El Ateneo. 503 p.
Folklore concepts and facts are explained alphabetically. A number of articles deal with popular speech forms, including *lunfardo*. See *HLAS, no. 14, 1948*, item 470.

2472. Cuervo, Rufino José. Diccionario de construcción y régimen de la lengua castellana (*Bol. inst. Caro y Cuervo*, año 6, no.

1, enero-abril, p. 97-100; no. 2, mayo-agosto, p. 269-270; no. 3, sept.-dic., p. 447-450).
Words registered: (no. 1) empeorar; (no. 2), emperezar; (no. 3) empero.

2473. ————. Disquisiciones sobre filología castellana. Edición, prólogo y notas de Rafael Torres Quintero. Bogotá, Instituto Caro y Cuervo (Publ. no. 4). xvi, 666 p.
A noteworthy edition of Cuervo's so-called minor works published previously under the editorship of Luis Alfonso in *El castellano en América* (see *HLAS, no. 13, 1947*, item 1973) and in *Disquisiciones sobre filología castellana*, Buenos Aires, El Ateneo, 1948, in addition to some others of less importance, hitherto unpublished.

2474. Dávila Garibi, J. Ignacio. Algunas observaciones acerca de la lengua Opata o Tegüima, rica en vocablos de interés para el estudio de la flora y de la fauna regionales. México. 46 p.

2475. Davis, Jack Emory. The *americanismos* in *El inglés de los güesos* (*Hispania*, v. 33, no. 4, Nov., p. 333-337).
Some 300 *americanismos* are found in Benito Lynch's novel. [F. Aguilera]

2476. Donnell, Albert L. El lenguaje del "Pensador Mexicano." México. 111 p.
The aim is laudable: a comparison of early 19th-century Mexican speech, as expressed in Fernández de Lizardi's works, with that of today. But can a single author be conclusive proof? Some lack of scientific method. Fails to acknowledge sources of many statements taken directly from others. Thesis, University of Mexico.

2477. Flórez, Luis. Cuestiones del español hablado en Montería y Sincelejo (*Bol. inst. Caro y Cuervo*, t. 5, 1949, i.e. 1950, p. 124-162).
Linguistic material gathered in sections of northern Colombia during a ten-day visit: phonology, morphology, vocabulary (fauna, flora, occupations, commerce, dwellings, food, dress, place names, etc.).

2478. ————. Del castellano en Colombia. El habla del Chocó (*Bol. inst. Caro y Cuervo*, año 6, no. 1, enero-abril, p. 110-116).
Brief notes compiled during a 17-day sojourn (1948) in the Colombian department of Chocó bordering on Panama and the Pacific. Local pronunciation will be treated more fully in the author's forthcoming work, *Pronunciación del español en Bogotá*. Of interest are final *m* (*tambiém, deciam*, etc.), preservation of *cúyo* (*¿Esto cúyo es?*), etc.

2479. Fogelquist, Donald F. The bilingualism of Paraguay (*Hispania,* v. 33, no. 1, Feb., p. 23-27).
Miscellaneous remarks on the nature of Guaraní and why the average Paraguayan prefers it to official Spanish.

2480. García Blanco, M. Voces americanas en el teatro de Tirso de Molina (*Bol. inst. Caro y Cuervo,* t. 5, 1949, i.e. 1950, p. 264-283).
A list of 39 words of American origin culled, with extracts, from the plays *Amazonas en las Indias* and *La lealtad contra la envidia.* (Tirso lived in Hispaniola, 1616-1618.)

2481. Giese, Wilhelm. Hispanismos en el mapuche (*Bol. filol.,* t. 5, 1947-1949, i.e. 1950, p. 115-132).
Spanish words current in popular Mapuche at the turn of the last century, listed in phonetic script according to concept groups (food, drinks, dress, plants, etc.). Sketchy and insufficiently documented. In a following note to the article (p. 133-135) the editor of the journal, Rodolfo Oroz, adds the principal divergencies of pronunciation and vocabulary that have crept into Mapuche speech in the last 40 years.

2482. González de la Calle, Pedro Urbano. "Lo compramos con él" (*Bol. inst. Caro y Cuervo,* año 6, no. 2, mayo-agosto, p. 282-292).
Discusses the psychological basis of the construction *lo compramos con él,* meaning "He and I bought it."

2483. Grases, Pedro. La idea de "alboroto" en castellano (*Bol. inst. Caro y Cuervo,* año 6, no. 3, sept.-dic., p. 384-430).
Interesting notes on the semantic development of the words *bululú* and *mitote* in particular, and on 26 other words expressing "alboroto" in Spain and Spanish America.

2484. ————. Locha. Nombre de fracción monetaria en Venezuela (*Bol. inst. Caro y Cuervo,* t. 5, 1949, i.e. 1950, p. 112-123).
Postulates the formation: *la ochava > lochava > locha > la locha.*

2485. Hoge, Henry W., and Walter Poesse. A bibliography of articles treating of certain lexical and grammatical aspects of Spanish (*Hispania,* v. 33, no. 4, Nov., p. 342-347).
Useful list of 170 entries selected from 13 principal journals in the Hispanic field from 1900 to July 1950. Many of the items deal with American-Spanish divergencies.

2486. Kahane, Henry, and Renée Kahane. The position of the actor expression in colloquial Mexican Spanish (*Language,* v. 26, no. 2, April-June, p. 236-263).
Attempts to show that the position of the subject follows a (flexible) system, depending on number and position of other elements in the ex-

pression (*Juan viene mañana; mañana viene Juan*), its own form (noun or pronoun), kind of action (imperfective: *los pájaros cantan;* perfective: *cantan los pájaros*), impersonal (*se me ocurre una idea*), reflective passive (*se ven los cerros,* but *las calabazas se cuecen en dos horas*), etc. This contribution to descriptive grammar offers some interesting findings, but classification seems unduly complicated.

2487. Krüger, Fritz. Etimologías hispánicas (*An. inst. ling.,* Mendoza, t. 4, p. 82-113).
Among other words deals extensively with *pingo,* "horse," as derived from *pinga,* "drop."

2488. Kunath, K. La casa rural en el este de Guatemala (*An. inst. ling.,* Mendoza, t. 4, p. 140-156).
A "words and things" article, with 14 drawings and 9 photographs, on rustic homes in eastern Guatemala: *la casa, la puerta, la cama, la cocina, el horno.*

2489. MacCurdy, Raymond R. The Spanish dialect in St. Bernard Parish, Louisiana. Albuquerque, New Mexico, The University of New Mexico Press (University of New Mexico Publications in Language and Literature, no. 6). 88 p.
Part of a doctoral dissertation (1948) based on phonograph-recorded texts spontaneously related by natives. Contents: the land and the people, descendants of early Spanish settlers from the Canary Islands (p. 14-25), phonology and morphology (p. 26-44), vocabulary (p. 45-88). The dialect belongs to the Caribbean linguistic zone and contains many gallicisms, Canary Island dialectalisms, and archaisms. For restrictions, see L. B. Kiddle's review in *Hispania,* v. 34, no. 2, May, p. 221.

2490. Malaret, Augusto. Antología de americanismos (*Bol. inst. Caro y Cuervo,* t. 5, 1949, i.e. 1950, p. 214-226).
A fragment of the author's work of similar title, containing 100 items with illustrative examples culled from Colombian authors.

2491. ————. Lexicón de fauna y flora (*Bol. inst. Caro y Cuervo,* año 6, no. 1, enero-abril, p. 81-96; no. 2, mayo-agosto, p. 253-268; no. 3, sept.-dic., p. 431-446).
Continuation: (no. 1) *escribano* to *guabá,* (no. 2) *guabairo* to *guas,* (no. 3) *guasa* to *huanque.*

2492. Malmberg, Bertil. Études sur la phonétique de l'espagnol parlé en Argentine. Lund, Sweden, Alf Lombard (Études Romanes de Lund, 10). 290 p.
The first extended study on the phonetics of spoken Spanish in Argentina, with special reference to Buenos Aires and the River Plate region. A critical examination of limited studies and scattered references by previous scholars (Tiscornia, Miguel de Toro, Maspero, Henríquez Ureña, Alonso, Rosenblat, Capdevila, Castro, and others), together with the results of the author's own observations and experiments conducted *in loco* from April to August, 1946.

Contains 15 pages of transcribed phonetic texts, a helpful index of cited words and forms, and a lengthy bibliography. An excellent contribution to American-Spanish studies.

2493. Meier, Harri. Esp. *garúa*, port. *caruja* (*Nueva rev. filol. hisp.*, año 4, no. 3, julio-sept., p. 270-274).
This note suggests a modification in Corominas' derivation of *garúa* from a Latin source (as against the indigenous source proposed by previous scholars).

2494. Moder Pérez de Valenzuela, Stella. Chilenismos de Maitencillo (*Bol. filol.*, t. 5, 1947-1949, i.e. 1950, p. 379-422).
A study of the vocabulary current among fishermen on the Chilean coast of Maitencillo, not registered in local dictionaries. Contains photographs and drawings of local instruments.

2495. Oroz, Rodolfo. Metáforas relativas a las partes del cuerpo humano en la lengua popular chilena (*Bol. inst. Caro y Cuervo*, t. 5, 1949, i.e. 1950, p. 85-100).
A list of slang designations for parts of the body, especially with humorous or unfavorable implications.

2496. Otero D'Costa, Enrique. Mestizajes del castellano en Colombia (*Bol. inst. Caro y Cuervo*, año 6, no. 1, enero-abril, p. 15-80).
Continuation (see *HLAS, no. 12, 1946*, item 2351). Tells how *tainismos* penetrated into the heart of Colombia, and discusses some 48 Quechua words common in present-day Colombian speech. Especially detailed treatment of *Cundinamarca, papa, pisco, quina.*

2497. Patín Maceo, M. A. Notas gramaticales (*Bol. acad. dom. lengua*, año 10, no. 34, abril, p. 3-13).
Continuation.

2498. Pino Saavedra, Yolando. Crónica de un soldado de la guerra del Pacífico (*Bol. filol.*, t. 5, 1947-1949, i.e. 1950, p. 7-114).
A linguistic study of a hitherto unpublished manuscript (formerly the property of Rodolfo Lenz) detailing the military adventures in Peru of the Chilean soldier Hipólito Gutiérrez, who departed from Chillán in 1879 and returned to Valparaíso in 1881. The historical document represents popular speech of the central-southern Chilean zone, much of it current today. The study of the language (p. 14-58: orthography, phonetics, morphology, syntax, vocabulary) is followed by the complete text (p. 59-95) with its original spellings. Of interest and value to American-Spanish dialectology. Also published separately.

2499. Rabanales Ortiz, Ambrosio. Uso tropológico, en el lenguaje chileno, de nombres del reino vegetal (*Bol. filol.*, t. 5, 1947-1949, i.e. 1950, p. 137-243).
A lengthy and instructive study of the metaphorical application of names of plants to physical and mental aspects of man and animals, to objects, actions, games, and general concepts. 20 drawings, helpful indices.

2500. Ragucci, Rodolfo M. Neologismos de mis lecturas (*Bol. acad. arg. let.*, t. 19, no. 71, enero-marzo, p. 37-48; no. 72, abril-junio, p. 143-168).
Continuation: (no. 71) *altos* to *amalevarse;* (no. 72) *amalhayado* to *americanada.*

2501. Robledo, Emilio. Orígenes castizos del habla popular de Antioquia y Caldas (*Bol. inst. Caro y Cuervo*, t. 5, 1949, i.e. 1950, p. 176-191).
A partial list of popular forms gleaned from the classics and still current in regions of Colombia. Most of them, to be sure, may be heard anywhere.

2502. Rodríguez Demorizi, Emilio. Refranero dominicano. Roma, G. Menaglia. 274 p.
A collection of proverbs, most of them of peninsular origin, and other popular sayings and idioms. Includes items, from the unpublished *Refranero criollo* of the Dominican J. A. Puig Rodríguez, of some 350 proverbs glossed by Puig in rustic speech, with an approximate phonetic transcription (without phonetic symbols).

2503. Rosenblat, Ángel. Vacilaciones y cambios de género motivados por el artículo (*Bol. inst. Caro y Cuervo*, t. 5, 1949, i.e. 1950, p. 21-32).
Discusses words like *el hambre, la hambre; el arte, la arte; el azúcar, la azúcar*, etc., with their changing genders in Spain and America.

2504. Sánchez Arévalo, Francisco. Notas sobre el lenguaje de Río de Oro (*Bol. inst. Caro y Cuervo*, año 6, no. 2, mayo-agosto, p. 214-252).
Principally a list of words and expressions current in the Provincia del Sur capital, Departamento del Magdalena.

2505. Selva, Juan B. Sufijos americanos (*Bol. inst. Caro y Cuervo*, t. 5, 1949, i.e. 1950, p. 192-213).
Lists many words current in America (often of questionable etymology) with the deprecatory suffixes *-ango, -anga, -engo, -enga, -ingo, -inga, -ongo, -onga, -ungo, -unga.* Based on a chapter of the author's *Crecimiento del habla.*

2506. ———. Trascendencia de la gramática de Bello y el estado actual de los estudios gramaticales. Buenos Aires, Kapelusz. 245 p.
Shows how the Academy grammar has in many instances adopted Bello's points of view; but occasionally it improves on Bello, as in certain matters of classification and nomenclature.

2507. Sequera Cardot, Juan. Estudio sobre el "que." Caracas, Ávila Gráfica. 84 p.

A brief essay on the well-known expletive *que* and the so-called gallicist *que*, repeating the theories of Bello and Cuervo, with many new examples, but no definite source references. The so-called gallicist *que* is probably of peninsular Spanish origin.

2508. Solá, José Vicente. Diccionario de regionalismos de Salta (República Argentina). [3rd edition.] Prólogo del doctor Carlos Ibarguren. Buenos Aires, Amorrortu. 366 p.

This new edition (on 2nd edition see *HLAS, no. 13, 1947*, item 2019) has fifty additional pages of new material. It received the first prize of the Comisión Nacional de Cultura.

2509. Speratti Piñero, E. S. Los americanismos en *Tirano Banderas* (*Filología*, año 2, no. 3, sept.-dic., p. 225-291).

A capable appraisal of the style and atmosphere in *Tirano Banderas*, by Valle Inclán (who visited Spanish America in 1892, 1910, and 1921), followed by a list of 187 items, *americanismos*, gleaned from his well-known novel. The entries contain local dictionary meanings followed by Valle Inclán's usage of the word, and frequently by that of Spanish American authors.

2510. Tejera, Emiliano. Palabras indíjenas de la isla de Santo Domingo (*Bol. acad. dom. lengua*, año 10, no. 34, abril, p. 30-34).

Continuation: *guayero* to *hagueigabón.*

2511. Wagner, Max Leopold. Apuntaciones sobre el caló bogotano (*Bol. inst. Caro y Cuervo*, año 6, no. 2, mayo-agosto, p. 181-213).

Explains the origin of over 100 words (a sampling of Colombian thieves' slang) supplied to him by the Instituto and prepared by police officials in Bogotá. Some of the words are peninsular, some American, and many Argentinian. A complete list of Colombian argot is a desideratum.

2512. ————. El sufijo hispanoamericano -*eco* para denotar defectos físicos y morales (*Nueva rev. filol. hisp.*, año 4, no. 2, abril-junio, p. 105-114).

Stresses interferences of the deprecatory suffixes -*eta*, -*eto*, -*eco*, -*enco*, -*engo*, etc. Suggests that -*eco*, prevalent in the Náhuatl linguistic zone (Mexico, Central America), is an imitation of the Náhuatl adjectival ending -*ic*, influenced by Spanish -*eto*, and by -*eco* (<Náhuatl -*ecatl*, denoting provenience).

2513. Zappacosta de Willmott, M. E. Problemas del hispanoamericano (*An. inst. ling.*, Mendoza, t. 4, p. 127-139).

Sketches some of the linguistic problems involved in the study of American Spanish, especially as envisaged in recent publications of Max Leopold Wagner, Bertil Malmberg, and Charles E. Kany.

Spanish American Literature

GENERAL

2514. Arango H., Rubén. Mi literatura. Crítica de literatura colombiana. Medellín, Colombia, Imprenta Departamental. 350 p., tables.
Superficial survey of Colombian letters from Jiménez de Quesada to *piedracielismo*. [A. Flores]

2515. Arenas Luque, Fermín V. Dos poetisas místicas de América, Sor Juana Inés de la Cruz y María Raquel Adler. Buenos Aires. 94 p.
Two articles serving as sketchy introductions to selected poems by two poetesses forcibly coupled together. [F. Aguilera]

2516. Sánchez, Luis Alberto. Nueva historia de la literatura americana. Asunción, Guarania. 598 p.

Fifth edition, nearer the "definitive" stage than the preceding ones. First published in 1937 as *Historia de la literatura americana, desde los orígenes hasta 1936* (Santiago, Ercilla); the next two editions (1940 and 1942, same publisher) had the subtitles, respectively, *Desde los orígenes hasta nuestros tiempos* and *Desde los orígenes hasta nuestros días*. The fourth edition bore a new title, *Nueva historia de la literatura americana* (Buenos Aires, Americalee, 1944), and was described by its author as "una refundición total . . . casi una obra nueva." [F. Aguilera]

2517. ————. La tierra del quetzal. Santiago, Ercilla. 217 p.
Informative, readable essays on diverse aspects of Guatemalan literature, from the *Popol-Vuh* to Arévalo Martínez. [A. Flores]

THE COLONIAL PERIOD

IRVING A. LEONARD

AN ever widening base for the study of colonial literature is the continuing publication of inedited works and the reprinting of rare and inaccessible books of the period. The additions of such texts in 1950 are fairly numerous and are of considerable importance, particularly those relating to the dramatic literature of the colonial centuries (items 2518, 2521, 2527). The inclusion of a new minor figure in the pantheon of Peruvian letters is facilitated by the third volume of the valuable *Clásicos peruanos,* edited by the indefatigable Jesuit scholar, Father Vargas Ugarte.

In the comparably modest output of studies during 1950 the number of essays and documentary materials relating to that first American writer, the Inca Garcilaso de la Vega, is a notable feature indicating the steadily increasing attention the Peruvian mestizo chronicler claims as a literary figure (items 2528, 2529, 2531, 2533, 2534). Among the works of a more generalized character the excellent synthesis of the cultural history of colonial Mexico by Jiménez Rueda stands out as one of the most valuable contributions.

TEXTS

2518. Aguilar, Cristóbal de. Selección dramática de . . . , autor de la Córdoba colonial. Prólogo y notas por J. Luis Trenti Rocamora. Buenos Aires, Comisión Nacional de Cultura, Instituto Nacional de Estudios de Teatro. 144 p.

The text of four lively sainetes, *Venció al desprecio el desdén, El premio de la codicia, Los niños y los locos dicen verdades,* and *La industria contra la fuerza,* together with a short drama, *El triunfo de la prudencia y oficios de la amistad,* all by an 18th-century writer who, though born in Spain, spent nearly all his eighty years in Córdoba, Argentina. He wrote an unknown number of plays, apparently more for reading than performance. A valuable addition to the growing repertory of colonial creole drama.

2519. Balli, Juan Bautista. Oración en elogio de la jurisprudencia pronunciada en la Real Universidad de México en el año del Señor de 1596. México, Jus. 89 p.
Facsimile edition of an unrecorded product of the colonial Mexican press found in a collection of books from Lima, Peru. Text is a discourse by a lawyer son of a local printer of Mexico City. Daniel Kuri Breña adds a careful analysis and Salvador Ugarte a bibliographical note. An edition of 125 copies of this work in Latin.

2520. Carvajal y Robles, Rodrigo de. Fiestas de Lima por el nacimiento del Príncipe Baltasar Carlos, Lima, 1632. Prólogo y edición de Francisco López Estrada. Sevilla. 194 p.
A contemporary versified description in sixteen *silvas* of the festivities in Lima celebrating for months the birth of the short-lived prince. This is one of the few *relaciones* of this sort in the colonial period to have literary merit; it presents a colorful account of the varied program of spectacles enjoyed by the *limeño* public. Reprinted with brief introduction, synopses of each *silva,* and index of names and places.

2521. Johnson, Harvey L. La *Historia de Comberción de San Pablo,* drama guatemalteco del siglo XVIII (*Nueva rev. filol. hisp.,* año 4, no. 2, abril-junio, p. 115-160).
Discussion and text of a manuscript play of 1,280 verses dated December 22, 1772 and signed José Aroche, which was written and performed in Guatemala. Its version of the Biblical incident is simple and direct and ". . . al alcance de todos encierra en pequeño espacio una acción sencilla sagrada y profana, notable por lo declamatorio y lo pintoresco del estilo." Carefully edited and with a discerning introduction, it offers a curious example of the survival of religious drama in the 18th century.

2522. Juana Inés de la Cruz, Sor. Poesías líricas. Segunda edición. Edición y prólogo de Joaquín Ramírez Cabañas. México, Editorial Porrúa (Col. de Escritores Mexicanos, 1). 270 p.

2523. Muñoz, Diego. Descripción de la Provincia de San Pedro y San Pablo de Michoacán, en las Indias de la Nueva España. Crónica del siglo XVI. Introducción de José Ramírez Flores. Guadalajara, México, Imprenta Gráfica (Ediciones de la Junta Auxiliar Jalisciense de la Sociedad Mexicana de Geografía y Estadística), 1950 [cover 1951]. 75, iii p.
This 16th-century ecclesiastical chronicle was also published serially in the *Boletín de la Junta Auxiliar Jalisciense de la Sociedad Mexicana de Geografía y Estadística.*

2524. El perico y la rabia (*Bol. arch. gen.,* México, t. 21, no. 2, p. 303-318).
A keenly satirical literary document of the late 18th or early 19th century, subtitled *Diálogo entre un médico y un consultor,* of possible attribution to Fernández de Lizardi.

2525. Ripalda, Hieronymo de. Texto de la edición considerada como príncipe de la *Doctrina Cristiana* con una exposición breve. Prólogo de José Bravo Ugarte. México, Editorial Buena Prensa. 69 p.
Written by the Jesuit Gerónimo de Ripalda (1535-1618), this *Doctrina Cristiana* was the most universally used in Hispanic countries from its first edition in 1591 to the present. Reprintings in many languages and dialects total many million copies.

2526. Rivas Sacconi, José Manuel. Romance de la defensa de Cartagena (*Rev. Indias,* v. 36, no. 112, p. 37-51).
A ballad of 1741.

2527. Vargas Ugarte, Rubén (ed.). Obras de don Lorenzo de las Llamosas. Introducción y notas de . . . . Lima, Tipografía Peruana (Clásicos Peruanos, v. 3). 215 p.
Writings of a Peruvian creole (1665?-1705?) who went to Spain in 1691 and, after a checkered career in the Peninsula, including imprisonment, and in France and Italy, apparently died in his forties. An obscure writer in prose and verse, much of which has remained unpublished, he is represented by an epic poem in ten cantos, *Demofonte y Filis,* of considerable merit, a brief elegy on the death of Sor Juana Inés de la Cruz, and a "comedia zarzuela," *También se vengan los dioses.* Excisions in text and omission of other writings limit value of this volume for a full study of a minor figure.

INDIVIDUAL FIGURES

2528. Aguilar Priego, Rafael. El hijo del Inca Garcilaso. Nuevos documentos sobre Diego de Vargas (*Bol. real acad. cien., bellas letras, nobles artes,* v. 21, no. 63, p. 45-48).
Data from notarial records relating to the natural son of the mestizo author of *Los comentarios reales.*

2529. Antolínez, Gilberto. Agonística vida de Garcilaso El Inca (*Cult. univ.,* no. 20-21, julio-oct., p. 59-68).
A heavily Freudian analysis in turgid prose of the Peruvian mestizo chronicler.

2530. Canedo, Lino G. Un cronista peruano en el siglo XVII, Fr. Diego de Córdoba Salinas (*Rev. Indias*, Madrid, v. 4, año 10, no. 41, julio-sept., p. 477-505).

2531. Durand, José. El Inca Garcilaso, historiador apasionado (*Cuad. amer.*, año 9, v. 52, no. 4, julio-agosto, p. 153-168).
The Inca Garcilaso, disillusioned by his fortunes in Spain, turned to recreating the history of his Peruvian culture, ". . . movido por la íntima necesidad de hacer un poco de luz sobre su propia vida." This article is the text of a lecture summarizing investigations of the author to appear in a volume.

2532. Hernández de Alba, Guillermo. José Celestino Mutis, poeta latino (*Bol. inst. Caro y Cuervo*, v. 5, 1949, i.e. 1950, p. 386-405).
The celebrated scientist who spent a large part of his life in colonial Colombia not only used Latin in his scientific writing but also composed short poems in the classical medium, examples of which are appended in facsimile.

2533. Martí-Abelló, Rafael. Garcilaso Inca de la Vega, un hombre del Renacimiento (*Rev. hisp. mod.*, año 16, no. 1-4, enero-dic., p. 99-112).
An admirably documented essay placing the Peruvian mestizo chronicler (1539-1616) well within the currents of the Spanish Renaissance. The increasing importance of the individual in his own peculiar character together with the prevailing utopianism and theories of religious conversion and of the "just war," with all of which the Inca Garcilaso preoccupies himself in his writings, clearly identify him with his contemporaneous artistic and intellectual movement.

2534. Porras Barrenechea, Raúl. El Inca Garcilaso de la Vega en Montilla. La familia de San Francisco Solano. Un documento cervantino. Conferencia pronunciada por . . . en el Teatro Garnelo de Montilla el día 14 de marzo de 1950. Montilla, Spain. 36 p.
From notarial records of Montilla, Spain, the author learns that El Inca Garcilaso lived in that town from 1561 to 1591, with interruptions in 1564 and 1570 for military service; he moved to Córdoba in 1591. In 1563 he changed his name from Gómez Suárez de Figueroa to Gómez Suárez de la Vega, and later to Garcilaso de la Vega. This lecture, with slightly different title, is printed also in *Bol. real acad. cien., bellas letras, nobles artes*, v. 21, no. 63, p. 15-44. (The second and third parts of the booklet do not refer to Garcilaso.)

2535. Porras Muñoz, Guillermo. Nuevos datos sobre Bernardo de Balbuena (*Rev. Indias*, Madrid, año 10, no. 39, enero-marzo, p. 591-595).
Reproduces text of document discovered in the Archive of the Indies at Seville, a petition of Balbuena for a *licencia* to go to the Indies

(New Spain), with supporting data regarding himself. The latter indicates that he was unmarried, that his father was in Nueva Galicia, and that he was a native of Valdepeñas, living there until he was twenty-one years of age.

2536. Rubio Orbe, Gonzalo. Francisco Eugenio Javier de Santa Cruz y Espejo. Biografía. Quito, Talleres Gráficos Nacionales. 294 p., illus.
A biography of the 18th-century Ecuadorean rationalist and writer which was awarded a national prize in 1943.

2537. Zertuche, F. M. Evocación de Gutierre de Cetina (*Universidad*, Monterrey, no. 8-9, julio, p. 49-62).
Reproduces documents relating to the proceedings at Puebla de los Ángeles in 1554 growing out of the fatal wounding of the celebrated Spanish poet. The provenance of these documents is not clearly indicated.

CRITICISM, TRANSLATIONS, MISCELLANEOUS STUDIES

2538. Arrom, José J. Estudios de literatura hispanoamericana. Habana, Úcar García. 159 p.
Collection of six lectures and essays, of which the following three deal with colonial subjects: *Las letras en Cuba antes de 1608*, p. 11-31, first published in *Rev. cub.*, 1944; *Consideraciones sobre "El príncipe jardinero y fingido Cloridano,"* p. 33-70, a Cuban play by Santiago de Pita published about 1733, and based on an Italian operatic piece of Giacenti A. Cicognini (1606-1660) with borrowings from Lope de Vega, Calderón, Moreto, Sor Juana Inés de la Cruz, and Cervantes; and *Entremeses coloniales*, p. 71-91, a brief survey of short skits surviving from colonial theater. The last-mentioned was also published in *Mem. cuarto cong. inst. int. lit. iberoam.*, under the title *Sainetes y sainetistas coloniales*.

2539. Balaguer, Joaquín. Colón, precursor literario (*Bol. inst. Caro y Cuervo*, v. 5, 1949, i.e. 1950, p. 372-385).
In the pages of Columbus's diary describing the tropical beauty of the islands discovered in the New World the author perceives a mystic feeling for nature and a poetic impression of landscapes which have points of contact with later writers such as Chateaubriand, Bernardin de Saint-Pierre, Victor Hugo, and others of the Romantic period and possibly influenced them.

2540. Castagnino, Raúl H. Esquema de la literatura dramática argentina (1717-1949). Buenos Aires, Instituto de Historia del Teatro Americano. 125 p.
A booklet manual with schematic bibliographical outline of Argentine theater history, of which chapters 2 to 4 refer to periods 1717-1810 ("Dramática colonial") and 1810-1820 ("Expresiones dramáticas de la Revolución").

2541. Cook, Pauline (trans.). The pathless grove. Sonnets of Sor Juana Inés de la Cruz

(1651-1695), "The Tenth Muse of Mexico." Prairie City, Illinois, Decker Press. 53 p.

Sensitive translations of twenty-two sonnets and an extract from Sor Juana's famous prose *Respuesta a Sor Filotea*, prefaced by an excellent biographical sketch.

2542. Fligelman, Frieda (trans.). The discovery of the New World by Christopher Columbus. A comedy in verse by Lope de Vega (1562-1635). Prose translation by . . . . Berkeley, California, Gillick Press. 62 p.

El nuevo mundo descubierto por Cristóbal Colón, one of the great Spanish dramatist's less inspired plays, said to be the first play written about America, is rendered into English for the first time.

2543. Forero, Manuel José. Hallazgo de un libro de Jiménez de Quesada (*Bol. inst. Caro y Cuervo*, Bogotá, v. 5, 1949, i.e. 1950, p. 411-421).

A copy of a manuscript work written by the conqueror of New Granada against the history of Paulo Giovio and defending Spain was discovered recently in the library of the University of Valladolid in Spain. Long paragraphs from it are quoted in this descriptive article.

2544. Gandía, Enrique de. El liberalismo colonial (*Rev. cub.*, v. 26, enero-junio, p. 90-111).

From the pages of that curious work *El lazarillo de ciegos caminantes* of Concolorcorvo (1773), the author extracts much data disproving the alleged tyranny, repression, and intolerance of Spanish rule. He says the satirical references to religious and other matters indicate a freedom of thought and expression believed non-existent in colonial Hispanic America. The author seems to overlook the apparent need to publish this work under a pseudonym and the false indication of a press at Gijón when it was printed surreptitiously in Lima.

2545. Jiménez Rueda, Julio. Historia de la cultura en México. El virreinato. México, Cultura. xv, 335 p.

An excellent synthesis of cultural history, broadly defined to include all products of human activity in colonial New Spain, by the foremost cultural historian of Mexico. This work is part of a trilogy of similar surveys of the pre-Hispanic and republican periods of Mexican history.

2546. Leonard, Irving A. Caviedes, José Hernández, and the 'under dog'; a parallelism (*Hispania*, v. 33, no. 1, Feb., p. 28-29).

A note of protest with similar phrasing in behalf of the underprivileged is observed in the brief poem *Privilegios del pobre* of the 17th-century *limeño* satirist, Juan del Valle Caviedes, and in Canto VIII, verses 1343-1348, 1367-1384 of the 19th-century gaucho epic, *Martín Fierro*.

2547. Lohmann Villena, Guillermo. Las comedias del Corpus Christi en Lima en 1635 y 1636 (*Mar del sur*, año 2, v. 4, no. 11, mayo-junio, p. 21-23).

The mystery plays *La margarita del Cielo* and *Las dos columnas de Hércules* were performed by sixteen actors under the direction of Cristóbal López de Rodas and Gonzalo de Aguilar, "autores de comedias."

2548. ————. Romances, coplas y cantares en la conquista del Perú (*Mar del sur*, v. 3, no. 9, enero-feb., p. 18-40).

The chronicles and other accounts and documents of the Conquest yield numerous references and even the text of ballads and songs known by the conquistadors and of some that grew out of their feats.

2549. López Cámara, Francisco. El cartesianismo en Sor Juana y Sigüenza y Góngora (*Fil. letras*, t. 20, no. 39, julio-sept., p. 107-132).

Clear traces of Descartes's ideas are perceptible particularly in the *Libra astronómica* of the 17th-century Mexican savant, Carlos de Sigüenza y Góngora (1645-1700), and in the long poem *Primero sueño* of his famous contemporary and friend, Sor Juana Inés de la Cruz (1651-1695). and both writers were precursors of the 18th-century Enlightenment in New Spain.

2550. Mata Gavidia, José. Introducción a la *Rusticatio mexicana*. Guatemala, Imprenta Universitaria. 112 p.

A fairly comprehensive exegesis of Landívar's famous Latin poem of late 18th-century Guatemala, with brief, documented biography of author, the genesis of his work, and its virtues and human elements, together with an appendix of tributes by distinguished critics.

2551. Millares Carlo, Agustín. Investigaciones biobibliográficas iberoamericanas. Época colonial. México, Universidad Nacional Autónoma de México, Instituto de Historia (Publicaciones, primera serie, no. 17). 153 p., illus.

A collection of eight revised and expanded bibliographical articles on: José de Anchieta, 16th-century Brazilian missionary; two Dominican friars named Alonso de Espinosa; Bishop Zumárraga's library; Bartolomé de las Casas; Bernardo de la Vega; Juan Ruiz de Alarcón; and Sancho de Muñón.

2552. Miró, Rodrigo. La cultura colonial en Panamá. México, B. Costa-Amic. 69 p.

A reprinting of three articles: *De la vida intelectual en la colonia panameña* (p. 11-36); *La educación colonial panameña* (p. 37-60); and *"La política del mundo," primera manifestación del teatro nacional* (p. 61-69). Many celebrated writers stopped briefly in Panama, the crossroads of the Hispanic American world, while others born there distinguished themselves elsewhere. Education was private, mainly by religious orders. *Política del mundo* was a verse tragedy of Víctor de la Guardia y Ayala, written and performed in Panama in 1809, its theme reminiscent of Shakespeare's *Julius Caesar.*

2553. **Robles, Oswaldo.** Filósofos mexicanos del siglo XVI. México, Librería de Manuel Porrúa (Biblioteca Mexicana, 4). 142 p., illus.

A chapter each is devoted to Alonso de la Vera Cruz, who introduced philosophic studies into New Spain, Tomás de Mercado, translator of Aristotle, and the Jesuit Antonio Rubio, peripatetic philosopher. The concluding chapter treats more briefly Bishop Zumárraga, Las Casas, and Vasco de Quiroga.

2554. **Romero de Terreros y Vinent, Manuel.** La biblioteca de Luis Lagarto. México, Imprenta Aldina. 39 p., illus.

A collection of 72 books of a renowned painter of miniatures and illuminator of books of early 17th-century Mexico as recorded in document found in Archivo General de la Nación. Works in Portuguese, Italian, and Castilian are chiefly of devotion but include literary writings of Lope de Vega, Camoens, Garcilaso de la Vega, Mateo Alemán, Bernardo de Balbuena, Juan de la Cueva, and a few pastoral novels. Full identification of individual works and facsimile reproductions of title pages of several.

2555. **Schons, Dorothy.** The Moore Collection of Araucaniana *(Library Chronicle,* University of Texas, v. 4, no. 1, fall, p. 43-46).

2556. **Torre Revello, José.** Un teatro porteño de los comienzos del siglo XIX: el Teatro del Sol *(Filología,* año 2, no. 2, mayo-agosto, p. 176-188).

Reproduces documentation relating to a short-lived theater house in which an *empresario,* José Cortés, wished to give vaudeville performances of "volatines, sombras chinescas, pantomimas, bailes y cantos" in 1807. The structure of the playhouse was so obviously a fire trap that permission for such entertainments was soon withdrawn.

2557. **Trenti Rocamora, J. Luis.** El repertorio de la dramática colonial hispanoamericana. Buenos Aires, Alea. 110 p.

A reprint in booklet form of bibliographical article published in *Bol. estud. teatro,* año 7, t. 7,

no. 26, julio-sept., p. 104-125 (see *HLAS, no. 15, 1949,* item 2173).

2558. UNIVERSIDAD DE SAN CARLOS. Estudios Landivarianos. Guatemala, no. 21, oct.-dic. (edición extraordinaria). 246 p.

These *Estudios Landivarianos* in honor of the 18th-century Jesuit Latin poet, Rafael Landívar, author of the *Rusticatio Mexicana,* are divided into four parts: 1, "Onorate l'altissimo poeta," a series of eulogies by modern critics; 2, "Documenta Landivariana," some eight archival documents, including a *partida de nacimiento;* 3, "Retorno a la patria," concerning the return of the poet's remains to Guatemala; and 4, "Antología Landivariana," with translations in various languages of the salutation to Guatemala in the opening verses of the poem, and of other fragments of the *Rusticatio.*

2559. **Vidal Martínez, Leopoldo.** El Ollantay incaico y el Ollantay colonial *(Mar del sur,* v. 3, no. 9, enero-feb., p. 42-51).

Author finds by internal evidence that the well-known play written in Quechua was 18th-century work of Father Antonio Valdez. Apparently this critic is unaware of an investigation, made by the late Professor E. C. Hills over thirty years ago, reaching similar conclusions through internal evidence, particularly the versification, which corresponded to that of the Spanish *comedias.* See E. C. Hills, *Hispanic Studies,* Stanford University Press, 1929.

ADDENDUM

2560. **León Pinelo, Diego de.** Semblanza de la Universidad de San Marcos por . . . (1648). Traducida del latín por Luis Antonio Eguiguren. Lima (Biblioteca del IV Centenario de la Fundación de la Universidad Nacional Mayor de San Marcos 1551-1951), 1949. 152 p.

The *Hypomnema apologeticum* of the learned Diego de León Pinelo, the famous *converso* of Peru, written in defense of the University of San Marcos, which was omitted from consideration by Justo Lipsio (Joest Lips) in his treatise on institutions of higher learning. This seldom consulted work is useful for an understanding of the university organization and the cultural and intellectual life of 17th-century Peru.

THE NINETEENTH AND TWENTIETH CENTURIES

ÁNGEL FLORES, CONCHA MELÉNDEZ, FRANCISCO AGUILERA, AND JOSÉ JUAN ARROM

GENERAL

ATTEMPTS at panoramic surveys (e.g., Martínez' Mexican literature and Arango's Colombian literature) were on the whole not very successful. There were, however a provocative period appraisal (*La literatura uruguaya del 900* by Ardao and others) and excellent critical studies of individual writers: Larra's *Artl,* Morales' *Echeverría* and Rodríguez Monegal's *Rodó.* [A. Flores]

PROSE FICTION

EN la producción novelesca de 1950, la novela de análisis psicológico y carácter urbano prevalece sobre las llamadas "novelas de la tierra," aunque aparecieran con predominante elemento de naturaleza, *Viento fuerte* de Miguel Ángel Asturias y *El mar es como un potro* de Antonio Arráiz. Esta última es una nueva edición de Losada de la novela *Daniel Velázquez*. Eduardo Barrios con *Los hombres del hombre* y, sobre todo, Eduardo Mallea en *Los enemigos del alma* representan el análisis de psicologías, o mejor, la creación de ellas. *Personas en la sala,* de Norah Lange, es la más original y perfecta novela artística de este género, hermosamente trabajada, teniendo como inteligencia central la psicología de una adolescente de diecisiete años. De esas novelas de atmósfera e intención clarísimas, pasamos a nuevas y audaces concepciones influídas por las últimas corrientes novelescas europeas. La novela de Enrique Araya, *El caracol y la diosa,* y la de Carlos Onetti, *La vida breve,* están sumergidas en un mar surrealista de difícil navegación. La tradición de la novela proletaria se continúa en un buen número de las de este año, en que son muy valiosas *Huelga blanca* de Héctor Raúl Almanza y *Viento fuerte* de Miguel Ángel Asturias.

Hay unos cuantos intentos de novelar la historia: el mejor de ellos, *El viento sobre el río* de Josefina Cruz, evocación de Buenos Aires en los primeros tercios del siglo XIX. Rafael Ulises Peláez ha escrito una especie de crónica novelesca sobre la generación boliviana anterior a la guerra del Chaco y su destino en esa guerra. La sátira y crítica de la civilización del siglo XX es motivo de la novela de Enrique Araya mencionada antes y de los cuentos de Próspero Morales Pradilla, *Cianuro y otras bebidas.* Pero los cuentos más bellos de este año son los folklóricos: *Los cuentos del tío Doroteo* de Francisco Izquierdo Ríos, y *Hermanos míos* de Jesús María Pereyra, leyendas y figuras indias de Santiago del Estero. Son notables también dentro de la literatura "de la tierra" los siete cuentos del vino, de Luis Durand, y *Hombres de Reloncaví* de Julio Silva Lazo.

En la crítica surgió de nuevo el viejo tema del criollismo, con aspectos de polémica, en la copiosa crítica que tuvo en Chile la novela *Frontera* de Luis Durand. Intervinieron con sensatas consideraciones, en la revista *Atenea* del año 1950, Manuel Rueda y Mario Osses, sobre todo Rueda, previniendo sobre el confusionismo anecdótico y microscópico que termina en "garrulería botánica o mercaderil."

Dos obras de desigual valor, pero de mucho interés en la historia de nuestra novela, se reeditaron en este año: *La aritmética del amor* de Blest Gana y *Raza de bronce* de Alcides Arguedas. El valor de esta novela de Arguedas, precursora de tantos caminos en nuestra novelística, se hará evidente ahora, con esta edición de Losada, que la hace accesible a quienes no tuvieron la suerte de leer la primera edición. [C. Meléndez]

POETRY

THE mid-century year of 1950 would have been virtually unrepresentative of a great half-century of Spanish American poetry had it not been for the publication of Pablo Neruda's *Canto general.* The mass production of verse continued unabated, but without a reasonable quota of distinguished accomplishments. Among the latter we must mention without further delay the works of the Costa Rican Alfredo Cardona Peña, the Mexicans Rosario Castellanos and Enriqueta Ochoa, and the Peruvian Percy Gibson. The decline of the Afro-Antillean genre, as exemplified by Félix B. Caignet, was made all the more apparent by the reissue of Luis Palés Matos' classic of 20 years ago. Felipe Arias Larreta's gallant effort seemed to show an *indigenismo* on the wane. The traditional themes and conventional rhetoric of some estimable poets who are sated with *nerudismo* and other isms failed to improve matters. Is it, one wonders, that a great period is at a close and we must wait patiently for *el que vendrá?*

There were the usual exhumations, commendable from the viewpoint of literary history, or at least historical curiosity: Evaristo Carriego, Rafael García Goyena, Salomé Ureña de Henríquez, Bartolomé Hidalgo, José Joaquín Palma, José Antonio Soffia. Six poems by Gabriela Mistral from a book in preparation appeared in an unpretentious selection of her own making. A number of fine poems by Jorge Carrera Andrade were published in English translation in London. No major anthology came to our notice. (Included in the present report as an addendum is a 1949 item which we consider a model of its kind, *Nueva poesía nicaragüense.*) Biography worthy of being noted as conscientious and informative dealt with Manuel Acuña (item 2743), Remigio Crespo Toral (item 2744), Rubén Darío (item 2763), Alejandro Guanes (item 2766), Mariano Melgar (item 2756), and Gabriela Mistral (item 2752). Arturo Berenguer Carisomo's essay on *Martín Fierro* and Antonio Fernández Spencer's article on César Vallejo were discerning and challenging evaluations. [F. Aguilera]

DRAMA

EL panorama teatral de 1950 es muy halagador. Por una parte, la renovación escénica que hemos venido señalando en años anteriores ha culminado este año en obras de alta calidad. Deben destacarse entre estas piezas *Algún día . . .* , de Andrés Terbay, estrenada con resonante éxito en Chile; *Como por arte de magia,* del uruguayo Dardo Fabregat Cúneo, que obtuvo excelente recepción en el Teatro Solís de Montevideo, y *Mañana es una palabra,* exquisito monólogo de la joven cubana Nora Badía. Por otra parte, la búsqueda laboriosa en nuestro pasado, para tener clara conciencia de lo que hemos hecho y afirmar el rumbo de lo que hemos de hacer, ha resultado en estimables obras de investigación: el valioso estudio sobre el teatro en Puerto Rico, de Antonia Sáez, la sintética historia de la literatura dramática argentina, de Raúl Castagnino, y varios artículos sobre temas similares en México, son cumplida muestra de la creciente importancia de estas tareas de erudición y de crítica.

En cuanto a la producción artística, hay tres hechos que convendría subrayar. Uno de estos es la vitalidad con que está reapareciendo el monólogo. Otro hecho evidente es que las obras de importancia estrenadas en 1950 se han escrito al calor de movimientos experimentales, de donde han pasado luego al teatro comercial. Y no es de menos interés observar el acusado contraste entre esta producción y la de hace algunos años, pues mientras entonces se escribían numerosas obras en verso de chato prosaísmo conceptual, las mejores de hoy, en prosa, son de elevado vuelo poético en la concepción y hasta en los matices de la expresión.

Consignemos, finalmente, la desaparición de tres importantes figuras en nuestro campo: la del argentino Alberto Gerchunoff, acaecida el 2 de marzo, la del cubano Salvador Salazar, el 10 de octubre, y la del mexicano Xavier Villaurrutia, el 25 de diciembre. [José Juan Arrom]

GENERAL

ÁNGEL FLORES

2561. Abreu Gómez, Ermilo (ed.). Escritores de Costa Rica. Joaquín García Monge, Roberto Brenes Mesén, Carmen Lira. Washington, Unión Panamericana, Departamento de Asuntos Culturales (Escritores de América). 123 p.

Not very impressive excerpts from the writings of Brenes Mesén (1874-1947), García Monge (b. 1881), and Carmen Lira (1888-1949).

2562. ÁBSIDE. México. V. 14, no. 1-2, enero-junio.

Memorial number devoted in its entirety to Gabriel Méndez Plancarte (1905-1949), humanist, poet, and founder-editor of this highly regarded "revista de cultura mexicana." See also item 1540. [F. Aguilera]

2563. Arabena Williams, Hermelo. Don Enrique Nercasseau y Morán, 1854-1925.

Ensayo crítico-anecdótico sobre el primer filólogo e hispanista chileno, seguido de una breve antología con la labor literaria del maestro. Santiago, Editorial Universitaria. 199 p.
Excerpts from the writings of a Chilean literary scholar, with a tribute to him and a brief biographical sketch.

2564. Arce, David N. Presencia y prosa de Alfredo Maillefert. México, Herber. 41 p.
Lyrical evocation of a talented Mexican writer (1889-1941).

2565. Arce de Vázquez, Margot. Impresiones. Notas puertorriqueñas. San Juan, Puerto Rico, Yaurel. 148 p.
Miscellaneous essays on the language and landscape of Puerto Rico and on some of its leading writers: Hostos, Palés Matos, Lloréns Torres, *et al.*

2566. Borges, Jorge Luis. Aspectos de la literatura gauchesca. Montevideo, Rosgal. 35 p.
Urban impact and influence of urban writers (Juan Cruz Varela, Francisco Acuña de Figueroa, etc.) in the formation and development of a gaucho theme and a literary tradition.

2567. Botelho Gosálvez, Raúl. Reflexiones sobre el cincuentenario del *Ariel* de José Enrique Rodó. La Paz, Centenario. 30 p.
A Bolivian novelist reinterprets Rodó's *Ariel,* showing the Arielism of the United States and Latin America and the Calibanism of the Soviet Union.

2568. Bueno, Salvador. 1950: un año en la literatura cubana (*Rev. cub.*, v. 27, julio-dic., p. 42-74).
Selective survey, with special emphasis on the novelist Enrique Labrador Ruiz and the poet Cintio Vitier. [F. Aguilera]

2569. Caballero Calderón, E. Diario de Tipacoque. Bogotá, ABC. 284 p., illus.
Vignettes evoking the section of Colombia which inspired Caballero Calderón to write his famous novel *Tipacoque.*

2570. Caso, Francisco, Ricardo Caso, and Pedro Caso. Tres hermanos. Prólogo de Ventura García Calderón. Lima, Tipografía Peruana. 459 p.
Collective autobiography of three distinguished Peruvians: a journalist, a painter, and a statesman, brothers with a wide range of interests in the arts and sciences.

2571. Córdova, Federico. Vida y obras de Germán Arciniegas. Habana, Ministerio de Educación, Dirección de Cultura (Contemporáneos, 1). 409 p.
Sympathetic biocritical study of the Colombian author Arciniegas (b. 1900); book-by-book summarization of his works.

2572. Donoso, Ricardo. La sátira política en Chile. Santiago, Imprenta Universitaria. 221 p., illus.
The political life of Chile as mirrored in the caricatures, cartoons, and satires of its outstanding periodicals from the early *El Espectador Chileno,* founded in 1829, to *La Raspa,* founded in 1949.

2573. Gómez Naranjo, Pedro A. Faro de cinco luces. Perfiles de Centro América. Bucaramanga, Colombia, Imprenta del Departamento. 185 p.
A former Colombian diplomat collects his periodical contributions dealing with the most diverse aspects of Central America.

2574. Grases, Pedro. Doce estudios sobre Andrés Bello. Buenos Aires, Nova. 181 p., port.
Essays dealing with Bello as poet and as teacher. Exhaustive bibliography.

2575. ————. Fuentes generales para el estudio de la literatura venezolana (*Rev. nac. cult.*, año 11, no. 81, julio-agosto, p. 86-99).
The author says: "He distribuído el material en tres grandes capítulos: Antologías, Estudios generales y Bibliografías; con una nota adicional relativa a las publicaciones periódicas, las cuales exigen un estudio monográfico." [Ed.]

2577. Izquierdo Ríos, Francisco. Vallejo y su tierra. Lima, Selva. 1950? 78 p.
Two essays describing the landscape, life, and lore of Santiago de Chuco, Department of La Libertad (northern Peru), and showing how these influenced the great Peruvian poet and novelist César Vallejo.

2578. Larra, Raúl. Roberto Artl, el torturado. Buenos Aires, Futuro. 158 p.
The first and only biocritical study dealing with the gifted playwright and novelist Artl (1900-1942); first-hand information, deeply felt tribute.

2579. La literatura uruguaya del 900. Montevideo, Número. 340 p.
Reprint of the special issue of *Número* (año 2, no. 6-8, enero-junio), commemorating the fiftieth anniversary of the publication of *Ariel.* Contributors are: Arturo Ardao, Mario Benedetti, Sarandy Cabrera, Manuel Arturo Claps, José Enrique Etcheverry, Antonio Larreta, José Pereira Rodríguez, Carlos Real de Azúa, Emir Rodríguez Monegal, Jorge Augusto Sorondo, Idea Vilariño. Important articles on Rodó and other towering Uruguayan writers of the so-called "1900 generation"—Carlos and María Eugenia Vaz Ferreira, Agustini, Herrera y Reissig, Reyles, Viana, Quiroga, and Sánchez. Additional articles on literary magazines edited by members of this brilliant group. Well documented. [F. Aguilera]

2580. Martínez, José Luis. Literatura mexicana, siglo XX, 1910-1949. Segunda parte. Guías bibliográficas. México, Ro-

bredo (Clásicos y Modernos, Creación y Crítica Literaria, 4). 202 p.
Bibliographies of Mexican writers and magazines between 1900 and 1949, with a supplementary section by Francisco Giner de los Ríos on the 1939-1949 publications of Spanish poets living in Mexico. Part I was a collection of reviews. See *HLAS, no. 15, 1949*, item 2238.

2581. **Merino Brito, Eloy G.** José Antonio Saco. Su influencia en la cultura y en las ideas políticas de Cuba. Habana, Molina. 266 p.
This biocritical study, which was awarded the Bacardi Prize for 1949, deals with "el cubano más real y útil de su tiempo," the statesman and sociologist Saco (1797-1879).

2582. **Montero Bustamante, Raúl.** Iniciación del Uruguay en el modernismo literario (*Rev. nac.*, Montevideo, t. 46, año 13, no. 137, mayo, p. 173-212).
Important article on the forerunners of modernism in Uruguay and the decisive role played between 1895 and 1900 by *Revista Nacional de Literatura y Ciencias Sociales, La Revista, Revista del Salto,* and *Revista Literaria.* [F. Aguilera]

2583. **Morales, Ernesto.** Esteban Echeverría. Prólogo de Enrique Herrero. Buenos Aires, Claridad (Biblioteca Hombres e Ideas, 2. serie, v. 1). 217 p., illus., port.
Well-rounded biography and critique of the romantic poet and thinker Echeverría; fine summary of all known facts.

2584. **Nesbit, Louis.** The Jewish contribution to Argentine literature (*Hispania,* v. 33, no. 4, Nov., p. 313-319).
On Alberto Gerchunoff, Bernardo Verbitsky, Enrique Espinoza (pseudonym of Samuel Glusberg), Carlos Grünberg, César Tiempo, Lázaro Liacho, Samuel Eichelbaum. [F. Aguilera]

2585. **Paz, Octavio.** El laberinto de la soledad. México, Cultura (Ediciones Cuadernos Americanos, 16). 195 p.
Eight essays dealing with the idiosyncratic roots of the Mexican—an existentialist viewpoint.

2586. **Quinteros Delgado, Juan Carlos.** Un gran literato olvidado, Amadeo Almada. Prólogo de Rodolfo Almeida Pintos. Montevideo, Florensa y Lafón. 76 p.
Not very successful attempt to resurrect a Uruguayan journalist who on May 31, 1909, delivered an eloquent lecture on Rodó's *Motivos de Proteo.*

2587. **Quiroga, Horacio.** Diario de viaje a París de . . . . Introducción y notas de Emir Rodríguez Monegal. Montevideo, El Siglo Ilustrado. 137 p., port.
Quiroga's diary covering part of his Paris sojourn (March 21-June 10, 1900); mostly about his impressions of the Universal Exposition and the one absorbing passion of the time: bicycle races.

2588. **Rodó, José Enrique.** Ariel. Montevideo, Uruguaja Esperanto-Societo. 157 p.
A Latin American classic in an excellent Esperanto translation.

2589. **Rodríguez Monegal, Emir.** José E. Rodó en el novecientos. Montevideo, Número. 99 p.
Five pithy essays dealing with Rodó as critic and creative writer and showing his influence on his generation.

2590. **Saldarriaga Betancur, Juan Manuel.** De sima a cima, o Marco Fidel Suárez ante la conciencia colombiana. Medellín, Colombia, Dirección de Educación Pública, Extension Cultural (Biblioteca de Autores Antioqueños, v. 3). 509 p.
Homage, by various hands, to the Catholic intellectual leader Marco Fidel Suárez (1855-1927) whom Valera once called "el Cervantes moderno."

2591. **Sánchez, Luis Alberto.** La literatura en el Perú contemporáneo (1915-1918) (*Rev. nac. cult.,* año 11, no. 80, mayo-junio, p. 57-77).
Fascinating account of literary activities, amusements, and political vicissitudes. Particularly important is the history of some literary reviews which have become famous. [F. Aguilera]

2592. ———. Recuerdo de Augusto d'Halmar (*Rev. América,* v. 20, no. 61, feb., p. 163-165).
Random notes on the Chilean man of letters Augusto d'Halmar (1881-1949).

2593. **Serra Rojas, Andrés.** Antología de la elocuencia mexicana, 1900-1950. México, Manuel Porrúa. 343 p.
Speeches of the last fifty years by outstanding Mexican orators from Justo Sierra (1848-1912) to the anthologist (b. 1906), who is at present a professor in the Law School.

2594. **Serrano, Miguel.** Ni por mar, ni por tierra . . . . Historia de una generación. Santiago, Nascimento. 398 p.
Autobiographical notes by a Chilean who began his literary career in 1936; his pet aversions are the Masons and his uncle Vicente Huidobro; his ideal is to go as journalist to the Antarctic.

2595. **Urbina, Luis G.** Crónicas. Prólogo y selección de Julio Torri. México, Universidad Nacional Autónoma (Biblioteca del Estudiante Universitario, 70). xx, 301 p.
Sundry newspaper contributions by a well-known Mexican poet; travel notes from Europe and the Western Hemisphere.

2596. **Valle, Rafael Heliodoro.** Amigos cubanos de Ricardo Palma (*Rev. cub.,* v. 26, enero-junio, p. 52-75).

An interesting chapter in the history of American intellectual cooperation. [F. Aguilera]

2597. ————. Ermilo Abreu Gómez: notas bibliográficas (*Hispania*, v. 33, no. 3, Aug., p. 230-232).
Born in Mérida, Yucatán, in 1894, Abreu Gómez has distinguished himself in various literary fields. [F. Aguilera]

ADDENDA

2598. Alba, Alfonso de. Antonio Moreno y Oviedo y la generación de 1903. México, Biblioteca de Autores Laguenses, t. 10, 1949. 182 p., illus., group ports.
Cultural life in the Mexican town of Lagos de Moreno at the beginning of the century and the influence exerted upon it by a lofty cultural leader, Antonio Moreno y Oviedo.

2599. Altamirano, Ignacio Manuel. Obras completas. T. 1. Discursos. Edición, prólogo y notas de Agustín Yáñez. México, Secretaría de Educación Pública, 1949. xvi, 313 p.
The first volume of Altamirano's complete works consists of speeches on political and cultural matters, demonstrating his patriotic zeal and democratic ideology.

2600. González, Manuel Pedro. Ficha bio-bibliográfica de Alfonso Reyes (*Rev. iberoamer.*, t. 15, no. 29, feb.-julio, 1949, p. 13-28).
"En estos apuntes provisionales . . . sólo se ha recogido lo publicado en forma de libro o folleto. . . ." Comprehensive biographical information. [F. Aguilera]

2601. Lugones, Leopoldo. Antología de la prosa. Selección y comentario inicial de Leopoldo Lugones (hijo). Buenos Aires, Centurión (Col. Ulises, 15), 1949. 509 p.
Lugones' son collects many lectures and articles by his illustrious father, some of them published here for the first time.

2602. Palma, Ricardo. La Bohemia de mi tiempo. Lima, Ediciones Hora del Hombre (Biblioteca del Pensamiento Peruano, Col. Literatura, Ensayos, 2), 1948. 102 p.
Written in 1886, this essay is a revealing discussion of a group of Peruvian writers who flourished between 1847 and 1860 and left a significant production.

2603. Saz Sánchez, Agustín del. Resumen de historia de la novela hispanoamericana. Prólogo de José María Castro y Calvo. Barcelona, Atlántida (Col. Intelecto), 1949. 238 p.
Although elementary, repertorial, and unoriginal, these essays cover fairly well the main trends and highlights of Latin American fiction.

PROSE FICTION

CONCHA MELÉNDEZ

NOVELS, SHORT STORIES, PROSE SKETCHES

2604. Almanza, Héctor Raúl. Huelga blanca. México, Impresora Veracruz. 283 p.
Las tierras algodoneras mexicanas que lindan con el Río Bravo son el medio envolvente de esta bella novela proletaria, que presenta la oposición que hacen los hacendados a los inspectores del gobierno enviados para proteger a los campesinos. Engañando a los campesinos sobre el propósito del gobierno, los hacendados los inducen a una huelga en contra de sus propios intereses, la cual se resuelve revocando la disposición gubernamental que protegía a los campesinos. El protagonista, Felipe García, quien descubre y denuncia el engaño, muere herido por la espalda por uno de los agentes de los hacendados. La vida de los humildes sembradores de algodón se presenta en su digna sencillez, destacándose Severo Martínez y Ambrosio Ginés como símbolo del honor y el trabajo honrado, aunque para ellos, infecundo. También es notable la figura de Sabina, que sirve de enlace con la crítica del tipo vano y presuntuoso de la clase privilegiada en la ciudad: el catrín innoble.

2605. Alonso, Carmen. Y había luz de estrellas . . . . Santiago, Flor Nacional. 73 p.
Cuentos de asunto campesino. La prosa, en dos niveles: bellos paisajes descriptivos, brevísimos, y habla ruda, expresión de los hombres y mujeres. La autora sabe mantener la unidad tonal.

2606. Araya, Enrique. El caracol y la diosa. Santiago, Zig-Zag. 154 p.
Novela humorística donde se hace la crítica de la civilización del siglo XX. El autor en su prefacio sitúa el punto de vista en un joven loco, Sebastián Apablaza, y lo presenta advirtiéndonos que son sus memorias las que leeremos. "La humanidad está enajenada," dice Sebastián al autor cuando se le pide permiso para publicar sus memorias. Excelente comentario de Mario Osses en *Atenea*, año 27, t. 99, no. 305-306, nov.-dic., p. 376-387.

2607. Arráiz, Antonio. El mar es como un potro (Dámaso Velázquez). Buenos Aires, Losada. 293 p.
Con tono de vigorosa poesía y en el escenario de la isla Margarita, Arráiz presenta la figura de Dámaso Velázquez, contrabandista, terrateniente, hombre de mar bravío y astuto con rasgos de generosidad que le hacen admirado y amado por todos los que trabajan bajo sus órdenes. La biografía del Caribe y sus islas, el mar con su belleza de color y su fauna de maravilla, las bellas mujeres de Margarita, forman una serie de frescos luminosos que contrastan al fondo con la feroz venganza de Dámaso Velázquez en la persona de su hermosa mujer Rosario y su amante, auditor de Dámaso. El folklore de las islas en boca de negros e indios embellece esta novela, continuadora de las novelas de la naturaleza de América y original en la creación

del protagonista, quien aparece en presencia en las últimas escenas, pero cuya figura se agiganta desde el comienzo del libro con lo que dicen de él quienes le conocen y con lo que acerca de él tejió la leyenda.

2608. Asturias, Miguel Ángel. Viento fuerte. Buenos Aires, Losada. 205 p.

En esta novela el autor supera las anteriores, *El señor Presidente* y *Hombres de maíz.* En la historia del choque entre una compañía explotadora del banano en Centroamérica y los trabajadores nativos, Asturias consigue un equilibrio justo entre verdad y belleza; entre su maravillosa fantasía y su sentido de un mundo que avanza, dolorosamente, es cierto, hacia tiempos de nueva justicia.

2609. Barrios, Eduardo. Los hombres del hombre. Santiago, Nascimento. 317 p.

Vuelta de Eduardo Barrios al tono y técnica de su más valiosa novela, *El hermano asno.* El diario como convención, el estilo confidencial y poético, el conflicto del narrador participante como centro de la novela, la acercan a aquella creación ya lejana. El título lo explica el mismo Barrios: "¿Cómo no ha descubierto antes el ser humano que una muchedumbre lo forma? Compleja e indivisible multitud. Perturban desde la infancia estos fantasmas que se nos incorporan. Sobre todo, algunos, esos que representan a hombres que hubiéramos querido ser y nunca fuimos y que perduran embrollando nuestra pluralidad de suyo numerosa." El conflicto del hombre en esta novela: duda de la fidelidad de su mujer, de su paternidad del hijo único ante el testamento del amigo inglés, millonario, que les deja sus millones, es enfocado de distinto modo por cada uno de los hombres interiores; pero es la voz de Francisco, el cristiano y sereno, quien le señala la illusión de su hijo como sostén vital, porque "las ilusiones de los hombres no difieren para la mirada de los cielos." Acertado comentario de Mario Osses en *Atenea*, año 27, t. 99, no. 304, oct., p. 103-106.

2610. Belmar, Daniel. Oleaje. Santiago, Ediciones Flor Nacional. 75 p.

Un título que se suma a la ya larga tradición naturalista de la novela chilena. El oleaje de la vida pecadora de Bruma hace bajar el oleaje de la vida del médico a quien cuenta sus errores, en un gesto de perdón para la mujer que le traicionó, al mismo tiempo que siembra una esperanza de buen amor en la que ha ido a consultarle. Comentario de Mario Osses en *Atenea*, año 27, t. 99, no. 305-306, nov.-dic., p. 372-373, que, aunque contiene elogios desmedidos, afirma un punto de vista que coincide con la mejor crítica de hoy: "La riqueza vivencial y literaria no reside tanto en el contenido sino en el recorrido."

2611. Benavides, Rodolfo. La vertiente. México, Editorial Iberoamericana. 368 p.

Novela de la ocupación francesa en México centrada en el pueblo minero de Real del Monte y de los años que siguieron hasta el comienzo de la revolución de 1910. Sólo en dos momentos se logran escenas de afecto perdurable: las de la resistencia de los habitantes y las de la vida dura de los mineros y el comienzo de su descontento y protesta. La "vertiente" es el cambio político que inicia la revolución.

2612. Blest Gana, Alberto. La aritmética del amor. Santiago, Zig-Zag. 508 p.

Nueva edición de la primera novela de Blest Gana, publicada en 1860, donde se describen costumbres de Santiago de Chile alrededor de intrigas amorosas a base de interesadas miras.

2613. Braida, Lisímaco. El gualicho del Molino Viejo. Montevideo, Florensa y Lafón. 161 p.

El autor ha definido y valorado certeramente estos relatos al decir en la introducción: "Apuntes y esbozos que salen a la luz pública, sin más trascendencia que referir pedazos de vida de los gauchos troferos, crónicas de bailes, sucedidos y anécdotas ya antañadas."

2614. Camacho Guerrero, Abel. Alma California. México, El Fénix. 294 p.

Se critica en esta novela el regionalismo estrecho y falso de los habitantes del territorio mexicano de California durante el breve período de la gobernación del General Francisco J. Múgica. El alma de la nueva generación que despierta al deber de servicio y mejoramiento del pueblo, se presenta en una joven enfermera, California. El programa de Múgica fracasa por las intrigas de los regionalistas. La sátira social alcanza interés pero la novela se desarrolla sin que el autor logre la artística presentación del asunto, es decir, el hábil manejo de lo significativo.

2615. Castera, Pedro. Carmen. Memorias de un corazón. México, Editorial Porrúa. 309 p.

Precedida de un prólogo de Carlos Gónzalez Peña sobre la novela mexicana en el siglo XIX, que en el aspecto sentimental sólo por excepción aparece en México, se publica esta quinta edición de *Carmen.* Se trata de una de las muchas imitaciones de la *María* de Jorge Isaacs. La novela de Castera no resiste, como *María*, un examen ceñido.

2616. Castro, Baltazar. Un hombre por el camino. Santiago, Cultura. 240 p.

Rosendo Arriaza es centro de esta novela. A través de su vida vemos el destino de los trabajadores chilenos en las compañías explotadoras de cobre o constructoras de vías férreas. La novela, bien estructurada, termina con la muerte de Rosendo en la región de viñedos donde nació. Su vuelta sugiere la aceptación de las faenas de la tierra como restauradoras del alma en el fracaso de la ambición.

2617. Castro, Óscar. Llampo de sangre. Santiago, Editorial del Pacífico. 233 p.

El "espíritu minero" característico de los chilenos se objetiva en el ansia de hombres buscadores y explotadores de minas que se mueven en una escala que va del ingeniero al obrero envueltos en la misma obsesión de que ya no han de libertarse. El verdadero protagonista es un niño, Gilberto, creación de intenso relieve, endurecido en su tránsito de niño a minero por la experiencia heroica que salva a los perseguidos por la justicia humana.

2618. Cruz, Josefina. El viento sobre el río. Buenos Aires, Emecé. 314 p.

Una novela histórica es la reconstrucción panorámica de un tiempo, una atmósfera, un clima vital. Vale por la calidad de la interpretación personal del autor y su habilidad en la presentación de lo histórico y lo novelesco en proporciones artísticas. Josefina Cruz, aunque no siempre ha vitalizado su relato hasta evitar los pasajes de "materia muerta" en que resume historia, evoca a Buenos Aires en los primeros tercios del siglo XIX, los años finales de la presidencia de Mitre y los primeros de la de Sarmiento, recreando con finura y gracia psicologías en sus hondos y triviales sentimientos, en sus vidas apasionadas. El punto de vista del negro en el personaje Matías y del indio ante el blanco en la dramática creación de la india Mauleo, casi eclipsan al centro de narración, el doctor Salcedo, actor en dos episodios decisivos en su transformación moral: la guerra del Paraguay y la epidemia del cólera en Buenos Aires.

2619. Darío, Rubén. Cuentos completos. México, Fondo de Cultura Económica. 357 p.

Por primera vez se publican en un volumen todos los cuentos y esbozos de cuentos de Rubén Darío, precedidos de una muy valiosa introducción crítica de Raimundo Lida, que es el mejor estudio estilístico de la prosa rubeniana escrito hasta ahora.

2620. Durand, Luis. Sietecuentos. Santiago, Nascimento (Col. Araucaria). 196 p.

La región chilena de vinos tintos y bodegas colmadas es marco y fondo de estos cuentos. En *Vino tinto*, *La carreta de Juan Mardones* y *La picada*, la fascinación del vino termina en la muerte. En este último y también en *Mi amigo Pidén*, Durand se revela como hábil creador de figuras de animales. El perro Calluza y el Pidén, magnífica presentación de un caballo, aparecen en relación conmovedora con el hombre en un nivel de comprensión casi humana. Comentario de Mario Osses en *Atenea*, año 27, t. 99, no. 305-306, nov.-dic., p. 368-372.

2621. García Rodríguez, José. Alma rústica. México, Stylo. 154 p.

Escrita en 1902, según la fecha al final de la última página, esta novela de costumbres rurales en el escenario de una hacienda mexicana sigue el estilo realista de la novela española al finalizar el siglo XIX, y presenta con acierto a Francisco Rojas, el "alma rústica" que destruye la vida de la hija de su patrón, enloquecido por el desengaño y los celos.

2622. González, José Luis. Paisa. Un relato de la emigración. México, Fondo de Cultura Popular. 71 p.

En la "dirección realista, humana y social," sitúa Luis Enrique Délano esta novela breve que presenta con intensidad dramática y habilidad técnica, el problema de los emigrantes puertorriqueños en Nueva York. Tres personajes encarnan el tema: "el otro," el instigador sin escrúpulos; Perucho, noble protector e inspirador de los suyos, y Andrés, el protagonista, arrastrado por la desesperación del desempleo a la colaboración con "el otro" en un asalto a una bodega de Harlem. La novela comienza en medio del drama y en retrospecciones alternadas

con el presente, aparece la niñez de Andrés en el seno de su familia jíbara, el traslado al arrabal La Perla en San Juan, la muerte del padre aplastado por un fardo en la bodega de un buque y la dispersión de la familia que lleva a Andrés niño al hogar de su padrino en Nueva York. El estilo directo, resuelto en un vocabulario desnudo, apenas atenuado por un toque de poesía, coloca a José Luis González en el clima naturalista de la novela proletaria. El procedimiento es escénico en la complicación y solución.

2623. González Vera, José Santos. Vidas mínimas. Santiago, Ercilla. 111 p.

Tercera edición "corregida y disminuída" de las dos novelas breves *El conventillo* y *Una mujer*, escenas y pasiones de gentes de arrabal en Santiago y Valparaíso, en que el autor, según su prologuista, es a la vez observador y participante. González Vera ha obtenido en 1950 el Premio Nacional de Literatura. Véase el estudio críticobiográfico por Ernesto Montenegro en *Rep. amer.*, t. 46, año 31, no. 18, sept. 30, p. 273-275.

2624. Goyanarte, Juan. El ventisquero. Buenos Aires, Emecé. 99 p.

Los editores de *Lago argentino*, la bella novela de Goyanarte aparecida en 1946 (véase *HLAS no. 12, 1946*, párrafo 2534), reproducen el segundo capítulo en la colección *Cuadernos de la quimera*.

2625. Gutiérrez, Benigno A. Gente maicera. Mosaico de Antioquia la Grande. Medellín, Colombia, Bedout. 303 p.

En esta original compilación de tradiciones, anécdotas y poesías de autores de Antioquia, Colombia, se incluyen algunos cuentos de subido mérito como *La vaca sorda* de Eduardo Arias Suárez y *El machete* de Julio Posada.

2626. Gutiérrez, Joaquín. Puerto Limón. Santiago, Nascimento. 280 p.

Las variaciones de la vida en un puerto de Costa Rica donde una compañía frutera norteamericana exporta los bananos del interior, sirven de fondo a una multitud de personajes, todos hundidos en la atmósfera cálida, de pobreza moral desconcertante. Silvano Rojas, el adolescente sencillo, pudo ser la inteligencia central que diera a la novela un punto de vista ordenador de los materiales con que Gutiérrez, usando del método de narrador en primera persona, no logra darnos un sentido preciso a que atenernos en la interpretación del libro. Comentario de Mario Osses en *Atenea*, año 27, t. 98, no. 302-303, agosto-sept., p. 302-305.

2627. Heredia, José María. Trabajos desconocidos de . . . (*Rev. cub.*, v. 26, enerojunio, p. 271-285).

Published in 1840-1841 in *Repertorio de Literatura y Variedades*, México, these three stories have apparently remained unknown to professional *heredianos*. [F. Aguilera]

2628. Izquierdo Ríos, Francisco. Cuentos del tío Doroteo. Montevideo, Selva. 77 p.

Brevísimos apuntes de sucesos imaginados, en que los personajes son con frecuencia pájaros, animales o duendes, presentan el folklore y el paisaje del Oriente peruano. El estilo, lleno de gracia poética, es siempre de cautivadora sencillez, si bien cuando el que habla es el tío Doroteo alcanza un nivel artístico que contrasta con la manera llana de la abuela u otro narrador, sazonada con palabras evocadoras del folklore quechua. Adviértense curiosas equivalencias con las metamorfosis ovidianas o la mitología griega. El breve libro tiene estructura armoniosa y unidad total, creadoras del encanto particular de su atmósfera.

2629. Jugo, Román. Los límites del hombre. San José, Borrase. 166 p.

El centro de esta novela es Roberto Santacruz, sabio médico y escritor a quien el narrador en primera persona viene a proponer la edición de sus obras. Pero sólo puede asistir al entierro de quien vino a visitar. La vida noble y dolorosa de Santacruz se presenta a través de los diferentes puntos de vista de una vieja sirvienta, un amigo burgués y mediocre, un discípulo brillante y agradecido, un compañero de profesión a quien protegió y un delator envidioso que causó su desprestigio e indirectamente su muerte a destiempo. Este original procedimiento de contrapunto se completa con dos cartas que aclaran el secreto amor de Santacruz y un capítulo final en que el narrador participante aclara el título de la novela.

2630. Labatón, José. El Gringo. México, Gráficos Guanajuato. 247 p.

Contrabandistas bajo el mando de Santiago González, "El Gringo," son los personajes de esta novela, llena de riesgos y encuentros con la policía.

2631. Labrador Ruiz, Enrique. La sangre hambrienta. Habana, Ayón (Col. Nuevas Novelas Cubanas). 232 p.

Más que una novela limitada a la elaboración de un tema que aclare su actitud ante el complejo asunto elegido, Labrador Ruiz ha creado una atmósfera, una temperatura social de la vida cubana en el caos revolucionario de 1933. El relato presenta, primero, una casa de huéspedes en la Habana, con un abigarrado grupo de inquilinos, y, luego, una serie de *apuntes,* descripción de un pueblo cubano, el de la niñez del narrador, ambiente de plebeyez y monotonía en que resaltan figuras y circunstancias que hubieran sido, tratadas aparte como cuentos, creaciones de efectos muy sugestivos. El tono, humorístico y satírico, tiene también por momentos ternura y conmiseración. El habla criolla da sazón muy cubana a escenas y descripciones. Comentario de Raimundo Lazo en *Abril,* año 1, no. 5.

2632. Lange, Norah. Personas en la sala. Buenos Aires, Editorial Sudamericana. 216 p.

Una adolescente de diecisiete años, inteligencia central de esta novela, aunque escribe sus recuerdos da la impresión de que aún es muy joven al escribirlos, pues no se descubre el reajuste del punto de vista, como sucede en las memorias. El estilo, de una sencillez insinuante, sabia, es de calidad que podría describirse con las palabras con que la narradora describe las de sus protagonistas: "aunque dijeran *calle* o *estación* esas palabras adquirían siempre una

calidad distinta." Esa calidad es belleza envolvente, gracia, feminidad profunda.

2633. Luquín, Eduardo. Águila de oro. México, B. Costa-Amic. 149 p.

Historia del pistolero Mardegal desde que abandona su pueblo hasta que, enriquecido, se pasea por Chapultepec vestido de charro. Pero el personaje más importante es Lacimar, quien al fin se deja convencer por la mujer que ama a abandonar su vida de bandolero y a alejarse con ella y su hijo a comenzar una vida nueva.

2634. Mallea, Eduardo. Los enemigos del alma. Buenos Aires, Editorial Sudamericana. 363 p.

En esta hermosa novela Mallea vuelve a la presentación de vidas confinadas en espacios limitados, concentrando el interés en el análisis del drama violento que a cada paso agita la superficie como un torbellino o hierve sordo en los pensamientos. Mario Guillén y sus hermanas Déborah y Cora, pertenecen a la familia de personajes, que como Ágata y Nicanor Cruz, en *Todo verdor perecerá,* han sido creados por Mallea entrechocándose dentro de una casa que en la novela alcanza categoría simbólica. La historia de Mario, Déborah y Cora—mundo, demonio y carne—se entrecruza hábilmente con la de Ortigosa y su mujer Consuelo, creando también en esta última, una psicología femenina profunda y fina. El escenario es las ciudad provinciana de la niñez de Mallea, Bahía Blanca, cuya atmósfera de vientos invernales y luminosa primavera aprovecha el novelista como fondo de discreta poesía. Como en sus otras novelas, es Mallea el narrador omnisciente con breves pasajes ensayísticos que nos recuerdan la tendencia del autor a acercar sus ensayos a la novela y sus novelas al ensayo.

2635. ————. La torre. Buenos Aires, Editorial Sudamericana. 421 p.

Con esta obra Mallea acentúa en la novelística hispanoamericana las novelas en torno a una familia en las vidas de sucesivas generaciones. *La torre* es, según una nota del autor, el segundo libro en que presenta el mundo de los Ricarte, continuación de *Las águilas* en donde el castillo exótico, monstruo de arquitectura, es símbolo de la riqueza y decadencia desarraigada del sentido de la tierra. En *La torre* "el campo domina al intruso edificio concebido por León Ricarte, bajándolo a golpes de verde a nivel de la tierra: la casa tragada por su propia llanura." El nieto, Roberto Ricarte, busca angustiosamente un camino, construye una íntima torre donde razona, titubea y sueña, sano ya de vanidad y falsedades huecas, pero sin fortaleza consistente para la acción. Mallea promete un tercer libro, *La tempestad,* en que su personaje superará las circunstancias y luchará con su destino en acción directa y libre.

2636. Mancisidor, José. La primera piedra. México, Stylo. 228 p.

Compilación de cuentos de variada temática y desiguales efectos técnicos, no siempre eficaces. Sobresalen sin embargo por su creación firme a través del personaje central, los cuentos inspirados en la Revolución Mexicana: *Tierra y pan* y *El destino.*

2637. Martínez Orozco, Alfredo. La brecha. México, Stylo. 118 p.

El tema es el de la esterilidad de una mujer joven y sensible por impotencia congénita del marido. La novela comienza en la Escuela de Medicina en donde aparecen como estudiantes los dos personajes importantes del relato: Ernesto Esponda y Pablo Santacruz. La protagonista, Cristina, sufre una crisis muy honda al no realizar su deseo de ser madre: el profesor Baralt aconseja a Esponda que deje que Cristina conciba un hijo de otro hombre. La solución se realiza: Santacruz es padre del hijo de Cristina. Cómo se llevó a cabo el consejo del médico, no lo sabemos ni lo sabe Cristina hasta que Pablo Santacruz se lo dice. Después de la conmoción que tal revelación le causa, Cristina, quien ama profundamente a su esposo, afirma que todos los hijos nacen del alma. La escena final aclara esta actitud del autor ante su tema.

2638. ———. La voz de la tierra. México, Stylo. 310 p.

Tercera edición de la que hasta ahora resulta la mejor novela del autor. Sin embargo ¿cuál es el tema de esta novela? ¿La vida recia y valiente de los hacheros colombianos? ¿El despertar de un hacendado culto, Roberto Vélez, a "la voz de la tierra"? ¿Las convenciones sociales que limitan el destino de la mujer colombiana? El primero de esos temas, magníficamente presentado por el autor, hubiera bastado para una novela.

2639. ———. Yajángala. México, Stylo. 168 p.

Relato poético de una leyenda de los indios paeces de Colombia recogida y enviada al autor por el padre misionero, Juan David, de la orden de San Lázaro. Los personajes, evocados con romántica visión que recuerda un modelo lejano de obras de este género (*Atalá* de Chateaubriand), expresan las creencias y tradiciones de su raza.

2640. Merino Fernández, Carlos. Retablos de Huehuetlán. México, Talleres Gráficos de la Nación. 237 p.

Esta divertida novela en donde el autor asegura que ha querido pintar cuadros a manera de los milagros o retablos pintados por artistas populares anónimos mexicanos, tiene como modelo algunas de las aventuras de don Quijote aunque es algo muy diferente: la vida en el pueblo de Huehuetlán, pueblo que "toma a broma todos los males que le hacen y juzga como payasos a sus esbirros y políticos profesionales." El personaje central es foco de las burlas más exageradas, pero también aparecen en caricaturas grotescas el cura, el médico y otros personajes. El autor promete una segunda parte.

2641. Miró, Rodrigo. El cuento en Panamá. Estudio, selección, bibliografía. Panamá, Imprenta de la Academia. 203 p.

El estudio que precede a esta selección de cuentos panameños es un completo y preciso resumen. Es, además, una buena crítica del cuento como arte y se detiene con acierto en algunas de sus particularidades. Y hay afirmaciones tan dignas de reflexión como ésta: "En América Hispana el tema sobra, limitando, por

lo mismo, las necesidades de la invención. Para el artista americano lo difícil es saber mirar." Las selecciones, ordenadas según un criterio cronológico, comienzan con unas páginas del Conquistador González de Oviedo, seguidas de cuentos románticos, realistas, vanguardistas y, desde 1928, de tendencia nativista.

2642. Molina Massey, Carlos. La montonera de Ahuancruz. Buenos Aires, Editorial América Gaucha. 265 p.

Esta novela reconstruye las postrimerías de la dictadura de Rosas, en forma panorámica que abarca los ataques indios a las haciendas fortificadas de la frontera, las montoneras destacadas por Rosas para sojuzgarlos y la ciudad de Buenos Aires bajo el terror de la Mazorca. El relato, a pesar de seguir la forma tradicional de la novela histórica del siglo pasado, acentúa con habilidad la invención sobre la historia, sin deformarla.

2643. Morales Pradilla, Próspero. Cianuro y otras bebidas. Bogotá, A. B. C. 138 p.

En tono irónico humorístico, Morales Pradilla presenta en estos cuentos situaciones y psicologías del siglo XX. El cuentista aparece como espectador de lo que cuenta, exagerando a veces las figuras a proporciones caricaturescas o en irónico drama, como en *Las manos del vecino* y *Narciso Rey*. El conjunto denota una rica imaginación y una técnica original, que se destaca particularmente en *Gran cacao* y *Peter Polk*.

2644. Mosquera, Marta. La cuarta memoria. Buenos Aires, Emecé. 50 p.

Muy original por su tema y procedimientos, esta breve novela nos presenta la psicología de un joven belga participante en la segunda guerra mundial. La técnica enlaza los apuntes de un maestro de Ongamira, Córdoba, con las memorias de Georges Van Helz, que el maestro traduce y transcribe.

2645. Oliveira, Cézar R. L. de. Hombres 40, caballos 8. Buenos Aires, Editorial Sudamericana. 259 p.

Crea el autor el ambiente dramático de la segunda guerra mundial en París y Berlín, y el de las prisiones alemanas de la Francia ocupada, a través de las experiencias de Roque Ernesto Ribeira, joven abogado argentino corresponsal de guerra. El tema es la transformación de Ribeira al ver desmoronarse sus convicciones totalitarias después de meses de prisión en Toulouse y Tarbes. La evasión del vagón en donde con otros prisioneros Ribeira era trasladado a un campo de concentración en Alemania, es un episodio narrado con eficacia artística.

2646. Onetti, Carlos J. La vida breve. Buenos Aires, Editorial Sudamericana. 390 p.

Bajo este sencillo título se desarrolla una novela compleja en sentido y procedimientos. El protagonista, Juan María Brausen, proyecta en tres planos fases de su secreto mundo mental: lo subconsciente y lo imaginado, en aquella parte grosera, cruel y viciosa en que vive como Arce; en el doctor Díaz Grey, personaje central de la novela para cinematógrafo que va creando, y en las peripecias de la vida que vive como Juan María Brausen, casado con Gertrudis y despedido por economía de la agencia donde trabajaba.

2647. Peláez C., Rafael Ulises. Cuando el viento agita las banderas. 2 v. La Paz, Universo. 262, 244 p.

Se aproxima esta novela a la crónica novelesca. El primer volumen presenta la generación anterior a la Guerra del Chaco en el pueblo boliviano de San Felipe de Austria. Aficionados a la literatura, lectores de Joyce, Proust, Cendrars, Pearl Buck, aparecen como artistas abúlicos con aspiraciones y sueños que sólo son pretextos de conversación. El segundo volumen relata la participación de estos jóvenes en la Guerra del Chaco; el tránsito violento de la vida muelle y sin sentido al dolor y miserias de una guerra en que El Chaco se vuelve "infierno verde," escenario de lodo y fuego que conocemos ya en las novelas y cuentos de Toro Ramallo, Augusto Guzmán, Óscar Cerruto y Augusto Céspedes. Con habilidad para crear psicologías y dramatizar escenas, con estilo sobrio y tono que va de la ironía y el humorismo a la patética visión de muchas escenas de guerra, el autor no logra seleccionar y ordenar sus materiales en un conjunto abarcable: la atención se desvía con digresiones demasiado largas o exceso de información histórica. Es decir, sucede lo que el crítico Carlos Gregorio Taboada señala como un valor de la novela: "dejando de ser ficción, se ha convertido en historial de sucesos documentados."

2648. Pereyra, Jesús María. Hermanos míos. Buenos Aires, J. Héctor Matera. 118 p.

Precedido de breve autobiografía del autor aparecen estos relatos y semblanzas de hechos heroicos de la historia argentina y leyendas y figuras indias de Santiago del Estero llenas de la poesía y folklore rural de esa región tan influída por la herencia quechua. El narrador, nacido en la fundación El Rosario, casi dentro de la selva, se mezcla en los relatos, presentándolos como recuerdos.

2649. Quiroz, Alberto. Los ladrones. México, Editorial Iberoamericana. 145 p.

Escrita con miras a la adaptación cinematográfica, no pierde por eso esta novela su valor artístico. Comienza como una novela picaresca en que dos jóvenes casi adolescentes, Enedino y Remigio, se disponen a regresar al pueblo del primero, en donde vive la viuda de grandes riquezas doña Romualda. La técnica escénica, un poco esperpéntica, subraya la sátira con hábil arte.

2650. Ribera Chevremont, Evaristo. El niño de arcilla. San Juan, Puerto Rico, Imprenta Venezuela (Bibl. de Autores Puertorriqueños). 145 p.

Aunque el autor llama a este libro novela, es en verdad una autobiografía poetizada desde la primera infancia en la vieja ciudad aún envuelta en tradiciones y atmósfera colonial, hasta su regreso de España enriquecido por la nueva estética de la poesía de la primera post-guerra. *El niño de arcilla* es lectura necesaria para aclarar el sentido de la valiosa obra poética de Evaristo Ribera Chevremont.

2651. Rodríguez Tomeu, Humberto. El hoyo. Habana, Editorial Luz Hilo. 172 p.

A través de cuentos de absurdos asuntos y matiz surrealista, casi todos alrededor de un tema de crítica a la naturaleza humana, Rodríguez Tomeu no logra en algunos aclarar su sentido. Otros quedan en mero esbozo.

2652. Samayoa Chinchilla, Carlos. Madre Milpa. Guatemala, Tipografía Nacional. 462 p.

La riqueza de las tradiciones indias de Guatemala, la mezcla de supersticiones prehistóricas vivas aún y el catolicismo en el indio de hoy, en un fondo de naturaleza de resplandeciente trópico es el asunto de un grupo de cuentos—a mi ver los mejores—de este hermoso libro. *El novillo careto, La llamada* y *La manga* son por su arte y sentido, creaciones admirables. Entre las evocaciones coloniales—casi todas leyendas —*Noche de sarao* alcanza la categoría del cuento estructurado con modernidad.

2653. Silva Lazo, Julio. Hombres de Reloncaví. Santiago, Nascimento (Col. Araucaria, 3). 190 p.

Sencillos relatos casi siempre alrededor de campesinos del sur del valle central de Chile. El narrador en primera persona crea la atmósfera de cerros y nieves, lluvia y sol, árboles nativos, en sus cuentos. Sobresale el titulado *Una mujer, un diálogo y un paisaje.*

2654. Téllez, Hernando. Cenizas para el viento y otras historias. Bogotá, Litografía Colombia. 216 p.

Variada temática que abarca también múltiples puntos de vista: el narrador como protagonista o el autor como narrador—en una ocasión es una adolescente quien narra—da interés a este libro en donde se presentan escenas de revolución nacional y escenas de tragedia universal contemporánea, como *Sangre en los jazmines* y *Victoria al atardecer.* Sobresale por su hábil presentación del conflicto y original solución *Espumas y nada más.*

CRITICISM AND BIOGRAPHY

2655. Alegría, Fernando. *Cuentos de viento y agua* por Juan Marín (*Atenea,* año 27, t. 96, no. 297, marzo, p. 303-307).

Se considera a Juan Marín como uno de los más notables cuentistas de Hispanoamérica. Sus *Cuentos de viento y agua* no son tan poéticos o dramáticos como los de Baldomero Lillo o Manuel Rojas, pero están mejor construídos y son "lo mejor de su obra literaria en el campo de la aventura y el misterio."

2656. Arguedas, José María. La novela y el problema de la expresión literaria en el Perú (*Mar del sur,* año 2, v. 3, no. 9, enero-feb., p. 66-72).

Andean ecology as mirrored in the Peruvian novel. [A. Flores]

2657. Ayala, Francisco. Notas sobre *Don Segundo Sombra* (*Asomante,* año 6, v. 6, no. 2, abril-junio, p. 28-33).

Güiraldes' technique: to present his hero through the eyes of a child, thus lending him an aureole of mystery dear to young people. [A. Flores]

2658. Benedetti, Mario. Los temas del novelista hispanoamericano (*Número*, año 2, no. 10-11, sept.-dic., p. 491-502).
Brilliant analysis of the thematic diversity in the Spanish American novel. [A. Flores]

2659. Cañas, Salvador. Homenaje a Miguel Ángel Asturias (*Rep. amer.*, t. 46, año 30, no. 6, marzo 1., p. 81-83).
Resumen estas páginas la valoración que algunos escritores argentinos, entre ellos Norah Lange y Pablo Rojas Paz, así como el peruano Xavier Abril, han hecho de la admirable obra novelesca de Miguel Ángel Asturias.

2660. ————. Salarrué o la fantasía profusa (*Rep. amer.*, t. 46, año 30, no. 8, marzo 20, p. 125-126).
Resumen global de la obra del artista salvadoreño autor de *Cuentos de barro*.

2661. Carrión, Benjamín. La novela ecuatoriana contemporánea (*Cuad. amer.*, año 9, v. 50, no. 2, marzo-abril, p. 261-274).
Interpretación ideológica más que analítica de la novela ecuatoriana contemporánea. Señala en ella como tema general "el reclamo de justicia, denuncia y protesta permanentes"; como defectos, el convencionalismo, el "cartelismo," la ausencia de la ternura y la piedad, la falta de hondura psicológica y superficial descripción de lo sexual. Estos defectos aparecen en los novelistas ecuatorianos de la primera época y van siendo abolidos tanto en novelas como *Las cruces sobre el agua* de Gallegos Lara y *La fuente clara* de Humberto Salvador como en los cuentos de Ángel F. Rojas, *Banca*.

2662. Cotto-Thorner, Guillermo. Manuel Gálvez y su trilogía de la guerra uruguaya (*Rev. iberoamer.*, v. 16, no. 31, feb.-julio, p. 79-89).
Examen de la crítica sobre la trilogía de Gálvez y consideraciones sobre la novela histórica según el ensayo de Amado Alonso sobre *La gloria de don Ramiro*. El autor acepta casi toda la crítica negativa que se ha hecho a estas novelas, pero encuentra que el conjunto posee "méritos indiscutibles." Estos méritos, según la cita de Tristán Valdaspe que aparece en seguida, son vida y poder de evocación, y según Spell, el hecho de ser "documento viviente" de la guerra del Paraguay y el tirano López. Esto último destruye la selección, simplificación y sobriedad, ausentes de las novelas "por afán de realismo y exactitud." Damos razón a la severa crítica de José Bianco, quien asegura que Gálvez no ha realizado las novelas que intentó.

2663. Díaz-Plaja, Guillermo. Raíz hispánica de Eduardo Mallea (*Cuad. hispanoamer.*, v. 6, no. 17, sept.-oct., p. 231-239).
Sostiene el autor que la ortodoxia lingüística y el sobrio estilo del novelista argentino son de raíz hispánica inconfundible. [F. Aguilera]

2664. Englekirk, John E., and Gerald E. Wade. Bibliografía de la novela colombiana (*Rev. iberoamer.*, v. 15, no. 30, agosto, 1949-enero, 1950, p. 309-411).
"Sobre la novela colombiana . . . no hay bibliografía ni crítica que sirva para el estudio que ya merece. . . . A otros les tocará completar el cuadro que aquí ofrecemos como guía. . . ." Annotated whenever possible. Occasionally, critical references considered little known are included. An integral part of this guide is *Introducción a la novela colombiana*, by Wade and Englekirk, in pages 232-251 of the same issue, based on Wade's essay, first published in English in *Hispania*, v. 30, no. 4, Nov., 1947, p. 467-483. [F. Aguilera]

2665. Fabbiani Ruiz, José. Los cuentos de Blanco Fombona (*Rev. nac. cult.*, año 12, no. 82-83, sept.-dic., p. 35-41).
"Blanco Fombona," asegura Fabbiani, "desnaturaliza el cuento para convertirlo en panfleto político o diatriba personal." Su estilo se caracteriza por diminutivos despectivos, con los que deforma la realidad. Su solución es siempre el engaño del hombre. Si Blanco Fombona fué un escritor notable, no lo fué en el arte del cuento. Se lo impidieron su egolatría y sus pasiones sin cauce.

2666. ————. La obra narrativa de Pedro-Emilio Coll (*Rev. nac. cult.*, año 11, no. 80, mayo-junio, p. 41-45).
Analysis of a Venezuelan master of the short story. [A. Flores]

2667. L. D. Augusto d'Halmar (*Atenea*, año 27, t. 96, no. 295-296, enero-feb., p. 7-9).
Semblanza de Augusto Goemine Thompson, escritor chileno que firmó sus libros con el seudónimo de Augusto d'Halmar, muerto en enero de 1950. En ella se valora brevemente la producción novelesca de d'Halmar, desde *Juana Lucero*, su primera novela, de concepción y estilo naturalista. Véase descripción, por Gustavo Labarca Garat, de una visita a d'Halmar, en *Atenea*, año 27, t. 97, no. 298, abril, p. 7-9.

2668. Laso Jarpa, Hugo. María Elena Aldunate, una revelación (*Atenea*, año 27, t. 99, no. 304, oct., p. 143-146).
Comentario de la novela poemática *Candia* que sitúa a María Elena Aldunate en el clima novelesco de María Luisa Bombal. Véase comentario de Luis Durand en *Atenea*, año 27, t. 99, no. 305-306, nov.-dic., p. 403-405.

2669. Lazo, Raimundo. "El Lugareño" y la literatura cubana (*Rev. cub.*, v. 26, enero-junio, p. 45-51).
Breve comentario del libro *Escenas cotidianas* de Gaspar Betancourt Cisneros, escritor cubano de mediados del siglo XIX, quien firmó sus cuadros de costumbres camagüeyanas con el seudónimo de El Lugareño.

2670. Leo, Ulrich. *Doña Perfecta* y *Doña Bárbara*. Un caso de ramificación literaria

(*Rev. iberoamer.*, v. 16, no. 31, feb.-julio, p. 13-25).
Estudia este ensayo el paralelismo entre la trama de la novela de Galdós y la de Gallegos, y la opuesta solución que dan estos novelistas a las tensiones que establecen en sus novelas. Aunque paralelismos y contrastes están bien trazados, este trabajo no tiene el interés interpretativo de otros de Ulrich Leo, ya que todo el análisis se basa en el problema social que presentan ambos libros, más que en los recursos novelescos que los autores manejan.

2671. Llerena, Mario. Función del personaje en la novela cubana (*Rev. hisp. mod.*, año 16, no. 1-4, enero-dic., p. 113-122).
Caracteriza la novela cubana, según Llerena, la ligazón con el desarrollo histórico de Cuba. En su costumbrismo se funden ficción y sociología. Llerena comprueba sus ideas en las novelas *Cecilia Valdés* de Cirilo Villaverde, *Juan Criollo* de Carlos Loveira y *El Dios maltrecho* de J. F. Esares Don. En la tercera y cuarta parte del ensayo, Llerena estudia las novelas contemporáneas de Labrador y Luis Felipe Rodríguez. Las conclusiones de la parte quinta son hondas y originales: arte inspirado y condicionado por el drama real del pueblo no es arte "en el sentido del puro goce estético."

2672. Martínez, Carlos. El premio "Atenea" en la Universidad de Concepción (*Atenea*, año 27, t. 99, no. 304, oct., p. 149-153).
Discurso de entrega del premio otorgado por la Universidad de Concepción a Luis Durand por su novela *Frontera*. Véanse comentarios sobre *Frontera* por Olga Acevedo, Manuel Rueda y Jorge Jobet, respectivamente, en *Atenea*, año 27, t. 96, no. 295-296, julio, p. 156-158; t. 98, no. 301, julio, p. 139-144; no. 302-303, agosto-sept., p. 341-344.

2673. Massiani, Felipe. Heroísmo y ensueño de Jorge Isaacs (*Rep. amer.*, t. 46, año 30, no. 9, abril 20, p. 137-138).
Estudio biográfico de Jorge Isaacs y su tiempo, en relación con las transformaciones violentas del momento que sigue a la independencia de la América Hispana.

2674. Mata, Ramiro W. El gaucho en Javier de Viana (*Rev. nac.*, Montevideo, año 13, t. 47, no. 141, sept., p. 410-426).
Treatment of the gaucho in the short stories of the Uruguayan master Javier de Viana (1872-1927). [A. Flores]

2675. ————. José Eustasio Rivera. Su vida y su obra (*Rev. nac.*, Montevideo, año 13, t. 45, no. 133, enero, p. 95-126).
Superficial laudatory article by an Argentine critic. [A. Flores]

2676. Moretié C., Yerko. *Raza de bronce* de Alcides Arguedas (*Atenea*, año 27, v. 99, no. 304, oct., p. 131-140).
Losada hizo este año la quinta edición de la novela de Arguedas publicada en 1919, pre-

cursora, en su presentación del indio y la naturaleza, de toda la serie que logra más altos valores en *El mundo es ancho y ajeno* de Ciro Alegría. Moretié encuentra débil la creación de personajes y señala la falta de protagonista. Acierta diciendo que en esta novela el protagonista es el indio boliviano. Alaba los pasajes históricos "de indignado patriotismo" como admirables; también las descripciones del altiplano. De la extensa nota crítica trasciende un comentario exacto: Arguedas manejó con desigual maestría los materiales de su novela. A pesar de esto, ella debe incluirse entre las novelas valiosas hispanoamericanas.

2677. Nautilus. Reflexiones del medio siglo (*Atenea*, año 27, t. 96, no. 295-296, enero-feb., p. 1-6).
En este balance de medio siglo de literatura chilena se incluye un sucinto juicio sobre la novela chilena desde Blest Gana hasta Eduardo Barrios y Luis Durand.

2678. Pereda Valdés, Ildefonso. La novela picaresca y el pícaro en España y en América. Montevideo, Medina. 141 p.
Los capítulos 12 y 14 comentan *El periquillo sarniento* de Fernández de Lizardi y los personajes Picardía y Vizcacha de *Martín Fierro*, señalando las diferencias entre el pícaro español y el de América. El capítulo 15 comenta el libro de Calixto Bustamante Carlos Inca (Concolorcorvo) señalando lo picaresco en este regocijado libro que pertenece más bien a los relatos de viaje que tienen por antecedente gran número de nuestras crónicas coloniales.

2679. Piper, Anson C. El yanqui en las novelas de Rómulo Gallegos (*Hispania*, v. 33, no. 4, Nov., p. 338-341).
On the Mr. Builder of *La trepadora*, Mr. Danger of *Doña Barbara*, Mr. Davenport of *Canaima*, and Mr. Hardman of *Sobre la misma tierra*. [F. Aguilera]

2680. Porras Cruz, Jorge Luis. La vida y la obra de Luis G. Inclán. México. 296 p.
Doctoral dissertation, University of Mexico, on the 19th-century Mexican novelist Inclán, showing the Mexican background of his books, the psychology of his characters, his technique, his style. [A. Flores]

2681. Rodríguez Monegal, Emir. Objetividad de Horacio Quiroga, con textos inéditos. Montevideo, Número, 32 p.
Piensa el autor de este ensayo que Quiroga vivió, parcial o simbólicamente, los asuntos de sus cuentos. El horror, la dureza de sus creaciones, fueron horror y dureza de su vida. Haber sabido presentarlas en el arte de sus cuentos es lo que llama Rodríguez Monegal "objetividad de Horacio Quiroga." El ensayo va seguido de cartas de Quiroga a Ezequiel Martínez Estrada y Julio E. Payró, en donde se resumen las ideas del cuentista sobre la creación de su arte y sobre la muerte. Apartado de *Número*, año 2, no. 6-8, enero-junio. Véase no. 2579.

2682. **Sánchez, José.** El cuento hispano-americano (*Rev. iberoamer.*, v. 16, no. 31, feb.-julio, p. 101-122).
Útil ensayo informativo más que crítico, sobre la historia del cuento hispanoamericano. Convendría, sin embargo, aclarar la diferencia entre la "tradición" y el cuento tal como lo concebimos hoy. En las tradiciones de Ricardo Palma, en las del puertorriqueño Coll y Toste, el material histórico o legendario está contado con frecuentes rasgos agudos o humorísticos pero no elaborado estrictamente como cuentos. Ricardo Palma creó un género narrativo, la "tradición," que tuvo imitadores en todos nuestros países. Pero no son cuentos, como no lo son muchas aproximaciones al cuento de cronistas como Bernal Díaz o Gonzalo de Quesada.

2683. **Sánder, Carlos.** Río loco, por Lautaro Silva (*Atenea*, año 27, t. 97, no. 298, abril, p. 93-100).
Nota sobre los cuentos de Lautaro Silva en donde se señala como valor principal la interpretación del campesino chileno.

2684. **Wade, Gerald E., and William H. Archer.** The *indianista* novel since 1889 (*Hispania*, v. 33, no. 3, Aug., p. 211-220).
Excellent survey complementing Concha Meléndez' *La novela indianista en la América hispana, 1832-1889* (Madrid, 1934). [F. Aguilera]

2685. **Zaldumbide, Gonzalo.** Enrique Larreta: de Ávila a la pampa (*Cuad. hispanoamer.*, no. 13, enero-feb., p. 25-48).
Admirativa valoración de *Zogoibi* como obra de arte ajena a todo pretendido gauchismo. [F. Aguilera]

ADDENDA

2686. **Garro, J. Eugenio.** Jorge Icaza: vida y obra (*Rev. hisp. mod.*, t. 13, no. 3-4, julio-oct., 1947, i.e., 1949, p. 193-235).
Estudio completo de la obra de Icaza con énfasis en sus cuentos y novelas. Bibliografía.

2687. **Nemtzow, Mary.** Motivos de ironía y sátira en Ricardo Palma (*Mem. cuarto cong. inst. int. lit. iberoam.*, 1949, p. 293-312).
Typical characters and themes that were the butt of Palma's irony or ridicule. [F. Aguilera]

POETRY

FRANCISCO AGUILERA

BOOKS OF VERSE

2688. **Abella Caprile, Margarita.** Lo miré con lágrimas. Buenos Aires, Losada. 90 p.
Sixth book of verse since 1919 by a distinguished Argentine poet.

2689. **Adler, María Raquel.** Veneración. Buenos Aires. 65 p.
Ballads inspired by José de San Martín and his wife, María Remedios Escalada. Adler's usual religiousness (called mysticism by many) defers here to patriotism on the occasion of the San Martín Centennial.

2690. **Arias Larreta, Felipe.** El surco alucinado. Lima, Ediciones Trilce. 61 p.
Nativism combined with an attempt at metrical formality.

2691. **Arteche, Miguel.** El sur dormido. Santiago, Neira. 85 p.
A new voice in Chilean poetry, or rather a voice that seems new because it is a reversion to a traditional type of "pure" poetry.

2692. **Barrios, Gilberto, and Gabriel Urcuyo G.** Antología poética rivense. Managua, Tipografía Progreso. 62 p.
Eleven poets born in Rivas, Nicaragua. Only one, Alberto Ordóñez Argüello, seems to be more than a local celebrity.

2693. **Bedregal, Yolanda.** Nadir. La Paz, Universo. 177 p.
A significant book. Bedregal is no longer a "promise."

2694. **Blanco, Andrés Eloy.** Poda. Saldo de poemas 1923-1928. 3. ed. Caracas, Las Novedades. 270 p.
First published in 1934 and for the second time in 1942, this significant book includes the *Canto a España* which was awarded a grand prize by the Spanish Academy in 1923.

2695. **Blomberg, Héctor Pedro** (ed.). Poetas que cantaron al indio de América. Antología. Buenos Aires, Ángel Estrada y Cía. (Col. Estrada, 60). 187 p.
Useful anthology.

2696. **Cabrera, Rafael.** Presagios. 3. edición. México. 170 p.
Considerably enlarged new edition of the single book of a poet highly regarded in the second decade of the present century, and with good reason. Cabrera (1884-1943) entered the foreign service of his country a few years after the publication of his book (1912).

2697. **Caignet, Félix B.** A golpe de maracas. Poemas negros en papel mulato. Habana, Editorial Casín. 80 p.
No attempt at artistry or social message in these products of a born entertainer.

2698. **Campero Echazu, Octavio.** Voces. Tarija, Bolivia, Universidad Juan Misael Saracho. 112 p.
Many felicitous moments in the flow of this gentle verse.

2699. **Cardona Peña, Alfredo.** Poemas numerales, 1944-1948. Guatemala, Editorial

del Ministerio de Educación Pública. 131 p.
Awarded the Premio Centroamericano for 1948, this is the work of a Costa Rican poet living in Mexico. González Martínez' high praise in the prologue is fully justified.

2700. Carriego, Evaristo. Poesías. Misas herejes. La canción del barrio. Prólogo de Jorge Luis Borges. Nota preliminar de José Edmundo Clemente. Buenos Aires, Renacimiento. 197 p.
All the poems of an unpretentious poetaster (1883-1912), who somehow had the knack of appealing to the sentimentalism of the inhabitants of that large metropolis, Buenos Aires. Useful compilation.

2701. Castellanos, Rosario. De la vigilia estéril. México, Ediciones de América, Revista Antológica. 65 p.
Impressive performance by a woman with a unique poetic personality.

2702. Castro Zagal, Óscar. Rocío en el trébol. Santiago, Nascimento. 138 p.
Posthumous work of a gifted Chilean poet (1910-1947). See review by R. Louvel in *Atenea*, año 27, t. 99, no. 305-306, nov.-dic., p. 390-400.

2703. Centeno, Fernando. Signo y mensaje. Ilustraciones de Francisco Amighetti. San José, Ediciones del Repertorio Americano. 31 p.
Sensitively lyrical notwithstanding moments of near grandiloquence.

2704. Cunha, Juan. En pie de arpa. Montevideo, Ediciones Del Pie en el Estribo. 121 p.
Old poems (published in 1929-1945) and new ones. But the former have been rewritten to such an extent that they require a new appraisal.

2705. Donoso, Francisco G. Trasparencia. Santiago, Imprenta Chile. 108 p.
A poet who for over thirty years has been experimenting joyfully, and successfully, with forms that others consider outworn.

2706. Fernández Moreno, Baldomero. Suplementos. Buenos Aires, El Balcón de Madera. 34 p.
Posthumous work of a Spanish-born Argentine poet who died in 1950.

2707. Figueira, Gastón. Isla sin nombre. Montevideo, Gaceta Comercial. 82 p.
A score of original poems revealing a new facet of Figueira's poetic talent, followed by translations from the English of Kipling and Tagore.

2708. Flores Aguirre, Jesús. México esdrújulo. Buenos Aires, Ediciones López Negri. 232 p.
Selections from several books published in Mexico between 1925 and 1947 by "un poeta de sangre provinciana," as Pedro de Alba calls him in a note at the end of this compilation.

2709. Franco Oppenheimer, Félix. El hombre y su angustia, 1945-1950. Prólogo de Luis Palés Matos. Río Piedras, Puerto Rico, Editorial Yaurel (Col. Yaurel). 86 p.
First book by a member of the latest Puerto Rican *cénacle*, the Grupo Transcendentalista. The sincerity and simplicity of this verse excludes any contrived "ism."

2710. García Goyena, Rafael. Fábulas. Guatemala, Ediciones del Gobierno de Guatemala (Col. Los Clásicos del Istmo). lvi, 167 p.
First published in Guatemala, 1825. Later editions in 1836 (Paris), 1859 and 1886 (Guatemala), and 1894 (Madrid). García Goyena (1766-1823) was born in Guayaquil; when he was about 12 years old he joined his father in Guatemala, where he lived until the day of his death. Informative introduction, bibliography, and notes by Carlos Samayoa Chinchilla.

2711. Gibson, Percy. Yo soy. Bielefeld, Germany. 25 p.
A poets' poet, born in Arequipa, Peru, gives us his credo with an originality and technique unparalleled in current poetry.

2712. Hidalgo, Bartolomé. Cielitos y diálogos patrióticos. Con un estudio sobre el origen de la poesía gauchesca de Lázaro Flury. Buenos Aires, Ciordia y Rodríguez (Col. Ceibo, 19). 149 p.
The Uruguayan Hidalgo (1788-1823) wrote patriotic verses in gaucho idiom.

2713. Incháustegui Cabral, Héctor. Versos, 1940-1950. México, Stylo. 301 p.
Selections from five books published from 1940 to 1946 by a distinguished poet born in the Dominican Republic in 1912. Additional poems dated 1950.

2714. Jiménez Sierra, Elisio. Sonata de los sueños. Caracas, Ávila Gráfica. 100 p.
A miscellany of moods and themes and an uneven performance, with occasional felicitous moments.

2715. López Bermúdez, José. Canto a Cuauhtémoc. México, Universidad Nacional Autónoma de México. Unpaged.
Noble theme and treatment.

2716. Machado de Arnao, Luz. La espiga amarga. Caracas, Ávila Gráfica. 72 p.
Fine talent somewhat dissipated in the pursuit of words, words, words. Not an isolated case in present Spanish American poetry.

2717. Martán Góngora, Helcías. Océano. Popayán, Colombia, Universidad del Cauca (Biblioteca de Autores Caucanos, v 1). 115 p.
Spontaneous writing, often engaging. The

aquatic theme is overdone and the method repetitious.

2718. Martínez, José de Jesús. La estrella de la tarde y otros poemas. México, Nuevo Mundo. 83 p.
Disconcerting contrast between mature pieces, artistically speaking, and others which seem amateurish.

2719. Mistral, Gabriela. Pequeña antologia de . . . . Selección hecha por Gabriela Mistral. Santiago, Escuela Nacional de Artes Gráficas. 153 p.
The students of the National School of Graphic Arts were given the privilege of including six poems from *Lagar*, a still unpublished book of Gabriela Mistral.

2720. ————. Poemas de las madres. 63 dibujos de los cuadernos diarios de André Racz. Con un estudio crítico por Antonio R. Romera. Santiago, Cuadernos del Pacífico. Unpaged.
A collector's item. Romera's study of the Rumanian painter Racz fills half of the book.

2721. Muñoz Larreta, Helena. Sonetos en carne viva. Buenos Aires, Editorial Sudamericana. 159 p.
Interesting remarks about the sonnet by Juan Ramón Jiménez in his introduction. Helena's sonnets, however, hardly conform to the fluidity prescribed by the Spanish poet.

2722. Neruda, Pablo. Canto general. México. 567 p., illus.
First planned as a *Canto general de Chile* this work grew thematically in scope. Now the original Chilean "canto" is but one of 16 main subdivisions, some of which had seen independent publication in recent years (for instance, "Alturas de Macchu Picchu" and "Que despierte el leñador"). For years it will be maintained by some that this is Neruda at his best; others, though admiring the work, will insist that it is marred by the poet's avowed intention to mix poetry and politics. The copy here reviewed is one of a limited edition of 500, extravagantly large, heavy, and sumptuous, with colored illustrations on lining papers by Diego Rivera and David Alfaro Siqueiros. A smallsize facsimile edition for popular consumption was issued at about the same time. See also item 2742.

2723. ————. Peace for twilights to come. With a pen portrait of the poet by Ilya Ehrenburg. Bombay, People's Publishing House. 46 p.
English version, by "Waldeen," of Neruda's *Que despierte el leñador*. Issued by the All-India Peace Committee on the occasion of the poet's visit to India. See *HLAS, no. 14, 1948,* item 2877.

2724. Noguera Mora, Neftalí (ed.). La generación poética de 1918. Bogotá, Editorial Iqueima (Cuadernos Venezolanos, Publicaciones de la Embajada de Venezuela, 6). 88 p.
Twenty-eight poets. Among them: Antonio Arráiz, Andrés Eloy Blanco, Jacinto Fombona Pachano, Fernando Paz Castillo, Manuel F. Rugeles.

2725. Ochoa, Enriqueta. Las urgencias de un Dios. México, Ediciones Papel de Poesía. 55 p.
An outstanding newcomer, richly endowed and valiant, struggling to define her own idiom.

2726. Palés Matos, Luis. Tuntún de pasa y grifería. Prólogo de Jaime Benítez. San Juan, Puerto Rico, Biblioteca de Autores Puertorriqueños. 140 p.
New edition of a modern classic, preceded by an introduction on Palés Matos and pessimism in Puerto Rico (written 1938).

2727. Palma, José Joaquín. Poesías. Tercera edición. Guatemala, Ediciones El Libro de Guatemala (Col. Los de Ayer). xxxii, 283 p.
For a biography of this Cuban poet who spent the second half of his life in Honduras and Guatemala, see *HLAS, no. 14, 1948,* item 2893. Poems are preceded by letters from Darío, Martí, and others.

2728. Pérez, Saúl. Homo-ciudad. Montevideo, Ciudadela. 44 p.
Enthusiastic prologue by "Jesualdo." Young Pérez runs the risk of being one of those prodigies who overextend themselves.

2729. LOS POETAS ARGENTINOS CANTAN AL LIBERTADOR. Buenos Aires, Guillermo Kraft. 184 p.
Thirty-seven leading poets of the 19th and 20th centuries are represented by one poem each, inspired by José de San Martín.

2730. Ruiz, Carlos H. Manifiesto. Guatemala, Hispania. Unpaged, illus.
Often deliberately prosaic, these poems succeed in expressing the noble intentions of a poet who believes in "dynamic democracy."

2731. Sánchez Lavid, Aníbal. Siete recuerdos breves a la memoria de Federico García Lorca. Buenos Aires, Cuadernos Literarios Ánfora. 58 p.
Imitations of some external aspects of García Lorca's verse. To continue indulging in *lorquismo* is a disservice to the poet of Granada.

2732. Silva, Víctor Domingo. Aún no se ha puesto el sol. Santiago, Nascimento. 242 p.
More poems from an indefatigable and versatile writer (verse, prose fiction, and drama), whose first book of verse appeared in 1905. Present book does not show his usual selectivity.

2733. Soffia, José Antonio. Poemas y poesías. Selección y estudio crítico de Raúl Silva Castro. Santiago, Imprenta

Universitaria (Biblioteca de Escritores de Chile, 17). cii, 466 p.
Scholarly introduction. In addition to more than a hundred poems, there is included a brief paper on the Brazilian poet A. Gonçalves Dias. Soffia was born in 1843 and died in 1886.

2734. Umaña Bernal, José. Nocturno del Libertador. Bogotá, Voluntad. 33 p.
A long poem to Bolívar, restrained, grave, and inspired. Eduardo Caballero Calderón's praise of it in his prologue seems to us somewhat exaggerated.

2735. Ureña de Henríquez, Salomé. Poesías completas. Ciudad Trujillo, Impresora Dominicana (Biblioteca Dominicana, serie 1, v. 4). 351 p.
Issued by the Ministry of Education and Fine Arts to commemorate the 100th anniversary of the birth of this noted Dominican poet and educator. Based on the 1920 Madrid edition prepared by her son, the late Pedro Henríquez Ureña, it includes a conscientious critical introduction and notes by Joaquín Balaguer. It contains 11 poems not present in the Madrid edition.

TRANSLATIONS

2736. Carrera Andrade, Jorge. Visitor of mist. Introduction and translations by G. R. Coulthard. London, Williams & Norgate. 74 p.
Selections from the distinguished Ecuadorean poet. Five of the translations are the work of Kathleen Nott. The present volume "is intended largely as a complement to the English translations [by Muna Lee] published [in 1946] by Macmillan in New York under the title of Secret Country."

2737. Llona, Teresa María. Intersection. Translated by Marie Pope Wallis. Dallas, Texas, The Story Book Press. 64 p.
Translation of a Peruvian poet's unimportant book, Encrucijada. See HLAS, no. 4, 1938, item 4046.

CRITICISM AND BIOGRAPHY

2738. Ayestarán, Lauro. La primitiva poesía gauchesca en el Uruguay. T. 1, 1812-1838. Montevideo, Imprenta El Siglo Ilustrado. 245 p., illus.
Scholarly 60-page introduction followed by a selection of cielitos, diálogos, etc., many anonymous.

2739. Bajarlía, Juan Jacobo. Notas sobre el barroco. Undurraga y la poesía chilena. Gongorismo y surrealismo. Buenos Aires, Santiago Rueda. 71 p.
Baroque elements underlying the poetry of Antonio Undurraga and other Chileans. A 20-page essay followed by eleven poems (three of them inedited until now), and some notes. The essay appeared earlier in the year in Atenea, año 27, t. 98, no. 301, julio, p. 88-106.

2740. Berenguer Carisomo, Arturo. La estilística de la soledad en el Martín Fierro (Rev. univ. Buenos Aires, 4. época, año 4, no. 14, abril-junio, p. 315-389).
Original approach, persuasively argued, to the immortal Gaucho's personality—antisocial, anarchic, destructive—and to the author's artistic intuition. One of the year's enduring essays.

2741. Canton, Wilberto. Posiciones. México, Imprenta Universitaria (Serie Letras, no. 4). 174 p.
Biocritical articles of varying length on various writers. Outstanding because of the unusual information they contain are those on two Chilean poets, Pablo Neruda and Alberto Rojas Giménez.

2742. Cardona Peña, Alfredo. Pablo Neruda. Breve historia de sus libros (Cuad. amer., año 9, no. 6, nov.-dic., p. 257-289).
Not a bibliographer's but a keen poet-critic's account, enriched by information supplied by Neruda himself. Especially interesting revelations about Residencia en la tierra and Canto general.

2743. Castillo Nájera, Francisco. Manuel Acuña. México, Imprenta Universitaria. 201 p.
Searching study of the man and his poetry, painstakingly documented. The author's experience as a physician and his poetic talent explain the rare virtues of this work.

2744. Chacón, Jorge. Perfil literario de Remigio Crespo Toral. Prólogo de Gonzalo Zaldumbide. Quito, Editorial Ecuatoriana. xx, 422 p.
Crespo Toral (1860-1939) was a revered "national poet," virtually unknown outside Ecuador. This exhaustive study is an impassioned defense of his right to be recognized as one of the major poets of Spanish America. A good portion is devoted to Crespo Toral's works in prose.

2745. Coulthard, G. R. El sentimiento de la naturaleza en la poesía hispanoamericana (Atenea, año 27, t. 99, no. 305-306, nov.-dic., p. 267-298).
Rapid survey, from the inadequacy of Pedro de Oña to the cosmic breadth, deeply rooted in the American soil, of Neruda.

2746. Diego, Gerardo. Vicente Huidobro (Atenea, año 27, t. 96, no. 295-296, p. 10-18).
Brief but significant statement on Huidobro's influence, by a leading poet of Spain.

2747. Fernández Spencer, Antonio. César Vallejo o la poesía de las cosas (Cuad. hispanoamer., no. 14, marzo-abril, p. 387-398).
Discerning statement on the "conversational," "every-day" tone of Vallejo's idiom, which is one of the reasons why his poetry is "lo más avanzado que existe en la lírica de hoy."

2748. García, Serafín J. El tiempo en la poesía de "El Viejo Pancho" (*Rev. nac.*, Montevideo, año 13, t. 45, no. 134, feb., p. 222-234).
"El Viejo Pancho" is the pen name of José Alonso y Trelles (1860-1925), who cultivated gaucho subjects in Uruguay.

2749. Gastaldi, Santiago. En torno de la obra de Vasseur (*Rev. nac.*, Montevideo, año 13, t. 48, no. 143, nov., p. 260-275).
Unstinted praise of Álvaro Armando Vasseur as a poet.

2750. Gómez Paz, Julieta. Los antisonetos de Alfonsina Storni (*Cuad. amer.*, año 9, no. 3, mayo-junio, p. 224-232).
Sensitive evaluation of the compositions in Storni's last book, *Mascarilla y trébol*.

2751. Guillén, Pedro. Tras la huella de Porfirio Barba Jacob (*Cuad. amer.*, año 9, no. 1, enero-feb., p. 261-265).
Interesting footnote to a puzzling life.

2752. Iglesias, Augusto. Gabriela Mistral y el modernismo en Chile. Ensayo de crítica subjetiva. Santiago, Editorial Universitaria, 1949, i.e. 1950. 452 p.
As complete an account of the Chilean phase of Mistral's career as seems possible at the present time, with copious discussion of her work and that of many Chilean contemporaries of hers. The story of her successful candidacy for the Nobel Prize is a most interesting chapter. The author's familiarity with the literary scene in Chile results in a rich picture of the modernist movement in that country, with many a human interest story. The chattiness of the style blends well with the digressive method followed in the composition of the book. Iglesias is usually complimentary in the evaluation of Gabriela's contemporaries, and lavish of praise in her case.

2753. Llambías de Azevedo, Alfonso. El modernismo. Montevideo, La Casa del Estudiante. 31 p.
Searching inquiry into the meaning of *modernismo* as defined and understood by its principal practitioners and critics.

2754. Machado Bonet, Ofelia. Circunstanciales. II. Montevideo, Rosgal. 233 p.
One of the items (p. 175-192) in this miscellany of newspaper articles and lectures deals with the Uruguayan poet María Eugenia Vaz Ferreira (1875-1924).

2755. Méndez Plancarte, Alfonso. Primor y primavera del hai-kai (*Ábside*, v. 14, no. 4, oct.-dic., p. 495-531).
A good deal about this Japanese verse form in Spanish American poetry. Justified praise of José Juan Tablada and Jorge Carrera Andrade.

2756. Miró Quesada S., Aurelio. Mariano Melgar, estudiante y maestro (*Mar del sur*, año 3, no. 13, sept.-oct., p. 1-17).

Well documented study correcting flagrant biographical errors with regard to the forerunner of Peruvian romanticism.

2757. Monner Sans, José María. Los temas poéticos de Julián del Casal (*Cuad. amer.*, año 9, no. 1, enero-feb., p. 246-260).
Leopardi, Huysmans, Poe, and numerous French poets of the 19th century, as well as some contemporary Spanish American poets, influenced the Cuban poet.

2758. NERUDA EN GUATEMALA. Guatemala, Ediciones Saker-Ti. 45 p.
Articles on the Chilean poet published in the Guatemala City press on the occasion of his second visit to the country.

2759. Osorio Lizarazo, J. A. Dos poetas malditos de América (*Rev. América*, no. 62, marzo, p. 317-332).
On the Colombian Porfirio Barba Jacob (1880-1942) and the Venezuelan Carlos Borges (1867-1932). The account of the latter's preposterous conduct is a valuable biographical contribution.

2760. Pedroso, Margarita de. Influencia de Rubén Darío en la poesía española (*Atenea*, año 27, t. 97, no. 300, p. 297-320).
A Spaniard recognizes Darío's influence on Spanish poets of all magnitudes.

2761. Pereira Rodríguez, José. Las revistas literarias de Julio Herrera y Reissig (*Rev. nac.*, Montevideo, t. 48, año 13, no. 143, nov., p. 178-189).
Continuation of article mentioned in *HLAS, no. 15, 1949*, item 2419.

2762. Phillips, Allen W. La metáfora en la obra de Julio Herrera y Reissig (*Rev. iberoamer.*, v. 16, no. 31, feb.-julio, p. 31-48).
An attempt to capture the essence of this poet's salient characteristic as a prodigious master of metaphor.

2763. Quintana González, Octavio. Apreciaciones y anécdotas sobre Rubén Darío. León, Nicaragua. 150 p.
Even in a book as naïvely written as this, one finds interesting facts. The author is well intentioned and honest in his reporting.

2764. Rega Molina, Horacio. Proyección social del *Martín Fierro*. Buenos Aires, Presidencia de la Nación, Subsecretaría de Informaciones. 31 p.
The thesis is that José Hernández advocated in 1872 social reforms which Perón carried out 72 years later.

2765. Reyes, Alfonso. Tertulia de Madrid. Buenos Aires, Espasa-Calpe Argentina (Col. Austral). 145 p.

Anecdotes and other marginalia relating to Rubén Darío are to be found on pages 116-145 under the titles: *R. D. en México, La glorieta de R. D.,* and *Cartas de R. D.*

2766. Rodríguez-Alcalá, Hugo. Alejandro Guanes. Vida y obra *(Rev. hisp. mod.,* t. 14, no. 1-2, enero-abril, 1948, i.e. 1950, p. 1-50).
Paraguayan poet (1872-1925) who enjoyed much local prestige around 1910. Well documented.

2767. Vilariño, Idea. Julio Herrera y Reissig. Seis años de poesía. Montevideo, Número. 48 p.
Herrera's work produced between 1904 and 1910, the year of his premature death, constitutes his truly significant contribution, according to this perceptive critic. First published in *Número,* año 2, no. 6-8, enero-junio, p. 118-161.

2768. ————. *La torre de las esfinges* como tarea *(Número,* año 2, no. 10-11, sept.-dic., p. 601-609).
Herrera's manuscripts show that he was a painstaking artificer.

2769. Ycaza Tijerino, Julio. Rubén Darío y Pedro Salinas *(Cuad. amer.,* año 9, no. 5, sept.-oct., p. 298-303).
À propos Salinas' book reviewed in *HLAS, no. 14, 1948,* item 2936. Trenchant statement on Darío's authentic Hispano-Americanism as opposed to cosmopolitanism.

2770. Zanela, Catalina. Rafael López, poeta modernista. México, Ediciones Studium. 99 p.
Master's thesis which marshals all the facts about a poet who played a secondary but estimable role in the Mexican modernist movement. Born at Guanajuato in 1873, he died in 1943 at Mexico City.

ADDENDA

2771. Fierro, Humberto. El laúd en el valle *(Casa cult. ecuat.,* t. 3, no. 8, enero-junio, 1949, p. 179-227).
Reproduction of a significant book of verse published at Quito in 1919. Introduction by Hugo Alemán.

2772. Goldsack, Hugo. En torno a cierto fuego. Santiago, Ediciones Diógenes (Serie Nuevos Valores Líricos, 2), 1949. 31 p.
Goldsack is unquestionably a "nuevo valor."

2773. NUEVA POESÍA NICARAGÜENSE. Introducción de Ernesto Cardenal. Selección y notas de Orlando Cuadra Downing. Madrid, Instituto de Cultura Hispánica, Seminario de Problemas Hispanoamericanos (Col. La Encina y el Mar), 1949. 512 p.

Highly selective anthology, a model of its kind. Darío is followed by 13 poets representative of three groups or generations: "Los continuadores de Rubén" (Azarías Pallais, Salomón de la Selva, Alfonso Cortés), "Vanguardia" (José Coronel Urtecho, Pablo Antonio Cuadra, Joaquín Pasos), and "Los novísimos" (Ernesto Mejía Sánchez, Carlos Martínez Rivas, Ernesto Cardenal, Ángel Martínez, Ernesto Gutiérrez, Fernando Silva, Rodolfo Sandino). Excellent 90-page introduction; adequate notes.

2774. Prado, Pedro. Antología. Las estancias del amor. Santiago, Editorial del Pacífico, 1949. 158 p.
Selections from the second phase of Prado's poetry, covering the years 1934-1949. Compilation prepared by Raúl Silva Castro on the occasion of the award to Prado of the National Literary Prize for 1949. Prado died early in 1952.

2775. Rodríguez-Alcalá, Hugo. Los *Recuerdos* de Alejandro Guanes *(Rev. hisp. mod.,* t. 13, no. 3-4, julio-oct., 1947, i.e. 1949, p. 249-262).
Article superseded by a more extensive treatment (see item 2766).

2776. Santos, Ninfa. Amor quiere que muera. México, Ediciones América, Revista Antológica, 1949. 50 p.
Deeply felt love poetry, artistically restrained, by a woman born in Costa Rica but closely identified with the literary life of Mexico.

2777. Solari, Armando. Fábula y canto. Valparaíso, Victoria, 1949. 89 p., illus.
Includes a poem in memory of Miguel Hernández, of ambitious proportions and memorable quality.

2778. Valle, Rafael Heliodoro. Poemas desconocidos de Martí *(Rev. hisp. mod.,* t. 13, no. 3-4, julio-oct., 1947, i.e. 1949, p. 305-309).
Two poems that appeared in *El Eco de Ambos Mundos,* Mexico City, in 1876. Same article appears in *Arch. José Martí,* no. 14, enero-dic., 1949, i.e. 1950, p. 444-448.

2779. Vera, Pedro Jorge. Túnel iluminado. Quito, Casa de la Cultura Ecuatoriana (Biblioteca de Poetas Ecuatorianos, no. 3), 1949. 83 p.
Verse written in Chile and Ecuador between 1939 and 1948 by one of Guayaquil's finest poets.

2780. Xammar, Luis Fabio. Obras completas. I. Poesía. Lima, Ministerio de Educación Pública (Ediciones de la Dirección de Educación Artística y Extensión Cultural), 1949. 188 p.
Xammar's (1911-1947) scant but significant contribution in the field of poetry.

DRAMA

JOSÉ JUAN ARROM

PLAYS

2781. Amorim, Enrique. La segunda sangre. Pausa en la selva. Yo voy más lejos. Buenos Aires, Conducta (Col. Maese Pedro). 167 p.
Un prestigioso novelista busca laureles en las tablas sin lograrlos plenamente. De estas tres obras, la más satisfactoria es la última, donde el autor se desenvuelve en el ambiente rural uruguayo que él conoce bien (lo ha tratado con éxito en *El caballo y su sombra*), pero la estructura resulta algo desarticulada y la trama innecesariamente artificiosa y melodramática.

2782. Ayala Michelena, Leopoldo. Teatro seleccionado. Prólogo de Luis Peraza. Caracas, El Creyón. xvi, 430 p.
Doce piezas de un fervoroso cultivador del género. La deficiente cultura literaria del autor marra el mérito de estas producciones.

2783. Badía, Nora. Mañana es una palabra (*Nueva gen.*, año 1, no. 2, feb., p. 5-9).
Excelente monólogo en el cual se desarrolla en increíble concisión de minutos un delicado, veraz y tiernísimo análisis de una alma femenina. Iguala, y para algunos tal vez aventaje, a las obras maestras de este género, tales como *La más fuerte*, de Strindberg, *La voz humana*, de Cocteau, y *Antes del desayuno*, de O'Neill.

2784. Bengoa, Juan León. La espada desnuda. Drama histórico en 10 cuadros. Montevideo, Letras. 182 p.
Discreta escenificación de la vida de Artigas, de interés muy reducido fuera de las fronteras nacionales.

2785. Cantón, Wilberto. Saber morir. Pieza en tres actos (*Cuad. amer.*, v. 51, no. 3, mayo-junio, p. 233-288).
La publicación de esta obra por *Cuadernos Americanos* es ya garantía de su alta calidad. En ella se escenifica la dramática situación de un joven idealista que, condenado a la última pena por un asesinato político, huye hacia el único fin posible: la muerte. Hay diálogos brillantes y momentos de gran teatralidad; por lo contrario, algunas motivaciones, por muy freudianas que parezcan, dejan lugar a serias dudas.

2786. Fabregat Cúneo, Dardo. Como por arte de magia (*Rev. nac.*, Montevideo, v. 47, no. 139, julio, p. 85-120; no. 140, agosto, p. 250-272).
Feliz ensayo de teatro de ideas, loable no sólo por el adecuado manejo de los elementos dramáticos sino por la agudeza del diálogo y la desasosegante actualidad del tema analizado: la cada vez más peligrosa eficacia de los actuales medios de propaganda en manos de los simuladores de patriotismo que se erigen en árbitros de los destinos de un pueblo.

2787. Flores Chinarro, Francisco. Cuidado con las jaranas. Lima, Taller de Linotipia. 71 p.
Comedia de costumbres en dos actos y en verso, estrenada en Ica en 1861 y ahora publicada por primera vez.

2788. Godoy, Emma. Caín, el hombre. Misterio trágico. México, Ábside. 65 p.
Pieza que no acaba de plasmar ni en filosofía, ni en poesía, ni en teatro.

2789. Macau, Miguel A. Obras dramáticas. La justicia en la inconsciencia. Julián. La partida. El triunfo de la vida. México. 184 p.
Reimpresión de cuatro obras estrenadas entre 1909 y 1914.

2790. Perrín, Tomás. México en escena. Prólogo de Margarita Michelena. México, Excélsior. 132 p.
Contiene *Foro de México, o el drama de una comedia*, amena obra de carácter popular, llena de sátira política y abundancia de chistes en que la ironía y los dobles sentidos juegan parte principal.

2791. Porto, Miguel Antonio. En la pasión el martirio. Drama en tres actos, en verso. Habana, Belascoaín (Col. Cultura Ariguanabense, v. 2). 73 p.
Impresión de una obra inédita, del siglo XIX, de escaso mérito.

2792. Sáenz, Carlos Luis. Dramatizaciones. San José, Ediciones del *Repertorio Americano*. 86 p.
Quince piececitas infantiles, la mayor parte basadas en temas folklóricos y desarrolladas en un estilo delicado y atrayente.

2793. Sarah, Roberto. Algún día . . . . Comedia dramática en tres actos y un epílogo. Santiago. 108 p., illus.
Con los hechos aparentemente intrascendentes del vivir cotidiano y el lenguaje sencillo, vivo y suelto de la vida misma, el autor teje las ilusiones y desencantos de una familia y logra una pieza honda, sentida y sumamente humana. A la sobriedad y eficacia del diálogo van unidos el cuidado de los pormenores, una fina observación y el constante dominio de la escena, de todo lo cual resulta una obra de notables méritos como espectáculo teatral y como creación literaria. Roberto Sarah es el seudónimo de Andrés Terbay.

2794. Villaurrutia, Xavier. La tragedia de las equivocaciones. México, Gráficos Guanajuato. 19 p.
Última creación teatral del fino dramaturgo recientemente fallecido. Es un monólogo esencialmente trágico a pesar de su enfoque humorístico, que revela el ingenio e inventiva del autor a más de su consumada pericia de escritor.

TRANSLATION

2796. Drago-Bracco, Adolfo. Colombine wants flowers. Translated by Willis Knapp Jones (*Poet lore*, v. 56, no. 2, summer, p. 144-162).

Traducción de una pieza infantil, *Colombina quiere flores*, del guatemalteco A. Drago-Bracco (nacido en 1894).

CRITICISM AND BIOGRAPHY

2797. Castagnino, Raúl H. Esquema de la literatura dramática argentina, 1717-1949. Buenos Aires, Instituto de Historia del Teatro Americano. 125 p.

Este libro aparece, después de las extensas obras sobre el mismo tema por Ernesto Morales (1941) y Luis Ordaz (véase *HLAS, no. 12, 1946*, párrafo 2422), a manera de útil ensayo de selección y síntesis.

2798. ———— (and others). Martín Coronado (*Bol. estud. teatro*, t. 8, no. 29-30, abril-sept.).

Estos números están dedicados totalmente a conmemorar el primer centenario del dramaturgo argentino Martín Coronado (1850-1919). Contienen artículos de Raúl H. Castagnino, Joaquín Linares y Arturo Berenguer Carisomo y la reimpresión de *El granadero*, pieza en un acto y en verso, del propio Coronado, estrenada en 1916.

2799. Dos años y medio del INBA. V. 3. Fundación del Departamento de Teatro. México, Secretaría de Educación Pública, Instituto Nacional de Bellas Artes. 100 p.

Informe presentado por el Instituto Nacional de Bellas Artes sobre las actividades realizadas por los departamentos de Teatro y Literatura y de Producción Teatral, de enero, 1947, a junio, 1949.

2800. Hernández, José A. Notas sobre teatro peruano contemporáneo (*Mar del sur*, año 2, no. 10, marzo-abril, p. 62-74).

Ojeada impresionista, a veces levantada a líricos ditirambos y a veces reducida a meras listas, de la producción dramática peruana desde comienzos del siglo XIX hasta el momento actual.

2801. Jones, Willis Knapp. Latin America through drama in English. A bibliography. Washington, Pan American Union, Division of Philosophy, Letters and Sciences. 12 p.

Nueva edición de la útil bibliografía publicada en la revista *Hispania*, v. 28, no. 2, mayo, 1945. A las traducciones consignadas por el profesor Jones hay que agregar las de dos piezas de

capital importancia: *El güegüence*, comedia-ballet indígena, traducida por D. G. Brinton, Filadelfia, 1883, y *Corona de sombra*, del mexicano Rodolfo Usigli, traducida por William F. Stirling, Londres, 1946 (véase *HLAS, no. 12, 1946*, párrafo 2768a).

2802. Lemos, Martín F. Tres figuras inolvidables del viejo sainete criollo (*Bol. estud. teatro*, t. 8, no. 28, enero-marzo, p. 13-24).

Las tres figuras son Nemesio Trejo, Carlos M. Pacheco y Luis Vittone, todas de principios del siglo XX.

2803. María y Campos, Armando de. El programa en cien años de teatro en México. México, Ediciones Mexicanas (Enciclopedia Mexicana de Arte, 3). 62 p., 57 illus.

Monografía profusamente ilustrada sobre un aspecto poco estudiado de la historia teatral americana.

2804. Monzón, Antonio. El teatro porteño en el histórico año de la Revolución de Mayo (*Bol. estud. teatro*, t. 8, no. 28, enero-marzo, p. 3-12).

Pormenores sin trascendencia de la vida teatral de Buenos Aires en 1810.

2805. Pérez Leyva, María de los Ángeles. Fernando Calderón y su teatro. México. 108 p.

Estudio, todavía inseguro, de uno de los más destacados dramaturgos mexicanos del período romántico. Tesis, Universidad Nacional Autónoma de México.

2806. Rosa-Nieves, Cesáreo. Notas para los orígenes de las representaciones dramáticas en Puerto Rico (*Asomante*, año 6, v. 6, no. 1, enero-marzo, p. 63-77).

Consigna aisladas actividades teatrales desde 1644 hasta 1856.

2807. Sáez, Antonia. El teatro en Puerto Rico. Notas para su historia. Río Piedras, Editorial Universitaria (Cuadernos de la Universidad de Puerto Rico, Departamento de Estudios Hispánicos, no. 5). 185 p.

Valioso ensayo de ordenación de la producción dramática puertorriqueña durante los siglos XIX y XX. Contiene una buena bibliografía y listas de actores y compañías.

2808. Spell, Jefferson Rea. *Indulgencia para todos* in Austria and Germany (*Hisp. rev.*, v. 18, no. 2, April, p. 158-163).

Consigna el continuado éxito de la referida pieza de Manuel Eduardo de Gorostiza, 1789-1851, en tierras germánicas cuando ya estaba poco menos que olvidada en el mundo hispánico.

2809. Wogan, Daniel. The Indian in Mexican dramatic poetry (1823-1918) (*Bull. hisp. stud.*, v. 27, no. 107, July-Sept., p. 163-171).

Documentado estudio que señala la presencia en
el teatro mexicano del indio como personaje
heroico. Las principales figuras dramatizadas
son Xicotencatl, durante los primeros lustros, y
luego Guatémoc, que ha seguido siendo el más
popular de todos.

2810. Wyatt, James Larkin. La obra dra-
mática de Rodolfo Usigli. México. 111 p.
Tesis (Universidad Nacional Autónoma de
México) muy informativa, con numerosas citas

de Usigli y de varios críticos que hacen la lectura
interesante y amena.

ADDENDUM

2810a. Albán Mosquera, Ernesto. Estampas quiteñas. Quito, Editorial Fray Jodoco
Ricke, 1949. 303 p.
Colección de entremeses populares, de carácter
costumbrista y abundantes alusiones locales.

Brazilian Literature and Language

RALPH EDWARD DIMMICK

DURING 1950, publishers and critics alike continued to speak of a "crisis" in Brazilian letters. Falling sales may in part have been owing to the rapidly rising cost of living, which has made a book a luxury for the great majority of the population, but they may also reflect the decline in writing lamented by the critics. Thus it will be noted that a truly outstanding work, such as the first part of Veríssimo's *O tempo e o vento,* which appeared at the end of 1949, could become one of the greatest best-sellers in Brazilian history, despite its relatively high price. The stagnation which seems currently to characterize literary production in the country doubtless represents nothing more than a natural reaction to the great creative outburst of the thirties and early forties.

If, in prose, one notes little more than a continuation of the novels of social protest and introspection, dominant for fifteen years and more, among the younger poets there seems to be a trend toward Parnassianism—great preoccupation with words and with form, but little appeal to the emotions. As examples of this tendency, one might cite the names of Haroldo de Campos *(Auto do possesso),* José Escobar Faria *(Poemas de câmera),* and Ruy Affonso Machado *(Rumo enxuto).* The finest work of the year, however, was produced by others. *O irmão* of Alphonsus de Guimaraens Filho was awarded the Manuel Bandeira Prize in a contest sponsored by *Jornal de Letras,* and Cassiano Ricardo, the leader of the *verde-amarelistas* of the twenties, achieved in *A face perdida* a new depth and beauty of expression. Another notable event of 1950 was the publication of the complete *Obra poética* of Jorge de Lima, another *modernista* to show remarkable growth with the passage of years.

In prose fiction, 1950 was marked by the pre-eminence of the short story. A number of distinguished collections appeared, among the best being Leonardo Arroyo's *Viagem para Málaga* and Lúcia Benedetti's *Vesperal com chuva.* Even the best "novel" of the year, Fran Martins' *O cruzeiro tem cinco estrêlas,* is in reality a group of long short stories, within a rather artificial frame. Other important narrative works of 1950 were José Geraldo Vieira's novel *A ladeira da memória,* Jorge de Lima's *Guerra dentro do beco,* and Antônio Olavo Pereira's *Contra-mão.* César Arruda Castanho's *Um pingo no mapa* constituted perhaps the most promising debut.

Notable collections of *crônicas* were brought out by Alceu Amoroso Lima *(Manhãs de São Lourenço)* and Fernando Tavares Sabino *(A cidade vazia);* the latter is of peculiar interest to American readers.

The great flowering of the theater which has come about in Brazil since the war has been nourished chiefly by translations of foreign works, old and new, but Helena Silveira's expressionist drama *No fundo do poço* evoked much comment and controversy.

1950 saw the publication of the first volumes of two works of utmost importance to scholars. Lúcia Miguel-Pereira's *Prosa de ficção, 1870-1920* forms part of the long-heralded *História da literatura brasileira* being brought out under the general editorship of Álvaro Lins. Augusto Magne's *Dicionário da língua portuguesa*, when complete, should approximate in proportion and scope the *Oxford English Dictionary*.

The Brazilian Academy, in a sudden burst of energy, awarded its 1949 and 1950 prizes for 1948 and 1949 productions, respectively, whether published or unpublished. The 1949 prizes went to Agripa de Vasconcelos for *Suor e sangre*, poetry; Dirceu Quintanilha, *Novos mundos em Vila Teresa*, short stories; Roberto Alvim Corrêa, *Anteu e a crítica*, criticism (see *HLAS, no. 14, 1948,* item 3008); Lúcia Benedetti, *O casaco encantado*, drama; Humberto Bastos, *A economia brasileira e o mundo moderno*, scholarly work (see *HLAS, no. 14, 1948,* item 1090); Mário Graciotti, *A Europa tranquila*, miscellaneous.

The prize-winners in 1950 were: Domingos Carvalho da Silva, *Praia oculta*, poetry; Dinah Silveira de Queiroz, *As noites do Morro do Encantado*, short stories; A. L. Nobre de Melo, *Mundos mágicos*, criticism; J. B. de Melo e Sousa, *Meninos de Queluz*, social history; Guilherme de Figueiredo, *Um deus dormiu lá em casa*, drama; Theo Brandão, *Folclore de Alagoas*, folklore; Otón Xavier de Brito Machado, *Dicionário indiolálico*, scholarly work; Antônio Loureiro de Souza, *Bahianos ilustres* (see *HLAS, no. 15, 1949,* item 1822), biography, and Maluh de Ouro Prêto, *Crônicas de Paris*, travel (see *HLAS, no. 16, 1950,* item 2930).

The Machado de Assis Prize for "conjunto de obra" went to Eugênio Gomes, and the award of the Felipe de Oliveira Society, again for the whole of a writer's production, to Augusto Meyer. The only deaths of the year to be noted were those of Mário Sette and the poet Antônio Francisco da Costa e Silva.

BIBLIOGRAPHY AND LANGUAGE

2811. Azevedo, Francisco Ferreira dos Santos. Dicionário analógico da língua portuguesa. Ideias afins. São Paulo, Companhia Editôra Nacional. xxvi, 685 p.
Patterned directly upon Roget's *Thesaurus*, this admirable volume fills an important gap for Portuguese. The care bestowed upon organization and revision and the scope of the book (over 20,000 entries in the index), as well as its nature, combine to make it a reference aid indispensable to all students of Portuguese.

2812. Englekirk, John E. A literatura norteamericana no Brasil. México. 181 p.
Extensive bibliography of American works in Portuguese translation (including social and natural sciences), and of Brazilian criticism of American literature, preceded by an essay on Brazilian interest in American authors and the influence of the latter upon writers in the southern republic.

2813. Fernandes, Francisco. Dicionário de regimes de substantivos e adjectivos. Pôrto Alegre, Globo. 357 p.
This work, showing with copious examples from classic and modern authors the sequent constructions required by nouns and adjectives in common use, is invaluable to all students of Portuguese syntax. For Fernandes' *Dicionário de verbos e regimes*, see *HLAS, no. 13, 1947,* item 2262.

2814. Fichário. Resenha da bibliografia brasileira. Rio de Janeiro, Pongetti. Ano 1, no. 1, jan.-fev.
Bimonthly publication covering all books being published in Brazil, classified according to the Dewey decimal system. Extremely useful to all interested in keeping up with current bibliography.

2815. Machado Filho, Aires da Mata. Português & literatura. Belo Horizonte, Editôra Minas Gerais. 164 p.
This volume, giving the author's eminently sensible views on all aspects of good usage, is the fruit of his wide reading and deep meditation on linguistic problems.

2816. Magne, Augusto. Dicionário da língua portuguesa, especialmente dos períodos medieval e clássico. V. 1, *A-Af*. Rio de Janeiro, Ministério da Educação e Saúde, Instituto Nacional do Livro. lxxvi, 578 p.
First volume of what is intended as a monumental etymological dictionary of the Portuguese language. Emphasis on earlier periods; much attention to verbal constructions. First volume already contains 2 supplements. Brazilianisms included insofar as possible. Done with great care; should prove an invaluable tool to students of linguistics and of the Portuguese language in general.

2817. Neto, Serafim Silva. Introdução ao estudo da língua portuguesa no Brasil. Prefácio de Augusto Magne. Rio de Janeiro, Instituto Nacional do Livro (Biblioteca Popular Brasileira, 29). 286 p.
This book is, as the title indicates, a mere introduction to the subject of the Portuguese language in Brazil: it states problems rather than resolves them. Concerned chiefly with the ex-

ternal history of the language, based almost entirely upon previous studies, it offers a useful synthesis, and shows the work of a careful scholar.

2818. Netto, João Amoroso. "O Oitenta e Nove" (*Bol. bibliog.*, São Paulo, v. 16, p. 105-108).
Concerning a newspaper published by São Paulo law students in 1889.

2819. Safady, Jamil. História da imprensa árabe no Brasil (*Bol. bibliog.*, São Paulo, v. 14, p. 163-178).
Information concerning the activities of the Arab-language press in Brazil.

2820. Silva, António de Morais. Grande dicionário da língua portuguesa. Décima edição, revista, corrigida, muito aumentada e actualizada segundo as regras do acordo ortográfico lusobrasileiro de 10 de agôsto de 1945 por Augusto Moreno, Cardoso Júnior e José Pedro Machado. V. 2, Arma de alcance-Cestina. Lisboa, Confluência. 1114 p.
For v. 1, see *HLAS, no. 15, 1949*, item 2476.

2821. Sodré, Nelson Werneck. A pequena imprensa na Regência e no Império (*Rev. arq. mun.*, ano 17, no. 134, julho-agôsto, p. 69-86).
Concerning printed pasquinades of the 1830's.

2822. Tilden, J. (ed.). Dicionário inglês-português. Con pronúncia figurada e inúmeras expressões idiomáticas. São Paulo, Brasil Editôra. 381 p.
Many helpful hints on translation of idioms, but usage is English, rather than American, and while there is an entry for *doctors-commons, airplane (aeroplane)* is not included.

2823. Voigtlander, Maria Leonor. Bibliografia de história da literatura brasileira (*Bol. bibliog.*, São Paulo, v. 14, p. 103-116).
Bibliography of histories of Brazilian literature in general, and of literary histories of the various States.

CRITICISM AND BIOGRAPHY

2824. Alves, Joaquim. A propósito de movimentos literários (*Clã*, ano 3, no. 10, julho, p. 72-76).
Brazil lacks a tradition and a culture of its own: its culture is all imported from abroad. Literary activity in the provinces is confined to small groups, seldom of more than local importance.

2825. ANHEMBI. São Paulo. V. 1, no. 1, dez.
Excellent new monthly review, edited by Paulo Duarte, and dedicated chiefly to literary and sociological matters.

2826. Barros, Francisca de. Alguns aspectos da linguagem de Euclides da Cunha (*Brasília*, v. 5, p. 29-50).
Felicities and infelicities of Euclides' style.

2827. Belo, José Maria. Machado de Assis. Introdução a um ensaio crítico. O homen e o meio. Ascenção (*Jorn. letras*, ano 2, no. 10, abril, p. 11; no. 13, julio, p. 15; no. 18, dez., p. 4).
Aspects of Machado which should be covered in any critical study; influence on him of the milieu in which he grew up; his activities as a political reporter.

2828. Castello, José Aderaldo. Apontamentos para a história do simbolismo no Brasil (*Rev. univ. São Paulo*, ano 1, no. 1, jan.-março, p. 111-121).
Useful data concerning the introduction of the symbolist movement in Brazil.

2829. Cordeiro, José Pedro Leite. Ezequiel Freire (*Rev. arq. mun.*, ano 16, no. 131, fev., p. 47-51).
Short study of a minor romantic and his work.

2830. Costa, Afonso. Gregório de Matos no ambiente da terra natal (*Bol. bibliog.*, São Paulo, no. 16, p. 95-103).
". . . no cenário da Bahia intelectual, Gregório de Matos era um inadaptado, um odiado e, por isso, mais ainda, um odiento."

2831. Coutinho, Afrânio. Aspectos da literatura barroca. Rio de Janeiro, A Noite. 140 p.
Study of the origins, characteristics, and manifestations of the baroque in literature. Largely condensed from works by foreign scholars.

2832. Freire, Ezequiel. Trabalhos em prosa de . . . (*Rev. arq. mun.*, ano 16, no. 131, fev., p. 59-76).
Brief selections from his articles. See also items 2829, 2833, 2851.

2833. Freire, Hilário. Uma ressurreição literária. Sôbre o "Livro Póstumo" de Ezequiel Freire (*Rev. arq. mun.*, ano 16, no. 131, fev., p. 7-16).
Concerning a minor Paulista literary figure of the past century. See items 2829, 2832, 2851.

2834. Girão, Raimundo. Três gerações. Fortaleza, Clã. 135 p.
Essays on three literary figures of Ceará: Antônio Papi Júnior, Leonardo Mota, and Fran Martins. This last is especially interesting for the light it throws on an outstanding figure of the rising generation. See item 2889.

2835. Haddad, Jamil Almansur. Introdução a Anacreonte (*Rev. arq. mun.*, ano 17, no. 137, out.-dez., p. 39-50).
A leading poet of today studies a great Greek poet and his influence on Brazilian poetry of the 18th century.

2836. Lima, Alceu Amoroso. Manhãs de São Lourenço. Rio de Janeiro, Agir. 242 p.
Writing with a city-dweller's nostalgia for the bucolic, and with the perception of a keen observer and a meditative spirit, Sr. Lima has produced a volume of sketches of country life, both thought-provoking and possessing unusual poetic beauty.

2837. Lopes, Silvino. Maconha. Crônicas. Recife, EDM, 1950? 198 p.
Humorous articles, chiefly concerned with events and personalities of the day.

2838. Lopes, Waldemar. G.W.B.R. (*Nordeste*, ano 5, no. 1, jan.-fev., p. 1, 12, 19).
The Pernambuco railway in the literature and life of the Nordeste.

2839. Luso, João. Quatro conferências. Raimundo Correia visto de perto. A poesia em Eça de Queirós. Mestre Teófilo. Em louvor de Martins Fontes. Rio de Janeiro, Departamento de Imprensa Nacional. 109 p.
Of the two lectures on Brazilian subjects, the one devoted to Martins Fontes is a mere panegyric; that on Raimundo Correia, despite its title, is chiefly a study of his poetic art. "João Luso" is the pen name of Armando Erse.

2840. Mariz, Vasco. A renovação artística e literária no Brasil contemporâneo (*Brasília*, v. 5, p. 487-499).
Modernism and post-modernism in literature and art.

2841. Marques, Oswaldino. Canto grosso e a emergência de um novo realismo (*Clã*, ano 3, no. 10, julho, p. 58-66).
Study of the poetry of Emílio Correia Guerra, which the author finds identified with the aspirations of the collectivity.

2842. Melo, Gladstone Chaves de. A língua e o estilo de Rui Barbosa. Rio de Janeiro, Organização Simões (Col. Rex). 52 p.
The author says that Rui was a master of the language in an artistic sense, but no philologist. As a model of style, Rui represents a peril, in that his preciosity, rather than his more solid qualities, has been the object of imitation.

2843. Miguel-Pereira, Lúcia. História da literatura brasileira. V. 12. Prosa de ficção de 1870 a 1920. Sob a direção de Álvaro Lins. Rio de Janeiro, Olympio (Col. Documentos Brasileiros, 63). 338 p.
The first volume published in what is planned as a monumental history of Brazilian literature, Sra. Miguel-Pereira's contribution is a model for those to come. No mere compilation of previous works, this study represents great original research, careful scholarship, and excellent judgment. Indispensable to all students of Brazilian literature.

2844. Milliet, Sérgio. Dados para uma história da poesia modernista (1922-1928) (*Anhembi*, v. 1, no. 1, dez., p. 68-92).
Under a somewhat misleading title, Milliet analyzes the essential qualities of Mário de Andrade, Oswald de Andrade, Guilherme de Almeida, Menotti del Picchia, Cassiano Ricardo. Milliet's full name is Sérgio Milliet da Costa e Silva. Article is continued.

2845. Monteiro, Adolfo Casais. O romance e os seus problemas. Lisboa, Portugal, Livraria-Editôra da Casa do Estudante do Brasil (Biblioteca de Cultura Contemporânea, 1). 322 p.
Figuras do novo Brasil, p. 137-188, contains Monteiro's highly perceptive criticism of novels by Lins do Rêgo, Jorge Amado, Lúcio Cardoso, Amando Fontes, J. A. de Almeida, Ciro dos Anjos. Interesting transatlantic view of Brazilian novelistic production in the late 30's and early 40's.

2846. Monteiro, Clóvis. O romantismo no Brasil (*Correio da manhã*, suplemento de literatura e arte, julho 9, p. 5).
Domingos José Gonçalves de Magalhães and Antônio Gonçalves Dias as the initiators of romanticism in Brazil.

2847. Moog, Clodomir Vianna, e Alceu Amoroso Lima. Mensagem de uma geração. Discursos pronunciados na Academia Brasileira de Letras na posse do sr. Vianna Moog. Pôrto Alegre, Globo, 1950? 53 p.
Within the limitations of the occasion, Vianna Moog makes a profession of faith; and an interesting appreciation of his work is offered by Lima.

2848. A NATURALIDADE DE CASIMIRO DE ABREU E MAIS FALSIDADES, ERROS E MISTIFICAÇÕES DE UM BIÓGRAFO. Niterói, Academia Fluminense de Letras. 47 p., illus.
Contains Academy's reply to Nilo Bruzzi (see *HLAS, no. 15, 1949*, item 2481), characterized as "o homem-hiena" and "o metodista da confusão," refuting the arguments that Casimiro was born in Capivari and that he was lacking in filial piety, showing that the school Bruzzi had him attend did not exist at the time, and demonstrating that the descriptions of Casimiro and his associates are inaccurate.

2849. Pena, Cornélio. "Detesto a poesia" (*Jorn. letras*, ano 2, no. 16, out., p. 1, 7).
Views on literature of a writer who lives somewhat on the margin of the general current.

2850. Queiroz, Dinah Silveira de. Floradas na serra (*Jorn. letras*, ano 2, no. 14, agôsto, p. 2).
A popular woman novelist discusses the origin of her first and greatest success.

2851. Queiroz, Wenceslau de. Ezequiel Freire. À guisa de prefácio (*Rev. arq. mun.*, ano 16, no. 131, fev., p. 17-45).

Study of Freire's literary production. See items 2829, 2832, 2833.

2852. Rebêlo, Marques. "Nossa literatura está de rastros" (*Jorn. letras,* ano 2, no. 17, nov., p. 8, 14).
A well-known novelist and short-story writer gives his views on practically everything, in his own inimitable style. "Marques Rebêlo" is the pen name of Edy Dias da Cruz.

2853. Rezende, Carlos Penteado de. Interpretação biográfica de Fagundes Varela (*Investigações,* ano 2, no. 16, abril, p. 27-43).
An explanation of the title of the *Cântico do Calvário* and facts concerning the life of one of Brazil's great romantic poets.

2854. Ribeiro, Leonídio. Afrânio Peixoto. Rio de Janeiro, Condé. xx, 442 p., illus.
Contrary to what one might expect, this is not a biography of the man who for forty years occupied a prominent place in Brazilian medicine, teaching, politics, and literature. It is, however, an indispensable source of information, containing extensive quotations from Peixoto's unpublished memoirs, and reminiscences and appreciations by his numerous associates.

2855. Rosa, João Guimarães. *Sagarana* (*Jorn. letras,* ano 2, no. 15, set., p. 8-9).
Concerning the genesis of a notable collection of short stories.

2856. Sabino, Fernando. A cidade vazia. Crônicas. Rio de Janeiro, O Cruzeiro. 232 p.
Impressions of the author's stay in the United States. Brilliantly written; wry humor. Unfortunately, Sabino seems to have found no point of spiritual contact with the American people, even as the title suggests.

2857. Schmidt, Augusto Frederico. Paisagens e seres. Rio de Janeiro, Livros de Portugal. 196 p.
Sentimentality and banality are the leading characteristics of this highly disappointing book of sketches.

2858. A SEMANA DA ARTE MODERNA EM 1922 (*Letras e artes,* suplemento de *A Manhã,* ano 4, no. 153, fev. 5, p. 8-9, 14).
Interesting factual account of a literary and artistic event which has assumed the proportions of a legend.

2859. Silva, H. Pereira da. Graciliano Ramos. Ensaio crítico-psicanalítico. Rio de Janeiro, Aurora. 134 p.
An attempt to fathom the "mystery" of Ramos' personality from the characters in his novels. Thought-provoking, but essentially guesswork.

2860. Silveira, Brenno. Samuel Putnam, 1892-1950. Notas bio-bibliográficas. São Paulo, União Cultural Brasil-Estados Unidos. 32 p.

Notes on a leading interpreter of Brazilian culture to the American public, the former editor of this section of the *HLAS.*

2861. Tavares, José. O Brasil nas *Cartas* do Padre Antônio Vieira (*Brasília,* v. 5, p. 443-451).
Interesting aspects of colonial Brazil signalized by the great 17th century Portuguese writer.

2862. Veiga, Gláucio. Os concursos de Sílvio Romero (*Nordeste,* ano 5, no. 1, jan.-fev., p. 4, 6).
Official competitions in which Romero took part.

2863. Viana, Hélio. Um intelectual português na côrte de D. Pedro II (*Brasília,* no. 5, p. 465-486).
Information concerning José Feliciano de Castilho and his rather prominent role in the Brazilian literary scene of the mid-19th century.

2864. Vieira, José Geraldo. O autor fala de sua personagem J.L.C. (*Jorn. letras,* ano 2, no. 16, out., p. 1, 15, 6).
Important information concerning the genesis of many of the characters created by one of Brazil's leading novelists.

FOLKLORE

2865. Araújo, Christovam. Os bichos nos provérbios. Prefácio de C. F. de Freitas Casanovas. Rio de Janeiro, Ronega. 113 p.
Brazilian popular sayings involving animals, arranged by subject. It is interesting to note that the dog and the hen are those figuring in the greatest number of entries.

2866. Cordeiro, José. Perseguição de Lampião pelas forças legais (*Jorn. letras,* ano 2, no. 13, julho, p. 3, 13).
The story of a famous bandit, in verse, as it circulates among the people.

2867. Guimarães, Ruth. Os filhos do mêdo. Pôrto Alegre, Globo (Col. Autores Brasileiros, v. 34). 231 p.
This study of the present concept of the devil in the popular tradition of Brazil gathers oral material from northern São Paulo, southern Minas Gerais, and western Rio de Janeiro. Shows wide reading by the author, but is confused in organization.

2868. A MALHAÇÃO DE JUDAS. UMA PESQUISA DE ALUNOS (*Correio paul.,* set. 10, p. 10, 19).
A study of the custom of burning an effigy of Judas on Easter eve, as it is practiced in the State of São Paulo.

2869. Melo, José Maria de. Enigmas populares. Coletânea e classificação de adivinhas. Estudo de folclore comparado. Prefácio de Manuel Diegues Jr. Rio de Janeiro, A Noite. 385 p.

Vast collection of riddles, chiefly Brazilian, but with many foreign variants. Some attempt at classification by types, but two-thirds of the book are comprised in the chapter "Adivinhas comuns."

2870. Mussolini, Gioconda. Os "pasquins" do litoral norte de São Paulo e suas peculiaridades na ilha de São Sebastião *(Rev. arq. mun.,* ano 17, no. 134, julho-agôsto, p. 7-68).
Folk poems about local events of communal interest. Introduction, numerous examples.

2871. Silva, José Calasans Brandão da. O ciclo folclórico do Bom Jesus Conselheiro. Contribuição ao estudo da campanha de Canudos. Bahia, Tipografia Beneditina. 97 p.
Study of verses in circulation among the people, concerning the famous Antônio Conselheiro and the military campaign against him (1896-1897).

2872. Vianna, Antônio. Casos e coisas da Bahia. Bahia, Secretaria de Educação e Saúde (Publ. do Museu do Estado, no. 10). 165 p.
Reminiscences of Bahian festivals and customs 50 years ago.

2873. Vidal, Ademar. Lendas e superstições. Contos populares brasileiros. Rio de Janeiro, O Cruzeiro. 626 p., illus.
Vast collection of tales of popular origin from the Brazilian Northeast. Well written, but popular flavor has been lost. No scientific pretensions.

PROSE FICTION

2874. Araújo, J. A. dos Santos. Contos que a vida contou . . . . Rio de Janeiro, A Noite. 185 p.
Most of life's tales are ones of impossible love affairs, ending in renunciation.

2875. Arroyo, Leonardo. Viagem para Málaga. Rio de Janeiro, Olympio. 187 p.
These scenes of lower middle-class and proletarian life are less stories than evocations of moods. Pleasing in manner but a bit thin in substance. Winner of the Fábio Prado Prize for 1949.

2876. Austregésilo, Antônio. Almas desgraçadas. 2. edição. Rio de Janeiro, Pongetti. 169 p.
The hero of this novel of socio-philosophical overtones fancies himself a great moralist and a superior being; his misfortunes, however, are the result of constantly cutting off his nose to spite his face. Author's full name is Antônio Austregésilo Rodrigues Lima.

2877. Barreto, Lima. Numa e a ninfa. Rio de Janeiro, Gráfica Editôra Brasileira. 306 p.

Ostensibly the story of a politician who owes his rise in Congress to speeches written by his wife's lover, this is in reality but a thinly-veiled satire of the maneuvering by which the government of Brazil brought about the election of Hermes da Fonseca to the presidency in 1910. Highly defective as a narrative whole, this "novel" offers a series of brilliant sketches of political types, with delightfully ironic accounts of their finagling. This is the first printing of the author's final revision of the text, and by including in an appendix As aventuras do Dr. Bogoloff, from which many episodes of the novel are drawn, it permits an interesting view of Barreto's processes of composition.

2878. Beltrão, Luiz. Os senhores do mundo. Recife, Fôlha da Manhã. 175 p.
The *romance nordestino* continues, but nothing new is added. Sr. Beltrão has written a series of episodes in the lives of the poorest (and semi-criminal) classes of Recife, quite after the style of Amando Fontes or the earlier Jorge Amado.

2879. Benedetti, Lúcia. Vesperal com chuva. Rio de Janeiro, Gráfica Tupy. 150 p.
This collection of tales won the Brazilian Academy's Alfonso Arinos Prize for 1949. The best are ones like the title story, "Meu Tio Ricardo," and "Carnaval em Niterói," in which everyday happenings are described simply but eloquently, rather than those in which the author has consciously sought for dramatic effect.

2880. Carvalho, Jarbas de. Dez noites de amor. Rio de Janeiro, A Noite, 1950? 229 p.
The author has a notable gift of narrative invention and a little of the spirit of Maupassant—there are a variety of situations, surprise endings, good humor. Unfortunately the stories are not told with sufficient art: they need greater development.

2881. Castanho, César Arruda. Um pingo no mapa. São Paulo, Editôra Brasiliense. 224 p.
Story of a year in the life of a small town in the State of São Paulo. Emphasis on social evils, but no attempt to indicate cause or remedy. Hero is aware of the evils, but apparently will become resigned to them.

2882. Cavalcanti, Pedro de Oliveira. Perigo, escavações na linha. Rio de Janeiro, Cruzeiro. 249 p.
Using a technique reminiscent of Dos Passos, Cavalcanti tells the story of a spendthrift's descent to poverty and hard work, with a satirical view of Rio society in the 40's. This novel won honorable mention in the contest sponsored by O Cruzeiro.

2883. Coaracy, Vivaldo. O contador de histórias. São Paulo, Melhoramentos. 94 p.
"V. Cy." is justly known as one of Brazil's most distinguished and delightful *cronistas*. The present volume contains a series of fables for our time, whose concision, clarity, brilliance, and

mordant irony make them seem the work of a modern—and essentially indulgent—Voltaire.

2884. Cox, Dilermando Duarte. Os párias da Cidade Maravilhosa. Rio de Janeiro, Olympio. 232 p.
Though the literary value of this novel is slight, it has the distinction of being the first to concern itself with the people of Rio's hilltop slums, the *favelas*. The depictions and denunciations of conditions there doubtless have their worth as a social document.

2885. Furtado, Celso. De Nápoles a Paris. Contos da vida expedicionária. Rio de Janeiro, Zélio Valverde, 1950? 103 p.
These tales by a member of the Brazilian Expeditionary Force deal chiefly with civilian aspects of the war, the main interest lying in the differing views of the world entertained by the persons of various nationalities who come into contact one with another.

2886. Jobim, Rubens Mário. Sargento Fortuna e outros contos. Rio de Janeiro, Aurora (Biblioteca do Exército, v. 153). 204 p.
Short stories, chiefly military episodes, set in Rio Grande do Sul.

2887. Kelly, Celso. Temperamentos. Rio de Janeiro, Edições Gráfica Tupy Limitada, 1950? 167 p.
Short stories, each based on a trait of human nature. Unusual psychological situations interestingly presented, in a manner slightly suggestive of Pirandello. The writing, however, is undistinguished.

2888. Lima, Jorge de. Guerra dentro do beco. Rio de Janeiro, A Noite. 285 p.
This novel of a couple, physically united, but spiritually divorced, is obviously intended as a symbol of our warring world; but whatever message the author may have meant to convey is far from clear.

2889. Martins, Fran. O cruzeiro tem cinco estrelas. Fortaleza, Clã. 342 p.
Essentially a collection of short stories, rather than a novel, this work presents in the completely independent tales of five brothers a broad panorama of life in post-war Brazil. The episodes of the rubber worker and the labor agitator seem of literary rather than personal inspiration, but the other stories, especially that of the budding politician, display Martins' unusual narrative gifts to great advantage.

2890. Paim, Alina. A sombra do patriarca. Pôrto Alegre, Globo. 265 p.
Coming after *Simão Dias*, this novel is a disappointment. Srta. Paim attempts too many themes in too short a space: the feudal life of the sugar plantation, a family portrait, the revolt of a repressed personality, the unsuspected birth of love in a young woman. None of these stories is sufficiently developed; they are at times mutually incompatible. There is also melodramatic exaggeration. Srta. Paim is too good a narrative

artist to write a dull book, but one expects better of her and hopes that she will return to the greater simplicity and realism of her earlier work.

2891. Pereira, Antônio Olavo. Contramão. Rio de Janeiro, Olympio. 183 p.
This excellent study of one of society's misfits won the Fábio Prado prize for 1949. Originally written in 1937, it was reworked by the author to his greater satisfaction.

2892. Sant'Ana, Nuto. Satanás. São Paulo, Rossolillo. 202 p.
Novel of a Don Juan who eventually falls victim to matrimony. Some attempt at social satire.

2893. Schmidt, Afonso. Saltimbancos. São Paulo, Saraiva (Col. Saraiva, 21). 229 p.
First-person novel of an alcoholic magician. Poorly constructed, but gives interesting glimpses of the Bohemian existence of circus performers and vaudeville artists.

2894. Torres, Mário Brandão. Acauã. Páginas regionalistas. Prefácio de Gilberto Freyre. Rio de Janeiro, A Noite. 260 p.
The chief interest of this novel is for the sociologist and dialectologist, by reason of its detailed description of all phases of the *sertanejo's* life and of its attempt at a faithful reproduction of his mode of speech.

2895. Vieira, José Geraldo. A ladeira da memória. São Paulo, Saraiva (Col. Saraiva, 19). 319 p.
Though marred by Vieira's usual defects of poor construction and an idle display of ill digested erudition, his latest novel possesses uncommon psychological and sentimental interest. The story, strongly reminiscent of that of Tristram and Iseult, is relived in memory by the hero, after his beloved's death, as he tries to reconcile himself to living.

VERSE

2896. ANTOLOGIA DE POETAS DA NOVA GERAÇÃO. Prefácio de Álvaro Moreyra. Rio de Janeiro, Pongetti. 166 p.
Except for the use of free verse, the members of this particular generation might have been "new" fifty years ago. Hackneyed themes, pedestrian treatment.

2897. Azeredo, Carlos Magalhães de. Verão e outono (1920-1935). Rio de Janeiro, Jornal do Commércio (distribuição da Editôra Aurora). 184 p.
Sonorous but vapid poems by one who, despite occasional ventures into free verse, is still essentially a tardive Parnassian.

2898. Bairão, Reynaldo. O primeiro dia. Poemas em prosa. Rio de Janeiro, Orfeu. 59 p.
The intensely personal lyrics of a poet who seems to be seeking a way in life.

2899. Barroso, Antônio Girão. Novos poemas (*Clã,* ano 3, no. 10, julho, p. 43-54).
Pleasing lyrics on everyday themes.

2900. Benevides, Artur Eduardo. A valsa e a fonte. Fortaleza, Clã. 70 p.
Felicity of expression, musicality, and a strongly personal note mark these lyrics, whose themes are love, death, and the relation of the poet to his art.

2901. Campos, Haroldo de. Auto do possesso. São Paulo, Cadernos do Clube de Poesia (no. 3). 38 p.
Great formal beauty, but little emotional appeal, because of excessively hermetic language. "Os poemas me deixam indiferente; os versos me comovem," said the critic Sérgio Milliet.

2902. Faria, José Escobar. Poemas de câmera. São Paulo, Martins. 69 p.
Faria seems to represent a neo-Parnassian tendency in contemporary Brazilian poetry: his verses are carefully turned; great attention has been given to vocabulary; a certain preference being shown for the unusual; and expression of personal feeling is kept to a minimum. This is poetry to be admired, rather than felt.

2903. Freire, Ezequiel. Flores do campo (*Rev. arq. mun.,* ano 16, no. 131, fev., p. 77-186).
Reprint of poems published in 1874—the work of a minor romantic. See items 2829, 2832, 2833, 2851.

2904. Guimaraens Filho, Alphonsus de. O irmão. Rio de Janeiro, Agir. 109 p.
Verse of religious inspiration, chiefly mystical in character, showing at times a kinship with the poetry of San Juan de la Cruz. Sincerity and simplicity of expression characterize this work, which was one of the best productions of the year.

2905. Lima, Jorge de. Mira-coeli. Buenos Aires, Sociedad Editora Latino-Americana. 150 p.
Spanish translation (by Florindo Villa Álvarez?) of Lima's latest collection of mystical verse.

2906. ————. Obra poética. Edição completa, em um volume, organizada por Otto Maria Carpeaux. Rio de Janeiro, Getúlio Costa. xvi, 659 p.
Though Lima has long been recognized as one of Brazil's greatest poets, much of his verse, including the famous poems on Negro themes, has been out of print for years. The present volume reprints all previous collections and adds a long new section, "Anunciação e encontro de Mira-Coeli." Indispensable to students of the long and curious evolution of a poetic personality of first rank.

2907. Lousada, Wilson (ed.). Cancioneiro do amor. Os mais belos versos da poesia brasileira. Arcades—românticos—parnasianos. Rio de Janeiro, Olympio (Col. Rubáiyát). 202 p.
Well chosen anthology of love lyrics, from Gregório de Matos to the Parnassians. No living poets included.

2908. Machado, Ruy Affonso. Rumo enxuto. São Paulo, Martins. 121 p.
In much of this verse, the author seems to have been concerned with the mere sound of words, but in some of the shorter poems there is a clearness of thought and image suggestive of the hai-kai.

2909. Malta, Tostes. Luz distante. Rio de Janeiro. 94 p.
In his first volume of verse in 20 years, Malta shows himself more successful as a poet of *saudade* than as a reviver of *indianismo.*

2910. Martins, Luís. Cantigas da rua escura. São Paulo, Martins. 74 p., illus.
Covering ten years of poetic production, this slim volume shows that Martins' last work is definitely his best. He is a poet of night, with its weariness, its mystery, and the ugliness it partly conceals. This ugliness sometimes arouses the poet to revolt, sometimes to satire, but there is always an underlying tenderness. Incisive style with curious reminiscences of popular verse forms.

2911. Mello, Cezario de. Cantos da hora undécima. Recife, Editôra Nordeste. 116 p.
Saudade for his childhood, the very memory of which he realizes is fading, characterizes the majority of Mello's poems. Stylistically, they are composed of a rapid succession of images, connected in thought but not in syntax: there is an almost total lack of finite verbs.

2912. Pirajá, Nair Miranda. Poemas. Rio de Janeiro, Olympio. 63 p.
This handful of short lyrics (chiefly inspired by love) is marked by genuine passion and shows a true poetic gift.

2913. Rezende, Edgard (ed.). Os cem melhores sonetos brasileiros. 2. série. Rio de Janeiro, Freitas Bastos. 263 p.
Second-rate productions by writers of the late 19th and early 20th century.

2914. Ricardo, Cassiano. A face perdida. Rio de Janeiro, Olympio. 177 p.
The author, once a *verde-amarelista* in the vanguard of the modernist movement, has become introspective, simple, and concise in mode of expression. The experience of man, matured by inevitable suffering, is the dominating line of the present collection. The poet's full name is Cassiano Ricardo Leite.

2915. Veloso, Natércia Cunha. Teia de sonhos. Pôrto Alegre, Globo. 147 p.
Verse generally exceedingly banal, but a few compositions inspired by the sorrows of love reach the level of genuine poetry.

DRAMA

2916. Anchieta, José de. *Na vila de Vitória e Na visitação de Santa Isabel.* Peças em castelhano e português, do século XVI, transcritas e comentadas por Maria de Lourdes de Paula Martins. São Paulo, Museu Paulista (Bol. 3, ano 2-3, Documentação linguística, 3). 159 p., illus.
Two religious plays, presumably by Brazil's first literary figure, who used the theater for didactic purposes. Original text, and transcription in modern Spanish or Portuguese on opposite pages. Careful editing.

2917. Machado, Lourival. Raquel (*Anhembi*, v. 1, no. 1, dez., p. 100-116).
This play, intended for reading rather than acting, tells the story of Jacob's reconciliation with Leah after his discovery of Laban's deception.

2918. Silveira, Helena. No fundo do poço. Colaboração de Jamil Almansur Haddad. São Paulo, Martins. 102 p.
Expressionist drama concerning a degenerate family. Son kills mother and two sisters (pretexting euthanasia) so he can marry and have his own home. Loud-speaker used to represent voice of conscience, or of objects in the house.

ADDENDA

2919. Accioly, Breno. Cogumelos. Contos. Prefácio de Gilberto Freyre. Rio de Janeiro, A Noite, 1949? 100 p., illus.
A superbly developed atmosphere of nightmare characterizes these tales of moral degeneration. Despite morbidity, they form a distinguished production.

2920. Albano, José. Rimas de José Albano. Edição organizada, revista e prefaciada por Manuel Bandeira. Rio de Janeiro, Pongetti, 1948. 261 p.
Though Albano died only in 1917, he was, as Graça Aranha said, "um antigo." In no sense an imitator, or a cultivator of the archaic, he was a spiritual contemporary of Camões, and his verse is worthy of the best poets of the Portuguese Renaissance. The present, collected edition is the first to make Albano's work available to the general public, only the most limited of editions having been published during his lifetime.

2921. Anchieta, José de. Auto representado na festa de São Lourenço. Peça trilíngüe do século XVI, transcrita, comentada e traduzida, na parte tupi, por M. de L. de Paula Martins. São Paulo, Museu Paulista (Bol. 1, ano 1, Documentação Linguística, 1), 1948. 142 p., illus.
See also item 2916.

2922. Bandeira, Manuel (ed.). Antologia dos poetas brasileiros da fase romântica. 3. edição. Revisão crítica, em consulta

com o autor, por Aurélio Buarque de Hollanda. Rio de Janeiro, Ministério da Educação e Saúde, Instituto Nacional do Livro (Biblioteca Popular Brasileira, 27), 1949. 389 p.
New, revised edition of a work which is a "must" for any library of Brazilian literature, however small.

2923. Barros, Leitão de. Como eu vi Castro Alves e Eugénia Câmara no vendaval maravilhoso de suas vidas. Lisboa, Livros de Portugal, 1949. 219 p., illus.
The producer of the film *Vendaval maravilhoso* explains its inception and evolution, and gives a complete scenario.

2924. Borges, José Carlos Cavalcanti. Padrão G. Rio de Janeiro, Agir, 1948. 154 p.
The stream-of-consciousness technique (employed in all these sketches, rather than stories, of lower middle class characters) is something of a novelty in Brazilian literature, but Borges' use thereof is questionable. The situations not being well defined, the reader is frequently at a loss as to what is going on.

2925. CADERNO DE CONTOS. Recife, Edições A.A.B.B., 1949? 91 p.
Short stories by Arnaldo Cavalcanti de Aragão, Olavo Oliveira Melo, Manuel Arthur de Souza Leão, and Berlando Rapôso Torres, prize-winners in a contest sponsored by the Associação Atlética do Banco do Brasil, Recife.

2926. Coaracy, Vivaldo. Couves da minha horta. Rio de Janeiro, Olympio, 1949. 281 p.
This collection of *crônicas* is divided into two sections: 1, recollections of the author's early years, with emphasis on figures prominent in journalism at the turn of the century; 2, sketches of life on the island of Paquetá. Written with great charm, and occasional ironic reflexions on the ills of modern Brazil.

2927. Fagundes, Ligia. O cacto vermelho. Rio de Janeiro, Mérito, 1949. 261 p.
Short stories. Awarded prize by Brazilian Academy of Letters. See *HLAS, no. 15, 1949*, p. 216. [Ed.]

2928. Faria, Octavio de. Tragédia burguesa. I. Mundos mortos. 2. edição, revista. Rio de Janeiro, Olympio, 1949. 324 p.
New, revised edition of the first part of Faria's great, unfinished *roman fleuve*. Information concerning its genesis and gestation is given by the author in *Jorn. letras*, ano 2, no. 16, p. 9.

2929. Ferreira, H. Lopes Rodrigues. Castro Alves. V. 1. Rio de Janeiro, Pongetti, 1947? 456 p., illus.
Highly lyrical biography of great 19th-century poet. Information concerning friends and family. Abundant quotations from poetry used to illustrate *a vida do coração*.

2930. Ouro Preto, Maluh de. Crónicas de Paris. Rio de Janeiro, A Noite, 1949? 106 p.
These accounts of a girl's first brief visit to Paris, though superficial as observations, are delightful in their naturalness, and reveal a writer of genuine charm. Brazilian Academy prize.

2931. Passos, Alexandre. Castro Alves, arauto da democracia e da república. Rio de Janeiro, Pongetti, 1949? 35 p.
Brief account of the democratic movements of the mid-nineteenth century, and of Castro Alves as their herald in Brazil.

2932. Peixoto, Afrânio. Bugrinha. Rio de Janeiro, Cem Bibliófilos do Brasil, 1948. 248 p., illus.

De luxe edition of a popular success of thirty years ago.

2933. Requião, Hermano. Itapagipe. Minha infância na Bahia. Contribuição ao quarto centenário da cidade do Salvador. Rio de Janeiro, Olympio, 1949? 128 p., illus.
These recollections of a childhood 30 years ago in a suburb of Bahia, though utterly unpretentious, are completely charming, and form a valuable document for the social historian.

2934. Silva, Domingos Carvalho da. Praia oculta. São Paulo, Brasiliense, 1949. 93 p.
Silva is a neo-romantic of the best type. For him poetry is neither a vehicle of thought nor a sensual evocation, but the communication of an emotion which has been lived. Few writers of the new generation have, moreover, Silva's feeling for poetic language. A notable book.

Haitian Literature and Language

MERCER COOK

IN 1950 the Haitian spotlight was once again on politics, as the Estimé Government fell, exactly as its predecessor had fallen four years earlier. This resulted, as in 1946, in a brief stewardship by a military junta, a new Constitution, and new elections.

Notable literary works were few in number. By far the most ambitious project was the 635-page anthology of Haitian verse edited by Carlos St. Louis and Maurice A. Lubin. Other interesting publications included the first volume of M. Jérémie's *Mémoires*, and the pamphlet *Haïti et Chicago* by the same author.

Another brochure of special interest to North Americans was *Marian Anderson*, written by the poet Jean F. Brierre and historian René Piquion on the occasion of the contralto's first visit to Haiti. Wendell Phillips' famous oration on Toussaint Louverture was translated into French by Max Bissainthe, director of Haiti's National Library, though the translator modestly refrained from signing his name. This booklet, published by the Imprimerie de l'État on January 1, 1950—the anniversary of Haitian independence—is prefaced by a discussion of Toussaint's extraordinary appeal to foreign authors. In the United States alone, "more than 300 books and pamphlets have been published" about this great Negro leader.

At Howard University Walter B. Williams wrote a master's thesis, not yet published, on *La Relève: focal point of Haitian literature*. This is a study and index of an important literary magazine founded by Jacques C. Antoine and edited by him from 1932 to 1939. "With one or two notable omissions, its collaborators include the leading Haitian intellectuals of several generations." The author is librarian at Miner Teachers College, Washington, D. C.

PROSE

2935. **Brierre, Jean F.** Les Aïeules. Famous women in Haitian history. Port-au-Prince, Henri Deschamps. 20 p.
This one-act sketch was first performed in 1946 at the Lycée de Jeunes Filles, then directed by an Oregonian, Dorothy Kirby. Poet Jean Brierre introduces seven historic women, including Mme. Toussaint, Mme. Dessalines, and Défilée la Folle. The sketch is printed in French and English versions, as originally presented.

2936. ———, and **René Piquion**. Marian Anderson. Port-au-Prince, Henri Deschamps. 13 p.
Jean Brierre's moving poem on Marian Anderson and René Piquion's brief biography are designed to introduce the singer to the Haitian public.

2937. **Casséus, Maurice.** Mambo. Port-au-Prince, Imprimerie du Séminaire Adventiste. 120 p.
A classroom edition of a poetic short story by a Haitian novelist, with illustrations by Geo. Remponneau. The avowed purpose of the text is to provide material with Haitian background for lycée French classes.

2938. **Chevallier, André F., and Luc Grimard.** Bakoulou. Audience folklorique. Port-au-Prince, Société d'Édition et de Librairie. 202 p.
This interesting novel attacks unscrupulous vodun priests who exploit their superstitious, gullible victims. One of the authors, Luc Grimard, is a noted poet, former editor of the Catholic daily, *La Phalange*, and at present *recteur* of the Université d'Haïti.

2939. Guéry, Fortuna. Témoignages. Port-au-Prince, Henri Deschamps. 108 p.

A collection of articles and lectures by a well-known Haitian educator. Also included is a one-act dramatization of the creation of the Haitian flag. Mme. Guéry writes with nostalgic charm of the old Port-au-Prince. Reviewed in *Jour. negro hist.*, v. 35, no. 3, July.

2940. Hyppolite, Michelson P. Littérature populaire haïtienne. Port-au-Prince, Imprimerie de l'État. 129 p.

Riddles collected in various parts of Haiti by a graduate of the Institut d'Ethnologie, and presented in Creole and literal and literary French translation, with commentaries and photographs of persons consulted. Reviewed in *Conjonction*, no. 31, fév., 1951.

2941. Jérémie, J. Haïti et Chicago. Port-au-Prince, Henri Deschamps. 57 p.

The author is a distinguished nonagenarian, who has held high political office and has long been a prominent Catholic layman. On the maternal side he is a descendant of the Dessables family (Chicagoans usually spell the name Du Sable), and in this pamphlet he sketches the career of the Haitian who founded the Illinois metropolis.

2942. Lemaire, Emmeline Carriès. Coeur de héros—coeur d'amant. Port-au-Prince, Imprimerie Le Matin. 157 p.

Best known as a poet, Mme. Lemaire is an ardent admirer of Bolívar. Like most Haitians, she is justifiably proud that her country aided the Liberator when he needed it most. "This novelette, woven around an historical theme, is pure fantasy." Nevertheless, the book contains frequent quotations from the public and private papers of her hero.

2943. Steiner, Mia. Black dawn. Port-au-Prince, Henri Deschamps. 205 p.

A foreigner residing in Haiti is the author of this exciting novel of life in Saint-Domingue on the eve of the Revolution. The historical background is excellently portrayed; love interest is provided by a romance between a free mulatto girl and a slave freshly arrived from Africa. The novel is written in English.

VERSE

2944. Dorismond, Jacques. La Terre qui s'ouvre. Port-au-Prince, Imprimerie de l'État. 39 p.

These poems were reviewed in *Conjonction*, no. 29, Oct., 1950.

2945. St. Louis, Carlos, and **Maurice A. Lubin.** Panorama de la poésie haïtienne. Port-au-Prince, Henri Deschamps. vi, 635 p.

Selections from 150 Haitian poets are included in this *Panorama*, the most inclusive anthology of Haitian poetry yet to appear. Though some of the poets quoted might well have been omitted by a more critical selection, the reader is none the less impressed by the evidence of the important place that poetry has occupied in the history of Haitian letters. The volume is all the more useful because of the biographical notes on each of the poets. Editors St. Louis and Lubin are also responsible for *La Carte de la poésie haïtienne*, a map of Haiti grouping the poets according to birthplace.

ADDENDA

2946. Bec, Marie. La Fille de l'esclave. Drame pour jeunes filles. Port-au-Prince, Dandin Frères, 1949? 42 p.

First presented at the Théâtre Rex on July 13, 1949, this little drama in three acts takes us back to the days of the Haitian War of Independence. The slave's daughter saves the brutal master's widow and daughter, instead of avenging her father.

2947. Hyppolite, Michelson P. Les Origines des variations du créole haïtien. Port-au-Prince, Imprimerie de l'État, 1949? 85 p.

In this brief study, the author traces differences in Creole as spoken in the north, south, and west of Haiti. Using the Laubach transcription, with certain modifications, he shows how various words differ from region to region. The volume contains interesting observations on the French, Spanish, English, and African contributions to Haiti's unofficial language. Also included are six maps indicating graphically how intonation, the definite article, possessive adjectives, possessive pronouns, etc., vary as one travels through the country.

2948. Najac, Paul E. Amours, délices et orgues. Port-au-Prince, Imprimerie du Séminaire Adventiste, 1949? 38 p.

Twenty-eight poems by a young Haitian poet, with a preface by Eric Neff, former director of the Haitian-American Institute.

Law

Law

HELEN L. CLAGETT

COLLECTIONS OF LAWS, COMPILED WORKS, AND BIBLIOGRAPHIES

2949. Chile. Universidad de Chile. Facultad de Ciencias Jurídicas y Sociales. Memorias de licenciados. V. 1-12. Santiago, Editorial Jurídica de Chile. Various pagings.
In 1950 the Law School of the University of Chile began the practice of compiling theses of law students and binding six to eight per volume under the common subject matter, such as labor law, agricultural law, civil law (contracts), civil law (persons), etc.

2950. ESTUDIOS EN HOMENAJE A DON DALMACIO VÉLEZ SÁRSFIELD. Córdoba, Universidad Nacional de Córdoba, Biblioteca del Boletín de la Facultad de Derecho y Ciencias Sociales. 654 p.
The drafter of the first Argentine civil code, whose notes still accompany the text today, was honored by the compilation of various essays and studies of jurisconsults of outstanding authority.

2951. Guernik, Miguel. Derecho práctico. Buenos Aires, Librería Americana. 170 p.
A compilation of legal and judicial forms in handbook style.

2952. Jiménez Mejía, Rodrigo. Conferencias. Bogotá, Universidad Nacional de Colombia, Sección de Extensión Cultural. 153 p.
A collection of addresses, lectures, and essays on legal topics delivered at various universities by the author.

2953. Pérez Lobo, Rafael, and Jesús Pérez Bustamente (eds.). Diccionario de legislación cubana, 1930-1948. La Habana, Editorial Librería Selecta. 1328 p.
A useful index to eighteen years of legislation, with notes as to status of each legal provision in 1950, that is, whether it has been repealed, amended, or clarified in any manner. Another useful element is the notes pointing out which laws have been declared unconstitutional by the courts.

2954. Peru. Cámara de Diputados. Dirección General Administrativa. Compilación de la legislación peruana (concordada). V. 1. Lima. 480 p.
An official compilation of nearly 5,000 laws covering the years 1904 to 1924 is found in this first volume. A system of cross-references to related, implementary, and amendatory laws enhances the value of the work.

PHILOSOPHY OF LAW, HISTORY OF LAW, JURISPRUDENCE

2955. Castejón, Federico. Unificación legislativa iberoamericana. Madrid, Seminario de Problemas Hispanoamericanos (Cuadernos de Monografías, 10). 162 p.
Covers international attempts to accomplish unification, including work of various organizations and publications. Bibliographical aids are also discussed.

2956. Eder, Phanor J. A comparative study of Anglo-American and Latin American law. New York, New York University Press. 258 p.
A published version of the author's lectures delivered at the Inter-American Academy of International and Comparative Law in Habana, 1949. About one-third of the book is devoted to a bibliography of comparative law, including works in French, German, Spanish, and English.

2957. Gusmão, Paulo Dourado de. Curso de filosofia do direito. Rio de Janeiro, Livraria Freitas Bastos. 196 p.
A general work on legal philosophy to be used as a textbook. Excellent bibliography, p. 141-188.

2958. Kunz, Josef L. Latin-American philosophy of law in the twentieth century. New York, Inter-American Law Institute. 120 p.
Discussion of the various doctrines and schools developed and followed by the better known legal philosophers in Latin America.

2959. Laplaza, Francisco P. Antecedentes de nuestro periodismo forense hasta la

aparición de *La Revista Criminal* (1873) como introducción a la historia del derecho penal argentino. Buenos Aires, Depalma. 285 p.
A useful contribution to legal bibliography, limited to the field of penal law.

2960. Planas Suárez, Simón. Páginas de preocupacion y patriotismo (1936-1941). Buenos Aires, J. Pellegrini. 532 p.
A compilation of the author's articles, addresses, and studies on topics of law, politics, and government.

2961. Reyes Nevárez, Salvador. Proyecciones del existencialismo sobre el derecho. México. 80 p.
Although the policy has been to exclude from this bibliography the usual run of law school theses, the present work is included because of its treatment of a different type of subject matter seldom found in a work of this kind—the influence of existentialism on law. Thesis, University of Mexico.

2962. Sagastume Franco, Edmundo. Penetración jurídica de España en América. Guatemala. 64 p.
A thesis of unusual interest from the University of San Carlos, showing the influence of Spanish law in the American colonies as it still persists today.

2963. Vázquez Gayoso, Jesús. Apuntes de historia del derecho. Esquema para una exposición. Caracas, El Compás. 97 p.
A collection of notes and outlines for a general history of law and sources of law in Venezuela rather than a treatise or monograph on the subject.

COURTS AND JUDICIAL PROCEDURE

(CIVIL AND CRIMINAL)

ARGENTINA

2964. Ayarragaray, Carlos Alberto. Sentencias obligatorias. Buenos Aires, Compañía Impresora Argentina. 84 p.
The fact that provision was made in the new constitution of 1949 for *stare decisis* to be established in decisions of the Supreme Court, in specified types of cases, forms the basis of the comments of the author, an expert in procedural matters.

2965. CÓDIGO DE PROCEDIMIENTO PENAL DE LA PROVINCIA DE CÓRDOBA. Ley no. 3831, de agosto 28 de 1939, según la edición oficial, con la exposición de motivos. Córdoba, Assandri. 304 p.
Dr. Marcelo Finzi wrote the preface to and compiled valuable indices of sources and subject matter for this provincial code, adopted in 1939.

2966. CÓDIGO DE PROCEDIMIENTOS EN LO CIVIL Y COMERCIAL DE LA PROVINCIA DE BUENOS AIRES. Buenos Aires, Lajouane. 225, 59 p.
Contains text of code and an appendix covering the laws on the various periods in the procedural materials, such as time limits in which to place an action and obtain legal counsel, and periods in which the Supreme Court and other courts shall be in session.

2967. CÓDIGO DE PROCEDIMIENTOS EN LO CRIMINAL PARA LA JUSTICIA FEDERAL Y LOS TRIBUNALES DE LA CAPITAL Y TERRITORIOS NACIONALES. Buenos Aires, Lajouane (Códigos y Leyes Usuales de la República Argentina). 128 p.

BRAZIL

2968. Barbosa, Ruy. O júri sob todos os aspectos. Texto de Ruy Barbosa sôbre a teoria e a prática da instituição. Rio de Janeiro, Editôra Nacional de Direito. 133 p.
The centenary of the birth of Brazil's great jurist Ruy Barbosa brought the reprinting of many of his works as well as publications about him. Drs. Roberto Lyra and Mario César de Silva have collected herein the various writings of Dr. Barbosa on all aspects of juries and jury trials.

2969. Castro, Augusto Olympio Gomes de. Ementário de jurisprudência. Rio de Janeiro. 363 p.
A complete digest of the 2400 decisions issued by the Tribunal Superior Eleitoral on electoral and political party matters.

2970. Cruz, João Claudino de Oliveira e. Do recurso de agravo. Rio de Janeiro, Revista Forense. 421 p.
A detailed discussion of appellate procedure in Brazil.

2971. Ferreira, Nelson Martins. O judiciário na luta democrática. Rio de Janeiro, Tipografia Baptista de Souza. 79 p.
Discusses the place and work of the judicial power in furthering the cause of democracy.

2972. Franco, Ary Azevedo. O júri e a constituição federal de 1946. Rio de Janeiro, Freitas Bastos. 438 p.
The law of 1948 affecting trial by jury is the subject of comment and criticism.

2973. Nunes, José de Castro. Da fazenda pública em juízo (tribunal federal de recursos—juízo dos feitos). 1. edicão. Rio de Janeiro, Freitas Bastos. 581 p.
A treatise on jurisdiction and judicial interpretation in the field of public finance, chiefly as accomplished by the Appeals Court of the federal judiciary, only recently established.

2974. Tolomei, Victorio (ed.). Nova juris-prudência criminal. Acordãos de todos os tribunais do Brasil. Rio de Janeiro, Editôra Nacional de Direito. 189 p.
The decisions of all courts of Brazil dealing with criminal cases digested and classified.

2975. Vasconcellos, Cesar C. L. de (ed). Código de processo civil. Rio de Janeiro, Gráfica Editôra Aurora. 510 p.
Notes contain excerpts from learned opinion, legislation, and case-law in point. An appendix includes the complete text of individual laws which amended or repealed provisions of the Code proper.

MEXICO

2976. CÓDIGO DE PROCEDIMIENTOS CIVILES DEL ESTADO LIBRE Y SOBERANO DE DURANGO. Puebla, J. M. Cájica, Jr. (Col. de Leyes Mexicanas, Serie Leyes Federales y para el Distrito y Territorios Federales). 207 p.
Text of code of civil procedure now in force.

2977. Muñoz, Luis (ed.). Nuevo código de procedimientos civiles, con prontuario alfabético. México, Lex. 304 p.
The subject index is a valuable aid.

2978. Trueba Urbina, Alberto (ed.). Ley de amparo reformada. Doctrina, legislación y jurisprudencia. México, Porrúa. 286 p.
Annotated text of the newly revised law on the writ of *amparo,* which has developed into a unique institution under Mexican law.

OTHER COUNTRIES

2979. Arlas, José A. La cosa juzgada penal y su eficacia sobre la materia civil. Montevideo, Universidad de Montevideo (Biblioteca de Publicaciones Oficiales de la Facultad de Derecho y Ciencias Sociales, Sección 3, 52). 220 p.
Discussion of the procedural subject of *res judicata* in a criminal case preventing the bringing of a tort action for the same injury.

2980. Casarino Viterbo, Mario. Manual de derecho procesal. Derecho procesal orgánico. V. 1–2. Santiago, Editorial Jurídica de Chile (Manuales Jurídicos, no. 24–25).
One of the series of handbooks issued for use as textbooks in all fields of law. Each item is contributed by an outstanding authority in the field.

2981. CÓDIGO DE PROCEDIMIENTO CIVIL DE LA REPÚBLICA DE NICARAGUA. 2. edición oficial, ordenada por Víctor M. Román y

Reyes y Modesto Salmerón. Contiene origen de las disposiciones, reformas, concordancias y referencias a la jurisprudencia de la excelentísima Corte Suprema de Justicia. V. 1–2. Managua, Talleres Heuberger. 550 p.
The first official edition of this code made its appearance in 1904, and there was a dire need for the present work before it was finally completed. Approximately 120 pages at the end are devoted to implementary and related legislation.

2982. Galté Carré, Jaime. Manual de organización y atribuciones de los tribunales. Santiago, Editorial Jurídica de Chile (Manuales Jurídicos, no. 26). 521 p.
A textbook on the organization of judicial and administrative organs dispensing justice in Chile. Matters of jurisdiction and details of administration are included.

2983. Maza y Rodríguez, Emilio. En defensa de la acción pública. Recurso presentado ante el Tribunal de Garantías Constitucionales y Sociales contra la Ley núm. 7 de 1949, que creó dicho Tribunal. Habana, Montero (Monografías Jurídicas, v. 69). 66 p.
Although only a pamphlet insofar as the number of its pages is concerned, this work throws much light on the right of the people in Cuba to question judicially the constitutionality of legislation enacted by the Congress. This particular study is in connection with an action against the law which created the new Court of Constitutional Guarantees, set up to hear, among other actions, this type of popular action alleging unconstitutionality.

2984. Núñez y Núñez, Eduardo Rafael. Dictámenes de la jurispericia. Habana, Montero (Monografías Jurídicas, v. 71). 114 p.
Treats of administrative tribunals and civil procedure matters under Cuban law.

2985. Oblitas Poblete, Enrique. Procedimiento criminal de Bolivia. La Paz, Imprenta Norkita. 1000 p.
An exhaustive treatise with much detail.

2986. Pardo, Antonio J. Tratado de derecho procesal civil. V. 1. Medellín, Colombia, Imprenta de la Universidad de Antioquia. 502 p.
Extensive study of civil procedure, giving origin and historical sources. Very interesting on Colombian procedural legislation and on that of the other Latin American countries.

2987. Río L., Pedro Eliécer del (ed). Doctrinas del Tribunal Superior de Bogotá. Sala Civil. V. 1. Bogotá. 425 p.
The first volume of a useful digest of civil case-law compiled from decisions rendered by the highest local court in Bogotá. This volume covers only subjects from *A* through *D*.

ADMINISTRATIVE LAW
(INCLUDING TAXATION)

ARGENTINA

2988. Bello, Juan E., and Carlos M. Giuliani Fonrouge (eds.). Código tributario. Compilación de las disposiciones impositivas con sus respectivas reglamentaciones actualizadas, concordadas y anotadas con la jurisprudencia administrativa y judicial. V. 1. Buenos Aires, Depalma (Códigos Anotados Depalma). 959 p.
A section is allocated to each type of tax, such as income, excess profits, stamp, excise, and so on. In each instance the texts of the basic law and regulation are given. The annotations by the joint editors consist mainly of occasional judicial or administrative interpretation.

2989. Biondi, Mario. La ley nacional de sellos. Buenos Aires, Editora Argentina. 398 p.
A lengthy commentary on the stamp law in force.

2990. Carámbula, Adhémar H. Elementos para la formación del derecho tributario notarial. Buenos Aires, Depalma. 120 p.
The tax and economic aspects in the notarial profession are discussed here.

2991. Ministerio de Hacienda. Dirección de Impuestos y Contribuciones. Jurisprudencia administrativa en materia fiscal. Impuesto de sellos. Buenos Aires. 240 p.
A collection of administrative decisions in connection with the application and interpretation of the stamp tax legislation.

BRAZIL

2992. Accioly, Aristophanes. Contribuição de melhoria e valorização imobiliária. Rio de Janeiro, Edições Financeiras, 1950? 118 p.
Deals with special assessments on real estate and land taxation.

2993. Boucher, Hercules. Estudos de impôsto de renda e contabilidade. Tributação das pessoas jurídicas. Rio de Janeiro, Freitas Bastos. 460 p.
An important commentary on the taxing of business associations and on tax accounting. An appendix of over 100 pages contains forms for tax returns and case-law in point. The text of the income tax law and its regulations occupies over 80 pages.

2994. Brandão, Alonso Caldas. Código de obras e legislação complementar. Rio de Janeiro, A. Coelho Branco (Col. de Códigos e Leis Vigentes, 7). 773 p.
A compilation of the basic decree of 1937 with all amendatory and related legislation in the field of administration of the Federal District of Rio de Janeiro, whether enacted by federal or local authorities. The contents include materials on zoning and planning, waters, public works, local finance, construction of buildings and roads, sanitation, rentals, and other related subjects.

2995. Carneiro, Eryma. O balanço fiscal no direito e na contabilidade. Rio de Janeiro, Instituto de Organização e Revisão de Contabilidade. 96 p.
A handbook on law of accounting, including its use in tax matters.

2996. Figueiredo, Paulo Poppe de. Estatuto dos funcionários públicos civis da União, atualizado até junho de 1950. Rio de Janeiro, Gráfica Editôra Aurora. 124 p.
A compilation of current civil service laws and regulations.

2998. Instituto de Previdência e Assistência dos Servidores do Estado. Manual do segurado do IPASE, elaborado de acôrdo com a portaria n. 625, de 2 de maio de 1949. Rio de Janeiro, Serviço de Publicidade e Estatística do IPASE. 128 p.
A handbook on civil service regulations in connection with retirement, pensions, salaries, etc.

2999. Mello, Waldomar Guena (ed.). Páginas elucidativas sôbre impôsto de consumo. São Paulo, Editôra do Brasil. 550 p.
Contains text of the basic decree of 1949 concerning tax on articles of consumption and excise taxes, and commentaries on phases of the internal revenue law. Forms are also included.

3000. NORMAS GERAIS DE DIREITO FINANCEIRO. Rio de Janeiro, Edições Financeiras (Finanças em Debate, 1). 104 p.
A collection of debates, recommendations, and papers presented at a national conference on public finance. One of series published by Affonso Almiro.

3001. Santos, J. Pantaleão. Alfândegas, legislação e prática de serviço (fiscais aduaneiros). Rio de Janeiro, di Giorgio. 79 p.
A collection of law and administrative provisions on customs administration.

3001a. Sousa, Rubens Gomes de. Estudos de direito tributário. São Paulo, Saraiva. 318 p.
A series of studies on various aspects of tax law.

3002. Viana, Arruda. O município e a sua lei orgânica. São Paulo, Saraiva. 370 p.
The author comments on the 1947 basic law on municipalities and gives background references of interest. A fine index and forms add to the value of the work.

OTHER COUNTRIES

3003. ARANCEL DE ADUANAS. Decreto 2218 de 1950, julio 10. *Diario Oficial* no. 27359. Edición oficial. Bogotá, Banco de la República. 291 p.
An official edition of the text of the new Colombian tariff law and schedule.

3004. Carámbula, Adhémar H. Bases para la estructuración y estudio del derecho tributario notarial uruguayo. Montevideo, Asociación de Escribanos del Uruguay. 33 p.
This work was presented at the Second Notarial Conference held at Paysandú on September 10-11, 1949. The author published a general work on the same subject (item 2990).

3005. Castillo, Juan Lino. El derecho presupuestario en el Perú. Lima, Editorial P. T. C. M. 89 p.
A work on the budget containing tables and a fair bibliography.

3006. Charad Dahud, Emilio, and Víctor Sergio Mena Vergara. Derecho financiero. Santiago, Editorial Universitaria. (Col. Apuntes). 454 p.
A textbook on public finance prepared by the joint authors from notes taken in the course given by Prof. Felipe Herrera Lane.

3007. CÓDIGO ADMINISTRATIVO DEL ESTADO DE CHIHUAHUA. Contiene también la constitución política de la entidad. México, La Impresora. 675 p., loose leaf.
Chihuahua is the first of the 29 Mexican states to enact an administrative code.

3008. Cover, Gilbert Grace (tr.). Venezuelan income tax law of 1948, and regulations of the same law decreed in 1949. Caracas, Ávila Gráfica. 141 p.
Both the translated text of the law and regulation and the original Spanish are given, together with a useful index.

3009. Lardé y Larín, Jorge. Recopilación de leyes relativas a la historia de los municipios de El Salvador. San Salvador, Ministerio del Interior. 459 p.
The development of municipal corporations from the legal point of view.

3010. LEY GENERAL DE POBLACIÓN CON SUS REFORMAS Y REGLAMENTO DE LA MISMA. México, Secretaría de Gobernación. 112 p.
A new law on population including provisions on aliens and immigration was adopted in 1947. The text of this basic law and of its amendments and implementary regulation of 1950 are here published officially.

3011. Méndez, Aparicio. La jerarquía. Montevideo, Universidad de Montevideo, Facultad de Derecho y Ciencias Sociales (Biblioteca de Publicaciones Oficiales, Sección 3, no. 51). 152 p.
A monograph on administrative procedure, dealing in particular with the appeal within the administrative structure, rather than in special courts.

3012. Pérez Cubillas, José María. Curso de derecho fiscal. V. 1. 1. edición. Habana, Molina. 444 p.
This first volume by an outstanding tax and economics authority is intended for both lawyers and economists. The greater part is general and comparative in character, with incidental applications to Cuban law. The following volume or volumes will probably be more local in character.

3013. Rencoret Bravo, Álvaro. Derecho tributario. El impuesto sobre la renta. Santiago, Editorial Jurídica de Chile (Col. de Estudios Jurídicos y Sociales, v. 4). 404 p.
A useful textbook on income tax, as legislated on and practiced in Chile.

3014. Reyes Cardona, Julio Antonio. Derechos y acciones de los empleados y trabajadores del estado. Guatemala, Tipografía Nacional (Publ. de la Magistratura de Coordinación de Trabajo y Previsión Social). 79 p.
The rights of government workers under Guatemalan labor law and the constitution are set forth and interpreted in this little book published by the Coordinating Judge of the Labor Courts. See also item 2400.

3015. Tinoco, Pedro R. Comentarios de la ley de impuesto sobre la renta de Venezuela. Temas fiscales. Caracas, Ávila Gráfica. 283 p.
A fine exposition of the various aspects of income taxation in Venezuela, which had appeared previously as a series of articles in local newspapers.

CONSTITUTIONAL LAW

ARGENTINA

3016. Congreso. Cámara de Diputados. División Archivo, Publicaciones y Museo. Digesto constitucional de la Nación Argentina. Buenos Aires, Imprenta del Congreso de la Nación. 559 p.
Contains texts of the 1949 revised national constitution and of the various provincial charters.

3017. CONSTITUCIONES DE LA PROVINCIA DE CÓRDOBA. Introducción del Dr. Carlos R. Melo. Córdoba, Universidad Nacional de Córdoba, Dirección General de Publicidad (Biblioteca de Derecho Público Provincial Argentino, 3). ccxxxvi, 290 p.
A collection of the provincial charters.

3018. Marianetti, Benito. Nosotros y la constitución. 1. edición. Mendoza, D'Accurzio. 231 p.

The constitution under discussion here is the 1949 provincial charter of Mendoza. Comparison is made with earlier constitutions and the discussions of the Constituent Congress are commented on at great length.

3019. Melo, Carlos Rito. Introducción a las constituciones de la Provincia de Córdoba. Córdoba, Imprenta de la Universidad. 236 p.

A treatise on constitutional history of the province, through the adoption of several charters.

3020. Poviña, Jorge Raúl. Costumbres y usos constitucionales. Tucumán, Universidad Nacional de Tucumán, Instituto de Derecho Público (Publ. no. 495). 144 p.

Prof. Poviña gives a complete examination, sources, and classification of constitutional uses and customs in an admirably written essay.

3021. La reforma de la Constitución nacional, sancionada por la Convención Nacional Constituyente, el 11 de marzo de 1949. V. 1-2. Buenos Aires, Secretaría de la Presidencia, Subsecretaría de Informaciones y Prensa. 729 p.

Congressional debate as well as discussion of the necessary amendments to the constitution which took place in the Constitutional Convention are included in this exhaustive work. It contains also comparative constitutional provisions in other Latin American countries and texts of implementary and related legislation prior to and subsequent to adoption of the new Constitution.

3022. Riéffolo Bessone, José F. Los derechos sociales de la mujer. Cartas a mi amigo Bover. Sufragismo y feminismo. Perón y Evita. Buenos Aires, El Ateneo. (Biblioteca del Ciudadano, 1). 231 p.

Civil, social, and political rights of women in Argentina and in various European countries are discussed in the form of correspondence between the author, an Argentine diplomat abroad, and his friend Bover. Roman and Greek practice are included in background discussion.

3023. Sastre, Pastor. Instrucción cívica. Manual de la Constitución (de conformidad con el nuevo plan) para los colegios nacionales, liceos, escuelas normales y de comercio. Buenos Aires, Ciordia y Rodríguez. 320 p.

An elementary guide on the subjects of constitution and government.

3024. Vigo, Salvador C. Reforma constitucional argentina. Santa Fe, Editorial Nueva Impresora. 540 p.

This work consists of three parts and an appendix. In the first the fundamental concepts of constitutional law are explained; the scientific character of constitutional law is developed in five chapters, covering its method, object and subject, basic elements of the State, sources of constitutional law, powers of the State and its forms of government, political constitutions, etc. The second and third parts develop the main topic of this work, which is the constitutional amendments of 1949 in general. The 15 chapters of the third part analyze the new basic law, from the preamble to the provisions on the provincial governments.

3026. Vogel, Carlos Alfredo, and Eugenio Vélez Achaval. Historia argentina y constitución nacional. Buenos Aires, Perrot. 481 p.

Beginning with the Hispanic colonial period, the authors trace the development and history of constitutional government in Argentina through the periods of revolution, independence and dictatorship, to the present constitution of 1949.

Brazil

3027. Azorim, Nestor, and Luzio Araújo (eds.). Novo manual eleitoral. Rio de Janeiro. 110 p.

Contains the text of the new electoral code as promulgated by Law 1164 of July 24, 1950, together with annotations and interpretative and administrative resolutions of the Tribunal Superior Eleitoral on all electoral matters and political parties.

3028. Baleeiro, Aliomar. Alguns andaimes da Constituição. Rio de Janeiro, A. M. de Oliveira. 199 p.

Likening constitutions to buildings, the author entitles his work "The scaffold of the constitution of 1946" and shows how it was planned and constructed by the Constituent Assembly and its various committees.

3029. Brandão, Alonso Caldas. Legislação de estrangeiros. 1. edição. Rio de Janeiro, A. Coelho Branco (Col. de Códigos e Leis Vigentes, 5). 277 p.

Administrative and legislative enactments relative to aliens have been collected in the present volume, which includes also constitutional and treaty provisions in point. Among subjects covered are immigration, passports, extradition and nationality.

3030. ————, and Delcilio Palmeira. Repertório eleitoral. Rio de Janeiro, A. Coelho Branco. 546 p.

Following the promulgation of a new electoral code in early 1950, the joint authors of this work collected into a single volume all pertinent provisions in this field. In the second half of the book they collect administrative and judicial decisions, including the decision of 1947 rendered by the Electoral Court in which the registration of the Communist Party as a political party was ordered cancelled. Background materials and individual opinions in this particular case are included.

3031. Carvalho, A. Dardeau de. Nacionalidade e cidadania. Rio de Janeiro, Freitas Bastos. 311 p.

A commentary on the law enacted on September 18, 1949 revising the regulation of nationality and citizenship.

3032. CÓDIGO ELEITORAL. Lei n. 1.164, de 24 de julho de 1950 (substitui o Código eleitoral). São Paulo, Saraiva (Legislação Brasileira, Biblioteca da Livraria Acadêmica). 119 p.

Text of newly enacted electoral law and of other related laws, in codified form.

3033. ESTRANGEIROS. V. 1-2. Rio de Janeiro, Ministério da Justiça e Negocios Interiores, Serviço de Documentação. 831 p.

A complete compilation of laws and decrees pertinent to aliens in Brazil from 1808 to 1949. A useful bibliography and index increase the value of this work, as do the numerous cross-references to other legislation in point.

CHILE

3034. Amunátegui, Gabriel. Manual de derecho constitucional. Santiago, Editorial Jurídica de Chile (Manuales Juridicos, no. 28). 528 p.

Handbook for use in courses on constitutional law.

3035. Grimaldo Carles, Rodrigo. La nacionalidad en la Constitución panameña de 1946. Estudio crítico y comparado con el derecho chileno. Santiago. 83 p.

Interesting from the point of view of comparative law. The author of this thesis was a Panamanian law student at the Faculty of Law in the University of Chile.

3036. Heise González, Julio. Historia constitucional de Chile. Esquema de las explicaciones dadas en clase. Santiago, Editorial Jurídica de Chile (Col. de Apuntes de Clases, no. 3). 149 p.

A textbook compiled from class lectures and notes.

OTHER COUNTRIES

3037. Borja y Borja, Ramiro. Derecho constitucional ecuatoriano. V. 1-3. Madrid, Cultura Hispánica. 845, 748, 748 p.

An eminent jurist of Ecuador published in Spain this monumental treatise on the constitutional law of his country. The first two volumes, divided into "books," cover general constitutional law and philosophy with application to Ecuador, through provisions of the various charters adopted by this country. The third volume is an appendix containing the literal texts of the 18 constitutions that have regulated Ecuador since 1812.

3038. Demicheli, Alberto. El poder ejecutivo. Génesis y transformaciones. Buenos Aires, Depalma. 207 p.

The background and development of the executive power in Uruguay with comparative notes referring to basic systems of France, Great Britain, and the United States. The work includes a description of the pluripersonal executive as tried twice in Uruguay.

3039. Gidel, Gilbert Charles. La plataforma continental ante el derecho. Translated from the unpublished French original by A. Herrero Rubio. Valladolid, Spain, Universidad de Valladolid. 169 p.

Discussion of a subject of very present interest. Refers to recent declarations made by various American governments as to sovereignty over continental shelf and marginal seas.

3040. Infiesta, Ramón. Derecho constitucional. Habana, P. Fernández. 338 p.

Following generalities on constitutional law, the author restricts himself to the dogmatic portion of the Cuban charter, that is, the organization, duties, and rights of the three powers. He also devotes one chapter to the theory of "freedom" in a democracy.

3041. LEY DE EXTRANJEROS. Caracas, Imprenta Nacional. 56 p.

An unannotated official edition in pamphlet form of the law regulating aliens in Venezuela.

3042. Noguera Laborde, Rodrigo. Constitución de la República de Colombia y sus antecedentes documentales desde 1885. Bogotá, Universidad Católica Javeriana (Publ. del Fondo Rotatorio, 2). 263 p.

Extensively annotated. See also item 1353.

CIVIL LAW

ARGENTINA

3043. Boffi Boggero, Luis María. Algunos aspectos de la instrumentación pública en el proyecto de reformas al Código Civil. La Plata, Escuela de Artes y Oficios. 26 p.

A discussion of the proposed amendments to the Civil Code extensively circulated and commented upon in 1936.

3044. Cejas, Horacio E. Sucesiones. V. 1. Buenos Aires, Macchi, 352 p.

A standard text on wills and succession as regulated by the provisions of the civil code. This work is perhaps more detailed and better documented than the usual run of works of this kind. The present volume does not cover intestate succession, a subject apparently left to be covered in a second volume.

3045. Cejas, Horacio E., and Horacio W. Bliss. Contratos del derecho civil. Buenos

Aires, Editorial Ciencias Económicas.
245 p.
A textbook on formal contracts as differentiated
from obligations. This is used in a second year
course in economics where the law overlaps into
that discipline.

3046. Landó, Juan Carlos. Hacia la protección integral de la minoridad. Buenos
Aires, Depalma. 211 p.
A commentary on protection of children and
minors in both civil and criminal law fields.

3047. Lapa, Eduardo L. La propiedad en
la función del martillero. Buenos Aires,
Hachette. 327 p.
An elucidative treatise on property rights and
ownership in transactions and sales carried out
through services of an auctioneer.

3048. Parry, Adolfo E. Efectos de la quie-
bra y el concurso civil en las obligaciones
y en los contratos. Buenos Aires, Tipografía Editora Argentina. xxxi, 764 p.
A well written treatise on the effect of bankruptcy and liquidation on existing contracts.

3049. Pizarro, Néstor A. El código civil
argentino y el código civil de Luisiana.
Estudio sobre las fuentes legislativas del
código civil. Córdoba, Imprenta de la
Universidad (Cuadernos de Derecho Civil,
14). 144 p.
Many of the provisions of the Argentine civil
code of 1871, still basically in force at present,
were adopted from the Louisiana code of 1824
in this field, based on the Napoleonic code of
1808. Other provisions of the American code
are cited as reference and consultation sources.
The author comments in detail on the influence
of the North American on the South American
code.

3050. Rezzónico, Luis María. Estudio de
los contratos en nuestro derecho civil.
Buenos Aires. 434 p.
Covers various types of contracts, including
sales, and other transfers of property as regulated by Argentine national law.

BRAZIL

3051. Altamira, A. F. d' (ed.). Da locação
de imóveis. Rio de Janeiro, Editôra Nacional de Direito (Col. de Direito Usual).
246 p.
A collection of legislation, case law, and articles
on leases and rentals of real property.

3052. Ribeiro, Zeferino. O tabelionato.
Rio de Janeiro, Freitas Bastos. 300 p.
A monograph on notarial law and practice, including some forms for use in contracts, wills,
and deeds.

CHILE

3053. Rosende Subiabre, Hugo. Derecho
civil: sucesiones por causa de muerte.
Santiago, Editorial Universitaria (Col.
Apuntes). 301 p.
Compilation of class lectures delivered by the
professor on wills and succession. This type of
work is useful in the absence of a principal
textbook on the subject.

3054. Somarriva Undurraga, Manuel. In-
división y partición. V. 1-2. Santiago,
Editorial Jurídica de Chile (Col. de Estudios Jurídicos y Sociales, v. 5-6). 313,
450 p.
A learned professor of civil law turns out this
textbook on a very special phase of property
rights, including joint ownership, joint tenancy,
undivided rights, partition and other aspects,
positive and procedural, of the same topic.

3055. Stitchkin Branover, David. El
mandato civil. Santiago, Editorial Jurídica
de Chile (Col. de Estudios Jurídicos y
Sociales, v. 1). 588 p.
A comparative treatment of relations between
principal and agent in civil law from its beginnings in Roman Law to its present practice.

MEXICO

3056. Bazarte Cerdán, Wildebardo (ed.).
Leyes sobre arrendamientos para el Dis-
trito Federal y Estados de la República.
Prórroga de contratos de locales ocupados
por talleres, comercios . . . . México,
Botas (Col. de Leyes Mexicanas). 62 p.
A collection of laws of local enactment in the
field of landlord and tenant.

**3057. CÓDIGO CIVIL DEL ESTADO LIBRE Y
SOBERANO DE DURANGO.** Puebla, J. M.
Cájica, Jr. (Col. de Leyes Mexicanas, Serie
Leyes del Estado de Durango), 1950?
433 p.
Text of civil code which became effective in
1948.

3058. Schoenrich, Otto (tr.). The civil
code for the Federal District and Territories of Mexico, and the Mexican laws
on alien landownership. New York, Baker,
Voorhis. 627 p.
Translation of entire code text, including new
copyright law, with addition of restrictive legislation on land ownership by aliens.

3059. Serrano Trasviña, Jorge. Aporta-
ción al fideicomiso. México, Universidad
Nacional Autónoma de México, Escuela
Nacional de Jurisprudencia (Publ. del
Seminario de Derecho Mercantil y Ban-
cario, Serie A, no. 32). 382 p.

A thesis of interest because it describes the implantation of a common law concept in a civil law doctrine.

PERU

3060. Cornejo Chávez, Héctor. Derecho familiar peruano. V. 1. Arequipa, Editorial Universitaria. 351 p.

The first volume of an exhaustive treatise on domestic relations in Peru, commencing with a history of the legal background of the subject matter. Covers only marital relations from the personal and property angles.

3061. Echecopar García, Luis. Derecho de sucesiones. Examen del libro tercero del código civil peruano de 1936. Lima, Sanmartí. 345 p.

An erudite treatise on wills and succession in Peru.

3062. León Barandiarán, José. Manual del acto jurídico. Lima, Gil. 119 p.

Discusses all aspects of the so-called juridical or legal act, generally covered in the basic civil code provisions.

3063. Pacheco Medina, Miguel. Código civil. Jurisprudencia. Fasc. 1. Lima, Talleres Gráficos de Editora Médica Peruana. 103 p.

The case-law of 1950 on the various matters covered in the civil code has been collected, digested, and indexed chronologically and by subject matter, making a useful reference tool. It is to be hoped that this work will be continued, since there is little published of this nature.

OTHER COUNTRIES

3064. Cano Llopis, Manuel. Derecho de familia y derecho de sucesiones. Conjunto de temas sobre estas materias con adaptación de la legislación positiva vigente en Panamá. 1. edición. Panamá, Imprenta Nacional. 354 p.

The professor of the courses on domestic relations and wills found it necessary to write his own textbook in view of total lack of other texts in this field. Very useful in interpreting many of the changes adopted in this field in the past decade.

3065. CÓDIGO CIVIL. Edición oficial. Caracas, Ministerio de Relaciones Interiores. 485 p.

A current edition of the Venezuelan civil code adopted in 1942.

3066. CÓDIGO CIVIL DE LA REPÚBLICA DEL ECUADOR. Edición hecha por la Comisión Legislativa en uso de la facultad consignada en el Art. 77 de la Constitución Política. Quito, Talleres Gráficos Nacionales. 556 p.

Substantial recent changes in the laws of marriage and divorce, adoption, rights of children, property and others contributed to the need for a revised basic civil code, and the recodification was accomplished by a Legislative Commission in June, 1950.

3067. Granadillo C., Víctor Luis. Tratado elemental de derecho civil. T. 1. Caracas, Ávila Gráfica. 303 p.

This work is complete in three volumes, the second and third having been published in 1951 and 1952 respectively. All aspects of Venezuelan civil law are discussed, the present volume being devoted entirely to persons and domestic relations.

3068. Machado, José (ed.). Comentarios al Código Civil. 2 v. in 1. Guanabacoa, Cuba, Puga. 496, 422 p.

The individual code provisions are followed by commentaries and annotations by the author, with frequent reference to Cuban and Spanish case-law. Citation is made also to pertinent parts of treatises by well-known scholars.

3069. Ortega Torres, Jorge (ed.). Código civil, con notas, concordancias, jurisprudencia de la Corte Suprema y normas legales complementarias. Bogotá, Temis (Biblioteca de Derecho Civil). 1091 p.

A heavy volume containing copious notes, commentaries, and pertinent case-law following the individual code provisions. The full texts of related laws and decrees are also given.

3070. Rodríguez C., Fabio T. (ed.). Código civil de la República Dominicana. Leyes que lo modifican y lo completan. Ciudad Trujillo, Montalvo. 534 p.

A current revised text of the civil code, with full text of laws which have served to amend or repeal provisions therein, as well as of laws which implement the text.

3071. Saavedra, María Josefa. Régimen jurídico de la menor edad en Bolivia. Estudios, informes, proyectos, legislación. La Paz, Universidad Mayor de San Andrés, Escuela de Derecho y Ciencias Políticas (Publ., cuaderno no. 5). 199 p.

An eminent woman lawyer, whose principal interest has been in the rights of minors and juvenile delinquency, has compiled in the present work a number of studies and reports in the field of her specialization. Bills and laws considered by the legislature of Bolivia are incorporated in the collection.

CRIMINAL LAW

ARGENTINA

3072. Brebbia, Roberto H. El daño moral. Buenos Aires, Editorial Bibliográfica Argentina. 303 p.

Following a general discussion of the legal theory of damages, the author deals with legislation, case-law, and learned opinion on moral damages.

3073. CÓDIGO PENAL DE LA NACIÓN ARGENTINA. Edición corregida de acuerdo con la Ley de Fe de Erratas. Buenos Aires, Lajouane (Códigos y Leyes Usuales de la República Argentina). 93 p.
An unannotated edition of the criminal code.

3074. Jiménez de Asúa, Luis. Tratado de derecho penal. V. 1. Buenos Aires, Losada. 1129 p.
Invaluable work which will consist of five volumes. Exhaustive information and data on legislation, bibliographies, and sources of comparative criminal law. One section concerns penal law in Latin America.

3075. Presidencia. Subsecretaría de Informaciones. Dirección General del Registro Nacional. Abastecimiento y represión del agio. V. 1. Buenos Aires. 628 p.
An important contribution of official literature on price control and rationing. Also contains measures to repress speculation, which is made punishable as a crime. The first volume contains texts of three basic laws and other regulations, as well as related legislation between 1939 and 1948. The second volume will carry on the chronological compilation from 1948 until the date of its publication.

3076. Ure, Ernesto J. El delito de incumplimiento de los deberes de asistencia familiar. Ley no. 13.944. Buenos Aires, Editorial Ideas. 93 p.
The offense of non-support as punishable under Argentine law is discussed first, and comparison with practice in several European countries follows. The remaining brief chapters cover details of the crime itself and the procedural details involved in prosecuting persons guilty of the offense. An appendix contains the text of the foreign law provisions in Spanish translation.

MEXICO

3077. Baeza y Acévez, Leopoldo. Endocrinología y criminalidad. México, Imprenta Universitaria. 371 p.
A general treatise on the effect of glands and glandular secretions on crime, specially in connection with insanity. Although written by a lawyer and expert on forensic medicine, the work treats more of the psychological, medical, and sociological aspects than of the legal. An excellent bibliography, including domestic and foreign authors.

3078. Bernaldo de Quirós y Pérez, Constancio. Derecho penal, parte especial. Puebla, José M. Cájica, Jr. (Publ. de la Universidad de Puebla). 367 p.
A Spanish criminologist is the author of a general treatise on criminal law.

3079. Fernández del Valle y Rincón Gallardo, Justo. La responsabilidad civil del porteador de personas y el seguro obligatorio. México. 101 p.
Tort liability for carriers of persons and compulsory insurance is a new field for a Latin American author. Thesis, University of Mexico.

OTHER COUNTRIES

3080. Bramont Arias, Luis. La ley penal. Curso de dogmática jurídica. Lima, R. Meza Simich. xxxiii, 309 p.
A general treatise on criminal law and criminology.

3081. CÓDIGO PENAL DE LA REPÚBLICA DE NICARAGUA. Anotado y comentado por Manuel Escobar H. Edición oficial con todas sus reformas. Masaya, Nicaragua, El Espectador. viii, 195 p.
A much needed new edition of the penal code with its amendatory and complementary legislation. The code was adopted in 1891 and naturally many changes have occurred since that date. The extensive notes of the commentator add much to the reference value of the work.

3082. Coral Luzzi, Pascual Federico. Código de honor, con las leyes relativas al duelo, ajustado a la codificación penal de las Repúblicas O. del Uruguay, Argentina e iberoamericanas. Montevideo, A. Monteverde. 114 p.

3083. LA EXTRADICIÓN A LA LUZ DE LA LEGISLACIÓN VENEZOLANA. Caracas, Academia de Ciencias Políticas y Sociales. 117 p.
As a prelude to being admitted to membership in the Academy of Political and Social Sciences, Dr. Héctor Parra Márquez delivered a discourse on extradition under Venezuelan law. His speech and the reply of Dr. Ángel Francisco Brice are published together.

3084. Gumiel Terán, Pedro. Cuadro sinóptico para el estudio del código penal. Potosí, Bolivia, Imprenta Universitaria. 209 p.
The first part is devoted to the development of the penal code, and the second to the study of the penal legislation outside the code. A valuable contribution to the Bolivian bibliography on penal legislation.

3085. Jiménez de Asúa, Luis. Defensas penales en América. Habana, Montero (Biblioteca Jurídica de Autores Cubanos y Extranjeros, v. 145). 278 p.
A distinguished Spanish jurist adds another book to his already extensive list of works in the field in which he has specialized for so long. The present work is applied to Latin America, where he has spent many years as a political refugee.

3086. Lozano y Lozano, Carlos. Elementos de derecho penal. Bogotá, Universidad Nacional de Colombia. 610 p.

An eminent Colombian jurist treats the oft-covered field of penal law with unusual clarity and detail.

3087. Paredes Luna, Héctor. El delito deportivo ante el sistema jurídico-penal guatemalteco. Guatemala. 43 p.

An unusual topic has been selected as subject matter of this thesis (University of San Carlos), concerning assault and battery committed during activities in the field of sports.

3088. Pérez, Luis Carlos. Criminología. La nueva concepción naturalista del delito. Bogotá, Universidad Nacional de Colombia. 415 p.

A novel approach to the concept of a crime, taught by the author in his courses on criminal sociology.

3089. Ruiz-Funes García, Mariano. Criminologia de guerra. São Paulo, Saraiva. 396 p.

A translation into Portuguese of the treatise of a well-known Mexican criminologist.

COMMERCIAL LAW

ARGENTINA

3090. Bosch, Felipe (comp.). Legislación de seguros (privados). Buenos Aires, Lys. 366 p.

A collection of insurance laws and decrees as found in the commercial code, international rules, and the CIF and FOB contracts. The comments of various authorities are also included.

3091. Garo, Francisco J. Sociedades de responsabilidad limitada. Buenos Aires, La Facultad. 476 p.

A monograph on limited liability or private companies in Argentina compared to the institution as developed in other countries, particularly in France.

3092. Guernik, Miguel. Derecho práctico. Buenos Aires, Librería Americana. 170 p.

A manual of forms for commercial and private contracts, following in each case the pertinent provisions of law to which they apply.

3093. Sasot Betes, Miguel A. Directores de sociedades anónimas. Derechos, obligaciones, responsabilidad. Buenos Aires, Cía. Impresora Argentina. 331 p.

Every possible aspect of the rights and duties of corporation directors is discussed in this work, first published as series of articles in *Rev. Cien. Jur. Soc.*

3094. Satanowsky, Marcos. Estudios de derecho comercial. V. 1-2. Buenos Aires, Editora Argentina. 395, 393 p.

A sponsor of unification in the field of private law, the author discusses in this comprehensive treatise commercial law subjects which not only are regulated by the commercial code, but also fall into the field of the civil code, special legislation, and the administrative field. A portion of the first volume is generally historical and theoretical in nature. Some specific subjects covered are civil and commercial contracts and obligations, bankruptcy, negotiable instruments, corporations, and money.

3095. Solá Cañizares, Felipe de. Tratado de sociedades de responsabilidad limitada en derecho argentino y comparado, con la colaboración de Enrique Aztiria. V. 1. Buenos Aires, Editora Argentina. 709 p.

The Spanish author has specialized for many years in the subject of commercial organizations and has published many works on all phases thereof. The present volume is the first of a detailed treatise on a type of association rapidly growing in popularity in Argentina. The discussion is comparative in nature, with Argentine law and practice as a basis for the comparison.

MEXICO

3096. ANTEPROYECTO DEL LIBRO CUARTO DEL CÓDIGO DE COMERCIO. México, Secretaría de Economía. 105 p.

A much-needed revision of the commercial code is taken through the first step of a preliminary draft. Book 4 deals with commercial contracts.

3097. Caso, Ángel, and Javier Tercero. Documentación mercantil y aduanal. México, Ediciones Mexicanas (Col. Comercial, 1). 423 p.

The first volume of a new series of commercial handbooks intended for use not only by merchants and businessmen, but also as a textbook. Contains many forms, including those for all types of negotiable instruments, bonds, certificates, insurance, powers of attorney, etc.

3098. Vásquez del Mercado, Óscar. Fusión de sociedades mercantiles. México, Porrúa. 113 p.

Covers in detail the subject of consolidation and merger of corporations in general, and as practiced in Mexico in particular.

OTHER COUNTRIES

3099. CÓDIGO DEL COMERCIO DE NICARAGUA, CONCORDADO Y ANOTADO. Edición puesta al día. Managua, Asel. 270 p.

A badly needed revision of the commercial code of 1914, which became effective in 1916, has received treatment in the form of notes, cross-references and citations which brings its text up to date. See item 3107.

3100. **Cover, Gilbert Grace** (ed.). Venezuelan commercial code and civil code (código de comercio y código civil) on companies and registry. English-Spanish. Caracas, Translation Service. 135 p.
An important reference work which brings together in English the provisions of both basic codes relating to business associations.

3101. **Fábrega P., Jorge** (tr.). Corporation law of the Republic of Panama. Printed in Spanish and in English. Panamá, La Moderna. 52 p.
A fine translation of the text of the corporation law without additional notes or comments.

3102. **Labarca Salas, Leopoldo.** Manual jurídico-práctico del comerciante minorista. Santiago, Escuela Tipográfica Salesiana. 71 p.
A brief guide to elementary law and practice in the commercial field for use of small business men. Thesis, Law School, University of Chile.

3103. LEY DE CONTROL DE LAS TRANSACCIONES INTERNACIONALES. Reglamento de las operaciones en el mercado libre e índice de las categorías de artículos de importación. San José, Imprenta Nacional. 71 p.
Unannotated text of the Costa Rican law.

3104. LEYES BANCARIAS. Tegucigalpa, Ariston. 61 p.
A collection of the texts of four national decrees dealing with banks and banking law, including organization of the National Bank of Honduras in 1950.

3105. **Olavarría Ávila, Julio.** Manual de derecho comercial. V. 1. Santiago, Editorial Jurídica de Chile (Manuales Jurídicos, no. 29). 473 p.
One of a series of textbooks for the various fields of law covered in the curriculum of the law schools. Each contribution is by an outstanding expert in the field, the present work by the professor of mercantile law.

3106. **Santos, Antero, and Roberto Vetter.** Propriedade industrial no Brasil. Legislação vigente. Rio de Janeiro, G. Carneiro. 240 p.
A compilation of national and international legal provisions on patents and trademarks.

3107. **Solórzano, Aníbal.** Glosas al Código de Comercio de Nicaragua, concordancias y jurisprudencia. Managua, Asel. 770 p.
The extensive notes, commentaries, and digests of pertinent case-law which the editor has inserted following the individual articles of the code make this work an indispensable reference tool for the research worker on this particular field of commercial law. The annotated edition mentioned in item 3099 does not attempt to do more than give cross-references and citations to foreign code provisions and authorities, but

incidentally these same notes in exactly the same type and form are included in the present unofficial work, in addition to comprehensive commentaries. There is no doubt that there was some coordination here, inasmuch as both volumes were published within ten days of each other by the same publisher.

3108. **Villa Uribe, William.** Sociedades anónimas. Régimen legal en Colombia. Bogotá, Pax (Publicación de la Revista Trimestral de Derecho Comercial). 159 p.
A new codification on corporations was enacted in July, 1950. The present volume gives, in addition to the text of the new law, the original provisions on this subject that were scattered in the civil and commercial codes, as well as in a number of special laws and decrees. The 1950 law makes an orderly codification of all these provisions.

PRIVATE INTERNATIONAL LAW

3109. **Albónico Valenzuela, Fernando.** Manual de derecho internacional privado. V. 1-2. Santiago, Editorial Jurídica de Chile (Manuales Jurídicos, no. 32-33). 336, 378 p.
The author is professor on conflict of laws, at both the University of Chile and the Catholic University, Santiago.

3110. **Alfonsín, Quintín.** Régimen internacional de los contratos. Montevideo, Universidad de Montevideo, Facultad de Derecho y Ciencias Sociales (Biblioteca de Publicaciones Oficiales, Sección III, 54). 190 p.
An excellent treatise on the conflict of laws with relation to contracts. Copious references are made to national and foreign authorities. The practical aspects are supplied from the author's experience as legal counsel in the Ministry of Foreign Relations.

3111. **Corvalán Contardo, Enrique.** El derecho internacional privado aéreo. Santiago. 82 p.
A thesis (University of Chile) of interest because the subject matter has not received much attention from Latin American authors.

3112. **Duncker Biggs, Federico.** Derecho internacional privado. Santiago, Editorial Jurídica de Chile (Col. de Estudios Jurídicos y Sociales, v. 9). 464 p.
One of a series of textbooks undertaken in 1948-1950.

3113. TRATADOS DE MONTEVIDEO DE 1889 SOBRE EL DERECHO INTERNACIONAL PRIVADO. Montevideo, Universidad de Montevideo, Facultad de Derecho y Ciencias Sociales (Biblioteca de Publicaciones Oficiales, Sección II, 1). 63 p.
Reprinted texts of the various conventions signed in 1889.

PUBLIC INTERNATIONAL LAW

3114. Asturias Colom, Óscar. Los derechos del hombre ante el racionalismo y el historicismo. Guatemala. 63 p.
A law school thesis (University of San Carlos) of unusual depth emphasizes the right to a fair criminal trial and appeal under the writ of *amparo*.

3115. Colombia. Ministerio de Relaciones Exteriores. El derecho de asilo ante la Corte Internacional de Justicia. Bogotá, Imprenta Nacional. 42 p.
The Colombian point of view on the asylum case of Haya de la Torre as decided by the International Court is officially published.

3116. DECLARACIONES FUNDAMENTALES DE LOS DERECHOS HUMANOS. Texto de trascendentales documentos jurídicos sobre reconocimiento de atributos de la persona, aparecidos en el curso de la evolución social. Sucre, Bolivia, Universidad Mayor de San Francisco, Facultad de Derecho, Ciencias Políticas y Sociales. 113 p.

3117. Ferrer Vieyra, Enrique. Notas sobre privilegios e inmunidades en organismos internacionales y en especial en la Organización de los Estados Americanos. Córdoba, Imprenta de la Universidad. 165 p.
An interesting study of the development of the extension to international organizations of diplomatic privileges and immunities once limited to personnel of diplomatic and consular missions.

3118. Mello, Rubens Ferreira de (ed.). Textos de direito internacional e de história diplomática de 1815 a 1949. Rio de Janeiro, Imprensa Nacional. 881 p.
A selective collection of texts of treaties and of international and diplomatic documents which, in the editor's opinion, best demonstrate progress in the field of international law. These were selected from the period 1815-1949, from among those affecting Brazil or in which this country took part. The collection, with the editor's commentaries, includes such documents as the final act of the Vienna Congress, the Monroe Doctrine, the various multi-national conferences on private international law held in this hemisphere, various peace treaties, and the more recent United Nations and UNESCO documents, the North Atlantic Pact and similar historical instruments.

3119. Moreno Quintana, Lucio M., and **Carlos M. Bollini Shaw.** Derecho internacional público. Buenos Aires, Librería del Colegio. 837 p.
Two well-known internationalists have written an up-to-date text on public international law, showing the great development which has taken place in the past twenty years.

3120. Pan American Union. Inter-American juridical yearbook, 1949. Washington. 389 p.
This volume covers the second year of publication. The contents in three languages, according to the origin of the article, note, or document, treat of many aspects of Latin American law, with emphasis on international rather than on private law. Book reviews and lists of articles of hemispheric interest are also included.

OTHER TOPICS

3121. Berguido, Carlos, Jr., and **Jorge Fábrega.** Leyes marítimas panameñas. Panamá, Estrella de Panamá. 199 p.
A useful compilation of laws governing ships flying the flag of Panama.

3122. Caso, Ángel. Derecho agrario. Historia, derecho positivo, antología. México, Porrúa. xxx, 751 p.
An exhaustive history of agrarian law in Mexico by a well-known authority in the field.

3123. Catalano, Edmundo Fernando. Legislación de minas y régimen legal del petróleo. Buenos Aires, La Facultad. 500 p.
Comprehensive work, covering all aspects of Argentine mining and oil legislation.

3124. CÓDIGO DE MINERÍA DE LA REPÚBLICA ARGENTINA. Buenos Aires, Lajouane (Códigos y Leyes Usuales de la República Argentina). 110 p.
A compilation making current the national legislation in the field of mining.

3125. CÓDIGO DE MINERÍA PROMULGADA EL 12 DE MAYO DE 1950. Decreto ley no. 11357. Lima, Ministerio de Fomento y Obras Públicas. 112 p.
The mining legislation of Peru was in need of revision and codification. The implementary regulation to this new law appeared in 1951.

3126. CÓDIGO SANITARIO DE LOS ESTADOS UNIDOS MEXICANOS. Puebla, Mexico, José Cájica, Jr. (Col. de Leyes Mexicanas, Serie Leyes Federales). 122 p.
An English translation is noted in item 3142.

3127. Cortés Mendizábal, Francisco. ¿Son o no ciudadanos mexicanos, los ministros de los cultos religiosos? México. 110 p.
An interesting discussion in view of Mexico's policy of complete separation of church and state. Thesis, University of Mexico.

3128. Cuadra Vásquez, Humberto. Régimen jurídico de los deportistas profesionales (*Mem. licenciados,* v. 1, p. 391-423).
An unusual article on the legal regulation of professional and amateur sportsmen, which involves some aspects of labor law. Thesis, University of Chile.

3129. Diez, Manuel María. Servicio público de la radiodifusión. Buenos Aires, V. Abeledo. 362 p.

A very interesting treatise on radio law, covered from the viewpoints of jurisdiction, unfair competition in the commercial field, freedom of speech, copyright law, administrative restrictions, and international aspects. Very few comprehensive works on this subject have been published in Latin America. The chapters on copyright include discussion of playing of recorded music, a relatively new phase of the law in Argentina.

3130. DIGESTO DE SALUD PÚBLICA. V. 1. Buenos Aires, Ministerio de Salud Pública de la Nación, Sección Publicaciones. 527 p.

An official publication on public health laws and regulations. The first volume, in addition to generalities, contains the text of the basic sanitary code and of legislation pertinent to the field of public health over a 58-year period to 1943. The second and third volumes, when published, will cover 1943–1946 and 1946–1949 respectively, 1949 being the last year of the administration of the Minister who authorized the publication.

3131. Duarte Pereira, Osny. Direito florestal brasileiro. Rio de Janeiro, Borsoi. 573 p.

A treatise on forestry law. Bibliography, p. 543–547.

3132. Estévez Gazmuri, Carlos. Manual del abogado; recopilación. Santiago, Editorial Jurídica de Chile (Manuales Jurídicos, no. 34). 336 p.

On the 25th anniversary of the foundation of the Colegio de Abogados, the Law School of the University of Chile authorized the compilation of materials concerning or of interest to the legal profession, including the actual texts of laws dealing with the constitution and organization of the bar, the code of professional ethics, and pensions and fees applicable to attorneys in Chile.

3133. Gay de Montellá, Rafael. Principios de derecho aeronáutico. Buenos Aires, Depalma. 725 p.

A general treatise on comparative aeronautical law, including the public and private law aspects of the subject. The law of the United States, Great Britain, France, and other European countries is compared with that of Latin America and Spain. A goodly portion of the work refers to international law as it affects the various subdivisions of the subject matter.

3134. Hamilton, Eduardo. Manual de derecho aéreo. Santiago, Editorial Jurídica de Chile (Manuales Jurídicos, no. 35). 539 p.

The subject matter is approached from a general viewpoint, with discussion of international steps taken in this field.

3135. Llaguno, Pedro Pablo. Código notarial y legislación complementaria. Habana, J. Montero (Col. Legislativa de Bolsillo, v. 8). 317 p.

A small handbook for use of notaries.

3136. Manzanos Bonifaz, Alfonso. Sistemas penitenciarios militares y el régimen disciplinario para los prisioneros de guerra. México. 155 p.

The subject of military prisons and prisoners of war is treated from comparative and international law viewpoints. Thesis, University of Mexico.

3137. Padilla, Francisco E. Curso de derecho minero argentino. Tucumán, Argentina, Universidad Nacional de Tucumán, Instituto de Derecho Público (Publ. no. 496). 327 p.

A textbook for use in administrative law courses.

3138. Pinto, Paulo J. da Silva. Moratória e reajustamento da pecuária. Rio de Janeiro. 166 p.

Various laws enacted in 1948 and 1949 granting a special moratorium on civil and commercial debts of cattlemen and cattle owners receives critical comment by the author, who believes the legislation to have been unconstitutional. Court decisions in point are also discussed.

3139. Río, Jorge del. Introducción al derecho de la energía. Hechos generadores de esta nueva rama de las ciencias jurídicas. Buenos Aires, Caporaletti. 107 p.

A series of lectures in a course delivered by the author at the Institute of Agrarian and Mining Law of Buenos Aires University. Interesting, since this is relatively new subject matter in the teaching of law.

3140. Ríos Aponte, Luis E. (ed.). Régimen legal de aguas y fuerza hidráulica en Colombia. Legislacion y jurisprudencia. V. 1. Bogotá, Pontificia Universidad Católica Javeriana (Publ. del Fondo Rotatorio). 271 p.

In a summarized form, the editor has collected all legal provisions and case-law in the field of regulation of waters and hydraulic power. The provisions of law have never been enacted in a single code, and it was necessary to extract them from the general and special legislation in which they are disseminated.

3141. Ruiz de Esparza Salazar, Ignacio. Prontuario de la ley de la industria eléctrica, de su reglamento y de la clasificación uniforme de cuentas. México, Ocampo. 263 p.

A subject-matter arrangement of all legislation concerning the electric power industry is the unusual contribution of the compiler. A second part gives opinions and decisions rendered by the Comisión de Tarifas Eléctricas y Gas between 1945 and 1950.

3142. SANITARY CODE OF THE REPUBLIC OF MEXICO. México, "Traducciones." 26 p.

A translation into English of the outstanding provisions of this new basic law on public health. See item 3126.

3143. **Sarría, Eustorgio** (ed.). Código de minas y leyes del petróleo, con la jurisprudencia del Ministerio del ramo, del Consejo de Estado y de la Corte Suprema de Justicia. Bogotá, Crítica Jurídica. 433 p.
Annotated text of a collection of mining and petroleum laws. The annotations consist of full administrative and judicial decisions in point.

NEW LEGAL PERIODICALS

3144. EL FORO. Guatemala, Colegio de Abogados de Guatemala. Año 1, no. 1, nov.-dic.
This journal appears as the official organ of the Bar Association of Guatemala and follows the general trend of other law periodicals.

3145. LATIN AMERICAN JOURNAL ON POLITICS, ECONOMICS AND LAW. Buenos Aires. V. 1, no. 1, Jan.-March.
Dr. Enrique Bledel, well-known for his interest in Anglo-American and comparative law, is the editor of this publication. The coverage is for the entire continent, and the language is English, a combination which makes the contribution valuable as well as unique. Personal comments by the editor on trends of law are found in both English and Spanish.

3146. REVISTA ARGENTINA DE DERECHO PRIVADO. Buenos Aires. Año 1, no. 1, abril.
This periodical, edited by Dr. Roberto Pecach, covers many fields including labor, tax, and commercial law, as well as other branches.

3147. REVISTA DE DIREITO MERCANTIL. Rio de Janeiro. V. 1, no. 1, nov.-dez.

As the title implies, this periodical is devoted to the subject of commercial law. The initial issue contains a series of brief articles or reprinted addresses by various eminent attorneys, on an outline presented for a new commercial code. This journal is particularly complete as to its case law, devoting sections to the decisions of the Supreme Federal Tribunal, the Federal Appellate Tribunal, state courts, and special courts, respectively.

3148. REVISTA DE LA FACULTAD DE DERECHO Y CIENCIAS SOCIALES. Montevideo. Año 1, no. 1, abril.
Published under the able direction of Prof. Enrique Sayagues Laso, this new periodical includes the publication of studies of great interest by well-known professors and authors, from Uruguay and from other Latin American countries as well. Has sections on commentaries, jurisprudence, and book reviews and bibliographies. One section is assigned to commentaries on foreign laws.

3149. REVISTA JURÍDICA DEL PERÚ. Lima, Imprenta Editora Médica Peruana. Año 1, no. 1, enero-abril.
This periodical appeared as an organ of the Peruvian Committee of the Society of Comparative Legislation of Paris. Has sections on commentaries, cases, book reviews and bibliography. In this first number are found also the by-laws of this Committee and three notes: one on the outline of the organization or a declaration for a constitution of an Internal Association of Comparative Law under the auspices of the UN; the second is a summary of the topics to be debated at the International Congress of Private Law in Rome, July, 1950; the third contains a report on the 3rd International Congress on Comparative Law (London, August, 1950).

Music

CHARLES SEEGER

THE year was notable for the appearance of the *Boletín de Música y Artes Visuales* published monthly by the Pan American Union (in Spanish only) giving for the first time a fairly comprehensive picture of current music activity in the New World. Among other items it was noted that 132 bona fide conservatories of music instruction could be listed for 18 countries. (None were reported for Haiti, Honduras and Puerto Rico.) Concert life in the large urban centers continued the spectacular increase of recent years. 54 symphonic orchestras gave concerts in 17 countries. (None were reported from Haiti, Honduras, Nicaragua and Paraguay.) Argentina led with 105 symphony concerts in the capital city, 49 more than in 1949. Of the 254 works performed, 25 were by Argentine composers.

Recordings of works by Latin American composers began to appear on LP discs in the United States: Villa-Lobos' *Chôros No. 10* (Capitol) and *Uirapurú* (Columbia), and Roig's *Cecilia Valdés* (Cetra-Soria). Recordings of concert music made in Latin America were still virtually unobtainable in the United States. The Pan American Union began to sponsor weekly radio programs of Latin American popular music, using concert music to the extent that materials were available. A list of current "hits" and old favorites began to appear in *Américas* (English edition only), published monthly by the Pan American Union. Pérez Prado's *Mambo,* a hybrid of Afro-Cuban folklore and Harlem jazz, had a considerable vogue in Cuba, New York, and Mexico.

Perhaps a word of explanation of the glosses used in the listing of music in this section of the Handbook is in order. "For concert use" designates composed works in the learned or fine art of the Occidental music-community requiring executants of concert calibre; "For general use," the same type of idiom (unless otherwise specified) and performable at the concert level, but within the range of ability of good amateur and school groups. Attention should be called as usual to the omission of many titles in the field of folk music already included in the folklore bibliographies of R. S. Boggs published annually in the March number of the *Southern Folklore Quarterly.* A new quarterly *Revista Interamericana de Bibliografía,* with a highly selective music section, was launched by the Pan American Union in 1951. It is regretted that in *HLAS, no. 15, 1949,* item 2823, the nationality of the Bolivian composer Antonio González Bravo (b. 1885 in La Paz) was incorrectly given.

Periodicals received during the year by the Pan American Union were:

Ars. Revista de Arte. Director: I. Schlagman, Rodríguez Peña 335, Buenos Aires, Argentina. Founded: 1939? Irregular.

Boletim de SBACEM. Sociedade Brasileira de Autores, Compositores e Editores de Música. Rua Buenos Aires, 58-A, 1° andar, Rio de Janeiro, Brasil. Founded: 1949. Quarterly.

Boletín del Conservatorio Nacional de Música. Director: Carlos Sánchez Málaga. Secretario de Redacción: Rodolfo Holzmann. Calle Minería 180, Lima, Perú. Founded: 1944, as the *Boletín de la Academia Nacional de Música "Alcedo."* Irregular.

Conservatorio. Órgano Oficial del Conservatorio Municipal de Música. Director: Raúl G. Anckerman, Calles Rastro y Lealtad, Habana, Cuba. Founded: 1943. Published three times a year.

Do Re Mi. Órgano Oficial del Club Musical "Mozart," perteneciente al Instituto Musical "Margot Díaz Dorticós." Calle 23, No. 960, Vedado, Habana, Cuba. First received: Año 4, no. 5-6, sept.-oct., 1950. Monthly.

Educación Musical. Revista de Orientación y Superación Cultural. Órgano Oficial de la Confederación Nacional de Conservatorios y Profesionales de la Música. Director: Maestro Joaquín Rodríguez Lanza. Dirección: Ave. Central, No. 3, Depto. Kohly, Marianao, Cuba. Founded: 1948? Monthly.

Fantasía Musical; revista, cancionero. Dirección: Hotel Suiza, Cartagena, Colombia. Founded: 1950. Irregular.

Guión. Director: Luis Pons Vila, Apartado 2334, Habana, Cuba. Founded: 1940. Monthly.

México en el Arte. Secretaría de Educación Pública. Instituto Nacional de Bellas Artes. Consejo Técnico Consultivo. Coordinador: Jaime García Terrés. México, D. F., México. Founded: 1948. Irregular.

La Música. Publicada en La Habana por la Sociedad de Ediciones Cubanas de Música. Dirección: Ave. Pres. Menocal, 1452, Apt. 6, Habana, Cuba. Founded: 1948? Irregular.

Música Sacra. Diretor: João de Castro Abreu Magalhães. Caixa Postal, 23, Petrópolis, Estado do Rio de Janeiro, Brasil. Founded: 1941. Monthly.

Música y Artes Visuales. División de Música y Artes Visuales. Unión Panamericana, 17th & Constitution Ave., N.W., Washington 6, D. C. Founded: 1950. Monthly.

El Músico. Órgano Oficial del Sindicato Único de Trabajadores de la Música. Dirección: San Ildefonso, 42, México, D. F., México. Founded: 1950. Monthly.

Noticiario Ricordi. Boletín Mensual de Informaciones Musicales de la Editorial "Ricordi Americana, S. A." Cangallo 1570, Buenos Aires, República Argentina. Founded: 1938. Monthly.

Nuestra Música. Published quarterly by Ediciones Mexicanas de Música. Madero Eje Oriente, 715 (antes, Av. Juárez 18), Despacho 206, México, D. F., México. Founded: 1946.

Orientación Musical. Órgano del Ateneo Musical Mexicano. Director: Estanislao Mejía. Apartado Postal 8858, México, D. F., México. Agent in U. S.: Dewey Amner, Kent State University, Kent, Ohio. Founded: 1941. Monthly.

Polifonía. Director: Jorge Óscar Pickenhayn. Córdoba 664, II° Piso, Buenos Aires, Argentina. Founded: 1944. Monthly.

Pro Arte Musical. Órgano Oficial de la Sociedad Pro Arte Musical de Cuba. Director: Mariá T. Velasco de González Gordon. Calzada 510, Habana, Cuba. Founded: 2a. época, año 1, no. 2, marzo-abril, 1949. Quarterly.

Revista Musical al Servicio del Arte y la Cultura. Director: Ismael Cortés B. Dirección: Colegio Los Angeles, al Sur y 50 al Oeste, San José, Costa Rica. [Library has only año 4, no. 6, diciembre de 1950.]

Revista Musical Chilena. Published bimonthly by the Instituto de Extensión Musical, Universidad de Chile, Agustinas 620, Santiago de Chile. Bimonthly. Founded: 1945.

Revista de Estudios Musicales. Universidad Nacional de Cuyo. Instituto Superior de Artes. Departamento de Musicología. Mendoza, República Argentina. Founded: 1949. Irregular.

SADAIC. Revista de la Sociedad Argentina de Autores y Compositores de Música. Lavalle 1547, Buenos Aires, Argentina. Founded: 1936. Irregular.

Schola Cantorum. Director: Miguel Bernal Jiménez. Jardín Luis G. Gutiérrez, 347, Morelia, Michoacán, México. Founded: 1939. Monthly.

La Silurante Musical (El Torpedero Musical). Revista redactada únicamente por su fundador, Víctor de Rubertis. Dirección y administración: Sanabria 1350, Buenos Aires, Argentina. Founded: 1933? Published twice a year.

MUSIC

GENERAL

3150. CANCIONERO POPULAR AMERICANO. 75 canciones de las 21 repúblicas americanas. Washington, Unión Panamericana. 127 p.
Published for distribution in Latin America only. Copies presented to large music libraries elsewhere.

ARGENTINA

3151. **Eitler, Esteban.** Divertimiento 1950, para orquesta de cámara. Buenos Aires, Ediciones Politonia. 32 p.
For concert use. Brief biographical note by J. C. P.

3152. ————. Policromía 1950, para orquesta de cuerdas. Buenos Aires, Ediciones Politonia. 16 p.
For concert use; composed 1950. Brief biographical note by J. C. P.

3153. **Forte, Vicente** (arr.). El cancionero criollo. No. 3, La firmeza. No. 4, Triste entrerriano. No. 5, La tumba gaucha. Estilo pampeano. No. 6, Triste pampeano. No. 7, Paloma ingrata. Canción cuyana. No. 8, Bailecito. El nido. 2, 2, 2, 2, 2, 2 p.
Arranged for piano and voice. For general use.

CUBA

3154. **Gramatges, Harold.** 2 danzas cubanas. Montuna. Sonera. New York, Circle Blue Print Co., 1950? 4, 4 p.
Black-line print of composer's autograph. For concert use. Composed 1949.

3155. ————. Dos décimas (*Rev. Lyceum,* no. 21, feb., p. 39-46).
1, *Isla y mar;* 2, *Caribe.* Words by Rafaela Chacón Nardi. Composed in 1947, for sopranos, tenors, and basses, unaccompanied.

3156. ————. Tres danzas. Homenaje a Ignacio Cervantes (*Conservatorio,* no. 8, supplement, 4 p.).
For concert use; piano solo.

MEXICO

3157. **Bal y Gay, J.** Leñador, no tales el pino. Para coro a cappella. México, Ediciones Mexicanas de Música. 4 p.
Words by Rafael Alberti. For general use.

3158. **Chávez, Carlos.** Sinfonía india. New York, G. Schirmer (G. Schirmer's Edition of Study Scores of Orchestral Works and Chamber Music, no. 56). 82 p.
For concert use. Composed in New York, 1935-1936.

3159. **Galindo, Blas.** Sonata para violín y piano. México, Ediciones Mexicanas de Música. 45 p. Violin part separate.
For concert use. Composed 1945.

3160. **Halffter, Rodolfo.** Once bagatelas, para piano solo, op. 19. México, Ediciones Mexicanas de Música. 26 p.
For concert use.

3161. **Sandi, Luis.** Quisiera te pedir, Nísida, cuenta. Para coro a cappella. México, Ediciones Mexicanas de Música. 15 p.
Words by Miguel de Cervantes. English version by Noel Lindsay. For concert use.

3162. ————. The rabbit. El conejo. For four-part chorus of mixed voices, a cappella. Boston, The Boston Music Co. 8 p.
For general use.

PERU

3163. **Holzmann, Rudolph.** Remembranzas, para piano. Lima, Trítono. 7 p.
Three short pieces, for concert use. Composed 1949.

3164. **Sánchez Málaga, Carlos.** Cinco canciones, para canto y piano. Lima, Trítono. 11 p.
For concert use.

OTHER COUNTRIES

3165. **Amengual, René.** Diez preludios pequeños, para piano. Santiago, Casa Amarilla, 1950? 10 p.

3166. CANCIONES DE NAVIDAD. Música recopilada por María Luisa Muñoz, Departamento de Educación. San Juan? Puerto Rico. Unpaged.
20 music notations of folk-popular *aguinaldos* and *villancicos* on one staff.

3167. Jaegerhuber, Werner A. Complaintes haïtiennes recueillies et harmonisées. Haitian folklore songs. Canciones del folklore haitiano. 2. édition. Port-au-Prince. Unpaged, illus.
Six songs with piano accompaniment. Biographical note about author by Roger E. Savain and a tribute to him by Jean F. Brierre.

3168. Villa-Lobos, Heitor. Ave Maria no. 17. Four part chorus a capella. New York, Villa-Lobos Music Corporation. 5 p.
For general use.

PUBLICATIONS

GENERAL

3169. Boggs, Ralph Steele. Folklore bibliography for 1949 (*South. folk. quart.*, v. 14, no. 1, March, p. 1-77).
Ballad, song, dance, game, music, verse, as related to Latin America, p. 44-50. References to music are found also under other headings.

3170. Duran, Gustavo. Recordings of Latin American songs and dances. An annotated selective list of popular and folk-popular music. Second edition, revised and enlarged by Gilbert Chase. Washington, Pan American Union, Department of Cultural Affairs, Division of Music and Visual Arts (Music Series no. 3). xii, 91 p.
Nearly three hundred items are given brief descriptions; listings of available and unavailable discs. Preference is for materials showing traces of oral tradition. Upwards of 60 music notations showing metrical patterns. Bibliography.

ARGENTINA

3171. Devoto, Daniel. Las hojas (1940-1949). Buenos Aires, Aldabahor. 207 p.
A collection of 30 critical articles previously printed, some of them relating to Latin American music.

3172. Wilkes, Josué T. La antigua tonada tucumana (*Rev. estud. musicales,* año 1, no. 3, abril, p. 11-42).
A critical study of the notation and antiquity of the *Vidala de la Virgen Generala.*

BRAZIL

3173. Alvarenga, Oneyda. Babassuê. Discos FM. 39 a FM. 51. São Paulo, Prefei-tura do Município, Discoteca Pública Municipal (Registros Sonoros de Folclore Musical Brasileiro, IV). 136 p.
Continuation of the documentation and transcription of v. 3 of these dics (see *HLAS, no. 15, 1949,* item 2799). No music notations.

3174. ————. Catálogo ilustrado do Museo Folclórico. V. 2. São Paulo, Prefeitura do Município, Discoteca Pública Municipal. xviii, 295 p., 235 (plates).
Continuation of the model archiving and reporting techniques of this institution (see *HLAS, no. 14, 1948,* item 3360). Plates 135-173 are of musical instruments. See also item 554.

3175. ————. Música popular brasileira. Com 133 exemplos musicais (85 inéditos) e 52 fotografias inéditas. Rio de Janeiro, Globo. 330 p.
First published in Spanish by the Fondo de Cultura Económica, México (see *HLAS, no. 13, 1947,* item 2681); now in Portuguese. There has been some substitution and rearrangement of music notations and some additions, so that the numbering does not agree. The exact source of each notation is, however, given here.

3176. Barros, C. Paula. O romance de Villa-Lobos. Rio de Janeiro, Editôra A Noite. 1950? 220 p., illus.
Chatty, journalistic, and familiar. A catalogue of Villa-Lobos' works has the same general form as that in Vasco Mariz (see *HLAS, no. 15, 1949,* item 2805), but there are copious discrepancies.

3177. Lange, Francisco Curt. Estudios brasileños (Mauricinas). I. Manuscritos en la Biblioteca Nacional (*Rev. estud. musicales,* año 1, no. 3, p. 99-194).
Biobibliographical list of a considerable number of source materials. 24 fine plates, many of music mss.

3178. ————. Vida y muerte de Louis Moreau Gottschalk en Rio de Janeiro (1869). El ambiente musical en la mitad del Segundo Imperio (*Rev. estud. musicales,* año 2, no. 4, agosto, p. 45-147, plus plates).
A substantial monograph of original research, mostly in Brazilian sources, well documented and entertainingly written. The plates (50 pages) are excellent, reproducing photographs, drawings, cartoons, music, etc.

3179. Lavenêre, L. Nossas cantigas. 2. edição. Maceió, Brazil, privately published. Unpaged.
About 70 hectographed music notations of melodies, mostly very short.

CHILE

3180. ESTUDIOS SOBRE FOLKLORE EN CHILE Y LABOR DEL INSTITUTO DE INVESTIGACIONES MUSICALES. Santiago, Universi-

dad de Chile, Instituto de Investigaciones Musicales. 16 p., illus.
History and achievement of this Institute, 1943-1949, including list of 68 field trips. Six photographs, three of folklore interest.

3181. Lavín, Carlos. La tirana. Fiesta ritual de la provincia de Tarapacá (*Rev. musical chil.*, año 6, no. 37, otoño, p. 12-36).
Careful account of this festival, with confirmation of "casos sorprendentes de degradación de música quechua y aymará, en el lapso de los cuatro años corridos entre 1944 y 1948; tendencia y corriente que se acentúa cada día más y siempre a favor de un colorido eminentemente regional." Four photographs; four music notations (melodies only, with drumming). Map.

3182. REVISTA MUSICAL CHILENA, año 6, no. 39, primavera. 125 p.
The issue is mainly devoted to the Second Festival of Chilean Music, held Nov. 24 to December 10, 1950.

CUBA

3183. Ortiz, Fernando. La africanía de la música folklórica de Cuba. Habana, Ministerio de Educación, Dirección de Cultura. 477 p.
An exhaustive study of the frame and manner in which Afro-Cuban music has been cultivated and still is. Copiously annotated. Extensive bibliography. 83 *figuras*, mostly music notations, many of them drumming, some polyphonic. Music-technical work by Maestro Gaspar Agüero, aided by the drummers Raúl Díaz and Trinidad Torregrosa.

3184. ————. El kinfuiti. Un tambor para "jalar" muertos (*Bohemia*, año 42, no. 35, agosto 27, p. 20-21, 131, 140).
A variety of friction drum, played in a sitting posture by rubbing a piece of wood attached by a thong to the membrane of the drum. Used in the Afro-Cuban congo cult. Illus.

3185. Vega, Aurelio de la. The negative emotion. An essay on modern music. Habana, privately printed. 37 p.
Author finds little to admire in 20th-century concert music and practically nothing in that of the Americas.

EL SALVADOR

3186. Baratta, María de. Ensayo sobre música indígena de El Salvador (Cuzcatlán) (*Rev. estud. musicales*, año 1, no. 3, abril, p. 61-74).
A composer struggles with the problem of indigenism in music in an area where no basic research has been done. Nine music notations, including the *Danza de la yegüita* (dated July, 1939).

3187. González Sol, Rafael. Datos históricos sobre el arte de la música en El Salvador (*An. mus. nac.*, t. 1, no. 4, oct.-dic., p. 42-68).
Band (from 1841), orchestra (from 1860), publication (from 1870), school (from 1864), composers, performing groups, indigenous and other instruments, briefly mentioned. Author states that El Salvador does not have "música propia o regional."

MEXICO

3188. Comisión Central de Música Sacra de México. Anuario. Memoria del primer congreso interamericano (1949). Tulancingo, Mexico. 206 p., illus.

3189. Instituto Nacional de Bellas Artes. Dos años y medio del INBA. 3 v. México, Instituto Nacional de Bellas Artes. 166, 98, 100 p., illus.
Organizational structure; activity explained in detail with aid of diagrams, tables, etc. V. 1 deals with General Direction and Administration; v. 2, with the Department of Music; v. 3, with the foundation of the Department of Theater (including opera and ballet).

3190. López Alonso, David. Manuel M. Ponce. Ensayo biográfico. Prologado por Alejandro Quijano. Grabados de Francisco Díaz de León. México, Talleres Gráficos de la Nación. ix, 83 p.
Unpretentiously written. Two music notations, one of them of an unpublished *Preludio romántico* composed in 1934.

3191. Mendoza, Vicente T. Una adoración de pastores en Chilpancingo. Teatro tradicional (*An. inst. invest. estét.*, no. 18, p. 35-62).
15 music notations of complete melodies taken at dictation from informant "que se ha dado al trabajo de alentar esta clase de representaciones religiosas . . ." and who possessed the written (speech) text of this *adoración*.

3192. ————. La cachucha en México (*Nuestra música*, año 5, no. 20, 4. trimestre, p. 289-310).
This dance seems to have been introduced to the United States and Mexico by the famous composer of *tonadillas*, Manuel García, in the 1820's. Ten music notations.

3193. ————. Música indígena de México (*Méx. en el arte*, no. 9, p. 55-64).
Maintains thesis that pre-Conquest music traditions still survive. Brief review of study since Lumholtz (1904). Five plates, three in color, two of them being copies of frescoes at Bonampak. Six music notations. Bibliography.

3194. ————. El tango en México (*Nuestra música*, año 5, no. 18, 2. trimestre, p. 138-154).
Discussion. 14 music notations.

3195. Romero, Jesús C. Efemérides de Manuel M. Ponce. Aportación preliminar (*Nuestra música*, año 5, no. 18, 2. trimestre, p. 164-202).
Chronology (with documentation of composer's baptism on December 12, 1882); list of published and unpublished works, writings by and about the composer (d. 1948).

3196. Spell, Lota M. La música en la catedral de México en el siglo XVI (*Rev. estud. musicales*, año 2, no. 4, agosto, p. 218-255).
Translation into Spanish of a paper published in the *Hisp. am. hist. rev.*, v. 26, no. 3, Aug., 1946 (see *HLAS, no. 12, 1946*, item 1838). Well documented. Three plates of the grand organ.

VENEZUELA

3197. Liscano, Juan. Folklore y cultura. Caracas, Ávila Gráfica (Col. Nuestra Tierra, 2). 266 p., illus.
People, their folk-poetry, dances, festivals, musical instruments, and music described by a poet and philosopher who has studied all for over a decade, venturing into remote places and finally presenting in Caracas, before an audience of 15,000, "La Fiesta de la Tradición," to a description of which the last 100 pages are devoted. Many fine photographs fairly well reproduced.

3198. Ramón y Rivera, Luis Felipe. Nuestra música tradicional. Los cantos de trabajo. Caracas, *El Nacional*, mayo 28.
Brief description of songs of herding, grinding, and coffee-picking in Venezuela. One notation of the tune of a milking song.

OTHER COUNTRIES

3199. Ayestarán, Lauro. El minué montonero (*Rev. fac. hum. cien.*, no. 6, p. 225-237).
Brief history of a colonial descendant of the European minuet, 1820-1850. Nine manuscripts are documented and reproduced in fair facsimile. One schema of the formula of accompaniment. Also published as a separate. Eight plates.

3200. Cadilla de Martínez, María. La histórica danza de Puerto Rico en el siglo XVI y sus evoluciones (*Rev. musical chil.*, año 6, no. 37, otoño, p. 43-77).
Comparative study of the *cueca, zamacueca, seis regional*, and the *contradanza puertorriqueña*, with a view to their connection with the long-lost *el puertorrico*. Nine music notations.

3201. Delgadillo, Luis A. La música indígena y colonial en Nicaragua (*Rev. estud. musicales,* año 1, no. 3, abril, p. 43-60).
A composer treats lightly of a subject only too rarely written about. Fourteen music notations, most of them incomplete. There is a brief ap-pendix on the history of the *güegüence,* by Daniel G. Brinton.

3202. Denis, Lorimer. Quelques aspects de notre folklore. Port-au-Prince, Bureau d'Ethnologie (Série 2, no. 7). 48 p., illus.
Emphasizes the role of singing, both ritual and secular. Two types of jongleur (*espringeor, danseur*) are distinguished: *jongleurs de geste* and *jongleurs-histrions*. Nine reproductions of photographs, 15 music notations (melodies only), with words.

3203. Fonseca, Julio. Referencias sobre música costarricense (*Rev. estud. musicales,* año 1, no. 3, abril, p. 75-97).
A leading composer has dealt with folklore in one section and with activity of "artistic" groups in another. Nine music notations.

3204. Vásquez A., Rafael. Historia de la música en Guatemala. Guatemala, Tipografía Nacional. 346 p.
Arranged by categories: nationalism, indigenism, competitions, conservatory, bands, theater, societies. Covers mainly the period 1850-1925.

ADDENDA

MUSIC

3205. Espinosa, Francisco (arr.). Melodías regionales. San Salvador (Folklore Musical Salvadoreño), 1949. 29 p.
29 *sones, tonadas, alabados, canciones,* and *piñaleras* in simple piano arrangement (*piñaleras* on one staff).

3206. Graetzer, Guillermo. Grave, para violín solo. Buenos Aires, Editorial Argentina de Música, 1949. 2 p.
For concert use.

3207. Perceval, Julio. Te Deum, para coro, solista, órgano y orquesta. Obra premiada por la Comisión Nacional de Cultura, producción 1944-1945. Mendoza, Argentina, Universidad Nacional de Cuyo, Conservatorio de Música y Arte Escénico, 1948. Partitura, 54 p.
For either liturgical or concert use. Instrumentation omits woodwind.

3208. Sánchez Málaga, Carlos. Acuarelas infantiles, para piano. Lima, Trítono, 1949. 12 p.
Five short pieces. Composed 1933.

3209. Sanmartino, Luis R. Pampa, sierra y sol. Canciones y danzas de mi tierra. Buenos Aires, Editorial Saraceno, 1948. 26 p.
Six songs with words by Juan Bautista Grosso: *triste; gato; tonada; huella; zamba; vidala.*

PUBLICATIONS

3210. Almeida, Renato. Compêndio de história da música brasileira. Rio de Janeiro, F. Briguiet, 1948. 183 p., illus., facsims.
A condensation of the second edition of the author's *História da música brasileira,* for pedagogical use and translation into other languages. 16 illus., three of them of music mss.

3211. Barwick, Steven. Sacred vocal polyphony in early colonial Mexico. 2 v. in 3. Cambridge, Mass., 1949. 220, 271 p.
Doctoral dissertation (Harvard, 1949). V. 2, devoted to scores, is in two parts. Cathedral archives examined were: Mexico, Puebla, Guadalajara, Morelia, Oaxaca. 271 large pages of black-line print transcriptions from partbooks. Composers represented are: Fernando Franco, Pedro Hernández, Fructos del Castillo, Pedro Bermúdez, Francisco López, Juan Padilla, Bernardo de Peralta. Bibliography.

3212. Carrillo, Julián. Técnica musical. México, Secretaría de Educación Pública (Biblioteca Enciclopédica Popular, 3. época, 207), 1949. 124 p.
Résumé of the author's theories in relation to music education. Brief autobiography appended.

3213. Chávez, Carlos. La música mexicana. México, Secretaría de Educación Pública, 1949. 32 p.
The composer feels that indigenous (Indian) music is a reality of contemporaneous Mexican life and that its acculturation with European tradition is forming a Mexican music *sui generis.*

3214. Corte, A. della, and **G. M. Gatti.** Diccionario de la música. Con un apéndice, Música y músicos de América, por Néstor R. Ortiz Oderigo. Buenos Aires, Ricordi Americana, 1949. 633 p.
Translation into Spanish of the well-known Italian biographical *Dizionario di musica.* The appendix runs from p. 567 to p. 633.

3215. Lavín, Carlos. Nuestra Señora de las Peñas. Fiesta ritual del norte de Chile. Santiago, Universidad de Chile, Facultad de Ciencias y Artes Musicales, Instituto de Investigaciones Musicales (Col. de Ensayos, no. 5), 1949? 25 p.
Detailed account of this festival in the extreme north of Tarapacá. Instrumentation and origin of the participating bands. Five photographs; 14 music notations, some fragmentary.

3216. Matos Romero, Manuel. Conceptos sobre el origen histórico y evolución y desarrollo de la música en el Zulia. Maracaibo, Tipografía Criollo, 1948. 73 p.
Provincial history in the style of "popular antiquities."

3217. Mendoza, Vicente T. La canción chilena en México. Santiago, Universidad de Chile, Facultad de Bellas Artes, Instituto de Investigaciones Musicales (Col. de Ensayos, no. 4), 1949? 15 p.
Brief report of research done in 1948. Eight music notations in piano arrangement.

3218. Ponce, Manuel María. Nuevos escritos musicales. México, Stylo, 1948. 214 p.
A collection of 22 short essays in the gentle and appreciative style of the composer (1882-1948). Ten are "de nuestro ambiente," the rest on European music and musicians.

3219. Ramón y Rivera, Luis Felipe. La polifonía popular de Venezuela (Separata de la *Rev. inst. nac. tradición,* año 1, entrega 2, julio-dic., 1949, p. 168-208). Buenos Aires, 1949. 46 p.
Analytic study, with 16 pages of notations of three-voice polyphonic singing, phonographically recorded by the author and his wife, Isabel Aretz, in 1947. The zones investigated are shown on a map of the country.

3220. Trenti Rocamora, José Luis. El teatro en la América colonial. Prólogo de Guillermo Furlong. Buenos Aires, Huarpes, 1947. 534 p., illus.
Contains copious references to music, musicians, and related subjects. See *HLAS, no. 13, 1947,* item 2074.

3221. Zamudio G., D. El folklore musical en Colombia (*Rev. Indias,* v. 35, no. 109, mayo-junio, 1949, suplemento no. 14, 30 p.).
12 music notations, some fragmentary.

Philosophy

ANÍBAL SÁNCHEZ REULET

LA filosofía latinoamericana, al cumplirse la primera mitad del siglo XX, se halla en un período de rápida expansión. Cincuenta años atrás eran muy pocos los que se dedicaban en América Latina al cultivo de las disciplinas filosóficas. En la mayoría de los países no existían siquiera estudios regulares. La producción bibliográfica era escasa o inexistente.

La situación fué cambiando poco a poco desde 1910. A los nombres del cubano Enrique José Varona y del peruano Alejandro Deustua—los más altos representantes de la filosofía latinoamericana hasta entonces—se fueron uniendo otros no menos significativos: Alejandro Korn y José Ingenieros, en Argentina; Farias Brito, en Brasil; Enrique Molina, en Chile; Antonio Caso y José Vasconcelos, en México; Carlos Vaz Ferreira, en Uruguay. La obra más importante de estos pensadores se publicó, justamente, entre los años de 1910 y 1930. A ese período pertenece, también, el primer órgano especializado que se editó en América Latina: la *Revista de Filosofía* de Ingenieros.

El cambio fué más notable a partir de 1930, cuando hizo su aparición una nueva generación de pensadores en cuya avanzada se destacaban las figuras de Samuel Ramos, Mariano Iberico, Honorio Delgado y, muy especialmente, de Francisco Romero. Y hacia 1940, como resultado de las convulsiones políticas de Europa, América Latina recibió una nueva aportación—de notable efecto en algunos países— con la llegada de profesores emigrados de España, Italia y Alemania. Cabe recordar aquí la influencia ejercida por Joaquín Xirau, José Gaos e Eugenio Imaz, en México; por Juan David García Bacca, en Ecuador y Venezuela; por Rodolfo Mondolfo, en la Argentina.

En los últimos años el volumen y la calidad de la producción filosófica ha mejorado considerablemente. Hoy se editan no menos de diez revistas dedicadas exclusivamente a la filosofía, se han establecido facultades e institutos donde antes no existían y se han constituído sociedades o grupos profesionales en muchos países. La literatura filosófica cuenta, además, con un vasto público, más allá del estricto círculo de los intereses académicos. Así se explica la atención que las grandes editoriales y la prensa periódica dedican actualmente a la filosofía en sus colecciones y suplementos literarios.

Pero quizás el cambio más decisivo en los últimos cincuenta años haya sido la progresiva diversificación de escuelas y tendencias si se la compara con la casi absoluta hegemonía que el positivismo y el cientificismo tenían hacia 1900. América Latina ha estado abierta en años recientes a todas las posibles influencias de Europa y de los Estados Unidos, desde la neoescolástica hasta el empirismo lógico. A la estrechez sectaria y provinciana de comienzos del siglo ha sucedido una atmósfera de sofisticación cosmopolita.

El mismo interés por salir al mundo, y recibir de él cuanto sea posible, se advierte claramente en el orden de las relaciones internacionales. Hasta hace poco los países latinoamericanos no estaban representados, o lo estaban sólo ocasionalmente, en reuniones y congresos internacionales de filosofía. Francisco García Calderón y Coriolano Alberini fueron por muchos años los embajadores solitarios de la filosofía latinoamericana. Desde la última guerra, en cambio, los lationamericanos no sólo han participado más activamente en reuniones internacionales, sino que han organizado sus propios congresos. En ese sentido los Congresos Interamericanos de Filosofía que se realizaron en Haití (1944) y en Nueva York (1947), por iniciativa de la American Philosophical Association, y el Congreso Nacional de Filosofía convocado por la Universidad Nacional de Cuyo (Mendoza, Argentina) en 1949, contribuyeron a facilitar el acercamiento de los filósofos latinoamericanos con los de otras regiones del mundo y a establecer relaciones más permanentes entre ellos.

El hecho más saliente del año 1950 fué, precisamente, la realización de otros dos congresos: el Tercer Congreso Interamericano de Filosofía, realizado en la ciudad de México bajo los auspicios de la Universidad Nacional Autónoma, y el Primer Congreso Brasileño de Filosofía, organizado en San Pablo por el Instituto Brasileño de Filosofía. Al Congreso de México concurrieron representantes de Argentina, Bolivia, Colombia, Cuba, Estados Unidos, México, Perú, República Dominicana y Venezuela. Se resolvió, entre otros asuntos, fundar una Sociedad Interamericana de Filosofía que una en su seno a los distintos grupos nacionales. El Congreso de San Pablo, por su parte, aunque de alcance más limitado, tuvo la virtud de reunir por vez primera los filósofos de las diferentes regiones del Brasil.

Otro hecho significativo es la aparición, en 1950, de dos nuevas revistas: la *Revista de Filosofía,* cuya publicación ha iniciado el Instituto de Filosofía de la Facultad de Humanidades y Ciencias de la Educación de la Universidad Nacional de La Plata (Argentina), bajo la dirección del P. Octavio Nicolás Derisi, y la *Revista de Historia de las Ideas,* que ha empezado a editar la Universidad Nacional de Tucumán (Argentina) y cuyo director es el Dr. Rogelio Labrousse. Al mismo tiempo, otras publicaciones han regularizado su aparición.

El centenario de la muerte de Descartes fué conmemorado de distintas maneras en las universidades latinoamericanas. Varias revistas publicaron números especiales, entre ellas *Filosofía y letras* de México (t. 20, no. 39, julio-sept.), la *Revista de filosofía* de Santiago de Chile (v. 1, no. 4, dic.), la *Revista cubana de filosofía* de la Habana (v. 1, no. 6, enero-dic.), y *Cursos y conferencias* de Buenos Aires (v. 37, no. 219, junio).

Finalmente, corresponde destacar la publicación de nuevas colecciones de textos filosóficos. El Instituto de Filosofía de la Facultad de Humanidades y Ciencias de la Educación de La Plata (Argentina) ha iniciado una biblioteca de clásicos de la filosofía cuyo primer volumen corresponde al *Proslogion* de San Anselmo (texto latino y traducción castellana). La Sociedad Peruana de Filosofía, a su vez, ha comenzado a editar una colección titulada *Plena luz, pleno ser.* El primer volumen es una obra de Alberto Wagner de Reyna, *La filosofía en Iberoamérica.* Por su parte la Sección de Psicología del Instituto de Filosofía de la Universidad de Buenos Aires (Argentina) ha empezado a publicar una serie de Monografías Psicológicas, paralela a la que publica la Sección de Filosofía del mismo instituto. El primer trabajo aparecido es una *Introducción a la psicopatología* por el Dr. Honorio Delgado.

Hasta la presente edición del *Handbook* se incluían en esta sección tan sólo obras y artículos originales de autores latinoamericanos y estudios relativos al pensamiento y la filosofía en América Latina. Quedaban excluídas deliberadamente, por lo tanto, todas las publicaciones que tuvieran por objeto estudiar doctrinas o pensadores ajenos a la América Latina. Esta clase de trabajos se mencionaba, sin comentario, en un apéndice al final de la sección. De acuerdo con el nuevo criterio que se ha adoptado para la preparación de esta bibliografía, figurarán en adelante obras y artículos escogidos de autores latinoamericanos, cualquiera que sea el tema que traten, y de autores no latinoamericanos, pero que traten temas relacionados con el pensamiento y la filosofía de América Latina. Todos los trabajos relacionados con la filosofía latinoamericana se agrupan en un apartado especial de la subsección de *Estudios críticos*. Las reediciones de obras clásicas del pensamiento latinoamericano figuran en la subsección de *Obras generales*. Los estudios que se refieran a aspectos no estrictamente filosóficos del pensamiento latinoamericana aparecen bajo el título *Historia de las ideas*. Con el propósito de dar una visión más completa de lo que se está publicando en América Latina, se incluirá, en el *Apéndice,* una lista mínima de nuevas traducciones de obras clásicas o contemporáneas importantes.

OBRAS GENERALES Y MISCELÁNEA

3222. ACTAS DEL PRIMER CONGRESO NACIONAL DE FILOSOFÍA. MENDOZA, ARGENTINA, MARZO 30-ABRIL 9, 1949. T. 1-3. Buenos Aires, Universidad Nacional de Cuyo. 2197 p.

El t. 1 contiene, en su primera parte, los documentos oficiales del Congreso, la nómina de autoridades y miembros, los discursos pronunciados en las sesiones de apertura y clausura, los mensajes de adhesión y las ponencias finales. En esta primera parte se destaca la conferencia pronunciada por el Presidente de la República Argentina, General Juan Domingo Perón, exponiendo su filosofía política. La segunda parte del t. 1 incluye los trabajos leídos en las sesiones plenarias en que se discutieron los siguientes temas: la filosofía en la vida del espíritu, la persona humana, el existencialismo, la filosofía contemporánea y la filosofía y la ciudad humana. La sexta sesión plenaria estuvo dedicada a conmemorar los centenarios de Suárez, Goethe, y Varona y a rendir homenaje a la memoria de Félix Krueger, Guido de Ruggiero y Martín Grabmann. Los t. 2 y 3 recogen las contribuciones presentadas a las trece sesiones particulares. Han sido agrupados bajo los siguientes títulos: metafísica, situación de la filosofía actual, filosofía de la existencia, lógica y gnoseología, axiología y ética, psicología, estética, epistemología y filosofía de la naturaleza, filosofía de la historia, la cultura y la sociedad, filosofía de la educación, filosofía del derecho y la política, historia de la filosofía y filosofía argentina y americana. El t. 3 contiene, además, un índice alfabético de autores, un índice de autores por países y un índice general de los tres tomos. Las contribuciones se publican en la lengua original en que fueron presentadas (castellano, portugués, inglés, francés, alemán o italiano), pero los trabajos en inglés y alemán van acompañados de la respectiva traducción al castellano impresa en tipo menor. La publicación de estas actas ha estado al cuidado del profesor Luis Juan Guerrero de la Universidad de Buenos Aires. Por el número de los participantes y de los trabajos presentados (185 en total), éste ha sido el congreso de filosofía más importante entre los realizados hasta ahora en América Latina. Aunque se denominó Congreso Nacional, participaron o enviaron contribuciones gran número de filósofos no argentinos: entre los europeos más conocidos, Blondel, Croce, Garrigou-Lagrange, Marcel, Hartmann, Jaspers, Klages, Lavelle, Le Senne, Russell y Von Uexküll; entre los americanos, Carneiro Leão, Ferreira da Silva y Luis Washington, del Brasil; Charles de Koninck, del Canadá; Nieto Arteta, de Colombia; Walter Cerf y Karl Löwith, de Estados Unidos; José Vasconcelos, Francisco Larroyo y Oswaldo Robles, de México; Honorio Delgado, Mariano Iberico, Francisco Miró Quesada y Alberto Wagner de Reyna, del Perú, y Llambías de Azevedo, del Uruguay. El mayor número de contribuciones corresponde, sin embargo, a la Argentina, aunque se nota la ausencia de algunos nombres significativos, como el de Francisco Romero.

3223. ANAIS DO PRIMEIRO CONGRESSO BRASILEIRO DE FILOSOFIA. Promovido pelo Instituto Brasileiro de Filosofia sob os auspícios da Reitoria da Universidade de São Paulo. V. 1-2. São Paulo. 1-331, 335-652 p.

Contiene los documentos oficiales, actas, discursos, comunicaciones y resoluciones del Primer Congreso Brasileño de Filosofía realizado en San Pablo desde el 22 al 26 de marzo. Las comunicaciones (37 en total) están divididas en cuatro secciones. La primera reúne estudios sobre la filosofía en Brasil, de interés para el conocimiento de los antecedentes ideológicos del país. En ese sentido son especialmente valiosos los trabajos de Ivan Lins (*O positivismo no Brasil*); Miguel Reale (*O culturalismo na Escola do Recife*); y Renato Cirell Czerna (*Panorama filosófico brasileiro*). La segunda sección está dedicada a la metafísica, la filosofía de los valores y la estética e incluye, entre otras, contribuciones de Delfim Santos (*Temática existencial*); Italo Betarello (*A lógica poética de Vico*); Oscar Lorenzo Fernández (*O método metafísico e a noção de categoria*) y Renato Cirell Czerna (*Verdade e historicidade*). La tercera sección comprende las comunicaciones sobre gnoseología y lógica, entre las cuales se destacan dos estudios de Euryalo Cannabrava (*Juizos analíticos e juizos sintéticos* y *Dois aspectos da teoria do conhecimento*). La última sección agrupa trabajos dedicados a historia de la filosofía de la cultura, entre los cuales cabe señalar los de Alexandre Correia (*Noção de análise na filosofia grega*); Ivan Lins (*Aspectos do pensamento de Tomas Jefferson*) y Luis Pinto Ferreira (*S. Alexander e a renovação científica da filosofia*). En el primer volumen figuran, también, cuatro conferencias pronunciadas durante la realización del Congreso por Leonardo Van Acker (*Reflexões sôbre a objetividade da filosofia*); Miguel Reale (*Posição de Rui Barbosa no mundo de filosofia*); Pontes de Miranda (*O significado do Congresso*) y Arthur Versiani Velloso (*Acêrca do ensino da filosofia no Brasil*). Con excepción de tres trabajos en italiano y uno en alemán, las comunicaciones están escritas en lengua portuguesa.

3224. Belaunde, Víctor Andrés. El existencialismo cristiano (*Arch. soc. per. fil.*, v. 3, p. 71-84).
Analiza las raíces del existencialismo cristiano en San Agustín y Pascal.

3225. Francovich, Guillermo. El mundo, el hombre y los valores. La Paz, Fénix. 120 p.
Contiene nueve ensayos sobre temas relacionados con el problema antropológico y la teoría de los valores. Frente a la antropología naturalista, el autor propugna una antropología filosófica que tome en consideración el mundo de los valores.

3226. García Bacca, Juan David. La importancia de ser filósofo (*Fil. letras*, t. 19, no. 37, enero-marzo, p. 63-85).
Comentario de tono personal sobre la significación de la tarea filosófica. Parte de una afirmación que hace Heidegger, en su *Brief über den Humanismus*, acerca de la actualidad de la filosofía.

3227. ————. Siete modelos de filosofar. Caracas, Universidad Central, Facultad de Filosofía y Letras. 168 p.
Serie de conferencias públicas pronunciadas en la Universidad de Caracas en 1946. García Bacca expone a Platón, Aristóteles, Santo Tomás, Descartes, Kant, Husserl y Heidegger, como arquetipos de siete maneras diferentes de filosofar.

3228. Lima, Alceu Amoroso. O existencialismo e o mundo moderno (*Rev. arq. mun.*, ano 17, no. 137, out.-dez., p. 3-22).
Breve exposición del existencialismo. El autor señala doce notas características. Cree que ofrece una contribución positiva en la medida en que tiende a restituir a la naturaleza personal del hombre lo que las filosofías de la falsa abstracción le quitaron. Pero en todo aquello en que el existencialismo tiende a divinizar al hombre, o a aniquilar a Dios, está condenado al olvido.

3229. Luz y Caballero, José de la. Elencos y discursos académicos. Estudio preliminar por Roberto Agramonte. Habana, Universidad de la Habana (Biblioteca de Autores Cubanos, 16. Obras de José de la Luz y Caballero, v. 2). xlviii, 597 p.
Es el segundo volumen de las *Obras* de José de la Luz y Caballero. Contiene, principalmente, documentos relacionados con la organización de los estudios del Colegio de San Cristóbal de Carraguao y del Colegio del Salvador de la Habana, de los que Luz y Caballero fué director.

3230. Mendoza, Angélica. Fuentes del pensamiento de los Estados Unidos. México, El Colegio de México. 276 p.
Tesis doctoral presentada por la autora en la Universidad de Columbia (Nueva York). Estudia la evolución del pensamiento norteamericano en sus distintos componentes: vitales, históricos, religiosos, políticos y filosóficos. Los primeros cuatro capítulos muestran el desarrollo del puritanismo y su culminación intelectual en la obra de Jonathan Edwards. Los dos capítulos siguientes se ocupan de Franklin, como figura representativa de la Ilustración, y de Emerson, como portavoz de la reacción romántica. Los capítulos restantes tratan del crecimiento político, social y económico de la democracia americana, con sus nuevos problemas, y del influjo que, en el orden intelectual, tuvieron el pragmatismo y el idealismo.

3231. Mesa Rodríguez, Manuel I. Tres retratos de Luz y Caballero. Habana, El Siglo XX (Academia de la Historia de Cuba). 38 p.
Discurso leído en la Academia de la Historia de Cuba, el 11 de julio de 1950, para conmemorar el 150. aniversario del nacimiento de José de la Luz y Caballero. Son de gran interés los documentos iconográficos.

3232. Mondolfo, Rodolfo. Trabajo manual y trabajo intelectual desde la Antigüedad hasta el Renacimiento (*Rev. hist. ideas*, no. 1, p. 5-25).
Rectifica la creencia generalizada de que la antigüedad clásica despreciaba el trabajo manual. Testimonios de los filósofos e historiadores presocráticos prueban lo contrario. El desprecio por el trabajo mecánico y la exaltación de la actividad intelectual provienen, sobre todo, de Platón y Aristóteles. En la época posterior a Sócrates sólo los cínicos consideraron el trabajo en un plano de igualdad con el ejercicio de la inteligencia. La revalorización del trabajo manual se produce lentamente, con el advenimiento del cristianismo y tiene nueva expresión, durante el Renacimiento, en las obras de Alberti, Campanella y Moro.

3233. Romero, Francisco. Dos tesis recientes sobre el hombre (*Rev. fil.*, Santiago, v. 1, no. 3, agosto, p. 303-314).
Analiza dos tesis hoy muy generalizadas acerca del hombre: la de su radical historicidad y la de su soledad.

3234. ————. El hombre y la cultura. Buenos Aires, Espasa-Calpe Argentina. 147 p.
Catorce ensayos y artículos publicados previamente en diversas revistas y periódicos. El

primer ensayo, que da título al volumen, analiza las relaciones entre el hombre y el conjunto de los productos, actos y procesos en que consiste la cultura. El hombre, creador de la cultura, es al mismo tiempo conformado por ella. En *Unir y separar, o de la índole y límites de nuestra acción,* se señala que, tanto en la acción como en el pensamiento, el hombre realiza sólo dos operaciones fundamentales; análisis y síntesis. *Comunicación y situación* considera el problema de la vinculación entre el lenguaje y la situación concreta en que hablante y oyente se encuentran. El sentido y la posibilidad de la comunicación depende de los supuestos comunes que los dos posean. El *Positivismo y la crisis* discute el problema de la crisis espiritual e intelectual de la época presente, relacionándola con el derrumbe de la concepción del mundo representada por el positivismo y el evolucionismo de la segunda mitad del siglo XIX. *En torno a la idea de progreso* presenta una breve historia de la idea de progreso, desde el Renacimiento hasta nuestros días. Con el naufragio del positivismo la idea de progreso ha entrado también en crisis. El desenlace definitivo de esta crisis aún no está claro. El volumen contiene, además, estudios sobre Oswald Spengler y Manuel García Morente, sobre el filósofo uruguayo Carlos Vaz Ferreira y sobre el jurista argentino Sebastián Soler.

3235. **Roura Parella, Juan.** Tema y variaciones de la personalidad. México, Universidad Nacional Autónoma de México, Instituto de Investigaciones Sociales (Biblioteca de Ensayos Sociológicos, Cuadernos de Sociología). 240 p.
Consideraciones, de tono libre y personal, sobre el desarrollo y la esencia de la personalidad y sobre el problema del hombre y de su destino.

3236. **Schwartzmann, Félix.** El sentimiento de lo humano en América. Ensayo de antropología filosófica. T. 1. Santiago, Universidad de Chile, Facultad de Filosofía y Educación, Instituto de Investigaciones Histórico-Culturales. 289 p.
Es el primer volumen de una obra más extensa que comprenderá un segundo volumen. El autor declara, sin embargo, que este primer volumen, "al menos en ciertos aspectos, constituye un todo en sí mismo." La introducción está dedicada a exponer el método y señalar los límites de la investigación. La obra es concebida como una especie de "fenomenología de la experiencia del prójimo o de la variabilidad histórica del sentimiento de lo humano," independientemente de toda filosofía de los valores. Tiene más el carácter de una indagación psicológica que sociológica. El análisis se limita, por otra parte, al hombre latinoamericano o, como el autor prefiere designarlo, al "americano del sur." Se trata de descubrir los rasgos comunes que dan unidad espiritual al latinoamericano y que lo diferencian de otros tipos y modos de ser humanos. La primera parte de la obra, con la que concluye el primer volumen, analiza concretamente la manera cómo el latinoamericano vive su intimidad y se relaciona con el mundo de la naturaleza y la sociedad. Se utilizan, en este análisis, documentos literarios y estudios sociológicos de autores latinoamericanos y europeos. Los rasgos característicos del hombre americano son: discontinuidad, necesidad de prójimo, incapacidad para vincular lo ideal con lo temporal, cierto sentimiento de soledad, fuga de sí mismo y aislamiento.

3237. **El Tercer Congreso Interamericano de Filosofía.** Publicación auspiciada por la Dirección de Cultura del Ministerio de Educación. Habana, Editorial Cenit (Publ. de la Sociedad Cubana de Filosofía). 110 p.
Boletín informativo de la Sociedad Cubana de Filosofía sobre el Tercer Congreso Interamericano de Filosofía celebrado en México en 1950. Contiene: 1, información general acerca del Congreso; 2, los resúmenes de las comunicaciones presentadas; 3, el texto completo de las ponencias presentadas por los delegados de Cuba.

3238. **Washington, Luis.** Dicionário de filosofia (*Rev. arq. mun.,* ano 16, v. 130, jan., p. 31-67).
Contiene poco más de ciento cincuenta términos filosóficos correspondientes a la letra *A.* El autor ha utilizado como fuentes principales los diccionarios de Baldwin, Lalande, Eisler, Ranzoli, Franck, Goblot y Ferrater Mora. Se publicó también en tirada aparte.

ESTUDIOS CRÍTICOS

Filosofía Antigua y Medieval

3239. **Agoglia, Rodolfo M.** Arte y tragedia en Aristóteles (*Rev. fil.,* no. 1, p. 59-69).

3240. **Martínez, Agustín.** Introducción a la filosofía del espíritu de San Agustín (*Rev. fil.,* Santiago, v. 1, no. 3, agosto, p. 315-326).

Filosofía Moderna

3241. **Castro Turbiano, Máximo.** Presencia de Descartes en la filosofía contemporánea (*Rev. cub. fil.,* v. 1, no. 6, enero-dic., p. 33-41).

3242. **Ciudad Vázquez, Mario.** La certeza cartesiana y el problematismo contemporáneo (*Rev. fil.,* Santiago, v. 1, no. 4, dic., p. 397-418).

3243. **Estiú, Emilio.** La situación histórica de Herder y las bases de su filosofía (*Rev. fil.,* no. 1, p. 70-96).
Estudia la influencia del *Sturm und Drang* y de la obra de Hamann sobre la metafísica de Herder.

3244. **Fatone, Vicente.** La libertad creadora en Descartes (*Cursos y conferencias,* v. 37, no. 219, junio, p. 111-122).

3245. **Gallegos Rocafull, José M.** Las pruebas cartesianas de la existencia de Dios (*Fil. letras,* t. 20, no. 39, julio-sept., p. 23-39).

3246. **Gaos, José.** Actualidad de Descartes (*Fil. letras,* t. 20, no. 39, julio-sept., p. 9-21).

3247. **García Bacca, Juan David.** La determinación del ser central en la ontología fundamental, según Descartes (*Rev. fil.,* Santiago, v. 1, no. 4, dic., p. 509-522).

3248. **García Tudurí, Mercedes.** El cartesianismo y la crisis (*Rev. cub. fil.,* v. 1, no. 6, enero-dic., p. 23-24).

3249. **García Tudurí, Rosaura.** Descartes y el pensar (*Rev. cub. fil.,* v. 1, no. 6, enero-dic., p. 31-32).

3250. **González Ríos, Francisco.** Descartes, su mundo moral y religioso. Buenos Aires, Universidad de Buenos Aires, Facultad de Filosofía y Letras, Instituto de Filosofía (Serie Ensayos, no. 3). 50 p.
Breve estudio del pensamiento moral y religioso de Descartes.

3251. **Labrousse, Roger.** La influencia de Hobbes sobre la doctrina política de Pufendorf (*Rev. hist. ideas,* no. 1, p. 27-61).
El jusnaturalismo de Pufendorf constituye una respuesta y una rectificación de la doctrina de Hobbes, especialmente en lo que se refiere al concepto de soberanía. Mientras el pacto social tiene para Hobbes una validez ilimitada, en Pufendorf está condicionado—de acuerdo con la tradición del derecho natural—por normas eternas válidas. Al empirismo pesimista de aquel, se opone el racionalismo optimista de éste. En otros respectos, sin embargo, las tesis de Pufendorf se aproximan más a las de Hobbes. Menos rígido que Hobbes, pero partidario de la monarquía, Pufendorf hace sólo leves concesiones al liberalismo. Trata así de introducir, sin lograrlo plenamente, ciertas tesis de Hobbes dentro del cuerpo del jusnaturalismo tradicional. Esa es la razón de las incertidumbres y contradicciones que han hecho de su obra una fuente de inspiración para los pensadores posteriores, especialmente para Locke y Rousseau.

3252. **Martínez, Agustín M.** Fundamentos de la moral de Descartes (*Rev. fil.,* Santiago, v. 1, no. 4, dic., p. 419-435).

3253. **Miró Quesada, Óscar.** Copérnico. Su vida y su obra. Lima, Sociedad Peruana de Filosofía (Col. Plena Luz, Pleno Ser, 2). 191 p.
En la primera parte resume los sistemas geocéntricos hasta Tolomeo. En la segunda expone el sistema copernicano y sus consecuencias en la astronomía y cosmología modernas. El paso del geocentrismo al heliocentrismo es una etapa en el desarrollo de la objetividad científica que culmina, en nuestro siglo, con la teoría de la relatividad. El núcleo original de este estudio fué una conferencia pronunciada por el autor en conmemoración del centenario de Copérnico.

3254. **Mondolfo, Rodolfo.** Ensayos sobre el Renacimiento italiano. Tucumán, Argentina, Universidad Nacional de Tucumán, Instituto de Filosofía. 60 p.
Contiene dos estudios. El primero, titulado *La idea de cultura en el Renacimiento italiano,* considera el problema de la historia y de la cultura en la obra de los humanistas y pensadores, particularmente en Ficino y Bruno. El segundo lleva por título *El Renacimiento italiano y la filosofía moderna* y señala las contribuciones del pensamiento renacentista italiano al nacimiento de la filosofía moderna.

3255. **Piñera Llera, Humberto.** Descartes, el sentido común y la filosofía (*Rev. cub. fil.,* v. 1, no. 6, enero-dic., p. 7-16).

3256. **Roa, Armando.** El problema del ser en la filosofía de Descartes (*Rev. fil.,* Santiago, v. 1, no. 4, dic., p. 437-458).

3257. **Romero, Francisco.** Descartes en la filosofía y en la historia de las ideas (*Cursos y conferencias,* año 19, v. 37, no. 219, p. 89-110).

3258. ————. Sobre la oportunidad histórica del cartesianismo (*Rev. cub. fil.,* v. 1, no. 6, enero-dic., p. 4-6).

3259. **Wagner de Reyna, Alberto.** La certeza en Descartes (*Rev. fil.,* Santiago, v. 1, no. 4, dic., p. 459-468).

3260. **Xirau, Ramón.** Lo que no se lee en Descartes (*Rev. cub. fil.,* v. 1, no. 6, enero-dic., p. 17-22).

Filosofía Contemporánea

3261. **Delgado, Honorio.** Introducción a la filosofía de Jaspers (*Arch. soc. per. fil.,* v. 3, p. 21-32).

3262. **Derisi, Octavio N.** El existencialismo de Gabriel Marcel (*Sapientia,* año 5, no. 15, 1. trimestre, p. 41-52).
Después de exponer la metafísica de Marcel, a través de su obra *Position et approches concrètes du mystère ontologique,* critica el carácter anti-intelectualista de su filosofía. Marcel confunde el orden natural y el sobrenatural. Es necesario integrar conceptualmente los hallazgos de Marcel dentro de un sistema racional.

3263. **Gaos, José.** Caminos del bosque (*Cuad. amer.,* año 9, v. 53, no. 5, sept.-oct., p. 135-153).
Comentario sobre el libro de Heidegger del mismo nombre (*Holzwege*).

3264. ————. El ser y el tiempo de Martín Heidegger (*Fil. letras*, t. 19, no. 37, enero-marzo, p. 9-45).
Última parte de una exposición resumida—aunque muy próxima al texto original—de *Sein und Zeit*. Las dos primeras partes se publicaron con anterioridad en la misma revista (t. 16, no. 32, oct.-dic., 1948, p. 205-240; t. 17, no. 33, enero-marzo, 1949, p. 9-30).

3265. Miró Quesada, Francisco. Náusea, angustia y amor en la filosofía de Jean Paul Sartre (*Arch. soc. per. fil.*, v. 3, p. 43-70).

3266. Sánchez Villaseñor, José. Introducción al pensamiento de Jean Paul Sartre. México, Jus. 60 p.
Breve exposición de las ideas fundamentales de Sartre sobre la base de *L'Être et le néant* y de *L'Existentialisme est un humanisme?* Hay sólo escasas referencias a la obra literaria. El capítulo final está dedicado a la crítica y refutación de las ideas de Sartre. Breve bibliografía.

3267. Wagner de Reyna, Alberto. La filosofía existencial de Heidegger (*Arch. soc. per. fil.*, v. 3, p. 33-42).

FILOSOFÍA LATINOAMERICANA

3268. Agramonte, Roberto. Implicaciones de la polémica filosófica de la Habana (*Cuad. amer.*, v. 50, no. 2, marzo-abril, p. 87-116).
Estudio acerca de la polémica que sobre el eclecticismo sostuvo José de la Luz y Caballero con los hermanos González del Valle entre 1838 y 1840.

3269. Ardao, Arturo. Espiritualismo y positivismo en el Uruguay. Filosofías universitarias de la segunda mitad del siglo XIX. México, Fondo de Cultura Económica. 287 p.
Estudio documentado sobre la influencia que el espiritualismo ecléctico, el positivismo comteano y el evolucionismo de Spencer ejercieron sucesivamente en el Uruguay, a partir de la fundación de la Universidad de Montevideo, en 1849, hasta el último decenio del siglo XIX. Aunque estudia preferentemente la repercusión de estas doctrinas en la enseñanza universitaria, señala también su influjo en la vida política y cultural del país. Además compara la situación del Uruguay con la de otros países latinoamericanos: Argentina, Chile, México y Brasil.

3270. Claps, Manuel Arturo. Vaz Ferreira. Notas para un estudio (*Número*, t. 2, no. 6-8, p. 93-117).
Estudia diferentes aspectos de la personalidad y la obra de Vaz Ferreira: influencias, método, concepción de la filosofía, problema del conocimiento, valor práctico de la razón, legitimidad de la actitud religiosa, realidad del progreso moral. Se publicó también como tirada aparte.

3271. Costa, João Cruz. O desenvolvimento da filosofia no Brasil no século XIX e a evolução histórica nacional. São Paulo, Brasil. 403 p.
Tesis presentada para optar a una cátedra en la Facultad de Filosofía de São Paulo. Excelente estudio del desarrollo histórico de las ideas filosóficas en el Brasil. Aunque el autor dedica la mayor parte del libro al análisis del período positivista, nos da una visión total de las influencias filosóficas en la formación política y social del país. En la primera parte, considera los antecedentes coloniales: el período jesuítico, la Ilustración y las reformas de Pombal, la introducción del sensualismo (Verney). A continuación, presenta brevemente el influjo de la ideología y del espiritualismo ecléctico en la primera mitad del siglo XIX. Después, analiza las distintas etapas del positivismo en la segunda mitad del siglo, que coinciden con notables cambios sociales y políticos—entre otros, la ascensión de la burguesía y el advenimiento de la República. La última parte de la obra estudia la reacción antipositivista representada por Farias Brito. El libro, muy bien documentado, incluye una extensa y valiosa bibliografía.

3272. Farré, Luis. Diez años de filosofía argentina (*Rev. univ. Buenos Aires*, 4. época, año 4, no. 13, enero-marzo, p. 141-222).
Este trabajo está compuesto de una serie de pequeñas monografías en las que se estudian treinta autores contemporáneos en el campo de la actividad filosófica.

3273. Ferrater Mora, José. El problema de la filosofía americana (*Fil. letras*, t. 19, no. 38, abril-junio, p. 378-383).
Posibilidad de una filosofía característicamente americana.

3274. Frondizi, Risieri. Tipos de unidad y diferencia entre el filosofar en Latinoamérica y en Norteamérica (*Fil. letras*, t. 19, no. 38, abril-junio, p. 373-377).
Estudio comparativo del desarrollo de la filosofía en América Latina y los Estados Unidos. Afirma la unidad del pensamiento filosófico iberoamericano.

3275. García Bacca, Juan David. La filosofía del espíritu de Andrés Bello (*Rev. nac. cult.*, año 11, no. 80, mayo-junio, p. 46-56).
Capítulo inicial de un libro en preparación sobre el pensamiento filosófico de Bello.

3276. López Cámara, Francisco. El cartesianismo en Sor Juana y Sigüenza y Góngora (*Fil. letras*, t. 20, no. 39, julio-sept., p. 107-131).
See item 2549.

3277. Moreno, Rafael. Descartes en la filosofía de la Ilustración mexicana (*Fil. letras*, t. 20, no. 39, julio-sept., p. 151-169).

Estudia la influencia de Descartes a lo largo del siglo XVIII mexicano.

3278. Navarro, Bernabé. Descartes y los filósofos mexicanos modernos del siglo XVIII (*Fil. letras*, t. 20, no. 39, julio-sept., p. 133-149).
Sobre la influencia del cartesianismo en la enseñanza de Abad, Alegre, Clavijero y Díaz de Gamarra.

3279. Pauli, Evaldo. La nueva orientación filosófica del Brasil (*Sapientia*, año 5, no. 17, 3. trimestre, p. 196-207; no. 18, 4. trimestre, p. 282-297).
Estudio panorámico de las corrientes filosóficas contemporáneas.

3280. Peñalver, Patricio. La filosofía en Hispanoamérica. Antecedentes y situación actual (*Arbor*, t. 17, no. 57-58, sept.-oct., p. 65-84).
Complementa el trabajo *Tendencias actuales de la filosofía hispanoamericana* (párrafo 3281) dentro de un marco histórico más amplio. Adolece de errores de información. La mayor parte del trabajo está dedicada a la filosofía contemporánea.

3281. ————. Tendencias actuales de la filosofía hispanoamericana (*Estud. amer.*, v. 2, no. 6, mayo, p. 283-294).
Panorama incompleto de la filosofía hispanoamericana en los últimos treinta años. Contiene errores de información y valoración, al igual que el trabajo del mismo autor, párrafo 3280.

3282. Quiles, Ismael. Las primeras obras de filosofía impresas en América y su significado histórico (*Ciencia y fe*, año 6, no. 24, oct.-dic., p. 61-82).
Estudia las obras de Fray Alonso de la Veracruz impresas en México a mediados del siglo XVI.

3283. Robles, Oswaldo. Filósofos mexicanos del siglo XVI. México, Manuel Porrúa. 142 p., illus.
Estudia sucesivamente a Fray Alonso de la Veracruz (primer profesor de filosofía en la Universidad de México), Fray Tomás de Mercado (traductor de Aristóteles y comentador de Petrus Hispanus) y el Padre Antonio Rubio (autor de la llamada *Lógica Mexicana*). El último capítulo está dedicado a Fray Juan de Zumárraga, Fray Bartolomé de las Casas y Vasco de Quiroga, a quienes el autor considera las tres figuras más representativas del "humanismo teológico" del siglo XVI mexicano.

3284. Romero, Francisco. Indicaciones sobre la marcha del pensamiento filosófico en la Argentina (*Cuad. amer.*, año 9, v. 49, no. 1, enero-feb., p. 93-115).
La primera parte de este trabajo se publicó en la misma revista (año 8, no. 6, nov.-dic., 1949). En esta segunda parte, el autor estudia la reacción antipositivista y las nuevas tendencias filosóficas de la Argentina.

3285. Sánchez Reulet, Aníbal. Centenario de Varona. Washington, Unión Panamericana (La Filosofía en América, 2). 22 p.
Conferencia pronunciada, bajo los auspicios del Ateneo Americano de Washington, en un acto conmemorativo del centenario del nacimiento de Varona. Contiene una breve bibliografía.

3286. Washington, Luis. A filosofia no Brasil. São Paulo, Martins (Col. Natureza e Espírito, v. 3). 174 p.
Reúne trabajos escritos en diferentes épocas. No todos los estudios se refieren directamente a la filosofía brasileña. Pero la mayor parte del volumen está dedicado a presentar los momentos más significativos y las figuras más importantes del pensamiento filosófico en el Brasil. En ese sentido, son particularmente interesantes los ensayos reunidos bajo los siguientes títulos: *A filosofia no Brasil* (ojeada panorámica); *Nosso pensamento colonial; Momentos do pensamento brasileiro* (estudios sobre el P. Feijó, Euclides da Cunha, Farias Brito, Silvio Romero y Sérgio Buarque de Holanda) y *A filosofia atual no Brasil*.

ÉTICA Y FILOSOFÍA JURÍDICA Y POLÍTICA

3287. Aja, Pedro Vicente. Cuatro visiones de la libertad moral (*Rev. cub. fil.*, v. 1, no. 6, enero-dic., p. 62-66).

3288. Astrada, Carlos. Los modelos personales y la hipóstasis del valor. Sugestiones para un personalismo ético (*Cuad. fil.*, año 2, no. 5, nov., 1949-feb., 1950, p. 31-43).

3289. Bruera, José Juan. Estudios de filosofía del derecho. Rosario, Argentina, Editorial Rosario. 204 p.
Contiene una serie de ensayos y artículos publicados anteriormente en revistas o en forma de folleto. El autor adopta una actitud intermedia entre el formalismo jurídico y el historicismo extremo. La consideración histórica del derecho es indispensable a condición de no olvidar el carácter objetivo de las normas y de los valores trascendentes a que ellas apuntan.

3290. García Máynez, Eduardo. Los principios jurídicos de contradicción y tercero excluído (*Fil. letras*, t. 19, no. 37, enero-marzo, p. 47-62).

3291. Ojea Quintana, Julio M. La filosofía jurídica de Hans Kelsen (*Sapientia*, año 5, no. 16, 2. trimestre, p. 112-135).

3292. Reale, Miguel. Liberdade antiga e liberdade moderna (*Rev. univ. São Paulo*, ano 1, no. 1, jan.-março, p. 5-35).
Analiza las distintas interpretaciones de la libertad en Grecia y Roma (Maquiavelo, Rousseau, Constant, Fustel de Coulanges, Croiset, Jaeger, etc.), comparándolas con las concepciones modernas de la libertad.

HISTORIA DE LAS IDEAS

3293. Casullo de Carilla, Celina Ester. Lamennais y el Río de la Plata (*Rev. hist. ideas*, no. 1, p. 63-80).

Estudia la influencia de Lamennais sobre la generación romántica argentina (Echeverría, Alberdi, Gutiérrez) y sobre el chileno Francisco Bilbao.

3294. Horas, Plácido Alberto. Esteban Echeverría y la filosofía política de la generación de 1837. San Luis, Argentina, Universidad Nacional de Cuyo, Facultad de Ciencias de la Educación. 117 p.

Interesante estudio sobre la personalidad y el pensamiento político de Echeverría y su influjo en la generación romántica argentina. En el último capítulo se analiza con algún detalle la doctrina del *Dogma socialista*.

3295. Massuh, Víctor. Hostos y el positivismo hispanoamericano (*Cuad. amer.*, año 9, v. 54, no. 6, nov.-dic., p. 167-190).

Estudia el pensamiento de Hostos en sus aspectos morales, pedagógicos y políticos.

3296. Moreno, Rafael. Alzate y la filosofía de la Ilustración (*Fil. letras*, t. 19, no. 37, enero-marzo, p. 107-129).

Sobre la obra de Alzate como publicista y divulgador de las ideas de la Ilustración en México.

3297. Rexach, Rosario. El pensamiento de Félix Varela y la formación de la conciencia cubana. Editado por la Sociedad Lyceum. Habana, Lex. 130 p.

Biografía y exposición de las principales ideas filosóficas y políticas del prócer y pensador cubano.

3298. Varela Domínguez de Ghioldi, Delfina. Filosofía argentina. Vico en los escritos de Sarmiento. Pasión y defensa de la libertad. Buenos Aires. 101 p.

Estudia la influencia de Vico en la generación romántica argentina y, especialmente, en los escritos de Sarmiento.

3299. Zea, Leopoldo. La historia de las ideas en Hispanoamérica (*Fil. letras*, t. 19, no. 38, abril-junio, p. 365-372).

Sobre la importancia y necesidad de estudiar la historia de las ideas.

GNOSEOLOGÍA Y METAFÍSICA

3300. Derisi, Octavio Nicolás. La persona. Su esencia, su vida y su mundo. La Plata, Argentina, Ministerio de Educación, Universidad Nacional de La Plata, Facultad de Humanidades y Ciencias de la Educación, Instituto de Filosofía. 394 p.

El autor desarrolla su concepción de la persona dentro de una línea rigurosamente tomista. Frente al idealismo, el positivismo y el existencialismo, defiende una doctrina substancialista de la persona, en el sentido tradicional de aquel término. El capítulo inicial está dedicado a la fenomenología de la persona. Los dos capítulos siguientes tratan de la metafísica del conocimiento y del objeto de la voluntad moral. En los capítulos que siguen estudia las diferentes dimensiones de la persona humana en relación con el ámbito de la cultura y de la sociedad, y con los diferentes grados de la trascendencia: objetiva, real y divina. En el último capítulo discute los fundamentos de un posible humanismo personalista. Finalmente, en un epílogo, el autor se refiere a la perspectiva que, más allá de la filosofía de la persona, ofrece la trascendencia hacia Dios, fin último e inalcanzable de la existencia humana. "La persona humana queda así constituida en *persona de hijo de Dios*, por la gracia y el amor divinos en el tiempo, y por la visión beatificante y el amor de la Esencia divina en la eternidad."

3301. ————. La unidad del conocimiento humano (*Rev. fil.*, no. 1, p. 34-58).

Estudia el problema de la unidad del conocimiento desde el punto de vista de la filosofía aristitélico-tomista.

3302. Frondizi, Risieri. El problema del yo. Examen histórico y esquema para su interpretación. México. 1950? 201 p.

Disertación doctoral presentada por el autor a la Universidad Nacional de México. La primera parte está destinada a mostrar la desintegración de la doctrina substancialista del espíritu, tal como la formuló Descartes, como resultado de la crítica de Locke, Berkeley y Hume. A continuación, el autor expone su concepción personal del *Yo*, como estructura funcional. En apoyo de su tesis ofrece abundantes pruebas de caracter psicológico, inspirándose, sobre todo, en las conclusiones de la *Gestaltpsychologie*.

3303. González, Mario O. La crisis actual de los fundamentos de la matemática (*Rev. cub. fil.*, v. 1, no. 6, enero-dic., p. 25-30).

Analiza las posiciones logicistas, formalistas e intuicionistas. Se inclina a favor de esta última dirección.

3304. Gortari, Eli de. La ciencia de la lógica. Morelia, Mexico, Universidad Michoacana de San Nicolás de Hidalgo. 339 p.

Texto de introducción a la lógica para la enseñanza universitaria.

3305. Iberico, Mariano. La aparición. Ensayos sobre el ser y el aparecer. Lima, Universidad Nacional Mayor de San Marcos (Publ. del IV Centenario). 229 p.

Colección de ensayos, dividida en dos partes. La primera, que se titula "La mediación del lenguaje," reúne cuatro ensayos: 1, La poesía; 2, La transrealidad del objeto poético; 3, Lenguaje y metafísica; 4, La simbólica del aparecer y el sentimiento del destino. La segunda parte, titulada "Ser y aparecer," contiene dos ensayos: 1, El ser; 2, El aparecer. La tesis fundamental del libro es que el aparecer (mejor que la apariencia) no es una pura ilusión, ni "el velo de Maya" que oculta la verdadera realidad, sino el lenguaje universal en que se expresa el fondo existencial de las cosas. El autor analiza las relaciones y estructuras ontológicas del ser y del aparecer a través de sus típicos medios de expresión: el lenguaje, la poesía y el arte en general.

3306. Nicol, Eduardo. Historicismo y existencialismo. La temporalidad del ser y la razón. México, El Colegio de México. 373 p.

Se estudian conjuntamente, y en riguroso paralelismo, estas dos importantes direcciones del pensamiento contemporáneo, que tan íntimas conexiones tienen entre sí. Después de rastrear los antecedentes en el siglo XVIII y en Hegel—en quien, por primera vez, la categoría de lo histórico se da con plena claridad metafísica,—Nicol dedica sucesivos capítulos a Marx, Kierkegaard, Nietzsche, Bergson, Dilthey, Ortega y Gasset, y Heidegger. Aunque podrían ser ensayos independientes—escritos con soltura y libertad de estilo—los diferentes capítulos del libro se organizan alrededor de un tema único: las implicaciones ontológicas de las ideas de devenir y de individualidad y tiempo histórico.

ESTÉTICA Y TEORÍA DEL ARTE

3307. Mahieu, Jaime María de. Filosofía de la estética. San Luis, Argentina, Universidad Nacional de Cuyo, Facultad de Ciencias de la Educación. 101 p.

Breve tratado de estética orientado en el sentido de una psicología del arte. La primera parte se ocupa de la contemplación artística; la segunda, de la creación artística.

3308. Ramos, Samuel. Filosofía de la vida artística. Buenos Aires, Espasa-Calpe Argentina (Col. Austral). 145 p.

Este pequeño tratado de estética es una reelaboración de las lecciones dadas por el autor en su curso de la Facultad de Filosofía y Letras de México. En la primera parte, analiza el fenómeno artístico en relación con sus factores humanos: el creador, el espectador y el crítico. En la segunda parte, después de considerar el problema del objeto y de los valores estéticos, dedica los siguientes capítulos a estudiar la poesía, la música, las artes plásticas, la danza y la vinculación del arte con la vida y la sociedad.

ADDENDA

3309. Frankl, Víctor. Hispanoamérica y el pensamiento filosófico europeo (*Rev. Indias*, v. 35, no. 111, oct.-dic., 1949, p. 327-352).

Reflexiones acerca del destino de la filosofía europea en Hispanoamérica. Los países hispanoamericanos han logrado una expresión propia y original en el dominio del pensamiento filosófico. El mejor ejemplo lo constituye la obra de Vasconcelos.

3310. Montes de Oca y Silva, José. Teoría del conocimiento. Guadalajara, Mexico, 1949. 163 p.

Obra de texto destinada al "uso de los estudiantes de la Escuela Preparatoria de Jalisco."

3311. TEMAS DE FILOSOFÍA MODERNA SUSTENTADOS EN 1785 EN LA UNIVERSIDAD DE SAN CARLOS DE GUATEMALA. Edición bilingüe, traducida y anotada por José Mata Gavidia. Guatemala, Universidad de San Carlos de Guatemala, Facultad de Humanidades (Pensamiento Universitario Centroamericano), 1949. ix, 63 p.

Documentos relacionados con tesis de filosofía sostenidas en la Universidad de San Carlos de Guatemala en 1785. Útiles para el estudio de la enseñanza de la filosofía durante la época colonial.

3312. Wagner de Reyna, Alberto. La filosofía en Iberoamérica. Lima, Santa María, 1949. 112 p.

Comprende tres ensayos relativamente independientes. El primero considera el problema de la filosofía—como actitud espiritual, más que como ciencia—en relación con su propia historia. El segundo trata el tema de Iberoamérica considerada como unidad cultural dentro de la historia de Occidente. El tercer ensayo discute las posibilidades de desarrollo de la filosofía en Iberoamérica como una prolongación original de la filosofía europea.

3313. Zea, Leopoldo. Norteamérica en la conciencia hispano-americana (*Cuad. amer.*, año 7, v. 39, no. 3, mayo-junio, 1948, p. 161-183).

Se estudian las diferentes actitudes que los hispanoamericanos adoptaron, desde la Independencia, frente a los Estados Unidos y a su propia condición de hispanoamericanos.

APÉNDICE

TRADUCCIONES

3314. Collingwood, R. G. Idea de la naturaleza. Traducción y nota preliminar de Eugenio Imaz. México, Fondo de Cultura Económica. 211 p.

3315. Dewey, John. Lógica. Teoría de la investigación. Prólogo y traducción de Eugenio Imaz. México, Fondo de Cultura Económica. 599 p.

3316. Herder, J. G. Filosofía de la historia para la educación de la humanidad. Traducción de Elsa Tabernig. Buenos Aires, Nova. 148 p.

3317. Keller, Wilhelm. El concepto positivo de existencia y la psicología. Traducción de Ángela Molnos. Buenos Aires,

Universidad de Buenos Aires, Instituto de Filosofía, Sección de Psicología (Monografías Psicológicas, no. 3). 27 p.

3318. Lucrecio Caro, Tito. De la naturaleza de las cosas. Nueva traducción española por Lisandro Alvarado. Caracas, Ávila Gráfica (Publ. del Gobierno del Estado Lara). 285 p.
Traducción en prosa del poema de Lucrecio hecha por el erudito venezolano Lisandro Alvarado entre 1890 y 1904.

3319. Renouvier, Charles. Historia y solución de los problemas metafísicos. Traducción de Francisco González Ríos. Buenos Aires, Hachette (Col. Cultura Filosófica). 590 p.

3320. Riekel, August. Eidética. La memoria sensorial y su investigación. Traducción de J. Rovira Armengol. Buenos Aires, Universidad de Buenos Aires, Instituto de Filosofía, Sección de Psicología (Monografías Psicológicas, no. 2). 54 p.

3321. San Anselmo. Proslogion. Traducción castellana de Beatriz Maas. Prólogo de Guillermo Blanco. Buenos Aires, Ministerio de Educación, Universidad Nacional de la Plata, Instituto de Filosofía (Publ., Sección Textos, 1). 123 p.

3322. Scheler, Max. La esencia de lo trágico. Traducción de Ricardo Jacob Berindoague (*Rev. fil.*, Santiago, v. 1, no. 3, agosto, p. 281-302).
Es uno de los ensayos publicados en el volumen *Vom Umsturz der Werte.*

3323. Schelling, Federico Guillermo José. La esencia de la libertad humana. Buenos Aires, Ministerio de Educación, Universidad de Buenos Aires, Facultad de Filosofía y Letras, Instituto de Filosofía (Serie Textos Filosóficos, Filosofía Moderna, no. 4). 152 p.

3324. Schneider, Herbert W. Historia de la filosofía norteamericana. Traducción revisada por Eugenio Imaz. México, Fondo de Cultura. 621 p.

3325. Utitz, Emil. Caracterología. Traducción de J. Rovira Armengol. Buenos Aires, Universidad de Buenos Aires, Instituto de Filosofía, Sección de Psicología (Monografías Psicológicas, no. 4). 42 p.

Sociology

T. LYNN SMITH

EVENTS of the past thirty or forty years have stimulated the emergence of sociology as a separate discipline in Latin American studies. In recognition of this fact the *Handbook* initiates with the present number a section devoted to sociology as a distinct field of Latin American interest. The numerous publications here recorded bear eloquent testimony that the field is an active and growing one. It was not always so, although an interest in sociology has been intertwined throughout Latin American writings for nearly as long as we have records of the area.*

In an introduction to UNESCO's *International Social Study Bulletin* (v. 4, no. 3, 1952, special number devoted to Latin America) Dr. Paulo E. de Berredo Carneiro observes that sociology emerged in Europe as a discernible abstract discipline precisely at the time the nations of Latin America were beginning to achieve political independence. Under such challenging circumstances the men who guided the incipient republics were forced to turn their minds to the consideration of manifold and intricate problems. Whatever the point of view or emphasis it soon became evident that the exigencies of the time called for a scientific approach. The dearth of men and women qualified for so exacting a task, the enormous intellectual breadth which circumstances required of nineteenth-century leaders, and the very fact that sociology alone did not seem to provide a sufficient yardstick for a proper evaluation of social needs seem but a few of the reasons why so many of the men concerned with these questions were classified indiscriminately as "pensadores." They combined the role of sociologists, philosophers, political scientists, and even psychologists. Eugenio María de Hostos, the great Puerto Rican who singlehandedly did so much for cultural progress in various parts of Hispanic America, and Valentín Letelier, third rector of the University of Chile, for example, were both high in the ranks of the educators, philosophers, and social scientists. The Argentine José Ingenieros occupied a similar position in his time. Throughout the nineteenth century sociology had not achieved a status of its own nor had it yet, in Latin America, established a set of well-defined frontiers.

The twentieth century witnessed the rise of sociology in the area as a separate field of interest. It had ceased to be a vague and highly theoretical element among those related special disciplines characterized as "social." The Mexican Revolution of 1910, for instance, dramatized economic and social problems that called for the immediate application of sociological principles to concrete situations. On the other hand, the "Revolución Universitaria," which reoriented the University of Córdoba (Argentina) in 1918, imperatively demanded a total revision of higher education and investigative methods. From both these and parallel movements sociology derived

*This introductory note was prepared in the *Handbook of Latin American Studies* office.

279

a strong impetus. Events in other parts of the world, one shrunk through rapid communications, further stimulated interest in clear, definable, scientific treatment of national problems. The search for the necessary tools and methods was launched. The era of sociology as an aid in such matters as education, public health, land reform, housing, social security, international relations, and the good life in general had arrived.

It was owing to this clear comprehension of sociological factors and their significance in national life that such important undertakings as the Fondo de Cultura Económica in Mexico and the Escola de Sociologia e Política in São Paulo, Brazil, came into being. The former was established for the purpose of publishing in Spanish the basic works necessary for modernizing the study of sociology and the social sciences in general. It made available in Latin America the major sociological works originally written in Spanish, English, French, or German. This no doubt has contributed to improve the quality of teaching in the universities. The Escola de Sociologia e Política was the answer to a need felt by the progressive citizens of São Paulo for trained personnel in government projects and civic undertakings designed to strengthen the São Paulo area and to raise the standards of community life.

Along with these developments it is important to note the increased facilities for the teaching of sociology in the universities and specialized schools. Thus a discipline that used to be almost exclusively a part of the law curriculum is today taught in other professional schools of university rank, in the departments of philosophy and letters, in teacher training institutions, and even in the upper level of some pre-university schools.

The study of sociology has also given rise to journals of sociology, seminars, societies, congresses, and a wide range of international activities in this field. Those sponsored by UNESCO and the Organization of American States are especially notable and are generally recognized as having already done much to enhance interest in applied sociology. The work of the Inter-American Social and Economic Council, the Inter-American Institute of Indian Affairs, the Inter American Statistical Institute, and the Inter-American Institute of Agricultural Sciences is noteworthy. In addition there are numerous community studies of the type carried on in Brazil (Donald Pierson's study of Cruz das Almas, for instance) and an increasing emphasis on social anthropology (a subject closely related to sociology) as an aid in social progress. All these have unquestionably raised the standing of sociology among Latin Americanists. Furthermore, the growing demand for community and field studies as prerequisites to social planning and the constant search for Latin American solutions of Latin American problems (with the help, of course, of principles which have found universal application) have endowed sociology with a vitality it did not have in the earlier days of academic theorizing and facile generalization. These attitudes are reflected in the publications listed and annotated in this newly created section of the *Handbook of Latin American Studies*.

GENERAL

3326. Azevedo, Fernando de. A sociologia na América Latina, e particularmente no Brasil (*Rev. hist.*, São Paulo, ano 1, no. 3, julho-set., p. 339-361).
An important contribution to a fuller understanding of the history of sociological writing and teaching in Latin America, with emphasis upon developments in Argentina, Mexico, Peru, and Brazil.

3327. Nelson, Lowry. Rural Cuba. Min-neapolis, Minn., University of Minnesota Press. x, 285 p., charts and diagrams.
This is among the most fundamental contributions made by sociologists from the United States in the field of Latin American studies. Included are analyses of the population, the relations of man to the land, social stratification and the class system, the family, education and the schools, and the level of living.

3328. Willems, Emilio. Dicionário de sociologia. Pôrto Alegre, Brazil, Globo. xi, 156 p.

Definitions of many of the principal terms used in sociology along with brief biographical entries for well-known sociologists of various nationalities.

POPULATION

3329. Bernardes, Nilo. A colonização no município de Santa Rosa, Estado do Rio Grande do Sul (*Rev. bras. geog.*, ano 12, no. 3, julho-set., p. 383-390, plates, fold. map).

3330. Carneiro, Edison (ed.). Antologia do negro brasileiro. Pôrto Alegre, Brazil, Globo. xix, 432 p.
Selections from the writings of Brazilian scholars, and a few of other nationalities, who have dealt with subjects relating to the Brazilian Negro. Slavery, abolition, Negro revolts, folklore, religion, biographies of outstanding Brazilian Negroes, and the Negro in recent times are the principal subdivisions of the volume.

3331. Carneiro, J. Fernando. Imigração e colonização no Brasil. Rio de Janeiro, Faculdade Nacional de Filosofia, Cadeira de Geografia do Brasil (Publ. Avulsa no. 2). 60 p., folding maps, plates, table.
A skillful and courageous analysis of the immigration problem in Brazil, followed by a thought-provoking examination of European settlement in the States of Rio Grande do Sul and Santa Catarina. The number of immigrants of different stocks who entered Brazil from 1819 to 1947 is presented in tabular form. Appendix by Arthur Hehl Neiva and J. Fernando Carneiro. Abstract in English, French, and German. [H. O. Sternberg]

3332. Instituto Brasileiro de Geografia e Estatística. Estatística municipal. Distribuição da população brasileira, segundo o domicílio. Rio de Janeiro. 292 p., tables.
Further results of the 1940 census. For each county, there is shown the urban, suburban, and rural population. For the whole of Brazil, these figures were 9, 4, and 28 million, respectively. [H. W. Spiegel]

3333. ————. Estudos de estatística teórica e aplicada. Estatística demográfica, no. 11. Estudos sôbre a composição da população do Brasil segundo a côr. Rio de Janeiro, Serviço Gráfico do Instituto Brasileiro de Geografia e Estatística. 153 p., tables.
Demographic studies showing the ethnic composition of the Brazilian population. [H. W. Spiegel]

3334. Rios, José Arthur. Mudança na distribuição racial no Estado do Rio (*Sociologia*, v. 12, no. 2, maio, p. 130-147).
An analysis of available data relative to changes in the proportions of whites, Negroes, and mixed-bloods in the State of Rio de Janeiro. Since 1872 the percentage of whites has been increasing, largely because of a higher rate of natural increase.

3335. Uslar-Pietri, Arturo. De una a otra Venezuela. Caracas, Ediciones Mesa Redonda, 1950? 171 p.
The first part of this volume is devoted to the problems arising in and from the petroleum industry, the second is an analysis of population problems, and the third deals with educational problems, from the crisis in the national university to the deficiencies of rural schools.

3336. Ventura, Ovidio S., y Federico A. Moratorio Coelho. Síntesis demográfica de la capital federal. Buenos Aires, Ministerio de Salud Pública de la Nación, Dirección Nacional de Investigaciones Demológicas, Instituto de la Población (Publ. no. 8-E-1). 78 p., graphs, tables.
Summary materials relating to the characteristics of the population, the vital processes, and marriages in the city of Buenos Aires.

3337. Willems, Emilio. Einwanderungsprobleme Brasiliens (*Kyklos*, v. 4, fasc. 1, p. 60-68).
A brief treatment of Brazilian immigration problems, with emphasis upon the period since 1934.

COMMUNITY AND NEIGHBORHOOD

3338. Crist, Raymond E. The personality of Popayán (*Rural soc.*, v. 15, no. 2, June, p. 130-140).
The natural history of a small urban community in southern Colombia, showing the retarding effects of extreme social stratification, arising from "prestige land-holding," upon industrial and commercial development. See item 1140.

3339. Pierson, Donald. O estudo de Cruz das Almas (*Sociologia*, v. 12, no. 1, março, p. 33-43).
The first of a series of articles giving in Portuguese some of the materials from the study of the Brazilian village of Cruz das Almas. See items 3357, 3376, 3377.

3340. Siegel, Bernard J. Algumas considerações sôbre o estudo de uma vila brasileira (*Sociologia*, v. 12, no. 2, maio, p. 148-160).
Largely a discussion of the reasons why the author chose the *município* of Itapecerica da Serra, São Paulo, as the site for his study of the relation between the value system and human behavior in a Luso-Brazilian rural society. A few important observations about the impact of contacts with modern society upon the members of the lower classes and the antiquated systems of agriculture are included.

DIFFERENTIATION AND STRATIFICATION

3341. Acosta, César R. La población rural del Paraguay (*Mater. estud. clase media amér. latina*, v. 3, p. 93-108).
Brief discussions of the ethnic composition of the Paraguayan population, the sex ratio, private colonization ventures as socio-economic factors, and the social structure.

3342. Bagú, Sergio. La clase media en la Argentina (*Mater. estud. clase media amér. latina*, v. 1, p. 34-65).
This study includes a discussion of the concept of social class and the history of the middle class in Argentina, with sections on its social and economic position, its mentality, and its literature.

3343. Biesanz, John. The middle class in Panama (*Mater. estud. clase media amér. latina*, v. 4, p. 1-15).
A definition of the middle class, its relative importance in the population of Panama, and its composition, along with an analysis of the factors affecting its development and certain conditions, such as social mobility, which affect middle class people particularly.

3344. Campbell, Carolina de, and Ofelia Hooper. The middle class of Panama (*Mater. estud. clase media amér. latina*, v. 4, p. 38-75).
Definition and importance of the middle class, its development and changes, and its social and psychosocial characteristics.

3345. Carreño, Alberto María. Las clases sociales de México (*Rev. mex. soc.*, año 12, no. 3, sept.-dic., p. 333-350).
The bases of social stratification in Mexico, the origin of the present classes, the critical position of the present middle class, and the low level and standard of living of the lower classes.

3346. Carvajal, Juan F. Observaciones sobre la clase media en Cuba (*Mater. estud. clase media amér. latina*, v. 2, p. 30-44).
Discussions of the concept of social class, the role of the economic factor in class formation, the characteristics of the middle class, the old and new middle classes, and the organization of labor.

3347. Crevenna, Theo R. (ed.). Materiales para el estudio de la clase media en la América Latina. V. 1, La clase media en Argentina y Uruguay; v. 2, La clase media en Bolivia, Brasil, Chile y Paraguay; v. 4, La clase media en Panamá, El Salvador, Honduras y Nicaragua. Washington, Unión Panamericana, Oficina de Ciencias Sociales. 100, 98, 117, 128 p.
Articles are separately entered in this section.

3348. Germani, Gino. La clase media en la Argentina con especial referencia a sus sectores urbanos (*Mater. estud. clase media amér. latina*, v. 1, p. 1-33).
A summary of the results of an attempt to determine the absolute and relative importance of the middle and lower classes in Argentina. No account is taken of an upper class, except to indicate that its numbers would not be large. Of the total population, 55.2 per cent is placed in the *clase media* and 44.8 per cent in the *clase obrera*.

3349. Gordon, Maxine W. Cultural aspects of Puerto Rico's race problem (*Amer. soc. rev.*, v. 15, no. 3, June, p. 382-392).
A wealth of detail relative to discriminations based upon color or race in Puerto Rico. The historical perspective is ample.

3350. Grompone, Antonio Miguel. Las clases medias en el Uruguay (*Mater. estud. clase media amér. latina*, v. 1, p. 76-91).
A discussion of the organization and evolution of agriculture, stockraising, industry, and commerce in Uruguay, with the conclusion that the bulk of the population of the country belongs to the middle classes.

3351. Guandique, José Salvador. Noción y aspectos de la clase media en El Salvador (*Mater. estud. clase media amér. latina*, v. 4, p. 113-119).
A few brief summary statements about the middle class in El Salvador. The author believes there is a middle class in the country, that it constitutes about 30 percent of the population, and that it is increasing with industrialization.

3352. Hermann, Lucila. Classe media em Guaratinguetá (*Mater. estud. clase media amér. latina*, v. 3, p. 18-59).
Extracts from the author's doctoral dissertation at the University of São Paulo. The various social classes, including the middle class, were studied in relation to social organization in general. Much attention is devoted to the changes from one period to another.

3353. Jiménez de López, Georgina. La clase media en Panamá (*Mater. estud. clase media amér. latina*, v. 4, p. 16-37).
Brief expositions relating to the origin, make-up, and importance of the middle class in Panama, with an enumeration of the factors responsible for its development and some of the characteristics of its members.

3354. López Villamil, Humberto. Estudio de la clase media en Honduras (*Mater. estud. clase media amér. latina*, v. 4, p. 76-89).
Factors contributing to the development of a middle class and measures favorable to its growth.

3355. Nelson, Lowry. The social class structure in Cuba (*Mater. estud. clase media amér. latina,* v. 2, p. 45-72).
A penetrating study which traces the development of Cuban class structure, analyzes the relationship between national origins, color, and income and position in the social scale, and then questions the actual existence of any real middle class in Cuba.

3356. Palza S., Humberto. La clase media en Bolivia. Nota para el estudio y comprensión del problema (*Mater. estud. clase media amér. latina,* v. 3, p. 1-17).
The relation of race to social status, with an analysis of the factors affecting the development of a middle class and a brief discussion of some of the social and psychosocial characteristics of its members.

3357. Pierson, Donald. Status e prestígio em Cruz das Almas (*Sociologia,* v. 12, no. 2, maio, p. 113-129).
Cruz das Almas is said to be "a rather typical rural community in the State of São Paulo." Here an attempt is made to relate such factors as age, sex, family affiliation, ownership of land, race, color, and national origin to social status and prestige.

3358. Poviña, Alfredo. Concepto de la clase media y su proyección argentina (*Mater. estud. clase media amér. latina,* v. 1, p. 66-75).
Brief discussions of the concept of social class, the concept of the *clase media,* and the middle class in Argentina. According to the author, the middle class consists of professional men, public and private employees who receive salaries, small proprietors, small merchants and industrialists, and even "el agricultor o campesino que vive de su trabajo del campo."

3359. Pressoir, Catts. Étude sur la classe moyenne à Port-au-Prince, capitale de la République d'Haïti (*Rev. soc. haïtienne hist. geóg.,* v. 21, no. 77, avril, p. 1-10).
Dr. Pressoir insists that the middle class in Port-au-Prince (which he postulates as being 25 per cent of the total population) has considerable influence on the social, religious, and political life of the country. This percentage might seem too high to many students. [R. E. Crist]

3360. Raggi Ageo, Carlos Manuel. Contribución al estudio de las clases medias en Cuba (*Mater. estud. clase media amér. latina,* v. 2, p. 73-89).
A study of the importance of the middle class in Cuba, the factors in its development, and the basic characteristics of this class.

3361. Salvatierra, Sofonías. Ensayo sobre la clase media en Nicaragua (*Mater. estud. clase media amér. latina,* v. 4, p. 90-112).
The author doubts that racial differences, cultural differences, or variations in economic capacities justify one in asserting the existence of various social classes. Nevertheless, he concludes that the bulk of the Nicaraguan population belongs to the proletariat or lower class; and that the middle class is made up of doctors, lawyers, teachers, and other professionals.

3362. Vega, Julio. La clase media en Chile (*Mater. estud. clase media amér. latina,* v. 3, p. 60-92).
A discussion of the differences between class and caste, followed by brief treatments of the origins of the social classes in Chile and the present situation of the middle class in that country.

3363. Whetten, Nathan L. The rise of the middle class in Mexico (*Mater. estud. clase media amér. latina,* v. 2, p. 1-29).
One of the more adequate discussions of the concept of a middle class, followed by an analysis of the factors influencing the growth of the middle class in Mexico, the presentation of evidence that the lower class is still predominant in numbers, and a brief treatment of the rise of the middle class.

SOCIAL INSTITUTIONS

3364. Azevedo, Fernando. A sociologia da educação (*Sociologia,* v. 12, no. 2, maio, p. 106-112).
The preface to the second edition of the author's noted volume, *Sociologia educacional,* one of the most important works in contemporary sociology. Azevedo contends that French sociologists have not distinguished educational sociology from the comparative history of educational theories and that United States sociologists have not differentiated it from sociology applied to education. He conceives of educational sociology as the study of educational processes and systems, educational theories, and the relation of social organization to educational processes.

3365. Bastide, Roger. Medicina e magia nos candomblés (*Bol. bibliog.,* São Paulo, v. 16, p. 1-34).
An important contribution to the sociology of religion. The author analyzes in some detail the perpetuation of African ceremonies and materia medica in the treatment of various ailments, by specially prepared intermediaries between man and the supernatural, with particular emphasis upon the *candomblés, xangôs,* and *catimbós* in Brazil.

3366. Biesanz, John. Inter-American marriages on the isthmus of Panama (*Soc. forces,* v. 29, no. 2, Dec., p. 159-163).
The extent of intermarriage, with an analysis of the factors involved and the biosocial characteristics of the parties involved.

MAN-LAND RELATIONSHIPS

3367. Biesanz, John. Social forces retarding development of Panama's agricultural resources (*Rural soc.,* v. 15, no. 1, March, p. 148-155).

Rural traditions of communal land ownership, mutual aid, an easy satisfaction with grandiose paper plans, and concentration of land ownership and control, along with other social and economic factors, retard development.

3368. Caldeira, Clovis. Arrendamento rural no Brasil (*Obs. econ. fin.,* ano 15, no. 172, maio, p. 57-62, 243-244).
Geographical distribution of farm tenancy in Brazil, according to the 1940 census. Reprinted in *Bol. geog.,* ano 8, no. 86, maio, 1950, p. 203-215. [H. O. Sternberg]

3369. Flores Vilchis, Othón. El problema agrario en el estado de Morelos. México. 114 p.
A monograph of importance for those interested in the relation of man to the land or in rural sociology generally. Of the 11 chapters, seven are devoted to historical backgrounds, communications, population, property, credit, education, and the conclusions. Emphasis is upon agrarian reform and especially on the work of Zapata and Cárdenas. Thesis, Law School, University of Mexico.

3370. Guevara, Luis Alfredo. Granjas comunales indígenas. Lima, Empresa Periodística, 1950? 51 p., charts, illus.
A description of communal farming and related activities in the Indian villages of present-day Peru.

3371. Keller, Frank L. Finca Ingavi. A medieval survival on the Bolivian altiplano (*Econ. geog.,* v. 26, no. 1, Jan., p. 37-50).
A detail of a larger study (see item 1240). Map. [G. M. McBride]

3372. Meggers, Betty J. Caboclo life in the mouth of the Amazon (*Primitive man,* v. 23, no. 1-2, Jan.-April, p. 14-28).
Descriptive. [P. E. James]

3373. Souza, João Gonçalves de. Relações do homem com a terra em quatro communidades rurais do médio São Francisco (*Bol. soc. bras. geog.,* ano 1, no. 1, julho-agôsto, p. 15-25).
An important contribution in the field of rural sociology. The author presents the results of one of the few empirical studies of the social aspects of land tenure in Latin America.

SOCIAL PROCESSES

3374. Galvão, Hélio. Assistência mútua entre as populações rurais do Nordeste brasileiro (*Sociologia,* v. 12, no. 4, out., p. 289-311).
A significant study of mutual aid in Brazil's great, semi-arid, pastoral Northeast. The analysis of non-contractual forms of cooperation in agriculture, stock-raising, fishing, hunting, and religious and recreational activities is excellent.

3375. Mortara, Giorgio. Immigration to Brazil. Some observations on the linguistic assimilation of immigrants and their descendants in Brazil (In *Cultural assimilation of immigrants,* papers presented to the International Union for the Scientific Study of Population, First General Assembly, Geneva, 1949, under the auspices and published with the assistance of UNESCO on behalf of the Population Investigation Committee, London, Cambridge University Press, p. 39-44).
Level of education, group settlement, politics, and imperialist designs of the mother countries are factors affecting the assimilation of immigrants.

3376. Pierson, Donald. Caipira versus "cidadão" em Cruz das Almas (*Sociologia,* v. 12, no. 4, out., p. 312-322).
A study of the extent (which is considerable) to which the members of the lower classes residing in the open-country districts (the *caipiras*) constitute social groups distinct from the "citizens" who live in the small Brazilian town of Cruz das Almas. This is a valuable contribution to the study of town-country relationships.

3377. ————. Isolamento e contacto em Cruz das Almas (*Sociologia,* v. 12, no. 3, agôsto, p. 185-203).
A study of some of the social effects in a small Brazilian town of increasing contacts with the outside world. Not long ago the passing through of pack-train drivers offered the principal contacts with the greater society; later truck drivers, traveling pilgrims, newspapers, and the radio increased the frequency of contacts; as the study proceeded a bus line began serving the small center.

3378. Price, Paul H. Selected aspects of rural transportation in southern Brazil (*Int.-amer. econ. affs.,* v. 3, no. 4, spring. p. 31-40).
A study of the wagons, types of harness, and horses introduced into southern Brazil by immigrants from Poland and other European countries.

3379. Queiroz, Maria Isaura Pereira de. Assimilação de tres famílias em São Paulo (*Sociologia,* v. 12, março, no. 1, p. 22-32).
Case histories of a Japanese, an Armenian, and a Scot family, describing the changes in personality which eventually amounted to assimilation.

3380. ————. A estratificação e a mobilidade social nas comunidades agrárias do Vale do Paraíba entre 1850 e 1888 (*Rev. hist.,* São Paulo, ano 1, no. 2, abril-junho, p. 195-218).
An effective use of materials from historical documents in a sociological frame of reference to portray an important aspect of social structure in an historic part of the State of São Paulo.

OTHER TOPICS

3381. Bejarano, Jorge. Alimentación y nutrición en Colombia. Bogotá, Iqueima. 239 p.
The third edition of a volume devoted largely to technical aspects of diet and nutrition. Several chapters are of particular interest to sociologists: 6, "La costumbre alimenticia," 9, "Geografía y economía alimenticia en Colombia," 10, "La cuestión de la alimentación obrera," and 11, "Folklore alimenticio de Colombia." The first edition appeared in 1941.

3382. Figueroa Román, Miguel. An Argentinian stand on integral planning. A definition of planning. Tucumán, Argentina, National University of Tucumán, Institute of Sociography and Planning. 15 p.
Papers submitted to the National Planning Conference of the American Society of Planning Officials, Los Angeles, 1950. Included are summary statements about social planning in Argentina, with brief references to Point 4, the author's definition of planning, and his conception of the role of sociology in connection therewith.

3383. Masferrer, Alberto. El mínimum vital. Y otras obras de carácter sociológico. Guatemala, Ediciones del Gobierno de Guatemala (Col. Los Clásicos del Istmo). lix, 248 p.
A collection of the sociological writings of El Salvador's outstanding champion of the rights of the masses, prefaced by a lengthy treatment of Masferrer's life and work by Francisco Morán. *El mínimum vital* that every man should have consists of: 1, steady, honest, and fairly paid work under hygienic conditions; 2, food that is adequate, varied, nutritious, and healthful; 3, housing that is ample, well lighted and well ventilated; 4, good water and plenty of it; 5, clothing that is clean, well cut, and of the right weight; 6, medical attention and sanitary protections; 7, justice that is prompt and available to all; 8, effective primary and supplementary education which will form cordial personalities, expert workers, and conscientious heads of families; and 9, rest and recreation sufficient to restore the forces of the body and the mind. The first edition of the book appeared in 1925.

3384. Patín, Enrique. Observaciones acerca de nuestra psicología popular. Ciudad Trujillo, Montalvo. 45 p.
Observations and reflections upon the social psychology of the masses in the Dominican Republic. The approach is European, reminiscent of the work of Tarde and Le Bon. Influences from other countries in general, from the colonial period, from the geographical setting, from Haiti, from the various provinces, from the epoch of Concho Primo (19th century), and from the "Yankees" are all considered briefly. The volume concludes with an effort at delineating the principal characteristics of the "soul" of the common man in the Dominican Republic.

3385. Ramos, Alberto Guerreiro. Uma introdução ao histórico da organização nacional do trabalho. Ensaio de sociologia do conhecimento. Rio de Janeiro, Departamento Administrativo do Serviço Público, Serviço de Documentação (Publ. Avulsa no. 318).
An important pioneer work in the field of industrial sociology. The historical treatment is extensive and ample reference is made to the ways in which work is organized under the Taylor system and the Ford system, and in Germany.

3386. Szilard, Adalberto, e José de Oliveira Reis. Urbanismo no Rio de Janeiro. Rio de Janeiro, Construtor. 157 p., illus., maps.
A serious and well documented account of the problems created by recent building in Rio de Janeiro with specific solutions proposed. The text is divided into separate regions of the city by the authors, who are both engineers and town planners. [R. C. Smith]

ADDENDA

3387. Baldrich, Alberto. Libertad y determinismo en el advenimiento de la sociedad política argentina. Buenos Aires, Universidad de Buenos Aires, Facultad de Ciencias Económicas, Instituto de Sociología (Cuadernos de Sociología Política, Publ. no. 2), 1949. 19 p.
A rather philosophical analysis of the backgrounds (Spanish and English) of Argentina's political ideals.

3388. Maguire Ibar, Eugenia. Formación racial chilena y futuras proyecciones. Santiago, 1949. 71 p.
A thesis for the degree of Licenciado at the University of Chile. The work deals fully as much with political history and class conflict as with racial and other demographic matters.

3389. Montes de Oca y Silva, José. Prolegómenos a la sociología. Guadalajara, Mexico, Universidad de Guadalajara (Publ. del Departamento de Extensión Universitaria), 1949. 187 p.
An elementary treatment of a part of the frame of reference used in sociology. It is suitable for supplementary reading in introductory sociology courses.

3390. Ramos, Alberto Guerreiro, e Evaldo da Silva Garcia. Notícia sôbre as pesquisas e os estudos sociológicos no Brasil (1940-1949), com especial referencia a migrações, contatos de raça, colonização e assuntos correlatos. Rio de Janeiro, Conselho de Imigração e Colonização, 1949. 55 p.

A brief annotated bibliography of recent sociological research in Brazil prefaced by a short sketch of the development of empirical studies in that country. Important for all who wish to be acquainted with social science activities in Brazil.

3391. Rosario, José C., y José M. Zapata. Derivaciones pedagógicas de los problemas sociales y económicos de Puerto Rico. Río Piedras, P. R., University of Puerto Rico, College of Education (Monografías Pedagógicas, serie 1, no. 1), 1949. 134 p.

Following Robert E. Park's *An Outline of Sociology*, this book presents data on the origin, interrelationship, and intensity of the island's social and economic problems, suggests reasons for them, and proposes solutions, usually in terms of better informed public opinion. [H. Benjamin]

Abbreviations

Abril ....Abril. Habana, Cuba?

Ábside ....Ábside. México, D. F., Mexico.

Acta amer. ....Acta Americana. Inter-American Society of Anthropology and Geography. México, D. F., Mexico.

Actas cong. int. amer....Vigésimoséptimo Congreso Internacional de Americanistas. Actas de la Primera Sesión, Celebrada en la Ciudad de México en 1939. Tomo 2. México, D. F., Instituto Nacional de Antropología e Historia. 1947.

Agric. pecuária ....Agricultura e Pecuária. Rio de Janeiro, Brazil.

Agric. técnica ....Agricultura Técnica. Ministerio de Agricultura. Santiago, Chile.

Agron. jour. ....Agronomy Journal. Morgantown, W. Va.

Amer. anthrop. ....American Anthropologist. American Anthropological Association . . . . Menasha, Wis.

Amer. antiquity ....American Antiquity. Society for American Archaeology. Menasha, Wis.

Amer. arch. ....American Archivist. Society of American Archivists. Washington, D. C.

Amer. econ. rev. ....American Economic Review. Evanston, Ill.

Amér. indígena ....América Indígena. Instituto Indigenista Interamericano. México, D. F., Mexico.

Amer. jour. arch. ......American Journal of Archaeology. Archaeological Institute of America. Cambridge, Mass.

Amer. jour. sci. ....American Journal of Science. New Haven, Conn.

Amer. pol. sci. rev......American Political Science Review. American Political Science Association. Madison, Wis.

Amer. soc. rev...........American Sociological Review. American Sociological Society. College Park, Md.

Americanista ....Americanista. Buenos Aires, Argentina?

Americas ....The Americas. Academy of American Franciscan History. Washington, D. C.

An. acad. hist. Cuba....Anales de la Academia de la Historia de Cuba. Habana, Cuba.

An. acad. port. hist......Anais. Academia Portuguesa da Historia. Lisboa, Portugal.

An. amer. acad. pol. soc. sci. — The Annals of the American Academy of Political and Social Science. Philadelphia, Pa.

An. econ. estad. ....Anales de Economía y Estadística. Contraloría General de la República. Bogotá, Colombia.

An. estud. amer.........Anuario de Estudios Americanos. Universidad de Sevilla. Escuela de Estudios Hispano-Americanos. Sevilla, Spain.

An. fac. farm. odont.....Anais da Faculdade de Farmácia e Odontologia. Universidade de São Paulo. São Paulo, Brazil.

An. geog. estado Rio de Janeiro — Anuário Geográfico do Estado de Rio de Janeiro. Conselho Nacional de Geografia. Instituto Brasileiro de Geografia e Estatística. Niteroi, Brazil.

An. hist. revol. franc.....Annales Historiques de la Révolution Française. Société des Études Robespierristes. Paris, France.

An. inst. arte amer. invest. estét. — Anales del Instituto de Arte Americano e Investigaciones Estéticas. Universidad de Buenos Aires. Facultad de Arquitectura y Urbanismo. Buenos Aires, Argentina.

An. inst. étnico nac......Anales del Instituto Étnico Nacional. Ministerio del Interior. Buenos Aires, Argentina.

An. inst. invest. estét.....Anales del Instituto de Investigaciones Estéticas. Universidad Nacional Autónoma de México. México, D. F., Mexico.

An. inst. ling., Mendoza . Anales del Instituto de Lingüística. Universidad Nacional de Cuyo. Mendoza, Argentina.

An. instr. prim.........Anales de la Instrucción Primaria. Dirección de Enseñanza Primaria y Normal. Montevideo, Uruguay.

An. mus. imperial.......Anuário do Museu Imperial. Ministério da Educação e Saúde. Petrópolis, Brazil.

An. mus. nac. ....Anales del Museo Nacional "David J. Guzmán." San Salvador, El Salvador.

An. mus. paulista........Anais do Museu Paulista. São Paulo, Brazil.

An. prim. cong. hist. Anais do Primeiro Congresso de História da Bahia. Bahia, Brazil. Bahia

An. prov. Santo Evan- Anales de la Provincia del Santo Evangelio de México. Puebla, gelio de México Mexico.

An. serv. geog. exér. ....Anuario do Serviço Geográfico do Exército. Ministério da Guerra. Rio de Janeiro, Brazil.

An. soc. geog. hist. Anales de la Sociedad de Geografía e História de Guatemala. Guatemala Guatemala, Guatemala.

An. univ. cent. Ecuador . Anales de la Universidad Central del Ecuador. Quito, Ecuador.

An. univ. hispalense.....Anales de la Universidad Hispalense. Sevilla, Spain.

An. univ. Santo Anales de la Universidad de Santo Domingo. Ciudad Trujillo, Domingo Dominican Republic.

Anhembi ....Anhembi. São Paulo, Brazil.

Antrop. etnol. ....Antropología y Etnología. Consejo Superior de Investigaciones Científicas. Instituto Bernardino de Sahagún. Madrid, Spain.

Antrop. hist. ....Antropología e Historia de Guatemala. Ministerio de Educación Pública. Instituto de Antropología e Historia de Guatemala. Guatemala, Guatemala.

Arbor ....Arbor. Consejo Superior de Investigaciones Científicas. Madrid, Spain.

Arch. esp. arte.........Archivo Español de Arte. Consejo Superior de Investigaciones Científicas. Instituto Diego Velázquez. Madrid, Spain.

Arch. iberoamer. Archivos Iberoamericanos de Historia de la Medicina. Consejo hist. med. Superior de Investigaciones Científicas. Madrid, Spain.

Arch. pedia. Uruguay ...Archivos de Pediatría del Uruguay. Sociedad Uruguaya de Pediatría. Montevideo, Uruguay.

Arch. soc. per. fil........Archivos de la Sociedad Peruana de Filosofía. Lima, Peru.

Archaeology ....Archaeology. Archaeological Institute of America. Cambridge, Mass.

Architect. d'aujourd'hui .Architecture d'Aujourd'hui. Boulogne, France.

Architect. rev. ....Architectural Review. London, England.

Archiv für Völkerkunde . Archiv für Völkerkunde. Museum für Völkerkunde. Wien, Austria.

Arq. biol. tecnol.........Arquivos de Biologia y Tecnologia. Secretaria de Agricultura, Industria e Comércio. Instituto de Biologia e Pesquisas Tecnológicas. Curitiba, Paraná, Brazil.

Arquitectura, Habana ...Arquitectura. Colegio Nacional de Arquitectos. Habana, Cuba.

Art bull. ....Art Bulletin. The College Art Association of America. New York, N. Y.

Art news ....Art News. New York, N. Y.

Art quart. ....The Art Quarterly. Detroit Institute of Arts. Detroit, Mich.

Asomante ....Asomante. Asociación de Graduadas de la Universidad de Puerto Rico. San Juan, P. R.

Atenea ....Atenea. Universidad de Concepción. Concepción, Chile.

B. B. A. A.............Boletín Bibliográfico de Antropología Americana. Instituto Panamericano de Geografía e Historia. Comisión de Historia. México, D. F., Mexico.

Basic indus. Texas Basic Industries in Texas and Northern Mexico. The University north. Mexico of Texas. Institute of Latin-American Studies (Latin-American Studies, 9). Austin, Tex.

Belas artes ....Belas Artes. Academia Nacional de Belas Artes. Lisboa, Portugal.

Bermuda hist. quart. ....Bermuda Historical Quarterly. Hamilton, Bermuda.

Bohemia ....Bohemia. Habana, Cuba.

Bol. acad. arg. let. ......Boletín de la Academia Argentina de Letras. Buenos Aires, Argentina.

Bol. acad. dom. lengua . . Boletín de la Academia Dominicana de la Lengua. Ciudad Trujillo. Dominican Republic.

Bol. acad. nac. cien., Boletín de la Academia Nacional de Ciencias. Córdoba, Argentina.
Córdoba

Bol. acad. nac. hist. .....Boletín de la Academia Nacional de la Historia. Buenos Aires,
Argentina.

Bol. acad. nac. hist., Boletín de la Academia Nacional de Historia. Quito, Ecuador.
Quito

Bol. arch. gen., Caracas. .Boletín del Archivo General de la Nación. Caracas, Venezuela.

Bol. arch. gen., Ciudad Boletín del Archivo General de la Nación. Ciudad Trujillo,
Trujillo Dominican Republic.

Bol. arch. gen., México. .Boletín del Archivo General de la Nación. México, D. F., Mexico.

Bol. arch. nac., Habana. .Boletín del Archivo Nacional. Habana, Cuba.

Bol. arch. nac. hist.......Boletín del Archivo Nacional de Historia. Casa de la Cultura
Ecuatoriana. Quito, Ecuador.

Bol. bibl. univ. Coimbra. Boletim da Biblioteca da Universidade de Coimbra. Coimbra,
Portugal.

Bol. bibliog., Lima.....Boletín Bibliográfico. Universidad Nacional Mayor de San Marcos.
Biblioteca Central. Lima, Peru.

Bol. bibliog., São Paulo. .Boletim Bibliográfico. Biblioteca Pública Municipal de São Paulo.
Departamento de Cultura. São Paulo, Brazil.

Bol. cám. com. ind. Boletin de la Cámara de Comercio e Industrias de Tegucigalpa.
Tegucigalpa Tegucigalpa, Honduras.

Bol. carioca geog. ......Boletim Carioca de Geografia. Rio de Janeiro? Brazil.

Bol. estud. geog. ....Boletín de Estudios Geográficos. Universidad Nacional de Cuyo.
Instituto de Historia y Disciplinas Auxiliares. Mendoza,
Argentina.

Bol. estud. teatro.......Boletín de Estudios de Teatro. Comisión Nacional de Cultura.
Instituto Nacional de Estudios de Teatro. Buenos Aires,
Argentina.

Bol. filol. ....Boletín de Filología. Universidad de Chile. Instituto de Investigaciones Histórico-Culturales. Santiago, Chile.

Bol. geog. ....Boletim Geográfico. Conselho Nacional de Geografia. Instituto
Brasileiro de Geografia e Estatística. Rio de Janeiro, Brazil.

Bol. hist. antig..........Boletín de Historia y Antigüedades. Academia Colombiana de
Historia. Bogotá, Colombia.

Bol. hist. nat. soc. Boletín de Historia Natural de la Sociedad Felipe Poey. Universi-
F. Poey dad de la Habana. Museo Poey. Habana, Cuba.

Bol. inform. estud. soc. Boletín de Informaciones y de Estudios Sociales y Económicos.
econ. Instituto Nacional de Previsión. Quito, Ecuador.

Bol. inst. Caro y Cuervo. Boletín del Instituto Caro y Cuervo. Ministerio de Educación
Nacional. Bogotá, Colombia.

Bol. inst. estud. méd. Boletín del Instituto de Estudios Médicos y Biológicos. México,
biol. D. F., Mexico.

Bol. inst. hist. Ilha Boletim do Instituto Histórico da Ilha Terceira. Angra do
Terceira Heroísmo, Azores.

Bol. inst. intern. amer. Boletín del Instituto Internacional Americano de Protección a la
protec. infan. Infancia. Montevideo, Uruguay.

Bol. inst. nac. tec. ......Boletim do Instituto Nacional de Tecnologia. Rio de Janeiro(?),
Brazil.

Bol. inst. psicoped. nac... Boletín del Instituto Psicopedagógico Nacional. Lima, Peru.

Bol. inst. sudamer. Boletín del Instituto Sudamericano del Petróleo. Montevideo,
petról. Uruguay.

Bol. minas petról., Boletín de Minas y Petróleos. Ministerio de Minas y Petróleos.
Bogotá Bogotá, Colombia.

Bol. mus. nac., Rio .....Boletim do Museu Nacional. Ministério da Educação e Saúde.
Rio de Janeiro, Brazil.

Bol. mus. paraense Boletim do Museu Paraense Emilio Goeldi. Belém, Brazil.
Emilio Goeldi

Bol. paulista geog. ......Boletim Paulista de Geografia. Associação dos Geógrafos Brasileiros. São Paulo, Brazil.

Bol. real acad. cien., Boletín de la Real Academia de Ciencias, Bellas Letras y Nobles
bellas letras, nobles Artes. Consejo Superior de Investigaciones Científicas. Cór-
artes doba(?), Spain.

Bol. real acad. hist. .....Boletín de la Real Academia de la Historia. Madrid, Spain.

Bol. soc. arg. estud. Boletín de la Sociedad Argentina de Estudios Geográficos, Gaea.
geog. Gaea Buenos Aires, Argentina.

Bol. soc. bras. geog. ....Boletim da Sociedade Brasileira de Geografia. Rio de Janeiro, Brazil.
Bol. soc. chihuahuense ..Boletín de la Sociedad Chihuahuense de Estudios Históricos. Chihuahua, Mexico.
Bol. soc. mex. geog. estad.   Boletín de la Sociedad Mexicana de Geografía y Estadística. México, D. F., Mexico.
Brasília ....Brasília. Universidade de Coimbra. Instituto de Estudos Brasileiros da Faculdade de Letras. Coimbra, Portugal.
Brit. col. hist. quart. ....British Columbia Historical Quarterly. Provincial Archives. Victoria, British Columbia.
Brotéria ....Brotéria. Lisboa, Portugal.
Bull. Ga. acad. sci. .....Bulletin of the Georgia Academy of Science. University of Georgia. Athens, Ga.
Bull. hisp. stud. ....Bulletin of Hispanic Studies. Institute of Hispanic Studies. Liverpool, England.
Bull. inst. hist. res. ......Bulletin of the Institute of Historical Research. London, England.
Bull. Texas arch. paleon. soc.   Bulletin of the Texas Archaeological and Paleontological Society. Lubbock, Tex.

Cadernos ....Cadernos. Biblioteca da Academia Carioca de Letras. Rio de Janeiro, Brazil.
Calif. libr. bull. ....California Library Bulletin. California Library Association. Los Angeles, Calif.
Can. geog. jour. ....Canadian Geographical Journal. Canadian Geographical Society. Ottawa, Canada.
Carib. hist. rev. ....Caribbean Historical Review. Historical Society of Trinidad and Tobago. Port-of-Spain, Trinidad.
Carteles ....Carteles. Habana, Cuba.
Casa cult. ecuat. ....Casa de la Cultura Ecuatoriana. Quito, Ecuador.
Cath. hist. rev. ....Catholic Historical Review. American Catholic Historical Association. Washington, D. C.
Chron. bot. ....Chronica Botanica. Waltham, Mass.
Cien. nueva ....Ciencia Nueva. Tucumán, Argentina.
Ciencia ....Ciencia. México, D. F., Mexico.
Ciencia y fe............Ciencia y Fe. Colegio Máximo de San José. Buenos Aires, Argentina.
Clã ....Clã. Fortaleza, Brazil.
Clío ....Clío. Academia Dominicana de la Historia. Ciudad Trujillo, Dominican Republic.
College art jour. ....College Art Journal. New York, N. Y.
Comptes rendus cong. int. géog.   Comptes rendus du Congrès International de Géographie, Lisbonne, 1949. Union Geographique Internationale, 1950. Lisboa, Portugal.
Conserv. amer. ....Conservation in the Americas. Pan American Union in collaboration with the Pan American Section of the International Committee for Bird Preservation. Washington, D. C.
Conservatorio ....Conservatorio. Conservatorio Municipal de Música. Habana, Cuba.
Coop ....Coop. Departamento de Assistência ao Cooperativismo. Bahia, Brazil.
Cooperativismo ....Cooperativismo. Banco Nacional de Crédito Cooperativo. Rio de Janeiro, Brazil.
Correio da manhã .....Correio da Manhã. Rio de Janeiro, Brazil.
Correio paul. ....Correio Paulistano. São Paulo, Brazil.
Craft hor. ....Craft Horizons. American Craftsmen's Cooperative Council, Inc. New York, N. Y.
Cuad. amer. ....Cuadernos Americanos. México, D. F., Mexico.
Cuad. fil. ....Cuadernos de Filosofía. Universidad Nacional de Buenos Aires. Facultad de Filosofía y Letras. Buenos Aires, Argentina.
Cuad. hispanoamer. ....Cuadernos Hispanoamericanos. Seminario de Problemas Hispanoamericanos. Madrid, Spain.
Cuad. hist. prim. ....Cuadernos de Historia Primitiva. Madrid, Spain.
Cuad. inform. econ. ....Cuadernos de Información Económica. Corporación Venezolana de Fomento. Caracas, Venezuela.
Cuad. lit. ....Cuadernos de Literatura. Consejo Superior de Investigaciones Científicas. Instituto "Miguel de Cervantes" de Filología Hispánica. Madrid, Spain.

Cult. aliment. . . . . Cultura e Alimentação. Serviço de Alimentação da Previdência Social. Rio de Janeiro, Brazil.

Cult. univ. . . . . Cultura Universitaria. Universidad Central de Venezuela. Caracas, Venezuela.

Cultura, Rio de Janeiro . . Cultura. Ministério da Educação e Saúde. Serviço de Documentação. Rio de Janeiro, Brazil.

Cursos y conferencias . . . Cursos y Conferencias. Colegio Libre de Estudios Superiores. Buenos Aires, Argentina.

Documenta . . . . Documenta. Sociedad Peruana de Historia. Lima, Peru.

ECA . . . . ECA. Estudios Centro Americanos. San Salvador, El Salvador.

Ecology . . . . Ecology. Biological Society of America and the Duke University Press. Lancaster, Pa.

Econ. geog. . . . . Economic Geography. Clark University. Worcester, Mass.

Economía, Santiago . . . . . Economía. Universidad de Chile. Facultad de Economía. Santiago, Chile.

Estad. panameña . . . . Estadística Panameña. Contraloría General de la República. Dirección de Estadística y Censo. Panamá, Panama.

Estadística . . . . Estadística. Inter American Statistical Institute. Washington, D. C.

Estud. acad. lit. Plata . . . . Estudios de la Academia Literaria del Plata. Buenos Aires, Argentina.

Estud. amer. . . . . Estudios Americanos. Consejo Superior de Investigaciones Científicas. Escuela de Estudios Hispano-Americanos. Sevilla, Spain.

Estud. bras. . . . . Estudos Brasileiros. Rio de Janeiro, Brazil.

Estud. econ. . . . . Estudios Económicos. Universidad Autónoma Tomás Frías. Facultad de Economía y Finanzas. Potosí, Bolivia.

Estud. geog. . . . . Estudios Geográficos. Consejo Superior de Investigaciones Científicas. Instituto Juan Sebastian Elcano. Madrid, Spain.

Estud. hispanoamer. . . . . Estudios Hispanoamericanos. Homenaje a Hernán Cortés en el IV centenario de su muerte. Badajoz, Spain. Imprenta de la Diputación Provincial. 1948. 399 p.

Estud. hist. soc. España . . Estudios de Historia Social de España. Consejo Superior de Investigaciones Científicas. Madrid, Spain.

Estudios . . . . Estudios. Academia Literaria del Plata. Buenos Aires, Argentina.

Et caetera . . . . Et caetera. Guadalajara, Mexico.

Eugen. news . . . . Eugenical News. American Eugenical Society. New York, N. Y.

Fil. letras . . . . Filosofía y Letras. Universidad Nacional Autónoma de México. Facultad de Filosofía y Letras. México, D. F., Mexico.

Filología . . . . Filología. Universidad de Buenos Aires. Instituto de Filología. Buenos Aires, Argentina.

For. affs. . . . . Foreign Affairs. Council on Foreign Relations. New York, N. Y.

For the Dean . . . . For the Dean. Essays in anthropology in honor of Byron Cummings on his eighty-ninth birthday, September 20, 1950. Published by the Hohokam Museums Association, Tucson, Arizona, and the Southwestern Monuments Association. Santa Fe, N. Mex. 1950.

Formação . . . . Formação. Rio de Janeiro, Brazil.

Fortune . . . . Fortune. New York, N. Y.

Gac. med. bol. . . . . Gaceta Médica Boliviana. Universidad de Cochabamba. Facultad de Medicina y de las Escuelas de Odontología y Farmacia. Cochabamba, Bolivia.

Geog. helvetica . . . . Geographica Helvetica. Bern, Switzerland.

Geog. rev. . . . . The Geographical Review. American Geographical Society of New York. New York, N. Y.

Göteborgs Musei Arstryck . . . . Göteborgs Musei Arstryck. Göteborg, Sweden.

Habitat . . . . Habitat. São Paulo, Brazil.

Hac. econ. prev. . . . . Hacienda, Economía y Previsión. Ministerio de Hacienda, Economía y Previsión. Buenos Aires, Argentina.

HLAS . . . . Handbook of Latin American Studies. No. 1-13, 1935-1947. Cambridge, Mass., Harvard University Press, 1936-1951. No. 14-15, 1948-1949. Gainesville, Fla., University of Florida Press, 1951-1952.

Handbook of South American Indians
Handbook of South American Indians. V. 6. Smithsonian Institution. Bureau of American Ethnology, Bull. 143. Washington, D. C.

Hisp. amer. hist. rev.....Hispanic American Historical Review. Duke University Press. Durham, N. C.

Hisp. rev. ....Hispanic Review. University of Pennsylvania. Philadelphia, Pa.

Hispania ....Hispania. American Association of Teachers of Spanish and Portuguese. Wallingford, Conn.

Hispania, Madrid ....Hispania. Consejo Superior de Investigaciones Científicas. Instituto Jerónimo Zurita. Madrid, Spain.

Hist. tidskrift ....Historisk Tidskrift. Svenska Historiska Föreningen. Stockholm, Sweden.

Honduras rotaria ....Honduras Rotaria. Clubes Rotarios de la República de Honduras. Tegucigalpa, Honduras.

Horiz. econ. ....Horizontes Económicos. Buenos Aires, Argentina.

Hunt. libr. quart. ....Huntington Library Quarterly. San Marino, Calif.

Ilus. bras. ....Ilustração Brasileira. Rio de Janeiro, Brazil.

Imago mundi ....Imago Mundi. Stockholm, Sweden.

Impr. era ....The Improvement Era. Mutual Funds, Inc. Salt Lake City, Utah.

Ind. lab. ....Industry and Labour. International Labour Office. Geneva, Switzerland.

Ind. univ. publ. anthrop. ling.
Indiana University Publications in Anthropology and Linguistics. Memoir 4 and 5 of the International Journal of American Linguistics. Supplement to V. 16, no. 4, Oct., 1950 of this Journal. Bloomington, Ind.

Industriários ....Industriários. Instituto de Aposentadoria e Pensões dos Industriários. Rio de Janeiro, Brazil.

Infan. adoles. ....Infancia y Adolescencia. Consejo Venezolano del Niño. Caracas, Venezuela.

Int.-amer. econ. affs.....Inter-American Economic Affairs. Institute of Inter-American Studies. Washington, D. C.

Int. jour. amer. ling......International Journal of American Linguistics. Indiana University. Bloomington, Ind.

Int. lab. rev............International Labour Review. International Labour Office. Geneva, Switzerland.

Int. organ. ....International Organization. World Peace Foundation. Boston, Mass.

Int. ref. serv. ....International Reference Service. United States Department of Commerce. Office of International Trade. Washington, D. C.

Invest. econ. ....Investigación Económica. Universidad Nacional Autónoma de México. Escuela Nacional de Economía. México, D. F., Mexico.

Investigações ....Investigações. Departamento de Investigações. São Paulo, Brazil.

Isis ....Isis. History of Science Society. Cambridge, Mass. (Printed in Bruges, Belgium).

Jamaican hist. rev.......Jamaican Historical Review. The Jamaican Historical Society. Kingston, Jamaica.

Jorden runt ....Jorden Runt. Blasieholmstorg, Stockholm.

Jorn. letras ....Jornal de Letras. Rio de Janeiro, Brazil.

Jour. educ. soc. ....Journal of Educational Sociology. Payne Educational Sociology Foundation, Inc. New York, N. Y.

Jour. geog. ....The Journal of Geography. National Council of Geography Teachers. Chicago, Ill.

Jour. negro hist. ....Journal of Negro History. Association for the Study of Negro Life and History, Inc. Washington, D. C.

Jour. soc. amér. ....Journal de la Société des Américanistes. Publié avec le Concours du Centre National de la Recherche Scientifique et du Viking Fund. Paris, France.

Jus ....Jus. México, D. F., Mexico.

Kosmos ....Kosmos. Gesellschaft der Naturfreunde, Franckh'sche Verlagshandlung. Stuttgart, Germany.

Kulturgeografi ....Kulturgeografi. I Kommission hos Gyldendalske Boghandel. Nordisk Forlag. København, Denmark.

Kyklos ....Kyklos. Bern, Switzerland.

La. hist. quart. ....Louisiana Historical Quarterly. Louisiana Historical Society. New Orleans, La.
Language ....Language. Linguistic Society of America. Baltimore, Md.
Lingua posnaniensis ....Lingua Posnaniensis. Poznán, Poland.

Mag. art ....Magazine of Art. The American Federation of Arts. Washington, D. C.
A Manhã ....A Manhã. Rio de Janeiro, Brazil.
Mar del sur ....Mar del Sur. Lima, Peru.
Masterkey ....The Masterkey. Southwest Museum. Los Angeles, Calif.
Mater. estud. clase ⠀⠀⠀Materiales para el Estudio de la Clase Media en la América Latina.
⠀media amér. latina ⠀⠀Theo R. Crevenna [ed.]. 4 v. Washington, Unión Panamericana, 1950.
Md. hist. mag. ....Maryland Historical Magazine. Maryland Historical Society. Baltimore, Md.
Mem. acad. mex. hist....Memorias de la Academia Mexicana de la Historia. México, D. F., Mexico.
Mem. acad. nac. hist. ⠀⠀Memoria de la Academia Nacional de Historia y Geografía. México, D. F., Mexico.
⠀geog.
Mem. col. nac. ....Memoria de El Colegio Nacional. México, D. F., Mexico.
Mem. cuarto cong. inst. ⠀Memoria del Cuarto Congreso del Instituto Internacional de
⠀int. lit. iberoam. ⠀⠀⠀⠀Literatura Iberoamericana. Ministerio de Educación, Dirección de Cultura. Habana, Cuba. 1949.
Mem. inst. Oswaldo ⠀⠀Memórias do Instituto Oswaldo Cruz. Rio de Janeiro, Brazil.
⠀Cruz
Mem. licenciados ....Memorias de Licenciados. Universidad de Chile. Facultad de Ciencias Jurídicas y Sociales. Santiago, Chile.
Mem. Peabody mus. ⠀⠀Memoirs of the Peabody Museum of Archaeology and Ethnology.
⠀arch. ethnol. ⠀⠀⠀⠀⠀⠀Harvard University. Cambridge, Mass.
Mem. primer cong. ⠀⠀⠀Memoria del Primer Congreso de Historiadores de México y los
⠀hist. México ⠀⠀⠀⠀⠀⠀Estados Unidos Celebrado en la Ciudad de Monterrey, Nuevo León, México, del 4 al 9 de septiembre de 1949. Editorial Cultural. México. 1950. 420 p.
Mem. soc. cien. nat. ⠀⠀Memoria de la Sociedad de Ciencias Naturales La Salle. Caracas,
⠀La Salle ⠀⠀⠀⠀⠀⠀⠀⠀Venezuela.
Mercurio peruano ......Mercurio Peruano. Lima, Peru.
Mesoamer. notes ....Mesoamerican Notes. Mexico City College. Department of Anthropology. México, D. F., Mexico.
Méx. antiguo ....El México Antiguo. México, D. F., Mexico.
Méx. en el arte..........México en el Arte. Secretaría de Educación Pública. Instituto Nacional de Bellas Artes. México, D. F., Mexico.
Mid-America ....Mid-America. Loyola University. Institute of Jesuit History. Chicago, Ill.
Middle amer. research ⠀Middle American Research Records. The Tulane University of
⠀records ⠀⠀⠀⠀⠀⠀⠀⠀Louisiana. Middle American Research Institute. New Orleans, La.
Milit. eng. ....Military Engineer. Society of American Military Engineers. Washington, D. C.
Miss. valley hist. rev....Mississippi Valley Historical Review. Mississippi Valley Historical Association. Lincoln, Nebr.
Missionalia hispanica ...Missionalia Hispanica. Consejo Superior de Investigaciones Científicas. Instituto Santo Toribio de Mogrovejo. Madrid, Spain.
Mon. amer. ethnol. soc...Monographs of the American Ethnological Society. New York, N. Y.
The Month ....The Month. London, England.

Nat. hist. ....Natural History. American Museum of Natural History. New York, N. Y.
Nat. tax jour. ....National Tax Journal. National Tax Association. Lancaster, Pa.
New Mex. hist. rev......New Mexico Historical Review. Historical Society of New Mexico and University of New Mexico. Albuquerque, N. Mex.
Nimbus ....Nimbus. Sociedad Meteorológica de Bolivia. La Paz, Bolivia.
Nordeste ....O Nordeste. Fortaleza, Brazil.
Notes middle amer. ⠀⠀⠀Notes on Middle American Archaeology and Ethnology. Carnegie
⠀arch. ethnol. ⠀⠀⠀⠀⠀⠀Institution of Washington. Division of Historical Research. Washington, D. C.
Nuestra música ....Nuestra Música. México, D. F., Mexico.

Nueva era, Quito ....Nueva Era. Quito, Ecuador.
Nueva gen. ....Nueva Generación. Habana, Cuba.
Nueva rev. filol. hisp....Nueva Revista de Filología Hispánica. El Colegio de México y Harvard University. México, D. F., Mexico.
Nuevo educ. ....El Nuevo Educador. Ministerio de Educación Pública. Servicio Cooperativo Peruano–Norteamericano de Educación. Lima, Peru.
Número ....Número. Montevideo, Uruguay.

Obs. econ. fin. ....O Observador Econômico e Financeiro. Rio de Janeiro, Brazil.
Orientación musical .....Orientación Musical. Ateneo Musical Mexicano. México, D. F., Mexico.

Pac. disc. ....Pacific Discovery. California Academy of Sciences. Berkeley, Calif.
Pac. hist. rev. ....The Pacific Historical Review. The Pacific Coast Branch of the American Historical Association. Los Angeles and Berkeley, Calif.
Paideuma ....Paideuma. Deutsche Gesellschaft für Kulturmorphologie vom Frobenius Institut an der Johann Wolfgang Goethe-Universität. Frankfurt am Main, Germany.
Pet. geog. mitt. ....Petermann's Geographische Mitteilungen. Gotha, Germany.
Phylon ....Phylon. Atlanta University. Atlanta, Ga.
Poet lore ....Poet Lore. Boston, Mass.
Pol. sci. quart. ....Political Science Quarterly. Academy of Political Science. New York, N. Y.
Prev. soc., Ciudad   Previsión Social. Secretaría de Estado de Previsión Social. Ciudad
Trujillo   Trujillo, Dominican Republic.
Primitive man ....Primitive Man. Catholic Anthropological Conference. Washington, D. C.
Prob. agríc. indus.   Problemas Agrícolas e Industriales en México. México, D. F.,
México   Mexico.
Protec. soc., La Paz.....Protección Social. Caja de Seguro y Ahorro Obrero. La Paz, Bolivia.
Publ. soc. arqueol.   Publicaciones de la Sociedad Arqueológica de La Serena. La
La Serena   Serena, Chile.

IV cong. hist. nac. ......Quarto Congresso de História Nacional. Anais. Rio de Janeiro, Brazil.

Rep. amer. ....Repertorio Americano. San José, Costa Rica.
Repr. campechano ......El Reproductor Campechano. Departamento de Extensión Cultural. Campeche, Mexico.
Rev. acad. col. cien. ....Revista de la Academia Colombiana de Ciencias Exactas, Físicas y Naturales. Ministerio de Educación Nacional. Bogotá, Colombia.
Rev. acad. geog. hist.   Revista de la Academia de Geografía e Historia de Nicaragua.
Nicaragua   Managua, Nicaragua.
Rev. América ....Revista de América. Bogotá, Colombia.
Rev. arch. bibl. mus. ....Revista de Archivos, Bibliotecas y Museos. Consejo Superior de Investigaciones Científicas. Instituto Nicolás Antonio. Madrid, Spain.
Rev. arch. bibl. nac.,   Revista del Archivo y Biblioteca Nacionales. Sociedad de Geo-
Tegucigalpa   grafía e Historia de Honduras. Tegucigalpa, Honduras.
Rev. arch. nac.   Revista de los Archivos Nacionales de Costa Rica. San José,
Costa Rica   Costa Rica.
Rev. arq. mun. ....Revista do Arquivo Municipal. Prefeitura do Município de São Paulo. Departamento de Cultura. São Paulo, Brazil.
Rev. arqueol. etnol. .....Revista de Arqueología y Etnología. Habana, Cuba.
Rev. asoc. arg. diet. .....Revista de la Asociación Argentina de Dietología. Buenos Aires(?), Argentina.
Rev. asoc. méd. arg......Revista de la Asociación Médica Argentina. Buenos Aires, Argentina.
Rev. banco cent.   Revista del Banco Central de Costa Rica. San José, Costa Rica.
Costa Rica
Rev. banco rep.,   Revista del Banco de la República. Bogotá, Colombia.
Colombia

Rev. bibl. nac.,   Revista de la Biblioteca Nacional. Ministerio de Justicia e Instruc-
  Buenos Aires   ción Pública. Buenos Aires, Argentina.
Rev. bibl. nac., Habana..Revista de la Biblioteca Nacional. Habana, Cuba.
Rev. bim. cub. ....Revista Bimestre Cubana. Sociedad Económica de Amigos del
     País. Habana, Cuba.
Rev. branca ....Revista Branca. Rio de Janeiro, Brazil.
Rev. bras. estud. ped....Revista Brasileira de Estudos Pedagógicos. Ministério da Edu-
     cação e Saúde. Instituto Nacional de Estudos Pedagógicos. Rio
     de Janeiro, Brazil.
Rev. bras. geog. ....Revista Brasileira de Geografia. Conselho Nacional de Geografia.
     Instituto Brasileiro de Geografia e Estatística. Rio de Janeiro,
     Brazil.
Rev. bras. med. ....Revista Brasileira de Medicina. Rio de Janeiro, Brazil.
Rev. chil. hist. geog.....Revista Chilena de Historia y Geografía. Santiago, Chile.
Rev. cien. econ.,   Revista de Ciencias Económicas. Colegio de Doctores en Ciencias
  Buenos Aires   Económicas. Buenos Aires, Argentina.
Rev. cien. jur. soc. ......Revista de Ciencias Jurídicas y Sociales. Universidad Nacional del
     Litoral. Santa Fe, Argentina.
Rev. cub. ....Revista Cubana. Ministerio de Educación. Dirección de Cultura.
     Habana, Cuba.
Rev. cub. fil...........Revista Cubana de Filosofía. Universidad de la Habana. Habana,
     Cuba.
Rev. d'hist. amér. franç..Revue d'Histoire de l'Amérique Française. Institut d'Histoire de
     l'Amérique Française. Montreal, Canada.
Rev. d'hist. col..........Revue d'Histoire des Colonies. Société de l'Histoire des Colonies
     Françaises. Paris, France.
Rev. econ., Córdoba.....Revista de Economía. Banco de la Provincia de Córdoba. Cór-
     doba, Argentina.
Rev. econ., México......Revista de Economía. México, D. F., Mexico.
Rev. econ. arg...........Revista de Economía Argentina. Buenos Aires, Argentina.
Rev. econ. El Salvador..Revista de Economía de El Salvador. Ministerio de Economía.
     Instituto de Estudios Económicos. San Salvador, El Salvador.
Rev. educ., La Plata.....Revista de Educación. Dirección General de Escuelas de la
     Provincia de Buenos Aires. La Plata, Argentina.
Rev. educ. nac. ....Revista de Educación Nacional. Ministerio de Educación Pública.
     Lima, Peru.
Rev. española segur. soc..Revista Española de Seguridad Social. Ministerio de Trabajo.
     Instituto Nacional de Previsión. Madrid, Spain.
Rev. estud. jur. pol. soc..Revista de Estudios Jurídicos, Políticos y Sociales. Universidad
     Mayor de San Francisco Xavier de Chuquisaca. Sucre, Bolivia.
Rev. estud. musicales....Revista de Estudios Musicales. Universidad Nacional de Cuyo.
     Instituto Superior de Artes e Investigaciones Musicales. Men-
     doza, Argentina.
Rev. estud. pol..........Revista de Estudios Políticos. Instituto de Estudios Políticos.
     Madrid, Spain.
Rev. estud. yucatecos....Revista de Estudios Yucatecos. Mérida, Mexico.
Rev. fac. cien. econ.,   Revista de la Facultad de Ciencias Económicas. Universidad
  Buenos Aires   Nacional de Buenos Aires. Buenos Aires, Argentina.
Rev. fac. cien. econ.   Revista de la Facultad de Ciencias Económicas y de Administra-
  admin.   ción de Montevideo. Universidad de la República. Montevideo,
     Uruguay.
Rev. fac. cien. econ.   Revista de la Facultad de Ciencias Económicas, Comerciales y
  com. pol.   Políticas. Universidad Nacional del Litoral. Rosario, Argentina.
Rev. fac. cien. jur. soc.   Revista de la Facultad de Ciencias Jurídicas y Sociales de Guate-
  Guatemala   mala. Guatemala, Guatemala.
Rev. fac. hum. cien. ....Revista de la Facultad de Humanidades y Ciencias. Universidad de
     la República. Montevideo, Uruguay.
Rev. fil. ....Revista de Filosofía. Universidad Nacional de La Plata. Instituto
     de Filosofía. La Plata, Argentina.
Rev. fil., Santiago ......Revista de Filosofía. Sociedad Chilena de Filosofía y Universidad
     de Chile. Santiago, Chile.
Rev. filol. española .....Revista de Filología Española. Consejo Superior de Investiga-
     ciones Científicas. Instituto Miguel de Cervantes. Madrid,
     Spain.
Rev. geog. amer. ....Revista Geográfica Americana. Sociedad Geográfica Americana.
     Buenos Aires, Argentina.

Rev. geog. Chile ....Revista Geográfica de Chile. Comité Nacional de Geografía, Geodesia y Geofísica. Santiago, Chile.
Rev. hisp. mod. ....Revista Hispánica Moderna. Columbia University. Hispanic Institute in the United States. New York, N. Y.
Rev. hist., Islas Canarias.Revista de Historia. Universidad de La Laguna. Facultad de Filosofía y Letras. La Laguna de Tenerife, Canary Islands.
Rev. hist., Lima ....Revista Histórica. Instituto Histórico del Perú. Lima, Peru.
Rev. hist., Paris........Revue Historique. Paris, France.
Rev. hist., São Paulo....Revista de História. São Paulo, Brazil.
Rev. hist. amér. ....Revista de Historia de América. Instituto Panamericano de Geografía e Historia. México, D. F., Mexico.
Rev. hist. ideas..........Revista de Historia de las Ideas. Universidad Nacional de Tucumán. Tucumán, Argentina.
Rev. iberoamer. ....Revista Iberoamericana. Instituto Internacional de Literatura Iberoamericana. México, D. F., Mexico.
Rev. Indias ....Revista de las Indias. Ministerio de Educación Nacional. Bogotá, Colombia.
Rev. Indias, Madrid ....Revista de Indias. Consejo Superior de Investigaciones Científicas. Instituto Gonzalo Fernández de Oviedo. Madrid, Spain.
Rev. inst. econ. téc. publ.   Revista del Instituto de Economía y Técnica Publicitaria. Universidad Nacional de Córdoba. Córdoba, Argentina.
Rev. inst. etnol. nac. ....Revista del Instituto Etnológico Nacional. Ministerio de Educación Nacional. Bogotá, Colombia.
Rev. inst. hist. geog. bras.   Revista do Instituto Histórico e Geográfico Brasileiro. Rio de Janeiro, Brazil.
Rev. inst. nac. tradición   Revista del Instituto Nacional de la Tradición. Ministerio de Educación. Buenos Aires, Argentina.
Rev. jurídica ....Revista Jurídica. Universidad Mayor de San Simón. Facultad de Derecho, Ciencias Sociales, Políticas y Económicas. Cochabamba, Bolivia.
Rev. Lyceum ....Revista Lyceum. Lyceum y Lawn Tennis Club. Habana, Cuba.
Rev. meteorol. ....Revista Meteorológica. Junta Nacional de Meteorología. Montevideo, Uruguay.
Rev. mex. estud. antrop..Revista Mexicana de Estudios Antropológicos. Sociedad Mexicana de Antropología. México, D. F., Mexico.
Rev. mex. soc..........Revista Mexicana de Sociología. Universidad Nacional Autónoma de México. Instituto de Investigaciones Sociales. México, D. F., Mexico.
Rev. mus. paulista .....Revista do Museu Paulista. São Paulo, Brazil.
Rev. mus. reg. Ica......Revista del Museo Regional de Ica. Ica, Peru.
Rev. musical chil. ....Revista Musical Chilena. Universidad de Chile. Instituto de Extensión Musical. Santiago, Chile.
Rev. nac., Montevideo...Revista Nacional. Ministerio de Instrucción Pública. Montevideo, Uruguay.
Rev. nac. cult..........Revista Nacional de Cultura. Ministerio de Educación Nacional. Dirección de Cultura. Caracas, Venezuela.
Rev. peruana der. int. ...Revista Peruana de Derecho Internacional. Sociedad Peruana de Derecho Internacional. Lima, Peru.
Rev. soc. haïtienne hist. géog.   Revue de la Société Haïtienne d'Histoire et de Géographie. Port-au-Prince, Haiti.
Rev. trab. ....Revista del Trabajo. Secretaría del Trabajo y Previsión Social. México, D. F., Mexico.
Rev. univ., Cuzco......Revista Universitaria. Cuzco, Peru.
Rev. univ., Tegucigalpa..Revista de la Universidad. Universidad de Honduras. Tegucigalpa, Honduras.
Rev. univ. Buenos Aires.Revista de la Universidad de Buenos Aires. Buenos Aires, Argentina.
Rev. univ. nac. Córdoba.Revista de la Universidad Nacional de Córdoba. Córdoba, Argentina.
Rev. univ. São Paulo....Revista da Universidade de São Paulo. São Paulo, Brazil.
Rev. uruguaya geog......Revista Uruguaya de Geografía. Asociación de Geógrafos del Uruguay. Montevideo, Uruguay.
Rio ....Rio. Rio de Janeiro, Brazil.
Riv. agric. subtrop. trop..Rivista di Agricoltura Subtropicale e Tropicale. Instituto Agronomico per l'Africa Italiana. Firenze, Italy.

Riv. antrop. ....Rivista di Antropologia. Società Romana di Antropologia. Roma, Italy.
Romance phil. ....Romance Philology. University of California Press. Berkeley and Los Angeles, Calif.
Runa ....Runa. Universidad de Buenos Aires. Facultad de Filosofía y Letras. Buenos Aires, Argentina.
Rural soc. ....Rural Sociology. Baton Rouge, La.

Saeculum ....Saeculum. Freiburg-München, Germany.
Sapientia ....Sapientia. La Plata, Argentina.
Sci. month. ....The Scientific Monthly. American Association for the Advancement of Science. Washington, D. C.
II cong. indig.   Segundo Congreso Indigenista Interamericano. Anales. Lima. interamer.   1949.
Segur. soc. ....Seguridad Social. Caja Dominicana de Seguros Sociales. Ciudad Trujillo, Dominican Republic.
Segur. soc., Bogotá ....Seguridad Social. Instituto Colombiano de Seguros Sociales. Bogotá, Colombia.
Soc. forces ....Social Forces. University of North Carolina Press. Chapel Hill, N. C.
Sociologia ....Sociologia. São Paulo, Brazil.
Sombra ....Sombra. Rio de Janeiro, Brazil.
South. folk. quart.......Southern Folklore Quarterly. University of Florida and Southeastern Folklore Society. Gainesville, Fla.
Southw. jour. anthrop....Southwestern Journal of Anthropology. University of New Mexico and Laboratory of Anthropology, Santa Fe. Albuquerque, N. Mex.
Studio ....Studio. London, England.
Svensk geog. årsbok.....Svensk Geografisk Årsbok. Sydsvenska Geografiska Sällskapet. Lund, Sweden.

Tasks econ. hist. ....The Tasks of Economic History. A supplemental issue of *The Journal of Economic History*. The Economic History Association. New York University Press. New York, N. Y.
Tellus ....Tellus. Svenska Geofysiska Föreningen. Stockholm, Sweden.
Tópicos econ. ....Tópicos Económicos. Guatemala, Guatemala.
Tradición ....Tradición. Cuzco, Peru.
Trans. amer. philos. soc..Transactions of the American Philosophical Society. Philadelphia, Pa.
Trans. New York   Transactions of the New York Academy of Sciences. New York, acad. sci.   N. Y.
Travel ....Travel. New York, N. Y.
Trib. israelita ....Tribuna Israelita. México, D. F., Mexico.
Trim. econ. ....El Trimestre Económico. Fondo de Cultura Económica. México, D. F., Mexico.
Trópico ....Trópico. Secretaria da Educação e Cultura. Prefeitura Municipal de São Paulo. São Paulo, Brazil.

Unifruitco ....Unifruitco. United Fruit Company. New York, N. Y.
Uni-Ver ....Uni-Ver. Universidad Veracruzana. Jalapa, Mexico.
Univ. Antioquia ....Universidad de Antioquia. Medellín, Colombia.
Univ. Calif. publ. amer. University of California. Publications on Archaeology and Etharch. ethnol.   nology. Berkeley, Calif.
Univ. Habana ....Universidad de la Habana. Habana, Cuba.
Univ. México ....Universidad de México. Universidad Nacional Autónoma de México. México, D. F., Mexico.
Univ. mus. bull. ....University Museum Bulletin. University of Pennsylvania. The University Museum. Philadelphia, Pa.
Universidad, Monterrey .Universidad. Universidad de Nuevo León. Monterrey, Mexico.

Venezuela-up-to-date ...Venezuela-up-to-date. Venezuelan Embassy. Washington, D. C.
Verbum ....Verbum. Universidade Católica. Rio de Janeiro, Brazil.
Le vie del mondo ......Le Vie del Mondo. Consociazione Turistica Italiana. Milano, Italy.

World pol. ....World Politics. Yale University. Yale Institute of International Studies. New Haven, Conn.

World trade commod. ..World Trade in Commodities. United States Department of Commerce. Office of International Trade. Washington, D. C.

Yikal maya than ....Yikal Maya Than. Mérida, Mexico.

Zeit. ethnol. ....Zeitschrift für Ethnologie. Berliner Gesellschaft für Anthropologie, Ethnologie and Urgeschiche. Berlin, Germany.

Index

Kholla, 460. Kogi, 398. Krahó, 389. Maya, 157. Marcko (Peru), 465. Mehinaku, 464. Mérida (Venezuela), 410. Mixtec, 335. Montaña (Peru), 407. Motilón, 400. Muisca, 396a. Nicarindio, 359. Olmec, 163. Ona, 394. Otomí, 190, 327. Oyampi, 392. Pariukur, 378. Peru, 401. Quechua, 408. Siriono, 409. South America, 113, 372a. Taíno, 234. Tapajó, 417. Toltec, 163. Trumaí, 464. Tupi-Guarani, 385. Vapidiana, 391. Waurá, 384. Xingu, 379, 380, 383. Yámana (Yaghan), 394. Yaqui, 337.

Indians. *See also* Economics, History (by topics), Literature, *and* Maps.

Material culture—Costume, 195, 313. Engineering, 1230. Musical instrument, 277. Quipu, 312, 404. Tools, 307, 372. Weapons, 219a, 220a, 380.
   See also Artifacts.

Native sources — General, 215, 220. Guatemala, 205, 207. Mexico — Codices, 188, 192, 209, 220b. Texts, 187, 191, 193, 197, 208, 211, 212, 219, 326, 328.
   See also item 2517.

Sites—Argentina, 268, 270. Brazil, 246, 249, 250, 256. British Honduras, 178. Chile, 282. Colombia, 285, 290. Cuba, 230–232. El Salvador, 128, 134, 135, 147, 166, 172. Guatemala, 180, 181, 183. Mexico, 122, 146, 152, 154–156, 158, 176. Nicaragua, 118. Panama, 71. Peru, 296, 309, 310, 311, 316. Venezuela, 240, 257. West Indies, except Cuba, 237, 252, 253.

Anthropology, physical:
   General, 113.
   Anthropometry—Living, 426, 439, 440, 447, 451, 452, 456–458, 462, 464, 465. Skeletal, 426, 432, 435, 442, 452. Soft parts, 453.
   Deformity, trephining, mutilation, 429, 442, 444, 450, 460, 461.
   Physiological observations — General, 465, 466. Blood groups, 421, 445, 467. Blood pressure, 446. Disease, 431, 454. Metabolism, 433. Pigmentation, 428, 436, 437.
   Population, 332a, 430, 441, 448, 449.
   Racial groups—Classification, 114, 423, 455, 463. Mestizos, 427.
   Racial history, 455.
   Technique, 425, 468, 469.

Antolínez, Gilberto, 2529.
Antoni, Norberto, 1324.
Antunes, Paranhos, 569.
Arabena Williams, Hermelo, 2563.
Aragão, Arnaldo Cavalcanti de, 2925.
Aragão, Henrique de Beaurepaire, 1403.
Arango H., Rubén, 2514.
Arauco Camacho, Florencio, 460.

Araújo, Antônio Gomes de, 2018.
Araújo, Carlos da Silva, 2201.
Araújo, Christovam, 2865.
Araujo, Ely Goulart Pereira de, 1273.
Araújo, Heitor O., 2019.
Araújo, J. A. dos Santos, 2874.
Araújo, Luzio, 3027.
Araújo Mendizábal, Roberto, 1364.
Araya, Enrique, 2606.
Arbenz, Guilherme Oswaldo, 469.
Arcas, Juan Antonio, 1980.
Arce, David N., 2564.
Arce, José, 2257.
Arce de Vázquez, Margot, 2565.
Arce Ibarra, Roxana, 924.
Archer, William H., 2684.

Architecture:
   Argentina, 485, 486. Bolivia, 482, 488–491. Brazil, 482, 558–565, 567, 572, 573, 578, 580, 582, 584, 587, 591, 595. Chile, 492–494. Colombia, 482, 1704. Dominican Republic, 495–498. Ecuador, 482, 499. Guatemala, 482. Mexico, 482, 501, 503–505, 507, 509, 511–513, 1472, 1592. Panama, 482. Paraguay, 474. Peru, 482, 516–522. Southwest U. S., 480. Venezuela, 481, 482.

Arcila Farías, Eduardo, 808, 925, 1473.
Arcila Vélez, Graciliano, 284.
Arciniegas, Germán, 1962, 2571.
Ardao, Arturo, 1067, 2579, 3269.
Ardouin, Beaubrun, 1459.
Arenas Luque, Fermín V., 2008, 2515.
Arévalo, Juan José, 1362.
Arévalo Martínez, Rafael, 2517.
Argandoña Olivares, René, 2362.
Arguedas, Alcides, 2676.
Arguedas, José María, 2656.
Arias Larreta, Felipe, 2690.
Arias Solís, Enrique, 1404.
Arias Suárez, Eduardo, 2625.
Ariza, Alberto E., 1703.
Arlas, José A., 2979.
Armas, Fernando de, 1474.
Armas Arias, Guillermo, 599.
Armellada, Cesáreo de, 400.
Armillas, Pedro, 122–124, 185.
Armour Research Foundation, 626.
Arnal, Pedro, 1145.
Arnaud, Vicente Guillermo, 1749.
Arnold, J. R., 91a.
Aroche, José, 2521.
Arosemena, Mariano, 1893.
Arráiz, Antonio, 2607.
Arria Salas, Alberto, 2435.
Arriaga, Ponciano, 1806.
Arriagada, Próspero, 462.
Arroba, Gonzalo, 2338.
Arrom, José J., 2538.
Arroyo, Leonardo, 2875.
Arroyo, Luis, 1714.

Art:
   General, 471, 480, 482, 552.
   Catalogues and yearbooks—Argentina, 470. Brazil, 554, 577, 581, 596. Colombia, 529, 530. Mexico, 539.